THE YEARBOOK OF EDUCATION LAW 2022

Charles J. Russo, J.D., Ed.D. and Jeffrey C. Sun, J.D., Ph.D., editors

Published by Education Law Association
Philadelphia, Pennsylvania, USA

The Education Law Association improves education by promoting interest in and understanding of education law.

Join the social learning community at EducationLaw.org.

The opinions expressed in this publication are those of the authors and do not represent the official views of the Education Law Association.

© 2022 Education Law Association

All rights reserved. No part of this publication may be reproduced, distributed, or transmitted in any form or by any means, including photocopying, recording, or other electronic or mechanical methods, without the publisher's prior written permission, which may be sought by visiting EducationLaw.org.

ISBN-13: 978-1-56534-194-4
ISBN-10: 1-56534-194-5

EDITORS

Charles J. Russo, M.Div., J.D., Ed.D., is the Joseph Panzer Chair in Education in the School of Education and Health Sciences, Director of its Ph.D. Program, and Research Professor of Law in the School of Law at the University of Dayton. Dr. Russo served as 1998-99 President of the Education Law Association, and was the 2002 recipient of its McGhehey (Achievement) Award, the 2021 Distinguished Scholar Award from the American Educational Research Association's Special Interest Group on Religion & Education, and the 2021 Lifetime Achievement Award from the South African Education Law Association. Dr. Russo authored or co-authored more than 300 articles in peer-reviewed journals; authored, co-authored, edited, or co-edited 75 books, totaling nearly 1,200 publications. Dr. Russo also has spoken extensively on issues in education law in thirty-four of the United States and thirty-one other nations. In addition, he edits two journals and serves on over a dozen editorial boards.

Having spoken in thirty-four states and thirty-one nations outside the United States on all six inhabited continents, Russo taught summer courses in England, Spain, and Thailand. Internationally, he serves or has served as a Visiting Professor at the University of Notre Dame of Australia Faculty of Law in Sydney, Queensland University of Technology in Brisbane, and the University of Newcastle, Australia; the University of Sarajevo, Bosnia and Herzegovina; South East European University, Macedonia; the Potchefstroom and Mafeking Campuses of Northwest University, Potchefstroom, South Africa; the University of Malaya in Kuala Lumpur, Malaysia; the University of Sao Paulo, Brazil; Yeditepe University, Istanbul Turkey; Inner Mongolia University for the Nationalities, Tongliao, Inner Mongolia; and Peking University in Beijing, China. He is currently a Visiting Professor at Capital Normal University in Beijing.

Before joining the Faculty at the University of Dayton as Professor and Chair of the Department of Educational Administration in July 1996, Dr. Russo taught at the University of Kentucky in Lexington, Kentucky, from August 1992 to July 1996 and at Fordham University in his native New York City from September 1989 to July 1992. He taught high school for eight and one half-years, both prior to and after graduation from law school.

He received a Bachelor of Arts degree in Classical Civilization (1972), Juris Doctor Degree (1983), and Doctor of Education degrees in Educational Administration and Supervision (1989) from St, John's University in New York City. He received a Master of Divinity degree from the Seminary of the Immaculate Conception in Huntington, New York (1978). He received a Ph.D. Honoris Causa from Potchefstroom University, now the Potchefstroom Campus of Northwest University, in Potchefstroom, South Africa, in May 2004, for his contributions to the field of Education Law.

Jeffrey C. Sun, J.D., Ph.D., is Professor of Higher Education and Law, Distinguished University Scholar, Associate Dean for Innovation and Strategic Partnerships, and Director of the SKILLS Collaborative (a research and policy center examining workforce development and legal issues to career/ professional postsecondary education) at the University of Louisville. He is also Counsel at Manley Burke.

His research and practice areas focus on higher education law and professional/career education policies and practice. Dr. Sun has served as Project Director and Principal Investigator for over $25 million in grants and contracts.

He has published approximately 100 scholarly works and is co-author of ten books, including *Law, Policy, and Higher Education* (Carolina Academic Press, 2012); Law & Education Inequality: Removing Barriers to Educational Opportunities (Information Age Publishing, 2015); *Student Clashes on Campus: A Leadership Guide to Free Speech* (Routledge); and Academic Leadership and Governance of Higher Education: A Guide for Trustees, Leaders, and Aspiring Leaders of Two- and Four-Year Institutions (Stylus Publishing, 2nd Edition, 2022).

Dr. Sun received a BBA and an MBA from Loyola Marymount University, a law degree (J.D.) from the Moritz College of Law at The Ohio State University, and an M.Phil. and a Ph.D. from Columbia University.

CONTRIBUTORS

Jacob A. Bennett, Ph.D., COVID Testing & Outreach Manager, Simmons University, Boston, Mass.

Joy Blanchard, Ph.D., Associate Professor, Higher Education, School of Education, Louisiana State University, Baton Rouge, La.

Susan C. Bon, J.D., Ph.D., Faculty Fellow and Civility Advocate, Office of the President; Professor, Department Educational Leadership & Policies; Affiliate Professor, College of Law; University of South Carolina, Columbia, S.C.

Jyllian R. Bradshaw, J.D., Senior Associate, Porter Wright Morris & Arthur LLP, Dayton, Ohio, Adjunct Professor, University of Dayton, Dayton, Ohio

Amy L. Dagley, Ph.D., Assistant Professor, Educational Leadership, University of Alabama at Birmingham, Birmingham, Ala.

David L. Dagley, Ph.D., J.D., Professor Emeritus, Educational Leadership, University of Alabama, Tuscaloosa, Ala.

Todd A. DeMitchell, Ed.D., John & H. Irene Peters Endowed Professor Emeritus of Education Law & Labor, University of New Hampshire, Durham, N.H.

Joe Dryden, J.D., Ed.D., Associate Professor of Graduate Education, Texas Wesleyan University, Fort Worth, Tex.

Gillian Foss, Ph.D., School of Education, Louisiana State University, Baton Rouge, La.

Jeffrey S. Greenley, J.D., M.S., Superintendent, Belpre City Schools, Belpre, Ohio

Elizabeth T. Lugg, J.D., Ph.D., Associate Professor, Educational Law, Illinois State University, Normal, Ill.

Education Law Association

Raquel Muñiz, J.D., Ph.D., Assistant Professor, Lynch School of Education & Human Development; Assistant Professor, School of Law, Boston College, Boston, Mass.

Allan G. Osborne, Jr., Ed.D., Retired Principal, Snug Harbor Community School, Quincy, Mass.; *Education Law Into Practice* Editor, West's *Education Law Reporter*.

Patrick D. Pauken, J.D., Ph.D., Director and Professor, School of Educational Foundations, Leadership & Policy; Interim Chair, Higher Education and Student Affairs; Secretary, Board of Trustees, Bowling Green State University, Bowling Green, Ohio

Barbara Qualls, Ph.D., Associate Professor and Director, M.Ed.-Leadership/Advanced Certification Programs, Stephen F. Austin State University, Nacogdoches, Tex.

Andrea Schulewitch, J.D., M.Ed., Associate General Counsel, Washoe County School District, Reno, Nev.

Luke Stedrak, Ed.D., Associate Professor, Hibernia National Bank Endowed Professor, Department of Educational Leadership and Technology, Southeastern Louisiana University, Hammond, La.

Jeffrey C. Sun, J.D., Ph.D., Professor of Higher Education and Law, Distinguished University Scholar, Associate Dean for Innovation and Strategic Partnerships, and Director of the SKILLS Collaborative at the University of Louisville, Ky. He is also Counsel at Manley Burke.

CONTENTS

1 – School Governance 1

2 – School Employment 33

3 – Students in K-12 Schools 83

4 – Bargaining 125

5 – Students with Disabilities 136

6 – Torts 175

7 – Sports 247

8 – Higher Education Administration & Faculty 263

9 – Students in Higher Education 303

10 – Federal and State Legislation 339

Education Law Association

Chapter 1

SCHOOL GOVERNANCE

Barbara Qualls, Ph.D.[1] and Patrick Pauken, J.D. Ph.D.[2]

Introduction	2
Systemic Governance Issues	2
Constitutional Issues	2
Religion	2
Speech	3
Board Operations and Authority Issues	3
Taxation	6
Finance	10
Charter Schools	12
Administration of Charter Schools	12
Funding and Resources for Charter Schools	13
Other Charter School Cases	14
Localized Governance Issues	16
Bidding and Awarding of Contracts	16
School Construction and Land Issues	17
Breach of Contract	19
Property Rights and Use of Property	20
Open Records and Open Meetings	22
Student Residency and District Transfer	23
Conclusion	25
Alphabetical List of Cases	26
Cases by Jurisdiction	28

---

[1] Associate Professor and Director, M.Ed.-Leadership/Advanced Certification Programs, Stephen F. Austin State University, Nacogdoches, Tex.
[2] Director and Professor, School of Educational Foundations, Leadership & Policy; Interim Chair, Higher Education and Student Affairs; Secretary, Board of Trustees, Bowling Green State University, Bowling Green, Ohio.

Introduction

This chapter summarizes litigation concerning K-12 governance issues in 2021, with some cases decided in 2020 but reported in 2021. The organizational structure is in two sections: cases of system governance and cases of localized governance. The systemic governance section includes conflicts concerning constitutional issues of religion and speech; board operational issues; taxation; finance; and charter schools. The localized governance section contains cases of conflict on bidding and awarding of contracts; breach of contract; school construction and land issues; property rights and use of property; public records and Open Meetings; school boundaries; student residency; personnel and employment issues and other local issues.

Systemic Governance Issues

Constitutional Issues

Religion

The Second Circuit, in a case from Vermont, granted a preliminary injunction allowing a student attending a Catholic high school access to a state-sponsored dual enrollment program. The court reasoned that the injunction request based on a free exercise challenge was necessary to avoid irreparable harm to the senior student. The issue of access was further decided in favor of the student because she lived in an area where a public high school was not maintained.[3]

Three other religion cases involved First Amendment claims. In a New Jersey case, the district court determined that the public school district had a secular purpose in including the study of Islam in seventh-grade world cultures and geography courses. The decision recognized the necessary consideration of a parent's interest in managing their child's education and that there is a subtle but distinct difference between teaching religion and teaching about religion, thus did not violate the Establishment Clause.[4] In North Carolina, the district court also determined that the inclusion of the

---

[3] A.H. *ex rel.* Hester v. French, 985 F.3d 165, 385 Educ. L. Rep. 475 (2d Cir. 2021).
[4] Hilsenrath *ex rel.* C.H. v. Sch. Dist. of Chathams, 500 F. Supp. 3d 272, 390 Educ. L. Rep. 189 (D.N.J. 2020).

novel *The Poet X* had curricular value and that the parents' objection did not warrant an injunction to prohibit its use.[5] In Kentucky, the district court found that the governor overreached his authority in prohibiting all face-to-face instruction, even though his intent to mitigate the spread of the COVID-19 pandemic was secular. The religious school required in-person prayer and mentorship to fulfill its mission, a right that was recognized by the court.[6]

Speech

In Michigan, the Sixth Circuit affirmed that the treatment given to a speaker at a board meeting was not different from that given to others in similar situations. The plaintiff tried to speak in opposition to a possible decision on the use of public tax collections for property development. His litigation failed in all respects, including his claim of violation of equal protection in his speech during the public participation portion of a board meeting. The board's limitations on his protest speech were not found to be discriminatory.[7]

Board Operations and Authority Issues

In a New York case, the Second Circuit affirmed a lower court determination that a district's at-large system of election of school board members resulted in a dilution of minority voters' representation. Even though the community was demonstrably racially polarized, the court found that a successful claim of vote dilution does not require racial causation. The at-large system did violate the Voting Rights Act.[8] In Kentucky, the governor abolished the state board of education between sessions of the state legislature and created a new board. Members of the old board challenged his right to do so, claiming that their property and liberty rights were violated. The Sixth Circuit found that the governor had not exceeded his authority to reorganize the board between legislative sessions and that the members did not have a continuing property or liberty

---

[5] Coble v. Lake Norman Charter Sch., Inc., 499 F. Supp. 3d 238, 389 Educ. L. Rep. 784 (W.D.N.C. 2020).
[6] Danville Christian Acad., Inc. v. Beshear, 503 F. Supp. 3d 516, 390 Educ. L. Rep. 665 (E.D. Ky. 2020).
[7] Davis v. Detroit Pub. Schs. Cmty. Dist., 835 F. App'x 18, 386 Educ. L. Rep. 173 (6th Cir. 2020).
[8] Clerveaux v. E. Ramapo Cent. Sch. Dist., 984 F.3d 213, 385 Educ. L. Rep. 83 (2d Cir. 2021).

right to their former positions.⁹ In Wisconsin, a school district vendor was indicted on 21 of 22 counts for bribery designed to influence an official act when a board member accepted payments surrounding his advocacy for several votes of the board concerning contracts and the purchase of goods. The decision of the district court established that specific bribes do not need to be linked to other specific actions but rather that the "stream of benefits" theory applies in differentiating a gratuity from a bribe.¹⁰

In Ohio, new legislation was adopted geared toward the improvement of chronically failing schools. The new provision allowed an academic distress commission to install a single CEO who would assume complete operational, managerial, and instructional control of the school, replacing the authority of the board and administration. The board of one district objected, arguing that the legislation passed without the required three readings and that replacing or unseating a board violated the state's constitutional provision for city school boards. The state supreme court affirmed a lower court's decision that the statute violated neither the three readings rule nor the state constitution.¹¹

Three other state cases involved procedural questions about elections. In New Jersey, school district boards of trustees are either Type I (members appointed by mayors) or Type II (members elected by voters). A Type I district narrowly passed a resolution to hold a special election for voter approval to change to Type II. A series of procedural delays pushed the proposed election out for over a year. The summary decision was given by an appellate court with the determination that a trial court may not order a question concerning the reclassification of how board members are named, moving from Type I to Type II, on a special election date.¹² In a second New Jersey case, a group of citizens presented a petition to move the election of its board of education to the general election date. When the petition was rejected, the citizens sued. The appellate court affirmed a lower court's determination that how the petition was circulated, single question ballot initiative, insufficient number of signatures on the petition, and other anomalies were not sufficient to overturn an

---

⁹ Houchens v. Beshear, 850 F. App'x 340, 391 Educ. L. Rep. 138 (6th Cir. 2021).
¹⁰ U.S. v. Islam, 526 F. Supp. 3d 48, 395 Educ. L. Rep. 222 (E.D. Pa. 2021).
¹¹ Youngstown City Sch. Dist. Bd. of Educ. v. State, 161 N.E.3d 483, 386 Educ. L. Rep. 456 (Ohio 2020).
¹² Bd. of Educ. of E. Newark in Cnty. of Hudson v. Harris, 253 A.3d 664, 393 Educ. L. Rep. 372 (N.J. Super. Ct. App. Div. 2021).

election result.¹³ In Texas, a school board candidate attempted to have a competitor's name removed from the election ballot because of discrepancies in her address. Requirements for board candidacy included six-month continuous residence within the boundaries of the district. The responding candidate claimed that the discrepancy was only that she failed to update her official residency information. She provided voter records that indicated she had been in residence and that the discrepancy in her addresses was not challenged when she voted. The appeals court agreed with the responding candidate, stating in its decision that the complaining candidate had not provided sufficient evidence to warrant the requested writ of mandamus.¹⁴

In Pennsylvania, a group of landowners attempted to incorporate a new school district with the intent of annexing their property to an adjoining district. Their petition was denied, and on appeal, the case was remanded to the state secretary of education for merit examination. The petition was again denied because no students were living in the area. The last appellate court held that the argument of no students was not dispositive for a determination on the merits of the petition and that the refusal of the secretary to consider stipulations and testimony required another remand.¹⁵ In Oregon, a middle-school student was suspended and reprimanded for sexual harassment of two younger disabled students and theft of items from a teacher's desk. The student sued the district for defamation and negligence for having mishandled the disciplinary proceedings that resulted in damage to his reputation. The district's defense was the state's Anti-Strategic Lawsuits Against Public Participation law. The appeals court reversed and remanded the trial court's decision to allow the student's case to proceed, finding that the district had not engaged in discussions of his disciplinary history in a public place or other conditions as required for a defamation suit.¹⁶ A Mississippi school district's policy on names for its schools called for a proposed name change for a person must be posthumous and required a majority of votes from the board. A proposed name change was presented by the son of a former

---

¹³ Fuhrman v. Mailander, 248 A.3d 387, 389 Educ. L. Rep. 889 (N.J. Super. Ct. App. Div. 2021).
¹⁴ *In re* Dominguez, 621 S.W. 3d 899, 390 Educ. L. Rep. 833 (Tex. App. 2021).
¹⁵ Archer v. Rockwood Area Sch. Dist., 249 A.3d 617, 390 Educ. L. Rep. 698 (Pa. Commw. Ct. 2021).
¹⁶ C. R. v. Eugene Sch. Dist. 4J, 481 P.3d 334, 387 Educ. L. Rep. 349 (Or. Ct. App. 2021).

superintendent to change the name from the same as the town to his father's name. Over the course of several meetings, the board amended its policy to allow non-posthumous naming but required unanimous approval of the board. After the school's name was changed, several alumni objected, eventually suing the district. The chancery court denied the complaint finding that the process for appeals of a municipal authority was not followed. The appellate court affirmed, noting that the legal reasoning of the chancery court was inaccurate: the alumni lacked standing to sue the district as they could not provide evidence of harm that they would incur beyond that of any other member of the community. However, the correct result was achieved, so the chancery decision was affirmed.[17]

Taxation

The Eighth Circuit reversed a decision of a district court in determining that the corporation that is the Mayo Clinic is not an educational institution for purposes of taxation on passive income. An IRS audit charged $11,501,621 for passive income on the investment pool that the Mayo Clinic managed for its several subsidiaries. After paying the assessment, the Mayo Clinic filed for reimbursement, claiming exemption as an educational organization. The district court held for Mayo, but the decision was appealed. The Eighth Circuit found that educational organization status would apply only if the main function were education, with faculty, curriculum, and a student body. Even though the Mayo Clinic could cite several educational pursuits and charitable functions, those were not the primary functions of the corporation. The Circuit Court's opinion was that the Mayo Clinic was not eligible for the requested unrelated business income tax (UBIT) exemption.[18]

Three state supreme court cases examined issues of constitutionality. In Alabama, Jefferson County was under a federal desegregation order, and earlier attempts of communities to secede from the County district were unsuccessful because they could not provide evidence that their leaving the district would not hamper the desegregation effort. One community began the process of establishing a new district with a tax levy and the appointment of a board and superintendent. After the Eleventh Circuit again denied the proposal for a new district, a taxpayer filed suit for the return of

---

[17] Foster v. Sunflower Cnty. Consol. Sch. Dist., 311 So.3d 705, 388 Educ. L. Rep. 429 (Miss. Ct. App. 2021).
[18] Mayo Clinic v. U.S., 997 F.3d 789, 390 Educ. L. Rep. 479 (8th Cir. 2021).

the municipal levy to the community since the funding was not used for the planned new district. The appellate court affirmed the decision of the lower court, finding that Alabama's constitution concerning local amendments on school property tax did not prohibit the municipal ad valorem tax because the court recognized that there could be a point in the future when the community might propose a secession plan that would not impede the desegregation efforts.[19] In Arizona, a taxpayer and opposition group brought suit against the secretary of state in an attempt to block Proposition 208 by challenging the legality of the methods used to collect signatures for the Proposition 208 petitions. The county court held primarily in favor of the arguments of the opposition group, but the Arizona high court reversed that decision, clearing the way for Proposition 208 to be included on the general election ballot.[20]

Proposition 208 was passed with a slender majority and immediately came under attack by opposition groups. Proposition 208 was an income tax surcharge on high-income taxpayers whereby that revenue would be directly available to school districts. Part of the Proposition included a statement of exemption of Proposition 208 funds from a state constitutional law on local expenditure caps. The state supreme court approved the transfer of the appeal and heard the arguments presented by the opposition to Proposition 208. The state's high court held that the constitutionality of Proposition 208 was a case "ripe" for decision and that its provision that the monies collected from the Proposition were not local revenues was unconstitutional. The allocation provisions within the Proposition likewise exceeded the constitution's limits on expenditures. Finally, the allocation provision could not be separated from the remainder of the Proposition, making the revenue control limitations unconstitutional.[21]

Three other state supreme court cases examined other taxation issues. In Texas, a group of taxing entities, including a school district and a junior college district, challenged an appraisal review board's value on the mineral rights to land included in the jurisdiction of the entities. The ARB denied the appeal. The Texas high court heard the case on appeal by the property owners after two lower courts sided with the taxing entities. The entities were allowed to file an amended petition, but that was considered a new legal action that

---

[19] Campbell v. City of Gardendale, 321 So.3d 635, 393 Educ. L. Rep. 1004 (Ala. 2020).
[20] Molera v. Hobbs, 474 P.3d 667, 383 Educ. L. Rep. 475 (Ariz. 2020).
[21] Fann v. Arizona, 493 P.3d 246, 393 Educ. L. Rep. 851 (Ariz. 2021).

resets the statutory time for the property owners to file another Texas Citizens Participation Act (TCPA) to dismiss.[22] In one of two *In re* opinions, the Pennsylvania state supreme court vacated and remanded a decision by a lower court that denied an appeal by a school district concerning the appraised value of a specific property. The reasoning of the court in the decision to vacate was that the district's appeal was not barred by res judicata or by collateral estoppel.[23] In Colorado, the state high court responded to a question from the state General Assembly, inquiring whether it could require school districts to gradually eliminate temporary property tax credits without obtaining voter approval. The prevailing answer was that the Assembly could proceed with its planned legislation without conflict with the Taxpayer's Bill of Rights (TABOR), but the decision was not without dissent from the court's chief justice.[24]

Missouri's constitutional Hancock Amendment requires the state to refund money to payers of income tax when revenues are more than a percentage based on personal income. A taxpayer sued a school district both individually and on behalf of a class of property owners, contending that the school district levied taxes for six consecutive years at rates that violated the Hancock Amendment, although the district stopped just short of a levy that would have triggered voter approval. The county court judged in favor of the district, finding no violation of governing law, but the Court of Appeals reversed and remanded, finding that taxpayers were due refunds for the six years, whether they filed for injunctive relief or not, and that reasonable costs and attorney fees were also part of their relief.[25] In New Jersey, a large group of taxpaying entities challenged a city ordinance that levied a 1 percent tax on payroll expenditures that were attributable to nonresident employees. The levy was to be used exclusively to benefit the city's schools. On appeal, after the county court denied the entities' motion for summary judgment, the appellate court found that the payroll tax ordinance did not violate the obligation of the state to provide a thorough and efficient education system or any part of the other claims from the entities. The only area of mitigation concerning

---

[22] Kinder Morgan SACROC, LP v. Scurry Cnty., 622 S.W.3d 835, 391 Educ. L. Rep. 383 (Tex. 2021).

[23] *In re* Coatesville Area School Dist., 244 A.3d 373, 386 Educ. L. Rep. 835 (Pa. 2021).

[24] *In re* Interrogatory on House Bill 21-1164 Submitted by Colo. Gen. Assembly, 487 P.3d 636, 391 Educ. L. Rep. 360 (Colo. 2021).

[25] Blankenship v. Franklin Cnty. Collector, 619 S.W.3d 491, 388 Educ. L. Rep. 986 (Mo. Ct. App. 2021).

language about the application of the tax on the payment for work performed outside the taxing entities' boundaries but supervised from within.[26]

Two state appeals court cases concerned ad valorem taxes. In Texas, the Court of Appeals, Dallas, affirmed a county court decision that granted the request of the charter school operator for exemption from ad valorem taxation on the private property leased by the charter operator for use by the school.[27] In Georgia, a Tax Allocation District (TAD) in Atlanta was formed by entities contiguous to an area designated for redevelopment. The Atlanta Board of Education joined with other taxing entities to utilize portions of its ad valorem property tax in that TAD to redevelop a "blighted" area of the city. A group of taxpayers in opposition to the use of tax dollars for the venture intervened. The Court of Appeals affirmed the opinion of the county court in that the school board acted within its authority, did not need the approval of a project-specific resolution for the redevelopment, and the city was not required to produce a new or amended local law before using the school tax funds.[28] In Illinois, a school district voted for a special education tax of $30 million without seeking voter approval. The amount represented a rate of 0.913842 percent when equalized. The county reduced the levy to the legally permissible 0.8 percent. A group of intervenors objected to the levy, even though the county took a similar action every year since 2005. Their 13-count objection included a range of alleged violations, but only the one dealing with the requirement to submit a levy to voters for approval was in play in the case. The county court found for the school district and the county tax collector because the actual levy was within the 0.8 percent allowed by the Property Tax Extension Limitation Law (PTELL) and the appellate court affirmed.[29] A final case involving the contested use of tax money concerned a watchdog group that sued a former superintendent to recover $113,433 from a settlement agreement with a former employee that the superintendent approved. The superintendent's defense strategy included a request for bifurcation, seeking first to establish standing and second to consider merit. The county court granted his motion,

---

[26] Mack-Cali Realty Corp. v. State, 246 A.3d 847, 388 Educ. L. Rep. 895 (N.J. Super. Ct. App. Div. 2021).

[27] Dallas Cent. Appraisal Dist. v. Int'l Am. Educ. Fed'n Inc., 618 S.W.3d 375, 388 Educ. L. Rep. 388 (Tex. App. 2020).

[28] Franzen v. Atlanta, 857 S.E.2d 237, 390 Educ. L. Rep. 397 (Ga. Ct. App. 2021).

[29] John P. Sanfilippo & Sons, Inc. v. Rickert, 167 N.E.3d 277, 389 Educ. L. Rep. 924 (Ill. App. Ct. 2020).

ruling that the watchdog group did not have standing either as an association or as individual taxpayers and that the chief executive officer of the organization did not qualify as a resident of the district. The Court of Appeal affirmed the lower court's decision.[30]

Finance

The Second Circuit overturned a district court finding concerning a class action suit brought by investors in an educational services corporation, alleging fraud and misleading statements regarding the reported financial gains from the sale of a Chinese tutoring subsidiary and the revaluation of a second Chinese subsidiary. One accusation of fraud involved a sham sale and repurchase of a one-on-one tutoring service in Guangzhou, which was purported to represent $50 million in pre-tax income. The second accusation stemmed from a purported profit of $25.2 million from transactions with Beijing Shunshun Bida Information Consulting Co. Ltd., which provided counseling services to students seeking college abroad. The Second Circuit reversed the entire district court decision, finding that the investor group sufficiently alleged the false or misleading statements and their complaint sufficiently showed a loss.[31] A district court in California held that the final rule from the Department of Education concerning the allocation of the Coronavirus Aid, Relief, and Economic Security (CARES) Act conflicted with the intent of the Act. The rules-imposed conditions on how the CARES Act funds would be shared by public and private schools, in violation of the Administrative Procedure Act. The preliminary injunction sought by the plaintiff entities was necessary because the eight states, the District of Columbia, and the four municipal school districts that were named parties in the case would likely suffer irreparable harm without the injunction.[32] Ohio established a Quality Community School Support (QCSS) program that awarded substantial per-student funding for schools designated a "Community School of Quality" with a single student in attendance who was designated economically disadvantaged could create the possibility of $1,750 in additional funds. The application process for accessing the funds required the requesting school to be "in good standing" in all states where it operated schools. All the schools

---

[30] San Diegans for Open Gov't v. Fonseca, 279 Cal. Rptr. 3d 1, 390 Educ. L. Rep. 710 (Cal. Ct. App. 2021).
[31] Lea v. TAL Educ. Group, 837 F. App'x 20, 386 Educ. L. Rep. 667 (2d Cir. 2020).
[32] Michigan v. DeVos, 481 F. Supp. 3d 984, 386 Educ. L. Rep. 197 (N.D. Cal. 2020).

under the operation of one provider were denied funding because the corporation that managed the provider was not listed as a foreign corporation by the Ohio Secretary of State. The state's supreme court ruled that the requirement of "in good standing" was met by the operator being both qualified and effective. The writ of mandamus sought by the operator was granted as it related to the Ohio Department of Education but did not mandate that the governor and other state officials approve the schools' applications.[33]

Four other state cases dealt with funding issues. An appellate court in New York found for parents and others in a class action suit that alleged that the state's funding process violated the constitutional directive for serving at-risk students. Inadequacies in an identified high-needs district, an average-needs district, a district with a high rate of teenage pregnancy, and other districts all had inadequate funds to serve at-risk students. However, the court recognized in its opinion that its role was to define and safeguard protected rights while the state legislature was tasked with creating and implementing a remedy for the identified inadequate funding areas.[34] In Pennsylvania, a multi-campus charter school requested an injunction concerning its suit against the state's department of education concerning a redirection fee. By state law, funding for the charters in the suit flowed through the school district where the charter school was located. Each time a redirection of funds was requested, the state charged a fee to the charters. The charters' injunction request was countered by a preliminary objection from the state education department. The court determined that factual disputes existed concerning whether the state's administrative code authorized the redirection fee; whether it "usurped and infringed" on the legislative branch; and whether the redirection fee was too vague. The factual disputes in total constituted a viable claim for the court to deny the department's objection to the charter's request for a permanent injunction.[35] In another Pennsylvania case, a group of school districts, parents, and advocacy associations sought to depose the Speaker of the House concerning the legislative process of school funding. The long-running case was appealed to the state's highest court and remanded to the original court where the governor was

---

[33] State *ex rel.* Horizon Sci. Acad. of Lorain, Inc. v. Ohio Dept. of Educ., 172 N.E.3d 1019, 394 Educ. L. Rep. 332 (Ohio 2021).
[34] Maisto v. State, 149 N.Y.S.3d 599, 393 Educ. L. Rep. 750 (N.Y. App. Div. 2021).
[35] Pa. Virtual Charter Sch. v. Dept. of Educ., 244 A.3d 885, 386 Educ. L. Rep. 849 (Pa. Commw. Ct. 2020).

protected by chief executive privilege.³⁶ A state audit of a school district in Ohio revealed misappropriation of over $50,000. The state brought an action against the former chief executive officer and other school officials. The CEO appealed a lower court's summary judgment in favor of the state, claiming that he did not have control over the disbursement of funds. The appellate court reversed the decision and found for the former CEO, stating in its opinion that the CEO did not exercise control over the state allocations and that such monies were directed to the city's chief financial officer. The CEO did not supervise the financial officer. The appellate court reversed the earlier decision, and the case was remanded with instructions for entry of judgment in favor of the CEO.³⁷

Charter Schools

Administration of Charter Schools

A parent was arrested after a series of exchanges with charter school personnel about his presence in the school building. He sued the school, its charter operator, the municipality, and its police department, citing defamation, false arrest, false imprisonment, malicious prosecution, false imprisonment of a child, spoliation of evidence, breach of contract, and civil rights claim of deprivation of his Fourteenth Amendment protection rights. The federal district court determined that the portions of his suit relating to the school had no basis that would hold the parent company operators of the charter school responsible for the actions of the staff employed by a subsidiary. No implied contract between the parent and school was breached by the school sending the director of student services instead of the principal to meet with the father. The Eleventh Circuit affirmed the district court's summary judgment in favor of the defendant—the police department, charter operator, school, and municipality.³⁸ Two related cases in Pennsylvania involved a charter school operator that proposed to consolidate eight schools into one multiple-school corporation. The state department of education denied the request, which was appealed to the Charter Schools

---

[36] William Penn Sch. Dist. v. Dept. of Educ., 243 A.3d 252, 385 Educ. L. Rep. 872 (Pa. Commw. 2020).

[37] State *ex rel.* Ohio Atty. Gen. v. Burns, 156 N.E.3d 461, 383 Educ. L. Rep. 1068 (Ohio Ct. App. 2020).

[38] Turner v. Homestead Police Dept., 828 F. App'x 541, 383 Educ. L. Rep. 159 (11th Cir. 2020).

Appeal Board (CAB). Action by the CAB was determined by a majority of the Board. One seat on the seven-member board was vacant, and two other members recused themselves. With only four remaining members to vote, the question was whether any action of the CAB would be determined by a majority of the Board (4 of 7 or 6) or a majority of the members voting. The Commonwealth Court determined that only a majority is needed to act and that not all CAB members are obligated to vote.[39] In the same court, a related matter was decided that the charter operator could petition the court for a declaration validating the CAB 3-1 vote.[40]

Two Florida charter cases involved the termination of one charter and denial of the application of another. In the termination case, a public school was declared a charter by its district but almost immediately had difficulty in operation. A series of events occurred, including gross mismanagement of funds and presenting a danger to the health and safety of students. The district terminated the charter's contract after just one year. The Administrative Law Judge revoked the charter, returning the school to its status as a public middle school. The appellate court affirmed the actions of the school district and ALJ.[41] In the other Florida case, a sponsoring school district denied a charter operator's application, but the denial was reversed on appeal to the Charter School Appeal Commission. The district appealed the reversal, claiming that the record did not substantively support the reversal. The Commission's decision was affirmed with language in the appellate court's decision that expressly allowed the Commission to seek clarification and consider information outside the strict record.[42]

Funding and Resources for Charter Schools

In New Jersey, the nonprofit organization, Education Law Center (ELC) which represented a class of students in the state's poorest school districts, requested a judicial review of the applications for renewal or expansion of seven charter schools, which had been approved by the state's commissioner. The state's high

---

[39] Propel Charter Schs. v. Dept. of Educ., 242 A.3d 985, 385 Educ. L. Rep. 836 (Pa. Commw. Ct. 2020).

[40] Propel Charter Schs. v. Dept. of Educ., 243 A.3d 322, 385 Educ. L. Rep. 894 (Pa. Commw. Ct. 2020).

[41] Lincoln Mem'l Acad., Inc. v. Manatee Cnty. Sch. Bd., 309 So.3d 710, 386 Educ. L. Rep. 1084 (Fla. Dist. Ct. App. 2021).

[42] School Bd. of Volusia Cnty. v. Fla. East Coast Charter Sch., 312 So.3d 158, 388 Educ. L. Rep. 1043 (Fla. Dist. Ct. App. 2021).

court found that an analysis of the fiscal impact of a charter on the public schools in its area was needed even in former "Abbott" school districts. (Former "Abbott" districts are those districts designated as among the poorest in the state who were guaranteed a level of funding commensurate with richer districts as a result of the 1985 *Abbott v. Burke* case.) In addition, the court's review determined that the remand for the commissioner to conduct segregative-impact analysis five years after the grant of applications would not serve the interest of students and was not in the spirit of the commissioner's charge to make renewal application decisions based on circumstances at the moment.[43] A request for judicial review of a denial of a special exception to build a charter school and a religious facility in Florida resulted in an affirmation of the original denial. A court of appeals found that the building requestor was afforded procedural due process and was not due further consideration for second-tier certiorari review.[44] In another Florida case, a group of charter schools challenged their exclusion from the proceeds of a public school referendum from an *ad valorem* levy. On appeal, the District Court of Appeal of Florida found that the public school's referendum violated a state law requiring substantively equal funding for students in charter schools "the same as students enrolled in other public schools in the school district."[45] In New York, the mechanism for funding charter schools is by transfer of the amount of funding an individual student would generate for his public school to the charter school of his choice. A charter school notified the state that it was owed $588,466 in unpaid tuition, and the public school that owed the tuition was notified, but the public school sought judicial review of the decision to intercept. On appeal, the county court's dismissal of the public school's petition was affirmed.[46]

Other Charter School Cases

Female students sued a charter school and its operators concerning a dress code requirement that girls must wear skirts,

---

[43] *In re* Renewal Application of TEAM Acad. Charter Sch., 252 A.3d 1008, 392 Educ. L. Rep. 872 (N.J. 2021).
[44] Somerset Acad., Inc. v. Miami-Dade Cnty. Bd. of Cnty. Comm'rs, 314 So.3d 597, 390 Educ. L. Rep. 437 (Fla. Dist. Ct. App. 2020).
[45] Acad. for Positive Learning, Inc. v. Sch. Bd. of Palm Beach Cnty., 315 So.3d 675, 390 Educ. L. Rep. 440 (Fla. Dist. Ct. App. 2021).
[46] Lansingburgh Cent. Sch. Dist. v. N.Y. State Educ. Dept., 151 N.Y.S.3d 730, 394 Educ. L. Rep. 1053 (N.Y. App. Div. 2021).

jumpers, or skorts instead of pants or shorts. Their challenge included claims under both the Equal Protection Clause and Title IX. The district court found for the students on the equal protection claim but for the defendant charter school on the Title IX claim. On appeal, the Fourth Circuit reversed both decisions, with the opinion that the dress code of the charter school was not an act attributable to the state, so it did not trigger equal protection. The district court's dismissal of the Title IX claim as not applicable to dress codes was similarly reversed by the Fourth Circuit's recognition that claims of sex discrimination related to a dress code are not automatically excluded from the reach of Title IX.[47] In Rhode Island, a charter school sought a zoning decision that would allow expansion to a permanent location, but some factions of the city council opposed the request. The Supreme Court of Rhode Island confirmed approval of zoning that allowed the operation of a mayoral charter school as "municipal use" instead of a "nonprofit educational institution serving young children."[48] The New York City public school district provided COVID-19 screening tests. Charter schools petitioned for an order that would require the same screening tests for children who were residents of the city but attended charter schools. The county court that accepted the petition directed the board of education to provide the screening for students and staff of charter schools under the same terms and testing that was provided to public schools. On appeal, the Supreme Court, Appellate Division, found that the board was not required to provide testing for staff members or to children who attended nonparty charter schools.[49] In Wisconsin, a charter school was notified that it was in default concerning several performance metrics and that its contract with its partner public school would be terminated. The governance board of the charter brought an action against the district challenging the default status. The county court granted the requested declaratory and injunctive relief sought by the charter's board. On appeal by the public school district, the Court of Appeals affirmed the relief granted on the stated issues of default of academic standards, personalized learning plans for all students, and teaching core curriculum through project-based learning. However, the single area

---

[47] Peltier v. Charter Day Sch., Inc., 8 F.4th 251, 393 Educ. L. Rep. 493 (4th Cir. 2021).
[48] City of Woonsocket v. RISE Prep Mayoral Acad., 251 A.3d 495, 391 Educ. L. Rep. 326 (R.I. 2021).
[49] King v. Bd. of Educ. of City Sch. Dist. of City of New York, 151 N.Y.S.3d 34, 394 Educ. L. Rep. 323 (N.Y. App. Div. 2021).

that was reversed was enrollment. The terms of the charter's contract allowed the public school sole discretion in determining whether the charter maintained enrollment sufficient for continued operation. The case was remanded with instructions for consideration of whether the public school's determination of enrollment sufficiency was made on a reasonable basis and with a proper motive.[50] A years-long battle between a parent and a Florida charter school ended when the district court of appeal denied the parent's petition for writ of certiorari. The parent engaged in social media attacks against the charter school after his children were withdrawn from the school in favor of homeschooling. The charter school brought an action against the parent for tortious interference and the school successfully rebutted his claim of right to protection under the anti-SLAPP statute. His petition for writ of certiorari was denied by the appellate court.[51]

Localized Governance Issues

Bidding and Awarding of Contracts

Two state court cases concerning contracts came from Louisiana. In the first, the second lowest bidder was awarded the contract for facilities repair because the apparent lowest bidder was unresponsive to a key component of the bid specifications. The third lowest bidder brought suit, claiming that the second lowest bidder submitted documents with a name different from the company name registered with the state. The court found that the addition of "a Louisiana Limited Liability Company" following the licensed name instead of "LLC" is not a substantive or deceptive difference to invalidate the award of the contract.[52] The second Louisiana case also dealt with an unresponsive and unsuccessful bidder. A two-phase contract for asbestos removal was awarded to the second lowest bidder because the first bidder did not have the state license for asbestos abatement that was delineated in the bid documents. Over a month after the execution of the contract with the winning

---

[50] Friends of Maple Grove, Inc. v. Merrill Area Common Pub. Sch. Dist., 959 N.W.2d 362, 390 Educ. L. Rep. 739 (Wis. Ct. App. 2021).
[51] Baird v. Mason Classical Acad., Inc., 317 So.3d 264, 391 Educ. L. Rep. 988 (Fla. Dist. Ct. App. 2021).
[52] Core Constr. Servs., LLC v. Div. of Admin., Dept. of Facility Planning and Control, 310 So.3d 569, 387 Educ. L. Rep. 412 (La. Ct. App. 2020).

company and after the project commenced, the lowest contractor sought injunctive relief to halt the award of the bid. The parish court determined that the original low bid was nonresponsive to the license requirements and not entitled to the contract. On appeal, the court affirmed the parish court's determination and found that the action of the school board did not deny procedural due process to the unsuccessful contractor.[53]

A contract dispute heard in a New York state appellate court involved defining the responsible party when a school district contracted with a consulting company for therapists for special education students' services. A child was injured by a therapist while performing home services and the parents sued the district, the consulting company, and the therapist. The school district's motion to dismiss was denied at the county court and appellate level, with the holding that the existence of a contract between the district and the consulting company did not define the relationship between the district and the therapist as that of an independent contractor. The significant part of the reasoning was that the home services were performed in coordination with the student's classroom teachers at the direction of the district's special education committee.[54]

School Construction and Land Issues

Three construction and land issues were decided by their respective states' high courts. The state of Alaska has a debt reimbursement program that allows municipalities to receive reimbursement for certain construction and renovation bonds, but there are requirements related to the structure of the bond's payment plan. A municipality participated regularly in the program and after an absence of several years, reapplied for a new reimbursement. The state department of education denied the new request because the repayment structure did not meet the requirements for repayment. The municipality requested an administrative review, which upheld the department's decision. The appeals to a state court and the state's highest court likewise resulted in an affirmation of the original decision.[55] The subcontractor for electrical construction at an Alabama school sued

---

[53] Lathan Construction, LLC v. Webster Parish Sch. Bd. *ex rel.* Kennon, 317 So.3d 881, 391 Educ. L. Rep. 1010 (La. Ct. App. 2021).
[54] D.S. v. Positive Behavior Support Consulting and Psychological Resources, P.C., 151 N.Y.S.3d 690, 394 Educ. L. Rep. 1048 (N.Y. App. Div. 2021).
[55] North Slope Bor. v. State, 484 P.3d 106, 389 Educ. L. Rep. 525 (Alaska 2021).

a Florida supplier for failure to deliver lighting fixtures, claiming breach of contract, fraudulent misrepresentation, and conversion. The supplier and its sole shareholder filed a motion for dismissal, then a petition for a writ of mandamus, claiming that the Alabama courts did not have jurisdiction. The Supreme Court of Alabama agreed that the trial court did not have general jurisdiction over the Florida supplier, but that the contacts with Alabama that did exist constituted personal jurisdiction. In addition, the supplier's fiduciary-shield defense was not sufficient to preclude the trial court's personal jurisdiction designation. The supplier's writ of mandamus was denied.[56] A school district in Nebraska condemned half of a tract of land zoned for mixed industrial use to build a new high school. The corporate owner of the land challenged the offered price and the appraised value, claiming that zoning changes and other planned development in the area raised the value of the land in question and also damaged the value of the remaining part of the tract that was not sought by the school district. On appeal from the trial court, the Supreme Court of Nebraska found for the corporation, awarding almost double the appraised and offered value, as well as significant legal fees.[57]

Three state cases were decided in the New York Supreme Court, Appellate Division. In the first, the city's School Construction Authority filed for summary judgment concerning a student's injury claim after the student tripped on a crack in the concrete surface of the schoolyard. The SCA's motion was denied, but the denial was reversed on appeal after it established that the surface defect was trivial as a matter of law and the SCA had no duty of supervision for the student or duty of inspection or maintenance of the school premises.[58] In the second case, a private school was in dispute with a neighboring landowner about the use of a road that was included in the neighbor's property. The private school was granted a declaration of use for the road and an injunction that prohibited the neighbor from interfering with its use of the road. The neighbor joined with an abutter landowner in appeal but the Supreme Court, Appellate Division, affirmed the lower court decision, allowing the private school to continue its use of the road under its existing

---

[56] Ex parte LED Corporations, Inc., 303 So.3d 1160, 384 Educ. L. Rep. 571 (Ala. 2020).
[57] Douglas Cnty. Sch. Dist. No. 10 v. Tribedo, LLC, 950 N.W.2d 599, 383 Educ. L. Rep. 1146 (Neb. 2020).
[58] Augustine v. City of N.Y., 136 N.Y.S.3d 457, 385 Educ. L. Rep. 950 (N.Y. App. Div. 2020).

easement appurtenance.⁵⁹ Delays in the completion of a contract for accessibility and electrical upgrades resulted in a notice of claim by the contractor against the city's School Construction Authority (SCA). The county court dismissed the complaint and denied the contractor's cross motion. On appeal, the Supreme Court, Appellate Division, found that the contractor's notice of claim was not in compliance with requirements and not technical in nature, thus it affirmed the lower court decision.⁶⁰

Breach of Contract

Two federal cases decided breach of contract issues. In the Eighth Circuit, a school district and high school principal were sued by a teacher who claimed that her dismissal by reduction of force and non-rehire constituted retaliation because she filed an EEOC complaint against the principal for sexual harassment. The conflict arose concerning the execution of insurance coverage for the claim. The district court found for the insurer, stating that neither of the policies for the two years over which the claims extended provided coverage and that the district's contractual claim under the doctrines of waiver and estoppel was not applicable. On appeal to the Eighth Circuit, the district court's opinion was affirmed.⁶¹ In Nebraska, a software manufacturer sued a school district for breach of contract when it copied a software item and distributed it in a manner not clearly allowed in its contractual agreement. The software at issue was part of an identification program that was needed when the district was forced to put all its instruction into an online format during the COVID-19 pandemic. The company's claim for copyright infringement and violation of the Nebraska Trade Secrets Act was dismissed.⁶²

Three state court cases concerning contractual disputes covered an indicted general counsel, operation of a wind turbine, and loss of market. In New Jersey, the board terminated the employment contract of its legal counsel after he was indicted on several conspiracy and evidence tampering charges related to a charge of

---

⁵⁹ Northwood Sch., Inc. v. Fletcher, 140 N.Y.S.3d 297, 387 Educ. L. Rep. 319 (N.Y. App. Div. 2021).
⁶⁰ BG Nat. Plumbing & Heating, Inc. v. N.Y.C. Sch. Constr. Auth., 150 N.Y.S.3d 279, 393 Educ. L. Rep. 794 (N.Y. App. Div. 2021).
⁶¹ Pine Bluff Sch. Dist. v. Ace Am. Ins. Co., 984 F.3d 583, 385 Educ. L. Rep. 129 (8th Cir. 2020).
⁶² eScholar LLC v. Neb. Dept. of Educ., 497 F. Supp. 3d 414, 389 Educ. L. Rep. 70 (D. Neb. 2020).

fraud against the district and several board members concerning the administration of its National School Lunch Program. The terminated attorney was eventually cleared on all charges and sued the district for breach of his employment contract. The county court found for the terminated attorney but did not include the award of prejudgment interest. The appellate court found that the contact at issue did not contain language from the Rules of Professional Conduct that would have supported the district's action and that the attorney was entitled to both prejudgment wages and interest.[63] A wind turbine was installed on an Ohio school district's property, with a contract that obligated the district to purchase energy from the wind turbine company at a fixed rate. Several years after the installation, the turbine was struck by lightning and rendered inoperable. The district and the turbine company agreed that the strike constituted an act of nature. The company did not remove the inoperable turbine promptly, as was indicated in the contract, and the district sued. A required mediation process was initiated, but the company halted its participation. The appellate court reversed a lower court decision granting dismissal of the company's motion. The county district court found that the school district fulfilled its contractual obligation by initiating the required mediation during the one-year limitations period.[64] In New York, another case arose as a by-product of the pandemic. A bus company's claim of coverage under an all-risk commercial property insurance policy was denied. The governor's executive order closing all in-person schools resulted in a "loss of market" which was specifically listed as an exclusion in the policy.[65]

Property Rights and Use of Property

In Utah and Indiana, two cases involved eminent domain. A landowner sold his property to a school district when he was told that if he did not sell, the district would initiate an eminent domain lawsuit. Approximately ten years later, the district determined that it would not use the property and sold it to a property developer. The original owner sued the district for violation of his statutory right of

---

[63] Nelson v. Elizabeth Bd. of Educ., 246 A.3d 802, 388 Educ. L. Rep. 882 (N.J. Super. Ct. App. Div. 2021).
[64] Ada Exempted Vill. Sch. Dist. Bd. of Educ. v. Ada Wind, LLC, 157 N.E.3d 232, 383 Educ. L. Rep. 1105 (Ohio Ct. App. 2020).
[65] Visconti Bus Serv., LLC v. Utica Nat. Ins. Grp., 142 N.Y.S. 3d 903, 389 Educ. L. Rep. 435 (N.Y. Sup. Ct. 2021).

first refusal. A lower court dismissed his suit, finding that the original discussions about eminent domain did not rise to a "threat of condemnation" and the Court of Appeals of Utah affirmed.[66] [It should be noted that this case was subsequently reversed and remanded in 2022.][67] The Indiana case involved a dispute between a school district and the children who inherited a property after their mother's death. The property was adjacent to existing school property that housed both an elementary school and a middle school. The enrollment growth of the district was documented by planning boards and an architectural firm. After considering several options, the district determined that the construction of a new middle school was the best solution and that it should be built on the property adjacent to the then-current middle school. Negotiations with the heirs for the sale of the property were unsuccessful and the district filed a complaint of condemnation. A county court approved the appropriation of the property and the heirs appealed. The Court of Appeals of Indiana held that the school district documented a present need, not a future or speculative need and that the appropriation by eminent domain was within its authority.[68]

In New York City, a private company planned to establish a school on the second floor of a commercial building and entered into a lease contract with the building's owner. The tenant sued the landlord for a list of failures, including fraudulent concealment, conditions on the first floor that made the operation of a school on the second floor nonviable, interference with business relations, and actual and constructive eviction. A county court denied the landlord's motion for partial summary judgment. However, the appellate court reversed and remanded, finding that the tenant should have been aware of the first-floor conditions as a matter of public record, that the tenant did not establish any of the claims in his complaint, and that the contract could not be reformed.[69] A community center proposed a day school and camp but needed deferential zoning treatment to do so on the property it wished to use. The zoning board denied the zoning request and the community center challenged the decision with an amended petition. The county court denied the amended petition, thereby dismissing the case. The

---

[66] Cardiff Wales LLC v. Washington Cnty. Sch. Dist., 483 P.3d 1262, 388 Educ. L. Rep. 966 (Utah Ct. App. 2021).
[67] Cardiff Wales LLC v. Washington Cnty. Sch. Dist., 511 P.3d 1155, 404 Educ. L. Rep. 270 (Utah 2022).
[68] Krause-Franzen Farms, Inc. v. Tippecanoe Sch. Corp., 173 N.E.3d 694, 394 Educ. L. Rep. 1059 (Ind. Ct. App. 2021).
[69] Intern. Dev. Inst., Inc. v. Westchester Plaza, LLC, 149 N.Y.S.3d 3, 393 Educ. L. Rep. 398 (N.Y. App. Div. 2021).

community center's appeal to the Supreme Court, Appellate Division, was unsuccessful with the final decision that the community center's proposal was for neither religious nor educational use, so it did not qualify for deferential zoning.[70]

Open Records and Open Meetings

In five cases dealing with transparency issues in school governance, the first was decided by the Ohio Supreme Court while the others were decided in lower state courts. In 2019, Connor Betts killed nine people and injured 27 others in a shooting in Dayton, Ohio. He was shot and killed by police. Within hours of the shooting, news agencies requested student records for Betts from the school district where he graduated in 2013. The district through its superintendent and custodian of records, declined to produce the records, relying on both provisions of Ohio law and the Family Education Records and Privacy Act (FERPA). The Second District Court of Appeals denied the news agencies' writ of mandamus. On appeal, the state's Supreme Court affirmed the lower court's decision, finding that Ohio's Public Records Act (PRA) protected the records of adult students, even deceased former students. The issue of whether FERPA should apply was not further examined.[71]

The State Court of Appeals in Indiana affirmed a decision by a lower court where a television station sought an order to compel a district to produce the discipline records related to the paid administrative leave of a teacher. The point of law argued was whether there is a difference between a factual basis and a fact-based account. The district released a generic description of the policy that the teacher violated, but the television station reporter argued that a factual basis required a name and a specific incident report. Both courts accepted the personnel-file exception to the Access to Public Records Act.[72] [It should be noted that the Supreme Court of Indiana reversed this decision in 2022.] In Pennsylvania, an altercation between a student and a parent was captured on surveillance video. An open records request for the video from a television reporter was declined by the district because it was a

---

[70] Sid Jacobson Jewish Cmty. Ctr., Inc. v. Zoning Bd. of Appeals of Inc. Vill. of Brookville, 144 N.Y.S. 3d 54, 390 Educ. L. Rep. 389 (N.Y. App. Div. 2021).
[71] State *ex rel.* Cable News Network, Inc. v. Bellbrook-Sugarcreek Local Schs., 170 N.E.3d 748, 392 Educ. L. Rep. 941 (Ohio 2020).
[72] WTHR-TV v. Hamilton Se. Sch. Dist., 167 N.E.3d 301, 389 Educ. L. Rep. 932 (Ind. Ct. App. 2021).

protected education record under FERPA. The state's Office of Open Records overruled the school district's decision, and a county court affirmed the OOR on appeal. The Commonwealth Court affirmed the decision but the district's final appeal to the state Supreme Court resulted in a granted in part decision, with remand instructions to remove all personally identifiable information from the video before its release.[73] The New York City Department of Education received a request for five years of records concerning open records requests that the department denied because of the absence of a reasonable description; that included a reference to "needle in a haystack;" that referenced either of two key open records decisions; and those that referenced a specific advisory opinion. In addition, all affidavits that were provided as examples of how requests were found to be lacking sufficient description were requested. On the denial of the request, the original requestor appealed to a county court which upheld the department's decision. In the last appeal, the decision to deny due to lack of a reasonable description was affirmed by the Supreme Court, Appellate Division.[74]

An open meetings conflict in New Jersey involved a board's decision to hold a resolution certifying tenure charges against an employee in a closed meeting. The employee sued, claiming a violation of the notice provisions of the Open Public Meetings Act. The county court granted the employee's motion for summary relief, but the district's appeal overturned the county court's decision. The opinion recognized the inherent conflict between the "shall not be discussed at a public meeting" provision in personnel law and an employee's right to demand consideration in public. The decision concluded that discussion of personnel issues is one of the exceptions to the Open Public Meetings Act.[75]

Student Residency and District Transfer

After moving to a new home address, a family received mail from the school district that was intended for a different family. One piece of mail indicated that the different family had a son who was attending school in the district in violation of the district's residency

---

[73] Cent. Dauphin Sch. Dist. v. Hawkins, 253 A.3d 820, 393 Educ. L. Rep. 382 (Pa. Commw. Ct. 2021).

[74] Aron Law, PLLC v. N.Y.C. Dept. of Educ., 146 N.Y.S.3d 7, 391 Educ. L. Rep. 355 (N.Y. App. Div. 2021).

[75] Simadiris v. Paterson Pub. Sch. Dist., 245 A.3d 276, 387 Educ. L. Rep. 815 (N.J. Super. Ct. App. Div. 2021).

requirements. The parent who lived in the home notified the district that the nonresident student should be ejected from the district's schools. She also spoke at board meetings on the issue and continued her objection to the student's attendance for a year. The nonresident student was finally ejected from the school district. The plaintiff then sued the district for retaliation for her speech in violation of protected First Amendment rights, citing a list of incidents where her child was not given appropriate recognition for successful competition or where she was not given appropriate or timely parental information. The court granted the school district's motion to dismiss, noting that the plaintiff-parent was given ample opportunity to amend the errors in her original complaint concerning timelines, the need for a statement of harm, and other procedural problems.[76]

A school district in Ohio lobbied for and received a legislative rider concerning fast-track district transfer that was attached to the state's budget bill. The rider provided a new mechanism for schools to move all property and attendance zones from one district system to another. The relinquishing district successfully argued that the new law that had been attached to the budget bill was a violation of Ohio's one-subject rule concerning the construction of legislation and also violated equal protection and due process protections.[77]

---

[76] Morales v. Valley Stream Union Free Sch. Dist. 24, 527 F. Supp. 3d 470, 395 Educ. L. Rep. 291 (E.D.N.Y. 2021).

[77] Plain Local Sch. Dist. Bd. of Educ. v. DeWine, 486 F. Supp. 3d 1173, 386 Educ. L. Rep. 760 (S.D. Ohio 2020).

Conclusion

This year, constitutional issues appeared in litigation in systemic governance, but issues related to board operation and authority dominated. Charter school litigation covered a significant range of topics that reflect many of the issues other public schools face. Funding, finance, taxation, and other issues related to resource acquisition and management continued to provide material for education litigation. Localized governance issues were less prominent this year than in past years but remained varied in the issues covered across competitive bidding, school construction, and breach of contract. Public records laws were relatively active in the courts again this year, although there was only one case from open meetings law. Ultimately, school governance, while it is about systems, laws, and regulation, is primarily about the relationships among interested parties in public education.

Alphabetical List of Cases

A.H. ex rel. Hester v. French
Acad. for Positive Learning, Inc. v. Sch. Bd. of Palm Beach Cnty.
Ada Exempted Vill. Sch. Dist. Bd. v. Ada Wind, LLC
Archer v. Rockwood Area Sch. Dist.
Aron Law, PLLC v. N.Y.C. Dept. of Educ.
Augustine v. City of N.Y.
Baird v. Mason Classical Acad., Inc.
Bd. of Educ. of E. Newark in Cnty. of Hudson v. Harris
BG Nat. Plumbing & Heating, Inc. v. N.Y.C. Sch. Constr. Auth.
Blankenship v. Franklin Cnty. Collector
C.R. v. Eugene Sch. Dist. 4J
Campbell v. City of Gardendale
Cardiff Wales LLC v. Washington Cnty. Sch. Dist.
Cent. Dauphin Sch. Dist. v. Hawkins
City of Woonsocket v. RISE Prep Mayoral Acad.
Clerveaux v. E. Ramapo Cent. Sch. Dist.
Coble v. Lake Norman Charter Sch., Inc.
Core Constr. Servs., LLC v. Div. of Admin., Dept. of Facility Planning and Control
D.S. v. Positive Behavior Support Consulting and Psychological Resources, P.C.
Dallas Cent. Appraisal Dist. v. Int'l Am. Educ. Fed'n Inc.
Danville Christian Acad., Inc. v. Beshear
Davis v. Detroit Pub. Schs. Cmty. Dist.
Douglas Cnty. Sch. Dist. No. 10 v. Tribedo, LLC
eScholar LLC v. Neb. Dept. of Educ.
Ex parte LED Corporations, Inc.
Fann v. Arizona
Foster v. Sunflower Cnty. Consol. Sch. Dist.
Franzen v. Atlanta
Friends of Maple Grove, Inc. v. Merrill Area Common Pub. Sch. Dist.
Fuhrman v. Mailander
Hilsenrath ex rel. C.H. v. Sch. Dist. of Chathams
Houchens v. Beshear
In re Coatesville Area School Dist.
In re Dominguez
In re Interrogatory on House Bill 21-1164 Submitted by Colo. Gen. Assembly
In re Renewal Application of TEAM Acad. Charter Sch.
Intern. Dev. Inst., Inc. v. Westchester Plaza, LLC

John P. Sanfilippo & Sons, Inc. v. Rickert
Kinder Morgan SACROC, LP v. Scurry Cnty.
King v. Bd. of Educ. of City Sch. Dist. of City of New York
Krause-Franzen Farms, Inc. v. Tippecanoe Sch. Corp.
Lansingburgh Cent. Sch. Dist. v. N.Y. State Educ. Dept.
Lathan Construction, LLC v. Webster Parish Sch. Bd. ex rel. Kennon
Lea v. TAL Educ. Group
Lincoln Mem'l Acad., Inc. v. Manatee Cnty. Sch. Bd.
Mack-Cali Realty Corp. v. State
Maisto v. State
Mayo Clinic v. U.S.
Michigan v. DeVos
Molera v. Hobbs
Morales v. Valley Stream Union Free Sch. Dist. 24
Nelson v. Elizabeth Bd. of Educ.
North Slope Bor. v. State
Northwood Sch., Inc. v. Fletcher
Pa. Virtual Charter Sch. v. Dept. of Educ.
Peltier v. Charter Day Sch., Inc.
Pine Bluff Sch. Dist. v. Ace Am. Ins. Co.
Plain Local Sch. Dist. Bd. of Educ. v. DeWine
Propel Charter Schs. v. Dept. of Educ.
San Diegans for Open Gov't v. Fonseca
School Bd. of Volusia Cnty. v. Fla. East Coast Charter Sch.
Sid Jacobson Jewish Cmty. Ctr., Inc. v. Zoning Bd. of Appeals of Inc. Vill. of Brookville
Simadiris v. Paterson Pub. Sch. Dist.
Somerset Acad., Inc. v. Miami-Dade Cnty. Bd. of Cnty. Comm'rs
State *ex rel.* Cable News Network, Inc. v. Bellbrook-Sugarcreek Local Schs.
State *ex rel.* Horizon Sci. Acad. of Lorain, Inc. v. Ohio Dept. of Educ.
State *ex rel.* Ohio Atty. Gen. v. Burns
Turner v. Homestead Police Dept.
U.S. v. Islam
Visconti Bus Serv., LLC v. Utica Nat. Ins. Grp.North Carolina
William Penn Sch. Dist. v. Dept. of Educ.
WTHR-TV v. Hamilton Se. Sch. Dist.
Youngstown City Sch. Dist. Bd. of Educ. v. State

Cases by Jurisdiction

FEDERAL CASES

Second Circuit
A.H. *ex rel.* Hester v. French
Clerveaux v. E. Ramapo Cent. Sch. Dist.
Lea v. TAL Educ. Group

New York
Morales v. Valley Stream Union Free Sch. Dist. 24

Third Circuit

New Jersey
Hilsenrath *ex rel.* C.H. v. Sch. Dist. of Chathams
Pennsylvania
U.S. v. Islam

Fourth Circuit
Peltier v. Charter Day Sch., Inc.

North Carolina
Coble v. Lake Norman Charter Sch., Inc.

Sixth Circuit
Davis v. Detroit Pub. Schs. Cmty. Dist.
Houchens v. Beshear

Kentucky
Danville Christian Acad., Inc. v. Beshear
Ohio
Plain Local Sch. Dist. Bd. of Educ. v. DeWine

Eighth Circuit
Mayo Clinic v. U.S.
Pine Bluff Sch. Dist. v. Ace Am. Ins. Co.

Nebraska
eScholar LLC v. Neb. Dept. of Educ.

Ninth Circuit

California
Michigan v. DeVos

Eleventh Circuit
Turner v. Homestead Police Dept.

STATE & D.C. COURT CASES

Alabama
Campbell v. City of Gardendale

Alaska
Ex parte LED Corporations, Inc.
North Slope Bor. v. State

Arizona
Fann v. Arizona
Molera v. Hobbs

California
San Diegans for Open Gov't v. Fonseca

Colorado
In re Interrogatory on House Bill 21-1164 Submitted by Colo. Gen. Assembly

Florida
Acad. for Positive Learning, Inc. v. Sch. Bd. of Palm Beach Cnty.
Baird v. Mason Classical Acad., Inc.
Lincoln Mem'l Acad., Inc. v. Manatee Cnty. Sch. Bd.
School Bd. of Volusia Cnty. v. Fla. East Coast Charter Sch.
Somerset Acad., Inc. v. Miami-Dade Cnty. Bd. of Cnty. Comm'rs

Georgia
Franzen v. Atlanta

Illinois
John P. Sanfilippo & Sons, Inc. v. Rickert

Indiana
Krause-Franzen Farms, Inc. v. Tippecanoe Sch. Corp.
WTHR-TV v. Hamilton Se. Sch. Dist.

Louisiana
Core Constr. Servs., L.L.C. v. Div. of Admin., Dept. of Facility Planning and Control
Lathan Construction, LLC v. Webster Parish Sch. Bd. *ex rel.* Kennon

Mississippi
Foster v. Sunflower Cnty. Consol. Sch. Dist.

Missouri
Blankenship v. Franklin Cnty. Collector

Nebraska
Douglas Cnty. Sch. Dist. No. 10 v. Tribedo, LLC

New Jersey
Bd. of Educ. of E. Newark in Cnty. of Hudson v. Harris
Fuhrman v. Mailander
Mack-Cali Realty Corp. v. State
Nelson v. Elizabeth Bd. of Educ.
In re Renewal Application of TEAM Acad. Charter Sch.
Simadiris v. Paterson Pub. Sch. Dist.

New York
Aron Law, PLLC v. N.Y.C. Dept. of Educ.
Augustine v. City of N.Y.
BG Nat. Plumbing & Heating, Inc. v. N.Y.C. Sch. Constr. Auth.
D.S. v. Positive Behavior Support Consulting and Psychological Resources, P.C.
Intern. Dev. Inst., Inc. v. Westchester Plaza, LLC
King v. Bd. of Educ. of City Sch. Dist. of City of New York
Lansingburgh Cent. Sch. Dist. v. N.Y. State Educ. Dept.
Maisto v. State
Northwood Sch., Inc. v. Fletcher
Sid Jacobson Jewish Cmty. Ctr., Inc. v. Zoning Bd. of Appeals of Inc. Vill. of Brookville
Visconti Bus Serv., LLC v. Utica Nat. Ins. Grp.North Carolina

Ohio
Ada Exempted Vill. Sch. Dist. Bd. of Educ. v. Ada Wind, LLC
State *ex rel.* Cable News Network, Inc. v. Bellbrook-Sugarcreek Local Schs.
State *ex rel.* Horizon Sci. Acad. of Lorain, Inc. v. Ohio Dept. of Educ.
State *ex rel.* Ohio Atty. Gen. v. Burns
Youngstown City Sch. Dist. Bd. of Educ. v. State

Oregon
C.R. v. Eugene Sch. Dist. 4J

Pennsylvania
Archer v. Rockwood Area Sch. Dist.
Cent. Dauphin Sch. Dist. v. Hawkins
In re Coatesville Area School Dist.
Pa. Virtual Charter Sch. v. Dept. of Educ.
Propel Charter Schs. v. Dept. of Educ.
William Penn Sch. Dist. v. Dept. of Educ.

Rhode Island
City of Woonsocket v. RISE Prep Mayoral Acad.

Texas
Dallas Cent. Appraisal Dist. v. Int'l Am. Educ. Fed'n Inc.
In re Dominguez
Kinder Morgan SACROC, LP v. Scurry Cnty.

Utah
Cardiff Wales LLC v. Washington Cnty. Sch. Dist.

Wisconsin
Friends of Maple Grove, Inc. v. Merrill Area Common Pub. Sch. Dist.

Chapter 2

SCHOOL EMPLOYMENT

Jeffrey C. Sun, J.D. Ph.D.[1]

Introduction	35
Professional Conduct	35
Civil Rights	36
Free Speech	36
Due Process	39
Employment Discrimination	41
Race, Ethnicity, and National Origin	41
Disability Discrimination	46
Age Discrimination	49
Pregnancy Discrimination	50
Sexual-Orientation Discrimination	50
Unspecified/Other Discrimination	51
Hostile Work Environment	51
Class Action	53
Vicarious Liability	53
Fees Determinations	54
Court-Related Issues	55
Evidentiary Standards	55
Jurisdiction	56
Waiver	57
Frivolous Litigation	58
Statute of Limitations	58

---

[1] Professor of Higher Education and Law, Distinguished University Scholar, Associate Dean for Innovation and Strategic Partnerships, and Director of the SKILLS Collaborative at the University of Louisville, Ky.

 Recusal 59
 Res Judicata 59
 Immunity 60
Tenure/Continued Employment 61
Employment Classifications 64
Workplace Safety 64
Workers Compensation 64
Whistleblower 65
Employment Termination 65
Compensation and Benefits 67
 Federal Claims 67
 State Claims 68
Conclusion 73
Alphabetical List of Cases 74
Cases by Jurisdiction 77

Introduction

This chapter summarizes 114 cases addressing school employment matters. The issues include matters of professional conduct; employee speech; due process; employment discrimination; class action certifications; vicarious liability; court fees; procedural matters such as jurisdiction, statute of limitations, and res judicata; tenure/continued employment; employee classifications; workplace safety; workers' compensation; whistleblower coverage; employment termination; and compensation/benefits.

Professional Conduct

In Connecticut, a principal alleged that the state board improperly revoked her initial educator and professional educator certificates after it was discovered that the administration at her school had cheated during statewide standardized testing.[2] The Connecticut state appellate court rejected the claim because there was sufficient evidence that she directly participated in the cheating, did nothing to stop it, and, as the principal, had responsibility for the cheating incident.

In Illinois, a state appellate court reiterated that, when reviewing a school board's termination decision, Illinois appellate courts must consider whether the board's factual findings were against the weight of the evidence and whether the facts provided a sufficient basis to terminate the plaintiff.[3] In that case, the plaintiff/teacher's employment claim failed because there was sufficient evidence supporting the finding that she cheated on standardized testing by opening a test booklet ahead of time. That evidence included testimony from a student-teacher and a student who observed the incident.

In Wyoming, teachers may be suspended or dismissed for a variety of reasons, including neglect of duty, failure to perform duties satisfactorily, and any other good or just cause relating to the educational process.[4] Here, the plaintiff/teacher was terminated after a physical incident during school involving a student, who

---

[2] Moulthrop v. Conn. State Bd. of Educ., 258 A.3d 126, 395 Educ. L. Rep. 360 (Conn. App. Ct. 2021).

[3] Longanecker v. E. Moline Sch. Dist. No. 37, 159 N.E.3d 466, 385 . 320 (Ill. App. Ct. 2020).

[4] Mirich v. State ex rel. Bd. of Trs. of Laramie Cnty. Sch. Dist. Two, 481 P.3d 627, 387 Educ. L. Rep. 356 (Wyo. 2021).

happened to be the teacher's daughter. The Wyoming Supreme Court found the termination reasonable because there was substantial evidence of "good or just cause relating to the educational process" for the dismissal.

Civil Rights

Free Speech

During this period, 12 employment cases primarily challenging an educator's speech asserting employee speech principles of public institutions emerged. Seven federal appellate court cases addressed public educator claims for free speech. For a public employee, including an educator at a public school, to prevail in a First Amendment protection case, the employee's speech must be on a matter of public concern, and the employee must be speaking as a private citizen.

In two cases, the Second Circuit found that educators in New York failed to meet the standard of asserting claims arising from matters of public concern. In the first, a teacher failed to allege that he was retaliated against for exercising his First Amendment rights because his statements contained in internal union grievances did not address a matter of public concern.[5] In another case, the Second Circuit concluded that, because the plaintiff's statements alleging discrimination were personal complaints or grievances not of public concern, they were not entitled to First Amendment protection.[6]

In a case from Texas, the Fifth Circuit heard the appeal of a board's HVAC system manager alleging he was terminated in violation of his First Amendment rights due to statements made during an internal investigation of the school district's finances.[7] The plaintiff's claim failed because the statements were made as part of his official duties, so the speech was not protected.

Likewise, two Sixth Circuit cases also addressed claims of public school educators who spoke on matters pursuant to their official duties. In one case on appeal from a Tennessee federal district court, the plaintiff, who was the school principal, alleged she was terminated for exercising her First Amendment rights based on

---

[5] Agosto v. N.Y.C. Dep't of Educ., 982 F.3d 86, 384 Educ. L. Rep. 627 (2d Cir. 2020).
[6] Curry-Malcolm v. Rochester City Sch. Dist., 835 F. App'x 623, 386 Educ. L. Rep. 629 (2d Cir. 2020).
[7] Hawkland v. Hall, 860 F. App'x 326, 395 Educ. L. Rep. 180 (5th Cir. 2021).

statements she made at a school board work session regarding a proposed school mascot change.[8] The principal's claim failed because the speech in question was within the scope of her job, so it was not protected. Next, the Sixth Circuit affirmed an Ohio federal district court's denial of the teacher's claims who, after expressing concerns about classroom discipline and control, had an altercation with a student leading to her being placed on administrative leave.[9] When officials reassigned the plaintiff to five periods of study-hall duty, an hour of counseling duties, and lunch duty, she unsuccessfully claimed that they violated her First Amendment free speech rights. The Sixth Circuit agreed that, because the teacher's speech was within the scope of her duties and not made as a private citizen, her claim lacked merit. In a third Sixth Circuit case on appeal from Ohio, the court affirmed the denial of a custodian's claim that he was dismissed in violation of the Fair Labor Standards Act (FSLA) and that his right to free speech was violated after he expressed concerns over working conditions.[10] Because the speech represented internal complaints about official duties and not matters of public concern, the court agreed that the board had a legitimate, nondiscriminatory reason for his dismissal that he failed to rebut as a pretext.

Finally, the Ninth Circuit faced an athletic coach's claim of free speech as a public employee.[11] In that case, the speech at issue involved prayer that occurred while the plaintiff was standing in the middle of the football field, players were required to stand next to him, and fans watched. Thus, the plaintiff/coach's First Amendment claim failed because he was not speaking as a private citizen. However, the U.S. Supreme Court later reversed the decision holding that the coach's prayer was private speech with a rationale that the school district's policy unduly burdened the public employee's rights under the First Amendment's Free Exercise Clause.

Four cases asserted an educator's speech rights at the federal district court level. In Rhode Island, a federal district court

---

[8] Davidson v. Arlington Cmty. Schs. Bd. of Educ., 847 F. App'x 304, 389 Educ. L. Rep. 756 (6th Cir. 2021).
[9] Bushong v. Delaware City Sch. Dist., 851 F. App'x 541, 391 Educ. L. Rep. 599 (6th Cir. 2021).
[10] Grant v. Gahanna-Jefferson Pub. Sch. Dist., 850 F. App'x 431, 391 Educ. L. Rep. 147 (6th Cir. 2021).
[11] Kennedy v. Bremerton Sch. Dist., 991 F.3d 1004, 388 Educ. L. Rep. 101 (9th Cir. 2021)

addressed a claim of speech retaliation in its analysis.[12] The plaintiff/teacher alleged she was terminated in retaliation for exercising her First Amendment rights of free speech and free association based on her statements regarding union involvement in developing the COVID-19 distance learning plan and her participation in the union. To succeed on a retaliation claim based on the right to free association, the plaintiff must show retaliation sufficient to deter a person of ordinary firmness from exercising his constitutional rights, and a link between the association and retaliation. Here, the plaintiff's free speech claim survived the motion to dismiss because she was speaking on a matter of public concern, her interest in the protected activity outweighed the school's interest in restricting her speech, and her speech was a substantial factor in her termination. The plaintiff's free association claim survived the motion to dismiss as well because she sufficiently pled that her association with the union resulted in retaliation by the school.

Similarly, in Michigan, the plaintiff, who was the school principal, alleged she was placed on administrative leave in violation of her First Amendment free speech, free petition, and free association rights, and that it was based on race discrimination because she is White. Plaintiff's race discrimination claim failed because she did not allege that she suffered an adverse employment decision.[13] However, the plaintiff's First Amendment claim survived the motion to dismiss because her speech alleging corruption and discrimination against her concerned public matters considering her status in the community as principal. In the same court, a coach also raised an issue of employee free speech as a public employee.[14] In that case, the federal district court ruled that, while the plaintiff/coach was speaking as a private citizen in filing a civil lawsuit and speaking to the press, the civil lawsuit was not protected because his speech concerned the school's failure to renew his contract and was not on a matter of public concern. His statements to the press concerning alleged sexual misconduct with underage students did rise to the level of public concern, but the plaintiff failed to produce evidence that his statements to the press were relevant

---

[12] Mullen v. Tiverton Sch. Dist., 504 F. Supp. 3d 21, 390 Educ. L. Rep. 917 (D.R.I. 2020).

[13] Blick v. Ann Arbor Pub. Sch. Dist., 516 F. Supp. 3d 711, 393 Educ. L. Rep. 216 (E.D. Mich. 2021).

[14] Jordan v. Stroughter, 520 F. Supp. 3d 892, 394 Educ. L. Rep. 221 (E.D. Mich. 2021).

to the decision not to hire him over a year later, so the claim did not survive.

When a principal in Washington alleged she was wrongfully terminated primarily based on free speech retaliation, a federal trial court in Washington rejected her claim because she spoke out on a matter of public concern about possible violations of the FLSA in her capacity as a public employee rather than as a private citizen.[15] The court did allow the principal's disability discrimination claim to proceed because a question of fact existed whether she was covered by a state law on disability.

Only one case involving employee speech took place at the state level. A California state appellate court, considering a claim under the anti-SLAPP statute as a Strategic Lawsuit Against Public Participation, outlined that the defendant first bears the burden of establishing the challenged claim arises from a protected activity, or an activity underlying or forming the basis of the claim.[16] If the defendant succeeds, the burden then shifts to the plaintiff to establish a probability of success. Here, the plaintiff/teacher's discrimination and retaliation allegations were based on the district's decisions to reassign then terminate him, not on the investigation or any communications made during the investigation. Thus, the court reversed the dismissal of the plaintiff's claims under the anti-SLAPP statute because the district's decisions to place the plaintiff on leave and to terminate him are not protected activities under the statute.

Due Process

In 2021, five judicial opinions rested heavily on employee-based due process claims against public schools. The first of four federal cases evaluating the due process rights of public school employees arose in Kentucky, where a federal trial court ruled that the public educator's due process rights were not violated by the school district's decision for nonrenewal of employment.[17] The court explained that to state a successful due process claim, the plaintiff must show that the employee had a property or liberty interest in their continued employment. Here, the plaintiff/instructor was a

---

[15] Blackman v. Omak Sch. Dist., 466 F. Supp. 3d 1172, 383 Educ. L. Rep. 225 (E.D. Wash. 2020).
[16] Verceles v. L.A. Unified Sch. Dist., 278 Cal. Rptr. 3d 246, 390 Educ. L. Rep. 364 (Cal. Ct. App. 2021).
[17] Fisher v. Fletcher, 500 F. Supp. 3d 621, 390 Educ. L. Rep. 213 (E.D. Ky. 2020).

"volunteer" as opposed to an employee, so the plaintiff had no property interest in her continued employment.

With a slightly different issue, the federal trial court in Massachusetts also examined due process rights, which may concern either a property or liberty interest. Here, the plaintiff/teacher alleged that he was deprived of a property interest in his job and a liberty interest (i.e., reputation and professional status), so he was entitled to due process.[18] However, the court found that the plaintiff failed to sufficiently allege a property or liberty interest, so his due process claim failed. The court explained that the employee, who in this case was unwilling to follow the grievance procedures laid out in the collective bargaining agreement, had not met the general exhaustion requirement of administrative remedies or proceedings within the system.

In Pennsylvania, a federal trial court reaffirmed that due process claims may be brought for deprivation of a liberty or property interest.[19] Here, the plaintiff, who was a tenured teacher, alleged that he was constructively discharged without due process over statements he made, but his due process claim failed because he was suspended with pay and given an explanation of the evidence, which satisfied his property interest in continued public employment. The plaintiff's liberty interest in his reputation claim failed as well because the principal was entitled to qualified immunity.

In the Northern District of Illinois, a federal court examined the doctrinal rule that to prove a due process violation in a constructive discharge claim, the plaintiff must show that the defendant engaged in harassing behavior considered sufficiently severe or pervasive so much so that it alters the conditions of employment.[20] Here, the plaintiff/teacher alleged that the defendants falsely accused her of making negative comments about the principal, falsely told staff and the public that she went on leave due to pregnancy, changed her performance evaluation process and cycle, took away her keys and access to the district's network, and otherwise shunned and ostracized the plaintiff. The court found these events sufficient to allege due process violations under the constructive discharge theory

---

[18] Yourga v. City of Northampton, 474 F. Supp. 3d 408, 384 Educ. L. Rep. 260 (D. Mass. 2020).

[19] Suniaga v. Downingtown Area Sch. Dist., 504 F. Supp. 3d 430, 390 Educ. L. Rep. 932 (E.D. Pa. 2020).

[20] Smoler v. Bd. of Educ. for W. Northfield Sch. Dist. #31, 524 F. Supp. 3d 794, 394 Educ. L. Rep. 881 (N.D. Ill. 2021).

because her employer made her workplace conditions so intolerable, she had to resign.

Finally, in 2021, only one state court addressed a school employee due process case. A Georgia appellate court case ruled that the Georgia Fair Dismissal Act grants public employees fair notice, a meaningful opportunity to be heard, and an opportunity to be heard by a tribunal possessing some academic expertise and apparent impartiality.[21] Here, the defendant/teacher alleged she was terminated without proper due process because no tribunal was appointed. However, the court held that the Georgia Fair Dismissal Act applies to state level decisions offering a tribunal, and if this case had a tribunal, it would have been advisory to the local school board, which acted on the termination, not the state. In other words, the local board was not required to offer the same levels of due process as outlined under the Georgia Fair Dismissal Act.

Employment Discrimination

Race, Ethnicity, and National Origin

Thirteen cases presented issues in which the prevailing legal claim centered on school employment discrimination based on race, ethnicity, and/or national origin discrimination. One strand of these cases examines the circumstantial nature of these cases. Specifically, when there is no direct evidence of discrimination, the plaintiff bears the burden of establishing a prima facie case showing of discrimination, then the burden shifts to the defendant to provide a legitimate, nondiscriminatory reason. If the defendant does so, the burden shifts back to the plaintiff to show that the defendant's offered reason is pretext.

Three of these cases came from the Second Circuit. In one case on appeal from the Connecticut district court, the plaintiff/teacher alleged that she was terminated based on her race (Caucasian) and points to a few stray remarks by the principal as evidence.[22] However, the plaintiff's race discrimination claim failed because she did not sufficiently allege that she suffered the adverse employment action (i.e., termination) as a result of race discrimination. The case also addressed a hostile environment claim that was dismissed

---

[21] Rabun Cnty. Bd. of Educ. v. Randel, 864 S.E.2d 160, 396 Educ. L. Rep. 338 (Ga. Ct. App. 2021).
[22] Langlois v. Hartford Bd. of Educ., 831 F. App'x 548, 384 Educ. L. Rep. 756 (2d Cir. 2020).

based on a lack of evidentiary pleading. In another Second Circuit case arising from a New York district court, the federal district court had ruled that the teacher/plaintiff failed to demonstrate an adverse employment action.[23] In that case, the plaintiff/teacher alleged that she was given a negative evaluation under irregular circumstances, placed on an improvement plan, reassigned from a classroom to a cart, excluded from a master teaching program, removed as English Department chair, assigned to teach tenth grade while her cohorts moved on to eleventh, and passed over for an opportunity to teach Advanced English; further, the plaintiff alleged that, when she complained to the principal about this negative treatment, he agreed that her colleagues were intimidated because she was a Black woman, and stated that he was intimidated by her too. Because a jury could reasonably conclude that at least some of these acts constituted adverse employment actions because of race discrimination, the Second Circuit held that her claim survived the defendant's motion for summary judgment. In a third opinion, on appeal from a New York district court, the Second Circuit considered municipality liability for discrimination under § 1983, which requires the plaintiff to show that the discriminatory conduct occurred pursuant to municipal policy or custom.[24] Here, the plaintiff, a former teacher, alleged that he was terminated in retaliation for exercising his First Amendment rights and based on his race as an African American. He supported these allegations by alleging that the defendants targeted African American teachers who spoke out, often resulting in termination, while non-African Americans received lesser sanctions for similar conduct. According to the federal appellate court, the plaintiff failed to identify a formal policy of retaliation or disparate treatment, and his allegations about African American males engaging in certain speech were too conclusory to survive his discrimination claims.

In a Fifth Circuit case on appeal from Texas, the plaintiff, who in this case was a school principal, alleged that her contract was not renewed because of race discrimination as an African American, sex discrimination as a female, and age discrimination as a 55-year-old employee.[25] Plaintiff's race discrimination claim failed because the

---

[23] Carter v. Syracuse City Sch. Dist., 850 F. App'x 22, 391 Educ. L. Rep. 120 (2d Cir. 2021).
[24] Green v. Dept. of Educ. of City of N.Y., 16 F.4th 1070, 396 Educ. L. Rep. 56 (2d Cir. 2021).
[25] Ross v. Judson Indep. Sch. Dist., 993 F.3d 315, 388 Educ. L. Rep. 551 (5th Cir. 2021).

evidence showed she was treated the same as similarly situated individuals of other racial classes; her sex discrimination claim failed because she was replaced by three women; and lastly, her age discrimination claim failed because the school provided other, legitimate reasons for nonrenewal. In another Fifth Circuit case arising from Texas, the plaintiff, a district employee serving most recently as the Title I liaison, alleged she was discriminated against based on ethnicity as an Hispanic/Latinx person and retaliated against for exercising her First Amendment rights.[26] Plaintiff's ethnicity-based discrimination claim failed because her pleadings did not demonstrate how she was treated differently based on her heritage or ethnicity, and her First Amendment claim failed because she was not speaking on a public matter, so her speech was not protected.

In a Seventh Circuit case on appeal from Illinois, the plaintiff, who was most recently a library assistant, alleged racial discrimination based on her African American identity and age discrimination based on her age of 62 after being laid off.[27] The plaintiff's position was eliminated for budgetary reasons and was never filled by anyone of any race or age. Given the layoff rationale and non-filling of the position, she failed to allege that the school's non-continuation of her employment, even for other positions, was pretext for discrimination. The Seventh Circuit also reviewed an Illinois case addressing Title VII, under which an employer cannot fire or otherwise discriminate against a person based on race in regard to compensation, terms, conditions, or privileges of employment, nor can an employer limit, segregate, or classify employees or applicants in a way that would deprive them of employment opportunities based on race.[28] The plaintiffs, including a teachers' union and a class of African American teachers and paraeducators, alleged disparate treatment and disparate impact based on racial discrimination against African Americans following layoffs where 40% of laid-off union members were African American despite only making up 30% of the union as a whole. In this case, the plaintiffs' claims failed. Although the plaintiffs showed that layoffs disparately impacted African Americans, they failed to show a less

---

[26] Wright v. Arlington Indep. Sch. Dist., 834 F. App'x 897, 386 Educ. L. Rep. 160 (5th Cir. 2020).
[27] Chatman v. Bd. of Educ. of City of Chi., 5 F.4th 738, 393 Educ. L. Rep. 41 (7th Cir. 2021).
[28] Chicago Tchrs. Union v. Bd. of Educ. of the City of Chi., 14 F.4th 650, 395 Educ. L. Rep. 135 (7th Cir. 2021).

discriminatory alternative to the layoffs or that the layoffs were based on intentional discrimination.

On appeal from a federal district court in Georgia, the Eleventh Circuit presents another race discrimination case from a principal. In that case, the plaintiff, who was a school principal at the time, failed to state a claim for race discrimination based on his African American identity because he did not adequately allege that the school's non-discriminatory reasons were implausible or inconsistent so as to support a finding that they are a pretext for discrimination.[29] Specifically, he was replaced by someone of the same race, though not the same sex, and did not identify any similarly situated comparators. Additionally, the plaintiff did not deny the defendant's legitimate, nondiscriminatory reasons for his termination. The plaintiff also failed in his sex discrimination claim as a male principal. He failed to contest the proffered reasons for his termination (e.g., unprofessional email, failure to conduct formal observations of all teacher evaluations, school's performance with excessive numbers of out-of-school suspensions, his rating of "needs improvement"), but instead, the court concluded that the former principal largely faced quarrels and the lawsuit was simply an attempt to excuse the principal's misconduct. By contrast, in another Eleventh Circuit case from Florida, the court addressed race-based employment discrimination where the plaintiff, this time an assistant principal, alleged that his contract was not renewed based on race discrimination as a White educator.[30] The outcome of this case is different from the other Eleventh Circuit cases. This court found in favor of the plaintiff because the defendants offered the plaintiff a recommendation for the same type of job at a school with a different racial composition, and because the nonrenewal was at odds with the positive performance evaluations that the plaintiff, as assistant principal, had previously received by the school leadership. Therefore, a reasonable jury could conclude the school acted based on race. A third Eleventh Circuit case from Alabama involved similarly situated comparators. The plaintiffs, two White security guards, unsuccessfully sued the district for race discrimination.[31] The two plaintiffs – one male and one female – also asserted claims

---

[29] Ward v. Troup Cnty. Sch. Dist., 856 F. App'x 225, 393 Educ. L. Rep. 189 (11th Cir. 2021).

[30] Lewis v. Sch. Bd. of Palm Beach Cnty., Fla., 850 F. App'x 674, 391 Educ. L. Rep. 151 (11th Cir. 2021).

[31] Earle v. Birmingham Bd. of Educ., 843 F. App'x 164, 388 Educ. L. Rep. 625 (11th Cir. 2021).

of sex discrimination, but those claims also failed. The plaintiffs did not identify a similarly situated comparator who was treated more favorably to justify either of their claims.

In addition to the Circuit Courts of Appeals cases above, three federal district courts heard issues of race discrimination. In North Carolina, an African American teacher in a public school alleged that her reassignment and the non-renewal of her employment contract were based on racial discrimination and that the school retaliated against her for her claims of racial discrimination.[32] However, the federal district court in North Carolina found that the plaintiff's reassignment was not an adverse employment action, and the defendant offered legitimate, nondiscriminatory reasons for her termination, namely that she was not meeting her employer's legitimate expectations. Further, the plaintiff failed to show this reason was pretext for the alleged discrimination. Another federal district court in North Carolina heard a case brought by a Black school cafeteria worker who was denied a promotion based on her race. The board allegedly hired a less-qualified, non-African American applicant for the position instead. In order to state a failure to promote claim based on discrimination, a plaintiff must show that she was a member of a protected class who applied to a position she was qualified for but was rejected under circumstances that suggest unlawful discrimination. Here, the federal trial court denied the defendant's motion to dismiss the plaintiff/cafeteria worker's claims because she plausibly alleged that, as a member of a protected class, she applied for and was denied a promotion that she was qualified for under circumstances supporting an inference of discrimination.[33]

In the Western District of Louisiana, the plaintiff, an African American, female district employee serving as the director of federal programs, alleged she was discriminated against based on race and sex over trivial internal decisions and her placement on paid administrative leave.[34] The plaintiff's claims failed because being placed on paid administrative leave is not an adverse employment action, and, regardless, the school district offered a legitimate, nondiscriminatory reason (that any adverse employment actions were due to an investigation into her misconduct which took place in

---

[32] Cole v. Wake Cnty. Bd. of Educ., 494 F. Supp. 3d 338, 388 Educ. L. Rep. 696 (E.D.N.C. 2020).

[33] Stevens v. Cabarrus Cnty. Bd. of Educ., 514 F. Supp. 3d 797, 392 Educ. L. Rep. 669 (M.D.N.C. 2021).

[34] Hardison v. Skinner, 489 F. Supp. 3d 536, 387 Educ. L. Rep. 580 (W.D. La. 2020).

a federal program under the plaintiff's supervision). This case also addressed a challenge about due process; however, that claim was also dismissed.

Disability Discrimination

Disability discrimination in school employment often emerges based on state and federal laws protecting the rights of persons with disabilities. In a Seventh Circuit case from Illinois, the plaintiff, a school social worker, alleged that he was not promoted or given a position on an assessment team because of his disability.[35] The plaintiff's disability discrimination claim failed because the failure to promote him was not an adverse employment action, nor was its decision not to hire him for additional assessment teams that he was not fully qualified for.

In 2021, two employment discrimination cases based on disability in the Tenth Circuit weighed heavily on an analysis of the Americans with Disabilities Act (ADA) which bans discrimination based on disability when hiring, advancing, or dismissing employees. In the first of a pair of cases before it, the Tenth Circuit affirmed the Kansas district court's decision that, although a middle school teacher suffering from PTSD established a prima facie case, officials offered a legitimate, non-discriminatory reason for her termination and the burden shifted to her to show that their proffered reason was pretextual.[36] Although the teacher asserted how other, non-disabled colleagues were reprimanded or suspended, but not dismissed, for similar conduct, the court concluded that the plaintiff did not provide sufficient details alleging that she was similarly situated to the others. Likewise, in another Tenth Circuit case from New Mexico, the federal appellate court reiterated the rule that the ADA bars discrimination by employers against a person based on disability relating to application procedures, hiring, advancement, termination, employee compensation, job training, and other terms, conditions, and privileges of employment. In that case, the plaintiff, who was also a teacher, established issues of material fact as to whether she is regarded as having a disability because she provided evidence that she was diagnosed with PTSD, that her PTSD was not transitory and minor, and there is evidence

---

[35] Williams v. Bd. of Educ. of City of Chi., 982 F.3d 495, 384 Educ. L. Rep. 39 (7th Cir. 2020).
[36] Fisher v. Basehor-Linwood Unified Sch. Dist. No. 458, 851 F. App'x 828, 391 Educ. L. Rep. 606 (10th Cir. 2021).

the school knew of the PTSD.[37] Further, the plaintiff established a genuine issue of material fact as to whether her transfer was a demotion constituting adverse employment action; therefore, her disability discrimination claim survived.

In an Eleventh Circuit case from Georgia, the case applied both the ADA and Section 504 of the Rehabilitation Act in the public employment setting.[38] The general rule was that the ADA bars employers from discriminating based on disability relating to discharge and other terms, conditions, and privileges of employment. Likewise, the Rehabilitation Act bars federally funded programs from discriminating based on disability. In the case at issue, the plaintiff, a former middle school teacher, failed to assert her disability discrimination claim because the school offered a legitimate, nondiscriminatory reason for her termination—that the ADA does not require employers to allow dangerous behavior (e.g., former teacher allegedly threatened to kill herself and her son who was a student at the school, threatened school administrators, and consumed excessive amounts of anti-anxiety drug at school). Even if the behavior is the result of a disability, the plaintiff failed to show that the school's reason was pretext. This case also raised a Family Medical Leave Act claim arising from the teacher's non-renewal of employment, but again, the security risks would not support that claim either.

In a Washington D.C. federal district court case, a teacher's aide falsely registered her daughter as having residency in the District of Columbia so she could attend school there.[39] The federal trial court rejected her claim that the proffered reason for her dismissal was a pretext for disability discrimination because she failed to cast doubt on the reasonableness of the officials' belief that her having committed residency fraud warranted her dismissal. However, because the court was convinced that the board's re-investigation of the fraud claim, after nineteen-months of inactivity, constituted pretext for the discrimination claim, there was genuine issue of material fact as to whether the district's legitimate, non-retaliatory reason for the delayed investigation was pretextual.

In 2021, three cases centered primarily on state-based or defined territorial claims, including the District of Columbia Human Rights

---

[37] Neri v. Bd. of Educ. for Albuquerque Pub. Schs., 860 Fed. App'x 556, 395 Educ. L. Rep. 187 (10th Cir. 2021).
[38] Todd v. Fayette Cnty. Sch. Dist., 998 F.3d 1203, 390 Educ. L. Rep. 865 (11th Cir. 2021).
[39] Congress v. Dist. of Columbia, 514 F. Supp. 3d 1, 392 Educ. L. Rep. 634 (D.D.C. 2020).

Law. In the case addressing the District of Columbia Human Rights Act, the application of that law to a teacher who became disabled from the job was the central issue.[40] The D.C. appellate court ruled - a plaintiff may recover for failure to reasonably accommodate a disability if the complaint shows that the plaintiff has a disability and can perform the essential functions of her position with or without reasonable accommodation; if the plaintiff is successful, the burden shifts to the employer to show that it reasonably accommodated the plaintiff's disability. In this case, the plaintiff, a teacher, had been suffering from PTSD after being attacked by a student. The teacher could not perform the essential functions of her teaching job, even with reasonable accommodations. However, because there was reason to believe the plaintiff could return to work in a non-classroom position, the case was remanded to the Office of Human Rights to determine whether extended unpaid leave was a reasonable accommodation despite the plaintiff's request for reassignment.

In California, where a state appellate court encountered a case in which the plaintiff experienced "electromagnetic hypersensitivity" but the school district failed to accommodate her condition, and instead, retaliated against her in violation of the California Fair Employment and Housing Act.[41] In light of the allegations, the state appellate court drew on the rule that an employer cannot refuse to hire or discharge a person, nor can it discriminate against them in compensation, terms, conditions, or privileges of employment, based on physical disability. In that case, the plaintiff, a teacher in the district, alleged that the school discriminated against her based on and failed to accommodate her disability of electromagnetic sensitivity. Initially, the state trial court ruled in favor of the defendant/school district. On appeal, the plaintiff prevailed, having adequately pled her cause of action for failure to provide reasonable accommodation for her disability. The judgment on the alleged retaliation was affirmed.

In Michigan, a state appellate court emphasized that to show a violation of Michigan's Persons with Disabilities Civil Rights Act, the plaintiff must show that he is disabled, his disability is unrelated to his ability to perform his job duties, and he has been discriminated

---

[40] Turner v. D.C. Off. of Hum. Rts., 243 A.3d 871, 386 Educ. L. Rep. 396 (D.C. 2021).
[41] Brown v. L.A. Unified Sch. Dist., 275 Cal. Rptr. 3d 322, 387 Educ. L. Rep. 297 (Cal. Ct. App. 2021).

against in violation of the statute.[42] The plaintiff, who served as a school custodian, alleged he was discriminated against because of his ADHD and inability to read, but there is no evidence of anyone at the school ever refusing to read the plaintiff something upon request, the plaintiff never told the school he was disabled, and the plaintiff never requested an accommodation. At the end, the plaintiff's claim failed because he did not establish that the school's animosity towards him was related to his disability.

Age Discrimination

In 2021, the age discrimination cases within the school employment context often rested on a state claim and the Age Discrimination in Employment Act (ADEA). However, in the only case resting largely on federal law, a federal trial court in Utah acknowledged that under the ADEA, an employer cannot discriminate against employees who oppose age discrimination. The board ultimately dismissed its groundskeeper for refusing to fire two older coworkers because of their age.[43] The plaintiff's age discrimination claim survived the board's motion for summary judgment because he adequately alleged that he was subject to a materially adverse employment action due to his opposition to his employer's mandate, which he alleged amounted to age discrimination.

The two state law claims of age discrimination occurred in Minnesota and Missouri. A Minnesota appellate court found in favor for the complaining employee regarding age discrimination.[44] Under the Minnesota Human Rights Act, an employer cannot discriminate against a person based on age regarding hiring, tenure, compensation, terms, upgrading, conditions, facilities, or privileges of employment. Here, the plaintiff, a 57-year-old network technician who started in 1997, alleged that the school initiated several performance evaluations on him in less than a year when his last review took place more than two years prior, exaggerated his minor performance issues, placed him on an unachievable performance improvement plan (PIP) to cause resignation or termination, threatened termination for failing to comply with the unachievable

---

[42] Jewett v. Mesick Consol. Sch. Dist., 957 N.W.2d 377, 388 Educ. L. Rep. 950 (Mich. Ct. App. 2020).

[43] Johnson v. Salt Lake City Sch. Dist., 499 F. Supp. 3d 1126, 390 Educ. L. Rep. 100 (D. Utah 2020).

[44] Henry v. Indep. Sch. Dist. #625, 964 N.W.2d 667, 395 Educ. L. Rep. 411 (Minn. Ct. App. 2021).

PIP, reprimanded him more harshly than others, denied him a training session, and made comments that the department had problems because people were "too old." The court found this listing of actions sufficient to allege age discrimination by showing disparate treatment under the *McDonnell Douglas* framework.

By contrast, a Missouri appellate court applied the Missouri Human Rights Act, which bars an employer from discriminating against a person because of their age regarding compensation, terms, conditions, or privileges of employment.[45] In that case, the plaintiff, a school bus driver, alleged that students on her bus harassed her while driving, but she did not allege it was because of her age. Thus, the plaintiff's age discrimination claim failed because she did not present evidence sufficiently alleging her age was a contributing factor in the alleged harassment.

Pregnancy Discrimination

Under the New Jersey Law Against Discrimination, a plaintiff must establish a prima facie case of pregnancy discrimination by showing that she was pregnant, qualified, subject to adverse employment action, and there was a nexus between her pregnancy and the adverse employment action. Here, the plaintiff, an unmarried teacher at a faith-based school, was pregnant, but there were no issues with her performance.[46] Reversing an earlier order in favor of school officials, a state appellate court allowed her pregnancy discrimination claim to survive because the school could not base her dismissal solely on engaging in premarital sex.

Sexual-Orientation Discrimination

In 2021, one sexual orientation discrimination case emerged in a federal district court in Indiana against a Catholic school by its guidance counselor.[47] The plaintiff/guidance counselor alleged that she was terminated because of her same sex marriage. To plead sexual orientation discrimination under Title VII, the plaintiff must assert that the employer instituted a specific adverse employment action against the employee based on their sexual orientation. Here,

---

[45] Ickenroth v. Parkway Sch. Dist. C-2, 612 S.W.3d 247, 385 Educ. L. Rep. 402 (Mo. Ct. App. 2020).

[46] Crisitello v. St. Theresa Sch., 242 A.3d 292, 385 Educ. L. Rep. 812 (N.J. Super. Ct. App. Div. 2020).

[47] Starkey v. Roman Cath. Archdiocese of Indianapolis, Inc., 496 F. Supp. 3d 1195, 389 Educ. L. Rep. 140 (S.D. Ind. 2020).

the plaintiff/guidance counselor alleged that she was terminated because of her same-sex marriage. The plaintiff's sexual-orientation discrimination claim survived a motion for judgment on the pleadings because she adequately alleged that the school's environment was hostile toward homosexual students, faculty, and staff.

Unspecified/Other Discrimination

In 2021, one employment discrimination case within schools framed a rather unique claim. The Tenth Circuit noted an exception under Title VII for Indian tribes.[48] Here, the plaintiff, a school employee, alleged her employer discriminated against her under Title VII. However, the court held that her employer, a private corporation operating educational programs, was the Navajo Nation which constituted an "Indian tribe," so the exception to Title VII applied.

Hostile Work Environment

In 2021, five school-based employment cases claimed hostile work environment as the primary action at issue. In a case before the First Circuit from Rhode Island, a former school principal as the plaintiff brought a hostile work environment claim that included a wrongful retaliation claim.[49] For such case to prevail, the plaintiff must show that she engaged in protected conduct, suffered adverse employment action, and there was a causal connection between the protected conduct and the adverse employment action. Here, the female, African American plaintiff alleged that she was subjected to a hostile work environment as a result of her opinions on affirmative action. The plaintiff's claim failed because the school offered legitimate, non-discriminatory reasons for its actions.

Two cases emerged before the Second Circuit. In one of the cases, the central legal issue was a hostile environment allegedly arising to a constitutional violation under § 1983.[50] To succeed, the plaintiff must first establish a prima facie case of discrimination by showing she is a member of a protected class who is qualified for the position and suffered an adverse employment action, the circumstances of

---

[48] Jim v. Shiprock Assoc. Schs., Inc., 833 F. App'x 749, 385 Educ. L. Rep. 505 (10th Cir. 2020).
[49] Lima v. City of E. Providence, 17 F.4th 202, 396 Educ. L. Rep. 81 (1st Cir. 2021).
[50] Kunik v. N.Y.C. Dept. of Educ., 842 F. App'x 668, 388 Educ. L. Rep. 590 (2d Cir. 2021).

which support an inference of discrimination. Here, the plaintiff, a former public school teacher, alleged that she suffered an adverse employment action because the unsatisfactory performance review she received prevented her from getting to teach summer school or other optional work assignments. The court found that the unsatisfactory performance review did not result in an adverse employment action because the plaintiff had not applied to teach summer school or for additional work in the year she alleged discriminatory treatment, and she had not taught summer school in 10 years. Even if the school denied her those opportunities, the denial was insufficient to constitute a material loss of benefits; additionally, the plaintiff did not sufficiently allege that any adverse employment action was motivated by discrimination. Another case from the Second Circuit case highlighted that, in order to bring a successful § 1983 claim against a municipal entity, the plaintiff must allege that a violation occurred due to a municipal policy or custom.[51] A former teacher in New York alleged he was subject to a hostile work environment because of his Irish national origin in violation of his rights to equal protection. The former teacher's assertion that the board was deliberately indifferent by ignoring his complaint in the prior year failed because he failed to show that the outcome was anything other than bureaucratic inaction.

A federal trial court in South Carolina articulated the doctrinal rule that a Title VII hostile work environment showing requires the plaintiff to show there was unwelcome conduct based on her being a woman which was sufficiently severe or pervasive to alter the conditions of the plaintiff's employment and create an abusive work environment, and the conduct is imputable to the employer.[52] Here, the plaintiff, the former educational director of a prison school district, alleged that her employer was sometimes angry, confrontational, insulting, ridiculing, and berating, among other things. However, evidence shows that the employer treated all coworkers in a similar matter, so the plaintiff failed to establish that his conduct was sufficiently severe and pervasive.

In the sole state court case, a New York appellate court ruled that the plaintiff, who was a teacher, presented a viable hostile work

---

[51] O'Kane v. Plainedge Union Free Sch. Dist., 827 F. App'x 141, 383 Educ. L. Rep. 146 (2d Cir. 2020).
[52] Bouknight v. S.C. Dept. of Corrections, 487 F. Supp. 3d 449, 387 Educ. L. Rep. 180 (D.S.C. 2020).

environment claim based on sexual harassment.[53] That is, the pleadings survived the motion to dismiss because the teacher was repeatedly subjected to unwelcome sexual harassment that became physical at least once, and the defendants failed to investigate or take action after she reported the conduct.

Class Action

In 2021, one case addressed a class action issue. Prior to the appellate review, the district court, in conjunction with an appointed Special Master, had calculated class members' damages individually to reflect the possibility that (1) a class member would not have been appointed to a teaching position by the defendant even if they had passed the certification test required and (2) a class member would not have remained a teacher of the defendant through retirement or judgment.[54] Here, the plaintiffs, who were teachers in the district, successfully brought a class action alleging racial discrimination based on disparate impact of African American and Latinx identities in the certification test used. The court found that there was no abuse of discretion in the lower court's method of using individualized determinations to calculate backpay instead of a class wide pro-rata reduction.

Vicarious Liability

In 2021, one case rested on a vicarious liability claim in addressing a school employment matter. Under vicarious liability, an employer is liable for a tort committed by its employee if the employee is acting withing the course (i.e., time and place test) and scope (i.e., employment-related risk of injury test) of his employment at the time of the action. Here, the plaintiff, a student within the district, alleged that the school was liable for its janitor molesting and raping a special education student during school hours.[55] The Louisiana appellate court held that, because the assault occurred on school premises, during employment hours, and was reasonably

---

[53] Root v. Salamanca Cent. Sch. Dist., 145 N.Y.S.3d 691, 391 Educ. L. Rep. 340 (N.Y. App. Div. 2021).
[54] Munoz v. Bd. of Educ. of City Sch. Dist. of N.Y.C., 841 F. App'x 310, 388 Educ. L. Rep. 177 (2d Cir. 2021).
[55] Doe v. ABC Sch., 316 So.3d 1086, 391 Educ. L. Rep. 966 (La. Ct. App. 2020).

incidental to the janitor's employment duties, his actions were employment-related for vicarious liability purposes.

Fees Determinations

In 2021, two employment cases within the school context tackled questions of litigation-related fees. For instance, to award the defendant attorney fees in the plaintiff's Americans with Disabilities Act (ADA) suit, the court must find, at minimum, that after the claim was filed, circumstances changed to the extent that a reasonable person would conclude the claim was no longer viable. In a federal district court in Puerto Rico, the defendant moved to recover attorney fees under the ADA, but the court denied the motion because the plaintiff, a former school teacher, presented claims that were not clearly "unfounded, frivolous, or otherwise unreasonable."[56] Accordingly, the federal court noted that it could not reasonably conclude that the circumstances in this case changed following her deposition so as to make her ADA claim became meritless. Notably, the mere fact that she failed to establish a prima facie case does not automatically imply her suit was frivolous.

In Georgia, a state appellate court examined a challenge around arbitration fees.[57] Under the Federal Arbitration Act, arbitration agreements are valid, irrevocable, and enforceable unless there are grounds at law or in equity for revocation of any contract; any doubts in the arbitrability of an issue are resolved in favor of arbitration. In a case that started off as an employment discrimination challenge under Title VII, the appellate court concluded that the defendant/teacher's allegation regarding the fees charged for arbitration would be precluded from effectively vindicating her Title VII claims should be reheard. After considering how the defendant had not established that she actually had to pay the fees, the appellate court concluded that the trial court incorrectly applied the effective vindication defense.

---

[56] Lopez-Lopez v. Robinson Sch. Inc., 495 F. Supp. 3d 84, 388 Educ. L. Rep. 853 (D.P.R. 2020).

[57] Omnitech Inst., Inc. v. Norwood, 861 S.E.2d 145, 393 Educ. L. Rep. 883 (Ga. Ct. App. 2021).

Court-Related Issues

In 2021, 17 school-based employment cases centered around procedural issues regarding their outcomes. The procedural matters ranged from burden of proof standards, jurisdictional matters, res judicata, and waiver of rights.

Evidentiary Standards

While the standard of proof is a court-related matter, evidentiary rules are another court-related matter examining procedural determinations. In a federal appellate decision through the Fourth Circuit, on appeal from North Carolina, the court reviewed the lower court's decision on the admissibility of evidence for abuse of discretion. To be overturned, the lower court's decision must be arbitrary and irrational.[58] Here, it came out during discovery that the plaintiff, who was the school headmaster, misrepresented his credentials and employment history to the school during his recruitment, and the plaintiff argued that this evidence was inadmissible because it was more than a decade ago and not relevant. The lower court properly ruled that the evidence was relevant and, therefore, admissible.

In California, to state a breach of contract claim, it must be shown that a contract existed, the plaintiff performed or had an excuse for nonperformance, the defendant breached, and the breach resulted in damages to the plaintiff.[59] In this case, the plaintiff failed to offer evidence that additional efforts by the defendant would have resulted in higher sales. The Ninth Circuit ruled that the defendant made significant efforts to sell the plaintiff's courses, so the burden of proof was properly placed on the plaintiff for each element of his claim.

In cases involving the Public School Employees' Retirement Board, the party offering a fact bears the burden of proving that fact by a preponderance of the evidence.[60] That is, the party must show that the factual element is more probable than not to have occurred. Here, the plaintiff, a retired public school principal working in post-retirement as a charter school principal in the school district, was

---

[58] Benjamin v. Sparks, 986 F.3d 332, 386 Educ. L. Rep. 92 (4th Cir. 2021).
[59] Codding v. Pearson Educ., Inc., 842 F. App'x 70, 388 Educ. L. Rep. 198 (9th Cir. 2021).
[60] Lebron v. Pub. Sch. Employees' Ret. Bd., 245 A.3d 300, 387 Educ. L. Rep. 839 (Pa. Commw. Ct. 2020).

receiving the benefits of both his annuity and his salary. The court observed that he, as claimant, had to have a reasonable belief that his return to work must comply with the Retirement Code. Therefore, the plaintiff had the burden of proving that he reasonably believed that his return to work each school year was in compliance with the Retirement Code, then the burden shifted to the defendant to prove that the hiring company either did not exercise its judgment under the Retirement Code or that its judgment was not based on emergency or shortage of personnel. The case was vacated and remanded to make this determination.

Jurisdiction

Five cases raise jurisdictional issues within school employment claims. As a general rule, federal courts have jurisdiction over all civil actions that arise under the U.S. Constitution, federal laws, or treaties of the United States; they also have jurisdiction over state law claims that necessarily raise a federal issue that is actually disputed, substantial, and capable of resolution in federal court. One case arising out of Virginia involved a public school teacher bringing claims under the state constitution and state statutes following his termination. The Fourth Circuit ruled that the defendant's removal of the case to federal court was improper because the plaintiff/teacher did not raise any federal causes of action.[61] Earlier, a federal trial court in Virginia realized that no federal claims existed, questioning its jurisdiction over the case.[62] In this case, the plaintiff, a school teacher, brought claims under the Virginia Constitution, and the defendants attempted to remove the claims to federal court. The court found that the plaintiff's claim did not raise federal issues because he did not raise claims under Title IX, a federal law, and the Virginia Constitution claims did not necessarily raise federal issues. In light of these findings, the case could not be removed to federal court.

When appealing a denial of summary judgment on qualified immunity grounds, the court must accept that the evidence gives rise to factual disputes identified by the lower court, and the court can only review whether the version of those facts most favorable to the plaintiff's claim is sufficient to overcome qualified immunity. To that

---

[61] Vlaming v. West Point Sch. Bd., 10 F.4th 300, 394 Educ. L. Rep. 45 (4th Cir. 2021).
[62] Vlaming v. West Point Sch. Bd., 480 F. Supp. 3d 711, 385 Educ. L. Rep. 747 (E.D. Va. 2020).

end, a federal appellate court in the Fifth Circuit heard a case from Texas where the plaintiff was a student suing her teacher, among other individuals, after she attempted to make her recite the Pledge of Allegiance then retaliated against her when she refused.[63] The teacher moved for summary judgment based on qualified immunity which the federal district court denied, finding a genuine issue of material fact, so the teacher filed an interlocutory appeal; the Fifth Circuit denied this appeal for lack of jurisdiction.

According to a federal district court in New York, the general rule is that subject matter jurisdiction may be facial or fact-based, so long as it is shown affirmatively.[64] Also, jurisdiction cannot be made by merely drawing inferences from the pleadings favorable to the asserting party. Here, the plaintiff was a noncitizen teacher whose formerly approved "Immigrant Petition for Alien Workers" was revoked by U.S. Citizenship and Immigration Services, and her request to reopen was denied. The plaintiff/teacher's claim seeking judicial review was dismissed because the Immigration and Nationality Act deprived the district court of subject matter jurisdiction to review the U.S. Citizenship & Immigration Services substantive and discretionary decisions.

According to an Illinois appellate court, a plaintiff has standing when the claimed injury is distinct and palpable, fairly tracible to the defendant' actions, and substantially likely to be prevented or redressed by the requested relief.[65] Here, the plaintiffs, who were the local school council members, lacked standing to challenge the principal's suspension without pay because the Illinois School Code did not give them a right to protect the principal from dismissal, and because their alleged injuries could not be redressed.

Waiver

To consider whether an employment discrimination claim waiver was knowing and voluntary, courts consider the totality of the circumstances; factors include the clarity and specificity of release language, the plaintiff's education and business experience, the amount of time the plaintiff had to deliberate on the release before signing, whether the plaintiff knew or should have known her rights under the release, whether the plaintiff was encouraged to or

---

[63] Oliver v. Arnold, 3 F.4th 152, 391 Educ. L. Rep. 565 (5th Cir. 2021).
[64] Razi Sch. v. Cissna, 519 F. Supp. 3d 144, 393 Educ. L. Rep. 661 (E.D.N.Y. 2021).
[65] Beyer v. Bd. of Educ. of City of Chi., 160 N.E.3d 1086, 386 Educ. L. Rep. 440 (Ill. App. Ct. 2019).

did seek counsel, whether there was a chance for negotiation on the terms, and whether the consideration given for the waiver exceeds the benefits the employee was already entitled to by contract or law. Here, the plaintiff/teacher argued that she did not receive payment or any other benefit for the release of her claims so the last factor was not met; however, the defendant alleged that it promised the plaintiff it would not seek suspension of her teaching license, would tell future employment inquiries that she voluntarily resigned, and would make available to her copies of any in-service credits. The court found this to be adequate consideration, thus the plaintiff's waiver was valid.[66]

Frivolous Litigation

A federal court may impose sanctions against litigants who abuse the judicial process. Once a pattern of frivolous litigation has emerged, the district court may impose pre-filing injunctions. In a New York federal district court, the plaintiff, a former school employee, repeatedly alleged that she was discriminated against and ultimately terminated because of race and age, despite numerous warnings from the court.[67] Thus, the court held that the plaintiff was permanently enjoined from bringing any more pro se actions arising from her employment.

Statute of Limitations

During this period, three school employment cases contended with a statute of limitation concern. Under New York education law, there is a one-year statute of limitations. In New York, the state appellate court ruled that the plaintiff, a school bus driver who claimed First Amendment retaliation related to his March 2019 termination, met the statute of limitation.[68] The plaintiff's July 2019 motion for leave to serve the proposed petition/complainant was timely as the statute of limitations did not expire until March 2020.

Under Georgia law, public employees must bring retaliation claims within one year of discovering the retaliation or within three

---

[66] Miles v. Unified Sch. Dist. No. 500, Kansas City, Kan., 855 F. App'x 433, 393 Educ. L. Rep. 172 (10th Cir. 2021).
[67] Malcolm v. Ass'n of Supervisors and Adm'rs of Rochester, 532 F. Supp. 3d 114, 396 Educ. L. Rep. 103 (W.D.N.Y. 2021).
[68] Lilley v. Greene Cent. Sch. Dist., 134 N.Y.S.3d 503, 384 Educ. L. Rep. 978 (N.Y. App. Div. 2020).

years of the retaliation, whichever is earlier. According to a Georgia state appellate court, the statute of limitations on the plaintiff/teacher's Georgia Whistleblower Act claim began accruing on April 24, 2017, the date she was informed that her contract would not be renewed.[69] Because the plaintiff filed her complaint more than one year after April 24, 2017, her claims were time-barred.

Under Ohio law, a teacher may appeal her termination within thirty days of receipt of the notice for the termination. In an Ohio appellate case, the plaintiff/teacher's thirty-day window to file the appeal started when the plaintiff's attorney received notice of the final decision terminating her employment on September 20, 2019, but her notice of appeal was not filed until October 26, 2019.[70] Because there were thirty-six days between the plaintiff's receipt of the notice of termination and the filing of her appeal, her appeal was time-barred.

Recusal

Under Louisiana law, a judge should be recused when they are biased, prejudiced, or interested in the cause or its outcome, or if they are biased or prejudiced in favor of or against a party or a party's attorney or witness, to an extent they could not be fair and impartial.[71] Here, the plaintiff, who was a teacher in the district, brought a motion to recuse because the judge had represented the school board for twenty-four years prior to becoming a judge. The judge also presided over the criminal charges in this matter, which the plaintiff felt could taint his view of her evidence in this civil matter. The court found that the plaintiff was entitled to a hearing on her motion to recuse because she sufficiently alleged bias.

Res Judicata

In 2021, two cases examined the application of res judicata. The doctrine of res judicata precludes a plaintiff from bringing a suit when the action arises out of the same set of circumstances that have already been litigated. The Sixth Circuit determined that the

---

[69] Mimbs v. Henry Cnty. Schs., 857 S.E. 2d 286, 390 Educ. L. Rep. 406 (Ga. Ct. App. 2021).
[70] Vukovic-Burkhardt v. Dayton Bd. of Educ., 169 N.E. 3d 53, 390 Educ. L. Rep. 1227 (Ohio Ct. App. 2021).
[71] Wilson v. St. Landry Parish Sch. Bd., 311 So.3d 457, 388 Educ. L. Rep. 420 (La. Ct. App. 2020).

plaintiff, who worked as the supervisor of the district's online program, was barred by res judicata for a First Amendment case.[72] The rationale was because a Michigan court had already decided his defamation case on the merits, both actions involved the same parties, and the First Amendment issues could have been resolved in the defamation case.

A New York appellate court ruled that the plaintiff/employee's claim was barred by res judicata because he had already attacked in court the decision to give him a "U" rating and the refusal to let him rescind his resignation.[73]

Immunity

During this period, five cases examined qualified or sovereign immunity from lawsuits. Three cases applied state laws and two cases drew on general principles under federal law. To defeat qualified immunity under federal law, the plaintiff must show that the defendant violated another constitutional right and that the constitutional right was clearly established at the time of the violation. Here, the plaintiff/student alleged the assistant principal violated her equal protection rights under § 1983.[74] The federal district court in Colorado ruled that the assistant principal was not entitled to qualified immunity because the student adequately alleged how the assistant principal violated a constitutional right, and that constitutional right had been clearly established at the time of the violation.

Similarly, in Michigan, the plaintiffs' claim that the state waived immunity for their request for compensation failed after drawing on a federal analysis.[75] A state appellate court offered several reasons in concluding that the waiver did not take place. First, the federal Contracts Clause has not historically provided for damages. Second, the plaintiffs had alternative equitable claims they brought and recovered on. Third, there were no other circumstances supporting an award of damages for a Contracts Clause violation. Accordingly, the state was immune from the plaintiffs' damages claim.

---

[72] Codden v. Manistee Area Pub. Schs. Bd. of Educ., 842 Fed. App'x 985, 388 Educ. L. Rep. 616 (6th Cir. 2021).
[73] Miller v. Livanis, 137 N.Y.S.3d 15, 386 Educ. L. Rep. 430 (N.Y. App. Div. 2020).
[74] Doe v. Roaring Fork Sch. Dist., 510 F. Supp. 3d 971, 391 Educ. L. Rep. 759 (D. Colo. 2020).
[75] AFT v. State, 964 N.W.2d 113, 395 Educ. L. Rep. 396 (Mich. Ct. App. 2020).

The remaining cases focused on state laws. In Georgia, official immunity does not typically bar claims against state officers for injunctive and declaratory relief from the enforcement of unconstitutional laws, so long as the relief is only prospective, but suits for monetary damages and other retrospect relief are prohibited. In a Georgia appellate case, the plaintiff/teacher alleged that state and local officials violated Georgia's Fair Dismissal Act and sought relief in the form of a declaration about her termination and injunctive relief for reinstatement and backpay.[76] The plaintiff's claim for injunctive relief and reinstatement sought prospective relief, thus they were not barred by immunity, but her claim for backpay was barred.

In Missouri, the state recognizes official immunity as an affirmative defense, so public employees, such as those employed at public schools, are protected from liability for negligence for discretionary acts performed in the course of official duties. However, that protection does not extend to ministerial acts. Under the public duty doctrine in Missouri, public employees are not civilly liable for breaches of a duty owed to the general public, as opposed to an individual. In a Missouri appellate case, the defendant/teacher failed to demonstrate facts establishing his affirmative defense of official immunity or his argument that the public duty doctrine applied in a claim brought by the plaintiff/student after the defendant/teacher refused him restroom access.[77]

In general, sovereign immunity prohibits lawsuits against the state unless the state consents and waives immunity. In Texas, the defendant/principal alleged she was terminated because of racial discrimination as African American female.[78] The state appellate court held that the school did not waive immunity from suit by requesting disclosures or responding to discovery because discovery may be necessary to resolve issues surrounding jurisdiction.

Tenure/Continued Employment

During this period, seven cases dealt with issues around teacher tenure and continued employment. The Tennessee Teacher Tenure

---

[76] Barnes v. Bearden, 850 S.E.2d 181, 384 Educ. L. Rep. 564 (Ga. Ct. App. 2020).
[77] Doe *ex rel.* Doe Minor v. Garagnani, 614 S.W.3d 556, 386 Educ. L. Rep. 530 (Mo. Ct. App. 2020).
[78] Democratic Schs. Rsch., Inc. v. Rock, 608 S.W.3d 290, 383 Educ. L. Rep. 502 (Tex. App. 2020).

Act allows school boards to reduce the number of teaching and non-licensed positions when necessary due to a decrease in enrollment or other good reason. In a Tennessee federal district court case, the plaintiff/employee alleged the school violated Tennessee's Teacher Tenure Act when it pulled the funding for her program and terminated her, and she was entitled to damages.[79] Plaintiff's claim was successful, and the school was ordered to pay her backpay which could not be offset by any earnings from outside employment.

According to the Tennessee Tenure Act, a teacher's tenured status ends upon resignation, but the issue is whether constructive discharge is considered resignation under the Act.[80] Here, the plaintiff/teacher alleged that she was forced to resign due to stalking, bullying, and harassment, and the court noted that constructive discharge has been considered a firing under employment discrimination laws. However, the Supreme Court of Tennessee held that constructive discharge was not covered by the Tenure Act, and that the plaintiff did not abide by the Tenure Act, so her tenure status ended when she resigned.

A statute at issue in Colorado grants qualified teachers sole discretion to exercise their right of non-probationary portability. A qualified teacher is one who was employed by a school district, is later hired by another school district, and submits the required documentation. Here, the plaintiff/teacher sought relief from the school's requirement that teachers relinquish their right to non-probationary portability as a condition of employment through its online job application and employment contract.[81] The state appellate court found that the required relinquishing of non-probationary portability violated statutory rights.

Under Illinois statute, the school may suspend a teacher charged without pay, and if the teacher is not ultimately dismissed based on the charges, the teacher must be made whole for lost earnings.[82] In this case, the plaintiff/teacher had been suspended and reinstated. Although the school board drew on the disciplinary hearing officer's finding, the school board contested the hearing officer's finding that the teacher's version of her suspension was credible. The board

---

[79] Williams v. Shelby Cnty. Bd. of Educ., 479 F. Supp. 3d 721, 385 Educ. L. Rep. 635 (W.D. Tenn. 2020).
[80] Lemon v. Williamson Cnty. Schs., 618 S.W.3d 1, 387 Educ. L. Rep. 951 (Tenn. 2021).
[81] Stanczyk v. Poudre Sch. Dist. R-1, 490 P.3d 582, 393 Educ. L. Rep. 438 (Colo. App. 2020).
[82] Bd. of Educ. of City of Chi. v. Moore, 163 N.E.3d 190, 387 Educ. L. Rep. 326 (Ill. App. Ct. 2019).

instead concluded that the teacher's misbehaviors (e.g., failure of supervision, a failure to perform certain duties, and a failure to comply with board policies and state ethical and professional teaching standards) warranted 90-day time-served suspension, which was to be deducted from her net back pay. The Illinois appellate court agreed, and the plaintiff/teacher successfully argued that the school did not have the authority to deduct her 90-day suspension from her net back pay.

In Missouri, the Teacher Tenure Act applies to two types of teachers: permanent teachers who have been employed by the same school district for five consecutive years and continue to be employed thereafter, and probationary teachers who have been employed by the district for less than five consecutive years. According to state law, permanent teachers enjoy significantly more procedural protections than probationary teachers regarding termination.[83] Here, the plaintiff/teacher alleged that he was a permanent teacher, and the school violated the Teacher Tenure Act and breached his contract by failing to renew his contract. However, the plaintiff was not considered a permanent teacher, and thus had no right to contract renewal, because his prior teaching experiences had not been at public schools.

The plaintiff brought an Article 78 claim, which is a grievance process in New York, so as to appeal the ineffective rating he received on his annual performance review.[84] Here, the Department of Education of New York based the plaintiff/teacher's rating on an assessment of her students' growth compared to other similarly situated students based on criteria the school used. Therefore, the plaintiff's challenge of the Department's ineffective performance rating failed because the plaintiff failed to show the rating was made in bad faith or that it violated a lawful procedure or substantial right.

Under a New Jersey statute, the board of education may suspend a tenured teacher without pay for 120 days pending the determination on a charge; if the determination is not made within 120 days, the board must resume payment of the teacher's full salary.[85] In a New Jersey case, the plaintiff/teacher's employment as

---

[83] Welsh v. Kansas City Pub. Schs., 608 S.W.3d 751, 383 Educ. L. Rep. 546 (Mo. Ct. App. 2020).

[84] Francois v. Dept. of Educ. of City of N.Y., 138 N.Y.S.3d 25, 386 Educ. L. Rep. 917 (N.Y. App. Div. 2020).

[85] Ciripompa v. Bd. of Educ. of Bor. of Bound Brook, 247 A.3d 1, 389 Educ. L. Rep. 381 (N.J. Super. Ct. App. Div. 2021).

a bus driver and as an umpire was considered "substituted employment" during his suspension because his employment as a bus driver was inconsistent with his employment as a teacher since he could not have worked both jobs at the same time.

Employment Classifications

One case in 2021 presented a legal challenge about an employee classification. On appeal, the Supreme Court of West Virginia could only order relief to the petitioners if it found that the lower court incorrectly found the board's definition of "executive secretary" contradicted the statutory definition. The court concluded that the plaintiff/employee's claim for reclassification was successful because the current classification was clearly contrary to the legislative scheme and outside the school board's usual zone of discretion.[86]

Workplace Safety

Under a Florida firearm regulation statute, if a person is adversely affected by an ordinance, regulation, measure, directive, rule, enactment, order, or policy that is enforced in violation of the statute, he may file suit against a county, agency, municipality, district, or other entity in any court in the state with jurisdiction. Here, the plaintiff/teacher challenged school policy prohibiting him from having a firearm in his vehicle parked on campus. The court found in favor of Plaintiff because he was adversely affected by the school's policy.[87]

Workers Compensation

In Missouri, to establish that a plaintiff is a statutory employee under workers' compensation law, it must be shown that the work is performed under contract, the injury occurs on or about the premises of the alleged statutory employee, and the work is in the usual course

---

[86] McCann v. Lincoln Cnty. Bd. of Educ., 851 S.E.2d 512, 384 Educ. L. Rep. 1054 (W.Va. 2020).

[87] Forrester v. Sch. Bd. of Sumter Cnty., 316 So.3d 774, 391 Educ. L. Rep. 961 (Fla. Dist. Ct. App. 2021).

of the alleged statutory employer's business.[88] Here, the plaintiff/sign language interpreter had an agreement with the district forming a contract, her injury occurred at the school, and the district provided evidence that it hired sign language interpreters in the past meaning it was not unusual for its business. Thus, the plaintiff is a statutory employee and the only remedy available to her is under workers' compensation laws.

Whistleblower

During this period, two whistleblower cases emerged. In Alabama, the protections against retaliation provided by the Code of Ethics applied only when the public employee reports alleged violations of the Code to the Commission in the form of a complaint; it does not include notifying employers or other public officials by means other than a complaint.[89] Accordingly, state employees in Alabama are protected from employer retaliation when they make a sworn statement "blowing the whistle," but the statute at issue in this case applied only to the filing of a complaint. In this case before the Alabama Supreme Court, because the plaintiffs did not file a complaint with the Alabama Commission, they were not protected by the Code.

Under the Texas Whistleblower Act, there is an immunity waiver that allows a public employee alleging violation of the Whistleblower Act to sue their employer for relief, waiving sovereign immunity for the state or local government entity in this situation.[90] In a case before the Texas appellate court, the plaintiff/teacher alleged he was terminated in violation of the Whistleblower Act after making complaints with the Texas Division of Child Protective Services about other teachers. The plaintiff's claim survived the motion to dismiss because there was a question of fact as to whether his grievance satisfied the necessary requirements to qualify for protection.

Employment Termination

---

[88] Linkous v. Kirkwood Sch. Dist., 626 S.W.3d 889, 393 Educ. L. Rep. 952 (Mo. Ct. App. 2021).
[89] Craft v. McCoy, 312 So.3d 32, 388 Educ. L. Rep. 1030 (Ala. 2020).
[90] Herrera v. Dall. Indep. Sch. Dist., 609 S.W.3d 579, 383 Educ. L. Rep. 1168 (Tex. App. 2020).

During this period, six school-based employment termination lawsuits emerged. In a Seventh Circuit case on appeal from Indiana, the settlement agreement at-issue contained a non-disparagement paragraph prohibiting all parties from disparaging the other party, with disparage being defined as any communication, written or verbal, that is false or defamatory or communication made with reckless disregard to its truth or falsity.[91] The court ruled that the language in the disparagement paragraph is forward-looking and does not apply to a press release issued before the settlement agreement.

The federal trial court in Massachusetts ruled on a case about misrepresentation.[92] To state a claim for intentional misrepresentation, a plaintiff must show that the defendant made a false representation of material fact, the defendant knew the representation was false, the misrepresentation was made for the purpose of inducing the plaintiff to act on it, and the plaintiff relied on the representation to his detriment. Here, the plaintiff/employee's intentional misrepresentation claim arising from his termination survived the motion to dismiss because the plaintiff identified the time, place, and contents of misrepresentation, and the mayor's statements were declarative or definite for a reasonable factfinder to infer that they were material and definite enough to rely on.

Three of the cases resided in New York's state courts. In New York, when reviewing the penalty imposed pursuant to a disciplinary hearing, courts consider whether the punishment was so excessive or disproportionate that it shocks the court's sense of fairness. In the first case, the plaintiff/tenured guidance counselor was terminated for leaving school early on four days and leaving school without authorization one day for lunch at a time that was not her designated lunch period; her pay had been docked accordingly for those five days.[93] The state trial court found that the plaintiff's termination based on this conduct shocked the conscience, noting there was no evidence that she falsified records, engaged in fraud, or affected the financial well-being of the department with her conduct. Also in New York, a probationary employee can be terminated without a hearing for any reason or for no reason, as long

---

[91] Pack v. Middlebury Cmty. Schs., 990 F.3d 1013, 387 Educ. L. Rep. 471 (7th Cir. 2021).
[92] Khelfaoui v. Lowell Sch. Comm., 496 F. Supp. 3d 683, 389 Educ. L. Rep. 113 (D. Mass. 2020).
[93] Caroli v. N.Y.C. Dept. of Educ., 132 N.Y.S.3d 517, 383 Educ. L. Rep. 1041 (N.Y. 2020).

as the termination is not unlawful or in bad faith.[94] In this New York appellate case, the plaintiff/probationary teacher's termination was based on his declining performance evaluations and disciplinary misconduct. The court found his termination was not unlawful or in bad faith, therefore, the termination was lawful. In the third case, under New York education law, a member of the retirement system who is retired on disability should be placed on a preferred eligible list with the district of their last employment should their disability retirement be rescinded.[95] Here, the plaintiff/teacher was entitled to recall rights after being granted disability retirement benefits that included a hearing before his termination.

In Ohio, a state law prohibits a teacher's contract from being terminated for reasons other than good and just cause, which the Supreme Court of Ohio has interpreted to mean a fairly serious matter; a teacher cannot be terminated for good and just cause where the teacher's physical conduct towards a student did not result in injury and where the teacher did not intend any harm to the student.[96] In an Ohio appellate court case, the plaintiff moved the student in a way that was intended to maintain control of the situation, not to harm the student in any way. The court found that the lower court did not abuse its discretion in holding that the board lacked good and just cause to terminate the plaintiff.

Compensation and Benefits

During this period, 19 cases addressed matters of school employee compensation and benefits. These cases often challenged regulations or statutes calculating or impacting the dollar values of compensation, insurance applications, or retirement benefits.

Federal Claims

Two cases in this section specifically pertained to the federal ERISA law, which governs retirement benefits. To state a claim for delinquent contributions under ERISA, the plaintiff must show that

---

[94] Verma v. Dept. of Educ. of City of N.Y., 146 N.Y.S.3d 20, 391 Educ. L. Rep. 358 (N.Y. App. Div. 2021).
[95] Grube v. Bd. of Educ. Spencer-Van Etten Cent. Sch. Dist., 149 N.Y.S.3d 575, 393 Educ. L. Rep. 426 (N.Y. App. Div. 2021).
[96] Fiedeldey v. Finneytown Loc. Sch. Dist. Bd. of Educ., 156 N.E.3d 1017, 383 Educ. L. Rep. 1095 (Ohio Ct. App. 2020).

the defendant has contribution obligations arising from a plan or a collectively bargained agreement and is an employer under the ERISA definition.[97] In a Second Circuit case on appeal from New York, a federal appellate court found that the plaintiff/fund failed to plausibly allege that the defendants had any obligation to contribute to the fund. Therefore, the plaintiff could not state a delinquent contribution claim under ERISA.

Also, to prove a delinquent-contributions claim, the plaintiff must first establish that the defendant had an obligation to contribute to a fund under the terms of their ERISA pension plan.[98] Here, the New York federal district court found that the plaintiff, who is the fund provider, failed to plausibly allege that the defendants had any obligation to contribute to the fund. In fact, the defendants had not signed the Trust Agreement or Plan Document, so they were not bound to their contents. Therefore, the plaintiff could not state a delinquent contribution claim under ERISA.

State Claims

The Michigan Retirement Health Benefit Plan at-issue in one Sixth Circuit case states that a member becomes vested according to either Schedule A or Schedule B, but neither schedule vests for life.[99] Therefore, the plaintiffs failed to show that the retiree health benefit plan contained clear, affirmative language that the benefits would vest for life.

Illinois law treats a charter school as a public, nonsectarian, nonreligious, non-home based, and non-profit school that operates within the Illinois public school system.[100] In a Seventh Circuit decision on appeal from Illinois, the federal court found that charter schools have enough public attributes to be considered governmental for Employee Retirement Income Security Act (ERISA) purposes. As examples, the court lists the fact that charter schools are funded by the school district in which they operate, must have governing bodies separate from the governing body of any charter or education management organizations, must be approved and reviewed by the

---

[97] Div. 1181 Amalgamated Transit Union-N.Y. Emps. Pension Fund v. N.Y.C. Dept. of Educ., 9 F.4th 91, 393 Educ. L. Rep. 535 (2d Cir. 2021).
[98] Div. 1181 Amalgamated Transit Union-N.Y. Emps. Pension Fund v. N.Y.C. Dept. of Educ., 527 F. Supp. 3d 455, 395 Educ. L. Rep. 276 (E.D.N.Y. 2020).
[99] Mich. Educ. Ass'n Fam. Ret. Staff Ass'n v. Mich. Educ. Ass'n, 856 F. App'x 580, 393 Educ. L. Rep. 582 (6th Cir. 2021).
[100] Graham v. Bd. of Educ., 8 F.4th 625, 393 Educ. L. Rep. 529 (7th Cir. 2021).

Illinois State Board of Education and the local school board, and approved charter schools receive state funding to cover start-up and ongoing operation costs.

Under the relevant Alabama statute, the Circuit Court of Montgomery County is the exclusive venue for review of a final decision by a claims administrator.[101] Here, because the plaintiff's complaint is that the PEEHIP claims administrator made a final decision denying his insurance claim which he is now contesting, then Montgomery County had exclusive jurisdiction over the matter.

In Arkansas unemployment insurance cases, the court is to review the evidence and make all reasonable inferences in the light most favorable to the board's findings of fact.[102] In a case before an Arkansas appellate court, the plaintiff/teacher was entitled to unemployment benefits for the summer term because she was a year-round employee who was furloughed during the summer term because of COVID-19. If she was not a year-round employee, then she would not have been entitled to unemployment benefits between academic terms so long as she worked during the first academic term and had a contract or reasonable assurance that she would be employed during the second academic term.

Under a California statute, final compensation was determined by the highest average annual compensation that a member could earn in any 12-month period.[103] In a case before the California appellate court, the defendant claimed that this period referred to a school year. The court agreed that the defendant's interpretation—that any period of 12 consecutive months referred to a school year—was within the range of reasonable statutory construction.

In a case before a Colorado appellate court, there was a question of fact as to whether the requested maintenance medical care was related, reasonable, and necessary to her work injury.[104] The court ruled that the evidence was sufficient to establish that the plaintiff had reached her pre-injury level of functioning where physicians testified to that performance level, including a physician who treated her prior to the injury. Thus, the plaintiff's need for continued care was no longer work-related.

---

[101] Ex parte Blue Cross & Blue Shield of Ala. v. Blue Cross & Blue Shield, 321 So.3d 682, 393 Educ. L. Rep. 1025 (Ala. 2020).
[102] Tucker v. Dir., Div. of Workforce Servs., 626 S.W.3d 132, 393 Educ. L. Rep. 906 (Ark. Ct. App. 2021).
[103] Rush v. State Tchrs.' Ret. Sys., 276 Cal.Rptr.3d 778, 388 Educ. L. Rep. 923 (Cal. Ct. App. 2021).
[104] Bolton v. Indus. Claim Appeals Off., 487 P.3d 999, 391 Educ. L. Rep. 934 (Colo. App. 2019).

Under the relevant statute for municipalities with under 500,000 people in Illinois, eligible employees are entitled to at least ten paid sick days per year; this was later amended to include birth, adoption, or placement for adoption as eligible for sick leave, and a doctor's note was required after thirty days of sick leave for birth.[105] In Illinois, the plaintiff/teacher argued that there was no limit on when paid sick leave for birth could be taken, and that it was unaffected by summer break. The court held that sick leave had to be contemporaneous with the event, and the plaintiff could only use her 30 days of paid sick leave for birth in the 30 days immediately following the birth, otherwise she must provide a physician's certificate.

In Louisiana, "earned compensation" refers to an employee's base pay for a given pay period, with base pay being defined as prescribed compensation for a full-time position not including any kind of overtime, per diem, differential pay, payment in kind, premium payment, or other allowance for expenses incident to employment.[106] In a case before the Louisiana appellate court, the plaintiff/retired university president argued that his salary supplements should have been included in his earned compensation. However, the plaintiff's claim failed because the statute does not include salary supplements in earned compensation.

Under Minnesota law, the workers' compensation judge can depart from the usual parameters in a rare case when such departure is necessary for proper treatment.[107] Further, the Workers' Compensation Court of Appeals can only review issues raised in the notice of appeal. Here, the plaintiff did not raise the rare case exception to the worker's compensation judge or in her Notice of Appeal, therefore she forfeited the exception.

Under Missouri law, a school district cannot form a contract unless the contract is within the scope of its powers or is expressly authorized by law.[108] Another state statute required school districts to offer health insurance benefits to its retirees at the same rate as active employees until the retiree became eligible for Medicare, at which point the school district could offer reduced coverage. In a case

---

[105] Dynak v. Bd. of Educ. of Wood Dale Sch. Dist. 7, 164 N.E.3d 1226, 388 Educ. L. Rep. 340 (Ill. 2020).
[106] Slaughter v. La. State Emps.' Ret. Syst., 322 So.3d 839, 394 Educ. L. Rep. 429 (La. Ct. App. 2021).
[107] Leuthard v. Indep. Sch. Dist. 912 – Milaca, 958 N.W. 2d 640, 389 Educ. L. Rep. 514 (Minn. 2021).
[108] Spiegel v. Ferguson-Florissant Sch. Dist., 625 S.W.3d 800, 393 Educ. L. Rep. 890 (Mo. Ct. App. 2021).

before the Missouri appellate court, the plaintiff alleged that the contract was not void even if the provision regarding the payment of his health insurance premiums was; because the provision used the word "shall" which implies a mandatory duty, the entire contract was void and unenforceable.

In New York, medical reports that do not substantially comply with the workers' compensation law cannot be admitted to show causation, diagnosis, degree of disability, and other related details about the injury or illness; however, there is an exception to this rule when the objecting party fails to raise their objection in a timely manner.[109] In a New York appellate case, the Workers' Compensation Board precluded the psychiatrist's reports and testimony based on the fact he was an independent medical evaluation (IME) examiner and not claimant's treating physician, and because he did not substantially comply with the requirements of an IME examiner. However, the appellate court held that the Workers' Compensation Board erred in precluding the psychiatrist's report because the employer did not raise any issue to these reports and testimony until years after it should have been addressed, thus their objections were untimely. Also, in New York, the standard for courts to review the Retirement System's decision is to determine whether it is arbitrary, capricious, or without a rational basis.[110] In an appellate court in New York, the denial of the plaintiff/teacher's application for disability retirement benefits was not irrational or arbitrary and capricious where both doctors who performed a medical examination concluded that the plaintiff was not totally and permanently disabled. Under New York's Retiree Health Insurance Moratorium Act, a covered employer cannot provide retirees with lesser health insurance benefits than it provides active employees.[111] A New York appellate court found that the discontinuation of income-related monthly adjustment amount (IRMAA) reimbursements violated the moratorium statute where the district claimed the IRMAA reimbursements were mistakenly disbursed for ten years because of administrative error because, even if the disbursements were made in error, they are still within the scope of the moratorium statute.

---

[109] Page v. Liberty Cent. Sch. Dist., 135 N.Y.S.3d 180, 385 Educ. L. Rep. 283 (N.Y. App. Div. 2020).

[110] Servedio v. Lee, 136 N.Y.S.3d 55, 385 Educ. L. Rep. 938 (N.Y. App. Div. 2020).

[111] Bailenson v. Bd. of Educ. of Chappaqua Cent. School Dist., 149 N.Y.S.3d 485, 393 Educ. L. Rep. 422 (N.Y. App. Div. 2021).

In Ohio, equivocal medical opinions cannot be evidence.[112] Equivocation happens when the doctor repudiates an earlier opinion, renders uncertain or contradictory opinions, or does not clarify an ambiguous statement. In a case brought by an allegedly disabled public school teacher, an Ohio appellate court found that because the physician's report, which observed the same physical findings as the patient's treating doctor but came to a different conclusion, was not ambiguous or contradictory, the trial court did not err in refusing to disregard the report.

Under Pennsylvania law, all payments that might artificially inflate compensation for the purpose of enhancing retirement benefits are excluded in the computation of an employee's final average salary.[113] Here, the Pennsylvania trial court found that the payment that the plaintiff/principal received from the settlement agreement was intended to be back pay, so the settlement agreement payment was considered retirement-covered compensation for calculating the plaintiff's final average salary. Also in Pennsylvania, a claimant under the state retirement plan meets the standard of "good cause" when their actions are justified or reasonable given the circumstances.[114] The court found that the plaintiff had good cause not to attend the hearing when his counsel had made his unavailability known prior to the hearing and the plaintiff's mother's open-heart surgery had been moved up to the hearing date due to emergent circumstances.

The seniority of a multi-classified service employee involved in a reduction-in-force will only be considered in connection with the particular classification being reduced.[115] After analyzing the classification schemas (i.e., the four aide classifications were considered a single classification, and the three early childhood classroom assistant teacher (ECCAT) classifications were considered a single classification), the Supreme Court of Appeals for West Virginia recognized that they were clearly treated as two separate and distinct classifications. Therefore, the two classifications accrued seniority independently of each other for reduction-in-force purposes.

---

[112] State ex rel. Ewart v. State Teachers Ret. Sys. Bd. of Ohio, 157 N.E.3d 866, 384 Educ. L. Rep. 496 (Ohio Ct. App. 2020).

[113] Whalen v. Pub. Sch. Employees' Ret. Bd., 241 A.3d 1242, 384 Educ. L. Rep. 921 (Pa. Commw. Ct. 2020).

[114] Madden v. Pub. Sch. Employees' Ret. Bd., 241 A.3d 507, 384 Educ. L. Rep. 398 (Pa. Commw. Ct. 2020).

[115] Webster Cnty. Bd. of Educ. v. Davis, 856 S.E. 2d 661, 389 Educ. L. Rep. 570 (W. Va. 2021).

Conclusion

In 2021, the number of cases involving school employees increased substantially from 64 in 2020 to 114 in 2021. This increase is likely a product of case declines due to COVID last year. The types of cases remain consistent; they ranged from civil rights to workplace safety issues. Many school employee cases raised both federal and state claims to challenge an incident, but most of the cases centered around issues involving state statutory and administrative provisions. The school employee cases also highlighted the contested terrain between employees (e.g., teachers and principals) and employers (e.g., districts, state education departments, or schools) as well as among other parties (e.g., state employee retirement boards).

Alphabetical List of Cases

AFT v. State
Agosto v. N.Y.C. Dept. of Educ.
Bailenson v. Bd. of Educ. of Chappaqua Cent. Sch. Dist.
Barnes v. Bearden
Bd. of Educ. of City of Chicago v. Moore
Benjamin v. Sparks
Beyer v. Bd. of Educ. of City of Chicago
Blackman v. Omak Sch. Dist.
Blick v. Ann Arbor Pub. Sch. Dist.
Bolton v. Indus. Claim Appeals Off.
Bouknight v. S.C. Dept. of Corrections
Brown v. L.A. Unified Sch. Dist.
Bushong v. Del. City Sch. Dist.
Caroli v. N.Y.C. Dept. of Educ.
Carter v. Syracuse City Sch. Dist.
Chatman v. Bd. of Educ. of City of Chicago
Chicago Tchrs. Union v. Bd. of Educ. of the City of Chicago
Ciripompa v. Bd. of Educ. of Bor. of Bound Brook
Codden v. Manistee Area Pub. Schs. Bd. of Educ.
Codding v. Pearson Educ., Inc.
Cole v. Wake Cnty. Bd. of Educ.
Congress v. D.C.
Craft v. McCoy
Crisitello v. St. Theresa Sch.
Curry-Malcolm v. Rochester City Sch. Dist.
Davidson v. Arlington Cmty. Schs. Bd. of Educ.
Democratic Schs. Rsch., Inc. v. Rock
Div. 1181 Amalgamated Transit Union-N.Y. Emps. Pension Fund v. N.Y.C. Dept. of Educ. (E.D.N.Y. 2020).
Div. 1181 Amalgamated Transit Union-N.Y. Emps. Pension Fund v. N.Y.C. Dept. of Educ. (2d Cir. 2021).
Doe *ex rel.* Doe Minor v. Garagnani
Doe v. ABC Sch.
Doe v. Roaring Fork Sch. Dist.
Dynak v. Bd. of Educ. of Wood Dale Sch. Dist. 7
Earle v. Birmingham Bd. of Educ.
Ex parte Blue Cross & Blue Shield of Ala. v. Blue Cross & Blue Shield
Fiedeldey v. Finneytown Loc. Sch. Dist. Bd. of Educ.
Fisher v. Basehor-Linwood Unified Sch. Dist. No. 458
Fisher v. Fletcher

Forrester v. Sch. Bd. of Sumter Cnty.
Francois v. Dept. of Educ. of City of N.Y.
Graham v. Bd. of Educ.
Grant v. Gahanna-Jefferson Pub. Sch. Dist.
Green v. Dept. of Educ. of City of N.Y.
Grube v. Bd. of Educ. Spencer-Van Etten Cent. Sch. Dist.
Hardison v. Skinner
Hawkland v. Hall
Henry v. Indep. Sch. Dist. #625
Herrera v. Dall. Indep. Sch. Dist.
Ickenroth v. Parkway Sch. Dist. C-2
Jewett v. Mesick Consol. Sch. Dist.
Jim v. Shiprock Assoc. Schs., Inc.
Johnson v. Salt Lake City Sch. Dist.
Jordan v. Stroughter
Kennedy v. Bremerton Sch. Dist.
Khelfaoui v. Lowell Sch. Comm.
Kunik v. N.Y.C. Dept. of Educ.
Langlois v. Hartford Bd. of Educ.
Lebron v. Pub. Sch. Emps. Ret. Bd.
Lemon v. Williamson Cnty. Schs.
Leuthard v. Indep. Sch. Dist. 912 – Milaca
Lewis v. Sch. Bd. of Palm Beach Cnty.
Lilley v. Greene Cent. Sch. Dist.
Lima v. City of E. Providence
Linkous v. Kirkwood Sch. Dist.
Longanecker v. E. Moline Sch. Dist. No. 37
Lopez-Lopez v. Robinson Sch. Inc.
Madden v. Pub. Sch. Emps. Ret. Bd.
Malcolm v. Ass'n of Supervisors and Adm'rs of Rochester
McCann v. Lincoln Cnty. Bd. of Educ.
Mich. Educ. Ass'n Fam. Ret. Staff Ass'n v. Mich. Educ. Ass'n
Miles v. Unified Sch. Dist. No. 500, Kan. City
Miller v. Livanis
Mimbs v. Henry Cnty. Schs.
Mirich v. State *ex rel.* Bd. of Trs. of Laramie Cnty. Sch. Dist. Two
Moulthrop v. Conn. State Bd. of Educ.
Mullen v. Tiverton Sch. Dist.
Munoz v. Bd. of Educ. of City Sch. Dist. of N.Y.C.
Neri v. Bd. of Educ. for Albuquerque Pub. Schs.
O'Kane v. Plainedge Union Free Sch. Dist.
Oliver v. Arnold
Omnitech Inst., Inc. v. Norwood

Pack v. Middlebury Cmty. Schs.
Page v. Liberty Cent. Sch. Dist.
Rabun Cnty. Bd. of Educ. v. Randel
Razi Sch. v. Cissna
Root v. Salamanca Cent. Sch. Dist.
Ross v. Judson Indep. Sch. Dist.
Rush v. State Teachers' Ret. Sys.
Servedio v. Lee
Slaughter v. La. State Emps. Ret. Syst.
Smoler v. Bd. of Educ. for W. Northfield Sch. Dist. #31
Spiegel v. Ferguson-Florissant Sch. Dist.
Stanczyk v. Poudre Sch. Dist. R-1
Starkey v. Roman Cath. Archdiocese of Indianapolis, Inc.
State *ex rel.* Ewart v. State Tchrs. Ret. Sys. Bd. of Ohio
Stevens v. Cabarrus Cnty. Bd. of Educ.
Suniaga v. Downingtown Area Sch. Dist.
Todd v. Fayette Cnty. Sch. Dist.
Tucker v. Dir., Div. of Workforce Servs.
Turner v. D.C. Off. of Hum. Rts.
Verceles v. L.A. Unified Sch. Dist.
Verma v. Dept. of Educ. of City of N.Y.
Vlaming v. West Point Sch. Bd. (4th Cir. 2021)
Vlaming v. West Point Sch. Bd. (E.D. Va. 2020)
Vukovic-Burkhardt v. Dayton Bd. of Educ.
Ward v. Troup Cnty. Sch. Dist.
Webster Cnty. Bd. of Educ. v. Davis
Welsh v. Kansas City Pub. Schs.
Whalen v. Pub. Sch. Emps.' Ret. Bd.
Williams v. Bd. of Educ. of City of Chicago
Williams v. Shelby Cnty. Bd. of Educ.
Wilson v. St. Landry Parish Sch. Bd.
Wright v. Arlington Indep. Sch. Dist.
Yourga v. City of Northampton

Cases by Jurisdiction

FEDERAL CASES

D.C. Circuit

Washington D.C.
Congress v. D.C.

First Circuit
Lima v. City of E. Providence

Massachusetts
Khelfaoui v. Lowell Sch. Comm.
Yourga v. City of Northampton
Puerto Rico
Lopez-Lopez v. Robinson Sch. Inc.
Rhode Island
Mullen v. Tiverton Sch. Dist.

Second Circuit
Agosto v. N.Y.C. Dept. of Educ.
Carter v. Syracuse City Sch. Dist.
Curry-Malcolm v. Rochester City Sch. Dist.
Div. 1181 Amalgamated Transit Union-N.Y. Emps. Pension Fund v. N.Y.C.
Dept. of Educ.
Green v. Dept. of Educ. of City of N.Y.
Kunik v. N.Y.C. Dept. of Educ.
Langlois v. Hartford Bd. of Educ.
Munoz v. Bd. of Educ. of City Sch. Dist. of N.Y.C.
O'Kane v. Plainedge Union Free Sch. Dist.

New York
Div. 1181 Amalgamated Transit Union-N.Y. Emps. Pension Fund v. N.Y.C.
Dept. of Educ.
Malcolm v. Ass'n of Supervisors and Adm'rs of Rochester
Razi Sch. v. Cissna

Third Circuit

Pennsylvania
Suniaga v. Downingtown Area Sch Dist.

Fourth Circuit
Benjamin v. Sparks
Vlaming v. West Point Sch. Bd.

North Carolina
Cole v. Wake Cnty. Bd. of Educ.
Stevens v. Cabarrus Cnty. Bd. of Educ.
South Carolina
Bouknight v. S.C. Dept. of Corrections
Virginia
Vlaming v. West Point Sch. Bd.
Hawkland v. Hall
Oliver v. Arnold
Ross v. Judson Indep. Sch. Dist.
Wilson v. St. Landry Parish Sch. Bd.
Wright v. Arlington Indep. Sch. Dist.
Louisiana
Hardison v. Skinner

Sixth Circuit
Bushong v. Del. City Sch. Dist.
Codden v. Manistee Area Pub. Schs. Bd. of Educ.
Davidson v. Arlington Cmty. Schs. Bd. of Educ.
Grant v. Gahanna-Jefferson Pub. Sch. Dist.
Mich. Educ. Ass'n Fam. Ret. Staff Ass'n v. Mich. Educ. Ass'n

Kentucky
Fisher v. Fletcher
Michigan
Blick v. Ann Arbor Pub. Sch. Dist.
Jordan v. Stroughter
Tennessee
Williams v. Shelby Cnty. Bd. of Educ.

Seventh Circuit
Chatman v. Bd. of Educ. of City of Chicago
Chicago Tchrs. Union v. Bd. of Educ. of the City of Chicago
Graham v. Bd. of Educ.

Pack v. Middlebury Cmty. Schs.
Williams v. Bd. of Educ. of City of Chicago

Illinois
Smoler v. Bd. of Educ. for W. Northfield Sch. Dist. #31
Indiana
Starkey v. Roman Cath. Archdiocese of Indianapolis, Inc.

Ninth Circuit
Codding v. Pearson Educ., Inc.
Kennedy v. Bremerton Sch. Dist.

Washington
Blackman v. Omak Sch. Dist.

Tenth Circuit
Fisher v. Basehor-Linwood Unified Sch. Dist. No. 458
Neri v. Bd. of Educ. for Albuquerque Pub. Schs.
Jim v. Shiprock Assoc. Schs., Inc.
Miles v. Unified Sch. Dist. No. 500, Kan. City

Utah
Johnson v. Salt Lake City Sch. Dist.
Colorado
Doe v. Roaring Fork Sch. Dist.

Eleventh Circuit
Earle v. Birmingham Bd. of Educ.
Lewis v. Sch. Bd. of Palm Beach Cnty.
Todd v. Fayette Cnty. Sch. Dist.
Ward v. Troup Cnty. Sch. Dist.
Todd v. Fayette County School District

STATE & D.C. COURT CASES

Alabama
Craft v. McCoy
Ex parte Blue Cross & Blue Shield of Ala. v. Blue Cross & Blue Shield

Arkansas
Tucker v. Dir., Div. of Workforce Servs.

California
Brown v. L.A. Unified Sch. Dist.
Verceles v. L.A. Unified Sch. Dist.
Rush v. State Teachers' Ret. Sys.

Colorado
Bolton v. Indus. Claim Appeals Off.
Stanczyk v. Poudre Sch. Dist. R-1

Connecticut
Moulthrop v. Conn. State Bd. of Educ.

District of Columbia
Turner v. D.C. Off. of Hum. Rts.

Florida
Forrester v. Sch. Bd. of Sumter Cnty.

Georgia
Barnes v. Bearden
Mimbs v. Henry Cnty. Schs.
Omnitech Inst., Inc. v. Norwood
Rabun Cnty. Bd. of Educ. v. Randel

Illinois
Beyer v. Bd. of Educ. of City of Chicago
Bd. of Educ. of City of Chicago v. Moore
Dynak v. Bd. of Educ. of Wood Dale Sch. Dist. 7
Longanecker v. E. Moline Sch. Dist. No. 37

Louisiana
Doe v. ABC Sch.
Slaughter v. La. State Emps' Ret. Syst.

School Employment   81

Wilson v. St. Landry Parish Sch. Bd.

Michigan
AFT v. State
Jewett v. Mesick Consol. Sch. Dist.

Minnesota
Henry v. Indep. Sch. Dist. #625
Leuthard v. Indep. Sch. Dist. 912 – Milaca

Missouri
Doe *ex rel.* Doe Minor v. Garagnani
Ickenroth v. Parkway Sch. Dist. C-2
Linkous v. Kirkwood Sch. Dist.
Spiegel v. Ferguson-Florissant Sch. Dist.
Welsh v. Kansas City Pub. Schs.

New Jersey
Crisitello v. St. Theresa Sch.
Ciripompa v. Bd. of Educ. of Bor. of Bound Brook

New York
Bailenson v. Bd. of Educ. of Chappaqua Cent. Sch. Dist.
Caroli v. N.Y.C. Dept. of Educ.
Francois v. Dept. of Educ. of City of N.Y.
Grube v. Bd. of Educ. Spencer-Van Etten Cent. Sch. Dist.
Lilley v. Greene Cent. Sch. Dist.
Miller v. Livanis
Page v. Liberty Cent. Sch. Dist.
Root v. Salamanca Cent. Sch. Dist.
Servedio v. Lee
Verma v. Dept. of Educ. of City of N.Y.

Ohio
Fiedeldey v. Finneytown Loc. Sch. Dist. Bd. of Educ.
State *ex rel.* Ewart v. State Tchrs. Ret. Sys. Bd. of Ohio
Vukovic-Burkhardt v. Dayton Bd. of Educ.

Pennsylvania
Lebron v. Pub. Sch. Employees' Ret. Bd.
Madden v. Pub. Sch. Employees' Ret. Bd.
Whalen v. Pub. Sch. Emps.' Ret. Bd.

Tennessee
Lemon v. Williamson Cnty. Schs.

Texas
Democratic Schs. Rsch., Inc. v. Rock
Herrera v. Dall. Indep. Sch. Dist.

West Virginia
McCann v. Lincoln Cnty. Bd. of Educ.
Webster Cnty. Bd. of Educ. v. Davis

Wyoming
Mirich v. State *ex rel.* Bd. of Trs. of Laramie Cnty. Sch. Dist. Two

Chapter 3

STUDENTS IN K-12 SCHOOLS

Joe Dryden, J.D., Ed.D.[1] and
Andrea Schulewitch, J.D., M.Ed.[2]

Introduction	85
First Amendment	86
Expression	86
Religion	88
Fourth Amendment	90
Excessive Force	90
Search & Seizure	92
Family Educational Rights and Privacy Act	96
Abuse, Harassment, and Bullying	97
Employee-on-Student Actions	97
Student-on-Student Actions	100
Substantive Due Process	104
Discrimination	108
Racial Discrimination	108
Desegregation	110
Sexual Discrimination	110
Transgender Students	110
Non-transgender Sex Discrimination Claims	111

---

[1] Associate Professor of Graduate Education, Texas Wesleyan University, Fort Worth, Tex.
[2] Associate General Counsel, Washoe County School District, Reno, Nev.

Student Discipline 113
Crimes.. 114
Miscellaneous Claims from COVID-19 Restrictions 115
Compulsory Attendance 116
Conclusion 116
Alphabetized Case List 117
Cases by Jurisdiction... 119

Introduction

This year's chapter on students is abbreviated because the previous entries covered additional volumes. This year's entry covers volumes 385 through 395 of West's Education Law Reporter to align with other chapters in *The Yearbook of Education Law*. Despite this abbreviated version, trends in case categories remain consistent.

First Amendment expression cases included a long overdue U.S. Supreme Court suit about off-campus student expression, a disagreement over essays on LGBT+ issues, transcriptions of the Pledge of Allegiance, political speech in a school parking lot, government speech on mandatory vaccine forms, threatening and bullying off-campus social media posts, and dress codes for graduation ceremonies. Cases on religion included free exercise challenges to mask mandates and school closures, cases over allegedly anti-Christian curricular content, and exclusion of religious schools in educational choice programs.

Fourth Amendment cases involved claims of excessive force and unlawful seizure, including against school resource officers (SROs) who allegedly went too far in securing out-of-control or violent students. Other Fourth Amendment cases involved searches for drugs and school visitors, strip searches, confiscating weapons, and the need for *Miranda* warnings.

As in previous editions, the part covering abuse and harassment, approximately 25 percent of the total, accounted for more cases than any other section as school officials perpetually work to protect students from predatory employees and abusive classmates. Title IX disputes included lawsuits by genotypic females against the participation of genotypic males in female sports.

Other cases examined the substantive rights of parents relating to state mandates for school closures, mask mandates and proof of immunization, unreasonable seizures by teachers, and curricular content. Other substantive due process suits examined the use of divisive and racist content in school curricula and the inclusion of religious content in required middle school courses. The chapter ends with a brief conclusion.

First Amendment

Expression

In *Mahanoy Area School District v. B. L. ex rel. Levy*,[3] the U.S. Supreme Court affirmed that officials in Pennsylvania violated the First Amendment rights of a high school cheerleader they suspended for posting a picture of herself and a friend with their middle fingers extended and a caption using a vulgar expression because she failed to qualify for the varsity team. The Justices agreed that officials failed to show that the student's posting created or was likely to make a substantial disruption of school operations and that although they were crude, they did not target members of the school community, identify it, or involve content that placed it outside of the umbrella of First Amendment protection.

The mother of a fourth-grade student in South Carolina failed in her Section 1983 action against her school board and principal after they refused to include her daughter's essay on equality for those who are LGBT+ in a class essay book. The Fourth Circuit affirmed the judgment of educators that because the content of the essay was not age-appropriate, they had legitimate pedagogical concerns insofar as the book was distributed under the school's auspices such that members of the public might reasonably have perceived that the material bore its imprimatur.[4] The court explained that because faculty members supervised the development of the essay book, was curricular in nature, and designed to impart specific knowledge to the students, the activity was curriculum-related.

The Fifth Circuit largely dismissed in favor of educators in Texas who allegedly compelled a student to transcribe the Pledge of Allegiance despite claims that the mother completed opt-out paperwork through the board.[5] A federal trial court found that most defendants were entitled to qualified immunity except the teacher who asked the student to transcribe the pledge. The panel decided it lacked jurisdiction to review fact-based challenges on denying a motion for summary judgment while refusing to award attorney fees.

In Missouri, parents objected to an official statement attached to a religious exemption form from mandatory vaccine requirements over their concern that the vaccine used embryonic tissue in its

---

[3] 141 S. Ct. 2038, 391 Educ. L. Rep. 19 (2021).
[4] Robertson v. Anderson Mill Elementary Sch., 989 F.3d 282, 387 Educ. L. Rep. 50 (4th Cir. 2021).
[5] Oliver v. Arnold, 3 F.4th 152, 391 Educ. L. Rep. 565 (5th Cir. 2021).

production. After the parents withdrew their children from school until the state-approved form was on file, they initiated litigation alleging violations of their rights to free expression, free exercise, and equal protection, along with a hybrid-rights claim. On further review of a dismissal in favor of the board, the Eighth Circuit affirmed. The court characterized the statement as government speech representing a substantial interest unrelated to the plaintiff's free expression rights, viewing the form as adopted pursuant to a valid and neutral law of general applicability that did not violate the parents' sincerely held religious beliefs.[6] Because the other constitutional claims were dismissed, the court agreed that the hybrid-rights doctrine lacked merit.

Parents in Louisiana sued their school board and superintendent on behalf of their daughter after officials had her painted image of President Donald Trump removed from her assigned parking spot. The board had a policy of allowing seniors to paint their parking spaces for a fee of $25 with prohibitions against offensive, negative, or rude symbols or language. A federal trial court granted the plaintiffs' motion for a preliminary injunction because the actions of the defendants violated the First Amendment insofar as the painting was not lewd, vulgar, or obscene; did not advocate for the use of drugs; did not create or pose a likelihood of creating a substantial disruption of school operations; and did not represent school-sponsored speech over which officials have greater editorial control.[7]

In Colorado, a school board and various officials successfully defended an action brought on behalf of students they expelled for posting antisemitic and threatening comments on Snapchat.[8] Parents claimed that officials violated their children's First Amendment and due process rights because the policy was vague and overly broad. A federal trial court granted the defendants' motion for summary judgment because *Tinker* affords officials the authority to punish off-campus speech that materially or substantially disrupts the school's work and interferes with the rights of others to be secure. The court observed that the policies were neither facially vague nor overly broad, nor did they pose a real danger of compromising the First Amendment rights of parties not before the court, and that officials provided adequate due process at both the suspension and expulsion stage where more formal procedures are required.

---

[6] B.W.C. v. Williams, 990 F.3d 614, 387 Educ. L. Rep. 462 (8th Cir. 2021).
[7] Thomas v. Varnado, 511 F. Supp. 3d 761, 392 Educ. L. Rep. 81 (E.D. La. 2020).
[8] C1.G. v. Siegfried, 477 F. Supp. 3d 1194, 385 Educ. L. Rep. 237 (D. Colo. 2020).

In another case involving off-campus student expression, the federal trial court in Massachusetts entered a judgment in favor of a school committee that suspended high school students for online bullying violating commonwealth law and its policy.[9] The facts revealed that the students repeatedly targeted a classmate, resulting in emotional harm to him. The bullied student needed mental health intervention, and, as a result, his participation on the school's hockey team declined. The court determined that officials may intervene to protect students from harassment and bullying and need not tolerate expression inconsistent with a school system's educational mission. It noted that neither the policy nor the underlying statute was impermissibly subjective nor prohibitive of a substantial amount of protected speech.

A high school student and her father, members of the Sioux Nation, sued their board, claiming violations of her equal protection, expression, and free exercise rights when they forbade her from wearing beads and feathers as a part of her graduation attire. The federal trial court in Arizona dismissed the father's claim as not cognizable and the student's equal protection charge as not plausible.[10] The court declared that the graduation dress code only incidentally burdened the plaintiff's free exercise rights and that rational basis was the proper standard of review to judge the actions of the board and officials who proffered content-neutral justifications.

Religion

The Second Circuit issued a writ of mandamus directing state and local officials in Vermont to allow students to participate in a tuition program, enabling them to attend the high schools of their choice, regardless of whether they are religiously affiliated. Reversing an earlier order to the contrary in light of recent U.S. Supreme Court precedent, the court reiterated the principle that denying a benefit of general applicability aid due to religious affiliations can only be tolerated if a state has a compelling interest, something it lacked here.[11]

---

[9] Doe *ex rel.* Doe v. Hopkinton Pub. Schs., 490 F. Supp. 3d 448, 387 Educ. L. Rep. 674 (D. Mass. 2020).

[10] Waln v. Dysart Sch. Dist., 522 F. Supp. 3d 560, 394 Educ. L. Rep. 635 (D. Ariz. 2021).

[11] *In re* A.H., 999 F.3d 98, 390 Educ. L. Rep. 896 (2d Cir. 2021).

In a case from Michigan, the Sixth Circuit initially affirmed the dismissal of a parental claim over a mask mandate for elementary-age children after a federal trial court ruled that any burden associated with the COVID-19 mask requirements on their religious practices was incidental.[12] The plaintiffs claimed violations of the Free Exercise Clause, equal protection, and their substantive rights as parents. The panel agreed that the mask mandate, described as neutral and generally applicable, was rationally related to the important government interest of reducing the spread of COVID-19. The court rejected the equal protection claim because the mask mandate applied to all educational institutions, both public and private, and the substantive due process claim was duplicative. The Sixth Circuit subsequently vacated the opinion and granted a request for a rehearing *en banc*,[13] dismissing the claim as moot because the mandate had been rescinded.[14]

Parents of a high school student petitioned a federal trial court in North Carolina for a temporary restraining order (TRO) to prevent their school board from including a book in the first-year curriculum due to concerns over profanity, sexual references, and anti-Christian bigotry in violation of the First Amendment. While the court expressed concern that officials included such a controversial book, it did not address the claim's merits, maintaining that the plaintiffs failed to present enough evidence to warrant a TRO.[15]

A mother in New Jersey sued her school board and various officials, claiming Establishment Clause violations due to instruction about Islam in her daughter's world cultures and geography class. The court granted the board's motion for summary judgment because the mother lacked standing to seek an injunction because her daughter no longer attended the school but did allow her case for nominal damages to proceed based on prior violations.[16] The court applied the *Lemon* test in granting the board's motion for summary judgment because the material had a secular purpose, did not have the effect of advancing Islam, did not constitute excessive entanglement, and a reasonable observer would not have perceived

---

[12] Resurrection Sch. v. Gordon, 507 F. Supp. 3d 897, 391 Educ. L. Rep. 201 (W.D. Mich. 2020).
[13] Resurrection Sch. v. Hertel, 11 F.4th 437, 394 Educ. L. Rep. 91 (6th Cir. 2021).
[14] Resurrection Sch. v. Hertel, 35 F.4th 524, 2022 WL 1656719 (6th Cir. 2022).
[15] Coble v. Lake Norman Charter Sch., 499 F. Supp. 3d 238, 389 Educ. L. Rep. 784 (W.D.N.C. 2020).
[16] Hilsenrath *ex rel.* C.H. v. Sch. Dist. of Chathams, 500 F. Supp. 3d 272, 390 Educ. L. Rep. 189 (D.N.J. 2020).

it as an endorsement of religion. The court also rejected the claim that any coercion was present.

Officials of a faith-based school in Kentucky successfully challenged the governor's executive order shutting down all public and nonpublic schools in response to the COVID-19 pandemic.[17] The court granted the preliminary injunction in light of officials' allegation that the executive order violated their rights to the free exercise of religion because it believed they were likely to succeed on the merits of their claim in that the order was not narrowly tailored to serve a compelling public health interest. The court granted the motion for the entire commonwealth because the order was not generally applicable: It did not apply to preschools, universities, law firms, laundromats, liquor stores, gun shops, and other activities where people were allowed to assemble in groups.

In New York, parents unsuccessfully disputed the exclusion of students from school if they could not provide proof of vaccination during a measles outbreak and local emergency declarations barring unvaccinated children from the public assembly.[18] The plaintiffs alleged that the directives violated various students' rights. Granting the defendant's motion for summary judgment, a federal trial court pointed out that the parents failed to raise a property or liberty interest protected by the Fourteenth Amendment or a genuine issue regarding whether the exclusion process was constitutionally inadequate, precluding the due process claim. Due to the contagious nature of measles, the court wrote that an emergency existed that did not reflect discriminatory animus such that any failure to provide pre-deprivation hearings was excused. The court concluded that the officials did not violate students' rights to equal protection, free exercise, or assembly.

Fourth Amendment

Excessive Force

A high school student and his mother in New York sued various board employees and school safety agents under Section 1983, alleging false arrest and excessive force following his arrest for

---

[17] Danville Christian Acad., v. Beshear, 503 F. Supp. 3d 516, 390 Educ. L. Rep. 665 (E.D. Ky. 2020).
[18] W.D. v. Rockland Cnty., 521 F. Supp. 3d 358, 394 Educ. L. Rep. 243 (S.D.N.Y. 2021).

disorderly conduct after resisting the efforts of the agents to escort him to the office. On further review of a grant of summary judgment in favor of the defense, the Second Circuit affirmed that the safety agents had probable cause to arrest the student for obstruction of governmental administration, precluding relief on the false arrest claim. [19] However, the court panel vacated and remanded partly because a reasonable fact finder could have ruled that the force was excessive—the crime leading to the arrest was minor. When tackled by two agents, the student sustained a concussion and was pinned to the ground by at least four agents, plus an administrator. The court remarked that factual issues over whether the student posed an immediate threat to safety agents or others precluded the defense's motion for summary judgment on his excessive force claim.

In a second case from New York, a father, on behalf of his son with a developmental disability, filed a Section 1983 action against a city department of education and a paraprofessional for unlawful seizure and excessive force, as well as state law claims for assault, battery, and false imprisonment. The father alleged that the paraprofessional took his son to the school's basement, out of view of security cameras and personnel, to beat him with a wooden stick. A federal trial court partially granted the defense's motion to dismiss because the father failed to file sufficient statutorily mandated prelitigation notice; additionally, he lacked standing to seek prospective declaratory relief as the paraprofessional no longer worked at the school.[20] The court refused to dismiss the respondent's superior claims premised on the student's underlying assault and battery claims because the father plausibly alleged sufficient facts that the paraprofessional acted within the scope of employment, insofar as staff members routinely used force to restrain and discipline students.

In Wisconsin, following an altercation between school personnel and her daughter, a mother sued a school board and its positive behavior support (PBS) coach under Section 1983 for unlawful seizure, and the use of excessive force in violation of the Fourth Amendment, as well as state law claims for battery and negligence. A federal trial court denied the defendant's motion for summary judgment because the unlawful seizure and excessive force claims were not subject to exhaustion of administrative remedies under the

---

[19] Concepcion v. N.Y.C. Dep't of Educ., 836 F. App'x 27, 386 Educ. L. Rep. 649 (2d Cir. 2020).
[20] A.W. by E.W. v. New York Dep't of Educ., 519 F. Supp. 3d 128, 393 Educ. L. Rep. 645 (E.D.N.Y. 2021).

Individuals with Disabilities Act (IDEA).[21] The court rejected the PBS coach's motion for summary judgment on the Fourth Amendment objective reasonableness standard because genuine issues of material fact existed as to whether the force he exerted effectuated an unlawful seizure and use of excessive force. The court allowed two claims to proceed—the state battery claim, as to whether the coach intentionally used force against the student, and on his discretionary immunity defense to the state negligence claim, as to whether his actions were malicious, willful, and intentional—because material issues of fact remained.

Search & Seizure

A high school student in Missouri brought a Section 1983 action against his school board, various employees, a school resource officer (SRO), and police officers alleging an unconstitutional seizure after being interrogated by two police officers for 20 minutes about a sexual assault that occurred at the house of a peer. In an interlocutory review of the denial of the SRO's motion to dismiss, premised on qualified immunity for his nominal role in escorting the student to the room and closing the door, the Eighth Circuit reversed and remanded in his favor.[22] The panel directed the trial court to dismiss the claim against the SRO because it failed to allege circumstances that a reasonable officer in the SRO's position would have known constituted a seizure.

In a second interlocutory appeal from Missouri before the Eighth Circuit, police officials successfully questioned an order denying their motion to dismiss a complaint based on qualified immunity.[23] Two high school students attending a football camp filed a Section 1983 suit against state university police officers alleging that they violated the Fourth Amendment by seizing them following an investigation of their having possibly taken photographs of a female as she undressed. The coaches, under the perceived authority and direction of the officers, interrogated the players for hours about the incident. Although the alleged seizure did not occur on traditional school grounds and was initiated by law enforcement, the court was satisfied that the officers were entitled to qualified immunity under

---

[21] Price *ex rel.* J.K. v. Mueller-Owens, 516 F. Supp. 3d 816, 393 Educ. L. Rep. 252 (W.D. Wis. 2021).
[22] L.G. *ex rel.* M.G. v. Columbia Pub. Schs., 990 F.3d 1145, 387 Educ. L. Rep. 488 (8th Cir. 2021).
[23] T.S.H. v. Green, 996 F.3d 915, 389 Educ. L. Rep. 713 (8th Cir. 2021).

the reasonableness standard because it did not violate the students' clearly established Fourth Amendment rights.

In Ohio, the mother of a third-grader suspended for ten days sued her school board and an SRO, alleging Fourth and Fourteenth Amendment violations under Section 1983 and state claims. The mother alleged that the SRO physically restrained and escorted her son to the principal's office following an emotional outburst and that, while there, she intentionally sprayed him in the face with a juice box. The court denied the defense's motion for summary judgment on the Section 1983 claim, alleging that the SRO violated the student's due process right to bodily integrity, thus rejecting the defense's claim for qualified immunity, but did dismiss the Fourth Amendment excessive force claim as duplicative because the seizure was reasonable.[24]

Four middle school students in New York who identify as racial minorities were strip-searched without a reason, notice, or consent from their guardians. The students, through their parents, sued the board, principal, and school nurse, among others, claiming unlawful searches violating the Equal Protection Clause, Title VI, the IDEA, and Section 504 of the Rehabilitation Act (Section 504). The court rejected the IDEA and Section 504 claims because the parents' focus was not on the appropriateness of their children's placements.[25] The court dismissed the claim against the nurse as not subjecting two students to a strip search violating the Fourth Amendment or Equal Protection Clause, thereby precluding Monell's liability. However, the court thought that the students presented a claim for Monell's liability against the board based on final-policymaker theory relating to the principal but dismissed the failure-to-train claim against it regarding the unlawful searches as not constituting deliberate indifference under Title VI, thereby precluding liability.

In Louisiana, a mother and her son, arrested for terrorizing under state statute, sued the arresting officer under Section 1983 for allegedly violating the student's Fourth Amendment rights, malicious prosecution, and defamation. The incident arose following a classroom discussion about school shooters where the student, allegedly as a joke, posed for a photograph in front of a likeness of himself containing the annotation about a future school shooter. While the criminal charges were dismissed, the court rejected the

---

[24] Kouider *ex rel.* Y.C. v. Parma City Sch. Dist. Bd. of Educ., 480 F. Supp. 3d 772, 385 Educ. L. Rep. 761 (N.D. Ohio 2020).
[25] I.S. *ex rel.* Disla v. Binghamton City Sch. Dist., 486 F. Supp. 3d 575, 386 Educ. L. Rep. 704 (N.D.N.Y. 2020).

student's Fourth Amendment claim on cross-motions for summary judgment because probable cause existed for the arrest.[26] The court reasoned that even if the officer lacked probable cause, he was not liable for malicious prosecution or defamation because the arrest was not objectively unreasonable.

School staff in Florida successfully defended against a Section 1983 claim by a guardian, on behalf of an eight-year-old with an individualized education program and positive behavioral intervention plan (PBIP), for alleged violations of the Fourth and Fourteenth Amendments. While the PBIP listed non-physical responses educators could use, a teacher attempted to move the child after the student refused to comply with directions. The court granted the defendants' motion to dismiss because staff members' having called law enforcement officials to school after the teacher reported that the student punched her was within the scope of their discretion and did not violate the child's established Fourth Amendment rights.[27] In addition, because the court specified that staff members neither had a duty to prevent the summoning of law enforcement nor a substantive due process duty to protect the student under the Fourteenth Amendment, insofar as no custodial relationship existed and their contacting the police was not conscience-shocking, they were protected by qualified immunity.

A juvenile in North Carolina adjudicated delinquent for the sale and delivery of marijuana successfully challenged an order denying his motion to suppress a confession obtained during an interview by a principal, with a silent SRO present. Reversing in favor of the juvenile, an appellate found that under the totality of the circumstances and in light of the SRO's presence, the interrogation was a coercive environment that exceeded restrictions typically imposed during school such that a reasonable student would have believed he was not free to leave. The court added that because the juvenile was in custody during the interview, he was entitled to a *Miranda* warning.[28]

In a juvenile delinquency petition where a student was charged with possession of marijuana, an appellate court in Florida affirmed an order suppressing evidence that the officials improperly seized from his backpack along with his post-*Miranda* incriminating

---

[26] Stokes v. Faber, 522 F. Supp. 3d 225, 394 Educ. L. Rep. 611 (E.D. La. 2021).
[27] Digennaro v. Malgrat, 522 F. Supp. 3d 1189, 394 Educ. L. Rep. 747 (S.D. Fla. 2021).
[28] *In re* D.A.H., 857 S.E. 2d 771, 390 Educ. L. Rep. 767 (N.C. Ct. App. 2021).

statements.[29] The panel asserted that the vice principal lacked reasonable suspicion to search and seize the juvenile's backpack and that the student did not knowingly and voluntarily waive his *Miranda* rights. The court emphasized that because the juvenile made his post-*Miranda* incriminating statements to police only after the vice principal discovered the marijuana, and his remarks resulted from the unlawful seizure, they had to be suppressed as the fruit of the poisonous tree.

In a second case from Florida, another appellate court affirmed that a county sheriff successfully petitioned for a Risk Protection Order (RPO) under a public safety statute after a student with autism became agitated at school and verbally threatened to shoot classmates.[30] Under the RPO, the sheriff sought to confiscate the student's firearms and ammunition. The court upheld the denial of the student's request for declaratory relief because, weighing the non-exhaustive list of fifteen factors in evaluating grounds for an RPO, it felt the student posed a significant danger to himself and others. The court rejected the student's claim that the statute was unconstitutionally vague on its face and as applied because it was convinced that "significant danger" has a plain meaning. The court agreed that the student's claim that the statute impermissibly delegated legislative authority to the executive and judicial branches and prosecutorial authority to law enforcement lacked merit.

A nonstudent was charged with three counts, including conspiracy to commit physical abuse of a child and possession of a firearm on school grounds. When a trial court denied the defendant's motion to suppress evidence of firearms discovered in his vehicle or post-arrest statements, he pled guilty to conspiracy. On further review of a matter of first impression in Wisconsin, an appellate court affirmed that the less-stringent *T.L.O.* "reasonableness, under all the circumstances" standards applied that permit searches on school grounds without probable cause or warrants.[31] The court was of the opinion that the standard applies to searches of nonstudents on school grounds when the subjects are reasonably believed to pose a threat to safety and extends to searches of vehicles. The court posited that it was permissible because the search was justified at its inception and reasonably related in scope to the circumstances.

In Texas, officials at a middle school administratively searched a student after receiving a tip, revealing that he had provided a

---

[29] State v. J.J.T., 310 So. 3d 455, 387 Educ. L. Rep. 410 (Fla. Dist. Ct. App. 2020).
[30] D.T.M. v. Judd, 310 So. 3d 986, 387 Educ. L. Rep. 975 (Fla. Dist. Ct. App. 2020).
[31] State v. Vang, 960 N.W. 2d 434, 436 390 Educ. L. Rep. 1267 (Wis. Ct. App. 2021).

controlled substance to a peer who possessed it a day earlier. Administrators met with the juvenile, who appeared to be under the influence, and commenced a search, leading to the discovery of a controlled substance in his backpack. On review of the denial of the student's motion to dismiss the charge of possession of a controlled substance on school property, an appellate court in Texas affirmed the adjudication of delinquency.[32] The court agreed that the search for controlled substances at school was justified at its inception, the only part of the two-prong test the juvenile questioned.

Family Educational Rights and Privacy Act

In a long-running suit, a board questioned an order granting a news station's Right-to-Know-Law (RTKL) request to obtain school bus surveillance video of an incident involving a high school basketball player and a parent. On remand from the Supreme Court of Pennsylvania, an appellate panel affirmed and remanded with instructions that because the video was directly related to the student and the board maintained it as part of its permanent records, it was an educational record under the Family Educational Rights and Privacy Act (FERPA) but was exempt from public access under the RTKL.[33] However, because the board lacked a policy or practice of releasing protected records or personally identifiable information without parental consent, and it failed to prove by a preponderance of the evidence that disclosure would have resulted in its loss of federal or commonwealth funds, would not have violated FERPA, or fell under RTKL's loss of funds exemption, the court ordered disclosure as long as all personally identifiable information could be redacted. The Supreme Court of Pennsylvania agreed to resolve whether the appellate panel committed reversible error by ordering disclosure and mandating redaction of the student's educational record that was exempt from public access under both FERPA and the RTKL.[34]

---

[32] *In re* I.O., 612 S.W.3d 637, 385 Educ. L. Rep. 427 (Tex. App. 2020).
[33] Cent. Dauphin Sch. Dist. v. Hawkins, 253 A.3d 820, 393 Educ. L. Rep. 382 (Pa. Commw. Ct. 2021).
[34] Cent. Dauphin Sch. Dist. v. Hawkins, 268 A.3d 376 (Pa. 2021).

Abuse, Harassment, and Bullying

Employee-on-Student Actions

The mother of a middle school student in Texas failed in her Title IX claim against her school board for sex discrimination following her daughter's prolonged sexual abuse by an SRO. After the mother learned of the abuse upon discovering sexually explicit text messages on her daughter's cell phone, the SRO was convicted of sexual assault of a child. When the civil case was removed from a state venue, a federal court granted the board's motion for summary judgment. The Fifth Circuit affirmed that although officials were on notice that the SRO and the student had a close bond, they were not liable because they lacked actual knowledge that she was at risk for sexual abuse at his hands.[35]

After a teacher was convicted of first-degree sexual assault and his board terminated his employment, parents, on behalf of a middle school student, filed suit alleging Title IX, Section 1983, and Nebraska tort claims against the board, the principal, and the teacher. Although officials only allowed same-sex pairings for one-on-one mentoring, when parents consented to allow their daughter to work with a teacher in the administrative office, he violated program guidelines by being alone with her in a classroom. On appeal of a grant of summary judgment in favor of the board and principal, as well as a default judgment against the teacher for $1.2 million in damages, the Eighth Circuit affirmed.[36] The court agreed that because the board and principal lacked actual notice of the teacher's alleged misconduct, the claim did not reach the deliberate indifference prong under Title IX and Section 1983.

In Maryland, parents alleged that a classroom aide sexually abused children as a paid employee and volunteer. At the same time, more than a dozen reports complained about his inappropriate behavior and sexual abuse. After the aide pled guilty to criminal charges, their parents sued, alleging Title IX violations against him, the board, and the principal. The federal trial court found that the principal was the appropriate person with authority to address the

---

[35] M.E. v. Alvin Indep. Sch. Dist., 840 F. App'x 773, 388 Educ. L. Rep. 168 (5th Cir. 2020).

[36] KD v. Douglas Cnty. Sch. Dist. No. 001, 1 F.4th 591, 391 Educ. L. Rep. 493 (8th Cir. 2021).

alleged discrimination and institute corrective measures.³⁷ Still, the court denied the board's motion for summary judgment because issues of fact remained as to whether the principal had actual notice after purportedly receiving three reports about the aide's inappropriate conduct, whether she acted with deliberate indifference as the board's proxy by failing to alter his authority over and access to students; and whether the harassment was so severe, pervasive and objectively offensive to create a hostile environment that had an adverse educational impact on the student.

A federal trial court in Mississippi granted motions to dismiss in favor of school defendants after a mother, on behalf of her son, filed suit under Section 1983 and the Fourteenth Amendment when a counselor allegedly sexually assaulted him after she informed officials about his behavior.³⁸ The court dismissed the official capacity claims against the counselor and principal without objection. Next, the court denied the claims against the board because the mother failed to allege plausibly that it had official policies which caused a violation of her son's right to bodily integrity, as required for Section 1983 municipal liability. The court was of the view that even if the board negligently failed to train employees about sexual abuse, it did not act with deliberate indifference, nor was it the moving force behind the counselor's alleged misbehavior. Finally, the court rejected the individual capacity claim against the principal due to qualified immunity because the mother failed to allege plausibly that she learned of facts or a pattern of inappropriate behavior leading to the counselor having sexually abused her son.

In a second case from Mississippi, a former student sued his school board and teacher under Section 1983 and the Fourteenth Amendment alleging failure to investigate properly, train, and supervise teachers, deliberate indifference, and negligence. The plaintiff claimed that board officials permitted unreasonably dangerous conditions to exist on the premises by allowing teachers to cover classroom windows. A federal trial court rejected the Section 1983 claim but only partially granted the defendants' motion for failure to state a claim.³⁹ The court held that the board was not vicariously liable for negligence for the teacher's alleged sexual

---

[37] Andrews *ex rel.* S.H. v. Bd. of Educ. of Prince George's Cnty., 513 F. Supp. 3d 648, 392 Educ. L. Rep. 202 (D. Md. 2021).
[38] Harris *ex rel.* Doe v. Parker, 512 F. Supp. 3d 714, 392 Educ. L. Rep. 101 (S.D. Miss. 2021).
[39] Rodgers v. Smart, 521 F. Supp. 3d 615, 394 Educ. L. Rep. 530 (N.D. Miss. 2021).

assault because it was outside the scope of his duties. The court declined to dismiss the negligence charge due to allegations that the former superintendent performed a discretionary function in failing to conduct a thorough background investigation when hiring the teacher. This was not time-barred under the state tort claims act.

A female high school student who allegedly was sexually harassed and abused by a teacher sued her county school board for violations of Title IX, Section 1983, and state law. The board terminated the teacher's employment upon learning this, leading to his arrest for sexual battery of a minor. A federal trial court in Florida denied the board's motion for summary judgment in part because genuine issues of material facts existed as to whether the board had actual notice of, and responded with deliberate indifference to, the teacher's prior sexual misconduct, his prior relationships with multiple former students, and the risk he ultimately posed to this plaintiff and others at the school.[40] The court did grant the board's motion in part on the Section 1983 claim in light of its policy of deferring to school police in cases of teacher harassment and abuse because this did not deprive the student of her constitutional rights.

The Supreme Court of Wyoming affirmed a board's dismissal of a teacher following an incident during school hours between him and a student who was his daughter.[41] Following an argument earlier in the day, the teacher was speaking with his daughter in a hallway and was seen on a video pulling her to the ground by her sweatshirt and pushing her against lockers. The court agreed that the board's bullying policies and professional conduct standards governing conflicts with students applied to the teacher, even though he was her parent. The court believed that the teacher was on notice of these policies and standards. Substantial evidence showed he violated them by using profanity and physically assaulting the student during the confrontations.

Parents of a special education student who allegedly was molested, raped, and permanently injured by a janitor in an elementary school bathroom filed a petition against the janitor and the board. After a trial court entered a default judgment against the janitor, it held that the board was independently and vicariously liable, awarding the plaintiffs general damages for past and future

---

[40] Doe v. Sch. Bd. of Miami-Dade Cnty., Fla., 521 F. Supp. 3d 1242, 394 Educ. L. Rep. 542 (S.D. Fla. 2019).
[41] Mirich v. State *ex rel.* Bd. of Trs. of Laramie Cnty. Sch. Dist. Two, 481 P.3d 627, 387 Educ. L. Rep. 356 (Wyo. 2021).

medical expenses. An appellate court in Louisiana affirmed that the board was vicariously liable because although it did not authorize the janitor's conduct, he had unsupervised proximity to students, which allowed him to assault isolated children in incidents that took place on school premises during class, and were reasonably related to his employment duties.[42] The court rejected the board's defense of discretionary act immunity because it was independently negligent at an operational level, and was liable for failing to exercise reasonable care by retaining the janitor following the return of his troublesome background check.

Student-on-Student Actions

In Virginia, a former student brought a Title IX action against his county board, alleging that the high school's administrators acted with deliberate indifference to reports that a peer sexually harassed her on a bus trip to perform at a band festival. On a challenge to a jury verdict in favor of the board, the Fourth Circuit reversed in favor of the plaintiff, ordering a new trial due to the lack of evidentiary support that the board did not have actual notice of the student's sexual assault allegations because officials had a report that could objectively have been understood as alleging sexual harassment.[43] Based on the evidence in the record, the court ascertained that a reasonable jury should resolve whether the board acted with deliberate indifference to the student's allegations and if the sexual harassment was so severe, pervasive, and objectively offensive that it deprived the plaintiff of equal access to educational opportunities or benefits.

In Illinois, two female students brought a Title IX action against a school board and various officials, alleging that they failed both to prevent or to make an appropriate response to sexual misconduct by a male peer. After the board insurers received notice of the suit and the board settled with the students, the insurers sought a declaration of their rights and obligations. Because the alleged misconduct occurred outside of the period of the sexual misconduct coverage, the board relied on its errors-and-omissions and general commercial liability coverage. After a federal trial court entered judgment on the pleadings against the insurers, the Seventh Circuit reversed in its favor because the sexual misconduct exclusion

---

[42] Doe v. ABC Sch., 316 So. 3d 1086, 391 Educ. L. Rep. 966 (La. Ct. App. 2020).
[43] Doe v. Fairfax Cnty. Sch. Bd., 1 F.4th 257, 391 Educ. L. Rep. 450 (4th Cir. 2021).

provisions in the error-and-omissions and general commercial liability coverage policies were not ambiguous, such that the student's claims fell outside of the scope of coverage.[44]

After an elementary school student allegedly was sexually violated by classmates, his mother, acting pro se, brought a civil rights action against board members alleging discrimination, retaliation, and harassment. A federal trial court in Florida granted the board's motion to dismiss and denied the mother's request for leave to amend the complaint. The Eleventh Circuit later affirmed that the mother, who was not an attorney, could not bring a pro se action on the child's behalf but could seek legal representation to do so.[45] The panel agreed that the trial court correctly dismissed the complaint for failing to state a plausible claim because federal criminal statutes do not provide for civil causes of action or remedies. Likewise, the court acknowledged that the complaint failed to state a claim of civil rights conspiracy against the board based on its handling of the incident. The panel added that the trial court did not abuse its discretion by denying the mother leave to amend the complaint, as the mother did not indicate how a viable claim could be more carefully drafted.

In Colorado, a high school student whom a classmate raped filed a Section 1983 claim against one of the school's assistant principals and a Title IX charge against the board alleging deliberate indifference due to their failure to respond to information about the assault, allowing the attacker to subject her to harassment and bullying. The federal trial court denied the assistant principal's motion to dismiss the Section 1983 claim on qualified immunity grounds because the amended complaint sufficiently presented a claim for deliberate indifference insofar as he knew of, acquiesced to, and did nothing to stop sexual harassment.[46]

The mother of a high school student, who claimed that she was sexually harassed and physically assaulted by a classmate during study hall within the line of sight of a teacher assigned to supervise the room, filed a Title IX action against the board and various officials. On removing the case from a state court to a federal venue in New York, it partially granted the defendants' motion to

---

[44] Netherlands Ins. Co. v. Macomb Cmty. Unit Sch. Dist. No. 185, 8 F.4th 505, 393 Educ. L. Rep. 524 (7th Cir. 2021).
[45] Grappell v. Carvalho, 847 F. App'x 698, 389 Educ. L. Rep. 778 (11th Cir. 2021).
[46] Doe v. Roaring Fork Sch. Dist., 510 F. Supp. 3d 971, 391 Educ. L. Rep. 759 (D. Colo. 2020).

dismiss.⁴⁷ The court observed that under state law, the mother neither stated a claim for negligent supervision of students nor negligent supervision, hiring, training, and/or retention of employees. The court rejected the Title IX liability claim as to the initial assault. Still, it allowed the mother to proceed with peer-to-peer harassment because officials failed to protect her daughter from further harassment after they were notified of the initial assault.

A high school student in Texas failed in his suit against his school board, alleging its failure to train and supervise staff properly about his complaints of bullying, harassment, discrimination, and retaliation due to his race, in violation of the Civil Rights Act and his Fourteenth Amendment due process rights. A federal trial court in Texas adopted the recommendation of a magistrate judge granting the board's motion to dismiss the Section 1983 claim as to supervisory liability attributed to it and an assistant superintendent because the latter was not the final policy maker.⁴⁸ The court dismissed the student's claim for failure to make a sufficient plea of deliberate indifference over the training policies under either the proof-by-pattern method or narrow single-incident exception.

In the first of a pair of cases from Ohio, a mother who alleged that her son was subjected to systemic student-on-student bullying in school while participating in a youth basketball program brought a Section 1983 action against the board, superintendent, principal, and coaches. A federal trial court granted the mother's motion for a protective order permitting her and her child to proceed in litigation by pseudonym. ⁴⁹ Although usually disfavored, the court considered the confidential nature of the information being compelled during discovery, coupled with the need to protect the child from bullying, plus the possibility that disclosure of his name could lead to more bullying and harassment, which could disrupt the student's educational opportunities.

The parents of a kindergarten student sued her teacher and school officials, alleging that she was bullied and assaulted by a peer, including being punctured by a sharp pencil. The parents claimed that the defendants allegedly acted recklessly or indifferently to known risks and reports about their child being bullied. On appeal

---

⁴⁷ AA by BB v. Hammondsport Cent. Sch. Dist., 527 F. Supp. 3d 501, 395 Educ. L. Rep. 298 (W.D.N.Y. 2021).
⁴⁸ Sneed v. Austin Indep. Sch. Dist., 487 F. Supp. 3d 584, 387 Educ. L. Rep. 213 (W.D. Tex. 2020).
⁴⁹ Doe v. Mechanicsburg Sch. Bd. of Educ., 518 F. Supp. 3d 1024, 393 Educ. L. Rep. 640 (S.D. Ohio 2021).

of an order in favor of the parents, the Supreme Court of Ohio reversed on behalf of the defendants because they were not on notice of a known risk that a peer would have physically harmed the child in light of a previous incident where the former allegedly pushed the plaintiff's daughter while waiting in a line.[50] The court reasoned that even if a known risk existed, there was no evidence that the defendants previously disregarded it. So, the court reinstated a grant of summary judgment in their favor.

In the first of two cases from North Carolina, the mother of three elementary school students sued the State Board of Education for violating their state constitutional rights by acting with deliberate indifference to ongoing harassment and bullying, preventing them from receiving sound primary education. In a challenge to the denial of the state board's motion for an interlocutory appeal, the state's highest court noted that the mother presented a colorable claim based on the officials' deliberate indifference to the hostile academic environment, which deprived her children of their fundamental educational rights.[51] The court ruled that sovereign or governmental immunity could not bar their claim because the plaintiffs lacked an adequate remedy under state law.

After a special education student was attacked by peers, partially with the encouragement of a bus driver, the students were adjudicated delinquent, and the bus driver was charged criminally. When the child was attacked in class two years later, the board succeeded in moving the case to a federal venue, where a trial court essentially granted the defendants' motions to dismiss.[52] The court rejected the claims of violations of the child's right to due process; equal protection due to municipal custom, policy, or practice; and failure to train, supervise, or monitor related to the deliberate indifference to student-on-student wrongdoing as insufficiently pled. The court did point out that because the mother sufficiently established that the board treated her son differently than other similarly situated students, the state law claims could be remanded.

Despite being warned against meeting with an ex-boyfriend, a high school student was killed during a murder-suicide at a friend's house. The student's mother sued the city, school board, and various officials, alleging that they breached their duty of care because they

---

[50] A.J.R. v. Lute, 168 N.E. 3d 1157, 390 Educ. L. Rep. 1182 (Ohio 2020).
[51] Deminski *ex rel.* C.E.D. v. State Bd. of Educ., 858 S.E.2d 788, 391 Educ. L. Rep. 943 (N.C. 2021).
[52] Sciacca v. Durham Cnty. Bd. of Educ., 509 F. Supp. 3d 505, 391 Educ. L. Rep. 651 (M.D.N.C. 2020).

knew of the dispute and that the ex-boyfriend was violent with another ex-girlfriend, resulting in a safety plan for the other female. After a trial court granted the defendants' motion for summary judgment against the mother, an appellate court panel affirmed in part and reversed in part. The Supreme Court of Arizona subsequently explained that while educators have the duty to protect students, it is limited by time and place considerations; they were not liable because this only applies when they fulfill their roles as custodians, land possessors, and quasi-parental figures.[53] According to the court, once students leave the safety of school officials' control, ending their unique relationship, officials are relieved of their affirmative duty to protect pupils from hazards they may encounter.

In Washington, after an ongoing conflict between high school students escalated from threats to assault, resulting in the accused shoving and injuring the victim, officials disciplined both of them. Still, they did not file criminal charges against the aggressor. On further review of an order granting the mother of the injured student an antiharassment protection order, an appellate court in Washington reversed and vacated because she lacked a factual basis for obtaining the relief she sought insofar as the statutory language contemplated granting such a request only after a student has been adjudicated or undergone criminal inquiry by law enforcement.[54]

Substantive Due Process

The parents of a first-grader in Texas diagnosed with attention deficit-hyperactivity disorder and functional defiance disorder unsuccessfully sued their school board and his teacher alleging an unreasonable seizure, plus violations of his rights to substantive due process and under Section 504 and the Americans with Disabilities Act (ADA). After an aide removed the child from class due to his disruptive behavior, when he tried to move forcibly past the teacher by pushing and kicking her, she placed the student on the ground, restraining him in a chokehold. While describing the teacher's behavior as ill-advised, the Fifth Circuit affirmed that it could not classify it as arbitrary, capricious, or unrelated to legitimate state

---

[53] Dinsmoor v. City of Phoenix, 492 P.3d 313, 393 Educ. L. Rep. 837 (Ariz. 2021).
[54] *In re* K.G.T., 483 P.3d 808, 388 Educ. L. Rep. 961 (Wash. Ct. App. 2021).

interests.⁵⁵ The court maintained that state law offered adequate alternative remedies for excessive corporal punishment. The court agreed that the teacher was entitled to qualified immunity on the Fourth Amendment claim because the law is not established when it is permissible to subdue a physically aggressive or violent student. The court upheld the denial of the disability discrimination claims, absent evidence that they were the reason the teacher reacted as she did.

Parents of elementary students in Ohio failed in their Section 1983 action against their school board, officials, and a police impersonator who convinced a principal, teachers, and parents that he was the head of a "scared-straight" program. The complaint included allegations of violating students' rights to equal protection under Section 504 and Title VI. The record revealed that the impersonator regularly intervened in discipline issues by inflicting corporal punishment and verbal abuse on students while restraining them in handcuffs. Once police officials, who had a contract with the board to provide support, realized the man was an imposter, they arrested him, charging him with more than fifty criminal violations. The Sixth Circuit affirmed that getting duped by a con man did not constitute an affirmative act which would have increased the danger associated with a known threat.⁵⁶ The court agreed that neither the teacher nor principal was liable for substantive due process violations and dismissed the equal protection claim because the plaintiff was unable to describe any similarly situated comparator.

Students in Rhode Island unsuccessfully sued state officials seeking a declaration that they had the right to meaningful civics education after the defendants failed to adopt laws and practices to ensure that they provided these opportunities. The federal trial court granted the defendants' motions to dismiss because the students lacked standing to allege violations under the Sixth and Seventh Amendments and the Jury Selection and Service Act due to their failure to plead that they experienced a present injury.⁵⁷ The court rejected the claims because although they did not allege a nonjusticiable political question, the students failed to allege adequately that they were discriminated against based on race or other discrete classification such that the questioned conduct was

---

⁵⁵ T.O. v. Ft. Bend Indep. Sch. Dist., 2 F.4th 407, 391 Educ. L. Rep. 534 (5th Cir. 2021).
⁵⁶ M.J. *ex rel.* S.J. v. Akron City Sch. Dist. Bd. of Educ., 1 F.4th 436, 391 Educ. L. Rep. 474 (6th Cir. 2021).
⁵⁷ A.C. v. Raimondo, 494 F. Supp. 3d 170, 388 Educ. L. Rep. 668 (D.R.I. 2020).

properly reviewed under, and met, rational basis review. The court concluded that civics education is neither a fundamental right under the Constitution nor implicit in the concept of ordered liberty.

An African American middle school student, through his mother, sued the school board in Virginia, various officials, and coaches, alleging substantive due process violations due to allegedly severe and persistent bullying he experienced in his school's football program. The student also brought claims of supervisor liability under Section 1983; racial discrimination under Title VI and Section 504; and negligence, including allegations of assault, racial slurs, and simulated sexual acts against him and others. The record revealed that once notified, the coaches and other officials allegedly took steps to minimize and hide the misbehaviors. The student eventually filed for a waiver to transfer to another school. A federal court denied the defendant's motion to dismiss because the substantive due process claim was such a close call that discovery should proceed.[58] The court allowed the complaints for supervisor liability, deliberate indifference, and Title VI violations to proceed as adequately pleaded. The court dismissed the Section 504 charge for failure to state a claim.

Parents unsuccessfully filed a Section 1983 class action on behalf of their children, challenging the constitutionality of New York's medical exemption requirements for mandatory school immunizations while seeking a TRO and a preliminary injunction to restrain the regulations' implementation and enforcement. A federal trial court recognized that while a showing of irreparable harm and the balance of hardship tipped in the parents' favor, the parents were unlikely to show that the regulations infringed on a fundamental right or liberty interest in parenting or the right to refuse medical procedures.[59] Moreover, the court thought that the parents were unlikely to succeed in their due process challenge allowing school administrators to require additional information in support of a medical exemption, as well as their claim that medical exemption forms and the requirement that they be reissued annually was overly burdensome. The court determined that the regulations' definition of "detrimental to the child's health" was not arbitrary or oppressive, as it related to public health and safety.

In another such case, defendants in New York moved to dismiss the complaint and requested a transfer of venue, while the parents

---

[58] DJ ex rel. Hughes v. Sch. Bd. of Henrico Cnty., 488 F. Supp. 3d 307, 387 Educ. L. Rep. 228 (E.D. Va. 2020).
[59] Doe v. Zucker, 496 F. Supp. 3d 744, 389 Educ. L. Rep. 123 (N.D.N.Y. 2020).

filed a motion to amend. A federal trial court rejected the motion to amend as futile because the proposed complaint could not survive.[60] As the court was persuaded that the parents' failure to comply with medical exemption requirements did not infringe a fundamental right, it evaluated their substantive due process claims under rational basis scrutiny, decreeing that they failed to present such a claim. Because the medical exemptions were issued for medical reasons based on nationally accepted evidence guidance, the court dismissed the equal protection claims.

After officials in New Mexico ordered school closures in response to the COVID-19 pandemic, parents and a local board of education sought injunctive relief under Section 1983, alleging violations of their rights to equal protection and substantive due process, as well as of the state constitution and the right to a free appropriate public education under the IDEA. The federal trial court partially denied the state's motion to dismiss because the plaintiffs suffered an injury-in-fact; additionally, there was a causal connection between and among the actions of the governor, secretary of education and the harm that a favorable order likely would have redressed.[61] The court did grant the motion in part when the plaintiffs voluntarily dismissed their claims against the state and secretary of the health department. The court indicated that the plaintiffs sufficiently stated Section 1983 claims alleging that the governor and education secretary participated in creating, implementing, and enforcing the COVID-19 reentry guidance and process.

In Louisiana, a high school student and her guardian filed claims of substantive due process violations against two teachers who used force to restrain her out-of-control, violent behavior as she fought with a peer. During the struggle, the plaintiff claimed to have suffered a concussion and post-traumatic stress syndrome. A federal trial court granted the teachers' motion for qualified immunity despite using aggressive language during the altercation, suggesting that the students had other avenues of a remedy under state law for intentional infliction of emotional distress, assault and battery, and abuse of a minor.[62]

When social workers in California interviewed children at school without parental consent, a federal trial court granted their motion for qualified immunity on substantive due process, and Fourth

---

[60] Doe v. Zucker, 520 F. Supp. 3d 217, 394 Educ. L. Rep. 154 (N.D.N.Y. 2021).
[61] Hernandez v. Grisham, 499 F. Supp. 3d 1013, 390 Educ. L. Rep. 54 (D.N.M. 2020).
[62] E.H. *ex rel.* Abron v. Barrilleaux, 519 F. Supp. 3d 328, 393 Educ. L. Rep. 668 (E.D. La. 2021).

Amendment claims.[63] The court was of the opinion that the parents stated a *Monell* claim against the county based on evidence that its social workers routinely made false representations and omitted exculpatory information during juvenile proceedings.

In Utah, the father of a deceased student unsuccessfully sued his police department, school board, and various officials, alleging substantive due process violations when he was not informed of his son's possible involvement with drugs. Despite the death of two of the plaintiff's son's friends, school officials never mentioned their suspicion to the father that his son might have been involved in drug use. The court granted the defendants' motion to dismiss based on qualified immunity because the right to be informed of dangerous drugs was not clearly established.[64] The court also asserted that neither the special relationship nor the state-created danger theories applied because inaction was not enough, the actions of those involved did not shock its conscience, and the requisite level of control did not exist to assign liability.

Discrimination

Racial Discrimination

Parents in Connecticut filed a suit challenging state standards regulating the racial composition of inter-district magnet schools, claiming equal protection violations because the standards required all such schools to enroll at least 25 percent non-Black and non-Hispanic students under the threat of a financial penalty. The group claimed to have incurred substantial expenses in its effort to educate parents around the state about the harmful effects of the state-wide racial quota regulations. On appeal of dismissal in favor of the state for lack of organizational standing, the Second Circuit affirmed that the alleged injury-in-fact did not directly interfere with the group's ability to carry out its core activities.[65]

The first of two cases from Texas involving high school students who are African American addressed a discrimination claim under

---

[63] Scanlon v. Cnty. of Los Angeles, 495 F. Supp. 3d 894, 388 Educ. L. Rep. 871 (C.D. Cal. 2020).
[64] Ainsworth v. Park City Police Dep't, 515 F. Supp. 3d 1182, 392 Educ. L. Rep. 835 (D. Utah 2021).
[65] Conn. Parents Union v. Russell-Tucker, 8 F.4th 167, 393 Educ. L. Rep. 483 (2d Cir. 2021).

Title VI alleging repeated incidents of peer-to-peer racial harassment. The complaint described incidents where the student was called racial slurs, subjected to loud music, including racial slurs, and treated with disdain and hostility by other students, mostly in band and classes. A federal trial court rejected the defense's motions for summary judgment regarding the existence of a racially hostile environment and deliberate indifference to the use of racial slurs by peers because material issues of fact remained.[66] The court did grant the defense's motions for summary judgment as to other incidents of harassment because officials did not act with deliberate indifference.

Another African American high school student in Texas filed suit seeking to prevent the enforcement of a board policy over hair length for males. The student, out of a desire to pay homage to his cultural roots, grew his hair into locks over three years, exceeding the allowable lengths described in the board policy such that he tied his hair up to comply. Despite these efforts, the complaint alleged that during his first year and a half of high school, the student was called out of class approximately once per week for an inspection of his hair. Halfway through the student's second year, the board added the words "when let down"[67] to the hair length policy for males, under which he was forced to either cut his hair or transfer to another district. On choosing the latter, he filed suit. A federal trial court granted the student's motion for summary judgment because it was likely to succeed on the merits of his equal protection claim based on sex, his First Amendment charge, the irreparable harm he faced outweighed the potential harm to the board, and that the public interest would not have been disserved.

A school board disputed an order from the Pennsylvania Human Rights Commission (HRC) to cease and desist the use of imagery negatively stereotyping Native Americans as constituting unlawful discrimination. Reversing in favor of the school board, an appellate court emphasized that while the HRC had jurisdiction to hear the complaint, its conclusion that the imagery harmed Native Americans was unsubstantiated and speculative.[68]

---

[66] Sneed v. Austin Indep. Sch. Dist., 490 F. Supp. 3d 1069, 387 Educ. L. Rep. 697 (W.D. Tex. 2020).
[67] Arnold v. Barbers Hill Indep. Sch. Dist., 479 F. Supp. 3d 511, 517, 385 Educ. L. Rep. 614 (S.D. Tex. 2020).
[68] Neshaminy Sch. Dist. v. Pa. Hum. Relations Comm'n, 257 A.3d 766, 394 Educ. L. Rep. 951 (Pa. Commw. Ct..2021).

Desegregation

An Arkansas school board, operating under a desegregation decree, succeeded in gaining an exemption from the state's Public School Choice Act banning segregative inter-district transfers as a federal trial court approved the request enabling it to make transfers on a case-by-case basis.[69] On further review of a challenge by the state Department of Education, the Eighth Circuit reversed and remanded in its favor.[70] The panel was of the view that the trial court abused its discretion and that the amendments to the Act did not constitute a change in circumstances supporting the modification to the decree because the board could not explain how the requested modification impacted the vestiges of segregation.

Sexual Discrimination

Transgender Students

Most courts examining transgender student bathroom usage policy have entered judgments in favor of the plaintiffs under equal protection and/or Title IX. In this year's only case, a transgender student in Florida sued the board, claiming that its unwritten bathroom usage policy, which prohibited the plaintiff from using the boys' restroom, violated equal protection and Title IX. The record described the plaintiff as a depressed and anxious child who suffered from gender dysphoria before transitioning from a female to a male through hormones and gender reassignment surgery. The first few months after transitioning, the plaintiff used the boys' restroom without complaints or concerns. Then, without reason, the board adopted a policy requiring students to use the bathrooms associated with the genders listed on their enrollment documents or one that was gender-neutral. On appeal of an injunction and damages in favor of the plaintiff, the Eleventh Circuit only examined the equal protection claim, commenting that the board's bathroom policy assigned students to bathrooms arbitrarily. This court vacated the

---

[69] U.S. v. Junction City Sch. Dist., 984 F.3d 608, 385 Educ. L. Rep. 142 (8th Cir. 2020).
[70] U.S. v. Junction City Sch. Dist., 14 F.4th 658, 395 Educ. L. Rep. 143 (8th Cir. 2021).

order when a majority of the active judges in the circuit voted to grant a rehearing *en banc*.[71]

At issue in Idaho was a challenge to the state's Fairness in Women's Sports Act which banned transgender females from participating in women's sports, established a gender verification process, created a private cause of action against school boards that violated its terms, and prevented retaliation against those who reported suspected violations. Transgender college and high school students sought to enjoin enforcement of the Act as violations of their equal protection and Title IX rights. The federal trial court granted the transgender students' motion because the claim would succeed on the merits, and the plaintiff would have suffered irreparable harm if the Act were enforced.[72] The court contended that an intervening cisgender student would likely succeed on the merits of her equal protection claim because males were not subjected to the invasive gender verification processes, which it believed would incentivize harassment and exclusionary practices.

Non-transgender Sex Discrimination Claims

A male high school student in Virginia sued his board, alleging Title IX, due process, and free speech violations due to a disciplinary process associated with sexual assault allegations. Three female students complained about inappropriate questions of a sexual nature, with one alleging that he touched her below her navel. Because the plaintiff admitted many of the allegations, the Fourth Circuit rejected his erroneous outcome claim while rebuffing his charge that a prior high-profile sexual assault scandal presupposed the board toward gender discrimination.[73] Next, the court decided that the board provided adequate due process and that cross-examination of the accusers was unnecessary, given the admissions. The court wrote that the plaintiff's vulgar comments were not constitutionally protected and the board's sexual harassment policy, which included terms such as "intimidating" or "offensive," was not overly broad.

Parents of female students in North Carolina sued a charter school corporation, members of its board, and its managing operator

---

[71] Adams v. Sch. Bd. of St. Johns Cnty., Fla., 3 F.4th 1299, 392 Educ. L. Rep. 538 (11th Cir. 2021), rehearing en banc granted, vacated, 9 F.4th 1369, 11th Cir. (Fla.), Aug. 23, 2021

[72] Hecox v. Little, 479 F. Supp. 3d 930, 385 Educ. L. Rep. 657 (D. Idaho 2020).

[73] Doe 2 *ex rel.* Doe 1 v. Fairfax Cnty. Sch. Bd., 832 F. App'x 802, 385 Educ. L. Rep. 215 (4th Cir. 2020).

claiming equal protection and Title IX violations arising from its dress code. The plaintiffs objected primarily to the requirement that females wear skirts, arguing that doing so limited their mobility; forced them to sit with their knees together, distracting them from their academic efforts; and sent a message that they were more delicate than males. On review of a grant of summary judgment in favor of the operator, the Fourth Circuit reversed and remanded because adopting the dress code was not attributable to the state.[74] The court reversed the Title IX claim because genuine issues of material fact remained as to whether the dress code excluded females from participating in or denied them the benefits of the school's educational program.

Female high school students in Utah unsuccessfully sued the state's athletic association, claiming that refusing to offer tackle football for girls violated their rights to equal protection under Title IX. Rejecting the claims, the federal trial court found no evidence of invidious discrimination, that any female was denied participation in tackle football, or that a policy or practice existed under which state officials failed to accommodate the athletic interests of females.[75] Conversely, the court acknowledged that there were nondiscriminatory reasons for the low participation rate of females in tackle football, such as fear of injury.

The Supreme Court of Nevada reversed and remanded an order in favor of parents for additional findings of fact on Title IX bullying and harassment. The parents alleged that classmates frequently called names and teased the sons regarding their sexual orientation. The plaintiff's son and his friend displayed signs of stress, avoided class, and stopped attending school. Eventually, both students enrolled in private schools. The court ruled that the homophobic name-calling the students experienced fell within the penumbra of Title IX, that officials had actual notice of severe and pervasive bullying, and had substantial control over the harasser but did not act with deliberate indifference to be subject to *Monell* liability.[76]

---

[74] Peltier v. Charter Day Sch., 8 F.4th 251, 393 Educ. L. Rep. 493 (4th Cir. 2021).
[75] Gordon v. Jordan Sch. Dist., 522 F. Supp. 3d 1060, 394 Educ. L. Rep. 704 (D. Utah 2021).
[76] Clark Cnty. Sch. Dist. v. Bryan, 478 P.3d 344, 385 Educ. L. Rep. 982 (Nev. 2020).

Student Discipline

Parents of a fourth-grader in Louisiana filed suit challenging his six-day suspension after a teacher in an online class observed a BB gun in the room that he shared with his brothers. The parents failed in seeking a writ of mandamus directing the board to review the suspension, or judicial review, claiming violations of Sections 1983 and 1985. After the board had the case removed to a federal trial court, while the parents sought a remand to a state venue, the court observed that the request did not involve a novel question of state law, arose from the same facts as the federal claims and the statute did not mandate litigation in state court. The court refused to apply the *Burford* abstention because the state law was clear, unambiguous, and not subject to ongoing state proceedings or complex administrative regulations. Likewise, the court refused to apply the *Younger* abstention due to a lack of state judicial proceedings, and it did not involve an important matter of state interest.[77]

A student in Pennsylvania with autism and Tourette syndrome sued his school board and various officials, claiming violations of his rights to expression under the First Amendment, due process, and equal protection, as well as of Section 504 and ADA, after being suspended for more than 60 days for posting offensive and threatening messages on social media. The concern arose because the student used racist language and images of weapons he claimed could smuggle weapons past school security guards. A federal trial court denied the defense's motion for summary judgment because genuine issues of material fact existed as to whether the student had a "kill list," whether he told others about the list, whether he made other threats of violence in school, and whether officials suspended him without a hearing due to his alleged in-school statements or online postings.[78] The court granted the defendants' motions for summary judgment based on qualified immunity because the policy under which the student was suspended was not unconstitutionally vague or overbroad, and there was no evidence of disability discrimination under Section 504.

After being adjudicated delinquent on charges of theft and second-degree assault, a student in Maryland unsuccessfully

---

[77] Harrison v. Jefferson Parish Sch. Bd., 502 F. Supp. 3d 1088, 390 Educ. L. Rep. 626 (E.D. La. 2020).

[78] Hewlette-Bullard on behalf of J.H-B. v. Pocono Mountain Sch. Dist., 522 F.Supp.3d 78, 394 Educ. L. Rep. 555 (M.D. Pa. 2021).

disputed the conditions placed on his probation, claiming that the order not to suspend him from school was unconstitutionally vague and lacking procedural safeguards. The Court of Special Appeals affirmed that the trial court did not abuse its discretion and that the conditions of probation were clear, definite, capable of comprehension, rationally related to the offenses, and infused with substantial procedural safeguards.[79]

Crimes

In the first of three cases dealing with terroristic threats, the Supreme Court of South Dakota reversed the adjudication of juvenile delinquency, where a principal sent a student to the office to agitate an emotionally disturbed peer. While in the office, the student spoke about a bomb and killing others with scissors. The panel admonished the lower court for not including additional findings of fact or conclusions of law, pointing out that the evidence was insufficient to classify any remarks as terroristic threats.[80]

A student in California unsuccessfully challenged his conviction for making terroristic threats upon being sentenced to six months of probation after posting pictures of a replica gun with captions about school attendance.[81] Analyzing the facts through the filter of telecommunications law, specifically the elements of the crime of making a criminal threat, an appellate court affirmed that the student intended to make an unequivocal, unconditional, immediate, and specific threat which caused classmates and teachers to have reasonable fears for their safety.

When a student in Alabama posted an image of a Columbine shooter on the Instagram page of an acquaintance who lived in a different state in a misguided effort to be funny—despite apologizing profusely, deleting the post, and begging for forgiveness—the acquaintance shared it with parents and others who added comments about school shootings. Given the widespread media coverage of events in another district two weeks earlier, concern over the post spread widely. The local police department received an alarming number of calls, and school operations were substantially disrupted for days. Despite a police search of the student's home, which uncovered nothing of concern, officials charged him with

---

[79] *In re* S.F., 245 A.3d 30, 387 Educ. L. Rep. 795 (Md. Ct. Spec. App. 2021).
[80] *In re* I.T.B., 962 N.W.2d 436, 392 Educ. L. Rep. 972 (S.D. 2021).
[81] *In re* A.G., 272 Cal. Rptr. 3d 602, 385 Educ. L. Rep. 272 (Cal. Ct. App. 2020).

making a terroristic threat, and he was adjudicated as delinquent. An appellate court reversed in favor of the student due to insufficient evidence revealing any intent to convey a message of harm or create a serious public inconvenience.[82]

Miscellaneous Claims from COVID-19 Restrictions

The Supreme Court of South Carolina reviewed a proviso of the state's appropriations act claiming that it forbade school officials from imposing mask mandates funded by the act and that it is setting a five percent cap for virtual education program enrollments was unconstitutional. The court noted that another proviso manifestly set forth the legislature's intent to prohibit mask mandates funded by the appropriations act. It did not violate the one-subject rule because it was reasonably and inherently related to raising and spending tax money.[83] The court rejected the claim that the proviso violated the state constitutional guarantee of equal protection or free education for students while rejecting the plaintiffs' request for an advisory opinion.

Parents in New York commenced a hybrid Article 78 proceeding, seeking a declaratory judgment against the governor and various officials challenging executive orders issued in response to the COVID-19 pandemic. The parents sought to compel school boards to offer full-time, in-person instruction and declarations that guidance issued under executive orders on social distancing was invalid arbitrary, and capricious. Alternatively, the parents sought a declaration that hybrid/remote learning models were unlawful. A trial court rejected the claim that the governor exceeded his authority in issuing and renewing the executive orders.[84] The court denied the parent's request for a TRO and a preliminary injunction because the parents could not demonstrate that students attending school through the hybrid/remote learning models were deprived of meaningful education. However, the court invalidated guidelines establishing disparate social distancing requirements for elementary and secondary students and the county-wide metric used for gauging the need for school closures as arbitrary and capricious.

---

[82] N.C. v. State, 309 So. 3d 629, 386 Educ. L. Rep. 1071 (Ala. Crim. App. 2020).
[83] Richland Cnty. Sch. Dist. 2 v. Lucas, 862 S.E.2d 920, 395 Educ. L. Rep. 439 (S.C. 2021).
[84] Hensley v. Williamsville Cent. Sch. Dist., 150 N.Y.S.3d 513, 393 Educ. L. Rep. 801 (N.Y. Sup. Ct. 2021).

Compulsory Attendance

A mother in Georgia failed to sue her superintendent and school board, seeking a writ of prohibition, a temporary restraining order, and temporary and permanent injunctions after her children were disenrolled for non-residency. An appellate court affirmed that the mother was not entitled to relief, that the order was not directly appealable, and that she failed to follow the procedures required to file an interlocutory challenge.[85]

Conclusion

The chapter represents an abbreviated version covering ten volumes of West's *Education Law Reporter,* 385-395. The cases include common themes seen in previous years, except disputes over the mandates associated with COVID-19. We anticipate additional cases in next year's chapter based on substantive due process and free-exercise claims. In addition, there will likely be an increase in cases where parents question curricular content, including Critical Race Theory and issues of sexual identity. There may also be an increase in cases of student discipline, student-on-student abuse, and harassment as the social-emotional impact of the government shutdowns and mask mandates play out in schools.

---

[85] Nance v. Houston Cnty. Sch. Dist., 857 S.E. 2d 97, 389 Educ. L. Rep. 589 (Ga. Ct. App. 2021).

Alphabetized Case List

A.C. v. Raimondo
A.G., *In re*
A.H., *In re*
A.J.R. v. Lute
A.W. by E.W. v. New York Dep't of Educ.
AA by BB v. Hammondsport Cent. Sch. Dist.
Adams v. Sch. Bd. of St. Johns Cnty., Fla.
Ainsworth v. Park City Police Dep't
Andrews ex rel. S.H. v. Bd. of Educ. of Prince George's Cnty.
Arnold v. Barbers Hill Indep. Sch. Dist.
B.W.C. v. Williams
C1.G. v. Siegfried
Cent. Dauphin Sch. Dist. v. Hawkins
Clark Cnty. Sch. Dist. v. Bryan
Coble v. Lake Norman Charter Sch.
Concepcion v. N.Y.C. Dep't of Educ.
Conn. Parents Union v. Russell-Tucker
D.A.H., *In re*
D.T.M. v. Judd
Danville Christian Acad.
Deminski *ex rel.* C.E.D. v. State Bd. of Educ.
Digennaro v. Malgrat
Dinsmoor v. City of Phoenix
DJ *ex rel.* Hughes v. Sch. Bd. of Henrico Cnty.
Doe 2 *ex rel.* Doe 1 v. Fairfax Cnty. Sch. Bd.
Doe *ex rel.* Doe v. Hopkinton Pub. Schs.
Doe v. ABC Sch.
Doe v. Fairfax Cnty. Sch. Bd.
Doe v. Mechanicsburg Sch. Bd. of Educ.
Doe v. Roaring Fork Sch. Dist.
Doe v. Sch. Bd. of Miami-Dade Cnty., Fla.
Doe v. Zucker
E.H. *ex rel.* Abron v. Barrilleaux
Gordon v. Jordan Sch. Dist.
Grappell v. Carvalho
Harris ex rel. Doe v. Parker
Harrison v. Jefferson Parish Sch. Bd.
Hecox v. Little
Hensley v. Williamsville Cent. Sch. Dist.
Hernandez v. Grisham
Hewlette-Bullard on behalf of J.H-B. v. Pocono Mountain Sch. Dist.

Hilsenrath *ex rel.* C.H. v. Sch. Dist. of Chathams
I.O., *In re*
I.S. *ex rel.* Disla v. Binghamton City Sch. Dist.
I.T.B., *In re*
K.G.T., *In re*
KD v. Douglas Cnty. Sch. Dist. No. 001
Kouider *ex rel.* Y.C. v. Parma City Sch. Dist. Bd. of Educ.
L.G. *ex rel.* M.G. v. Columbia Pub. Schs.
M.E. v. Alvin Indep. Sch. Dist.
M.J. *ex rel.* S.J. v. Akron City Sch. Dist. Bd. of Educ.
Mahanoy Area Sch. Dist. v. B. L. *ex rel.* Levy
Mirich v. State *ex rel.* Bd. of Trs. of Laramie Cnty. Sch. Dist. Two
N.C. v. State
Nance v. Houston Cnty. Sch. Dist.
Neshaminy Sch. Dist. v. Pa. Hum. Relations Comm'n
Netherlands Ins. Co. v. Macomb Cmty. Unit Sch. Dist. No. 185
Oliver v. Arnold
Peltier v. Charter Day Sch.
Price *ex rel.* J.K. v. Mueller-Owens
Resurrection Sch. v. Gordon
Resurrection Sch. v. Hertel
Richland Cnty. Sch. Dist. 2 v. Lucas
Robertson v. Anderson Mill Elem. Sch.
Rodgers v. Smart
S.F., *In re*
Scanlon v. Cnty. of Los Angeles
Sciacca v. Durham Cnty. Bd. of Educ.
Sneed v. Austin Indep. Sch. Dist.
State v. J.J.T.
State v. Vang
Stokes v. Faber
T.O. v. Ft. Bend Indep. Sch. Dist.
T.S.H. v. Green
Thomas v. Varnado
U.S. v. Junction City Sch. Dist.
W.D. v. Rockland Cnty.
Waln v. Dysart Sch. Dist.

Cases by Jurisdiction

FEDERAL CASES

U.S. Supreme Court
Mahanoy Area Sch. Dist. v. B. L. *ex rel.* Levy

First Circuit

Massachusetts
Doe *ex rel.* Doe v. Hopkinton Pub. Schs.
Rhode Island
A.C. v. Raimondo

Second Circuit
A.H. *In re*
Concepcion v. N.Y.C. Dep't of Educ.
Conn. Parents Union v. Russell-Tucker

New York
AA by BB v. Hammondsport Cent. Sch. Dist
A.W. by E.W. v. New York Dep't of Educ.
Doe v. Zucker
I.S. *ex rel.* Disla v. Binghamton City Sch. Dist.
W.D. v. Rockland Cnty.

Third Circuit

New Jersey
Hilsenrath *ex rel.* C.H. v. Sch. Dist. of Chathams
Pennsylvania
Hewlette-Bullard on behalf of J.H-B. v. Pocono Mountain Sch. Dist.

Fourth Circuit
Doe v. Fairfax Cnty. Sch. Bd.
Doe 2 *ex rel.* Doe 1 v. Fairfax Cnty. Sch. Bd.
Peltier v. Charter Day Sch.
Robertson v. Anderson Mill Elem. Sch.

Maryland
Andrews ex rel. S.H. v. Bd. of Educ. of Prince George's Cnty.
North Carolina

Coble v. Lake Norman Charter Sch.
Sciacca v. Durham Cnty. Bd. of Educ.
Virginia
DJ *ex rel.* Hughes v. Sch. Bd. of Henrico Cnty.

Fifth Circuit
M.E. v. Alvin Indep. Sch. Dist.
Oliver v. Arnold
T.O. v. Ft. Bend Indep. Sch. Dist.

Louisiana
E.H. *ex rel.* Abron v. Barrilleaux
Harrison v. Jefferson Parish Sch. Bd.
Stokes v. Faber
Thomas v. Varnado
Mississippi
Harris ex rel. Doe v. Parker
Rodgers v. Smart
Texas
Arnold v. Barbers Hill Indep. Sch. Dist.
Sneed v. Austin Indep. Sch. Dist.

Sixth Circuit
M.J. *ex rel.* S.J. v. Akron City Sch. Dist. Bd. of Educ.
Resurrection Sch. v. Hertel

Kentucky
Danville Christian Acad. v. Beshear
Ohio
Doe v. Mechanicsburg Sch. Bd. of Educ.
Kouider *ex rel.* Y.C. v. Parma City Sch. Dist. Bd. of Educ.
Michigan
Resurrection Sch. v. Gordon

Seventh Circuit
Netherlands Ins. Co. v. Macomb Cmty. Unit Sch. Dist. No. 185

Wisconsin
Price *ex rel.* J.K. v. Mueller-Owens

Eighth Circuit
KD v. Douglas Cnty. Sch. Dist. No. 001
L.G. *ex rel.* M.G. v. Columbia Pub. Schs.

T.S.H. v. Green
U.S. v. Junction City Sch. Dist.

Ninth Circuit

Arizona
Waln v. Dysart Sch. Dist
California
Scanlon v. Cnty. of Los Angeles,
Idaho
Hecox v. Little

Tenth Circuit

Colorado
C1.G. v. Siegfried
Doe v. Roaring Fork Sch. Dist.
New Mexico
Hernandez v. Grisham
Utah
Ainsworth v. Park City Police Dep't
Gordon v. Jordan Sch. Dist.

Eleventh Circuit
Adams v. Sch. Bd. of St. Johns Cnty., Fla.
Grappell v. Carvalho

Florida
Digennaro v. Malgrat,
Doe v. Sch. Bd. of Miami-Dade Cnty., Fla.

STATE & D.C. COURT CASES

Alabama
N.C. v. State

Arizona
Dinsmoor v. City of Phoenix

California
In re A.G

Florida
D.T.M. v. Judd
State v. J.J.T.

Georgia
Nance v. Houston Cnty. Sch. Dist.

Louisiana
Doe v. ABC Sch.

Maryland
In re S.F

Nevada
Clark Cnty. Sch. Dist. v. Bryan

New York
Hensley v. Williamsville Cent. Sch. Dist.

North Carolina
Deminski *ex rel.* C.E.D. v. State Bd. of Educ.
In re D.A.H.

Ohio
A.J.R. v. Lute

Pennsylvania
Cent. Dauphin Sch. Dist. v. Hawkins
Neshaminy Sch. Dist. v. Pa. Hum. Relations Comm'n

South Carolina
Richland Cnty. Sch. Dist. 2 v. Lucas

South Dakota
I.T.B., *In re*

Texas
I.O., *In re*

Washington
K.G.T., *In re*

Wisconsin
State v. Vang

Wyoming
Mirich v. State *ex rel.* Bd. of Trs. of Laramie Cnty. Sch. Dist. Two

Chapter 4

BARGAINING

Jeffrey S. Greenley, J.D., M.S.[1]

Introduction	126
Arbitration	126
Duty of Fair Representation	127
Fair Share Fees and Union Dues	127
Interpretation of CBAs and Statutes	129
Conclusion	131
Alphabetical List of Cases	132
Cases by Jurisdiction	132

---

[1] Superintendent, Belpre City Schools, Belpre, Ohio

Introduction

This chapter reviews K-12 cases involving collective bargaining published during 2021. The cases, which come from both state and federal courts, provide a glimpse of the status of the ever-changing process of collective bargaining. The chapter is divided by subject matter to better organize the various cases and their outcomes.

Arbitration

A New York teachers' union unsuccessfully brought a grievance. It sought a preliminary injunction to enjoin its school board from requiring teachers to report to work in person during the COVID-19 pandemic and for failing to respond to a demand for safe work environment information. After a hearing on the merits, a trial court held that the board's reopening of the schools was not arbitrable because it was a monumental question affecting the general public, such that a preliminary injunction would have deprived the state from exercising supervision over a constitutionally required obligation.[2] Moreover, the court observed that the union failed to meet any of the factors necessary to obtain a preliminary injunction, given the speculative nature of the union's concerns, combined with the proactive and protective steps school officials took to reopen the buildings.

Another case from New York illustrated that a grievance may still be arbitrable even if it is not derived from the language in a collective bargaining agreement (CBA). When a teachers' federation sought to compel arbitration because board employees disclosed confidential information to the public about the disciplinary charges two teachers faced in violation of a state code of ethics, an appellate court affirmed an order in its favor.[3] The court agreed that although there was no specific reference to the code of ethics in the CBA, arbitration provisions are to be interpreted broadly, finding that a reasonable relationship existed between the subject matter of the dispute and that of the CBA.

---

[2] Buffalo Tchrs. Fed'n v. Bd. of Educ. of City Sch. Dist. of Buffalo, 142 N.Y.S. 3d 736, 389 Educ. L. Rep. 419 (N.Y. Sup. Ct. 2021).
[3] Bd. of Educ. Yonkers City Sch. Dist. v. Yonkers Fed'n of Teachers, 135 N.Y.S.3d 422, 385 Educ. L. Rep. 307 (N.Y. App. Div. 2020).

Duty of Fair Representation

As reflected by a case from New York, claims over the duty of fair representation can be dismissed if not timely filed. The Second Circuit affirmed the dismissal of such a pro se claim where the employee failed to file her action alleging civil rights violations within the timeframes of both the state and federal statutes of limitations and had not exhausted administrative remedies.[4]

Fair Share Fees and Union Dues

Litigation continues in the wake of the U.S. Supreme Court's landmark judgment in *Janus v. American Federation of State, County, and Municipal Employees Council 31*,[5] which ended compulsory fair share fees for non-union public employees. In Illinois, a non-union teacher who refused to participate in a strike filed a class action suit challenging a state law requiring him to pay fair share fees, seeking to recover the monies he paid. On further review of the dismissal of the teacher's claim, the Seventh Circuit affirmed that because union officials acted in good faith under then-current law in collecting the fees, they did not have to return the dues.[6] Not long after that, the Fourth Circuit, in a similar fashion, affirmed that non-union teachers in Maryland could not recover the fair share fees they paid because even though the law under which they did so was struck down, officials acted in good faith in collecting the monies.[7]

After *Janus*, a union member may cease paying union dues, but only in accordance with the terms and conditions of the applicable CBA. In such a case, when a custodian in Illinois notified union officials that she wished to resign her membership and stop paying dues immediately, they allowed her to do so but only permitted her to opt out of payments after the window outlined in her union membership agreement lapsed. Affirming an earlier order in favor of the union, the Seventh Circuit agreed that because the custodian voluntarily decided to pay for the benefits of union membership, she

---

[4] Malcolm v. Ass'n of Supervisors and Adm'rs of Rochester, 831 F. App'x 1, 384 Educ. L. Rep. 733 (2d Cir. 2021).
[5] Janus v Am. Fed'n of State, Cnty., & Mun. Emps., Council 31, 138 S. Ct. 2448 (2018).
[6] Ocol v. Chic. Tchrs. Union, 982 F.3d 529, 384 Educ. L. Rep. 56 (7th Cir. 2020).
[7] Akers v. Md. State Educ. Ass'n, 990 F.3d 375, 387 Educ. L. Rep. 134 (4th Cir. 2021).

was bound by the terms and conditions of that contract, including its cancellation window.[8]

The Third Circuit, in a case from New Jersey with similar facts and legal arguments, affirmed that union members remained bound to the terms of their membership agreements after *Janus* and could only resign during the applicable windows outlined in their CBAs.[9] A federal trial court in Illinois reached the same outcome in a class action suit by teachers, granting their union's motion to dismiss their claim because by voluntarily agreeing to the terms of union membership, they could only cease paying dues during the window set forth in their CBA.[10]

Public school teachers and other employees in Minnesota unsuccessfully filed a class action suit seeking refunds for those who paid union dues and fair share fees. The federal trial court granted the union's motion to dismiss on the basis that the good faith defense did not obligate it to a refund of dues of those who paid fair share fees, adding that union members could only cease payments by complying with the cancellation window in their CBAs.[11]

In Nevada, the state's highest court affirmed that a local teachers' union did not breach the bylaws of its national affiliate by terminating its dues-transmittal agreement for payments in a dispute that arose when it sought to renegotiate its dues-collection service agreement with the state affiliate.[12] When, after notifying the state union at least three times of its intent to renegotiate, the local union stopped transmitting dues, the state and national affiliates filed suit arguing that, under their bylaws and constitutions, the local did not have the authority to cease payments. Ruling in favor of the local union, the court agreed that it was only bound by a contractual agreement to transmit dues, not the bylaws of the two outside organizations. It correctly terminated the agreement under its terms through the letters demanding renegotiate.

---

[8] Bennett v. Council 31 of the Am. Fed'n of State, Cnty., and Mun. Emps., AFL-CIO, 991 F.3d 724, 388 Educ. L. Rep. 67 (7th Cir. 2021).

[9] Fischer v. Gov. of N.J., 842 F. App'x 741, 388 Educ. L. Rep. 596 (3d Cir. 2021).

[10] Troesch v. Chic. Tchrs. Union, Local Union No. 1, Am. Fed'n of Tchrs., 522 F. Supp. 3d 425, 394 Educ. L. Rep. 627 (N.D. Ill. 2021).

[11] Hoekman v. Educ. Minn., 519 F. Supp. 3d 497, 393 Educ. L. Rep. 696 (D. Minn. 2021).

[12] Nev. State Educ. Ass'n v. Clark Cnty. Educ. Ass'n, 482 P.3d 665, 387 Educ. L. Rep. 938 (Nev. 2021).

Interpretation of CBAs and Statutes

According to the Supreme Court of New Jersey, school boards are permitted to pay the salary and benefits of teachers temporarily serving full-time in support of their union. The litigation arose when taxpayers sued their school board under multiple state statutes to prevent it from using public funds to compensate teachers for their full-time union work. Although a trial court originally dismissed the action, an intermediate panel reversed in favor of the taxpayers, rejecting the practice as improperly using public funds. On further review, the state's highest court reversed in favor of the board, explaining that the release provisions serve a public purpose insofar as they encourage cooperative labor relations, facilitate the early resolution of disputes, and support the district's management of the public schools pursuant to state law.[13]

At issue in Illinois was whether a union member dismissed for allegedly sexually harassing another employee had a legitimate property interest in employment derived from his CBA, entitling him to due process before the school board terminated his employment. Citing the board's "at-will" policy, officials did not provide the employee with due process before his dismissal, despite his CBA stating that employees "may be…discharged for reasonable cause."[14] The employee unsuccessfully sued the board in a federal trial court, claiming that the CBA afforded him a property right under the Fourteenth Amendment and the entitlement to due process. Conducting its analysis of the CBA and policy language, the Seventh Circuit reversed in favor of the employee, pointing out that the CBA created a protected property interest for which he was entitled to due process.

A similar case occurred in New York with a different result: a school board dismissed a probationary teacher for failing to report that another employee allegedly facilitated cheating by students during an examination. The teacher, citing a CBA provision, unsuccessfully argued that she was entitled to due process. Affirming in favor of the board, an appellate court examined the plain language of the CBA, deciding that although the teacher had the total number of years of service required by an applicable provision, she lacked the three years of service in the school before the language was activated. The court concluded that because the

---

[13] Rozenbilt v. Lyles, 243 A.3d 1249, 386 Educ. L. Rep. 816 (N.J. 2021).
[14] Cheli v. Taylorsville Cmty. Sch. Dist., 986 F.3d 1035, 1037 386 Educ. L. Rep. 129 (7th Cir. 2021).

CBA language was inapplicable, the board correctly terminated the teacher's employment.[15]

The second of three cases from New York revealed that union members must exhaust administrative remedies prior to bringing suits under statutes. A substitute teacher and bowling coach unsuccessfully sued his chancellor and others, seeking to restore his job and pay because he failed to bring and complete a timely grievance before filing suit. An appellate court affirmed the dismissal of the teacher's claim because he failed to exhaust administrative remedies under his CBA.[16]

Another case from New York demonstrates that courts typically uphold the actions of school boards as long as they are not arbitrary, unreasonable, irrational, or indicative of bad faith. The dispute here arose when a union challenged a board's action of decommissioning twenty bus routes and privatizing portions of others due to budgetary issues it faced. An appellate panel affirmed an order upholding the board's action because it had a rational basis and was neither arbitrary nor capricious.[17]

A dispute arose between a union and school board over CBA language governing excess health insurance premium dollars and a state law disallowing the retention of unexpended funds from year to year. State law allowed unspent monies to carry over only if obligations were encumbered by legally enforceable obligations, such as CBA provisions. They were attached before the end of the fiscal years in which they occurred. The union sought nonbinding arbitration to release excess healthcare funds to members generated over three fiscal years. After the arbitrator entered an order in favor of the union, the board sought a declaratory judgment disallowing the distribution of the excess funds, given the statutory language preventing such action. On further review of a judgment in favor of the board on the ground that the statutory exception had not been met, the Supreme Court of New Hampshire reversed on behalf of the union.[18] The court noted that the funds had not lapsed because they were properly encumbered by an enforceable obligation before the end of each fiscal year for which they were appropriated.

---

[15] Lin v. N.Y.C. Dep't of Educ., 142 N.Y.S.3d 10, 388 Educ. L. Rep. 931 (N.Y. App. Div. 2021).
[16] Katz v. Carranza, 132 N.Y.S.3d 126, 383 Educ. L. Rep. 1039 (N.Y. App. Div. 2020).
[17] Lucas v. Bd. of Educ. of E. Ramapo Cent. Sch. Dist., 136 N.Y.S.3d 369, 385 Educ. L. Rep. 942 (N.Y. App. Div. 2020).
[18] Mondadnock Sch. Dist. v. Monadnock Dist. Educ., 242 A.3d 789, 385 Educ. L. Rep. 824 (N.H. 2020).

The first of two cases from West Virginia illustrates that when asked to review statutory language, courts construe it in a manner giving effect to legislative intent. School aides classified in a new statutory category as early childhood classroom assistants filed a grievance with the agency seeking to carry over their seniority. When the employment agency refused because the plain language of the statute created an entirely new classification, the state's highest court affirmed in its favor.[19] The court reasoned that that statute's plain language evidenced the legislative intent to create a new classification not allowing seniority to transfer.

In the second case, the same court indicated that statutory language trumps board policy. School secretaries unsuccessfully sued their county board, seeking to be reclassified as Executive Secretaries, a step higher than their actual designations as Secretary III; the state employment administrative agency responded that their job duties fit squarely in the statutory classification of Secretary III. When the secretaries challenged this, an administrative law judge affirmed the agency's adjudication but ordered it to grant the secretaries back pay and place them in the new classification because they fit their local board's policy definition of executive secretary. On further review, the Supreme Court of Appeals of West Virginia affirmed an earlier order overturning the administrative law judge's action because, to the extent that the plaintiffs failed to meet the statutory definition of executive secretary, the local board's policy could not change state law.[20]

Conclusion

Similar to last year, there were fewer cases to review due to the ongoing impact of the worldwide COVID-19 pandemic on courts and schools across the United States. This year's chapter continued last year's section for fair share fee cases as the limits and details of *Janus* continue to be defined.

---

[19] Webster Cnty. Bd. of Educ. v. Davis, 856 S.E. 2d 661, 389 Educ. L. Rep. 570 (W. Va. 2021).
[20] McCann v. Lincoln Cnty. Bd. of Educ., 851 S.E.2d 512, 384 Educ. L. Rep. 1054 (W.Va. 2020).

Alphabetical List of Cases

Akers v. Md. State Educ. Ass'n
Bd. of Educ. Yonkers City Sch. Dist. v. Yonkers Fed'n of Teachers
Bennett v. Council 31 of the Am. Fed'n of State, Cnty, and Mun. Employees, AFL-CIO
Buffalo Teachers Fed'n v. Bd. of Educ. of City Sch. Dist. of Buffalo
Cheli v. Taylorsville Cmty. Sch. Dist.
Fischer v. Gov. of N.J.
Hoekman v. Educ. Minn.
Janus v. Am. Fed'n of State, Cnty., and Mun. Employees Council 31
Katz v. Carranza
Lin v. N.Y.C. Dep't of Educ.
Lucas v. Bd. of Educ. of E. Ramapo Cent. Sch. Dist.
Malcolm v. Ass'n of Supervisors and Adm'rs of Rochester
McCann v. Lincoln Cnty. Bd. of Educ.
Mondadnock Sch. Dist. V. Monadnock Dist. Educ.
Nev. State Educ. Ass'n v. Clark Cnty. Educ. Ass'n
Ocol v. Chicago Teachers Union
Rozenbilt v. Lyles
Troesch v. Chicago Teachers Union, Local Union No. 1, Am. Fed'n of Teachers
Webster Cnty. Bd. of Educ. v. Davis

Cases by Jurisdiction

FEDERAL CASES

U.S. Supreme Court
Janus v. Am. Fed'n of State, Cnty., and Mun. Employees Council 31

Second Circuit
Malcolm v. Ass'n of Supervisors and Adm'rs of Rochester

Third Circuit
Fischer v. Gov. of N.J.

Fourth Circuit
Akers v. Md. State Educ. Ass'n

Seventh Circuit
Bennett v. Council 31 of the Am. Fed'n of State, Cnty, and Mun. Employees, AFL-CIO

Cheli v. Taylorsville Cmty. Sch. Dist.
Ocol v. Chicago Teachers Union

Eighth Circuit

Minnesota
Hoekman v. Educ. Minn.

STATE & D.C COURT CASES

Nevada
Nev. State Educ. Ass'n v. Clark Cnty. Educ. Ass'n
New Hampshire
Mondadnock Sch. Dist. v. Monadnock Dist. Educ.

New Jersey
Rozenbilt v. Lyles

New York
Bd. of Educ. Yonkers City Sch. Dist. v. Yonkers Fed'n of Teachers
Buffalo Teachers Fed'n v. Bd. of Educ. of City Sch. Dist. of Buffalo
Katz v. Carranza
Lin v. N.Y.C. Dep't of Educ.
Lucas v. Bd. of Educ. of E. Ramapo Cent. Sch. Dist.

West Virginia
McCann v. Lincoln Cnty. Bd. of Educ.
Webster Cnty. Bd. of Educ. v. Davis

Chapter 5

STUDENTS WITH DISABILITIES

Allan G. Osborne, Jr., Ed.D.[1] and Susan C. Bon, J.D., Ph.D.[2]

Introduction	137
Entitlement to Services	138
Eligibility	139
Students in Nonpublic Schools	139
Procedural Safeguards	140
Child Find	141
Rights of Parents or Guardians	142
Developing Individualized Education Programs	142
Change in Placement	142
Dispute Resolution	143
Resolution Sessions and Mediation	145
Administrative Hearings	145
Exhausting Complaints Brought under Other Statutes	145
Exhausting Complaints Brought under the IDEA	147
Judicial Procedures	149
Standing to Sue	150
State Immunity	150
Placement	151
Appropriate Educational Placements	151
Private Facilities	153
Extended School Year	153

---

[1] Retired Principal, Snug Harbor Community School, Quincy, Mass.; *Education Law Into Practice* Editor, West's *Education Law Reporter*.
[2] Faculty Fellow and Civility Advocate, Office of the President; Professor, Department Educational Leadership & Policies; Affiliate Professor, College of Law; University of South Carolina, Columbia, S.C.

Remedies **154**
    Tuition Reimbursement 156
    Compensatory Services 158
    Attorney Fees 160
    Section 1983 161
Other IDEA Issues **162**
Discrimination Under Section 504 of the Rehabilitation Act and the Americans with Disabilities Act **162**
    Elementary and Secondary School Students 163
Conclusions **168**
Alphabetical List of Cases **169**
Cases by Jurisdiction **170**

Introduction

When Congress enacted the Education for All Handicapped Children's Act, now known as the Individuals with Disabilities Education Act (IDEA),[3] in 1975, it altered how public school officials deliver educational services to eligible students. Spurred in part by litigation,[4] this landmark legislation requires states to guarantee students with disabilities a free appropriate public education (FAPE) in the least restrictive environment (LRE). Today, school boards are charged with providing necessary educational services and programs for students with a wide array of disabilities in the face of many parental challenges to the services offered.

In the decades since the IDEA took effect, much of the litigation has focused on parental disagreements with their children's placements. While the underlying issue in most current cases is whether school boards offered students FAPEs, courts continue to adjudicate myriad procedural questions. Further, hearing officers and judges often must fashion equitable remedies when boards fail to live up to their statutory responsibilities. Not surprisingly, tuition reimbursement, compensatory educational services, and attorney fees remain oft-litigated topics.

The IDEA defines a FAPE as a program consisting of any needed special education and related services.[5] Yet, given the emphasis on individualization, the IDEA needs to establish clear-cut substantive standards to evaluate the adequacy of these services. The IDEA directs boards to afford students with disabilities specially designed instruction[6] as detailed in their individualized education programs (IEPs).[7]

In *Board of Education of Hendrick Hudson Central School District v. Rowley*,[8] the U.S. Supreme Court interpreted the IDEA as obliging school boards to furnish students with disabilities with personalized instruction, including support services, sufficient for them to benefit from the educations they receive consistent with their individual circumstances.[9] Simultaneously, the Justices

---

[3] 20 U.S.C. §§ *et seq.* 1400.
[4] *See, e.g.,* Pa. Ass'n for Retarded Children v. Pa., 343 F. Supp. 279 (E.D. Pa. 1972); Mills v. Bd. of Educ. of Dist. of Columbia, 348 F. Supp. 866 (D.D.C. 1972).
[5] 20 U.S.C. §§ 1401(9), 1412(a)(1)(A).
[6] 20 U.S.C. § 1401(29).
[7] 20 U.S.C. §§ 1401(14), 1414(d).
[8] Bd. of Educ. of Hendrick Hudson Cent. Sch. Dist., Westchester Cnty., v. Rowley, 458 U.S. 176, 5 Educ. L. Rep. 34 (1982).
[9] Endrew F. *ex rel.* Joseph F. v Douglas Cnty. Sch. Dist. RE-1, 580 U.S. 386 (2017).

cautioned lower courts not to impose their views of preferable educational methods on school personnel.[10] Nevertheless, hearing officers and judges must evaluate the level of services boards provide, and students need, to meet the IDEA's minimum standards.

Most of the litigation covered in this chapter focuses on the IDEA. Consistent with previous years, parties filed litigation on behalf of students with disabilities under Section 504 of the Rehabilitation Act (Section 504)[11] and the Americans with Disabilities Act (ADA).[12] The plaintiffs in these cases often alleged that students were subjected to discriminatory treatment based on their disabilities.

Entitlement to Services

As a condition of receiving federal funds under the IDEA, states must ensure that they make FAPEs available to each resident child with disabilities between the ages of three and twenty-one, inclusive.[13] However, the IDEA does contain two significant limitations to this requirement. First, states need not provide services to students between the ages of three through five and eighteen through twenty-one if doing so is inconsistent with state law, practice, or a court order over public education to children in this age range.[14] Second, states are not mandated to provide special education to youth between the ages of eighteen through twenty-one who are incarcerated in adult facilities if they had not been previously identified as having disabilities and lacked EPs when they were incarcerated.[15] Moreover, students who graduated from high school with regular diplomas are no longer eligible under the IDEA.[16]

The IDEA defines qualified students as those having at least one of a number of identified disabilities who, by reason thereof, need special education and related services.[17] The IDEA's regulations further define the identified disabilities.[18]

---

[10] Rowley, 458 U.S. 176.
[11] 29 U.S.C. § 794.
[12] 42 U.S.C. §§ 12101 *et seq.*
[13] 20 U.S.C. § 1412(a)(1)(A).
[14] 20 U.S.C. § 1412(a)(1)(B)(i).
[15] 20 U.S.C. § 1412(a)(1)(B)(ii).
[16] 34 C.F.R. § 300.102(a)(2)(B).
[17] 20 U.S.C. § 1401(3).
[18] 34 C.F.R. § 300.8.

As a separate group, students attending nonpublic schools are entitled to some IDEA benefits even though individual children do not have the rights to receive services. Under the IDEA, school boards need only spend only a proportionate share of their federal special education dollars to provide services to children whose parents placed them in nonpublic schools.[19]

Eligibility

The Second Circuit affirmed that a statute from Connecticut terminating boards' duties to provide FAPEs at the end of the school years in which children turned twenty-one violated the IDEA.[20] Noting that at least three of the state's adult education programs met the criteria of public education, the court found that because they excluded individuals with disabilities between the ages of twenty-one and twenty-two, the law was contrary to the IDEA's intent that its provisions be available to students until the age of twenty-two.

Students in Nonpublic Schools

In a case from Pennsylvania, the Third Circuit affirmed that a mother whose son attended a nonpublic school did not need to enroll him in a public school to receive an offer of a FAPE.[21] The court explained that the mother did have to request an evaluation and that an expression of interest did not constitute a request that her son be evaluated.

The Ninth Circuit agreed that the board of the district in which a nonpublic school student from California resided was required to offer her a FAPE when her parents requested that they do so.[22] The court observed that the child's nonpublic school was outside the district's boundaries and did not absolve the board of its responsibilities under the IDEA.

---

[19] 20 U.S.C. § 1412(a)(10)(A).
[20] A.R. v. Conn. State Bd. of Educ., 5 F.4th 155, 393 Educ. L. Rep. 28 (2d Cir. 2021).
[21] A.B. *ex rel.* K.B. v. Abington Sch. Dist., 841 F. App'x 392, 388 Educ. L. Rep. 183 (3d Cir. 2021), *aff'g* 440 F. Supp. 3d 428, 378 Educ. L. Rep. 345 (E.D. Pa. 2020).
[22] Bellflower Unified Sch. Dist. v. Lua, 832 F. App'x 493, 385 Educ. L. Rep. 197 (9th Cir. 2020).

Procedural Safeguards

The IDEA includes a system of due process safeguards to ensure that school board officials properly identify, evaluate, and place students with disabilities consistent with its mandates[23] while affording their parents or guardians opportunities to participate in developing their IEPs and placements.[24] The IDEA also obligates boards to provide written notice and obtain parental consent prior to evaluating children[25] or making initial placements.[26] Once students are placed in a special education setting, officials must provide parents with proper notice before initiating changes.[27] While administrative or judicial actions are pending, boards may not change students' placements without parental consent,[28] hearing officers' orders,[29] or judicial decrees.[30]

The IDEA imposes an affirmative obligation on school boards to identify, evaluate, and serve all children with disabilities residing within their districts.[31] This includes children whose parents enrolled them in nonpublic schools.[32] As to students in nonpublic schools, as highlighted above,[33] the IDEA's regulations place the child-find duty on the boards in the districts where their nonpublic schools are located.

School personnel must conduct initial evaluations before they place students in special education programs.[34] Evaluators must complete all assessments within sixty days of the dates when parents consented to the evaluations.[35] All evaluations must be multidisciplinary, meaning they must consist of various assessment tools and strategies to obtain relevant information in the suspected areas of disability.[36] Parents and students with disabilities may be entitled to independent evaluations at public expense if they

---

[23] 20 U.S.C. § 1415.
[24] 20 U.S.C. §§ 1414(d)(1)(B)(i), 1414(f).
[25] 20 U.S.C. § 1414(a)(1)(D).
[26] 20 U.S.C. § 1415(b)(3).
[27] 20 U.S.C. § 1415(b)(3)(A).
[28] 20 U.S.C. § 1415(j).
[29] 20 U.S.C. § 1415(k)(3)(B)(ii).
[30] Honig v. Doe, 484 U.S. 305, 43 Educ. L. Rep. 857 (1988).
[31] 20 U.S.C. § 1412(a)(3).
[32] 20 U.S.C. § 1412(a)(10)(A)(ii)(I).
[33] *See* Bellflower Unified Sch. Dist. v. Lua, 832 F. App'x 493, 385 Educ. L. Rep. 197 (9th Cir. 2020). *See also* 34 C.F.R. § 300.131.
[34] 20 U.S.C. § 1414(a)(1)(A).
[35] 20 U.S.C. § 1414(a)(1)(C)(i)(I).
[36] 20 U.S.C. § 1414(b)(2), (3).

disagree with school boards' evaluations.[37] Boards, too, can request independent evaluations via administrative hearings to deny parents independent evaluations at public expense if the initial evaluations are shown to be appropriate.[38]

The IDEA requires all IEPs to contain statements of students' current educational performance, annual goals, and short-term objectives, specific educational services they must receive, the extent to which they can participate in general education, the dates of initiation and duration of services, and evaluation criteria to determine if the objectives are being met.[39] In addition, IEPs must include statements addressing how students' impairments affect their abilities to be involved in and progress in general education curricula, as well as about modifications they may need to participate in general programs. IEP teams must review the situations of all students at least annually, or sooner if necessary,[40] and reevaluate them at least every three years unless their parents and school officials agree that doing so is unnecessary.[41]

Child Find

The Second Circuit affirmed an order of a federal trial court in New York that a school board did not deny a child a FAPE by failing to identify her as having a disability sooner.[42] The panel agreed that the child's mother had not adequately justified her claim that the alleged child-find violation deprived her daughter of educational benefits.

Similarly, the Third Circuit affirmed that officials in New Jersey did not violate their child-find obligation by failing to identify a child with a history of trauma earlier.[43] School personnel knew of the child's history because she was earning passing grades, but the court ruled that educators had little evidence that her disability interfered with her learning.

---

[37] 20 U.S.C. § 1415(b)(1).
[38] 34 C.F.R. § 300.502(b).
[39] 20 U.S.C. § 1414(d)(1)(A).
[40] 20 U.S.C. § 1414(d)(4)(A).
[41] 20 U.S.C. § 1414(a)(2).
[42] KB *ex rel.* SB v. Katonah Lewisboro Union Free Sch. Dist., 847 F. App'x 38, 389 Educ. L. Rep. 747 (2d Cir. 2021).
[43] Northfield City Bd. of Educ. v. K.S. *ex rel.* L.S., 847 F. App'x 130, 389 Educ. L. Rep. 751 (3d Cir. 2021).

Rights of Parents or Guardians

In Connecticut, the federal trial court held that a school board did not deny the parents of a student with learning disabilities their right to participate fully in the IEP process.[44] The court pointed out that the parents attended multiple IEP team meetings, including those conducted at their request, and the team attempted to reschedule sessions when they were unable to be present.

The federal trial court in the District of Columbia reasoned that the school board did not improperly exclude a mother from the decision-making process in choosing a FAPE for her son.[45] The court relied on evidence that the mother had substantial opportunities to participate in the IEP meetings, meaningfully taking part in developing her son's program. The court added that the mother had visited the proposed schools to observe their educational environments.

Developing Individualized Education Programs

A federal trial court in Pennsylvania decreed that school officials' failure to include behavioral support in a child's IEP was a procedural violation of the IDEA.[46] Without clear communication from county officials, the court declared that because the parents could not evaluate whether the program offered to their son was appropriate, they could not make an informed choice.

Change in Placement

In two cases from New York, the Second Circuit, applying its precedent, summarily indicated that when parents unilaterally transfer their children from one private placement to another, the new school does not become the pendant placement.[47] In a third case from New York, a federal trial court denied parental requests to order their school board to provide in-person educational services for

---

[44] Wong v. Bd. of Educ., 478 F.3d 229, 385 Educ. L. Rep. 537 (D. Conn. 2020).
[45] J.T. v. Dist. of Columbia, 496 F. Supp. 3d 190, 389 Educ. L. Rep. 89 (D.D.C. 2020).
[46] Montgomery Cnty. Intermediate Unit No. 23 v. A.F. *ex rel.* D.F. and J.F., 506 F. Supp. 3d 293, 390 Educ. L. Rep. 1126 (E.D. Pa. 2020).
[47] Soria *ex rel.* G.S. v. N.Y.C. Dep't of Educ., 831 F. App'x 16, 384 Educ. L. Rep. 739 (2d Cir. 2020); Neske *ex rel.* A.N. v. N.Y.C. Dep't of Educ., 824 F. App'x 81 (2d Cir. 2020). C*iting* Ventura de Paulino v. N.Y.C. Dep't of Educ., 959 F.3d 519, 377 Educ. L. Rep. 53 (2d Cir. 2020).

their children during the pandemic.[48] The court rejected the parents' allegation that closing the schools and instituting remote learning violated the IDEA's status quo provision because, insofar as the closing order applied equally to all students, it did not amount to a change in placement.

Reversing an order of the federal trial court in New Jersey, the Third Circuit was of the opinion that under state law, the school board in the district where a child lived was responsible for funding his private school placement during the pendency of administrative proceedings.[49] The lower court and an administrative law judge had ordered the charter school the child attended to pay the tuition. In a second case from New Jersey, the Third Circuit agreed that when a mother filed a due process complaint, her daughter's stay-put placement was general education.[50] Because the mother never accepted the proposed IEP, the court concurred that it was her projected placement, not her then-current one.

The Ninth Circuit affirmed that a child in California's original IEP was his stay-put IEP, not the one his school board proposed and to which his parents never agreed.[51] The court wrote that the child's last implemented IEP, which was in force when his parents filed the due process complaint, constituted his then-current educational placement under the IDEA.

Dispute Resolution

Congress envisioned cooperative efforts to develop IEPs. Still, because Congress recognized that disagreements between school officials and parents were possible, it incorporated a detailed mechanism into the IDEA to address the resolution of disputes between the parties that includes resolution meetings;[52] mediation;[53] administrative due process hearings;[54] and, as a final resort, appeals

---

[48] J.T. *ex rel.* D.T. v. de Blasio, 500 F. Supp. 3d 137, 390 Educ. L. Rep. 126 (S.D.N.Y. 2020).
[49] Hatikvah Int'l Acad. Charter Sch. v. E. Brunswick Twp. Bd. of Educ., 10 F.4th 215, 394 Educ. L. Rep. 31 (3d Cir. 2021).
[50] Northfield City Bd. of Educ. v. K.S. *ex rel.* L.S., 847 F. App'x 130, 389 Educ. L. Rep. 751 (3d Cir. 2021).
[51] E.E. *ex rel.* Hutchison-Escobedo v. Norris Sch. Dist., 4 F.4th 866, 392 Educ. L. Rep. 597 (9th Cir. 2021).
[52] 20 U.S.C. § 1415(f)(1)(B).
[53] 20 U.S.C. § 1415(e).
[54] 20 U.S.C. §§ 1415(f), (g).

to the courts.⁵⁵ The IDEA specifies that school officials must schedule resolution sessions with parents within fifteen days of receiving complaints. Although resolution sessions are mandatory unless waived by mutual consent, mediation is a voluntary next step that may not be used to deny or delay parents' rights to administrative hearings.

Parents may request impartial due process hearings if they disagree with the actions or recommendations of school personnel over proposed IEPs or any aspect of FAPEs. Parties must request hearings within two years of the dates they knew or should have known about the actions on which the complaints are based.⁵⁶ Parents can be excused from meeting this timeline if they can show that school officials misrepresented the problems about which they complained or withheld required information from them.⁵⁷

A party not satisfied with the final orders of administrative proceedings has the right to appeal to state or federal courts once administrative remedies are exhausted unless it is futile to do so. The IDEA obligates aggrieved parties to file judicial appeals within ninety days of final administrative orders.⁵⁸

In *Schaffer ex rel. Schaffer v. Weast*,⁵⁹ the U.S. Supreme Court placed the burden of proof in administrative proceedings on the parties challenging IEPs, effectively putting the onus on parents in most instances because they are the ones typically challenging IEPs. The IDEA empowers the judiciary to review the record of administrative proceedings, hear additional evidence, and "grant such relief as the court determines is appropriate" based on the preponderance-of-evidence standard.⁶⁰ The Justices did caution judges in lower courts not to substitute their views of proper educational methodology for that of competent school authorities.⁶¹ Parties appealing final administrative decisions have ninety days to do so unless state law dictates otherwise.⁶²

---

[55] 20 U.S.C. § 1415(i)(2)(A).
[56] 20 U.S.C. § 1415(f)(3)(C).
[57] 20 U.S.C. § 1415(f)(3)(D).
[58] 20 U.S.C. § 1415(i)(2)(B).
[59] Schaffer *ex rel.* Schaffer v Weast, 546 U.S. 49, 203 Educ. L. Rep. 49 (2005).
[60] 20 U.S.C. § 1415(i)(2)(C)(iii).
[61] Bd. of Educ. of Hendrick Hudson Cent. Sch. Dist., Westchester Cnty., v. Rowley, 458 U.S. 176, 5 Educ. L. Rep. 34 (1982).
[62] 20 U.S.C. § 1415(i)(2)(B).

Resolution Sessions and Mediation

In a dispute from New York involving tuition reimbursement, the Second Circuit emphasized that although the IDEA allows school personnel to propose changes to IEPs during resolution periods, it does not authorize them to amend them unilaterally during that period.[63] The court remarked that the resolution period is designed to foster a mutual process similar to the cooperative process for IEP development outlined in the IDEA.

Administrative Hearings

Exhausting Complaints Brought under Other Statutes

Parents sometimes attempt to sidestep the IDEA's exhaustion requirement by filing suit under statutes such as Section 504 or the ADA that do not have analogous standards. In *Fry v. Napoleon Community Schools*,[64] the U.S. Supreme Court was of the view that in such cases, exhaustion is not required when the crux of a suit is something other than a denial of a FAPE but is necessary if relief is available under the IDEA. Thus, if a complaint's gravamen seeks relief for denying a FAPE, the parties must first exhaust the IDEA's administrative remedies. Despite the U.S. Supreme Court's clarification, litigation has continued.

The Third Circuit agreed with a federal trial court in Pennsylvania that parents of a student with multiple disabilities who sought only monetary damages first had to exhaust the IDEA's administrative remedies.[65] The parents alleged that the child was restrained, placed in handcuffs, and locked in a bathroom in contravention of his action plan, but the courts agreed that the crux of the suit was that school officials denied the child a FAPE. In another case from Pennsylvania, the Third Circuit affirmed that they could not proceed with their unexhausted Section 504/ADA claims because they essentially sought a remedy for denying a FAPE.[66]

---

[63] Bd. of Educ. of Yorktown Cent. Sch. Dist. v. C.S., 990 F.3d 152, 387 Educ. L. Rep. 105 (2d Cir. 2021), *aff'g* 357 F. Supp. 3d 311, 363 Educ. L. Rep. 231 (S.D.N.Y. 2019).

[64] Endrew F. *ex rel.* Joseph F. v Douglas Cnty. Sch. Dist. RE-1, 580 U.S. 386 (2017).

[65] Ahearn v. E. Stroudsburg Area Sch. Dist., 848 F. App'x 75, 390 Educ. L. Rep. 506 (3d Cir. 2021).

[66] T.R. v. Sch. Dist. of Philadelphia, 4 F.4th 179, 392 Educ. L. Rep. 579 (3d Cir. 2021), *aff'g* 458 F. Supp.3d 274, 381 Educ. L. Rep. 834 (E.D. Pa. 2020).

After a hearing officer in Texas dismissed a due process complaint as untimely, the child's mother filed suit with the extra claim that the school board failed to provide her son with a safe, educational environment in violation of Section 504 and the ADA. A majority of the Fifth Circuit affirmed that the complaint sought redress for denial of a FAPE and needed to be exhausted.[67] The dissenting judge interpreted the complaint that a teacher had physically assaulted the child as one not needing exhaustion because claims alleging abuse, assault, or harassment, even when suffered by a student with disabilities, are not subject to this provision.[68]

A twenty-three-year-old student in Michigan with a hearing impairment who had been denied a diploma, but settled his IDEA claims, filed an ADA suit seeking compensatory damages alleging that the school board discriminated against him by not providing him with the resources necessary to participate fully in class. A divided Sixth Circuit affirmed that the student had to exhaust the IDEA's administrative remedies because his suit focused on the adequacy of his education.[69] However, the dissent believed the student's allegations that officials denied him effective communication access to services, teachers, instruction, and extracurricular activities because of his hearing impairment constituted a classic ADA claim of discrimination not requiring exhaustion.[70]

The mother of a child with disability-related behaviors whom school officials frequently sent home reached a settlement agreement with her board over her IDEA complaints but filed suit alleging violations of the ADA. A federal trial court in California dismissed for failure to exhaust remedies, but the Ninth Circuit reversed in favor of the mother because her suit was about her son's exclusion from the classroom, not the inadequacy of his IEP.[71]

According to the federal trial court in Maryland, the mother of a child with multiple disabilities did not have to exhaust the IDEA's administrative remedies before filing her disability-based discrimination claim.[72] The mother sued after a school administrator

---

[67] T.B. *ex rel.* Bell v. NW. Indep. Sch. Dist., 980 F.3d 1047, 384 Educ. L. Rep. 6 (5th Cir. 2020).
[68] *Id.* at 1054 (Higginson, J., dissenting).
[69] Perez v. Sturgis Pub. Schs., 3 F.4th 236, 391 Educ. L. Rep. 580 (6th Cir. 2021).
[70] *Id.* at 245 (Stranch, J., dissenting).
[71] D.D. *ex rel.* Ingram v. L.A. Unified Sch. Dist., 984 F.3d 773, 385 Educ. L. Rep. 160 (9th Cir. 2020).
[72] L.J. v. Baltimore Curriculum Project, 514 F. Supp. 3d 707, 392 Educ. L. Rep. 654 (D. Md. 2021).

allegedly grabbed her son, slung him over his shoulder, and smashed his face into a wall. The court was convinced that the suit met both elements of *Fry* and that the claim was not one over denying a FAPE.

An appellate court in Connecticut affirmed that a father who filed suit alleging that his kindergarten-aged son had not been in a fully inclusive placement under the terms of his IEP had to exhaust the IDEA's administrative remedies.[73] Applying Fry's analysis, the court concurred that the gravamen of the complaint was that school personnel failed to educate the child in the LRE, thereby denying him a FAPE. The court also thought that although the father sought monetary damages, which are unavailable under the IDEA, this did not excuse the exhaustion requirement.

Exhausting Complaints Brought under the IDEA

The Third Circuit agreed that the parents of multiple students with disabilities, who filed a class action suit in Pennsylvania alleging that their school board failed to provide appropriate translation and interpretation services to them in light of their limited English proficiency, had to exhaust the IDEA's administrative remedies individually.[74] The court posited that systemic exemptions to the exhaustion requirement apply when plaintiffs challenge policies threatening basic IDEA goals instead of components of special education programs. Whether parents receive translation or interpretation services, the court wrote, is best resolved by hearing officers.

Parents in California filed a class action suit alleging that their school board did not timely identify and evaluate their children with disabilities, along with failing to provide them with sufficiently individualized accommodations and services. The parents unsuccessfully charged that exhaustion was unnecessary because they sought systemic, district-wide reforms. The Ninth Circuit affirmed the denial of the parents' claim because they failed to identify any policy the administrative process could not address.[75] The court commented that describing problems as being broad and far-reaching was neither sufficient to meet the standard of systemic,

---

[73] Phillips v. Hebron, 244 A.3d 964, 387 Educ. L. Rep. 274 (Conn. App. Ct. 2020).
[74] T.R. v. Sch. Dist. of Philadelphia, 4 F.4th 179, 392 Educ. L. Rep. 579 (3d Cir. 2021), *aff'g* 458 F. Supp.3d 274,
381 Educ. L. Rep. 834 (E.D. Pa. 2020).
[75] Student A v. S.F. Unified Sch. Dist., 9 F.4th 1079, 394 Educ. L. Rep. 31 (9th Cir. 2021).

nor was their suit systemic just because it applied to numerous students and was framed as a class action.

In a case from New York City where parents contested the mayor's school closing orders during the COVID-19 pandemic, a federal trial court granted one motion to dismiss on exhaustion grounds but denied another.[76] The court maintained that the parents were not obligated to exhaust their claims that the orders violated the IDEA's status-quo provision because it fell within the exceptions outlined in the statute. Conversely, the court stated that the parents had to exhaust their FAPE-based claims, ascertaining that their contention that a backlog of administrative appeals existed did not demonstrate futility.

After the governor of New Mexico closed schools due to the COVID-19 pandemic, a school board member and parents, including the mother of a student with disabilities, filed suit against various officials claiming, among other things, that the closures violated their rights under the IDEA. The mother of the child with disabilities alleged that her daughter had not received many of her IEP services. The federal trial court asserted that the mother did not have to exhaust administrative remedies because doing so would have been futile under the circumstances.[77] On the other hand, in subsequent action in the same case, the court denied a motion to add another plaintiff-parent because he had not exhausted his administrative remedies.[78] The court was persuaded that a hearing officer could consider whether the state's reentry guidance prevented the child from receiving an in-person education and had the authority to make necessary alterations to the guidance. The court concluded that the administrative process could provide the father with the relief he sought because it was the type of issue a hearing officer could address.

The grandmother of a young child with multiple medical conditions challenged an order of an administrative law judge that she was not entitled to obtain an independent educational evaluation of the child at public expense. On appeal, the grandmother raised additional claims that a federal trial court in

---

[76] J.T. *ex rel.* D.T. v. de Blasio, 500 F. Supp. 3d 137, 390 Educ. L. Rep. 126 (S.D.N.Y. 2020).

[77] Hernandez v. Grisham, 494 F. Supp. 3d 1044, 388 Educ. L. Rep. 746 (D.N.M. 2020).

[78] Hernandez v. Grisham, 508 F. Supp. 3d 893, 391 Educ. L. Rep. 207 (D.N.M. 2020).

Washington summarily dismissed because they were related to the denial of a FAPE and so were subject to exhaustion.[79]

Judicial Procedures

In a case from Colorado, the Tenth Circuit dismissed and remanded an appeal for lack of jurisdiction because the federal trial court had not entered a final judgment.[80] Instead, because the trial court had remanded the dispute to an administrative law judge, the panel rejected the claim because it was not a final judgment.

The mother of a student in Washington, D.C., unsuccessfully filed a due process complaint alleging that officials denied her son a FAPE. Before the dispute reached the federal trial court, the mother and school officials agreed on a subsequent IEP. After the trial court rejected the mother's suit as moot because the challenged IEP was no longer in force and she had not sought retrospective relief, the Circuit Court for the District of Columbia affirmed the dismissal due to the lack of an effective remedy.[81]

When the parents of a student with autism from Massachusetts sought to supplement the record on appeal to the federal trial court, it allowed them to introduce an affidavit from their attorney about statements made at the hearing because there was no a transcript of the proceedings.[82] The court did refuse the parental request to admit copies of the IEPs of other students in the proposed program because, by failing to produce them at the administrative level, they waived the opportunity to put them in the record.

The federal trial court in Oregon granted a motion for class certification in a suit brought on behalf of four students with disabilities and a nonprofit advocacy agency alleging that the lack of state-level monitoring, enforcement, and assistance for school systems led to a pattern of boards misusing shortened school day schedules for students with disability-related behaviors.[83] The court granted the plaintiffs' motion because they met the numerosity,

---

[79] Smith ex rel. C.M. v. Tacoma Sch. Dist., 476 F. Supp. 3d 1112, 384 Educ. L. Rep. 859 (W.D. Wash. 2020).
[80] C.W. ex rel. B.W. v. Denver Cnty. Sch. Dist. No. 1, 994 F.3d 1215, 389 Educ. L. Rep. 32 (10th Cir. 2021).
[81] J.T. v. Dist. of Columbia, 983 F.3d 516, 385 Educ. L. Rep. 34 (D.C. Cir. 2020).
[82] Doe v. Newton Pub. Schs., 474 F. Supp. 3d 434, 384 Educ. L. Rep. 279 (D. Mass. 2020).
[83] J.N. v. Or. Dep't of Educ., 338 F. Supp. 3d 256, 391 Educ. L. Rep. 850 (D. Or. 2021).

commonality, typicality, and adequacy of representation requirements for class certification.

In New Mexico, the federal trial court rejected complaints brought by the parents of a child with disabilities as moot because school officials had developed a new IEP for her based on its instructions in an earlier order.[84] Previously, the court noted that the child's IEP misrepresented the state's guidance on in-person instruction during the COVID-19 pandemic.[85]

Standing to Sue

Multiple plaintiffs, including a school board member, parents, and the mother of a child with disabilities, sued state officials challenging New Mexico's school closure orders in response to the COVID-19 pandemic, alleging violations of the Equal Protection Clause, the Due Process Clause, and the IDEA. The federal trial court observed that only the mother of the student with disabilities met the IDEA's standing standards.[86] The court subsequently explained that the mother had standing to sue the governor because she alleged injuries in the form of denial of education and denial of FAPE that was fairly traceable to his actions.[87] The court conceded that a favorable judgment would have redressed the child's injuries because the governor may direct whether and to what extent schools must provide in-person education.

State Immunity

The federal trial court in New Mexico decreed that the state could not rely on sovereign immunity as a defense in the suit multiple parties filed over the state's school closure orders during the pandemic.[88] The court found that because Congress abrogated Eleventh Amendment immunity when states accepted federal IDEA funds, New Mexico waived its immunity.

---

[84] Hernandez v. Grisham, 508 F. Supp. 3d 893, 391 Educ. L. Rep. 207 (D.N.M. 2020).
[85] Hernandez v. Grisham, 494 F. Supp. 3d 1044, 388 Educ. L. Rep. 746 (D.N.M. 2020).
[86] Id.
[87] Hernandez v. Grisham, 499 F. Supp. 3d 1013, 390 Educ. L. Rep. 54 (D.N.M. 2020).
[88] Hernandez v Grisham, 508 R. Supp. 3d 1044, 388 Educ. L. Rep. 746 (D.N.M. 2020).

Placement

The IDEA regulations direct school boards to ensure a "continuum of alternative placements" to meet the needs of students with disabilities for special education and related services.[89] The continuum must range from placements in general education to private residential facilities and includes homebound services. All placements must be in the LRE, with removal from general education permitted only to the extent necessary to provide special education and related services.[90]

At the same time, placements must be made at public expense consistent with state educational standards.[91] IEP teams must review all placements at least annually and revise them when necessary.[92] In *Rowley*, the U.S. Supreme Court defined a FAPE as an education that complies with the IDEA's procedures and reasonably calculates to enable a child to receive educational benefits.[93] Later, though, in *Endrew F. ex rel. Joseph F. v. Douglas County School District RE-1*,[94] the Court clarified that IEPs should be appropriately ambitious in light of students' circumstances.

States, at a minimum, must adopt policies and procedures consistent with the IDEA. While states may provide greater benefits than the IDEA requires, if they do establish higher standards, courts consider them along with the IDEA when evaluating the appropriateness of IEPs.[95]

Appropriate Educational Placements

In a dispute from Texas, the Fifth Circuit determined that a school board provided a FAPE to a child with learning disabilities because she had mastered her IEP goals and demonstrated positive academic and nonacademic benefits.[96] Partially affirming an earlier order, the court discerned that during the two years in question, the

---

[89] 34 C.F.R. § 300.115.
[90] 20 U.S.C. § 1412(a)(5).
[91] 20 U.S.C. § 1401(9).
[92] 20 U.S.C. § 1414(d)(4).
[93] Bd. of Educ. of Hendrick Hudson Cent. Sch. Dist. v. Rowley, 458 U.S. 176, 5 Educ. L. Rep. 34 (1982).
[94] Endrew F. *ex rel.* Joseph F. v Douglas Cnty. Sch. Dist. RE-1, 580 U.S. 386 (2017).
[95] *See, e.g.*, David D. v. Dartmouth Sch. Comm., 775 F.2d 411, 28 Educ. L. Rep. 70 (1st Cir. 1985); Geis v. Bd. of Educ. of Parsippany-Troy Hills, 774 F.2d 575, 27 Educ. L. Rep. 1093 (3d Cir. 1985).
[96] P.P. *ex rel.* Pinault v. N.W. Indep. Sch. Dist., 839 F. App'x 848, 387 Educ. L. Rep. 499 (5th Cir. 2020).

student earned passing grades, mastered grade-level content, and performed in the top half of her class.

The Tenth Circuit, in an appeal from Colorado, insisted that the IDEA did not require school officials to employ particular teaching methodologies.[97] The court agreed that the IEP providing the child with consistent reinforcement, visual prompts, and utilizing various teaching strategies effectively addressed her behaviors and were reasonably calculated to provide her with educational benefits.

In Connecticut, the federal trial court declared that a school board provided a FAPE for a student with a visual impairment.[98] The court indicated that the child's IEP was individually tailored to meet his needs and allow him to progress, his report card grades were above average, and he exceeded expectations on standardized tests.

A federal trial court in Pennsylvania held that school officials failed to provide a FAPE for a child with autism.[99] The court elaborated that the IEP did not include the behavioral support the child needed or the services of a behavioral specialist, thus rendering it substantively inadequate.

Similarly, the federal trial court in Maryland invalidated an IEP that it deemed did not adequately address the behavior problems a child with multiple disabilities exhibited because it failed to include teacher consultation with a behavioral therapist.[100] In the court's opinion, the child's progress was inappropriate in light of her circumstances.

Like all states, New Mexico closed its schools, resorting to remote learning models during the COVID-19 pandemic. This led the mother of a child with learning disabilities to challenge the school closure orders alleging that officials did not provide her daughter with many of her IEP services. The federal trial court agreed that the closures denied the child a FAPE because by denying her access to sufficient specialized instruction and services, she suffered a lack of progress.[101]

---

[97] Elizabeth B. v. El Paso Cnty. Sch. Bd., 841 F. App'x 40, 388 Educ. L. Rep. 172 (10th Cir. 2020).
[98] Wong v. Bd. of Educ., 478 F. Supp. 3d 229, 385 Educ. L. Rep. 537 (D. Conn. 2020).
[99] Montgomery Cnty. Intermediate Unit No. 23 v. A.F. *ex rel.* D.F. and J.F., 506 F. Supp. 3d 293, 390 Educ. L. Rep. 1126 (E.D. Pa. 2020).
[100] S.S. v. Bd. of Educ. of Harford Cnty., 498 F. Supp. 3d 761, 389 Educ. L. Rep. 316 (D. Md. 2020).
[101] Hernandez v. Grisham, 494 F. Supp. 3d 1044, 388 Educ. L. Rep. 746 (D.N.M. 2020).

In the first of two cases from the District of Columbia, the federal trial court ruled that the school board offered a FAPE to a child with autism because the proposed school placements were capable of implementing his IEP.[102] The court remanded the second case to a hearing officer to address whether the board's proposed placement for a student with a behavior disorder and developmental delays could properly manage his aggressive behaviors.[103]

Private Facilities

A federal trial court in Iowa approved the private school placement a school board offered to a student diagnosed with reactive attachment disorder, anxiety, and cognitive delays who experienced behavior problems and poor academic progress.[104] The court pointed out that the school focused on the type of behavioral problems the child had and offered a well-structured program to address his at-school behavioral challenges. Further, the court was convinced that the school's staff had extensive experience with students with similar problems and was able to provide small classes and one-to-one instruction with a focus on developing life skills. The court rejected the parental request for a residential placement because the student's reluctance to go to school and the resulting conflict with them did not hinder his ability to progress.

Extended School Year

The Second Circuit agreed with a federal trial court in New York that a child who had been ill was not entitled to an extended school year program.[105] The court decided that the student had not lost any credits while hospitalized, remained on track to graduate, did not require an inordinate period of review to maintain her progress, and had not suffered regression.

In like manner, remarking that boards need only provide extended school year services if students need them to receive FAPEs, the Tenth Circuit affirmed that a child from Colorado with

---

[102] J.T. v. Dist. of Columbia, 496 F. Supp. 3d 190, 389 Educ. L. Rep. 89 (D.D.C. 2020).
[103] W.S. v. Dist. of Columbia, 502 F. Supp. 3d 102, 390 Educ. L. Rep. 540 (D.D.C. 2020).
[104] Banwart v. Cedar Falls Cmty. Sch. Dist., 489 F. Supp. 3d 846, 387 Educ. L. Rep. 605 (N.D. Iowa 2020).
[105] KB *ex rel.* SB v. Katonah Lewisboro Union Free Sch. Dist., 847 F. App'x 38, 389 Educ. L. Rep. 747 (2d Cir. 2021).

multiple disabilities was not entitled to such a placement because her IEP specified that she did not need such a placement and her parents failed to provide evidence that she did.[106]

Remedies

When school boards fail to provide FAPEs for students with disabilities, the IDEA empowers the courts to grant such relief as they deem appropriate.[107] Along with prospective relief, courts frequently award reimbursement of costs parents bear in unilaterally obtaining appropriate services for their children.

In *Burlington School Committee v. Department of Education, Commonwealth of Massachusetts*,[108] the U.S. Supreme Court recognized that school boards must reimburse parents for costs incurred in providing their children with special education and related services if they prevail in having their chosen placements deemed appropriate. Based on litigation that has been codified, the IDEA allows reimbursement awards to be limited when parents do not provide boards with prior notice of their dissatisfaction with their children's placements and their intent to enroll them in private schools.[109]

The U.S. Supreme Court emphasized in *Florence County School District Four v. Carter*[110] that parents can be reimbursed even if the facilities they chose are not state-approved as long as they offer otherwise appropriate programs. Later, in *Forest Grove School District v. T.A.*,[111] the Justices were of the view that reimbursements may be available even if students had not previously received services from the public schools. Courts often grant awards of compensatory education services when parents lack the financial means to obtain private services while litigation is pending.

Congress adopted the Handicapped Children's Protection Act in 1986 to allow parents who prevail in litigation pursuant to the IDEA

---

[106] Elizabeth B. v. El Paso Cnty. Sch. Bd., 841 F. App'x 40, 388 Educ. L. Rep. 172 (10th Cir. 2020).

[107] 20 U.S.C. § 1415(i)(2)(C)(iii).

[108] Sch. Comm. of Town of Burlington, Mass. v. Dep't of Educ. of Mass., 471 U.S. 359, 23 Educ. L. Rep. 1189 (1985).

[109] 20 U.S.C. § 1412(a)(10)(C)(iii).

[110] Florence Cnty. Sch. Dist. Four v. Carter By & Through Carter, 510 U.S. 7, 86 Educ. L. Rep. 41 (1993).

[111] 557 U.S. 230 (2009).

to recover their legal expenses.[112] Congress responded to the U.S. Supreme Court's opinion in *Smith v. Robinson*,[113] interpreting the original act as not allowing prevailing parents to recover attorney fees.

Buckhannon Board and Care Home v. West Virginia Department of Health and Human Resources,[114] a non-education case, generated a new line of attorney fees litigation under the IDEA. In *Buckhannon,* the U.S. Supreme Court struck down the catalyst theory as a means of recovering attorney fees, noting that to be reimbursed for legal expenses, plaintiffs must either receive enforceable judgments on the merits or court-ordered consent decrees. In *Arlington Central School District Board of Education v. Murphy*,[115] refusing to rewrite the statute, the Justices explained that parents could not recover expert witness fees under the IDEA because the act does not expressly call for such a remedy.

Congress later amended IDEA's attorney fees provisions, allowing school boards to seek reimbursement of their legal expenses when parental complaints are later deemed frivolous, unreasonable, or without foundation or when the litigation was continued after it clearly became frivolous, unreasonable, or without foundation. School boards may also seek awards when parents bring actions for improper purposes, cause unnecessary delays, or needlessly increase the cost of litigation.[116] Under this provision, awards are levied against their attorneys, not the parents.

The IDEA is not the exclusive avenue through which parents may enforce the rights of their children with disabilities. The IDEA clearly states that none of its provisions can be interpreted as restricting or limiting the rights, procedures, and remedies available under the Constitution, Section 504, or other federal statutes protecting the rights of students with disabilities.[117] Consequently, litigation is often filed under Section 504, the ADA, and Section 1983 of the Civil Rights Act of 1871,[118] along with the IDEA. Cases under Section 504 and ADA are discussed later in this chapter. Suits seeking remedies under Section 1983, the U.S. Constitution, or other federal legislation are discussed in this section.

---

[112] 20 U.S.C. § 1415(i)(3)(B)-(G).
[113] Thomas v Robinson, 468 U.S. 992, 18 Educ. L. Rep. 148 (1984).
[114] Buckhannon Bd. & Care Home Inc. v. W. Virginia Dep't of Health & Hum. Res., 532 U.S. 598 (2001).
[115] Arlington Cent. Sch. Dist. Bd. of Educ. v. Murphy, 548 U.S. 291 (2006).
[116] 20 U.S.C. § 1415(i)(3)(B)(i)(II), (III).
[117] 20 U.S.C. § 1415(l).
[118] 42 U.S.C. § 1983.

Tuition Reimbursement

Parents often seek private school tuition reimbursement after pursuing nonpublic educational services because they believe their public schools failed to provide FAPEs for their children. Suppose parents fail to inform IEP teams in a timely manner that they reject the placements they are offered and so plan to enroll their children in nonpublic schools. In that case, courts have the discretion to reduce the amount awarded pursuant to the IDEA. Moreover, courts generally deny reimbursement if parents refuse to make their children available to school personnel for evaluations or if their actions are unreasonable.[119]

Parents often raise tuition reimbursement claims after unilaterally enrolling their children in nonpublic school placements. To reiterate, courts often reject such claims if parents acted without first seeking evaluations and IEPs from the public schools. In one such case from Pennsylvania, the Third Circuit affirmed that a parent's general conversation and expression of interest in special education programming did not qualify as a request for an evaluation or an intent to reenroll their child in the public school.[120] The court thus disagreed that their board had the duty to evaluate, propose an IEP, or reimburse the parent for private school tuition.[121]

The Second Circuit, in a case from New York, agreed that the IDEA did not allow school officials to amend a student's IEP unilaterally during the resolution period after her parents filed a due process complaint.[122] The court was satisfied that per the IDEA, school personnel might suggest changes to IEPs, but parents have the right to reject proposed public placements and enroll their children in suitable private schools. When the IEP team sought to place the child in twelve-student classes and then fifteen, the parents rejected both as insufficient. A federal trial court decreed that in light of this error and unilateral IEP amendment, the board denied the child a FAPE because it promised what would not be done. The appellate panel then affirmed tuition reimbursement for the parents at the private school of their choice.

---

[119] 20 U.S.C. § 1412(a)(10)(C)(iii).
[120] A.B. *ex rel* K.B. v. Abington Sch. Dist., 841 F. App'x 392, 388 Educ. L. Rep. 183 (3d Cir 2021), A.B. *ex rel* K.B. v. Abington Sch. Dist. 440 F. Supp. 3d 428, 378 Educ. L. Rep. 345 (E.D. Pa. 2020).
[121] 20 U.S.C. § 1412(a)(10)(A)(i); 34 C.F.R. § 300.137(a).
[122] Bd. of Educ. of Yorktown Cent. Sch. Dist. v. C.S., 990 F.3d 152, 387 Educ. L. Rep. 105 (2d Cir. 2021), Bd. of Educ. of Yorktown Cent. Sch. Dist. v. C.S., 357 F. Supp. 3d 311, 363 Educ. L. Rep. 231 (S.D.N.Y. 2019).

When a school board violates its FAPE obligation, it may also be responsible for transportation and other costs associated with private school placement. In such a case, parents of an elementary school student with epilepsy and autism sued their school board in Colorado, challenging the denial of their claim for reimbursement of costs associated with unilaterally enrolling their child in a private school.[123] The Tenth Circuit affirmed the denial of the board's defense that the parents' appeal was moot due to a Medicaid waiver that covered their private school tuition because they had a reasonable claim for transportation costs that were not reimbursed.

On the other hand, if a school board has not denied a FAPE, parents will unlikely succeed in tuition reimbursement claims for their children's unilateral private school placements. For instance, as a federal trial court in Connecticut confirmed, it is unnecessary to consider whether a private placement is appropriate if a school board provided a FAPE because no remedy would be due.[124]

As in previous years, parents sought tuition reimbursement after placing their children in private school settings adhering to specialized applied behavior analysis principles designed for children with autism spectrum disorders. The federal trial court in Maryland, thinking that a school board denied a child a FAPE, proceeded to analyze whether the parents' chosen private school setting for their daughter with autism spectrum disorder, other cognitive impairments and disorders, and congenital heart disease were appropriate.[125] Despite the parents' failure to demonstrate clearly that a twelve-month program was necessary to ensure a FAPE, the court awarded tuition reimbursement on the basis that the board's failure to increase behavioral analysis consultation hours contributed to the denial of a FAPE. Additionally, the court believed that the student was flourishing and achieved significant progress in the private school setting.

After their daughter suffered intense bullying from classmates, the parents of a middle school student with learning difficulties related to the removal of a brain tumor unilaterally enrolled her in a private school and sought tuition reimbursement. On further review of the denial of the parents' reimbursement claim in their suit alleging that the school board violated the IDEA and Section 504 by

---

[123] Elizabeth B. v. El Paso Cnty. Sch. Dist., 841 F. App'x 40, 388 Educ. L. Rep. 172 (10th Cir. 2020).
[124] Wong v. Bd. of Educ., 478 F. Supp. 3d 229, 385 Educ. L. Rep. 537 (D. Conn. 2020).
[125] S.S. v. Bd. of Educ. of Harford Cnty., 498 F. Supp.3d 761, 389 Educ. L. Rep. 316 (D. Md. 2020).

failing to provide a FAPE—because the parents failed to give the officials the requisite ten-day notice of placing their daughter in a private school—the Third Circuit vacated and remanded in their favor.[126] The court wrote that because the child's IEP team failed to propose a placement until a month after school began, tuition reimbursement was appropriate insofar as the parents reasonably believed the placement being offered was inadequate or unsafe—or, as here, where no IEP had been prepared.[127]

On the other hand, a federal trial court in Maryland acknowledged that although school board officials delayed completing a functional behavioral analysis and failed to adjust a student's IEP, this did not amount to a FAPE violation. Consequently, the court denied the parental request for tuition reimbursement in a private school, related services, transportation expenses, or any other such expenses related incident to their claim.[128] The court observed that because the board's delay did not depart substantially from accepted professional judgment, practice, or standards, the parents failed to support their allegations that school personnel acted with deliberate indifference and intentionally discriminated against their daughter.

Compensatory Services

Compensatory education is an equitable remedy designed to provide access to benefits necessary for children to be put in the positions they would have been absent from their school boards' IDEA violations.[129] When boards fail to provide necessary special education programming, compensatory services are to be calculated in a reasonable manner to remedy officials' failure to adhere to the IDEA.[130] In *Florence County*,[131] the U.S. Supreme Court found that because lower courts may award equitable relief to parents of children with disabilities, they may be eligible for compensatory education and services if their boards failed to provide FAPEs.

---

[126] K.E. v. Northern Highlands Reg'l Bd. of Educ., 840 F. App'x 705, 388 Educ. L. Rep. 144 (3d Cir. 2020).
[127] 20 U.S.C. § 1412(a)(10)(C)(iv).
[128] S.S. v. Bd. of Educ. of Harford Cnty., 498 F. Supp.3d 761, 389 Educ. L. Rep. 316 (D. Md. 2020).
[129] 20 U.S.C. § 1401(9).
[130] 20 U.S.C. § 1415(b)(6)(A); 34 C.F.R. § 300.151(b)(1).
[131] Florence Cnty. Sch. Dist. Four v. Carter By & Through Carter, 510 U.S. 7, 86 Educ. L. Rep. 41 (1993); 20 U.S.C. 1415(i)(2)(C)(iii).

Other cases involved disputes between parents seeking compensatory education due to school boards' failure to provide FAPEs. To be awarded compensatory education, parents must prove, by a preponderance of the evidence, that their children were denied FAPEs. If the denial of FAPEs was in part due to the misfeasance or nonfeasance of board officials and is not attributable entirely to the unreasonable actions of parents or attorneys, compensatory education may be an equitable remedy.

In the first of two disputes from Connecticut, the Second Circuit affirmed that the mother of a student with autism was entitled to reimbursement for a behavior analyst's autism consulting services her son received pursuant to his autism-related behavioral issues.[132] The court refused to reimburse the mother for the aid she provided her son because doing so was precluded by terms of the settlement agreement she entered with the school board to provide the same services.

After judging that a school board failed to provide FAPE throughout elementary school to a student with disabilities, a hearing officer distinguished between the board's IDEA and Section 504 obligations. Rather than engage in a simple calculation of the total hours of occupational therapy or reading assistance needed to ensure that the child received accommodations, the federal trial court in Connecticut assigned an independent evaluator to consider how much compensatory education would put the child in the place he would have been in had officials consistently met their duties in the first place.[133]

On the other hand, as reflected by a case from Alabama, compensatory education is not a guaranteed remedy for procedural violations. The court maintained that compensatory education is not an automatic guarantee because it is designed to remedy a child's educational setbacks due to IDEA violations. The court commented that a final determination rests on whether compensatory services are necessary to address identified and evidence-supported educational deficits. Ultimately, the Eleventh Circuit affirmed that a mother in Alabama failed to provide evidence that the procedural

---

[132] Dervishi v. Dep't of Special Educ., Stamford Bd. of Educ., 846 F. App'x 10, 389 Educ. L. Rep. 728 (2d Cir. 2021).
[133] Wong v. Bd. of Educ., 478 F. Supp. 3d 229, 385 Educ. L. Rep. 537 (D. Conn. 2020).

child-find violation caused substantive educational harm that compensatory educational services could have remedied.[134]

Procedural violations, such as a short delay in the identification of an appropriate placement, are not automatic violations of the IDEA. In such a dispute, the federal trial court in the District of Columbia posited that a school board does not necessarily violate FAPE when it is unable to make an appropriate placement for a student immediately.[135] In the court's perspective, a short, discrete gap, rather than an indefinite time with no placement, qualifies as a reasonable time span not violating the board's FAPE duty so as to call for compensatory services.

Attorney Fees

Parents of students with disabilities frequently initiate claims for attorney fees seeking relief after administrative hearings or court orders in their favor over alleged IDEA violations. Courts set the amounts of awards depending on prevailing party status and reasonableness of the hours, rates, and award amount requested, given the nature of claims. Under the IDEA, parents qualify as prevailing parties if the relief they received in response to their claims materially alters the legal relationship between the parties.[136]

In calculating an appropriate award when parents obtain partial success, courts follow the U.S. Supreme Court's two-step analysis in *Hensley v. Eckerhart*[137] by considering the relationship between the successful and unsuccessful claims and then evaluating the significance of the relief granted in light of the reasonableness of hours spent on the litigation. Determining prevailing party status may be complicated when parents achieve limited success at the special education appeals level.

The Eleventh Circuit, in a case from Alabama, affirmed that limited successes do not automatically guarantee prevailing party status.[138] Relying on *Hensley*,[139] the court affirmed that at least some of the benefits sought in the claims must be achieved by a party to

---

[134] J.N. *ex rel.* M.N. v. Jefferson Cnty. Bd. of Educ., 12 F.4th 1355, 395 Educ. L. Rep. 74 (11th Cir. 2021).
[135] J.T. v. Dist. of Columbia, 496 F. Supp.3d 190, 389 Educ. L. Rep. 89 (D.D.C. 2020).
[136] 20 U.S.C. §1415(i)(3).
[137] Hensley v. Eckerhart, 461 U.S. 424 (1983).
[138] J.N. *ex rel.* M.N. v. Jefferson Cnty. Bd. of Educ., 12 F.4th 1355, 395 Educ. L. Rep. 74 (11th Cir. 2021).
[139] *Hensley, 461 U.S. 424.*

merit an award of attorney fees. Here, the primary benefit the mother achieved, an IEP, was unrelated to the litigation, and she did not receive any substantive benefit from the suit. As such, the court upheld the denial of fees because the mother failed to receive any substantive benefit from the litigation.

Similarly, the federal trial court in Massachusetts denied a school committee's motion to dismiss a mother's request for attorney fees.[140] The court conceded that the mother had a plausible claim based on a *de minimis* award at the special education appeals level, such that the impact of her limited success should be reflected in any fees she received.

Section 1983

Section 1983 is a federal civil rights statute authorizing monetary, declaratory, or injunctive relief remedies for federal statutory or constitutional rights violations.[141] Under Section 1983, individuals may seek monetary damages for civil rights violations by state actors, including public school boards or their employees. Pursuant to the U.S. Supreme Court's judgment in *Monell v. Respondent is Department of Services of City of New York*,[142] to succeed on such claims, plaintiffs must prove violations of a federal constitutional right due to state policies, customs, or practices. Still, plaintiffs may not circumvent the IDEA's exhaustion requirements to claim money damages through Section 1983 claims.[143]

After her daughter with disabilities was exposed to violence, including disruptive, obscene, and disturbing behavior by two peers, her mother unsuccessfully sued, claiming that officials violated her educational rights by knowingly creating a dangerous environment that caused emotional suffering and psychological damage in violation of Section 1983. The federal trial court in Massachusetts rejected the mother's allegations because she offered only conclusory and vague allegations, which were insufficient to state a plausible *Monell* claim.[144]

---

[140] del Rosario *ex rel.* Burke v. Nashoba Reg'l Sch. Dist., 502 F. Supp. 3d 623, 390 Educ. L. Rep. 575 (D. Mass. 2020).
[141] Civil Rights Act of 1871, 42 U.S.C. § 1983.
[142] Monell v Dep't of Soc. Servs. of City of New York, 436 U.S. 658 (1978).
[143] 20 U.S.C. 1415(i)(3)(B)(i)(I); 20 U.S.C. 1401(3)(A).
[144] del Rosario *ex rel.* Burke v. Nashoba Reg'l Sch. Dist., 502 F. Supp. 3d 623, 390 Educ. L. Rep.575 (D. Mass. 2020).

Other IDEA Issues

This section reviews cases that arise under the IDEA that cannot be classified and included in other parts of the chapter. In that respect, the section deals with a miscellaneous issue rarely litigated.

In ongoing litigation from California, a federal trial court conceded that the state passed the second implementation phase of a consent decree.[145] The court ascertained that state officials proposed a legally adequate system for monitoring school systems' use of mediation; identifying the boards needing intensive monitoring; assessing small districts' performance in educating students with disabilities; specifying which needed intervention; plus a method to identify, locate, and evaluate all eligible students within communities.

Discrimination Under Section 504 of the Rehabilitation Act and the Americans with Disabilities Act

Disability rights and protections are the focus of both Section 504 and the ADA, as amended in 2008. Section 504 prohibits exclusion and discrimination of individuals with disabilities, specifically "[n]o otherwise qualified individual with a disability... shall, solely by reason of her or his disability be excluded from participation in, be denied benefits of, or be subjected to discrimination under any program or activity receiving [f]ederal financial assistance...."[146] These protections apply both to services provided by an agency and to employment by an institution receiving federal funding.

Section 504 and the ADA regulations prohibit entities and individuals from discriminating against and excluding individuals with disabilities. Section 504 applies to federally funded programs and activities, while the ADA[147] covers all entities, regardless of whether they receive federal funds.

Originally enacted in 1990, the ADA has had a wide impact in both public and private sectors. According to the ADA Amendments Act of 2008, the term "disability" should be broadly interpreted both in the ADA and Section 504.[148] The amendments expressly sought to

---

[145] Emma C. v. Thurmond, 472 F. Supp. 3d 641, 384 Educ. L. Rep. 141 (N.D. Cal. 2020).
[146] 29 U.S.C. § 794.
[147] 42 U.S.C. § 12101 *et seq.*
[148] P.L. 110-325, 122 Stat. 3553 (2008).

clarify the meaning of a person with a disability while making it easier to qualify as such a person. Before the amendments, in *Sutton v. United Air Lines*,[149] the U.S. Supreme Court ruled that an individual who claimed to be regarded as disabled needed to show that the disability limited a major life activity.

Because the statutory constructions of Section 504 and the ADA are similar, courts often review these claims simultaneously.[150] In order to qualify as an individual with a disability under Section 504 and the ADA, one must demonstrate that a physical or mental impairment substantially limits one or more major life activities, have a record of such impairments, or be regarded as having such impairments.[151] The definition of major life activities is broadly interpreted as including "functions such as caring for oneself, performing manual tasks, walking, seeing, hearing, speaking, breathing, learning, and working."[152]

In two previous U.S. Supreme Court cases, *School Board of Nassau County v. Arline*[153] and *Southeastern Community College v. Davis*,[154] the Justices interpreted the definition of "otherwise qualified" as meaning an individual could meet all of the program requirements despite having the disability. Once officials in entities receiving federal financial assistance determine that an individual is otherwise qualified, they must make reasonable accommodations unless doing so would create an undue hardship.[155] Similarly, the ADA imposes the duty to provide reasonable accommodations for private entities.

Elementary and Secondary School Students

The Office for Civil Rights (OCR) has the authority and responsibility to enforce Section 504 and the ADA. Even so, parents typically litigate these claims in the federal courts, seeking relief from alleged discrimination by school boards and their employees. Additionally, parents may seek relief in the courts under Section 504, the ADA, and the IDEA. Despite some similarity across the

---

[149] Sutton v. United Airlines, 527 U.S. 471 (1999), superseded by statute, 42 U.S.C. § 12102(3)(A) (2008).
[150] *See* 42 U.S.C.§ § 12134(b), 12201(a).
[151] 42 U.S.C. §12102(1); 34 C.F. R. §104.3(j)(1).
[152] 34 C.F. R. § 104.3(j)(2)(ii).
[153] Sch. Bd of Nassau Cnty., Fla. v. Arline, 480 U.S. 273, 37 Educ. L. Rep. 448 (1987).
[154] Se. Cmty. Coll. v. Davis, 442 U.S. 397 (1979).
[155] 34 C.F. R. § 104.12(a).

three statutes, parental claims under Section 504 and the ADA may be distinct from suits pursuant to the IDEA.

A mother in Texas unsuccessfully filed suit alleging that school officials discriminated, under the ADA and Section 504, against her son, who had multiple physical and cognitive impairments due to his disabilities. As revealed in the record, the school board dismissed two employees after becoming aware of the student's alleged mistreatment and reassigned a verbally abusive school bus driver to ensure he would have no further interaction with the child. The Fifth Circuit affirmed that the board was not liable under the ADA or Section 504 because there was no indication or awareness of previous harm, injuries, or mistreatment of the student by either employee, such that no evidence supported the mother's claim that officials acted with deliberate indifference.[156]

In a case from Washington, the Ninth Circuit held that genuine issues of material fact over the reasonable accommodations parents requested for their daughter precluded a school board's motion for summary judgment on their Section 504 and ADA claims.[157] Because the court thought it was unclear whether officials knew the student needed accommodations in the form of supervision and gross motor activity, but failed to provide them, whether they demonstrated deliberate indifference remained in dispute.

A federal trial court, in the first of two cases from Pennsylvania, decided that a school board was responsible for providing reasonable Section 504 accommodations necessary for a student to benefit from the regular academic program because his impairments met the statute's standard of substantially affecting at least one major life function.[158] The court noted that the board's procedural violation of its child-find duty resulted in a substantive denial of FAPE throughout elementary school.

In a similar case, a federal trial court upheld a hearing officer in Pennsylvania's order that a school board's denial of a FAPE on procedural grounds met the elements of parental claims under the IDEA and the ADA.[159] The court did reject the parents' Section 504

---

[156] Harrison v. Klein Indep. Sch. Dist., 856 F. App'x 480, 393 Educ. L. Rep. 574 (5th Cir. 2021).

[157] R.D. *ex rel.* Davis v. Lake Washington Sch. Dist. 843 F. App'x 80, 388 Educ. L. Rep. 620 (9th Cir. 2021).

[158] E.P. *ex rel* Allison H.P. v. Twin Valley Sch. Dist., 517 F. Supp. 3d 347, 393 Educ. L. Rep. 319 (E.D. Pa. 2021).

[159] Montgomery Cnty. Intermediate Unit No. 23 v. A.F. *ex rel* D.F. and J.F., 506 F. Supp.3d 293, 390 Educ. L. Rep. 1126 (E.D. Pa. 2020).

claim because they failed to demonstrate that the program at issue received federal funding.

Parents of a student with autism, intellectual and language impairments, attention deficit hyperactivity disorder, development coordination disorder, anxiety, and congenital heart disease claimed officials discriminated against their daughter on the basis of her disability, in violation of Section 504 and the ADA. Despite parental allegations that board officials acted with bad faith and gross misjudgment, the federal trial court in Maryland was of the opinion that because they failed to put forward sufficient evidence of intentionally discriminatory actions, they did not meet the deliberate indifference standard under either statute.[160]

Parents of a high school student in Washington, D.C., with anxiety and depression, and who had been hospitalized for suicidal ideation, sued the board alleging the denial of a FAPE under the IDEA, disability discrimination under Section 504 and the ADA, and the District of Columbia Human Rights Act (DCHRA).[161] The parents alleged that officials removed their daughter from an elite school because she needed special education, while the latter responded that she did not qualify for special services. Under these circumstances, the court ruled that it was plausible for the parents to prove bad faith or gross mismanagement in support of their disability discrimination claim under Section 504, the ADA, and the DCHRA. The court concluded that it might be possible for the parents to demonstrate that the board had a policy or practice of exclusion, that adherence to it resulted in the denial of services, and that officials advised the student to leave school so they could avoid funding special education services for her needs.

The federal trial court in Connecticut dismissed parents' Section 504, and ADA claims on the ground that a school board discriminated against their son due to his disability, race, and national origin, while retaliating in response to their protected activity when they reported their concerns about his education.[162] The parents claimed retaliation, alleging that their communication with school staff was limited and their son was removed from the National Honor Society after being disciplined and suspended from school for a code of conduct violation. The court reasoned that

---

[160] S.S. v. Bd. of Educ. of Harford Cnty., 498 F. Supp.3d 761, 389 Educ. L. Rep. 316 (D. Md. 2020).

[161] Reid-Witt *ex rel.* C.W. v. Dist. of Columbia, 486 F. Supp. 3d 1, 386 Educ. L. Rep. 690 (D.D.C. 2020).

[162] Wong v. Bd. of Educ., 478 F. Supp. 3d 229, 385 Educ. L. Rep. 537 (D. Conn. 2020).

pursuant to state law, because the hearing officer's jurisdiction was limited to the IDEA claims, it was proper for her not to have reviewed the Section 504 and ADA claims. The court added that because the parents failed to offer sufficient evidence supporting their Section 504 and ADA claims, the hearing officer properly declined to review those charges.

Claims often implicate both Section 504 and the ADA due to similarities between these laws. Such allegations may also involve the IDEA. In fact, a claim under Section 504 will be subsumed within the IDEA if it fails to be sufficiently different from a claim under the IDEA. The federal trial court in Massachusetts rejected a Section 504 claim by the mother of a student with a disability because it was not separate or distinct from her IDEA charge.[163] Although the mother alleged that school officials retaliated under Section 504, the court rejected this allegation as completely devoid of any factual assertions supporting such a plausible charge.

Discrimination claims arose under Section 504 and the ADA for aggressive behaviors by other students and peer-to-peer harassment. For student-on-student harassment discrimination claims to be actionable under Section 504 and the ADA, the courts are guided by the five-part test the U.S. Supreme Court established in *Davis v. Monroe County Board of Education*,[164] using the following elements: boards and/or programs are recipients of federal financial aid; officials have control over the students and contexts within which harassment occurred; students were harassed due to their disabilities; the harassment was sufficiently severe or pervasive so as to have denied victims equal educational opportunities; school officials had actual knowledge of the harassment; and officials acted with deliberate indifference.

The first of three cases arose in Pennsylvania when the parents of a middle school student who experienced difficulties following the removal of a brain tumor filed suit alleged violations of the IDEA and Section 504 as a result of the intense bullying to which his classmates subjected him. Because the child's personality changed after his brain surgery, his classmates increasingly bullied him, culminating in shocking incidents leading to a grand mal seizure and a punctured anus with rectal bleeding. The Third Circuit permitted the parents' claim to proceed under Section 504 to consider whether officials could have provided a reasonable accommodation,

---

[163] del Rosario *ex rel.* Burke v. Nashoba Reg'l Sch. Dist., 502 F. Supp. 3d 623, 390 Educ. L. Rep. 575 (D. Mass. 2020).
[164] Davis v. Monroe Cnty. Bd. of Educ., 526 U.S. 629, 134 Educ. L. Rep. 477 (1999).

explaining that a 504 Plan was not in place because the parents refused to accept the board's offer of a revised one when they failed to check the "agree" box on the 504 Plan, instead making a handwritten request for accommodations on it.[165]

In the second case on peer bullying, a federal trial court in North Carolina dismissed the ADA and Section 504 claims of the parents of a student with disabilities who was physically attacked on a school bus by peers who were encouraged to do so by the bus driver.[166] Although the driver was immediately charged with a felony and dismissed, while the students were charged with juvenile delinquency, the parents claimed another attack by one of the bullying students during class two years after the bus attack caused pain, mental anguish, humiliation, and embarrassment. Because the parents failed to allege other incidents for two years after the bus incident, the court was not convinced that officials acted with deliberate indifference.

The third case of peer bullying involved a student from California with attention deficit disorder who was injured when he was assaulted at a high school football game. The injured student's parents unsuccessfully sought monetary damages under the ADA and Section 504, claiming officials had the duty to adhere to guidance issued by the U.S. Department of Education in various Dear Colleague Letters (DCLs) intended to prevent harassment that qualified as disability discrimination. Affirming the denial of the claim for failure to meet the elements necessary to support charges of intentional discrimination or deliberate indifference, the Ninth Circuit found that DCLs are not enforceable as distinct legal obligations or as binding law.[167] The court remarked that the DCLs do not obligate parties to demonstrate actual knowledge of prior harassment or support claims of clearly unreasonable responses. The court asserted that no supervision could completely neutralize the risk of peer-on-peer harassment or bullying and that DCLs are merely aspirational, non-binding guidance not altering the elements of ADA or Section 504 claims. As DCLs are non-binding, and a social-related accommodation was never requested or denied, the court

---

[165] K.E. v. Northern Highlands Reg'l Bd. of Educ., 840 F. App'x 705, 388 Educ. L. Rep. 144 (3d Cir. 2020).

[166] Sciacca v. Durham Cnty. Bd. of Educ., 509 F. Supp.3d 505, 391 Educ. L. Rep. 651 (M.D.N.C. 2020).

[167] Csutoras v. Paradise High Sch., 12 F.4th 960, 395 Educ. L. Rep. 40 (9th Cir. 2021).

emphasized there was a lack of evidence of a failure to accommodate because officials did not act with deliberate indifference.

Conclusions

A great deal of litigation continues under the IDEA, Section 504, and the ADA, even though it appears to have slowed down during the past year. Not surprisingly, cases challenging school board actions over the delivery of services to students with disabilities during the COVID-19 pandemic continued to emerge.

The U.S. Supreme Court's judgment in *Fry* notwithstanding, parents raising claims under Section 504 and the ADA must exhaust the IDEA's administrative remedies before filing suit continues. Much of this litigation revolves around claims that officials denied students access to educational programming. The issue is whether these are FAPE-based complaints or allegations of discriminatory treatment.

Parents continue to seek remedies such as tuition reimbursement, compensatory education, and attorney fees when hearing officers or judges agree that their children were denied FAPEs. Yet, fewer cases this year sought reimbursement of litigation costs than in the past.

Because students with disabilities have rights and protections under Section 504, the ADA, and the IDEA, it is not surprising that litigation continues under all three statutes. As in the past, though, courts are reluctant to find discrimination absent evidence of bad faith or gross negligence by school officials.

Alphabetical List of Cases

A.B. *ex rel.* K.B. v. Abington Sch. Dist.
A.R. v. Conn. State Bd. of Educ.
Ahearn v. E. Stroudsburg Area Sch. Dist.
Banwart v. Cedar Falls Cmty. Sch. Dist.
Bd. of Educ. of Hendrick Hudson Cent. Sch. Dist. v. Rowley
Bd. of Educ. of Yorktown Cent. Sch. Dist. v. C.S.
Bellflower Unified Sch. Dist. v. Lua
Buckhannon Bd. and Care Home v. W. Va. Dep't of Health and Hum. Resources
Burlington Sch. Comm. v. Dep't of Educ., Commw. of Mass.
C.W. *ex rel.* B.W. v. Denver Cnty. Sch. Dist. No. 1
Cedar Rapids Cmty. Sch. Dist. v. Garret F.
Csutoras v. Paradise High Sch.
D.D. *ex rel.* Ingram v. L.A. Unified Sch. Dist.
David D. v. Dartmouth Sch. Comm.
Davis v. Monroe Cnty. Bd. of Educ.
del Rosario *ex rel.* Burke v. Nashoba Reg'l Sch. Dist.
Dervishi v. Dep't Special Educ., Stamford Bd. of Educ.
Doe v. Newton Pub. Schs.
E.E. *ex rel.* Hutchison-Escobedo v. Norris Sch. Dist.
E.P. *ex rel* Allison H.P. v. Twin Valley Sch. Dist.
Elizabeth B. v. El Paso Cnty. Sch. Dist.
Emma C. v. Thurmond
Endrew F. *ex rel.* Joseph F. v. Douglas Cnty. Sch. Dist. RE-1
Florence Cnty. Sch. Dist. Four v. Carter
Forest Grove Sch. Dist. v. T.A.
Fry v. Napoleon Cmty. Schs.
Geis v. Bd. of Educ. of Parsippany-Troy Hills, Morris Cnty.
Harrison v. Klein Indep. Sch. Dist.
Hatikvah Int'l Acad. Charter Sch. v. E. Brunswick Twp. Bd. of Educ.
Hensley v. Eckerhart
Hernandez v. Grisham
Honig v. Doe
J.N. *ex rel.* M.N. v. Jefferson Cnty. Bd. of Educ.
J.N. v. Or. Dep't of Educ.
J.T. *ex rel.* D.T. v. de Blasio
J.T. v. Dist. of Columbia
K.E. v. Northern Highlands Reg'l Bd. of Educ.
KB *ex rel.* SB v. Katonah Lewisboro Union Free Sch. Dist.
L.J. v. Baltimore Curriculum Project
Mills v. Bd. of Educ. of Dist. of Columbia

Monell v. Dep't of Social Servs.
Montgomery Cnty. Intermediate Unit No. 23 v. A.F. *ex rel.* D.F. and J.F.
Neske *ex rel.* A.N. v. N.Y.C. Dep't of Educ.
Northfield City Bd. of Educ. v. K.S. *ex rel.* L.S.
P.P. *ex rel.* Pinault v. NW. Indep. Sch. Dist.
Pa. Ass'n for Retarded Children v. Pa.
Perez v. Sturgis Pub. Schs.
Phillips v. Hebron
R.D. *ex rel.* Davis v. Lake Washington Sch. Dist.
Reid-Witt *ex rel.* C.W. v. Dist. of Columbia
S.S. v. Bd. of Educ. of Harford Cnty.
Sch. Bd. of Nassau Cnty. v. Arline
Schaffer *ex rel.* Schaffer v. Weast
Sciacca v. Durham Cnty. Bd. of Educ.
Smith *ex rel.* C.M. v. Tacoma Sch. Dist.
Smith v. Robinson
Soria *ex rel.* G.lS. v. N.Y.C. Dep't of Educ.
Southeastern Cmty. Coll. v. Davis
Student A v. S.F. Unified Sch. Dist.
Sutton v. United Air Lines
T.B. *ex rel.* Bell v. NW. Indep. Sch. Dist.
T.R. v. Sch. Dist. of Philadelphia
Ventura de Paulino v. N.Y.C. Dep't of Educ.
W.S. v. Dist. of Columbia
Wong v. Bd. of Educ.

Cases by Jurisdiction

FEDERAL CASES

U.S. Supreme Court
Bd. of Educ. of Hendrick Hudson Cent. Sch. Dist. v. Rowley
Buckhannon Bd. and Care Home v. W. Va. Dep't of Health and Hum. Resources
Burlington Sch. Comm. v. Dep't of Educ., Commw. of Mass.
Cedar Rapids Cmty. Sch. Dist. v. Garret F.
Davis v. Monroe Cnty. Bd. of Educ.
Endrew F. *ex rel.* Joseph F. v. Douglas Cnty. Sch. Dist. RE-1
Florence Cnty. Sch. Dist. Four v. Carter
Forest Grove Sch. Dist. v. T.A.
Fry v. Napoleon Cmty. Schs.

Hensley v. Eckerhart
Honig v. Doe
Monell v. Dep't of Social Servs.
Schaffer *ex rel.* Schaffer v. Weast
Sch. Bd. of Nassau Cnty. v. Arline
Smith v. Robinson
Southeastern Cmty. Coll. v. Davis
Sutton v. United Air Lines

D.C. Circuit
J.T. v. Dist. of Columbia

District of Columbia
J.T. v. Dist. of Columbia
Mills v. Bd. of Educ. of Dist. of Columbia
Reid-Witt *ex rel.* C.W. v. Dist. of Columbia
W.S. v. Dist. of Columbia

First Circuit
David D. v. Dartmouth Sch. Comm.

Massachusetts
del Rosario *ex rel.* Burke v. Nashoba Reg'l Sch. Dist.
Doe v. Newton Pub. Schs.

Second Circuit
A.R. v. Conn. State Bd. of Educ.
Bd. of Educ. of Yorktown Cent. Sch. Dist. v. C.S.
Dervishi v. Dep't Special Ed., Stamford Bd. of Educ.
KB *ex rel.* SB v. Katonah Lewisboro Union Free Sch. Dist.
Neske *ex rel.* A.N. v. N.Y.C. Dep't of Educ.
Soria *ex rel.* G.lS. v. N.Y.C. Dep't of Educ.
Ventura de Paulino v. N.Y.C. Dep't of Educ.

Connecticut
Wong v. Bd. of Educ.
J.T. *ex rel.* D.T. v. de Blasio

Third Circuit
A.B. *ex rel.* K.B. v. Abington Sch. Dist.
Ahearn v. E. Stroudsburg Area Sch. Dist.
Geis v. Bd. of Educ. of Parsippany-Troy Hills, Morris Cnty.
Hatikvah Int'l Acad. Charter Sch. v. E. Brunswick Twp. Bd. of Educ.

K.E. v. Northern Highlands Reg'l Bd. of Educ.
Northfield City Bd. of Educ. v. K.S. *ex rel.* L.S.
T.R. v. Sch. Dist. of Philadelphia

Pennsylvania
E.P. *ex rel* Allison H.P. v. Twin Valley Sch. Dist.
Montgomery Cnty. Inter. Unit No. 23 v. A.F. *ex rel.* D.F. and J.F.
Pa. Ass'n for Retarded Children v. Pa.

Fourth Circuit

Maryland
L.J. v. Baltimore Curriculum Project
S.S. v. Bd. of Educ. of Harford Cnty.
North Carolina
Sciacca v. Durham Cnty. Bd. of Educ.

Fifth Circuit
Harrison v. Klein Indep. Sch. Dist.
P.P. *ex rel.* Pinault v. NW. Indep. Sch. Dist.
T.B. *ex rel.* Bell v. NW. Indep. Sch. Dist.

Sixth Circuit
Perez v. Sturgis Pub. Schs.

Eighth Circuit

Iowa
Banwart v. Cedar Falls Cmty. Sch. Dist.

Ninth Circuit
Bellflower Unified Sch. Dist. v. Lua
Csutoras v. Paradise High Sch.
D.D. *ex rel.* Ingram v. L.A. Unified Sch. Dist.
E.E. *ex rel.* Hutchison-Escobedo v. Norris Sch. Dist.
R.D. *ex rel.* Davis v. Lake Washington Sch. Dist.
Student A v. S.F. Unified Sch. Dist.

California
Emma C. v. Thurmond

Oregon
J.N. v. Or. Dep't of Educ.

Washington
Smith *ex rel.* C.M. v. Tacoma Sch. Dist.

Tenth Circuit
C.W. *ex rel.* B.W. v. Denver Cnty. Sch. Dist. No. 1
Elizabeth B. v. El Paso Cnty. Sch. Dist.

New Mexico
Hernandez v. Grisham

Eleventh Circuit
J.N. *ex rel.* M.N. v. Jefferson Cnty. Bd. of Educ.

STATE & D.C. COURT CASES

Connecticut
Phillips v. Hebron

Chapter 6

TORTS

Jeffrey C. Sun, J.D.,[1] Ph.D., Raquel Muñiz, J.D., Ph.D.,[2] and Luke Stedrak, Ed.D.[3]

Overview 177
Elementary and Secondary Education Cases 177
   Intentional Torts..177
      Assault and Battery..177
      Defamation..178
      Other Intentional Torts..181
   Negligence..183
      Duty Owed 183
      Assumption of Risk and Liability Waiver 186
      Negligent Supervision 188
      Premises Liability..193
      Vehicular Accidents...196
      Wrongful Death 197
      Damages..198
   Work-Related Injuries...199
   Vicarious Liability 201
   Procedural 203
   Immunity 207

---

[1] Professor of Higher Education and Law, Distinguished University Scholar, Associate Dean for Innovation and Strategic Partnerships, and Director of the SKILLS Collaborative at the University of Louisville, Ky.
[2] Assistant Professor, Lynch School of Education & Human Development; Assistant Professor, School of Law, Boston College, Boston, Mass.
[3] Associate Professor, Hibernia National Bank Endowed Professor, Department of Educational Leadership and Technology, Southeastern Louisiana University, Hammond, La.

Higher Education Cases 213
  Intentional Torts 213
    Battery 213
    False Imprisonment 213
    Misappropriation of Funds 214
    Tortious Interference 214
    Defamation 215
  Negligence 216
    Duty Owed 216
    Premises Liability 220
    Negligent Misrepresentation 220
    Medical Malpractice 220
    Wrongful Death 221
    Other Negligence Claims 222
    Indemnification 224
  Vicarious Liability 225
  Products Liability 225
  Class Action 226
  Evidentiary Matters 226
  Notice 228
  Other Procedural Matters 229
  Immunity 232
Conclusion 235
Alphabetical List of Cases 236
Cases by Jurisdiction 239

Torts

Overview

This chapter reviews the 144 reported tort cases in education as recognized in the 2021 West's *Education Law Reporter*. The cases in this chapter addressed negligence, intentional torts, work-related tort actions, vicarious liability, product liability, insurance challenges, procedural matters in tort claims, and case immunity.

In light of the distinction between levels for education-based tort claims, we separated the discussion between school-level cases (i.e., elementary and secondary education) and postsecondary education (i.e., higher education) level cases. The separation is instrumental as the duties owed to students are different, at times, by age group, and the structural designs of educational institutions are different between school and college contexts. For instance, postsecondary education may have medical units or hospitals with vastly different liability concerns than the health services in elementary schools. Generally speaking, the cases in 2021 highlighted significant rules of law (e.g., state-created danger doctrine, economic loss doctrine, indemnification policies, and state tort claims acts) when examining tort cases.

Elementary and Secondary Education Cases

Intentional Torts

Assault and Battery

Two cases involved a physical altercation alleging assault and battery claims arising from student bullying. A federal trial court in Virginia held that the plaintiff student sufficiently stated claims to survive dismissal under § 1983 and Title VI against the defendant school board, principal, football coach, and boys' locker room supervisor but failed to state a discrimination claim under the Rehabilitation Act.[4] The case stemmed from an incident in which the White football players at a middle school assaulted and physically battered Black teammates in the locker room, which they recorded and posted on social media. One player who was attacked filed a substantive due process claim against the football coach under the state-created danger doctrine, requiring him to show that the coach

---

[4] DJ ex rel. Hughes v. Sch. Bd. of Henrico Cnty., 488 F. Supp. 3d 307, 387 Educ. L. Rep. 228 (E.D. Va. 2020).

created or increased the risk of private danger directly through affirmative acts. The plaintiff alleged that the defendant and other school officials were made aware of the racially-based incident involving bullying and harassment of the Black members of the football team. The court found this reporting sufficient to survive a motion to dismiss under the state-created danger doctrine.

The Supreme Court of Ohio reversed the state appellate court's reversal of the summary judgment in favor of the appellants, including a teacher and officials, in a case involving a kindergartener being bullied.[5] The family alleged that the kindergarten student was subject to numerous forms of bullying, including name-calling, teasing, exclusion, and physical bullying. The parents repeatedly identified a particular student as a bully. The bullying peaked when the previously identified bully stabbed the plaintiff student in the face with a sharp pencil while seated at the same table. Under Ohio law, an employee of a political subdivision is immune from liability except in three situations, including if the employee acted recklessly. The court found no known risk that the identified bully would physically harm the plaintiff student because the bullying was primarily verbal, with only one pushing incident. Therefore, the appellate court ruled that the appellants were not reckless and were entitled to summary judgment.

Defamation

Five defamation cases arose during this period—three state- and two federal-level cases. The Fourth Circuit affirmed the South Carolina district court's grant of summary judgment in favor of the defendant charter school, city, and school resource officer in a suit involving privacy and defamation.[6] The defendant high school terminated the plaintiff, a finance department employee, when the school eliminated the finance department. The federal appellate court ruled that school personnel escorting the former employee off the campus as part of the termination steps, the security officer's display of the former employee and her husband's photos at the school security desk, and the effect of both the termination letter and officer's placement of photos did not constitute any form of defamation. Further, the security officer's placement of photographs

---

[5] A.J.R. v. Lute, 168 N.E. 3d 1157, 390 Educ. L. Rep. 1182 (Ohio 2020).
[6] McMichael v. James Island Charter Sch., 840 F. App'x 723, 388 Educ. L. Rep. 154 (4th Cir. 2020).

did not arise to display private information or demonstrate an invasion of privacy claim.

An Illinois federal district court granted the defendant board of education's motion to dismiss the plaintiff/teacher's defamation, breach of contract, and two of her due process claims but denied the dismissal for the plaintiff's due process claim under the constructive discharge theory and defamation per se.[7] The plaintiff was a tenured teacher with reports of unprofessional and negative interactions with a colleague. An internal investigation concluded against the plaintiff, finding that she falsely reported abuse and acted unprofessionally. The court ruled that board members were immune from civil liability on the defamation claim because the statements were made within the scope of their position. The plaintiff's due process claims under the coerced resignation theory failed. However, she did sufficiently allege constructive discharge by alleging that the defendants made false accusations about her, changed her performance evaluation process, removed her keys and access to the network, and shunned her. The plaintiff's defamation per se claim survived because the defendants failed to show that the Notice of Remedy could be innocently interpreted to qualify for the innocent construction rule.

In Washington, the state's supreme court reversed the trial court's decision ordering the secretary of state to edit out the allegedly defamatory line.[8] The secretary of state publishes a voter's guide pamphlet for all statewide offices, and candidates may submit a statement and photo for publication; the pamphlet includes a disclaimer that statements are not edited for factual or grammatical accuracy. The defendant, another candidate for superintendent, submitted a statement claiming the plaintiff, as the superintendent incumbent, ignored the parents and educators by leading a policy to teach sexual positions to fourth graders. The secretary of state notified the plaintiff superintendent of the defendant candidate's statement, and the plaintiff filed a petition to bar its publication. The court found that there was not a substantial likelihood that the plaintiff could show that the defendant's statement was false because he did encourage parents to review a book with their fourth graders at home that included two pages depicting different sexual positions. Further, because he is a public official, the plaintiff would

---

[7] Smoler v. Bd. of Educ. for W. Northfield Sch. Dist. #31, 524 F. Supp. 3d 794, 394 Educ. L. Rep. 881 (N.D. Ill. 2021).

[8] Reykdal v. Espinoza, 473 P.3d 1221, 383 Educ. L. Rep. 455 (Wash. 2020).

have to show that the statement was made with actual malice, which he fails to do.

In South Carolina, the state's highest court reversed the grant and affirmation of the respondents' motion to dismiss the petitioner/former teacher's defamation claim against the school district and high school and civil conspiracy claim against the principal and assistant principal.[9] The petitioner asserted that the respondents targeted her for an uncalled-for and invasive performance evaluation which caused her to be ostracized and terminated. The circuit court dismissed the petitioner's civil conspiracy claim because she failed to plead special damages; she now argues that the court should overrule the requirement of special damages. The court agreed that the special damages pleading requirement in civil conspiracy claims should be overturned; instead, a civil conspiracy claim requires "(1) the combination or agreement of two or more persons, (2) to commit an unlawful act or a lawful act by unlawful means, (3) together with the commission of an overt act in furtherance of the agreement, and (4) damages proximately resulting to the plaintiff." Thus, the case was reversed and remanded in light of the abolition of the special damages pleading requirement.

An appellate court in Oregon reversed the trial court's grant of the defendant school district's special motion to strike the anti-SLAPP claims, which are strategic lawsuits against public participation.[10] The plaintiff was involved in several behavioral matters at school, and he was suspended from middle school when he was twelve years old for sexually harassing two younger students. Through its employees, the defendant allegedly published defamatory statements to third parties about the plaintiff sexually harassing younger students with disabilities, indicating that the plaintiff was a ringleader and a thief. Aside from some procedural matters, the defendant's motion failed to demonstrate an applicable exception. Notably, the defendant failed to show that the plaintiff's discipline was a public event connected to an issue of public interest, and the defamatory statements were not confined to his disciplinary proceedings. Also, the defendants allegedly published defamatory comments to third parties. Thus, the defendant was not protected under the statute.

---

[9] Paradis v. Charleston Cnty. Sch. Dist., 861 S.E.2d 774, 394 Educ. L. Rep. 403 (S.C. 2021).

[10] C. R. v. Eugene Sch. Dist. 4J, 481 P.3d 334, 387 Educ. L. Rep. 349 (Or. Ct. App. 2021).

Other Intentional Torts

Five other intentional tort claims within the elementary and secondary education levels emerged during this period. Initially a Title IX claim, the Eighth Circuit affirmed an order in favor of a board and middle school principal who did not have actual notice of a teacher's sexual abuse of the student.[11] Also, the appellate court ruled that the defendants were immune from the intentional tort claim under the Nebraska Political Subdivision Tort Claims Act. The court agreed that the board and principal lacked notice of the teacher's sexual misbehavior. Although the principal received reports of questionable teacher conduct (e.g., the student in question visiting the teacher's floor, being in the teacher's classroom at lunchtime with dimmed lights, having the teacher tie her shoelace in the hallway, being absent on the same day as the teacher, having the teacher grab her phone out of the back pocket of her pants), the principal responded to each questionable report by sending a security officer to the classroom during the lunch period and calling the student's father verifying his daughter's illness. In light of the efforts and the immunity, the appellate court affirmed the summary judgment in favor of the district and principal.[12]

In an intentional misrepresentation case, which also included questions of due process, a federal district court in Massachusetts denied the defendant's public school committee and the mayor's motion to dismiss the plaintiff/former superintendent's intentional misrepresentation and due process claims.[13] The court found it reasonable to infer from the context that the mayor knew the plaintiff planned to interview elsewhere due to opposition from the school committee and made promises of support to persuade the plaintiff not to interview for the other position; thus, dismissal was not appropriate for the plaintiff's intentional misrepresentation claim. The plaintiff also alleged due process violations against the school committee. The court agreed with the plaintiff, concluding that dismissing the due process claim was inappropriate.

In Ohio, a state appellate court reversed a grant of summary judgment in favor of the plaintiff, the State of Ohio, against the defendant, the community school's chief executive officer (CEO), for

---

[11] K.D. v. Douglas Cnty. Sch. Dist. No. 001, 1 F.4th 591, 391 Educ. L. Rep. 493 (8th Cir. 2021).
[12] Douglas Cnty. Sch. Dist. No. 001, 1 F.4th at 603.
[13] Khelfaoui v. Lowell Sch. Comm., 496 F. Supp. 3d 683, 389 Educ. L. Rep. 113 (D. Mass. 2020).

misappropriation of public funds.[14] The defendant's contract for his position as CEO specified that he had general supervision and management authority over the school and all those employed by the school and the authority to approve budget expenditures for the school along with the chief fiscal officer (CFO). An audit revealed that, during the defendant's school year as CEO, more than $50,000 had been misappropriated. The defendant alleged that, while he was a public official, he did not have sufficient responsibility to be liable for misappropriation under state law. The court found that the defendant did not receive the funds at issue here; the CFO did. Further, the defendant was not the CFO's supervisor, nor did he oversee the CFO. Therefore, he did not receive or collect money under the statute, and the case was remanded for judgment in the defendant's favor.

An appellate court in New York affirmed a grant of summary judgment in favor of the defendant regarding the plaintiff's tortious interference claim.[15] The plaintiff, a former high school teacher, attacked the defendant's former employer's decision to give him a poor rating and her refusal to allow him to rescind his resignation. The court held that the plaintiff was precluded from challenging the employer's actions in this action under the doctrine of collateral estoppel due to his prior Article 78 proceeding. The court also affirmed summary judgment in favor of the defendant's employer on the merits. The plaintiff does not have a claim for tortious interference with the contract because, among other reasons, he did not adequately allege that he was party to a contract with a third party. The court explained that the collective bargaining agreement could not be the basis for tortious interference with a contract claim.

In Connecticut, a state appellate court affirmed the trial court's granting of summary judgment in favor of the defendant superintendent on the plaintiff coach's recklessness, intentional infliction of emotional distress, and libel claims.[16] The plaintiff's recklessness claim failed because the defendant had nothing to do with his termination. There was no evidence suggesting that the inaccuracies in the press statements were due to an extreme departure of reasonable care, and proper protocols were followed to terminate an at-will employee like the plaintiff. Further, the

---

[14] State ex rel. Ohio Att'y Gen. v. Burns, 156 N.E.3d 461, 383 Educ. L. Rep. 1068 (Ohio Ct. App. 2020).
[15] Miller v. Livanis, 137 N.Y.S.3d 15, 386 Educ. L. Rep. 430 (N.Y. App. Div. 2020).
[16] Ortiz v. Torres-Rodriguez, 255 A.3d 941, 393 Educ. L. Rep. 740 (Conn. App. Ct. 2021).

plaintiff's intentional infliction of emotional distress claim fails because the statement made to the press was not sufficiently extreme and outrageous to satisfy the requirements for deliberate infliction of emotional distress; the plaintiff was not mentioned by name, nor does it say his termination or anything about child abuse. Finally, the court granted summary judgment in favor of the defendant on the plaintiff's libel claim. The articles he cited were extrinsic to the press statement and did not support any claim that the plaintiff was a child abuser.

Negligence

Among the negligence cases within the elementary and secondary education levels, ten broad issues arose in 2021: duty owed, assumption of risk, negligent supervision, premises liability, public-duty doctrine, vehicular accidents, wrongful death, bystander/impact rule, the release of liability, and punitive damage determinations. To succeed in negligence claims, plaintiffs must prove by a preponderance of the evidence that the defendants owed them duties of care to protect them from foreseeable harms and that the defendants breached their duties by acting unreasonably, resulting in their being the proximate cause of the injuries the plaintiffs experienced. In attempting to limit or eliminate liability, defendants can contest any of the legal elements of the negligence claims by denying that they had duties, by raising other defenses such as immunity, or by relying on procedural defenses to prevent plaintiffs from moving forward with their claims.

Duty Owed

Seven cases from five state courts and one federal court examined the duty owed to the injured party. A California federal district court held that the allegations made by the school district were sufficient to allege a negligence claim against the manufacturer, tobacco companies, and its officers.[17] The school district alleged that the defendant intentionally appealed to young users with its product marketing which foreseeably led to problems for school districts, like the need to devote time and resources to addressing nicotine use and financial costs for e-cigarette detection and disposal. The court found this adequate to place school districts

---

[17] In re JUUL Labs, Marketing, Sales Practices, and Products Liability Litigation, 497 F. Supp.3d 552, 389 Educ. L. Rep. 189 (N.D. Cal. 2020).

in the "foreseeable zone of risk," the defendant owed a duty of care under five state laws. The defendants argued that the economic loss doctrine bars the negligence claims. Still, the school district alleged property damage through hazardous waste and alterations that became necessary to school property because of the defendant's products. Because the school district plausibly alleged that the defendants owed them a duty due to foreseeability and public policy considerations, the court held that the school district's negligence claims should not be dismissed based on the economic loss doctrine.

The Supreme Court of Arizona ruled that a high school did not owe a female student a duty to protect her from her ex-boyfriend, who shot and killed her at a friend's house after-school.[18] The female student had become entangled in a dispute regarding the boyfriend's ex-girlfriend. After-school, they decided to meet at a friend's house to discuss the matter. While there, the boyfriend shot and killed her and then killed himself. While the school personnel knew he had possibly threatened his ex-girlfriend and that the girlfriend would meet with him after-school, they were unaware that he posed a threat to the girlfriend. The girlfriend had also told the school safety officer that the boyfriend did not threaten her. Thus, a known and tangible risk of harm did not arise within the scope of the student-school relationship, and the school did not owe the female student a duty of care.

An Indiana appellate court held that a school was not negligent when it refused to pay for a high school student's advanced math class.[19] The family enrolled the student in the school and sought to place him in advanced math classes at the school. The school offered a few options to the family, but they insisted on enrolling the student in a university course, for which they paid and afterwards sought reimbursement. The court found that the state law dual credit requirement did not grant students a right to attend a university or college course of their choice, requiring the high school to pay the cost. The school satisfied the state dual credit requirement through the International Baccalaureate (IB) program. Through the program, they provided the student several options for math courses; therefore, the school was not negligent and did not owe the student a duty to pay for college courses. In another Indiana case, its state appellate court held that a basketball coach was engaged in conduct ordinary to basketball when the coach, while participating in

---

[18] Dinsmoor v. City of Phx., 492 P.3d 313, 393 Educ. L. Rep. 837 (Ariz. 2021).
[19] Poore v. Indianapolis Pub. Schs., 155 N.E.3d 643, 383 Educ. L. Rep. 442 (Ind. Ct. App. 2020), *vacated*, 164 N.E. 3d 130 (Ind. 2021).

practice, swatted, struck, and injured a student player.[20] The ball struck the student on the temple and caused a concussion. The student sued the school corporation. The school corporation argued that they were entitled to summary judgment because blocking a basketball shot, which led to the incident, was ordinary conduct in basketball. The plaintiff student conceded that the coach did not intentionally strike her. However, the plaintiff responded that the coach acted recklessly. The appellate court did not find that the coach engaged in reckless behavior and held that the coach did not breach her duty of reasonable care towards the student-athlete.

An appellate court in Louisiana held that a school board's duty did not extend to a student who experienced an asthmatic attack, which led to an anoxic ischemic brain injury that resulted in permanent disability.[21] The asthma attack began during school hours, and the teacher took the student to the office, where the principal provided an inhaler and called the student's aunt and grandmother after being unable to reach the mother. The aunt and grandmother picked up the child at school, and after about an hour and worsening symptoms, the child collapsed and suffered the injury. The court held that a school board may be liable only when it has actual custody of the student entrusted to its care, and here, the student was in the custody of the aunt, someone the parent had designated as an approved caretaker. Therefore, the board was not negligent and owed no duty of care to the student in the situation.

A New Jersey appellate court held that a bus company owed a duty of reasonable care to a special needs student and her mother to transport the student home safely.[22] The student, who functioned at a sixth- or seventh-grade level, was transported to and from school by a van for special needs students as part of her Individualized Education Plan. The student asked the van driver to drop her off close to, but not at, her apartment, and the driver did so without parental approval. The student later went to another location with a boy, where she was repeatedly sexually assaulted. The appellate court held that to determine whether a duty exists, the court must first consider the foreseeability of harm to a potential plaintiff. It must analyze whether accepted fairness and policy considerations would support the imposition of a duty. The court held that the bus

---

[20] Matter of C.G., 157 N.E.3d 543, 384 Educ. L. Rep. 480 (Ind. Ct. App. 2020).
[21] Raymond v. Iberia Par. Sch. Bd., 323 So. 3d 447, 395 Educ. L. Rep. 462 (La. Ct. App. 2021).
[22] S.H. v. K & H Transp., 242 A.3d 278, 385 Educ. L. Rep. 798 (N.J. Super. Ct. App. Div. 2020).

company did owe the student and her mother a duty of reasonable care because educators must take reasonable precautions to keep their students safe, including during school-provided transportation.

A New York appellate court found that there were triable issues of fact that precluded the court from granting a charter school summary judgment in a student's negligence case where the then 15-year-old old was sexually assaulted and raped by a 19-year-old student at the school.[23] The school's executive director testified that the classroom doors were supposed to be locked when no teachers were present in the rooms and that before his tenure, numerous students were found alone in the rooms. The plaintiff student stated that the school was chaotic, and the assaulter had a history of violence and fighting in school. The court found that the school had a duty to supervise the students adequately and was liable for foreseeable injuries proximately caused by the lack of supervision. The school did not prove that the rape was not foreseeable and that the failure to lock the classrooms was not the proximate cause of the rape. The school owed the student a duty of care.

Assumption of Risk and Liability Waiver

Assumption of risk presents an affirmative defense barring recovery of damages from the injured party. Five cases within four states analyzed the assumption of risk defense or a release of liability. The Georgia Court of Appeals held that the jury should have been instructed on an assumption of risk when a high school senior suffered injuries during a bubble soccer event.[24] Before the event, the gaming company briefed all participating students on safety rules, but the student plaintiff was not present. The student injured himself during the event, and the soccer coach called an ambulance. Doctors found multiple bone fractures in the student's forehead and brain damage to the frontal lobe causing cognitive impairment and permanent loss of taste and smell. The student sued the gaming company. At trial, the gaming company asked for jury instruction on the assumption of risk, but the trial court declined. The appellate court found sufficient evidence that the plaintiff had played soccer since a young age, was familiar with soccer safety rules, and knew the game followed the rules of soccer. Moreover,

---

[23] Doe v. Bronx Preparatory Charter Sch., 146 N.Y.S.3d 623, 391 Educ. L. Rep. 932 (N.Y. App. Div. 2021).
[24] Game Truck Ga., LLC v. Quezada, 859 S.E.2d 125, 391 Educ. L. Rep. 951 (Ga. Ct. App. 2021).

there was evidence that the gaming company had instructed the student not to engage in horseplay, but he admitted to intentionally running toward another player. The court should have instructed the jury on the assumption of risk.

An appellate court in New York found that the student plaintiff had assumed the risk in playing baseball and thus upheld summary judgment in favor of the school district.[25] The plaintiff, a member of his high school's varsity baseball team, suffered permanent injuries to his right eye after a baseball struck him in the face during an outdoor baseball practice. He argued that the defendant's negligence caused the injury when they conducted multiple infield drills (named the "Warrior Drills") with multiple balls without the proper equipment and caution. The defendants claimed that the student assumed the risk inherent in playing baseball. The court ruled that the student was an experienced baseball player, having played baseball from a young age, who knew the risks and their nature, and voluntarily assumed them. Similarly, another New York appellate court held that a school basketball player assumed the risk of injury in playing basketball in a case in which the player collided with retracted bleachers during a basketball drill during practice.[26] The basketball court did not use boundary lines. The student conceded that the bleachers were open and obvious and that they were aware of the bleachers. The appellate court explained that a person voluntarily assumes the inherent risks that arise out of the nature of a sport in which they participate. The plaintiff's mother argued that eliminating the boundary lines during the drill increased the inherent risks. Disagreeing with the mother, the court ruled that the failure to use boundary lines did not increase the inherent risk and, therefore, the defendant's motion for summary judgment should have been granted by the trial court.

The Ohio Court of Appeals affirmed that a high school junior varsity basketball team member had assumed the risk of injury when she stayed to watch the varsity game, at least until half-time, and was injured when she went to retrieve her belongings during halftime from the locker room next to the court.[27] As she was leaving the locker room, the game had resumed, and a varsity player crashed

---

[25] Grady v. Chenango Valley Cent. Sch. Dist., 141 N.Y.S.3d 513, 388 Educ. L. Rep. 324 (N.Y. App. Div. 2021).
[26] Secky v. New Paltz Cent. Sch. Dist., 151 N.Y.S.3d 202, 394 Educ. L. Rep. 327 (N.Y. App. Div. 2021).
[27] Miller v. Cardinal Mooney High Sch., 168 N.E.3d 1254, 390 Educ. L. Rep. 1189 (Ohio Ct. App. 2021).

into the door, causing the door to slam the student plaintiff's fingers. She sustained severe injury. The appellate court found that the student plaintiff assumed the risk: it was not unusual for a locker room to be placed adjacent to the basketball court; a player hitting the door was an inherent risk in playing basketball; the hazard posed by using the locker room during a game was open and obvious to the plaintiff; and though she was not aware the game had restarted, she entered the locker room during half-time knowing that the game would soon resume.

Finally, in a liability waiver case, a state court of appeals in Florida affirmed that a student-athlete signing a release of liability pre-game barred the student's negligence claim.[28] During a soccer game, another player attempting to score a goal hit the student plaintiff, sending the plaintiff into an unpadded cement barrier near the soccer field. The student-athlete had signed a release of liability form before playing, in which he and his father agreed to release the school board from any liability for any injury. The student sued the board for negligence and argued on appeal that the release form was ambiguous. The appellate court first held that the student plaintiff did not preserve the claims presented in the lower court. However, the court explained that even if the student had kept his claims, the release of liability was unambiguous and enforceable, releasing the school board from liability.

Negligent Supervision

In 12 cases, half of which occurred within New York, plaintiffs sued the school district or school for negligent supervision. These claims allege negligence based on an employee's actions in which the employer negligently supervised the employee leading to the injury. In New York, a federal trial court agreed with the defendants in a case where the plaintiff student, age fifteen, was sexually assaulted by a nineteen-year-old student who sat beside her during study hall.[29] The student sued the school and school district for negligent supervision of students. A teacher assigned to supervise students during study hall did not appear to notice or intervene. The defendants argued that the student did not demonstrate that the school was aware of any prior conduct by the older student that

---

[28] Elalouf v. Sch. Bd. of Broward Cnty., 311 So. 3d 863, 388 Educ. L. Rep. 437 (Fla. Dist. Ct. App. 2021).
[29] AA by BB v. Hammondsport Cent. Sch. Dist., 527 F. Supp. 3d 501, 395 Educ. L. Rep. 298 (W.D.N.Y. 2021).

would have made the assault foreseeable. Therefore, the plaintiff failed to state a claim. The court agreed with the defendants that the plaintiff could not state a claim. However, the court noted that the school subsequently placed the students in the same study hall, despite the harassed student having a protective order against the older student. At that point, the school was on notice. The court granted the plaintiff leave to amend her complaint regarding the subsequent study hall placement.

In Texas, a federal district court found that a student failed to plead that the school district was deliberately indifferent, a requirement for liability under the student's § 1983 failure-to-supervise claim.[30] The Black female student was severely harassed in school based on her race. White students repeatedly called her racial slurs and engaged in racist behaviors, and teachers did not intervene. The student suffered severe trauma and emotional distress due to the harassment. The student argued that the school district failed to supervise employees who should have intervened. The court disagreed with the student that the school district was liable. More specifically, the court found that the school district could not be held liable for the actions of the associate superintendent under the § 1983 claim. Further, the court concluded that the student did not plead sufficient facts to support that the school board was deliberately indifferent in creating or enforcing school policies regarding the supervision of its students.

In Oregon, a district court found that a football coach was not entitled to qualified immunity in a football player's § 1983 claim arising out of concussions the student suffered during a game.[31] The coach had him continue playing and practicing without medical clearance. A doctor recommended the student attend only two class periods a day with accommodations and severely limited his physical activities. He suffered from anxiety and attempted suicide because of the injuries. The student sued the coach, arguing that the coach knew that allowing the student to return to play and practice would violate his right to bodily autonomy. The court found that the state statute created a liberty interest and placed a clear mandate on coaches and school districts to not return players with known or suspected concussions without clearance so that a jury could reasonably conclude that the coach acted deliberately indifferent to

---

[30] Sneed v. Austin Indep. Sch. Dist., 487 F. Supp. 3d 584, 387 Educ. L. Rep. 213 (W.D. Tex. 2020).
[31] Martin for C.M. v. Hermiston Sch. Dist. 8R, 499 F. Supp. 3d 813, 389 Educ. L. Rep. 823 (D. Or. 2020).

a known or obvious danger by returning the student to practice and play. Therefore, the coach violated the statute and caused a violation of the student's fundamental right to bodily autonomy.

The Supreme Court of Vermont affirmed that a high school football player was not contributorily negligent.[32] The state's highest court reasoned that the fact that the high school student was aware of prior homophobic slurs previously used by team players against other players and that he had been injured during a consensual boxing match at an earlier dinner did not make it reasonably foreseeable that he would be sexually assaulted at a later off-campus team dinner. The team dinner took place at the residence of one of the players. The state supreme court also found that the fact that the student was aware of lax supervision at the dinners did not mean he was contributorily negligent either. The student argued that the school board failed to properly supervise the football team, resulting in sexual assault. The state supreme court affirmed the lower court's grant of the student's post-trial motion to set aside the jury's contributory negligence determination.

The Supreme Court of Appeals for West Virginia ruled in favor of the parents of a transgender student in a case where the assistant principal consistently harassed the student.[33] The family argued that the school board was negligent per se by failing to adopt an anti-harassment policy or adopting an inadequate one as required by law. The state supreme court found that the Torts Claims Act provided immunity to political subdivisions for failure to adopt a written policy. The family also argued that the board was negligent per se by violating its anti-harassment policy. The court reversed the lower court's ruling on this issue because the board may have breached its duty to the student by not adopting an adequate anti-harassment policy and breaching the policy in place. The latter observation was based on the board allowing the assistant principal's harassment to continue via multiple harassment incidents at school. The court found the parents had sufficiently pled their negligent retention claim after the board renewed the assistant principal's contract and allowed the interactions between the administrator and the student to continue.

The Supreme Court of Missouri, in a student's claim of intentional, negligent supervision against the student's high school, held that expert testimony created a fact issue regarding whether

---

[32] Blondin v. Milton Town Sch. Dist., 251 A.3d 959, 391 Educ. L. Rep. 906 (Vt. 2021).
[33] C.C. v. Harrison Cnty. Bd. of Educ., 859 S.E.2d 762, 392 Educ. L. Rep. 980 (W.Va. 2021).

the school knew that the counselor posed a risk of sexual abuse to the children and whether the school disregarded the known risk.[34] The sexual abuse occurred while the student was a high school senior at a faith-based school. The lower court granted summary judgment in favor of the school on the student's intentional failure to supervise the claim. However, the state supreme court found that using all the evidence before them, including Father Doyle's expert testimony regarding the code and norms the Catholic Church used to note knowledge of sexual misconduct, a jury could reasonably find that the school knew the risk that the counselor posed to the students at the school and disregarded the known risk. The court remanded the case.

The Supreme Court of Rhode Island affirmed that a school breached its duty to adequately supervise students in its care.[35] The state's highest court found that the school was on notice of the foreseeable assault, given the student's history of disruptive and aggressive conduct. The student had previously violated the high school's sexual harassment and anti-bullying policies. Though the school was aware of the past behavior and the school handbook required teachers to supervise the hallways, the high school did nothing to handle the hallway or the student as he followed another student (the plaintiff) and yelled profanities at him. He had also not received any punishment other than detention. Eventually, he assaulted the plaintiff in the hallway, breaking the student's jaw in two places and dislocating his teeth. The court found that the issue of proximate causation was an issue for the jury, and the plaintiffs had presented sufficient evidence for the jury to find that the school's failure to supervise the student was the cause of the student's jaw injuries. The state supreme court upheld the denial of the defendants' motion for a new trial.

A New York appellate court ruled that the dismissal of new claims was warranted in a case where the defendants (school district and school) sought to dismiss specific claims the student plaintiff brought against them after the plaintiff was bullied and injured while playing kickball during gym class.[36] The student sustained a dislocated wrist and a laceration above her eye, leaving a scar. The student who bullied the plaintiff had several past complaints against

---

[34] Doe 122 v. Marianist Province of the U.S., 620 S.W.3d 73, 389 Educ. L. Rep. 630 (Mo. 2021).
[35] Dextraze v. Bernard, 253 A.3d 411, 392 Educ. L. Rep. 933 (R.I. 2021).
[36] C.D. v. Goshen Cent. Sch. Dist., 131 N.Y.S.3d 40, 383 Educ. L. Rep. 414 (N.Y. App. Div. 2020).

them. The plaintiff argued that the defendants were liable for negligent supervision and followed the notice of claim with additional legal claims. The defendants filed a motion to dismiss the additional claims, contending that such claims were outside the scope of the initial suit notice. The court agreed that the new claims, which incorporated other bullying incidents and noted that the plaintiff suffered stress, anxiety, and depression, were predicated on contemporary theories of liability, which were not part of the initial notice of claim and, therefore, should be dismissed.

In a second New York appellate court decision, the court ruled that a school district was not entitled to summary judgment in a high school student's personal injury case because the school district failed to establish that the injury was not foreseeable.[37] The tenth-grade student was physically assaulted by another student when the other student pushed the student's head from behind into a bulletin board. The assaulted student had previously reported to a teacher that the other student had made prior threats. The teacher had also witnessed the student making a closed fist at the assaulted student at least once or twice before the assault. The teacher never did anything about the threats. Thus, the court found that the school district failed to establish prima facie that the event was unforeseeable given proper supervision.

In a third case, a New York appellate court held that the lower court erred in not granting the defendant school district summary judgment. The assistant principal in the case was informed that a student, a nonparty to the case, was planning to fight someone, though no target was mentioned.[38] The assistant principal warned the student and his mother about the consequences of fighting. The student denied he intended to fight anyone. Nonetheless, the assistant principal warned the head of school security about the rumor. The student subsequently physically assaulted another student. The assaulted student was sued for negligent supervision and training, arguing that the school district failed to provide supervision that would have protected the student from the assault. The court found that the assistant principal had taken reasonable steps to prevent the fight, even without knowing the target student. Moreover, the court found that the negligent training claim could not

---

[37] Nizen–Jacobellis v. Lindenhurst Union Free Sch. Dist., 143 N.Y.S. 3d 368, 389 Educ. L. Rep. 452 (N.Y. App. Div. 2021).
[38] Wienclaw v. E. Islip Union Free Sch. Dist., 144 N.Y. S. 3d 106, 390 Educ. L. Rep. 393 (N.Y. App. Div. 2021).

proceed because the assistant principal acted within the scope of his employment in responding to the rumored fight.

In a fourth New York appellate decision, the court held that a first-grade student's motion for summary judgment was not premature on the issue of liability because the court had all the evidence it needed to decide on the case.[39] In this case, the first-grade student ran up and down the stairs after the teacher sent her to go quickly up the stairs, retrieve an item from the classroom, and return quickly. While running up the stairs, she fell and hit her head, suffering injuries. The school district argued that they still needed to depose the teacher in the case, but the court found that the school district had personal knowledge of the relevant facts and could have submitted an affidavit from the teacher. The court also found that, while the motion for summary judgment was not premature, the plaintiffs failed to establish they were entitled to summary judgment in their favor on the liability issue.

A final New York appellate court decision held that the lower court erred in denying the school district summary judgment in a negligent supervision case in which the school district did not have prior specific notice or knowledge of a student's physically or sexually aggressive behavior.[40] The student's prior misconduct history was limited to issues of attendance, insubordination, inappropriate verbal outputs, using drugs and alcohol, possessing and selling drugs, and academic difficulties. The history did not include sexually aggressive behavior similar to the behavior which injured the plaintiff. The student sexually assaulted the plaintiff, a student at the school, while alone in a classroom. Given the facts of the case, the court ruled that the school district was not liable for negligent supervision; they were not on notice such that supervision could have prevented the student from sexually assaulting the plaintiff.

Premises Liability

Five cases presented the issue of premises liability. For instance, the Florida Court of Appeals found the lower court erred in granting final summary judgment on a seven-year-old's negligence claim that arose when the child raced through a makeshift indoor running

---

[39] Chen v. City of N.Y., 149 N.Y.S.3d 190, 393 Educ. L. Rep. 402 (N.Y. App. Div. 2021).
[40] Knaszak v. Hamburg Cent. Sch. Dist., 152 N.Y.S.3d 199, 395 Educ. L. Rep. 384 (N.Y. App. Div. 2021).

course and struck a pedestal table, losing her permanent teeth and sustaining other long-term injuries.[41] The appellate court ruled that there were disputed issues regarding where the table was placed during the incident, whether the table had been on the running course before, and whether the danger the table posed would be open and obvious as a matter of law to a reasonable seven-year-old. The court reasoned that a jury could determine that it was foreseeable that an inexperienced second grader running on a crowded course with a table nearby could strike the table and sustain significant injuries. The appellate court reasoned that the trial court erred in overlooking relevant evidence and foreclosing negligence theories.

A Georgia appellate court reversed the grant of summary judgment in favor of the defendant board of education because there were genuine issues of fact where a student slipped and fell on rainwater exiting a school bus, resulting in a broken ankle.[42] The defendant board of education seemingly did not have any procedures for when rainwater enters the bus. The court held that summary judgment was improper because a jury could reasonably find that the bus driver had constructive knowledge of the hazard because he was in the immediate area and could have seen and removed the water. The student was not necessarily negligent for failing to look where she stepped when the bus doors sealed the steps from the outside, she was wearing flat sneakers, and she was not rushing to exit the bus. Further, there was no evidence that the student was aware of the water on the step before stepping into it; thus, the court could not find that the student's knowledge of the hazard was equal to or greater than the defendant's knowledge.

A New York appellate court reversed the grant of summary judgment in favor of the defendants, the school district, and the school, where a pedestrian sustained injuries after slipping on ice in the school parking lot.[43] The defendants argued that they did not owe a duty to remove the hazardous icy condition because it occurred during an ongoing storm or at a reasonable time. It snowed on the fall date from the early morning through when the plaintiff fell. However, the defendants failed to establish any specific amount of snowfall on the fall date. The court noted that even assuming the

---

[41] Collias ex rel. Collias v. Gateway Acad. of Walton Cnty., 313 So. 3d 163, 389 Educ. L. Rep. 659 (Fla. Dist. Ct. App. 2021).
[42] Dupree v. Houston Cnty. Bd. of Educ., 849 S.E.2d 778, 384 Educ. L. Rep. 527 (Ga. Ct. App. 2020).
[43] Ayers v. Pioneer Cent. Sch. Dist., 133 N.Y.S.3d 355, 384 Educ. L. Rep. 478 (N.Y. App. Div. 2020).

defendants met their initial burden, the plaintiff produced evidence showing that the weather conditions in the days leading up to the fall would cause ice to form, the defendants' parking lot had been covered with thick ice since the day before, and the defendants' groundskeeper plowed down to the ice. The state appellate court found these facts sufficient to raise an issue of fact as to the defendants' constructive notice of the parking lot's icy condition. Also in New York, another appellate court affirmed that the defendants – consisting of the city, department of education, and operator of an after-school program – were entitled to summary judgment because the defective condition of the schoolyard pavement was trivial as a matter of law and nonactionable.[44] A seventh-grade student tripped and fell over a crack in the concrete surface of the schoolyard while sprinting in an after-school program and suffered injuries. The defendants established that the crack was from one-eighth to seven-sixteenth inch wide with no vertical height differential. Further, the trip and fall occurred during daylight hours on a clear day. Thus, the appellate court ruled that summary judgment in favor of the defendants was affirmed, dismissing the plaintiff's premises liability claim.

Another appellate court in New York affirmed that the defendant school district was not entitled to summary judgment because the district failed to establish that it did not have actual or constructive notice of the alleged black ice condition.[45] The plaintiff slipped and fell on a patch of black ice in the parking lot of a school. Two custodians at the school had inspected the parking lot earlier that day. The evidence presented demonstrated a puddle of water in the park during the first inspection and details what the custodian would have done upon seeing an icy condition. The district, however, did not demonstrate what the second custodian observed during the second inspection, which took place approximately one hour before the incident. Because triable issues of fact remained in the case—whether the icy conditions existed and were visible and apparent and whether the conditions existed with sufficient length of time for the defendant to discover and correct them—the trial court should have denied the district's motion for summary judgment.

---

[44] K.A. v. City of N.Y., 134 N.Y.S.3d 423, 384 Educ. L. Rep. 974 (N.Y. App. Div. 2020).
[45] Steffens v. Sachem Cent. Sch. Dist., 140 N.Y.S.3d 253, 387 Educ. L. Rep. 316 (N.Y. App. Div. 2021).

Vehicular Accidents

Three cases involved vehicular accidents in state courts. The Alabama Supreme Court granted a teacher's writ of mandamus directing the lower court to enter summary judgment in favor of state-agent immunity in a case where the teacher let a student leave the classroom at hours other than those reflected in the teacher handbook.[46] The student left to purchase food at McDonald's and was involved in a vehicular accident while driving. The other vehicle's driver (another teacher) died, and the driver's two passengers were seriously injured. The two passengers' father sued the teacher who allowed the student to leave the summer class to purchase McDonald's food. The father argued that the teacher failed to follow the policies and procedures of the school. The state's highest court found that the teacher acted within her discretion, which qualified her for state-agent immunity from the negligence and wantonness claims. The court reasoned that she did not work beyond her authority in supervising students when she allowed the student to leave, and the plaintiffs failed to show that there was a detailed rule the teacher failed to follow.

In Texas, a state appellate court reversed the county court's order of summary judgment in favor of the appellee-insured school district regarding injuries sustained by a minor riding the school district's golf cart driven by a district employee.[47] The insurance policy contained language defining an "auto" as "a land motor vehicle...designed for travel on public roads but does not include mobile equipment," with "mobile equipment" defined as "vehicles designed for use principally off public roads."[48] The insurer argues that golf carts are "mobile equipment" because they are primarily intended for use on a golf course under Texas code, so the accident is not covered. However, while this is generally true, some golf carts are advertised for use on the road and include features that would be unnecessary for a golfer but necessary for public road use. Therefore, the insurer was not entitled to summary judgment because not all golf carts are designed primarily for off-public road use.

The Supreme Court of Utah affirmed that a motorist was entitled to request that a jury determine the proportion of fault

---

[46] Ex parte Blunt, 303 So. 3d 125, 383 Educ. L. Rep. 560 (Ala. 2019).
[47] Tex. Pol. Subdivisions Prop./Cas. Joint Self Ins. Fund v. Pharr-San Juan-Alamo ISD, 628 S.W.3d 486, 395 Educ. L. Rep. 450 (Tex. App. 2019).
[48] *Pharr-San Juan-Alamo ISD*, 628 S.W.3d at 490.

attributable to the school district and to a bus driver driving a school bus filled with children who turned in front of the motorist's car and caused a crash.[49] The motorist sued the school district and the bus driver arguing that the school district was liable for negligently employing the driver involved in multiple prior vehicular accidents. The school district argued that the negligent employment claim was redundant with the negligence claim the driver faced individually and argued that the motorist was not entitled to pursue the negligent employment claim after the district conceded vicarious liability for the bus driver's negligence. The state's highest court found that the district court erred in granting the school district's motion because the motorist was entitled to the request.

Wrongful Death

In the first of two wrongful death cases from Washington, a federal trial court held that the minor siblings' adoption following their brother's death did not deprive them of their status as statutory beneficiaries to the brother's estate.[50] The deceased brother was a minor with two minor siblings and one adult sibling. At his death, the brother and minor children were wards of the state. The defendants—the Department of Social and Health Services, school district, and numerous state employees—argued that the minor siblings were not statutory beneficiaries under the wrongful death statute, which allows a wrongful death action to benefit the parents or siblings of the deceased, because the minor siblings were adopted after their brother's death. The defendants argued that the minor siblings' adoption severed their sibling relationship with the deceased. The court held that, under the Washington statute, the statutory beneficiaries' right to recover vests at the time of the wrongful death. Therefore, the minor siblings' rights as the deceased's statutory beneficiaries are vested at their brother's death and before their adoption.

Also, the Supreme Court of Washington affirmed that the estate of a high school student, who died after being hit by a vehicle during an off-campus walk with his physical education class, raised material issues concerning proximate causation in the case.[51] The student was in the back of the group walking on the sidewalk with his back to oncoming traffic. The driver of the vehicle that struck

---

[49] Ramon v. Nebo Sch. Dist., 493 P.3d 613, 393 Educ. L. Rep. 874 (Utah 2021).
[50] Davis v. Strus, 474 F. Supp. 3d 1163, 384 Educ. L. Rep. 304 (E.D. Wash. 2020).
[51] Meyers v. Ferndale Sch. Dist., 481 P.3d 1084, 387 Educ. L. Rep. 369 (Wash. 2021).

him fell asleep at the wheel, left the roadway, and struck four students; the plaintiff and one other student died, while the other two were severely injured. The estate sued the driver and school district for wrongful death. The trial court granted the school district summary judgment, but the state court of appeals reversed the judgment. The Washington Supreme Court found that the alleged acts of negligence on behalf of the school were not too remote to be the legal cause of the student's death. Ultimately, the state's highest court remanded the case to the trial court.

Damages

In one case, an Indiana appellate court remanded a dispute where a mother sufficiently pleaded economic damages after an instructional assistant allegedly sexually abused her child with disabilities.[52] The student was born with cerebral palsy, microcephaly, congenital quadriplegia, optic nerve hypoplasia, and epilepsy. She could communicate only nonverbally and attended a school where employees provided special assistance to the child. A school employee sexually abused the child while changing her diaper. The mother sued, arguing that she suffered emotional distress because of the sexual abuse her daughter suffered, and she had lost the ability to care for her daughter at home. She also incurred expenses for the placement of her daughter in a long-term care facility. The court found that the mother could not recover damages for emotional distress because she did not satisfy the bystander or impact rules, given that the perpetrator never touched the mother and did not witness the abuse. However, the court found that she sufficiently pled a claim for economic damages. The court remanded the case for further proceedings.

In California, a state appellate court granted a school district's petition to mandate the trial court to strike a student's treble damages request in a case where the student alleged that they were sexually assaulted after the school district had covered up a prior sexual assault.[53] The court found that treble damages were inappropriate in the case. The court reasoned that treble damages are primarily exemplary (i.e., to make an example out of the defendants) and punitive and that under the California Tort Claims

---

[52] K.G. ex rel. Ruch v. Smith, 164 N.E.3d 829, 388 Educ. L. Rep. 334 (Ind. Ct. App. 2021), *vacated*, 178 N.E.3d 300 (Ind. 2021).

[53] L.A. Unified Sch. Dist. v. Superior Ct. of L.A. Cnty., 279 Cal. Rptr. 3d 52, 390 Educ. L. Rep. 721 (Cal. Ct. App. 2021).

Act, the school district, as a state actor, maintained sovereign immunity from liability from exemplary and punitive damages.

Work-Related Injuries

Six cases posed work-related injuries from state court cases. The Supreme Court of Alaska affirmed the Workers' Compensation Board's decision, and the Workers' Compensation Appeals Commission affirmed that the aide's injury was not substantially caused by her work.[54] The appellant, a school aid with significant preexisting cervical spine issues, reported an injury to her cervical spine after repositioning a child with disabilities student in his wheelchair. Medical professionals disagreed about whether the incident involving the student in a wheelchair could have aggravated her preexisting issues. The court affirmed the commission's finding that the appellee rebutted the presumption that the appellant was entitled to compensation. That evidence supported the board's conclusion that the appellant's employment was not the cause of her disability and need for medical treatment. The state's supreme court affirmed the Commission's decision, finding no reversible error.

The Supreme Court of Minnesota reversed the Workers' Compensation Court of Appeals (WCCA) decision vacating the Workers' Compensation Judge's (WCJ) order against the respondent school cafeteria dishwasher.[55] The respondent reported neck pain and difficulty looking up, which a medical consultation determined was due to the repetitive stress of her job. After years of treatment, a doctor concluded that the administered treatments were not reasonable or necessary. Thus, the defendant notified the respondent that it would no longer reimburse her, but she continued treatment. The respondent requested authorization and payment from the Department of Labor & Industry, which denied her request. She requested a hearing with a WCJ, who also denied her claim because the treatments were not necessary or reasonable. She appealed to the WCCA, alleging that her case warranted an exception to the treatment parameters for the first time because she was not a candidate for surgery and all other treatments had failed. The WCCA found in favor of the respondent. The court found that

---

[54] Sumpter v. Fairbanks N. Star Borough Sch. Dist., 494 P.3d 505, 394 Educ. L. Rep. 1066 (Alaska 2021).
[55] Leuthard v. Indep. Sch. Dist. 912 – Milaca, 958 N.W.2d 640, 389 Educ. L. Rep. 514 (Minn. 2021).

the WCJ's findings were supported by adequate evidence, and the WCCA erred in vacating that decision.

The New York State appellate court affirmed the denial of summary judgment because there were genuine issues of material fact as to whether the plaintiff employee's injuries were covered, and it affirmed the grant of summary judgment in favor of the building owners because they were entitled to contractual indemnification by the school.[56] The plaintiff, who worked for the school, was removing trash bags from an elevated area requiring a ladder. While about six feet off the ground, the ladder slipped, and he fell and sustained injuries. The plaintiff sued the school and the building owners for his injuries. The court held that the plaintiff did not establish that he was entitled to judgment on the liability issue. The plaintiff was instructed to clean and prepare the elevated area to be painted the next day, but he did not establish that he was preparing the area for painting when he fell. However, the defendant's school also failed to establish whether the plaintiff's injury took place while he was engaged in the painting project or if it was a non-enumerated activity.

In a second New York appellate court decision, the court affirmed the denial of the plaintiff construction worker's motion for summary judgment regarding proximate cause and the grant of the defendant school district's motion for summary judgment because they were not violating regulations at the time of injury.[57] The plaintiff fell off an extension ladder while carrying a 10-foot metal piece to the second floor of a construction project and sustained injuries. The plaintiff sued the school district that owned the project. The court held that the plaintiff did not meet his burden under state labor law because his testimony reveals his refusal to use the available safety equipment and that he carried items up the ladder that he was specifically told not to, creating an issue as to whether his conduct was the sole proximate cause of his injuries. Therefore, summary judgment for the plaintiff was properly denied on his state labor law claim. Further, the defendants sufficiently established that they were not violating any regulations regarding the use of ladders at the time of injury.

A third New York appellate case affirmed the denial of the plaintiff's control technician's and the defendant school district's

---

[56] Mejia v. Cohn, 136 N.Y.S.3d 480, 385 Educ. L. Rep. 956 (N.Y. App. Div. 2020).
[57] Ward v. Corning Painted Post Area Sch. Dist., 145 N.Y.S.3d 700, 391 Educ. L. Rep. 345 (N.Y. App. Div. 2021).

motions for summary judgment.[58] The plaintiff alleged that he was working in a room above the pool office when his foot slipped off the ladder. He fell to the floor of the office below. The worker and his wife sued the school board and general contractor under the state labor law and common law negligence. The plaintiff told two school district employees that he forgot he covered the opening to the room he was working in with cardboard and stepped on it, causing him to fall. Thus, the court held that the plaintiff's motion for summary judgment on his labor law claim was properly denied because he could not establish a violation of the law or that he was not the sole proximate cause of his injuries. Further, the defendant was not entitled to summary judgment on the plaintiff's claims because it did not sufficiently establish "that it did not create or have constructive notice of the allegedly dangerous condition."[59]

The Supreme Court of Virginia vacated and remanded the Worker's Compensation Commission's award of benefits to the claimant teacher, overturning the appellate court's decision for applying the wrong legal standard.[60] The claimant was a high school teacher when she slipped and fell on a puddle in her classroom, resulting in multiple injuries. She filed for benefits with the Worker's Compensation Commission, which held that she suffered an "injury by accident" to her shoulder. To show a compensable injury by accident, the plaintiff must show an obvious sudden mechanical or structural change in the body. The court held that the appellate court erred in ruling that the teacher, as claimant, does not need to demonstrate obvious sudden mechanical or structural change in every body part affected by the obvious accident. Instead, the court held that the change is the injury, so without a structural or mechanical change in the body part, there can be no injury.

Vicarious Liability

Four cases examined claims of vicarious liability in which the injured party sought to hold the employer liable for the acts of one of its staff. The Eleventh Circuit affirmed a grant of summary judgment in favor of a Florida charter school and its parent

---

[58] Cain v. Ameresco, 150 N.Y.S.3d 109, 393 Educ. L. Rep. 789 (N.Y. App. Div. 2021).
[59] Cain, 150 N.Y.S.3d at 112.
[60] Alexandria City Pub. Schs. v. Handel, 848 S.E.2d 816, 383 Educ. L. Rep. 490 (Va. 2020).

company.[61] The school had a policy prohibiting "walk-ups." The plaintiff entered the school to pick up his daughter and was warned he was not allowed inside. He entered the school again and was barred. The plaintiff asked the officer to get his daughter for him; forty minutes later, he went in to find the officer. The plaintiff was arrested, but the charges were dropped. The plaintiff sued, claiming vicarious liability against the charter school's parent company for the actions of subsidiary school employees. The court noted, in Florida, parent companies and their subsidiaries are considered separate and distinct legal entities. The plaintiff would have to show it appropriate to pierce the corporate veil, which was not appropriate because the parent company had no supervision over the school or its employees, and there was no evidence the school was used for improper or fraudulent purposes. Thus, the charter school's parent company was not liable for the acts of employees of a subsidiary school.

The U.S. District Court for the Northern District of Mississippi granted the defendant school district's motion to dismiss the plaintiff former student's negligence claim because the school district was not vicariously liable.[62] The plaintiff alleged that his former teacher committed sexual abuse against him, including sexually explicit texts, forced oral sex, and payment to remain silent on the abuse. Under Mississippi law, an employee is not acting within the scope of employment, and a governmental entity is not liable for any conduct by the employee that constitutes "fraud, malice, libel, slander, defamation, or any criminal offense other than traffic violations." The court held that the teacher's sexual abuse constituted a criminal offense under the statute; therefore, it was outside the scope of employment. The school could not be vicariously liable.

A New York federal trial court found in favor of the plaintiff student with disabilities student on his assault and battery claim.[63] The plaintiff's disabilities caused him to disrupt class occasionally. He attended a public school for students with developmental disabilities, and employees were required to use physical force to restrain or separate disruptive students when necessary. One paraprofessional took the plaintiff outside the view of security cameras and allegedly beat him with a stick leaving large visible

---

[61] Turner v. Homestead Police Dep't, 828 F. App'x 541, 383 Educ. L. Rep. 159 (11th Cir. 2020).
[62] Rodgers v. Smart, 521 F. Supp. 3d 615, 394 Educ. L. Rep. 530 (N.D. Miss. 2021).
[63] A.W. by E.W. v. N.Y. Dep't of Educ., 519 F. Supp. 3d 128, 393 Educ. L. Rep. 645 (E.D.N.Y. 2021).

marks. When his father reported this, the principal promised to investigate and call him back, but he never did. The father filed a police complaint, resulting in the paraprofessional's arrest. The court found that the plaintiff sufficiently alleged the paraprofessional was acting within his scope of employment because he was on duty at the time of the alleged assault and battery, the school routinely used force to restrain and discipline students, and state courts routinely held that physical punishment by school staff is within the bounds of general foreseeability. Therefore, the plaintiff sufficiently alleged that the defendant could be vicariously liable for the paraprofessional's conduct.

Procedural

In 2021, nine cases stemmed from procedural matters such as the statute of limitations, adequacy of notice, preemption, arbitration, and evidentiary burden. Four of the nine instances examined the statute of limitations of tort claims involving elementary and secondary school students.

The Tenth Circuit affirmed the Utah federal district court's dismissal of the plaintiff/student's claims because it was barred by the statute of limitations.[64] The plaintiff was allegedly sexually abused by an employee at a residential treatment facility in Utah. The student sued the facility a decade later. The facility moved to dismiss, alleging the suit was barred by the Utah statute of limitations. The plaintiff responded that the suit was timely in California. The Tenth Circuit applied California's choice-of-law rule because that is where the plaintiff originally filed this case. Under California law, the court must determine each state's interest in applying its law to determine if an actual conflict exists and, if so, which jurisdiction's interest would be more damaged by applying the other jurisdiction's laws. There was an actual conflict between the statutes. The court found Utah's interest would be more damaged if its laws were not applied because the conduct occurred in Utah, so the Utah statute of limitations applied, and the plaintiff's claims were untimely. The court subsequently reheard the case and

---

[64] Gerson v. Logan River Acad., 11 F.4th 1195, 394 Educ. L. Rep. 486 (10th Cir. 2021), withdrawn and superseded by 20 F.4th 1263, 397 Educ. L. Rep. 543 (10th Cir. 2021).

withdrew the decision above, superseding it with a new order offering slightly different analyses.[65]

A California federal district court held that conflict preemption did not bar the school district's state-law tort claims against the operator of a metal scrap yard bordering a high school. The school district alleged that the scrap yard had many instances that could have resulted in "environmental and human disaster," including hazardous waste, routine inspection violations, runoff of contaminated stormwater, and stockpiling of junk vehicles and other materials exceeding the height of the retaining wall. The school district brought state-law tort claims for continuing trespass, continuing private nuisance, continuing public nuisance, negligence, negligence per se, common law equitable indemnity, and declaratory judgment, which the defendant argued were preempted by the Comprehensive Environmental Response, Compensation, and Liability Act (CERCLA) because "they conflict with CERCLA's liability scheme and because they constitute an impermissible 'challenge to a CERCLA clean up.'"[66] However, the court found that the defendant operator failed to show a specific conflict between the plaintiff's claims and CERCLA, nor did they provide any cases finding that negligence or nuisance generally conflict with CERCLA. Thus, the school district's claims were not preempted.

The Georgia Supreme Court partially reversed the appellate court decision reversing the trial court's dismissal of the plaintiff's wrongful death and personal injury claims on immunity and statute of limitations grounds. The plaintiff's daughter drowned on a school trip to Belize. Her mother filed this wrongful death action within Georgia's statute of limitations but after Belize's statute of limitations expired. Georgia follows the doctrine of *lex loci delicti* (torts are governed by the substantive law of the state where the tort was committed) and *lex fori* for procedural issues (forum state law applies). Because Belize has a law creating a wrongful death cause of action that imposes a one-year statute of limitations, Belize's substantive limitations period applies. Accordingly, the plaintiff's claim was untimely. The plaintiff argued that Georgia's public policy exception applied, which holds that Belize law would not apply "if it would conflict with Georgia's public policy."[67] However, Georgia does

---

[65] Gerson v. Logan River Acad., 20 F.4th 1263, 397 Educ. L. Rep. 543 (10th Cir. 2021).
[66] L.A. Unified Sch. Dist. v. S&W Atlas Iron & Metal Co., 506 F. Supp. 3d 1018, 1029, 390 Educ. L. Rep. 1161 (C.D. Cal. 2020).
[67] Auld v. Forbes, 848 S.E.2d 876, 896, 383 Educ. L. Rep. 495 (Ga. 2020).

not recognize wrongful death claims for deaths occurring outside of Georgia, so the plaintiff would not be able to pursue her claim under Georgia law. Thus, applying Belize's statute of limitations does not violate Georgia's public policy.

A New York trial court held that the plaintiff student's claims for breach of statutory duty to report abuse were revived under the Child Victims Act despite the statute of limitations expiring.[68] The plaintiff alleged that a teacher sexually assaulted him as a minor. Under state law, school officials are required to report suspected abuse "when they have reasonable cause to suspect that a child coming before them in their professional or official capacity is an abused or maltreated child." Anyone required to report under state law who knowingly and willingly fails to do so will be civilly liable for the damages they proximately caused. The statute of limitations on civil actions from a sexual offense committed against a minor may be brought "on or before the plaintiff or infant plaintiff reaches the age of fifty-five years." Therefore, the Child Victims Act revived the plaintiff's claims against the school district for breach of statutory duty to report abuse and not barred by the statute of limitations.

An Ohio appellate court held that a twelve-year statute of limitations applied to the plaintiff former student's gross sexual imposition and sexual imposition and-or attempt claims against a teacher, and a four-year statute of limitations applied to her invasion of privacy claims.[69] The state law governing the plaintiff's sexual imposition claims extends the statute of limitations to twelve years for "an action brought by a victim of childhood sexual abuse asserting any claim resulting from childhood sexual abuse." The extended statute of limitations can apply to the actor and other defendants that have allegedly violated a duty, making them liable. Because the trial court based its ruling on an erroneous interpretation of the law, the plaintiff's sexual imposition claims are remanded for reconsideration in light of the court of appeals' interpretation. However, the appellate court affirmed the grant of judgment on the pleadings for the plaintiff's invasion of privacy claims because the plaintiff's allegations were based on voyeurism and secret videotaping, which do not qualify as "childhood sexual abuse," so those claims were subject to a four-year statute of limitations.

---

[68] PB-36 Doe v. Niagara Falls City Sch. Dist., 152 N.Y.S.3d 242, 395 Educ. L. Rep. 389 (N.Y. App. Div. 2021).
[69] S.A.S. v. Wellington Sch., 158 N.E.3d 962, 384 Educ. L. Rep. 1021 (Ohio Ct. App. 2020).

In a case about notice, an appellate court in New York affirmed the lower court's denial of the claimant's application for leave to serve a late notice of claim. Under New York law, "[a] notice of claim must be served within 90 days after the claim accrues," although the court may grant an extension. [70] The claimant alleged that she slipped and fell on snow and ice in a school district-owned parking lot. The claimant alleged that she was unaware of her injury's severity, which caused her delayed notice. However, the court concluded that she did not provide medical evidence supporting her position or explaining why the severity of her injury was not immediately apparent. Further, the claimant did not establish that the respondent school district had actual knowledge of the essential facts of her claim promptly. Thus, the lower court correctly denied the claimant's application for leave to serve a late notice of claim.

When addressing a matter of recusal, an appellate court in Louisiana held that the plaintiff teacher was entitled to a hearing on her motion to recuse the trial judge for bias. [71] After being terminated from her coach and elementary school teacher position, the plaintiff filed suit alleging wrongful termination and defamation. She also filed a motion for recusal because the trial judge served as the school board's counsel for twenty-four years before becoming a judge. The trial judge denied the plaintiff's motion without a hearing or referral to another judge, and he denied that the school board previously employed him without addressing whether he had acted as the school's attorney for twenty-four years. The Louisiana appellate court held that the plaintiff was entitled to a "full and fair opportunity to present facts in support of her motion at a hearing" on her motion for recusal.

A Pennsylvania trial court held that the defendant boarding school had accepted the judicial process and waived its arbitration claim in a wrongful death and survival action.[72] The decedent was a student at the boarding school where all students had to participate in an organized sport, and she was allowed to join the ski team despite not satisfying the skill requirements. Despite her lack of ability, the student was ordered to ski down the most difficult trail, which resulted in her crashing into equipment and suffering fatal

---

[70] Mariani v. Wilson Cent. Sch. Dist., 145 N.Y.S.3d 708, 719, 391 Educ. L. Rep. 348 (N.Y. App. Div. 2021).
[71] Wilson v. St. Landry Parish Sch. Bd., 311 So. 3d 457, 464, 388 Educ. L. Rep. 420 (La. Ct. App. 2020).
[72] DiDonato v. Ski Shawnee, 242 A.3d 312, 385 Educ. L. Rep. 260 (Pa. Super. Ct. 2020).

injuries. The decedent's estate filed a wrongful death and survival action, and the defendant boarding school asserted an issue of arbitration. However, the court held that the defendant waived its arbitration claim and accepted the judicial process because it raised the issue of arbitration for the first time nearly a year after the complaint was filed, participated in pre-trial discovery on venue issues, filed preliminary objections on the basis of improper venue, and waited until the trial court had ruled on the preliminary objections and the federal court on the notice of removal before asserting its arbitration claim.

The Kentucky Supreme Court reversed an order that the Cabinet for Health and Family Services ("Cabinet") exceeded its statutory authority by investigating allegations that a teacher neglected children in her care because the Cabinet did not meet its burden of proof to substantiate its allegations. The teacher worked for an elementary afterschool program. The Cabinet substantiated neglect findings against the teacher; a hearing officer affirmed. The Court of Appeals *sua sponte* raised the issue of whether the Cabinet had the authority to investigate the teacher and concluded it did not. The state's highest court noted that the teacher acted as a babysitter without "custodial control or supervision over the children in the afterschool program." [73] However, she was a person in a position of "authority" and "special trust," so the Cabinet did not exceed its statutory authority in investigating. Further, "the Cabinet failed to prove that it was more likely than not that [she] failed to provide a child adequate supervision necessary for the child's well-being," and evidence showed that the teacher was providing adequate supervision.

Immunity

Eleven cases during this period raised questions about immunity to the lawsuit. Eight of the cases originated in state courts. The Sixth Circuit affirmed the Ohio district court's denial of the defendant principal and assistant principal's motion to dismiss because the plaintiff's parents adequately alleged reckless conduct after their third-grade student committed suicide two days after being knocked unconscious by other students at school.[74] The administrators

---

[73] Dep't for Cmty. Based Servs., Cabinet for Health & Fam. Servs. v. Baker, 613 S.W.3d 1, 5, 385 Educ. L. Rep. 444 (Ky. 2020).

[74] Meyers v. Cincinnati Bd. of Educ., 983 F.3d 873, 385 Educ. L. Rep. 47 (6th Cir. 2020).

argued they were entitled to governmental immunity on appeal. Governmental immunity shields public school officials from "damages for injury, death, or loss to person or property allegedly caused by any act or omission in connection with a governmental or proprietary function."[75] There is an exception when "[t]he employee's acts or omissions were with malicious purpose, in bad faith, or in a wanton or reckless manner." The court found that the plaintiffs sufficiently alleged repeated instances of the student being physically attacked at school and the administrators' failure to respond or make any efforts to increase supervision adequately. The court held that this indifference to the student's well-being and complete failure to protect students against known risks constituted recklessness, an exempted provision from Ohio's governmental immunity law.

A Louisiana federal district court granted the defendant teachers' motion for summary judgment because the teachers were entitled to qualified immunity from the plaintiff student's due process claim. One defendant had broken up an altercation at school and was escorting the instigating student away when the plaintiff attempted to re-engage, so the other defendant physically restrained her. She continued to fight, and another teacher had to help physically restrain her. The plaintiff was diagnosed with a concussion, PTSD, anxiety, and depression from the incident. She sued, alleging Fourteenth Amendment violations via § 1983. The defendants moved for summary judgment, alleging they were entitled to qualified immunity. For qualified immunity, the court must decide if the plaintiff has shown the violation of a constitutional right and, if so, "whether the right was 'clearly established' at the time of the defendant's conduct."[76] The court held the plaintiff did not state a claim because the Fifth Circuit previously held that injuries suffered incidental to corporal punishment are not subject to the due process clause; the defendants were entitled to qualified immunity.

The Maryland federal trial court held that a board of commissioners was entitled to sovereign immunity from state constitutional and common law tort claims, but the defendant principal was not entitled to any immunity.[77] The plaintiff's mother

---

[75] Meyers, 983 F.3d 873 at 880.
[76] E.H. ex rel. Abron v. Barrilleaux, 519 F. Supp. 3d 328, 337, 393 Educ. L. Rep. 668 (E.D. La. 2021).
[77] L.J. v. Balt. Curriculum Project, 514 F. Supp. 3d 707, 392 Educ. L. Rep. 654 (D. Md. 2021).

brought claims against a city board of school commissioners and others alleging that her son with disabilities was physically handled to a degree it constituted unlawful seizure and excessive force, state-law torts, and disability discrimination by the defendant school administrator. The board alleged it was entitled to immunity from state constitutional tort claims because it is a state agency. The court agreed and dismissed the claims against the board on sovereign immunity grounds. The principal alleged that he was entitled to qualified immunity because he was a public official performing a discretional function. However, in Maryland, qualified immunity only applies in limited circumstances, none of which apply to this type of intentional conduct. The principal also claimed public official immunity, but Maryland does not recognize this type of immunity in an intentional tort claim against an individual. Thus, the principal was not entitled to immunity.

The Alabama Supreme Court affirmed the lower court's decision granting summary judgment in favor of the defendant bus driver, an employee of the county's board of education, on state-agent immunity grounds. [78] After missing the bus, the student attempted to cross the road to board a school bus as it passed by her house, going the other way. The student was struck by an automobile crossing the road and died. The parent sued for wrongful death, alleging the bus driver negligently invited the student to cross the highway to board the bus. The bus driver claimed state-agent immunity, which requires the government employee's acts arise "from the performance of official duties and the exercise of discretion in the supervision of students."[79] Where the bus driver saw the student running towards the bus, turned on the warning lights, and started exiting the bus to escort the student across the highway when the child was hit by an automobile, she was performing supervisory duties as a bus driver. Further, the plaintiff did not establish any exceptions to state-agent immunity that would apply here.

A Florida appellate court reversed and remanded the lower court's denial of the appellant school board's motion for summary judgment on sovereign immunity grounds.[80] The appellee was a spectator at a high school basketball game, after which a crowd turned and started running back towards the school. He turned and

---

[78] Edwards v. Pearson, 309 So. 3d 1216, 387 Educ. L. Rep. 400 (Ala. 2020).
[79] Edwards, 309 So. 3d 1216 at 1222.
[80] Sch. Bd. of Broward Cnty. v. McCall, 322 So. 3d 655, 394 Educ. L. Rep. 423 (Fla. Dist. Ct. App. 2021).

ran with the crowd but fell and suffered injuries. The appellee sued the school board, alleging failure to provide adequate security and crowd control, and the school board moved for summary judgment on sovereign immunity grounds. Sovereign immunity protects "certain [quasi-legislative] policy-making, planning, or judgmental governmental functions" from tort liability but generally does not protect "decisions made at the operational level—decisions or actions implementing policy, planning or judgmental governmental functions." The court found that the security plan was necessary for the board's goal of teaching students, the plan required judgment and expertise, and the school board clearly had the authority to formulate and apply the plan. Therefore, the school district was protected by sovereign immunity from liability surrounding its security plan because it was a planning-level function.

A Georgia appellate court reversed the lower court's denial of the defendant employees' motion for summary judgment on official immunity grounds.[81] The plaintiff student sued school employees for negligence, alleging they breached a ministerial duty to verify automobile insurance. The plaintiff was standing in her parking spot when she was struck by another student without insurance. The plaintiff sued school employees for issuing a parking permit to the uninsured student. The employees alleged they were entitled to official immunity, which only allows suit against a public officer who "(1) negligently performed a ministerial duty, or (2) acted within actual malice or an actual intent to cause injury while performing a discretionary duty." A ministerial duty is "simple, absolute, and definite, arising under conditions admitted or proved to exist, and requiring merely the execution of a specific duty." The court found that, where the parking application language was unclear regarding specific people or roles, did not define "verify," and required interpretation of "proof of insurance" under Georgia law, the defendants were not engaged in a ministerial duty and were entitled to official immunity. Another Georgia appellate court reversed the lower court's dismissal on immunity grounds because there was a factual dispute as to whether there was a violation of a ministerial duty or a protected discretionary action.[82] The parents allege that their child was burned by food in the lunchroom, and the school district and employees were negligent by failing to keep food at a reasonable and safe temperature, supervise the student, serve food

---

[81] Erickson v. Walker, 859 S.E.2d 804, 392 Educ. L. Rep. 1011 (Ga. Ct. App. 2021).
[82] Parr v. Cook Cnty. Sch. Dist., 860 S.E.2d 114, 392 Educ. L. Rep. 1017 (Ga. Ct. App. 2021).

safely, and ensure students were not served excessively hot food in an unstable container. The defendants claimed they were entitled to immunity. Sovereign immunity "protect[s] governments at all levels from unconsented-to legal actions." The Georgia Tort Claims Act expressly excludes school districts from its limited waiver of sovereign immunity. Under official immunity, "a public officer or employee may be personally liable only for ministerial acts negligently performed or acts performed with malic or an intent to injure." The plaintiffs argued the determination of discretionary or ministerial duties required a fact-specific inquiry that could not be conducted until discovery was completed. The court agreed and held that official immunity was currently improper.

Two cases originating from Missouri applied the public-duty doctrine presenting an immunity from the negligence claim. A Missouri appellate court affirmed that a student plaintiff failed to state a negligence claim against her teacher.[83] The student reported to the teacher that another teacher was pursuing a relationship with the student, and the teacher failed to report the student's disclosure to any authorities. The student was subsequently sexually assaulted by the teacher pursuing a relationship. The state appellate court found that the mandated reporting law created a duty to the general public under the public-duty doctrine, not a duty to any particular student through a special, direct, and distinctive interest to the student. The student did not have a special, direct, and distinctive interest in the reporting requirements and, therefore, could not plead a negligence claim against the teacher who did not report the student's disclosure.

Similarly, another Missouri appellate court reversed a grant of judgment issued by the lower court in favor of a teacher who denied a student permission to leave the class due to an urgent restroom need and who consequently wet himself in front of his peers.[84] The teacher argued that They had official immunity and were immune from liability under the public-policy doctrine, which states that public employees are not civilly liable for the breach of duty owed to the general public. The teacher made a bare assertion of official immunity and the public-duty doctrine without factual support. The appellate court found that the teacher did not provide sufficient evidence to qualify for official immunity or satisfy a prima facie

---

[83] E.M. ex rel. McInnis v. Gateway Region Young Men's Christian Assoc., 613 S.W.3d 388, 385 Educ. L. Rep. 1052 (Mo. Ct. App. 2020).
[84] Doe ex rel. Doe Minor v. Garagnani, 614 S.W.3d 556, 386 Educ. L. Rep. 530 (Mo. Ct. App. 2020).

showing under the public-duty doctrine. Under a different analysis, a Missouri appellate court reversed and remanded the circuit court's grant of the defendant nurses and teachers' motion to dismiss because the allegations fell within the ministerial act exception to official immunity, and the petition did not clearly establish that the nurses were in a true emergency situation to qualify for official immunity.[85] The plaintiff's daughter had a tracheostomy requiring a daily care routine and was given an Individualized Education Program (IEP). Her IEP was violated, resulting in her death. Official immunity shields public officials from liability when the official acts (1) within the scope of one's official duties and (2) without malice, with an exception where the "public officer fails to perform a ministerial duty required by law." The court found because they violated the IEP and school policy, the defendants breached a ministerial duty barring them from official immunity. Furthermore, official immunity only protects publicly employed medical professionals in a "true emergency situation." Given the student's IEP, the court held they were not acting in a "true emergency situation" and were not entitled to official immunity.

An Ohio appellate court affirmed a grant of summary judgment in favor of a public school teacher, board of education, and city schools because the defendants were entitled to political subdivision immunity on the negligence claims.[86] The plaintiff was an elementary student diagnosed with autism and ADHD in the defendant's teacher's special education class. The plaintiff was asked if he wanted to wear a body sock to calm him. He accepted but quickly fell, and his face hit the floor, injuring his front teeth. To survive summary judgment, the plaintiff had to point to some exception to political subdivision immunity under which the defendants could be held liable. The only exception the plaintiff refers to is that he suffered an injury caused by a school employee on school grounds, and his injury resulted from a physical defect on the grounds. However, the court ruled that the only defect alleged by the plaintiff was that the body sock was used; they did not allege any physical defect on the grounds. Thus, the defendants were entitled to political subdivision immunity.

---

[85] Kemp v. McReynolds, 621 S.W.3d 644, 390 Educ. L. Rep. 819 (Mo. Ct. App. 2021).
[86] Shields v. Plummer, 163 N.E.3d 653, 387 Educ. L. Rep. 341 (Ohio Ct. App. 2020).

Higher Education Cases

Intentional Torts

Among the intentional tort cases within the higher education level, issues of battery, false imprisonment, misappropriation of funds, tortious interference, and defamation were the prominent claims.

Battery

An Illinois appellate court reversed and remanded the circuit court's dismissal of the plaintiff student's battery action against the university's board of trustees and a professor.[87] The plaintiff alleged that, due to students disrupting class, the defendant professor told the plaintiff to be quiet, and she told him she was not talking. In response, the professor dragged the plaintiff's desk several feet before grabbing her by the collar and arm to remove her from her desk and into the hallway; he then kicked her things onto the floor. The plaintiff student alleges that the professor acted within the scope of his university employment when this occurred. Courts use the source of duty test to determine if a state employee breached a duty owed to the public independent of his employment. Here, the state employee, a professor, committed the alleged battery while teaching a class at the university. Still, the plaintiff argued professor owed a duty independent of his employment not to commit battery. The court agreed that the professor acted independently of his employment, thus, he was subject to liability.

False Imprisonment

A federal trial court in California, held that the plaintiff student athletes sufficiently stated a claim for false imprisonment against the track and field coach under state law.[88] The plaintiffs alleged that the defendant coach falsely imprisoned them at the track meets, schools, and dinners where sexual abuse occurred, but the defendant coach argued that they could have left the location or transferred schools at any time. Under California law, false imprisonment is the

---

[87] Rideaux v. Winter, 155 N.E.3d 1120, 383 Educ. L. Rep. 1062 (Ill. App. Ct. 2020).
[88] Aldrich v. Nat'l Collegiate Athletic Ass'n, 484 F. Supp. 3d 779, 386 Educ. L. Rep. 324 (N.D. Cal. 2020).

"nonconsensual, intentional confinement of a person, without lawful privilege, for an appreciable length of time," as short as 15 minutes. Confinement can be physical or based on threats, physical barriers, or unreasonable duress. Here, the defendant was much older than the plaintiff's student-athletes and was in a position of power, so the plaintiffs felt they had no choice but to go to and stay in his home. Although the case also rested on procedural considerations around the statute of limitations and jurisdiction, the court notably concluded that the plaintiffs stated a viable claim for false imprisonment.

Misappropriation of Funds

The Fifth Circuit affirmed a Mississippi jury verdict that university officials lacked adequate cause to terminate the plaintiff coach for misappropriating funds.[89] After an internal audit of the plaintiff's coach, the internal auditor found that she misallocated and misused university funds and owed the university. The plaintiff, the former head women's basketball coach, was terminated with two years and the amount left on her contract. Although the case involved multiple claims, including invasion of privacy, the court held on the primary claim that the university could only fire the plaintiff under Mississippi law for misappropriating funds if the misappropriations were deliberate, serious, and willful violations of the employee's duties, or refusal or unwillingness to perform her duties in good faith. Here, the plaintiff provided evidence that she had engaged in the complained behavior before, as did the male coaches, who were not reprimanded. Thus, the court found that if she did violate any policy, it was not deliberate, serious, and willful, and the plaintiff had performed her duties in good faith.

Tortious Interference

The Seventh Circuit affirmed the Illinois district court's grant of the defendant's university and former department head's motions to dismiss and for summary judgment on the plaintiff's former professor's race discrimination and tortious interference claims.[90] The plaintiff's former professor was denied tenure after several concerns about his teaching by students and fellow faculty members.

---

[89] Taylor-Travis v. Jackson State Univ., 984 F.3d 1107, 385 Educ. L. Rep. 458 (5th Cir. 2021).
[90] Monroe v. Columbia Coll. Chi., 855 F. App'x 284, 393 Educ. L. Rep. 163 (7th Cir. 2021).

The plaintiff sued, alleging racial discrimination, a hostile work environment, intentional interference with the contract, and tortious interference with prospective economic advantage. The first element of a tortious interference claim is a reasonable expectation of entering a business relationship. Here, the business relationship in question was tenure. Because tenure is such a discretionary decision and there were consistent criticisms of the plaintiff throughout his employment, he did not have a reasonable expectation of tenure to constitute a viable tortious interference claim.

Defamation

In 2021, four defamation claims were addressed in higher education cases. A New York federal trial court granted the defendant university and university officials' motion to dismiss the plaintiff students' defamation claims. [91] The plaintiffs are three suspended students who participated in a fraternity roast that contained obscene and offensive skits and jokes. A video of the roast was posted to a members-only Facebook page, but a third party recorded the video and sent it to the university and a local newspaper. The plaintiffs alleged that three university officials defamed them when they knowingly, negligently, or recklessly published, distributed, and circulated false accusations and statements during a "roast" of the plaintiff. To establish a defamation claim under New York law, the plaintiff must show a false statement published to a third party without privilege or permission that causes harm, with some exceptions. The statements at issue were either nonactionable opinions, the plaintiff students failed to allege how the statements were false, or the plaintiff students failed to adequately plead when and to whom the statement was made.

A New York appellate court reversed the trial level court's denial of the defendant's attorney, law firm, college, and college's general counsel's motion to dismiss the plaintiff's prior employee's defamation claim.[92] The plaintiff had served as Chief of Staff for Policy and Governmental Affairs and Corporation Counsel for the city and in-house counsel for the Catholic college. The alleged defamatory statements were made in a prior Article 78 proceeding.

---

[91] Doe #1 v. Syracuse Univ., 468 F. Supp. 3d 489, 383 Educ. L. Rep. 298 (N.D.N.Y. 2020).
[92] Gill v. Dougherty, 136 N.Y.S.3d 383, 385 Educ. L. Rep. 946 (N.Y. App. Div. 2020).

The court held that statements made in a prior action/proceeding pertinent to that action/proceeding are protected by absolute privilege. Because the statements at issue here were made in a prior action/proceeding and were relevant to that action/proceeding, they were protected, and the plaintiff's former employee's claim fails. In another New York appellate case, the court affirmed the trial court's granting of the defendant/employer's motion to dismiss the plaintiff's breach of contract and defamation claims.[93] The plaintiff, a former university employee, specifically alleged that the warning letter from the defendant "essentially finding" the plaintiff had violated the employer's policy was defamatory. In New York, to plead defamation, the plaintiff must plead with particularity as to person and time. Here, the plaintiff paraphrased and misstated the contents of the allegedly defamatory letter. Further, the letter was protected under qualified privilege because the letter was written by the plaintiff's employer in the context of a workplace investigation.

The Supreme Court of Montana held that the plaintiff soccer coach's claims for defamation were grounded in tort law rather than contract, where the plaintiff was internally investigated following sexual misconduct allegations.[94] The defendant's university allegedly released confidential personnel information and phone records and publicized materially incorrect information about the plaintiff with the intent to damage his reputation and career. The court found that an action is a tort if it arises from the breach of a legal duty as opposed to a breach of contract. Here, the university made false accusations against the plaintiff, and that the university knew or should have known would tarnish the plaintiff's character and destroy his career. Because that is more than simply releasing allegedly confidential personnel information, the plaintiff's defamation claim survived the motion to dismiss.

Negligence

Duty Owed

In 2021, seven higher education cases involving negligence claims examined the question of duty owed. Five of these cases resided at the state court level. The Ninth Circuit affirmed the Oregon district court's decision granting summary judgment,

---

[93] DiCoby v. Syracuse Univ., 142 N.Y.S.3d 13, 388 Educ. L. Rep. 934 (N.Y. App. Div. 2021).

[94] Plakorus v. Univ. of Mont., 477 P.3d 311, 385 Educ. L. Rep. 363 (Mont. 2020).

dismissal, and judgment on the pleadings in favor of the defendant university, former teammate, orthopedic surgeon, head football athletic trainer, head coach, and other university employees where the plaintiff, who was a student-athlete, had been injured.[95] The plaintiff student-athlete sustained a left thumb injury during preseason football practice. Following his injury and an alleged cyberbullying incident, the plaintiff quit the football team and permanently withdrew as a student three weeks after transferring. In Oregon, to state a negligence claim, the plaintiff must allege that the defendant owed him a duty it breached. Here, the plaintiff failed to allege sufficiently that the defendants breached any duty of care to him, thus his negligence claim failed.

In Rhode Island, a federal district court held in favor of the plaintiff student after she was raped in school-provided housing that did not have lockable bedroom doors during a study abroad program.[96] The court found that the defendant college had a duty to exercise reasonable care in providing students with secure housing for the Ireland program, and that duty was increased by the fact that the same thing had happened three years before (i.e., a student in a foreign program was provided housing by the college without a bedroom lock and was raped). Further, the school did not take any steps to assess room security before or after students had arrived, nor did it train the people involved in the Ireland program on safety and security with student housing. Thus, the college breached its duty by failing to provide the plaintiff with housing that included a lockable bedroom door, and her rape was a foreseeable result of that breach.

A Louisiana appellate court reversed the trial court's decision, holding that it erred in its application of duties owed by respective drivers in holding the defendant liable when backing slowly out of his spot in a community college parking lot and awarding the plaintiff forward driver damages.[97] The defendant stopped when he saw the plaintiff coming, but the plaintiff did not stop and collided with the trailer hitch on the defendant's truck. The appellate court held that a driver backing out of a parking space has a limited view, and a vehicle's brake and reverse lights may serve as reasonable notice to traffic as long as the driver backs out slowly and stops periodically. A driver moving through a parking lot has a duty to

---

[95] Wani v. George Fox Univ., 856 F. App'x 672, 393 Educ. L. Rep. 589 (9th Cir. 2021).
[96] Doe v. R.I. Sch. of Design, 516 F. Supp. 3d 188, 393 Educ. L. Rep. 206 (D.R.I. 2021).
[97] Collins v. Creighton, 303 So. 3d 1114, 383 Educ. L. Rep. 1185 (La. Ct. App. 2020).

remain attentive and to travel at a low speed. Here, the plaintiff did not maintain a low speed, nor did he attempt to maneuver around the reversing truck or honk his horn to avoid a collision, while the reversing driver backed up slowly while stopping periodically. Thus, the plaintiff did not meet his burden of proving the defendant was at fault.

In Massachusetts, a state appellate court affirmed the district court's grant of summary judgment in favor of the defendant coach and university when the plaintiff, a softball player at the university, filed negligence, gross negligence, and recklessness claims against the university and coach.[98] The plaintiff was injured when a teammate's bat hit her on the head during practice. The plaintiff sustained a concussion and required four stitches. The court held that participants in athletic events and practices owe a duty to fellow participants to refrain from reckless misconduct. Recklessness requires that the actor knows, or should know, that the act creates a high degree of risk of physical harm to another and the actor deliberately acts or fails to act in conscious disregard or indifference to the risk. Because the plaintiff could not prove that the teammate saw her in time to prevent the injury, her teammate's actions were not deemed reckless.

A New Jersey appellate court held that the defendant social hosts did not owe a duty of care to the plaintiff/student who became intoxicated at a party and was subsequently injured in a car accident.[99] The plaintiff attended a party in a dorm and consumed alcohol after telling his parents and the party hosts that he planned to stay the night. However, the plaintiff woke up and left around 5:00 a.m. He was injured when he crashed his car shortly after. The plaintiffs sued, alleging the university and present students owed him a duty to prevent him from driving under the influence. Courts typically consider four factors to determine whether to impose a duty: the relationship between parties, nature of the risk, opportunity, ability to exercise care, and public interest in the proposed solution. The court did not find it appropriate to impose a duty where the plaintiff voluntarily drank alcohol, had expressed his plan to stay overnight, and was asleep when the party ended, meaning no one was aware the plaintiff would drive.

A New York state appellate court denied the defendant resident life employees' motion for summary judgment in a wrongful death

---

[98] Brandt v. Davis, 159 N.E.3d 191, 384 Educ. L. Rep. 1032 (Mass. App. Ct. 2020).
[99] Franco v. Fairleigh Dickinson Univ., 248 A.3d 1254, 390 Educ. L. Rep. 322 (N.J. Super. App. Div. 2021).

action.[100] The plaintiff's son died from a heroin overdose while living in a dorm. Before the overdose, the student told his roommate he had suicidal thoughts. His roommate contacted the student's father/plaintiff, who contacted the school's residential life office to report that his son was having suicidal thoughts and he was concerned for his well-being. The defendant checked on the student, who told her that, while he was suffering from depression, he was on anti-depressants and not presently experiencing suicidal thoughts. She concluded that the student had no present intentions to commit suicide. Later that evening, the student overdosed. The court found that a suicide risk assessment of a college student on campus is similar enough to a clinical evaluation of self-harm threats to be considered proprietary conduct, making the defendants subject to ordinary negligence principles. Therefore, the defendants had a duty to act reasonably while executing the policies designed to prevent students in crisis from acting on suicidal ideation.

In another mental health matter, the Supreme Court of Pennsylvania affirmed the lower court's decision denying her motion for certification.[101] The plaintiff, a psychiatric clinic receptionist at the Western Psychiatric Institute and Clinic, was among those injured when a patient went on a shooting spree that killed one person and injured several others. The Medical Health Procedure Act (MHPA) applies to inpatients and involuntary outpatients in Pennsylvania. For MHPA to apply under involuntary outpatient treatment, at least one of the mandatory prerequisites for involuntary emergency examination must be present, and the physician must file the required documentation for such examination. There are three mandatory prerequisites: "(1) certification of a physician; (2) warrant issued by the county administrator authorizing such examination; or (3) application by a physician or other authorized person who has personally observed actions indicating a need for an emergency application." Here, the physicians treated the patient on a voluntary outpatient basis, and none of the involuntary emergency examination prerequisites were present, thus, MHPA did not cover the treatment.

---

[100] Webb v. Muller, 135 N.Y.S.3d 224, 385 Educ. L. Rep. 289 (N.Y. App. Div. 2020).
[101] Leight v. Univ. of Pitt. Physicians, 243 A.3d 126, 140 385 Educ. L. Rep. 844 (Pa. 2020).

Premises Liability

In a premises liability case, the Louisiana Court of Appeals affirmed the district court's grant of summary judgment in favor of the defendant state through the university's board of supervisors after the plaintiff pedestrian tripped and fell due to an uneven sidewalk on campus while attending a family event.[102] The uneven sidewalk had an elevation difference of about two inches or slightly less, and the plaintiff pedestrian did not see the uneven sidewalk before she tripped. To show that a public entity is liable for damages caused by a defective thing, the plaintiff must show, among other factors, that the public entity had actual or constructive notice of the defect. Constructive notice is ordinarily proven by showing the defect at issue existed for long enough to establish that reasonable diligence would have led to discovery and repair. Because there had been no prior falls on that part of the sidewalk and no one responsible for maintenance or reporting was aware of the condition, the state was not liable.

Negligent Misrepresentation

In Florida, a federal district court granted the defendant subcontractor's motion to dismiss the plaintiff contractor's claim for negligent misrepresentation after the defendant subcontractors peer-reviewed the construction of an elevated pedestrian bridge on campus that later collapsed.[103] To state a claim of negligent misrepresentation, the plaintiff must allege the exact statements or misrepresentations made; the time, place, and speaker for the statements; the content and manner in which the statements misled the plaintiff; and what the speaker gained from the fraud. Here, the plaintiff's claim fails because he referred to the defendants collectively, group pleading is not allowed, and many of his allegations were based solely on information and belief.

Medical Malpractice

The Mississippi appellate court reversed the circuit court's grant of summary judgment in favor of the defendant university, dean, and faculty proctor for medical malpractice but affirmed summary

---

[102] Jefferson v. Nichols State Univ., 311 So. 3d 1083, 388 Educ. L. Rep. 446 (La. Ct. App. 2020).
[103] Magnum Constr. Mgmt., LLC v. WSP USA Sols., 522 F. Supp.3d 1202, 394 Educ. L. Rep. 760 (S.D. Fla. 2021).

judgment for the plaintiff medical student's negligent hiring, supervision, and-or training claim. The plaintiff started experiencing back pain after participating in a clinical skills assessment. Her pain persisted after a few treatments with the proctor and another university physician. The court first noted that medical malpractice principles applied because the faculty proctor "depended on his specialized knowledge and skill to render the sacral spring test to [her]."[104] It then found that the plaintiff sufficiently alleged issues of fact surrounding her medical malpractice claim, specifically that the faculty proctor inaccurately applied force, applied too much force, and miscalculated the necessary delivery of force. Additionally, an employer is liable for negligent hiring when an employee injures another person if the employer knew or should have known about the employee's incompetence. The court concluded that the plaintiff did not show that the faculty proctor was negligently hired, supervised, and-or trained because he was qualified when hired.

Wrongful Death

In 2021, two wrongful death cases occurred within the higher education context. A Louisiana federal district court denied the defendant board of supervisors and individual fraternity board members' motion to dismiss the plaintiff's parents' wrongful death action after their son died from a fraternity-related hazing incident.[105] During the incident, the deceased student was ordered to take at least ten to twelve "pulls" of 190-proof alcohol. Despite many fraternity members knowing his extremely intoxicated and unconscious state, the plaintiff was not given any medical attention until the following day. The court held that the fraternity executive board member had a duty not to engage in, encourage, authorize, or substantially support hazing activities and to prevent risks associated with the duty. Because the hazing incident occurred in the fraternity house, the court recognized that the board members knew of potential and likely harm that would occur to the deceased if they breached their duty, and they failed to protect the deceased from other members behaving dangerously, the plaintiff parents

---

[104] Murphy v. William Carey Univ., 314 So. 3d 112, 119, 389 Educ. L. Rep. 1003 (Miss. Ct. App. 2020).
[105] Gruver v. La. Through the Bd. of Supervisors of La. State Univ. and Agric. and Mech. Coll., 510 F. Supp. 3d 367, 391 Educ. L. Rep. 721 (M.D. La. 2021).

stated a wrongful death claim against the fraternity executive board member.

The North Carolina Supreme Court affirmed the appellate court's reversal and remand of the plaintiff pipefitter estate's wrongful death action, which had been dismissed.[106] The plaintiff's estate alleged that the defendant employees disconnected the power and water sources from a chiller and drained it without following the warnings. Later, metal flanges were secured to the ends of the chiller's water pipes before a hard freeze. The plaintiff subsequently tried to loosen the flanges, but the pressurized gas produced by the freeze caused it to fly off, striking the plaintiff and knocking off part of his skull. The plaintiff died. To establish probable cause in a wrongful death action, the plaintiff must show that the injury was a reasonably foreseeable result of the defendant's conduct. Here, the defendants allege that it was not reasonably foreseeable that a chemical reaction would result in a pressurized explosion because they failed to properly drain the chiller. However, the court disagreed, finding it reasonably foreseeable that water left in pipes subject to freezing temperatures might freeze and burst; the court also noted the warnings.

Other Negligence Claims

Three federal cases addressed a series of other negligence claims within higher education. An Iowa federal trial court granted the defendant university and university official's motion for summary judgment on the plaintiff student's negligent misrepresentation claim after his dismissal based on sexual misconduct allegations.[107] The plaintiff sued, alleging sex discrimination under Title IX and negligent misrepresentation based on the Title IX Coordinator's indicated intent "to reach a mutually agreeable resolution with the parties."[108] To succeed on a negligent misrepresentation claim affecting only intangible economic interests, the plaintiff must show "(1) [t]he defendant was in the business [] of supplying information to others; (2) the defendant intended to supply information to the plaintiff or knew that the recipient intended to [do so]; (3) the information was false; (4) the defendant knew or reasonably should have known that the information was false; (5) the plaintiff

---

[106] Est. of Long by and through Long v. Fowler, 861 S.E.2d 686, 394 Educ. L. Rep. 383 (N.C. 2021).

[107] Doe v. Grinnell Coll., 473 F. Supp. 3d 909, 384 Educ. L. Rep. 179 (S.D. Iowa 2019).

[108] Grinnel Coll., 473 F. Supp. 3d at 937.

reasonably relied on the information in the transaction that the defendant intended the information to influence; (6) and the false information was the proximate cause of damage to the plaintiff." The court found the Title IX Coordinator's statement was of future intent, not false information sufficient to state a negligent misrepresentation claim.

The Nebraska federal district court granted the defendants' motion to dismiss the plaintiff student's claim after an intoxicated fraternity pledge cut the student's neck following a fraternity event.[109] The pledge was given large amounts of alcohol and drugs by fraternity members and left alone on campus. At that point, he entered a dormitory and, eventually, the plaintiff's unlocked dorm room, where he cut her neck. The plaintiff sued the fraternity house's property manager, the national fraternity organization, and officers of the fraternity chapter for negligence in allowing and encouraging hazing, underage drinking, and drug use. To be held liable for negligence, the risk of harm must have been foreseeable during the alleged negligence. Here, there is no evidence that the fraternity officers knew of or personally witnessed aggressive behavior by the assailant, let alone knew he would enter a private dorm room and harm someone. The court found that it was not foreseeable that providing the assailant with alcohol would result in him entering a private dorm room and assaulting a student.

In Pennsylvania, a federal district court held that the plaintiff football player did not state a negligence per se claim against the university or football coach under the state's former anti-hazing statute or Title IX.[110] The plaintiff/football player alleged that he was sexually harassed, hazed, and assaulted by his teammates. At the same time, the coaching staff did nothing to protect him from the harassment and retaliated against him when he complained. The court held that Title IX does not establish a statutory standard that can substitute for the common law negligence standard. The plaintiff did, however, state a negligence per se claim sufficient to survive a motion to dismiss against the university under an antihazing law, which prohibits intentionally, knowingly, or recklessly promoting hazing.

---

[109] Spagna v. Park Ave. Phi Psi House, 478 F. Supp. 3d 813, 385 Educ. L. Rep. 578 (D. Neb. 2020).
[110] Humphries v. Pa. State Univ., 492 F. Supp. 3d 393, 387 Educ. L. Rep. 720 (M.D. Pa. 2020).

Indemnification

In the first of two negligence cases in the higher education sector raising questions of indemnification, the Eleventh Circuit vacated and remanded the Georgia federal district court's grant of summary judgment in favor of the defendant contractor in a wrongful death action surrounding the death of a sleep study participant at the clinic.[111] The plaintiff university alleged that it was entitled to indemnification, which requires the court to consider "(A) whether [the] University has a contractual right to indemnity as an 'affiliate' in the Amended Agreement, and (B) whether the indemnification bar doctrine precludes indemnification."[112] Under Georgia law, an affiliate is a corporation related to another corporation by shareholdings or other means of control, like a subsidiary, parent, or sibling corporation. Here, the university owns 100% of the entity that owns 100% of the clinic. Therefore, the university was the clinic's affiliate and had a right to indemnification by the defendant contractor.

In New York, an appellate court reversed a grant of summary judgment.[113] The plaintiff laborer was injured while renovating a university building when he hit his head on a scaffold's wooden support beam, which caused him to fall backward down the stairs. The laborer and his wife brought suit against the university building owner, general contractor, and subcontractor alleging hazardous work conditions violating the labor law, negligence, and loss of consortium. The defendants moved for summary judgment on the plaintiff's contractual indemnification claims on the basis that "indemnification provisions contained in construction contracts are void to the extent that they purport to indemnify parties for their own negligence."[114] The court found that the indemnification provision requiring indemnification for actual or alleged negligent acts" raised issues of fact about negligence by the university building owner. Thus, summary judgment was not appropriate for this claim.

---

[111] Emory Univ. v. Neurocare, 985 F.3d 1337, 386 Educ. L. Rep. 34 (11th Cir. 2021).
[112] Emory Univ., 985 F.3d at 1337.
[113] Edwards v. State Univ. Constr. Fund, 151 N.Y.S.3d 464, 394 Educ. L. Rep. 1036 (N.Y. App. Div. 2021).
[114] Edwards, 151 N.Y.S.3d at 474.

Vicarious Liability

The Minnesota federal district court granted the defendant university's motion to dismiss the plaintiff student's tort claims against the university after a professor allegedly posted a virtual class video online in which the plaintiff can be seen using the bathroom because she mistakenly believed her camera was off and she was muted.[115] The plaintiff/student alleged that the university was vicariously liable for the tortious acts of the professor, specifically the publication of private facts, intrusion upon seclusion, negligent infliction of emotional distress, and intentional infliction of emotional distress. An employer is vicariously liable for torts of its employee committed within the course and scope of employment. For intentional acts, the focus is on whether the employee's acts were foreseeable; because the adoption of confidentiality policies does not equal foreseeability, the plaintiff student's claim of vicarious liability for an intentional act fails. The court ruled that his vicarious liability for negligence claim fails because it is clear that the employee was not authorized to perform the conduct at issue, and the actions were not to further the employer's interest.

Products Liability

Two products liability cases in higher education emerged in 2021. In North Carolina, a federal district court granted the defendant manufacturers' motion to dismiss the plaintiff's mother's claim for products liability arising from asbestos-containing talc.[116] The plaintiff's daughter was a former university student who died from mesothelioma after being exposed to the defendant manufacturers' asbestos-containing talc product in ceramic materials she used at university. The plaintiff/mother sued the defendant manufacturers for negligent failure to warn, breach of an implied warranty, negligent design, gross negligence, and wrongful death. For the plaintiff/mother's products liability action to proceed, she must provide sufficient evidence to show that her daughter was regularly exposed to a specific product over some extended period in proximity to where the deceased worked. The court concluded that while the plaintiff/mother did present sufficient evidence that her

---

[115] Miles v. Simmons Univ., 514 F. Supp. 3d 1070, 392 Educ. L. Rep. 693 (D. Minn. 2021).
[116] Foushee v. R.T. Vanderbilt Holding Co., 507 F. Supp. 3d 654, 391 Educ. L. Rep. 190 (E.D.N.C. 2020).

daughter was exposed to asbestos in talc, the mother did not allege sufficient frequency, regularity, or proximity for her claims to survive a motion to dismiss.

In a state court case, the Supreme Court of North Carolina affirmed the superior court's grant of summary judgment in favor of the defendant subcontractor after the plaintiff property owner alleged negligence.[117] The subcontractor installed allegedly defective floor trusses in a number of the plaintiff's apartment buildings for students. The economic loss rule prohibits recovery in tort by a plaintiff against a promisor for failing to perform his contract, even though the failure to perform was due to negligence. Therefore, the court held that the economic loss rule barred the plaintiff's tort claim because it was a purely economic loss arising from a commercial transaction, thus, it was a breach of contract claim disguised as a negligence claim.

Class Action

An appellate court in Indiana reversed and remanded an earlier denial of the defendant university's motion for partial summary judgment on the plaintiff students' class-action complaint regarding mold growth in dorms. The plaintiffs are students who live in freshmen dorms on campus and have suffered continued injuries due to mold exposure from an infestation in the dorms. The university argued that the lower court erred in granting the plaintiff students' motion to certify the "Moldy Dorms and Noise Polluted Dorms Classes."[118] The burden of proof in class certification is on the plaintiffs, and decisions by the trial court to certify a class action are reviewed only for abuse of discretion. Here, where the class was certified based on claims not pled in the plaintiffs' amended complaint, the appellate court determined that the trial court abused its discretion and certification was improper.

Evidentiary Matters

In 2021, three tort cases within higher education examined evidentiary matters. A federal district court in New York reversed a magistrate's decision to disclose redacted versions of records from

---

[117] Crescent Univ. City Venture, LLC v. Trussway Mfg., 852 S.E.2d 98, 385 Educ. L. Rep. 395 (N.C. 2020).
[118] Ind. Univ. by and through Bd. of Trs. v. Thomas, 167 N.E.3d 724, 730, 389 Educ. L. Rep. 967 (Ind. Ct. App. 2021).

the university counseling center and mental health provider regarding the complainant.[119] The plaintiff/male student was expelled after an investigation for sexual misconduct and subsequently filed suit against the defendant university, board of trustees, and university officials, alleging Title IX violations, breach of contract, breach of the implied covenant of good faith and fair dealing, negligence, gross negligence, and violation of the state constitution. In New York, psychotherapist records are not covered by the psychotherapist-patient privilege if they are not made during diagnosis or if the patient reasonably expected them to be disclosed. Here, some records contained privileged material along with a number of records that were either not made in the course of diagnosis or the plaintiff reasonably expected them to be disclosed, or both, so those records were not protected by the privilege.

The Indiana appellate court reversed the grant of the plaintiff's motion for a new trial and vacated judgment against the defendant's university.[120] The plaintiff tripped, fell on a riser at the end of the court, and suffered injuries at a university basketball game. At deposition, a university employee testified that she believed there were tables and chairs on the riser. She later found video footage, informed the university's attorney that nothing was on the riser at that game, and testified to this at trial. The attorney failed to inform the plaintiff of this change. The plaintiff alleges disclosure was required, and this failure prevented her from fully and fairly presenting her case, causing prejudice. As a general rule, the court should not set aside final judgment unless the party can show that the misconduct substantially prejudiced the presentation of their case. Here, while the court agreed that the failure to correct deposition testimony before trial violated local rules and constituted misconduct, the plaintiff failed to establish that it substantially prejudiced her in presenting her case.

A Louisiana appellate court affirmed the trial court's grant of summary judgment in favor of the defendant university on the plaintiff elevator passengers' personal injury claims. The plaintiffs were injured after an elevator in a campus building malfunctioned, causing it to drop and abruptly stop. An unidentified university employee informed the plaintiffs that the same elevator had a similar issue the day before, but the trial court found this statement

---

[119] Doe v. Syracuse Univ., 481 F. Supp. 3d 66, 386 Educ. L. Rep. 186 (N.D.N.Y. 2020).

[120] Univ. of Notre Dame v. Bahney, 158 N.E.3d 809, 384 Educ. L. Rep. 988 (Ind. Ct. App. 2020).

to be inadmissible hearsay. The plaintiffs appealed this decision. "Hearsay is a statement, other than one made by the declarant while testifying at the present trial or hearing, offered in evidence to prove the truth of the matter asserted." [121] In Louisiana, hearsay is not admissible unless an exception applies, like when a declarant is unavailable as a witness. The appellate court affirmed that the plaintiffs failed to establish an applicable hearsay exception because they failed to follow up with any of the 25 employees the university identified that might know about the incident to attempt to find the unidentified employee.

Notice

In 2021, three state-level cases raised concerns about proper notice in tort claims within higher education. In Mississippi, a state appellate court affirmed the circuit court's grant of the defendant university's motion to dismiss the plaintiff invitee's claims under the Mississippi Tort Claims Act (MTCA) because the plaintiff did not comply with MTCA notice requirements.[122] Seven categories of information must be included in a notice of claim under the MTCA: circumstances bringing about injury, the extent of injury, time and place of injury, names of all known persons involved, amount of damages sought, and residence of the person making a claim at the time of injury and at the time of filing. Here, the plaintiff did not include the amount of damages sought, merely stating it exceeded the statutory cap of $500,000, nor did she include her address at the time of injury or at the time of filing. Therefore, she did not give adequate notice so as to substantially comply with the requirements of MTCA.

In Wisconsin, a state appellate court reversed and remanded the circuit court's entry of summary judgment in favor of the defendant city in the plaintiff instructor's personal injury claim because she did not provide it with formal notice of injury as required by statute, but the court ruled that there was a genuine issue of material fact as to whether the defendant city was prejudiced by that failure.[123] Under state law, plaintiffs in a personal injury suit against a city must

---

[121] Jackson v. Bd. of Supervisors of La. State Univ. and Agric. and Mech. Coll., 307 So. 3d 227, 232, 385 Educ. L. Rep. 1090 (La. Ct. App. 2020).

[122] Keever v. Miss. Instits. of Higher Learning, 309 So. 3d 460, 386 Educ. L. Rep. 1035 (Miss. Ct. App. 2019).

[123] Clark v. League of Wis. Muns. Mut. Ins. Co., 959 N.W.2d 648, 390 Educ. L. Rep. 756 (Wis. App. 2021).

generally bring two types of notice: notice of injury, a claim with the claimant's address, and an itemized list of the relief sought. Here, the plaintiff did not provide notice of injury. However, because the city had actual notice of the plaintiff's claim through her notice of claim form and an injury form completed shortly after the incident, there was a genuine issue of fact as to whether the lack of a notice of injury prejudiced the city.

A New Jersey appellate court reversed and remanded the superior court's denial of the plaintiff patient's motion for leave to file a late notice of claim under the New Jersey Tort Claims Act (TCA) and motion to reconsider because the plaintiff's cause of action accrued on the date he retained counsel in this suit, not on the date of his accident. [124] The plaintiff suffered severe injuries from a motorcycle accident, which he alleges were caused or significantly aggravated by professional negligence of the medical staff of the state or state university health center. The TCA requires a notice of claim be filed no later than 90 days after the cause of action accrues unless the claimant can show "(1) 'extraordinary circumstances' for his or her failure to file a timely notice of claim and (2) the public entity or employees involved have not been 'substantially prejudiced by the plaintiff's tardiness.'"[125] The court held that extraordinary circumstances, the plaintiff's extremely delicate emotional state, justified his cause of action timing to accrue on the date he retained legal counsel, not the date of his accident.

Other Procedural Matters

Seven other cases raised additional procedural matters based on tort claims in higher education. These matters included issues of jurisdiction, res judicata, joinder, amended petition, and jury instructions.

The Seventh Circuit affirmed the Illinois district court's decision entering judgment in favor of the defendants, the litigant in a guardianship proceeding and forensic accountant, relating to statements submitted to the law school about the plaintiff law professor's alleged conduct in probate court. [126] The plaintiff sued the litigant and forensic accountant, alleging defamation based on statements they submitted to the university regarding her conduct

---

[124] Jeffrey v. State, 255 A.3d 1204, 394 Educ. L. Rep. 312 (N.J. Super. App. Div. 2021).
[125] Jeffrey, 255 A.3d at 1206.
[126] Black v. Wrigley, 997 F.3d 702, 712, 390 Educ. L. Rep. 7 (7th Cir. 2021).

in probate court and the use of university letterhead. The plaintiff alleged that the lower court erred by not including a jury instruction on her defamation claim against the litigant. The federal appellate court held that the district court might have committed a plain error in omitting the defamation jury instruction against the litigant. Still, the plaintiff failed to show "that the outcome probably would have been different without the error."[127] Specifically, the jury found in favor of the forensic accountant on the defamation claim arising out of the same statements because the statements were true. Thus, the court concluded that the plaintiff failed to show the omission of defamation jury instructions against the defendant litigant violated a substantial right.

A federal district court in Texas granted the motion of the plaintiffs, parents of a deceased student, for remand after the defendant's flight school removed the action to federal court under federal question jurisdiction.[128] The plaintiffs' son attended the defendant's flight school, where he was regularly bullied, abused, and humiliated, along with the other Chinese students, by the staff. The plaintiffs allege their son committed suicide because of the school's abuse and discriminatory policies. The plaintiffs brought suit in Texas state court, but the defendant removed the case to federal court, alleging the claims presented substantial federal questions. Where a complaint only alleges state-law claims, federal courts will have federal question jurisdiction only where the state-law claim necessarily raises a federal issue or the state-law claims are completely preempted by federal law. Here, because the complaint alleges only state-law claims that do not necessarily raise a federal issue and the defendant did not cite any cases to support the allegation that plaintiffs' claims are completely preempted by federal law, the federal district court does not have jurisdiction.

A Pennsylvania federal district court held that the derivative jurisdiction doctrine did not deprive the federal court of subject matter jurisdiction over a third-party joinder complaint.[129] The plaintiffs, parents of a baby injured during a c-section, brought a medical malpractice claim in state court against the university hospital, physicians, and others, and the defendants filed a joinder complaint asserting crossclaims against the physician who

---

[127] Black, 997 F.3d at 712.
[128] Yan v. U.S. Aviation Group, 509 F. Supp.3d 642, 391 Educ. L. Rep. 675 (E.D. Tex. 2020).
[129] Da Silva v. Temple Univ. Hosp., 506 F. Supp.3d 318, 390 Educ. L. Rep. 1151 (E.D. Pa. 2020).

performed the c-section. The United States substituted itself as a defendant and removed this case to federal court, but the plaintiffs argue that it should be remanded to Pennsylvania state court because the derivative jurisdiction doctrine barred the university defendants' claims against the United States. The federal district court held that the derivative jurisdiction doctrine does not bar FTCA actions originally in state court against a federal employee. Here, the university defendants in state court filed a joinder against another individual while the U.S. was not yet a party. The United States did not substitute itself as a defendant until it removed the action, thus, the state court had subject matter jurisdiction over the joinder.

In a res judicata issue, an Indiana appellate court held that the plaintiff pedestrian had a history of frivolous filings that warranted filing restrictions.[130] The plaintiff pedestrian fell outside of the university library and brought suit. At one point in the suit, the plaintiff was sanctioned for filing frivolous motions and warned that if it continued, his suit would be dismissed; after this, the plaintiff filed an appeal despite the trial court declining to certify its orders for interlocutory appeal. The plaintiff filed frivolous, repetitive, and disjointed motions, and the trial court dismissed his suit. The plaintiff appealed. The doctrine of res judicata bars claims in which the claim or issue has already been previously litigated. Here, the plaintiff's claims were mere attempts to relitigate issues that had been conclusively litigated before, so his claims were precluded.

In another res judicata case, a Missouri appellate court held that the plaintiff students' claims for damages against the university for breach of contract, negligence, and state consumer protection laws were precluded because of the plaintiffs' previous voluntary dismissal.[131] The plaintiffs voluntarily dismissed their previous suit so they could re-file suit in Kansas to avoid the sovereign immunity law of Missouri. For res judicata to preclude a claim, the suit must involve the same claim, the same parties, claims that either were or could have been raised and a final judgment on the merits. Because a voluntary dismissal is considered an adjudication on the merits, the Missouri appellate court ruled that the prior voluntary dismissal of the plaintiff's claim constituted a final judgment on the merits precluding the claim.

---

[130] Holland v. Trs. of Ind. Univ., 171 N.E.3d 684, 393 Educ. L. Rep. 431 (Ind. Ct. App. 2021).
[131] Bell v. Curators of Univ. of Mo., 621 S.W.3d 179, 390 Educ. L. Rep. 795 (Mo. Ct. App. 2021).

The Louisiana Court of Appeals reversed and remanded the district court's decision, holding that the joinder of the state university hospital was unnecessary for adjudication of the medical malpractice suit against the state. [132] The plaintiffs sued after a patient died from surgical complications. A Medical Review Panel found an unknown someone breached the standard of care. The plaintiffs learned the identity of the two doctors at a later deposition but did not add them as defendants. The state alleged that, for vicarious liability, the university medical center that employed the doctors who breached a duty must be joined. Joinder is required in two scenarios: (1) when, otherwise, complete relief cannot be granted, or (2) when he claims an interest relating to the action and is in such a position that his absence might impair his ability to protect his interest or leave any of the parties subject to a substantial risk of incurring multiple or inconsistent obligations. Here, neither the state university nor its hospital would be responsible for paying a medical malpractice judgment; the state is responsible. Thus, the state's argument failed. In an amended petition case, the Louisiana Court of Appeals reversed and remanded the district court's dismissal of the plaintiff's amended petition in her defamation action against the defendant board of supervisors and director of the technical college.[133] The court held that because there was no evidence that the plaintiff's failure to amend was a willful refusal of the trial court's order, and the delay did not interfere with the orderly administration of justice nor did it prejudice the defendants, dismissal of the plaintiff's amended petition was not warranted.

Immunity

In 2021, five tort cases within the higher education context raised issues of immunity. The Fourth Circuit held that Eleventh Amendment immunity did not apply to the plaintiff, former Director of Broadcast Operations' wrongful termination, defamation, retaliation, and discrimination claims and remanded the case for the district court to determine whether state sovereign immunity applied.[134] The Eleventh Amendment bars a federal court from

---

[132] Farooqui v. BRFHH Shreveport, LLC, 316 So. 3d 579, 391 Educ. L. Rep. 400 (La. Ct. App. 2021).
[133] Henry v. Bd. of Supervisors of La. Cmty. and Tech. Coll. Sys., 313 So. 3d 1009, 389 Educ. L. Rep. 986 (La. Ct. App. 2020).
[134] Williams v. Morgan State Univ., 850 F. App'x 172, 391 Educ. L. Rep. 128 (4th Cir. 2021).

hearing any suit in law or equity that is commenced or prosecuted against one of the United States by citizens of another state or by citizens or subjects of any foreign state; a state may waive Eleventh Amendment immunity by voluntarily removing the case to federal court. Because the state removed the present case to federal court, it waived its Eleventh Amendment immunity. However, state sovereign immunity "bars all claims by private citizens against state governments and their agencies, except where Congress has validly abrogated that immunity or the state has waived it," state sovereign immunity is not waived by removal to federal court. Therefore, the Maryland district court must address the issue of state sovereign immunity on remand.

In Texas, the Fifth Circuit affirmed the district court's dismissal of the plaintiff postdoctoral fellow's tort, Texas Constitution, First Amendment, and Fourteenth Amendment claims against the defendant state university health science center and employees for failure to state a claim and lack of jurisdiction. The Eleventh Amendment protects state universities under Texas law, thus, the claims against the university health sciences center were properly dismissed, and the defendant was entitled to immunity. Further, under Texas law, if a suit is filed "against both a governmental unit and any of its employees, the employee shall immediately be dismissed on the filing of a motion by the governmental unit."[135] Because the plaintiff sued individuals for intentional torts arising from the same incidents for which it sued the university, the federal appellate court ruled that the Texas Torts Claims Act claim was properly dismissed.

In Florida, a state appellate court affirmed the circuit court's denial of the plaintiff/guardian's motion for summary judgment and granted the defendant university's cross-motion for summary judgment on sovereign immunity grounds.[136] The plaintiff brought a medical malpractice suit against a university, teaching hospital, and physician after the physician failed to prescribe anticoagulants to the patient, which resulted in disabilities. However, under Florida law, agents acting for the state cannot be held personally liable in tort or named as a defendant in action for injuries or damages suffered as a result of any act, event, or omission of action in the scope of their employment or function. Florida considers a private medical school and its physicians as state agents when the

---

[135] Huang v. Huang, 846 F. App'x 224, 230, 389 Educ. L. Rep. 737 (5th Cir. 2021).
[136] Lazzari v. Guzman, 314 So. 3d 374, 390 Educ. L. Rep. 434 (Fla. Dist. Ct. App. 2020).

institution is a nonprofit, independent college or university located and chartered in Florida and is owned/operated as an accredited medical school within the scope of and pursuant to guidelines established in the contract. Here, the Basic Affiliation Agreement clearly conferred sovereign immunity on the university for its patient treating services at the medical school.

In Missouri, a state appellate court affirmed the circuit court's dismissal of the plaintiff law school employee's assault, battery, negligence, and discrimination claims against the defendant supervisor because her supervisor was immune from negligence under the Kansas Tort Claims Act (KTCA).[137] While driving the plaintiff to a work-related event at a law firm, she and the defendant's supervisor got into a fight, culminating in the defendant yelling at her and crashing the vehicle into a concrete barrier. Under the KTCA, no government entity or employee acting within the scope of employment will be liable for any damages arising from an employee's claim for the tortious conduct of another employee if that claim is recoverable under the Kansas Workers Compensation Act. The court ruled that the plaintiff and the defendant worked for the same governmental entity, and the plaintiff's claim is recoverable under the Kansas Workers Compensation Act. Therefore, the defendant is immune from suit under the KTCA.

In North Carolina, a state appellate court affirmed the superior court's dismissal of the plaintiff college recruiter's wrongful discharge and tort claims against the university and coworkers on immunity grounds following alleged sexual harassment by coworkers that worked in his office.[138] The plaintiff was employed by a public university primarily in Alabama, but he worked at a recruiting office for the university in North Carolina. The plaintiff argued that the sovereign immunity law of North Carolina applied because that is where all tortious conduct took place. Still, the court held that the state where tortious conduct occurred was irrelevant. The issue is "whether one state has been 'haled involuntarily' into the courts of another state."[139] Thus, the Alabama sovereign immunity law applied. In Alabama, state universities are considered arms of the state entitled to the same sovereign immunity the state enjoys. Because the university in question is an Alabama state university, and Alabama does not recognize a business and

---

[137] Hill v. Freedman, 608 S.W.3d 650, 383 Educ. L. Rep. 537 (Mo. Ct. App. 2020).
[138] Farmer v. Troy Univ., 855 S.E.2d 801, 388 Educ. L. Rep. 975 (N.C. Ct. App. 2021).
[139] Troy Univ., 855 S.E.2d at 806.

commercial ventures exception to sovereign immunity, the defendant university was entitled to sovereign immunity.

Conclusion

In 2021, tort litigation in elementary/secondary education and higher education continued with the same general issues, such as intentional torts, negligence, product liability, procedural matters, and immunity. Significantly, the negligence cases dominated both levels of education ranging from questions of the school's duty, premises liability, vehicular accidents, and wrongful death. Across the tort litigation, most cases occurred at the state level, and New York state cases rose to the highest number of cases from a single jurisdiction. As cases continue in this area, incidents of racial bullying, sexual misconduct, alcohol consumption, suicide attempts, and adequacy of staff supervision represent unusual behaviors that are worth tracking as they may continue to escalate.

Alphabetical List of Cases

A.J.R. v. Lute
A.W. by E.W. v. N.Y. Dep't of Educ.
AA by BB v. Hammondsport Cent. Sch. Dist.
Aldrich v. Nat'l Collegiate Athletic Ass'n
Alexandria City Pub. Schs. v. Handel
Auld v. Forbes
Ayers v. Pioneer Cent. Sch. Dist.
Bell v. Curators of Univ. of Mo.
Black v. Wrigley
Blondin v. Milton Town Sch. Dist.
Brandt v. Davis
C.C. v. Harrison Cnty. Bd. of Educ.
C.D. v. Goshen Cent. Sch. Dist.
C.R. v. Eugene Sch. Dist.
Cain v. Ameresco
Chen v. City of N.Y.
Clark v. League of Wis. Muns. Mut. Ins. Co.
Collias ex rel. Collias v. Gateway Acad. of Walton Cnty.
Collins v. Creighton
Crescent Univ. City Venture, LLC v. Trussway Mfg.
Da Silva v. Temple Univ. Hosp.
Davis v. Strus
Dep't for Cmty. Based Servs., Cabinet for Health & Fam. Servs. v. Baker
Dextraze v. Bernard
DiCoby v. Syracuse Univ.
DiDonato v. Ski Shawnee
Dinsmoor v. City of Phx.
DJ ex rel. Hughes v. Sch. Bd. of Henrico Cnty.
Doe #1 v. Syracuse Univ.
Doe 122 v. Marianist Province of the U.S.
Doe ex rel. Doe Minor v. Garagnani
Doe v. ABC Sch.
Doe v. Bronx Preparatory Charter Sch.
Doe v. Grinnell Coll.
Doe v. R.I. Sch. of Design
Doe v. Syracuse Univ.
Dupree v. Houston Cnty. Bd. of Educ.
E.H. ex rel. Abron v. Barrilleaux
E.M. ex rel. McInnis v. Gateway Region Young Men's Christian Assoc.

Edwards v. Pearson
Edwards v. State Univ. Constr. Fund
Elalouf v. Sch. Bd. of Broward Cnty.
Emory Univ. v. Neurocare
Erickson v. Walker
Est. of Long by and through Long v. Fowler
Ex parte Blunt
Farmer v. Troy Univ.
Farooqui v. BRFHH Shreveport, LLC
Foushee v. R.T. Vanderbilt Holding Co.
Franco v. Fairleigh Dickinson Univ.
Game Truck Ga., LLC v. Quezada
Gerson v. Logan River Acad.
Gill v. Dougherty
Grady v. Chenango Valley Ctr. Sch. Dist.
Gruver v. La. Through the Bd. of Supervisors of La. State Univ. and Agric. and Mech. Coll.
Henry v. Bd. of Supervisors of La. Cmty. and Tech. Coll. Sys.
Hill v. Freedman
Holland v. Trs. of Ind. Univ.
Huang v. Huang
Humphries v. Pa. State Univ.
In re JUUL Labs, Marketing, Sales Practices, and Products Liability Litigation
Ind. Univ. by and through Bd. of Trs. v. Thomas
Jackson v. Bd. of Supervisors of La. State Univ. and Agric. and Mech. Coll.
Jefferson v. Nichols State Univ.
Jeffrey v. State
K.A. v. City of N.Y.
K.D. v. Douglas Cnty. Sch. Dist. No. 001
K.G. ex rel. Ruch v. Smith
Keever v. Miss. Instits. of Higher Learning
Kemp v. McMcReynolds
Khelfaoui v. Lowell Sch. Comm.
Knaszak v. Hamburg Cent. Sch. Dist.
L.A. Unified Sch. Dist. v. S&W Atlas Iron & Metal Co.
L.A. Unified Sch. Dist. v. Superior Ct. of L.A. Cnty.
L.J. v. Balt. Curriculum Project
Lazzari v. Guzman
Leight v. Univ. of Pitt. Physicians
Leuthard v. Indep. Sch. Dist. 912 – Milaca
Magnum Constr. Mgmt., LLC v. WSP USA Sols.

Mariani v. Wilson Cent. Sch. Dist.
Martin for C.M. v. Hermiston Sch. Dist. 8R
Matter of C.G.
McMichael v. James Island Charter Sch.
Mejia v. Cohn
Meyers v. Cincinnati Bd. of Educ.
Meyers v. Ferndale Sch. Dist.
Miles v. Simmons Univ.
Miller v. Cardinal Mooney High Sch.
Miller v. Livanis
Monroe v. Columbia Coll. Chi.
Murphy v. William Carey Univ.
Nizen–Jacobellis v. Lindenhurst Union Free Sch. Dist.
Ortiz v. Torres-Rodriguez
Paradis v. Charleston Cnty. Sch. Dist.
Parr v. Cook Cnty. Sch. Dist.
PB-36 Doe v. Niagara Falls City Sch. Dist.
Plakorus v. Univ. of Mont.
Poore v. Indianapolis Pub. Schs.
Ramon v. Nebo Sch. Dist.
Raymond v. Iberia Par. Sch. Bd.
Reykdal v. Espinoza
Rideaux v. Winter
Rodgers v. Smart
S.A.S. v. Wellington Sch.
S.H. v. K & H Transp.
Sch. Bd. of Broward Cnty. v. McCall
Secky v. New Paltz Cent. Sch. Dist.
Shields v. Plummer
Smoler v. Bd. of Educ. for W. Northfield Sch. Dist. #31
Sneed v. Austin Indep. Sch. Dist.
Spagna v. Park Ave. Phi Psi House
State ex rel. Ohio Att'y Gen. v. Burns
Steffens v. Sachem Cent. Sch. Dist.
Sumpter v. Fairbanks N. Star Borough Sch. Dist.
Taylor-Travis v. Jackson State Univ.
Tex. Pol. Subdivisions Prop./Cas. Joint Self Ins. Fund v. Pharr-San Juan-Alamo ISD
Turner v. Homestead Police Dep't
Univ. of Notre Dame v. Bahney
Wani v. George Fox Univ.
Ward v. Corning Painted Post Area Sch. Dist.
Webb v. Muller

Wienclaw v. E. Islip Union Free Sch. Dist.
Williams v. Morgan State Univ.
Wilson v. St. Landry Par. Sch. Bd.
Yan v. U.S. Aviation Group

Cases by Jurisdiction

FEDERAL CASES

First Circuit

Massachusetts
Khelfaoui v. Lowell Sch. Comm.

Rhode Island
Doe v. R.I. Sch. of Design

Second Circuit

New York
AA by BB v. Hammondsport Cent. Sch. Dist.
A.W. by E.W. v. N.Y. Dep't of Educ.
Doe v. Syracuse Univ.
Doe #1 v. Syracuse Univ.

Third Circuit

Pennsylvania
Da Silva v. Temple Univ. Hosp.
Humphries v. Pa. State Univ.

Fourth Circuit
McMichael v. James Island Charter Sch.
Williams v. Morgan State Univ.

Maryland
L.J. v. Balt. Curriculum Project
Virginia
DJ ex rel. Hughes v. Sch. Bd. of Henrico Cnty.
North Carolina
Foushee v. R.T. Vanderbilt Holding Co.

Sixth Circuit
Davis v. Detroit Pub. Schs. Cmty. Dist.
Houchens v. Beshear

Kentucky
Danville Christian Acad., Inc. v. Beshear
Ohio
Plain Local Sch. Dist. Bd. of Educ. v. DeWine

Fifth Circuit
Huang v. Huang
Taylor-Travis v. Jackson State Univ.

Louisiana
E.H. ex rel. Abron v. Barrilleaux
Gruver v. La. Through the Bd. of Supervisors of La. State Univ. and Agric. and
　Mech. Coll.
Mississippi
Rodgers v. Smart
Texas
Sneed v. Austin Indep. Sch. Dist.
Yan v. U.S. Aviation Group

Sixth Circuit
Meyers v. Cincinnati Bd. of Educ.

Seventh Circuit
Black v. Wrigley
Monroe v. Columbia Coll. Chi.

Illinois
Smoler v. Bd. of Educ. for W. Northfield Sch. Dist. #31

Eighth Circuit
K.D. v. Douglas Cnty. Sch. Dist. No. 001

Iowa
Doe v. Grinnell Coll.
Minnesota
Miles v. Simmons Univ.
Nebraska
Spagna v. Park Ave. Phi Psi House

Ninth Circuit
Wani v. George Fox Univ.

California
Aldrich v. Nat'l Collegiate Athletic Ass'n
In re JUUL Labs Marketing, Sales Practices, and Products Liability Litigation
L.A. Unified Sch. Dist. v. S&W Atlas Iron & Metal Co.
Oregon
Martin for C.M. v. Hermiston Sch. Dist. 8R
Washington
Davis v. Strus
Tenth Circuit
Gerson v. Logan River Acad.

Eleventh Circuit
Emory Univ. v. Neurocare
Turner v. Homestead Police Dep't

Florida
Magnum Constr. Mgmt., LLC v. WSP USA Sols.

STATE & D.C. COURT CASES

Alabama
Edwards v. Pearson
Ex parte Blunt

Alaska
Sumpter v. Fairbanks N. Star Borough Sch. Dist.

Arizona
Dinsmoor v. City of Phx.

California
L.A. Unified Sch. Dist. v. Superior Ct. of L.A. Cnty.

Connecticut
Ortiz v. Torres-Rodriguez

Florida
Collias ex rel. Collias v. Gateway Acad. of Walton Cnty.
Elalouf v. Sch. Bd. of Broward Cnty.
Lazzari v. Guzman
Sch. Bd. of Broward Cnty. v. McCall

Georgia
Auld v. Forbes
Dupree v. Hous. Cnty. Bd. of Educ.
Erickson v. Walker
Game Truck Ga., LLC v. Quezada
Parr v. Cook Cnty. Sch. Dist.

Illinois
Rideaux v. Winter

Indiana
Holland v. Trs. of Ind. Univ.
Ind. Univ. by and through Bd. of Trs. v. Thomas
K.G. ex rel. Ruch v. Smith (Ind. Ct. App. 2021)
K.G. ex rel. Ruch v. Smith (Ind. 2021).
Matter of C.G.
Poore v. Indianapolis Pub. Schs. (Ind. Ct. App. 2020)
Poore v. Indianapolis Pub. Schs. (Ind. 2021).
Univ. of Notre Dame v. Bahney

Kentucky
Dep't for Cmty. Based Servs., Cabinet for Health & Fam. Servs. v. Baker

Louisiana
Collins v. Creighton
Doe v. ABC Sch.
Farooqui v. BRFHH Shreveport, LLC
Henry v. Bd. of Supervisors of La. Cmty. and Tech. Coll. Sys.
Jackson v. Bd. of Supervisors of La. State Univ. and Agric. and Mech. Coll.
Jefferson v. Nichols State Univ.
Raymond v. Iberia Par. Sch. Bd.
Wilson v. St. Landry Par. Sch. Bd.

Torts 243

Massachusetts
Brandt v. Davis

Minnesota
Leuthard v. Indep. Sch. Dist. 912 – Milaca

Mississippi
Keever v. Miss. Instits. of Higher Learning
Murphy v. William Carey Univ.

Missouri
Bell v. Curators of Univ. of Mo.
Doe 122 v. Marianist Province of the U.S.
Doe ex rel. Doe Minor v. Garagnani
E.M. ex rel. McInnis v. Gateway Region Young Men's Christian Assoc.
Hill v. Freedman
Kemp v. McReynolds

Montana
Plakorus v. Univ. of Mont.
New Jersey
Franco v. Fairleigh Dickinson Univ.
Jeffrey v. State
S.H. v. K & H Transp.

New York
Ayers v. Pioneer Ctr. Sch. Dist.
C.D. v. Goshen Ctr. Sch. Dist.
Cain v. Ameresco
Chen v. City of N.Y.
DiCoby v. Syracuse Univ.
Doe v. Bronx Preparatory Charter Sch.
Edwards v. State Univ. Constr. Fund
Gill v. Dougherty
Grady v. Chenango Valley Cent. Sch. Dist.
K.A. v. City of N.Y.
Knaszak v. Hamburg Cent. Sch. Dist.
Mariani v. Wilson Cent. Sch. Dist.
Mejia v. Cohn
Miller v. Livanis
Nizen–Jacobellis v. Lindenhurst Union Free Sch. Dist.
PB-36 Doe v. Niagara Falls City Sch. Dist.

Secky v. New Paltz Cent. Sch. Dist.
Steffens v. Sachem Cent. Sch. Dist.
Ward v. Corning Painted Post Area Sch. Dist.
Webb v. Muller
Wienclaw v. E. Islip Union Free Sch. Dist.

North Carolina
Crescent Univ. City Venture, LLC v. Trussway Mfg.
Est. of Long by and through Long v. Fowler
Farmer v. Troy Univ.

Ohio
A.J.R. v. Lute
Miller v. Cardinal Mooney High Sch.
S.A.S. v. Wellington Sch.
Shields v. Plummer
State ex rel. Ohio Att'y Gen. v. Burns

Oregon
C.R. v. Eugene Sch. Dist.

Pennsylvania
DiDonato v. Ski Shawnee
Leight v. Univ. of Pitt. Physicians

Rhode Island
Dextraze v. Bernard

South Carolina
Paradis v. Charleston Cnty. Sch. Dist.

Texas
Tex. Pol. Subdivisions Prop./Cas. Joint Self Ins. Fund v. Pharr-San Juan-
    Alamo ISD

Utah
Ramon v. Nebo Sch. Dist.

Vermont
Blondin v. Milton Town Sch. Dist.

Torts 245

Virginia
Alexandria City Pub. Schs. v. Handel

Washington
Meyers v. Ferndale Sch. Dist.
Reykdal v. Espinoza

West Virginia
C.C. v. Harrison Cnty. Bd. of Educ.

Wisconsin
Clark v. League of Wis. Muns. Mut. Ins. Co.

Chapter 7

SPORTS

Gillian P. Foss, Ph.D.[1] and Joy Blanchard, Ph.D.[2]

Introduction 248
Discrimination.. 248
   Sexual Harassment and Misconduct 248
   Title IX and Sex Discrimination 249
   Discrimination-Based Employment Issues 251
Negligence 253
   Athlete Injury 253
   Sports Hazing Injuries to Students 254
   School Security and Spectator Injury 254
First Amendment Issues.. 255
NCAA Issues 256
Student-Athlete & Agent Conflict 258
Conclusion 259
Alphabetical List of Cases... 260
Cases by Jurisdiction... 260

---

[1] School of Education, Louisiana State University, Baton Rouge, La.
[2] Associate Professor, Higher Education, School of Education, Louisiana State University, Baton Rouge, La.

Introduction

This chapter reviews litigation from 2021 addressing sports in K–12 schools and higher education. Among the legal issues covered at the K–12 level are discrimination claims under Title IX of the Educational Amendments and Title VII of the Civil Rights Act, suits of negligence from student-athletes and spectators, and allegations of First Amendment violations. Although the higher education sector faced similar litigation patterns in 2021, legal issues of a financial nature—particularly those affiliated with the National Collegiate Athletic Association (NCAA)—also emerged in this arena. Given the intersecting topics (e.g., students in higher education, employees, and torts) with sports in the educational setting, some of the cases addressed in this chapter, at times, may also appear in other chapters to address the other dominant issues beyond the sports focus.

Discrimination

Sexual Harassment and Misconduct

The Eighth Circuit revived a Title IX sex discrimination case against a public university. In that case, ten African-American members of the university football team filed suit in a complex case related to an alleged sexual assault.[3] Six plaintiffs engaged in a consensual sex act with a White female student, and the remaining plaintiffs were in the same apartment at the time. As a result of the accusations levied against the student-athletes, the university suspended the players and prohibited them from participating in an upcoming bowl game. The plaintiffs claimed they were illegally targeted because of their race and sex. A federal district court dismissed all claims, but the federal appellate court reinstated the plaintiffs' claim of discrimination based on sex. The record indicated the university investigator failed to provide the plaintiffs equal access to review, respond to, or refute accusations from the accuser. Additionally, email correspondence from the investigator indicated that she believed the university had acted to cover up sexual assault allegations on the part of the football team back in 2015, and the

---

[3] Does 1-2 v. Regents of the Univ. of Minn., 999 F.3d 571, 391 Educ. L. Rep. 74 (8th Cir. 2021).

plaintiffs, in this case, alleged that her bias influenced her investigation of their case.

A group of female university swimmers filed suit in a federal district court in New York against the university, alleging they were subjected to a hostile environment at the hands of male teammates, and this hostile environment was condoned and ignored by the coaching staff.[4] One of the plaintiffs was not a swim team member but was allegedly raped by a male member of the team. The coach of the swimming team, as well as the university athletic director, failed to report the harassment, though, under Title IX regulations, he was required to do so. The trial court dismissed the university's motion to dismiss the claims against it. The court found that the university's indifference and culture of tolerating sexual harassment and intimidation likely "benefitted" the male athletes.

A federal district court in Michigan dismissed a basketball player's federal and state-level claims of sexual harassment following an incident in which his coach, frustrated and perturbed by a comment made by the plaintiff during a team huddle, grabbed his crotch and made lewd comments and gestures toward him.[5] Citing Title IX precedence, the court noted that a claim could only survive if the harassment were so severe and pervasive that it would prevent the plaintiff from benefits of access to the educational program—in this case, participation in athletics—but the coach's conduct in this single incident was not sufficiently severe to meet that standard.

Title IX and Sex Discrimination

At the collegiate level, a track athlete filed a Title IX claim alleging retaliation and sex discrimination after she was dismissed from the team.[6] The athlete was vocally supportive of her former coach, who had been investigated for sexual misconduct; the athlete claimed her participation in the investigation on behalf of her former coach led to her dismissal. In her filing, the plaintiff pointed to what she labeled as disparate treatment—such as not being able to utilize athletic facilities while considering transferring to a different

---

[4] Posso v. Niagara Univ., 518 F. Supp. 3d 688, 393 Educ. L. Rep. 623 (W.D.N.Y. 2021).
[5] Jones v. Univ. of Detroit Mercy, 527 F. Supp. 3d 945, 395 Educ. L. Rep. 353 (E.D. Mich. 2021).
[6] Du Bois v. Bd. of Regents of Univ. of Minn., 987 F.3d 1199, 386 Educ. L. Rep. 581 (8th Cir. 2021).

institution as well as not being eligible for a redshirt season while recovering from injury, which she claimed male athletes in other sports had been allowed to do. The federal district court in Minnesota dismissed the plaintiff's claims, finding she failed to demonstrate that she was treated differently because of her sex or that she had engaged in protected behavior. On appeal, the Eighth Circuit affirmed.

In another Eight Circuit case, a group of former athletes sued under Title IX after a university cut its women's hockey team but not its men's hockey team.[7] A federal district court in North Dakota granted the university's motion to dismiss; on appeal, that ruling was reversed. Title IX requires institutions to satisfy at least one aspect of a three-prong test regarding gender equity in sports: (1) provide athletic opportunities for women proportionate to the undergraduate student body; (2) demonstrate a continuing expansion of opportunity for women to participate in sports; or (3) demonstrate that all interest and ability have been accommodated. The plaintiffs relied on the third prong, arguing that hockey was the university's most popular women's sport. At the time of its discontinuance, the team was ranked sixth nationally. On remand, the Eighth Circuit instructed the district court to examine the case per the plain language of the statute's separate team regulation. The court was careful to instruct that the provision does not per se indicate that an institution must sponsor separate teams in every sport, but where "the provision of only one team would not 'accommodate the interests and abilities of members of both sexes.'"

In Utah, a group of high school parents unsuccessfully filed suit for their daughters after their three respective school districts refused to include women's tackle football in their high school sports offerings.[8] The parents claimed the lack of women's tackle football at the high school level violated the Equal Protection Clause and Title IX. Specifically, they argued vast gender disparities existed in a manner indicative of discrimination beset by the defendants' unwillingness to sanction an equivalent contact sport to men's tackle football for women. The federal district court disagreed, however, noting the Equal Protection Clause does not carry an inherent requirement to offer football teams for both men and women. Although many female students testified that school personnel acted to prevent or discourage their participation on the men's tackle

---

[7] Berndsen v. N.D. Univ. Sys., 7 F.4th 782, 393 Educ. L. Rep. 120 (8th Cir. 2021).
[8] Gordon v. Jordan Sch. Dist., 522 F. Supp. 3d 1060, 394 Educ. L. Rep. 704 (D. Utah 2021).

football team, the district handbook had longstanding and clear provisions allowing female athletes to participate, satisfying a significant consideration of the Equal Protection Clause claim. The court also noted that despite the plaintiffs' interest in a women's tackle football team, both district and broader data suggested the sustainability of a sanctioned league would be unlikely to the point of failing to meet Title IX requirements.

Discrimination-Based Employment Issues

A Connecticut middle and high school basketball referee filed a Title VII claim following several complaints to her hiring entities that the ranking system used to schedule referees between skill levels (and, subsequently, pay differentials) was discriminatory toward women.[9] After her complaints, the plaintiff also presented the argument for continued retaliation via low-level officiating appointments. The Second Circuit, however, dismissed the plaintiff's Title VII argument on the premise that non-school entities were in charge of referee hiring, scheduling, and ranking practices; therefore, the plaintiff did not succeed in arguing that she was a school employee of the extent that Title VII would apply.

In another Second Circuit case, a former male tennis coach filed a sexual discrimination lawsuit after he was terminated, claiming he was treated differently than other similarly situated female coaches.[10] A federal district court dismissed the suit, and the Second Circuit affirmed. The plaintiff held a full-time position elsewhere as a schoolteacher and was hired as a part-time tennis coach. Because of his obligations to the other job, the coach missed several practices and was 30 minutes late to every practice. Both courts found that this behavior caused his termination, not any alleged sex-based discrimination.

In Pennsylvania, a former varsity wrestling coach filed suit against the school district because, as a quadriplegic, unsatisfactory accommodations violated the Americans with Disabilities Act (ADA).[11] Although the alleged violations primarily involved an inaccessible practice facility, the plaintiff also argued that he faced

---

[9] Girard v. Int'l Ass'n of Approved Basketball Officials, Inc., 840 F. App'x 635, 388 Educ. L. Rep. 129 (2d Cir. 2021).
[10] Gagliardi v. Sacred Heart Univ., 855 F. App'x 1, 393 Educ. L. Rep. 157 (2d Cir. 2021).
[11] Belles v. Wilkes-Barre Area Sch. Dist., 843 F. App'x 437, 388 Educ. L. Rep. 629 (3d Cir. 2021).

a demotion (i.e., retaliation) and a hostile work environment in his coaching role after taking issue with the school's accommodation efforts. The Third Circuit affirmed the district court's ruling by dismissing such claims, however, noting the ADA claim was contingent largely on speculation; moreover, subsequent hiring decisions and work environments did not reflect harassment nor retaliation.

A former women's basketball coach sued for breach of contract, invasion of privacy, and Title VII and Title IX violations after being fired.[12] A jury awarded her damages for the remaining two years of her employment contract and awarded damages for violation of privacy after the university shared documents with a local newspaper. A federal district court dismissed the Title VII and Title IX employment claims. The Fifth Circuit upheld the jury verdict regarding the contract claims, finding the plaintiff did not willfully violate university policy and, thus, her actions did not constitute termination for cause. The court did, however, overturn the judgment for invasion of privacy. The records submitted to the newspaper included statements from the plaintiff to the university in which she complained that women's sports were not supported to the level of men's sports. The records also contained the university's notice to her of the alleged misdoing, which included misuse of funds—which the court found to be a matter of public concern and, thus, not an invasion of privacy. The Fifth Circuit upheld the dismissal of discrimination claims, failing to find a causal connection between her complaint of gender inequity and her dismissal.

In Minnesota, a university track coach resigned under threat of termination after members of her team complained that she made inappropriate comments of a sexual nature and discussed the athletes' weight and diet.[13] The coach filed suit under Title VII and Title IX, alleging she was subjected to a hostile environment and was treated differently than male coaches. A federal district court dismissed her claims, and the Eighth Circuit affirmed, finding her complaint did not sufficiently state an inference of disparate treatment based on sex as the cause of her termination.

---

[12] Taylor-Travis v. Jackson State Univ., 984 F.3d 1107, 385 Educ. L. Rep. 458 (5th Cir. 2021).
[13] Warmington v. Bd. of Regents of Univ. of Minn., 998 F.3d 789, 390 Educ. L. Rep. 494 (8th Cir. 2021).

Negligence

Athlete Injury

A Florida appellate court upheld a trial court ruling that a former high school soccer player's negligence claim was without merit following a game-related injury where another player shoved the athlete onto a cement block adjacent to the field.[14] According to the court, the language of a school district liability waiver was clearly defined despite not explicitly using the word "negligence." The smaller font of the potential injury provision and avoidance of the "negligence" term did not render the school liable for the athlete's injury, as the intent of the waiver was sufficiently understandable.

In New York, another unsuccessful negligence suit involving an athlete injury arose after a 14-year-old male student collided with bleachers and sustained an injury during his basketball practice.[15] His mother filed suit, claiming that the drill took place outside the typical boundaries of the basketball court and, therefore, the school assumed a heightened risk of harm from the retracted bleachers. The Supreme Court of New York disagreed and reversed the prior denial of summary judgment for the defendants. The court ruled that student-athletes automatically assume some risk of injury upon signing up to participate in sports, and a drill spanning beyond typical court boundaries was not nearly an egregious safety violation to the extent that it would satisfy the negligence claim. In a second New York case, a former high school baseball player argued that the permanent eye damage sustained from being hit with a baseball was due to school officials' negligence during the practice.[16] Although the drill involved multiple baseballs in play at one time—differing from a typical baseball game—the Supreme Court of New York affirmed summary judgment for the defendants, arguing that the experienced player was aware of risks during that particular drill and those generally in the sport. The defendants did not abandon their duty of care in this on-field situation.

A state appellate court in Ohio affirmed summary judgment on behalf of school officials after a high school junior varsity basketball

---

[14] Elalouf v. Sch. Bd. of Broward Cnty., 311 So.3d 863, 388 Educ. L. Rep. 437 (Fla. Dist. Ct. App. 2021).
[15] Secky v. New Paltz Cent. Sch. Dist., 151 N.Y.S.3d 202, 394 Educ. L. Rep. 327 (N.Y. App. Div. 2021).
[16] Grady v. Chenango Valley Cent. Sch. Dist., 141 N.Y.S.3d 513, 388 Educ. L. Rep. 324 (N.Y. App. Div. 2021).

player filed a negligence claim following a locker room injury.[17] The female student sustained the injury immediately after halftime of the varsity game when a player collided with the locker room door during a play, trapping the plaintiff's hand in the door. Still, the court argued that the risks of using that locker room door during a game were clear enough—particularly to an athlete who had used it before—and the school had taken measures to ensure the door was a feasible distance from the court to avoid immediate risk. As such, the plaintiff's claims did not satisfy the assumption of risk doctrine.

Sports Hazing Injuries to Students

The Supreme Court of Vermont upheld prior rulings of an extensive sports hazing case that arose after the plaintiff—then a high school football team member—was sexually assaulted at a dinner off-campus following a string of hazing injuries to other players in 2012.[18] Although the school district had presented the argument to the jury that the plaintiff was comparatively negligent in his awareness of toxic treatment by the upper-level students, the court disagreed, arguing the trial court's decision to award the student the full $466,666 in damages was accurate based on the fact that the student was fourteen years old and the assault was not foreseeable. The court did, however, rule in favor of the defendants' cross-appeal by ruling that the municipality had not violated the Vermont Public Accommodations Act in handling the case.

School Security and Spectator Injury

A Florida appellate court reversed and remanded an earlier trial court ruling over a school district's attempt to claim summary judgment via sovereign immunity.[19] The issue arose after a plaintiff, who had been a spectator at a high school basketball game, was injured by an unruly crowd. The legal issue was whether the security plan at that game demonstrated an error in planning or broader operational problems. The appellate court ultimately held that the security breakdown was a planning-level issue, satisfying the defendant's plea for summary judgment.

---

[17] Miller v. Cardinal Mooney High Sch., 168 N.E. 3d 1254, 390 Educ. L. Rep. 1189 (Ohio Ct. App. 2021).
[18] Blondin v. Milton Town Sch. Dist., 251 A.3d 959, 391 Educ. L. Rep. 906 (Vt. 2021).
[19] School Bd. of Broward Cnty. v. McCall, 322 So.3d 655, 394 Educ. L. Rep. 423 (Fla. Dist. Ct. App. 2021).

First Amendment Issues

The U.S. Supreme Court, in an 8–1 decision, ruled in favor of a high school cheerleader in Pennsylvania who faced a long-term suspension from the team after disparaging the team and school community via social media.[20] After failing to make the varsity cheerleading team, the plaintiff posted her profane communication. The Court affirmed earlier rulings that the speech, albeit uncouth, did not satisfy the material disruption standard set by *Tinker v. Des Moines*. Perhaps even more critical to the decision was that the plaintiff's social media use was conducted off school grounds and after-school hours. Although the Court refrained from fully resolving somewhat variable parameters on school officials' ability to discipline students for off-campus speech, they noted that the plaintiff's argument, in this case, satisfied three prongs of deliberation under these specific circumstances: (a) the lack of *in loco parentis* in schools, (b) the difficulties regulating non-school speech, and (c) the need for schools to remain "nurseries of democracy."

A group of African-American cheerleaders at a public university knelt to protest police brutality while the national anthem was presented before a football game. After that incident, the county sheriff and a state legislator called the university president, urging that this should be prevented from occurring again. The university instituted a policy for cheerleaders to wait in the stadium tunnel while the anthem played, but this policy was abolished after public outcry. One cheerleader filed suit, claiming her First Amendment rights had been violated.[21] She claimed the sheriff and state legislator conspired based on her race to prohibit her from exercising her rights of expression, and the sheriff conspired to deprive her of her rights because she was protesting the actions of law enforcement. A federal district court in Georgia dismissed her claims, and the Eleventh Circuit affirmed. In its ruling, the court cited a case prohibiting plaintiffs from basing § 1985(3) claims "on classes defined by the conduct the defendants oppose." The court also noted members of all racial classes on both sides of the debate regarding kneeling during the national anthem that was not based on animus toward a particular race.

In another unsuccessful First Amendment claim by a coach, the 9th Circuit upheld summary judgment in favor of the school district

---

[20] Mahanoy Area Sch. Dist. v. B. L. ex rel. Levy, 141 S. Ct. 2038, 391 Educ. L. Rep. 19 (2021).
[21] Dean v. Warren, 12 F.4th 1248, 395 Educ. L. Rep. 51 (11th Cir. 2021).

defendants after an assistant high school football coach refused to stop his post-game kneel prayer at the 50-yard line of the field.[22] School district personnel had repeatedly asked the coach to stop this practice, as it involved many members of the team and was a public spectacle to the point of violating the Establishment Clause; after initially resorting to alternate prayer timing, the coach announced (to both school officials and local media) that he would continue the original 50-yard line practice with the team. Upon suspension from his position, the plaintiff filed a First Amendment claim, but the court found that his publicized prayers occurred while in the capacity of a public employee—thus rendering his speech unprotected. Moreover, the defendants' efforts to accommodate the plaintiff's religious practices in a manner that would satisfy the Establishment Clause were narrowly tailored enough to pass judicial muster.

A free speech issue also arose in Michigan after a new high school principal failed to rehire the longstanding head coach of a men's basketball team.[23] The former coach—who had initiated and previously settled the case in civil court—filed a renewed complaint after not being rehired for the upcoming academic year. This time, the coach filed a First Amendment claim, arguing the decision not to rehire him was suggestive of retaliation from the original lawsuit and critical comments he had made to media entities about the school principal's decision-making. The district court found, however, that the coach's speech failed to meet the standard of a matter of public concern needed for a successful First Amendment claim.

NCAA Issues

In 2021, the U.S. Supreme Court ruled in yet another of the long line of antitrust lawsuits challenging the NCAA's authority to limit the benefits and compensation student-athletes may receive.[24] Previously, a California federal district court ruled to preserve the decades-old deference to the NCAA's amateurism rules but found that limiting benefits outside of the athletic context, such as

---

[22] Kennedy v. Bremerton Sch. Dist., 991 F.3d 1004, 388 Educ. L. Rep. 101 (9th Cir. 2021).

[23] Jordan v. Stroughter, 520 F. Supp. 3d 892, 394 Educ. L. Rep. 221 (E.D. Mich. 2021).

[24] Nat. Coll. Athletic Ass'n v. Alston, 141 S. Ct. 2141, 391 Educ. L. Rep. 45 (2021).

scholarships for graduate or vocational school, was illegal. The NCAA appealed, and the Court ultimately upheld the lower court rulings. In its opinion, the Court noted the NCAA's position as the sole entity in the marketplace for college-aged athletes and that the member institutions utilize their monopsony power to suppress competition and arbitrarily limit the amount and types of benefits permissible. For example, student-athletes can apply for support through the NCAA's "Student Assistance Fund" and "Academic Enhancement Fund" to cover costs such as travel expenses, clothing, magazine subscriptions, postgraduate tuition, and course-related supplies. The Court rejected the defense that these provisions preserved amateurism, finding that providing funds for educationally related expenses in no way could be confused as equating to a salary.

An appellate court in Indiana, where the NCAA is headquartered, reviewed a motion from the NCAA requesting the state adopt the apex deposition doctrine, which would preclude the plaintiffs in the more than 500 negligence lawsuits claiming the organization knew of the dangers associated with concussive head injuries yet failed to act appropriately from repeatedly deposing chief officials—specifically the president of the NCAA, its chief legal counsel, and its chief medical officer.[25] The court rejected the appeal, finding that information obtained through deposing top NCAA officials would be of value in gathering evidence to proceed with the lawsuits. In another case, an Indiana appellate court upheld a trial court's denial of injunctive relief for a broadcasting network, which had a multiyear exclusive contract with the NCAA to broadcast the "March Madness" men's basketball tournament and breached the contract after failing to make the second installment of annual payments when the 2020 tournament was canceled as a result of the COVID-19 pandemic.[26] The court found injunctive relief not to be a correct remedy. Still, it noted that other legal remedies could be pursued regarding the economic impact on the broadcasting network for its loss of the contract.

---

[25] Nat. Coll. Athletic Ass'n v. Finnerty, 170 N.E.3d 1111, 392 Educ. L. Rep. 957 (Ind. Ct. App. 2021).
[26] Westwood One Radio Networks, LLC v. Nat'l Coll. Athletic Ass'n, 172 N.E.3d 294, 393 Educ. L. Rep. 824 (Ind. Ct. App. 2021).

Student-Athlete & Agent Conflict

In 2021, the Second Circuit heard two cases related to a scheme in which agents paid the families and coaches of student-athletes to entice them to play with certain universities and then affiliate with particular sports agents should they reach the professional leagues. In the first case, the defendants—one an agent for Adidas and the other an upstart professional players agent—alleged that although they violated NCAA violations by providing inducements to student-athletes' families, they did nothing illegal.[27] A federal district court disagreed, and the appellate court affirmed that decision. In its opinion, the Second Circuit recounted the lengths the defendants went to conceal wire fraud payments and ruled the payments they funneled through certain universities equated to defrauding the government via federally funded institutions that could have used those resources to provide financial aid to other students. In the second case, the defendants were convicted by a jury of bribing university basketball coaches.[28] On appeal, the Second Circuit rejected the defendants' argument that the nexus between the enticements an agent of a federally funded entity (in this instance, the coaches) receives and the funds the government institution receives (here, the universities) must be commercial in nature. The court declined to broaden or abridge the language of 18 U.S.C. § 666, which prohibits bribery in federally funded programs, noting that Congress's intent in creating this law was to preserve the integrity of government agencies.

---

[27] U.S. v. Gatto, 986 F.3d 104, 386 Educ. L. Rep. 48 (2d Cir. 2021).
[28] U.S. v. Dawkins, 999 F.3d 767, 391 Educ. L. Rep. 88 (2d Cir. 2021).

Conclusion

The cases covered in this chapter involved student-athletes, facilities, coaches, spectators, and representative organizations at both the K–12 and higher education levels. Despite the narrow focus on sports, litigation from 2021 reflected broader patterns of persisting legal issues in the educational pipeline as a whole. Drawing from among these cases, one particular observation stands out: these cases presented a range of efforts to hold school personnel accountable for student safety. Some cases presented a strict line of accountability or restricted one's ability for free expression. In contrast, others allowed students, coaches, and other stakeholders to function with limited liability or wide freedoms to express themselves. Another legal observation from the cases in this chapter pertains to the higher education context. Several cases continue the longstanding debate as to whether intercollegiate amateurism is a recognized principle and to what extent courts will or should recognize that notion. Whether judicial precedent evolved or remained steadfast, many legal issues concerning sports in 2021 comprised situations where educational stakeholders must continually respond with equitable, intentional operations.

Alphabetical List of Cases

Belles v. Wilkes-Barre Area Sch. Dist.
Berndsen v. N.D. Univ. Sys.
Blondin v. Milton Town Sch. Dist.
Dean v. Warren
Does 1-2 v. Regents of the Univ. of Minn.
Du Bois v. Bd. of Regents of Univ. of Minn.
Elalouf v. Sch. Bd. of Broward Cnty.
Gagliardi v. Sacred Heart Univ.
Girard v. Int'l Ass'n of Approved Basketball Officials, Inc.
Grady v. Chenango Valley Ctr. Sch. Dist.
Gordon v. Jordan Sch. Dist.
Jones v. Univ. of Detroit Mercy
Jordan v. Stroughter
Kennedy v. Bremerton Sch. Dist.
Mahanoy Area Sch. Dist. v. B. L. ex rel. Levy
Miller v. Cardinal Mooney High Sch.
Nat. Coll. Athletic Ass'n v. Alston
Nat. Coll. Athletic Ass'n v. Finnerty
Posso v. Niagara Univ.
School Bd. of Broward Cnty. v. McCall
Secky v. New Paltz Ctr. Sch. Dist.
Taylor-Travis v. Jackson State Univ.
U.S. v. Dawkins
U.S. v. Gatto
Warmington v. Bd. of Regents of Univ. of Minn.
Westwood One Radio Networks, LLC v. Nat'l Coll. Athletic Ass'n

Cases by Jurisdiction

FEDERAL CASES

U.S. Supreme Court
Mahanoy Area Sch. Dist. v. B. L. *ex rel.* Levy
Nat. Coll. Athletic Ass'n v. Alston

Second Circuit
Gagliardi v. Sacred Heart Univ.
Girard v. Int'l Ass'n of Approved Basketball Officials, Inc.
U.S. v. Dawkins
U.S. v. Gatto

Sports

New York
Posso v. Niagara Univ.

Third Circuit
Belles v. Wilkes-Barre Area Sch. Dist.

Fifth Circuit
Taylor-Travis v. Jackson State Univ.

Sixth Circuit

Michigan
Jones v. Univ. of Detroit Mercy
Jordan v. Stroughter

Eighth Circuit
Berndsen v. N.D. Univ. Sys.
Du Bois v. Bd. of Regents of Univ. of Minn.
Does 1-2 v. Regents of the Univ. of Minn.
Warmington v. Bd. of Regents of Univ. of Minn.

Ninth Circuit
Kennedy v. Bremerton Sch. Dist.

Tenth Circuit

Utah
Gordon v. Jordan Sch. Dist.

Eleventh Circuit
Dean v. Warren

STATE & D.C. COURT CASES

Florida
Elalouf v. Sch. Bd. of Broward Cnty
School Bd. of Broward Cnty. v. McCall

Indiana
Nat. Coll. Athletic Ass'n v. Finnerty
Westwood One Radio Networks, LLC v. Nat'l Coll. Athletic Ass'n

New York
Grady v. Chenango Valley Cent. Sch. Dist.
Secky v. New Paltz Cent. Sch. Dist.

Ohio
Miller v. Cardinal Mooney High Sch.

Vermont
Blondin v. Milton Town Sch. Dist.

Chapter 8

HIGHER EDUCATION ADMINISTRATION & FACULTY

Jacob A. Bennett, Ph.D.[1] and Todd A. DeMitchell[2]

Introduction	265
Admissions	265
COVID-19	266
Discrimination Involving Faculty and Staff	266
Age	266
Disability	268
Pay	269
Racial/Ethnic/National Origin	270
Retaliation	273
Sex/Gender	275
Due Process	279
Employment	279
Faculty	280
Staff	283
Institutional Issues	284
First Amendment	288
Press	288
Religion	289
Speech	290
Labor Relations	291

---

[1] COVID Testing & Outreach Manager, Simmons University, Boston, Mass.
[2] John & H. Irene Peters Endowed Professor Emeritus of Education Law & Labor, University of New Hampshire, Durham, N.H.

Torts 293
Conclusion 295
Alphabetical List of Cases... 296
Cases by Jurisdiction... 297

Introduction

This chapter includes summaries of cases reported in 2021 that involved issues affecting higher education institutions (HEIs) and their administrators, staff, faculty, students, and families. The issues considered and decisions rendered suggest that high-profile issues like affirmative action and other race-conscious policies in admissions and elsewhere will continue to garner attention, that COVID-19 still played a role in the day-to-day operations of HEIs, if at a more moderate clip than the previous year; that discrimination cases regarding issues of race or sex were more prevalent than other forms; that pay equity continues to be a thorny issue; that decision to end or non-renew employment of faculty can be contentious; that unemployment claims for adjuncts face steep challenges baked into law and employment practice; and that the non-academic activities and operations of HEIs, including construction, sporting events, and fraternity parties, present significant risks to participants and institutions. These cases will be instructive to administrators, scholars, and policymakers involved in various issues affecting HEIs.

Admissions

The Connecticut federal district court considered a petition to intervene filed by a nonprofit membership organization opposing affirmative action in university admissions. The intervenor's proposed complaint would seek declaratory and injunctive relief, as did the United States in its original filing as plaintiff against the private university, alleging race and national origin discrimination under Title VI. The court considered two bases for intervention: as of right and by permission. Rule 24(a) of the Federal Rules of Civil Procedure provides that courts must permit intervention to anyone who timely files, can show an interest in the action, and demonstrate possible impairment of that interest based on the action and that no other party to the action adequately protects that interest. The court found the federal government provided adequate coverage of the stated interest. Rule 24(b) states that the court may permit intervention to anyone whose claim shares common questions of law or fact with the main action, and Second Circuit precedent holds that permissive intervention is within the discretion of the court and considers substantially the same factors as in of right claims. The district court denied the motion to intervene, and the U.S. withdrew its complaint following President Biden's inauguration.[3]

COVID-19

A university's interim president issued a directive on mask-wearing in campus buildings in response to the COVID-19 pandemic. The attorney general issued a letter stating that the directive of universal mask-wearing violated a state proviso. The interim president trimmed the requirement to only apply to university healthcare facilities and campus transportation. A professor petitioned the South Carolina Supreme Court for expedited review seeking a declaration that the state's proviso did not prohibit mandated universal mask-wearing at the university.[4] The court accepted the petition based on significant public interest. The court did not accept the attorney general's argument that the controversy presented a political question and was thus not a justiciable controversy, instead finding that the matter was a question of statutory interpretation. The court cited the clear and unambiguous language that the proviso prohibits discrimination against unvaccinated students, faculty, and staff and does not prohibit a universal mask mandate. The court sided with the professor, noting that the proviso prohibited state universities from requiring students receiving the COVID-19 vaccination to be on campus without a face covering but did not prohibit a universal mask mandate.

Discrimination Involving Faculty and Staff

Age

In a Seventh Circuit case from Illinois, the plaintiff was removed from his position as department chair because of a Title IX complaint brought against him.[5] The Title IX complaint was resolved through his dismissal as chair to address the department's toxic environment. The former chair brought an age discrimination suit against the university, alleging retaliation for his refusal to

---

[3] U.S. v. Yale Univ., 337 F.R.D. 35, 386 Educ. L. Rep. 358 (D. Conn. 2021).
[4] Creswick v. Univ. of S.C., 862 S.E.2d 706, 395 Educ. L. Rep. 434 (S.C. 2021).
[5] Sinha v. Bradley Univ., 995 F.3d 568, 389 Educ. L. Rep. 41 (7th Cir. 2021).

implement age-discriminatory policies against older employees. This case was rejected by an Illinois district court which stated that no discriminatory animus evidence was presented. Next, the plaintiff attempted to use a "cat's paw" theory invoked when a biased subordinate manipulated a decision-maker who did not harbor discriminatory animus. This approach failed. The Seventh Circuit affirmed the lower court's decision.

In Missouri, a former public safety director sued the university and her supervisor for a hostile work environment, tangible employment action, and retaliation based on age, gender, and color under state law.[6] A public university terminated the plaintiff for insubordination, failure to meet expectations, and lack of institutional fit. The state trial court entered judgment in favor of the plaintiff on her retaliation claim and awarded attorneys' fees, costs, and expenses, and denied the defendants' motion for judgment notwithstanding the verdict. The university appealed. The Missouri appellate court held that the university could be liable even if the supervisor was exonerated and the HR staffer resigned; sufficient evidence established discrimination and hostile work environment based on age or gender; sufficient evidence established termination was a reprisal for the plaintiff's engagement in a protected activity; and the plaintiff was entitled to attorneys' fees on appeal. The court affirmed the trial court's judgment and award of damages and attorneys' fees but reversed and remanded for further proceedings regarding litigation expenses.

In California, a female employee sued the university for age and gender discrimination and retaliation under state law.[7] The plaintiff claimed she had been overlooked for promotion and sidelined due to her age and gender, citing the ascent of a younger employee. After complaining to the university to no avail, the plaintiff asserts that the university punished her. She resigned and sued, and the trial court granted the defendant's motion for summary judgment. The plaintiff appealed to the California appellate court. The court found that evidence had been excluded at the trial court level presenting genuine issues of material fact as to whether the defendant's proffered legitimate rationale was pretextual and precluded summary judgment. The court pointed to three factors that cloud the pretext question: a discriminatory stray remark made by an influential advisor regarding "want[ing] someone younger" for a

---

[6] Sinha v. Bradley Univ., 995 F.3d 568, 389 Educ. L. Rep. 41 (7th Cir. 2021).
[7] Jorgensen v. Loyola Marymount Univ., 283 Cal. Rptr. 3d 737, 394 Educ. L. Rep. 1030 (Cal. Ct. App. 2021).

position, clear pay differentials between male and female associate deans, and other sources unrelated to the plaintiff had criticized management in question in this case. The appellate court reversed summary judgment, remanded for further proceedings, and awarded costs to the plaintiff/appellant.

Disability

A former employee filed charges against a public university, alleging disability discrimination and retaliation, violating the Americans with Disabilities Act (ADA), state human rights law, and Family and Medical Leave Act (FMLA). The plaintiff, diagnosed with atrial fibrillation in 2012, was terminated in 2017 after a series of poor performance evaluations. A federal district court in Texas dismissed all claims without prejudice, holding that they were barred by sovereign immunity. The Fifth Circuit heard the case on appeal and considered whether Congress validly abrogated state sovereign immunity for ADA and FMLA purposes and whether the state knowingly waived immunity in accepting federal funds. On the abrogation questions, the court held that while statutory language purported to allow both ADA and FMLA claims, Supreme Court decisions have held that Congress exceeded authority in such abrogation. Regarding the state waiving immunity, the Fifth Circuit held that neither the ADA nor FMLA required waiver under 42 USC § 2000d-7(a)(1), and state law required waiver of immunity in state courts but not in federal courts. The dismissals were all affirmed.[8]

A female adjunct professor brought an action against a community college and several officers in their official capacities, alleging violations of the ADA, Rehabilitation Act, § 1983, and state human rights law.[9] By clear and convincing evidence, a federal magistrate judge in New York found that the plaintiff had forged evidence crucial to her claimed disability and the accommodations sought. Rather than dismiss the case, a district court judge ordered the plaintiff to pay the defendants' attorneys' fees, and a $5,000 monetary sanction also precluded forged documents and included a negative inference instruction for future proceedings. The defendants moved for summary judgment, and the plaintiff moved for reconsideration of sanctions. Considering those motions and the

---

[8] Sullivan v. Tex. A&M Univ. Sys., 986 F.3d 593, 387 Educ. L. Rep. 43 (5th Cir. 2021).
[9] Esposito v. Suffolk Cnty. Cmty. Coll., 517 F. Supp. 3d 126, 393 Educ. L. Rep. 307 (E.D.N.Y. 2021).

plaintiff's additional problematic actions uncovered in *de novo* review, a federal district court in New York vacated the award of attorneys' fees, affirmed the monetary sanction, and dismissed the plaintiff's claims in their entirety. The defendants' motion for summary judgment was deemed withdrawn in light of the decision.

Pay

A Black male employee alleged gender-based discrimination claims under the Equal Pay Act (EPA) and race and gender-based discrimination and retaliation under Title VII. [10] The plaintiff worked as a compensation analyst at a public university and alleged discrimination as evidenced by the much higher starting salary, disparate increases offered to a White female colleague, and retaliation for actions taken after he filed a discrimination claim with the university. The Sixth Circuit heard the case and reversed the district court's grant of the university's motion for summary judgment. Finding that the university never articulated a legitimate, non-retaliatory reason for the adverse employment action and identifying significant factual inconsistencies in the university's rationale for the wage differences, the circuit court held that fact issues precluded summary judgment on the EPA and Title VII claims and remanded the case for further proceedings.

A tenured female professor filed suit against a public university, alleging violations of the EPA, Title VII, Title IX, Fourteenth Amendment's Equal Protection Clause, state law and state constitution Equal Rights Amendment, and breach of contract.[11] She based her claims on disparities between her salary and male professors in the department, and her assessment of the disparity was reinforced by other analyses performed by university staff. When the plaintiff requested a retroactive merit raise and was denied, she filed suit in district court, and the defendants sought summary judgment. When the Oregon district court granted summary judgment on all claims, the plaintiff appealed to the Ninth Circuit. Finding no genuine issue of material fact concerning claims under Title IX or state law or disparate treatment under Title VII, the Ninth Circuit affirmed the Oregon district court on those claims. On the claims under the EPA, state law, and disparate impact under Title VII, the court reversed and remanded for further proceedings.

---

[10] Briggs v. Univ. of Cincinnati, 11 F.4th 498, 394 Educ. L. Rep. 117 (6th Cir. 2021).
[11] Freyd v. Univ. of Or., 990 F.3d 1211, 388 Educ. L. Rep. 3 (9th Cir. 2021).

A separate opinion dissented in part and concurred in part, suggesting that all motions for summary judgment should be granted except the state law claim concerning salary discrimination.

Racial/Ethnic/National Origin

A Black female applicant filed charges against a public university's board of trustees, equal opportunity office, and an administrator in both official and individual capacities, alleging race discrimination in the university's decision not to hire her.[12] A White applicant was hired when four Black finalists were also under consideration by an all-White committee and despite the selected applicant failing to meet both required and preferred qualifications, which the plaintiff did meet. A federal district court in Massachusetts granted the defendants' motion for summary judgment, which the plaintiff appealed. The district court had adopted a magistrate judge's report that found no reasonable factfinder could find racial motivation in the decision not to hire. Still, the plaintiff had previously objected to the report on the grounds that it failed to view the record in the light most favorable to the plaintiff and failed to consider a statement and affidavit from the plaintiff alleging disputed facts. The First Circuit heard the appeal and held that fact remained concerning whether the university's proffered reason was pretextual. The underlying order was vacated, and the case was remanded for further proceedings.

An association of "faculty, alumni, and students opposed to racial preferences" sued a private university, its law school and law review, the United States, and the Secretary of Education, alleging Title VI and Title IX violations in selection processes for law review editors and articles, as well as in faculty hiring.[13] A federal district court in New York granted the defendants' motions to dismiss for lack of standing, which the plaintiffs appealed. The Second Circuit heard the appeal and affirmed the district court's ruling. While the plaintiffs argued that considerations of race and gender in the selection processes subjected their members to unlawful discrimination and possible "career-altering" harm resulting from rejecting their articles, the Second Circuit found that they failed to state an injury-in-fact and affirmed dismissal without prejudice. A concurring opinion observed that the defendants failed to satisfy the

---

[12] Taite v. Bridgewater State Univ. Bd. of Trs., 999 F.3d 86, 390 Educ. L. Rep. 884 (1st Cir. 2021).
[13] Faculty v. N.Y. Univ., 11 F.4th 68, 394 Educ. L. Rep. 79 (2d Cir. 2021).

first prong of Title III standing, requiring a showing of injury-in-fact, and that is enough to resolve the appeal.

A Black male professor sued a private college, alleging race discrimination in violation of Title VI.[14] Following denying his tenure bid, the plaintiff claimed the adverse tenure decision had been tainted by race discrimination; another contemporaneous order resolves several claims, leaving only the Title VI claim discussed here. An Illinois district court granted the defendants' motion for summary judgment based on a state statute of limitations. The plaintiff appealed, and the Seventh Circuit sought to determine whether a two-year or five-year state statute of limitations applied where no limitations period had been specified for Title VI claims. Addressing this question of first impression for the court, the court noted that every other circuit to do so had determined that courts should rely on the limitation's periods for personal injury tort when considering Title VI claims. The court held that Illinois' two-year limitation on personal injury suits applies and affirmed the lower court.

A tenured Black male professor from Nigeria appealed two issues to the Eighth Circuit after the Minnesota district court granted the defendants' motions to dismiss and for summary judgment with prejudice.[15] The plaintiff claimed discrimination regarding class schedules, resource allocation, and program participation and a retaliation claim for filing a 2012 lawsuit against the university. On appeal, the court upheld the summary judgment for individual defendants asserting that the suit could not be brought under 42 U.S.C. § 1981 and instead had to be brought under § 1983. The federal appellate court also held that the plaintiff failed to establish the prima facia case requiring a demonstration of causation of the but-for test, asserting the time between the protected activity and the discrimination was not close enough to raise an inference of causation.

A former instructor of software engineering at a state university sued that university for race discrimination and retaliation in violation of Title VII and state civil rights law.[16] The factual record established in an amended complaint from the plaintiff, a Black man, showed disparate treatment by his supervisor compared to the

---

[14] Monroe v. Columbia Coll. Chicago, 990 F.3d 1098, 387 Educ. L. Rep. 484 (7th Cir. 2021).
[15] Onyiah v. St. Cloud State Univ., 5 F.4th 926, 393 Educ. L. Rep. 66 (8th Cir. 2021).
[16] Baker v. Ferris State Univ., 516 F. Supp. 3d 735, 393 Educ. L. Rep. 240 (W.D. Mich. 2021).

treatment of other non-Black instructors in the same department. The university's board filed for judgment on the pleadings, a motion granted in part and denied in part by the district court in Michigan. The court held that the capacity to sue and be sued attaches to the board, the plaintiff could only sue the board and not the university itself, the board enjoys Eleventh Amendment immunity, the board has not waived that immunity by participating in litigation to this point, and the plaintiff had exhausted administrative remedies and could proceed on his claim for damages. The court dismissed two claims filed under state civil rights law but denied the board's motion to dismiss the remaining claims under Title VII.

A New York-based Israeli corporation with a primary purpose of fighting anti-Israeli discrimination was denied access to career services offered by a U.S.-funded university based in Lebanon, after which the Israeli corporation filed suit alleging national origin discrimination in violation of Title VI of the Civil Rights Act, as well as state and city laws.[17] The university moved for dismissal for lack of subject matter jurisdiction and failure to state a claim. A federal trial court in New York granted the motion and dismissed the case without prejudice, holding that the plaintiff's Title VI national origin discrimination claim was not sufficiently alleged and that supplemental jurisdiction over state and city law claims could not be exercised in this case.

A former community college police officer, who is White, sued the college and Black campus police chief, alleging racial discrimination, harassment, and retaliation. After the plaintiff expressed interest in a lateral opening on another campus, the chief said he planned to give him a promotion to backfill a supervisory position. The plaintiff did not apply for the new opening, but the chief hired someone else into the backfill position. The plaintiff alleged the new sergeant, a Black man, engaged in discriminatory practices after the plaintiff's EEOC complaint. The Ohio trial court denied the defendants' motion for judgment on the pleadings and motion to strike the plaintiff's request for punitive damages and attorneys' fees; the defendants then filed this appeal. The Ohio appellate court heard the appeal only to review alleged errors resulting in the denial of immunity. The appellate court affirmed that sovereign immunity applied to claims against the chief and the complaint sufficiently alleged conduct manifestly outside the scope of employment. A concurrence

---

[17] Bibliotechnical Athenaeum v. Am. Univ. of Beirut, 527 F. Supp. 3d 625, 395 Educ. L. Rep. 330 (S.D.N.Y. 2021).

discussed exceptions to immunity for employees of political subdivisions.[18] In another Ohio appellate case, a White adjunct professor filed a complaint of discrimination and harassment when a Black female law student allegedly challenged some of the course requirements. Dissatisfied with the university's handling of his complaint, the plaintiff filed a discrimination charge with the EEOC, which dismissed the complaint, and retaliation charges with the state's Civil Rights Commission. The instructor's contract was not renewed, leading to other judicial filings, including a third lawsuit for discrimination. The Ohio trial court dismissed all causes of action. The Ohio appellate court affirmed, citing absolute privilege and res judicata.[19]

Retaliation

A female professor sued a public university and two public university systems alleging sex discrimination, retaliation, and a hostile work environment.[20] The plaintiff was denied tenure at one university and subsequently was denied a new position at another university in the same public system. The denial of tenure was tied to reviewers' negative recommendations, but the plaintiff alleged it was because of sex discrimination and retaliation for complaining about her clinical workload. The new position was denied after her former supervisor responded to a reference check. The two suits were consolidated, and a federal district court in Texas granted summary judgment to the defendants. On appeal, the Fifth Circuit raised concerns about the district judge's conduct, including the judge's dismissive and prejudiced commentary. The appellate court held that the district court erred in dismissing claims against the state university systems *sua sponte*, that it abused discretion in refusing to allow the plaintiff to conduct sufficient discovery, and that a new judge should be appointed on remand.

A female emergency room physician filed suit against her private university employer, its hospital, and related divisions, seeking damages for gender-based discrimination and retaliation under Title VII, state human rights law, city ordinance, and

---

[18] Holmes v. Cuyahoga Cmty. Coll., 169 N.E. 3d 8, 390 Educ. L. Rep. 1213 (Ohio Ct. App. 2021).

[19] Newman v. Univ. of Dayton, 172 N.E.3d 1122, 394 Educ. L. Rep. 340 (Ohio Ct. App. 2021

[20] Miller v. Sam Houston State Univ., 986 F.3d 880, 386 Educ. L. Rep. 115 (5th Cir. 2021).

retaliation and interference under the Family Medical Leave Act.[21] The defendants moved for summary judgment. A federal district court in Pennsylvania held that the plaintiff's pretermination hearing conversations regarding gender disparities on campus constituted opposition activity protected by Title VII; the plaintiff established causal links between the protected activity and her termination; fact issues persisted concerning whether the defendants' proffered rationale was pretextual, whether the termination was gender-based, and whether the plaintiff's use of FMLA was a negative factor in her termination decision; and that emails sent by an administrator did not interfere with the plaintiff's FMLA benefits. All claims except FMLA interference may proceed to trial.

A female employee sued a public university, alleging sex discrimination and retaliation in violation of state human rights law.[22] The plaintiff was terminated during restructuring and declined to participate in the layoff and transition assistant program because it required releasing any employment-related claims. The plaintiff believed she was the victim of sex discrimination and retaliation but had not filed charges. Following termination, the plaintiff became employed by a nonprofit center within the university, an independent legal entity neither owned nor controlled by the university. The center laid off the plaintiff; she again received the layoff participation form, but this time signed, believing it only pertained to the center and not the university. The Missouri trial court entered judgment on the pleadings in favor of the university, stating that the plaintiff had released the defendants from liability. The plaintiff appealed, arguing an affirmative defense that the release on which the defendants relied resulted from a mutual mistake. The Missouri appellate court reversed and remanded for further proceedings, citing the material factual dispute as a bar to judgment on pleadings. In another Missouri appellate case, a university extension program was directed to move to a new office.[23] The supervisors experienced problems with a project director during the moving process, and program assistants complained about their supervisor. The supervisors asked the director to take paid leave in

---

[21] Mammen v. Thomas Jefferson Univ., 523 F. Supp. 3d 702, 394 Educ. L. Rep. 821 (E.D. Pa. 2021).
[22] McGruder v. Curators of Univ. of Mo., 617 S.W.3d 464, 387 Educ. L. Rep. 391] (Mo. Ct. App. 2021).
[23] Wille v. Curators of Univ. of Mo., 627 S.W.3d 56, 393 Educ. L. Rep. 980 (Mo. Ct. App. 2021).

response to the complaints, but the supervisors continued to receive complaints when she returned. The supervisors decided to terminate her. The director then had a work-related injury and took workers' compensation leave. Upon her return, she was terminated. She sued for retaliation for filing a workers' compensation claim. The Missouri trial court dismissed her claim because it was barred by sovereign immunity. The Missouri appellate court affirmed the dismissal and the denial of equitable relief because the termination decision was made before her accident.

Sex/Gender

A former female professor filed claims against a public college, alleging discrimination based on gender, national origin, and pregnancy, violating Title VII and state antidiscrimination law.[24] The plaintiff filed a motion to proceed anonymously, which a New Jersey district court denied. The Third Circuit heard the case on appeal under the collateral order doctrine that grants jurisdiction over certain non-final district court orders. The Third Circuit held that the district court did not abuse its discretion in denying the motion to proceed anonymously. While the plaintiff argued that using her real name would expose her to harassment, reputational damage, economic harm, and professional stigma, as well as to public scrutiny of personal information regarding her minor children, pregnancy, and miscarriage, the court found her arguments unconvincing.

A female coach filed charges against a public university, alleging sex discrimination and retaliation under Title VII and Title IX, and state claims of breach of contract, breach of the implied covenant of good faith and fair dealing, and invasion of privacy.[25] The plaintiff was the subject of several complaints made by team members. The university investigated, required repayment of misappropriated funds, and terminated the plaintiff. When a newspaper published a story about the termination, the plaintiff sued. A jury found in the plaintiff's favor on breach of contract but not Title VII or Title IX, and a Mississippi federal district court entered judgment in the plaintiff's favor for invasion of privacy. Both the plaintiff and the defendant appealed. The Fifth Circuit affirmed the breach of contract award, holding the plaintiff's termination was without

---

[24] Doe v. Coll. of N.J., 997 F.3d 489, 390 Educ. L. Rep. 470 (3d Cir. 2021).
[25] Taylor-Travis v. Jackson State Univ., 984 F.3d 1107, 385 Educ. L. Rep. 458 (5th Cir. 2021).

cause; reversed the invasion of privacy award, holding facts disclosed by the defendant were of legitimate public concern; affirmed that there was no cause of action under Title IX and denied retrial; and remanded with instruction to enter judgment in favor of defendant.

A male professor sued a public university and individuals, alleging a hostile work environment and gender discrimination violating Title IX and state law defamation and intentional infliction of emotional distress claims.[26] The plaintiff alleges that his relationship with a female international student was distorted by his supervisor and colleagues as inappropriate, compromising his ability to evaluate her impartially. The plaintiff pursued an internal investigation of a hostile work environment and discrimination and pressed charges when the investigation did not materialize. A Colorado federal district court granted summary judgment to the defendants on all counts. The Tenth Circuit heard the appeal on the Title IX judgment. Finding that the plaintiff decontextualized his account of what his supervisor said in the Title IX report against him, the Tenth Circuit affirmed the grant of summary judgment, finding that the plaintiff had not established a prima facie case for either hostile work environment or disparate treatment, failing to allege severe or pervasive acts of discrimination or any inference of discrimination based on gender.

In another Tenth Circuit case from Oklahoma, a female professor filed charges against a public university and state university system, alleging Title VII violations including sex discrimination, retaliation, and a hostile work environment.[27] The plaintiff, a transgender woman who transitioned after hire, filed charges after being denied tenure and the opportunity to reapply for tenure prior to, ultimately, being terminated. An Oklahoma federal district court denied the defendants' motion *in limine* and motion for summary judgment, granted the plaintiff's request for front pay, denied a motion for reinstatement and reconsideration, and applied a damages cap under Title VII. On appeal, the Tenth Circuit held the trial court did not abuse discretion in allowing a tenured expert to testify; the question of sex discrimination was for the jury; the trial court did abuse discretion in determining that extreme hostility made reinstatement infeasible and that this was a proper remedy; the trial court committed error in calculating front pay and abused

---

[26] Throupe v. Univ. of Denver, 988 F.3d 1243, 386 Educ. L. Rep. 615 (10th Cir. 2021).

[27] Tudor v. Se. Okla. State Univ., 13 F.4th 1019, 395 Educ. L. Rep. 99 (10th Cir. 2021).

discretion when determining roles at a state university and a community college was substantially equivalent; and the awards cap did not violate the Seventh Amendment Reexamination Clause.

After his termination, a male professor sued a private music college, alleging the college violated Title IX, Title VII, and state law.[28] He had been under Title IX investigation after a student filed a claim against him. The professor denied the claims and filed his own Title IX claim with the college. The college never issued a complaint against the student, suggesting that the professor's complaint may be retaliatory and falsely implying that no further action could be taken. The college issued its report, including various sanctions on the professor. After administrative leave, the plaintiff responded to questions from students about the investigation and shared his opinion that the college's process was unfair. His chair learned of the discussion and expressed disappointment before terminating the plaintiff. A Massachusetts federal district court held the employment discrimination claims brought under Title IX are not preempted by Title VII, the plaintiff had plausibly alleged causal links between a protected activity and his termination, and state law claims were preempted by § 301 of the Labor Management Relations Act.

A male former tenured professor sued a public university and individuals alleging Title VII and § 1983 claims. The plaintiff alleged his firing was discriminatory based on sexual orientation.[29] The plaintiff was placed on administrative leave for concerns over compliance issues but later received notice that the board sought his termination for "gross professional misconduct." The plaintiff sued in an Alabama federal district court, and the individuals and board moved to dismiss for failure to state a claim. The court granted the individuals' motion and held they exercised a discretionary function when firing the plaintiff. On the Title VII claims against the board, the court held that the plaintiff failed to show that the right to be free from discrimination based on sexual orientation was clearly established at the time of firing as *Bostock v. Clayton* was still pending[30] and granted the board's motion to dismiss retaliation

---

[28] Farzinpour v. Berklee Coll. of Music, 516 F. Supp. 3d 33, 393 Educ. L. Rep. 195 (D. Mass. 2021).

[29] Jones v. Bd. of Trs. for Ala. Agr. & Mech. Univ., 526 F. Supp. 3d 1100, 395 Educ. L. Rep. 264 (N.D. Ala. 2021).

[30] Bostock v. Clayton, 140 S. Ct. 1731 (2020) (declaring discrimination "because of" an employee's sex, includes discrimination for being homosexual or being a transgender person violates Title VII).

claims; the court did allow a Title VII disparate treatment claim to proceed.

A dean filed a sexual harassment claim with his university and with the state's Human Rights Commission (HRC) against his supervisor.[31] He alleged that her touching his arm and back was inappropriate and had occurred for several years before filing his complaints. The university's internal investigation found the claims unsupported. The HRC eventually found that the supervisor sexually harassed the plaintiff and awarded $80,000. Both the university and the plaintiff appealed the trial court's decision. The Montana Supreme Court reversed the lower court's order and instituted the awards for discrimination and retaliation. The dissent agreed with the retaliation finding but not the finding that the sexual harassment had not been proven by the plaintiff.

A female employee sued a community college alleging sexual orientation discrimination and that her termination violated state whistleblower law. The plaintiff alleged that she revealed that she is a lesbian to her supervisor and colleagues and, after that experienced hostile treatment.[32] She reported violations of a city ordinance against sexual orientation discrimination and was subsequently put on administrative leave before being terminated. A Texas trial court denied the defendants' motion to dismiss and a plea to jurisdiction, which the defendants appealed. A Texas appellate court considered the question of whether sexual orientation discrimination was barred by the state constitution, which does not enumerate "sexual orientation" as a protected category. However, after the trial court order, the U.S. Supreme Court determined that Title VII prohibitions on discrimination "because of … sex" applied to claims tied to sexual orientation. A separate opinion concurs with the result, and dissents due to the application of *Bostock* to state law, but the majority opinion reversed the jurisdiction plea, dismissed the whistleblower claim, and remanded for further proceedings under the state human rights law, deemed the exclusive remedy.

---

[31] Mont. State Univ.-Northern v. Bachmeier, 480 P.3d 233, 386 Educ. L. Rep. 949 (Mont. 2021).
[32] Tarrant Cnty. Coll. Dist. v. Sims, 621 S.W. 3d 323, 390 Educ. L. Rep. 805 (Tex. App.-Dallas 2021).

Due Process

A tenured professor and chair were removed from his chair position and terminated after his tenure was partly revoked for signing a property lease without authorization and his efforts to sell the department's medical practice. The university followed its procedures including an investigation and a two-day hearing in front of a faculty grievance committee, which upheld four grounds for dismissal but did not find whether termination was warranted. The professor sued in Kentucky federal district court, which upheld the dismissal decision. The professor appealed on due process grounds. The Sixth Circuit affirmed the lower court's holding, finding that the professor did not have a property interest in his chair position because administrative positions do not have a protected property interest. Furthermore, his due process rights and liberty interests of reputation and career options were not abridged, having all stated procedures afforded to him during his paid suspension.[33]

Employment

A surgeon had privileges at a private university hospital. After years of his privileges being renewed every two years, his privileges were not renewed. Hospital privileges are reviewed according to the university's procedures involving the Credentials Committee, Medical Executive Committee, and Quality and Safety Professional Affairs Committee.[34] The various committees upheld the nonrenewal. The surgeon sued the university hospital and individuals in their capacity and as agents of the hospital. The D.C. federal district court noted its limited review and that the hospital was immune by local law similar to the federal law, Health Care Quality Improvement Act, designed to promote effective professional peer review. The D.C. federal appellate court stated that the trial court erred and that the plaintiff could rebut the presumption of immunity at the evidentiary stage by proving that the review process was not reasonable.

---

[33] Kaplan v. Univ. of Louisville, 10 F.4th 569, 394 Educ. L. Rep. 60 (6th Cir. 2021).
[34] Kalan v. MedStar-Georgetown Med. Ctr., Inc., 253 A.3d 123, 392 Educ. L. Rep. 894 (D.C. 2021).

Faculty

A college president was terminated. She sued for due process and breach of contract claims in a Texas federal district court.[35] The trial court vacated the jury verdict for breach of contract and reduced the due process damages award from $12,500,000 to $1. The plaintiff appealed. On appeal, the Fifth Circuit affirmed that the plaintiff was only entitled to nominal damages because the asserted injury was the dismissal and not from an improper pretermination hearing. In addition, the appellate court reversed the breach of contract holding of the lower court, asserting that the public college could not assert constitutional immunity. In addition, the issue of attorneys' fees was remanded because the trial court abused its discretion by vacating the award.

An associate professor at a private university brought an action against the trustees of his institution.[36] Four causes of action remained after the defendant's motion to dismiss: breach of contract, breach of the covenant of good faith and fair dealing, promissory estoppel, and a violation of state law. The crux of the complaints was the alleged failure to protect the plaintiff from retaliation for filing a research misconduct complaint against a distinguished professor. The plaintiff partly based his suit on the failure to promote him to professor or division chief and the denial of his request for a joint appointment with another department. The defendants' motion for summary judgment was granted with prejudice. The New York federal district court held that there was no damage to the plaintiff's reputation and the university's policies are not contracts.

A visiting professor was appointed to a tenure-track position after signing a letter of employment terms and conditions. She received the same letter each year her contract was renewed, including information on the tenure policy. When she applied for tenure, her application was denied because of a lack of demonstrated proficiency in research. The professor filed suit one year after her written contract ended, claiming the university violated provisions of its policy manuals and her contract and did not give her adequate time to conduct the necessary research.[37] The Kentucky trial court found for the plaintiff, arguing that the suit was timely filed. The

---

[35] Tercero v. Tex. Southmost Coll. Dist., 989 F.3d 291, 387 Educ. L. Rep. 59 (5th Cir. 2021).
[36] Joshi v. Trs. of Columbia Univ. in City of N.Y., 515 F. Supp. 3d 200, 392 Educ. L. Rep. 723 (S.D.N.Y. 2021).
[37] Britt v. Univ. of Louisville, 628 S.W.3d 1, 394 Educ. L. Rep. 1101 (Ky. 2021).

Kentucky appellate court reversed. The State Supreme Court held that the yearly continuation letters constituted a valid contract setting out expectations for teaching, service, and research and that the terms were incorporated, but the suit was not timely filed. Time tolled from the contract's expiration and not with the cessation of employment activities. The court reversed the appellate court's denial of the university's motion for summary judgment.

A university health center's bylaws require faculty members to be evaluated annually by the department chairperson.[38] There are four evaluation categories, "not acceptable," marginal," "acceptable," and "superior." There is a process for reviewing the chair's evaluation. Following his annual review, a tenured professor requested access to files related to that review, citing the Freedom of Information Act.[39] The health center responded by sending the professor 908 pages of redacted documents. The professor appealed to the Freedom of Information Commission. The Commission found that the redacted portions of comments from the various review committees were exempted because the public interest in withholding the notes outweighed the public interest in disclosure, which may chill candid assessments. The Connecticut trial court dismissed the professor's complaint. The Connecticut appellate court held that the preliminary notes were protected from disclosure; however, the plaintiff was entitled to receive the final comments and ratings from committee members that were delivered to the dean.

The plaintiff was hired as a professor and chair of the Department of Ophthalmology. Years later, the American Academy of Ophthalmology commenced a confidential investigation in response to allegations of an ethics violation. The investigation found that the professor had engaged in misconduct and failed to provide all documents and correspondence concerning the investigation. The university suspended the professor, during which the professor entered a negotiation to leave the university. Part of the agreement required the professor to turn over all of his correspondence regarding the ethics investigation. The professor sued when the university refused to pay him an agreed-upon sum stating that he had not fulfilled the requirements of the separation agreement. He won at trial and the university appealed. The issue was whether the language of the agreement was ambiguous. The Florida appellate court found that the language was unambiguous.

---

[38] Lindquist v. Freedom of Info. Comm'n, 248 A.3d 711, 389 Educ. L. Rep. 907 (Conn. App. Ct. 2021).
[39] General Statutes § 1-200 et seq.

The professor did not fulfill the requirement to produce documents that were not in his possession in addition to those which were in his possession.[40]

An associate professor in a medical school brought a lawsuit for breaches of contract, implied contract, promissory estoppel, and implied covenant of good faith and fair dealing when she was denied promotion and tenure.[41] The Ohio trial court granted the university summary judgment, stating that state courts are reluctant to intrude on tenure decisions unless the administration has acted in bad faith, abused its discretion, violated constitutional rights, or acted fraudulently, and no evidence was presented to meet these criteria. On appeal, the Ohio appellate court held that it did not question the assessment of the plaintiff's qualification. However, the court found that genuine issues of fact existed regarding the breach of contract claim, specifically, lack of clarity of the hybrid tenure track criteria, failure to evaluate the plaintiff based on applicable contractual criteria, whether procedures were followed, and whether those failures prejudiced the plaintiff. The trial court's judgment was reversed and remanded for further proceeding.

A part-time adjunct faculty member filed for unemployment, asserting that she was a year-round employee after the department only offered her a single course to teach for the first summer session and none for the second, instead only offering an hourly rate of pay for non-teaching.[42] Due to her seniority, she could claim courses to teach during the summer if offered. Her employment contract included language stating that she had a reasonable assurance to perform a similar service from the year before during the fall semester. Upon review of her unemployment claim, the issue was whether the summer term constituted a regular term and not whether the claimant reasonably expected to teach during the summer term. The Pennsylvania trial court held that the summer term is not a regular term. It has a lower enrollment, lower course availability, and the catalog defined the fall and spring semesters as the major semesters. The claimant was not entitled to unemployment benefits.

---

[40] Bd. of Regents, Univ. of S. Fla. Bd. of Trs. v. Rowsey, 320 So.3d 954, 393 Educ. L. Rep. 993 (Fla. Dist. Ct. App. 2021).

[41] Pagano v. Case Western Reserve Univ., 166 N.E. 3d 654, 389 Educ. L. Rep. 460 (Ohio Ct. App. 2021).

[42] Prunty v. Unemp't Comp. Bd. of Review, 253 A.3d 349, 392 Educ. L. Rep. 906 (Pa. Commw. Ct. 2021).

Staff

Like many states, Arkansas does not normally approve unemployment benefits for employees of educational institutions for summer breaks in employment. The argument is that many school employees, who do not work during the summer, are not entitled to unemployment benefits because they have a reasonable expectation of employment at the start of the fall semester. This practice applies to employees with less than a ten-month position because they follow a ten-month school calendar. A director of a fitness center at a community college held a year-round position. When the COVID-19 pandemic hit, he was furloughed for two months. His application for unemployment benefits was denied because he had a reasonable assurance that he would perform the same services after the interruption. The board's decision was reversed on appeal, and benefits were awarded. The Arkansas appellate court held that the interruption was not due to a natural break in the academic cycle. The break in his year-round employment was due to the pandemic.[43]

A university employee received a warning letter, was directed to take anti-harassment training, and was later dismissed.[44] The state Division of Human Rights found for the university. The employee did not appeal the finding and instead brought a lawsuit for breach of contract and defamation, among other causes of action. The plaintiff lost and appealed. The New York appellate court held that the breach of contract claim fails. The employee was an at-will employee and thus was not owed a duty of good faith. Furthermore, the defamation claim failed. The employer's letter had a qualified privilege because it was made for supervisory purposes. Also, the plaintiff failed to adequately plead publication because the pleading was vague and undefined as to the requirement for the particularity of person and time for the publication.

The claimant was employed as a director. Three years after employment, the claimant's supervisor demoted him and notified him that he would be discharged in six months. Feeling humiliated, he soon left his employment, claiming he was offered a severance package if he resigned before the six months passed. He filed for unemployment benefits but was denied because he left his work voluntarily but not for a good cause. He appealed the decision. The

---

[43] Ballard v. Dir., Dept. of Workforce Servs., 625 S.W.3d 249, 393 Educ. L. Rep. 468 (Ark. App. 2021).
[44] DiCoby v. Syracuse Univ., 142 N.Y.S.3d 13, 388 Educ. L. Rep. 934 (N.Y. App. Div. 2021).

commission held that the claimant left the position voluntarily and that the state's employment law does not recognize constructive discharge. On the second point, the Missouri appellate court decided that the claimant had not demonstrated that he left for good cause. His pay was only reduced by 15.7%, and he was not demoted to an entry-level position. The commission's findings were affirmed.[45]

Institutional Issues

Two employees of a sports management company appealed their jury convictions on federal bribery charges, motioning to dismiss because the terms of the law were unconstitutionally vague as applied.[46] The Second Circuit took the case on appeal from a federal district court in New York. On the claim that the coaches were not "agents" of their institutions, the court relies on a plain reading of the text and Supreme Court precedent that construes employees as agents. On the claim that the coaches were not engaged in the business of their universities, the court referred to a Seventh Circuit decision that held the term "business" did not need to be narrowly construed in a commercial sense and also included intangible aspects of an organization. The court held the district court's application of the bribery law to be constitutional and affirmed the convictions.

In another Second Circuit case, a class of participants in a retirement plan administered by a private university sued the university, alleging violations of its fiduciary duties of loyalty and prudence and unreasonable performance losses for its defined benefits Faculty Plan and Medical Plan.[47] The district court dismissed all claims but one, and the plaintiffs requested reconsideration and leave to amend. Before the resolution of post-trial motions, it became public knowledge that the judge was leaving the bench for a position with her former firm. The plaintiffs filed for a new trial based on the judge's connection to the university through a colleague. The Second Circuit remanded two of the complaints, dismissed of their claim for breach of duty of prudence, and denial of leave to amend. The other claims were affirmed.

---

[45] Firmand v. Univ. of Mo., 628 S.W.3d 434, 395 Educ. L. Rep. 444 (Mo. Ct. App. 2021).
[46] U.S. v. Dawkins, 999 F.3d 767, 391 Educ. L. Rep. 88 (2d Cir. 2021).
[47] Sacerdote v. New York Univ., 9 F.4th 95, 393 Educ. L. Rep. 539 (2d Cir. 2021).

An Australian-based online global marketplace allows artists to sell their products through the website while the company aids in the oversight and execution of sales. An American university found products on the online marketplace that featured its trademarked images without approval. The university sued the marketplace for trademark infringement through vicarious liability, a federal statute, and a state statute on right-of-publicity. The federal district court in Ohio granted summary judgment in favor of the marketplace. The Sixth Circuit held that the university failed to preserve its vicarious liability claim under the Lanham Act. However, the court held that the Ohio district court was wrong to grant the marketplace summary judgment on the Lanham Act direct liability and state law right-of-publicity claims. Thus, the Sixth Circuit reversed and remanded[48]

A female student at a private university called the institution's security after a man approached her on campus and attempted entry into her residence hall. Security officers found the man still on campus, and while resisting being detained and handcuffed, he dropped a concealed firearm, which the officers retrieved. Charged with being a felon possessing a firearm, the defendant argued that the officers violated his Fourth Amendment rights and moved to suppress. The Eight Circuit heard the case on appeal from a Nebraska federal district court, which adopted the report and recommendation of a magistrate judge finding the Fourth Amendment inapplicable because the security officers were private individuals and were not coordinating with Omaha police. The Eighth Circuit affirmed.[49]

A recognized fraternity was located off campus and within the residential zoning district of the city. The city required that all fraternities and sororities in the district be sanctioned or recognized by the university. Before the end of the lease on a fraternity house within the zoning district, the university revoked its recognition, thus, no one could reside there. However, two residents remained, and the city cited the landowner for a zoning violation. The Board of Zoning affirmed, and the landowner sought judicial review asserting that the city impermissibly delegated its zoning authority to the university. The Indiana trial court granted relief, which was affirmed at the state appellate level. The Indiana Supreme Court reversed the trial court finding that the city did not delegate its

---

[48] Ohio State Univ. v. Redbubble, Inc., 989 F.3d 435, 387 Educ. L. Rep. 87 (6th Cir. 2021).
[49] U.S. v. Avalos, 984 F.3d 1306, 385 Educ. L. Rep. 472 (8th Cir. 2021).

legislative authority, instead it merely defined fraternities and sororities based on its relationship with the university.⁵⁰

A governmental entity of colleges and universities requested bids for a professional services contract to develop an online registration system for continuing education. Four vendors responded. Highlights were made on the plaintiff's proposal but were not saved. The proposal was disqualified because the required information was not provided. The plaintiff submitted multiple data requests under state law. He was dissatisfied with the information received, specifically requesting his highlighted proposal, which was not saved. The Administrative Law Judge, after a hearing, concluded that the state entity had not complied with the Data Practice Act and awarded $950 but had no authority to enforce the Officials Records Act. Eighteen months later, the plaintiff sued in a Minnesota trial court held that the Data Practice Act was settled and that there was no private cause of action for the Officials Records Act. The Minnesota appellate court affirmed. On appeal, the Minnesota Supreme Court reversed the state appellate court, granting a review of the complaint under the Data Practices Act but affirmed the holding that the Officials Records Act does not authorize a private cause of action.⁵¹

In another request for records, a university received a request under the Public Records Act for all emails between a retired professor and two journals on which he served as their editor and emails regarding his service on two advisory committees not affiliated with the university. The university responded that the requested emails are not "public records." The appeal to the university president failed, and the nonprofit health research organization filed suit in a Vermont trial court, granting summary judgment to the university. The research organization appealed. The Vermont appellate court held that the emails were not public records because they were not produced or acquired in the course of the public agency's business.⁵²

A city entered into an incentivizing plan to induce a private university to establish a branch campus within the city as part of its strategies to spur economic development. The city agreed to lease a building and pay $737,596 for renovating the building to meet the

---

⁵⁰ City of Bloomington Bd. of Zoning App. v. UJ-Eighty Corp., 163 N.E.3d 264, 387 Educ. L. Rep. 334 (Ind. 2021).
⁵¹ Halva v. Minn. State Colls. and Univs., 953 N.W.2d 496, 386 Educ. L. Rep. 491 (Minn. 2021).
⁵² U.S. Right to Know v. Univ. of Vt., 255 A.3d 719, 393 Educ. L. Rep. 727 (Vt. 2021).

needs of the private university's needs and paying the university $1,875,000 over three years to develop the campus. Both offers were contingent upon the university meeting specified performance goals. Taxpayers sued to enjoin the payments, asserting a violation of the Gift Clause. The Arizona Supreme Court dismissed the argument that, in applying the applicable two-prong test, deference must be given to the city, asserting that the bargained-for benefit must be proportionate to the market value of the benefit, which is an objective analysis, which the city failed.[53]

A State Board of Nursing terminated a nursing program for failure to meet the statutorily required passage rates on the National Council of State Boards of Nursing Licensing Examination. The college appealed the termination order, arguing that the board failed to conduct a formal hearing before terminating its program and did not provide necessary notice.[54] The Florida appellate court affirmed the program termination, finding that because there was no dispute of a material fact – the program did not meet the required passage rate – a formal hearing was not required, and, consequently, an informal hearing met due process requirements. Furthermore, the court concluded that the college's assertion regarding the passing rate was conclusory, thus, there was no factual dispute, and the argument regarding improper notice was rejected. The board's Notice of Intent to Terminate was sufficient.

A publishing company requested documents regarding the applicants for the president of a public university position under a state's open records act after a new president was appointed. The selected candidate was the only finalist for the position, which generated considerable criticism from the board of trustees. The university refused the request, and the publisher sued the university.[55] The Colorado trial court agreed with the plaintiff publisher and ordered the disclosure of the requested documents. The university appealed. In a split decision, the Colorado appellate court acknowledged that the trial court endeavored to bring clarity to the statutes to make them "better," but that was not the task before the court. The appellate court reversed the district court's judgment as well as its award of attorney fees and costs.

---

[53] Schires v. Carlat, 480 P.3d 639, 386 Educ. L. Rep. 979 (Ariz. 2021).
[54] Burnett Int'l Coll. v. Bd. of Nursing, 316 So.3d 763, 391 Educ. L. Rep. 957 (Fla. Dist. Ct. App. 2021).
[55] Prairie Mountain Pub. Co., LLP v. Regents of Univ. of Colo., 491 P.3d 472, 393 Educ. L. Rep. 455 (Colo. App. 2021).

This case involves a consortium of colleges, an "affiliated" school, and its land grant 1957 from the consortium. The deed contained two conditions, an Educational Use Clause and a First Offer Clause. The state appellate court reversed the California trial court opinion granting the action seeking to quiet title and ordered the enforcement of the First Offer and Educational Use Clauses as equitable servitude. The fact that the value of the land had appreciated did not materially alter the parties' allocation of risks, and contractual rights and responsibilities forfeiture was not applicable.[56]

At the relation of the attorney general, Missouri intervened in an action filed against a state university by a university employee who sought declaratory and injunctive relief from a rule prohibiting the storage of firearms in vehicles on campus property, seemingly in conflict with state law.[57] A trial court entered judgment in favor of the university, and the state appealed to the Missouri appellate court. The appellate court agreed with the state on whether state law preempted the rule, relying on a plain reading of the statute's language. Despite this, the court addressed and denied the other points raised by the state, finding that the burden of proof does rest with the state, that the rule was tailored narrowly to achieve a compelling government interest, and that, because of the determinations relative to strict scrutiny, the court need not come to a determination regarding the lay witness testimony provided by the president of the state university system. The court reversed on the question of preemption and remanded the remaining issues for further proceedings.

First Amendment

Press

An Arkansas newspaper that had contracted for years with one of the state's public colleges to run paid advertisements sued for violation of First and Fourteenth Amendment rights after the institution's denial of a new contract under Arkansas Act 710, "An Act to Prohibit Public Entities from Contracting with and Investing

---

[56] S. Cal. Sch. of Theology v. Claremont Graduate Univ., 274 Cal. Rptr. 3d 180, 386 Educ. L. Rep. 421 (Cal. Ct. App. 2021).
[57] State ex rel. Schmitt v. Choi, 627 S.W.3d 1, 393 Educ. L. Rep. 962 (Mo. Ct. App. 2021).

in Companies That Boycott Israel; and for Other Purposes."[58] The Arkansas federal district court denied the newspaper's motion for preliminary injunction and dismissed it for failure to state a claim. The Eighth Circuit reversed on appeal, finding the Act's language ambiguous. Specifically, the Act defines "Boycott Israel" and "boycott of Israel," in part, as "refusals to deal, terminating business activities, or other actions that are intended to limit commercial relations with Israel." Construing "other actions" as ambiguous, the court concluded that the phrase included both "commercial conduct," unprotected by the First Amendment, and "expressive conduct," which is protected. A dissenting opinion would apply a constitutionally-permissible interpretation and uphold the statute, arguing that under *ejusdem generis*, "other actions" should be construed as "commercial conduct" in line with the actions identified by the Act.[59]

Religion

An associate professor sued her employer and individuals for unlawful discrimination and retaliation, breach of contract, breach of the implied covenant of good faith and fair dealing, and tortious interference with contractual relations.[60] The issue was whether the college qualified as a "religious institution" for purposes of applying the ministerial exception and, if so, whether the plaintiff qualified for the exception. The college argued that the required "integration" of religious faith into instruction and scholarship meant that all faculty are ministers and all employees should be considered ministerial. The Supreme Court has emphasized a functional analysis to determine ministerial status and focused on what the plaintiff did and did not do. Unlike the plaintiffs in cases involving teachers in church-operated schools, the plaintiff here "was not required to, and did not, teach classes on religion, pray with her students, or attend chapel with her students." Determining that the Massachusetts trial court did not err in dismissing the defendants' affirmative defense of the ministerial exception, the Massachusetts supreme court remanded the case for further proceedings. The

---

[58] ARK. CODE ANN. § 25-1-503(a)(1).
[59] Arkansas Times LP v. Waldrip, 988 F.3d 453, 386 Educ. L. Rep. 588 (8th Cir. 2021).
[60] DeWeese-Boyd v. Gordon Coll., 163 N.E.3d 1000, 387 Educ. L. Rep. 902 (Mass. 2021), *cert. denied*, 142 S.Ct. 952, 399 Educ. L. Rep. 478 (2022).

defendants filed for a writ of certiorari from the Supreme Court of the United States, which was denied.

Speech

After violating policy requiring faculty to address students by "preferred pronouns" and having exhausted grievance procedures under the collective bargaining agreement, a professor sued the trustees and administrators of a public university, alleging violations of free speech and exercise rights, due process, and equal protection rights, and his employment contract.[61] The Ohio federal district court dismissed all federal claims and declined jurisdiction over state-law claims. The plaintiff appealed. On the free speech claim, the Sixth Circuit held that the plaintiff was speaking on a matter of public concern, and the university violated his rights by compelling him to use transgender students' pronouns and refusing to let him include language in his syllabi, clarifying his position. On the free exercise claim, the court held that the gender-identity policy was not neutral due to hostility expressed by university agents for the plaintiff's religious beliefs, and irregularities in the policy's application seemed geared to suppress those religious beliefs. The court disagreed that the policy was void for vagueness. The Sixth Circuit affirmed the dismissal of the due-process claim, reversed holdings finding no speech or exercise violations, vacated dismissal of the state-law claims, and remanded for further proceedings.

The plaintiff, an organization against using animals in scientific testing, sought to advertise on buses operated by the defendant, a public university, with images and text designed to provoke emotion surrounding the topic.[62] The defendant denied the advertising proposal for violating university policy against "political campaigns and viewpoints or endorsements." The plaintiff filed First and Fourteenth Amendment claims under § 1983, challenging the policy as facially unconstitutional, vague, and overbroad. The defendant argued that buses constitute a nonpublic forum requiring the university to show only that the policy is reasonable and viewpoint neutral and moved to dismiss. The plaintiff conceded that the transit system is a nonpublic forum, and the court agreed that it is plausible the policy constitutes an unconstitutional ban on the plaintiff's viewpoint as applied. The court also finds plausible the vagueness

---

[61] Meriwether v. Hartop, 992 F.3d 492, 388 Educ. L. Rep. 504 (6th Cir. 2021).
[62] People for Ethical Treatment of Animals v. Hinckley, 526 F. Supp. 3d 218, 395 Educ. L. Rep. 231 (S.D. Tex. 2021).

claim, as the policy does not define "political" nor how to determine whether an advertisement is "political." The Texas federal district court declines to conclude the overbreadth challenge until after the plaintiff is allowed discovery into the university's patterns of approval and rejection under the policy.

Labor Relations

A faculty union filed a grievance alleging violations of the collective bargaining agreement in the university's decisions to offer a one-year contract after a tenure denial and subsequently to non-renew the one-year contract.[63] The union filed a request for arbitration, which the D.C. trial court denied when it granted the university's motion to stay. The union appealed, and the D.C. appellate court held that neither the one-year contract offer nor its nonrenewal was arbitrable. Referring to the language of the collective bargaining agreement, the court noted that only grievances could be submitted for arbitration. The question was whether the one-year offer and nonrenewal represented violations, misinterpretations, or improper applications of the agreement. Finding that the one-year offer comported with a university policy on the Status of Faculty Members Denied Tenure and describing the decision as a "tenure decision" and thus not arbitrable under several articles of the collective bargaining agreement, the court affirmed the trial court ruling.

A state university sought judicial review of the holding by an administrative law judge (ALJ) in which a memorandum of understanding with the university police officers' union required ten hours of paid leave on holidays for officers working four ten-hour shifts per week.[64] The union was denied at the first two stages of the grievance procedure but successful in the third, where the ALJ found the issue of holiday leave is a matter of contract interpretation and, therefore, grievable. The ALJ concluded that the schedule change effectively redefined the workday and should be interpreted to redefine holiday leave, with all officers affected being credited accordingly. The university filed for review, and a Maryland trial court affirmed the ALJ's finding about the definition of the workday but reversed all other conclusions, holding that neither the court nor

---

[63] Univ. of the Dist. of Columbia Faculty Ass'n / Nat. Educ. Ass'n v. Bd. of Trs. of Univ. of the Dist. of Columbia, 257 A.3d 1026, 394 Educ. L. Rep. 1018 (D.C. 2021).

[64] Merryman v. Univ. of Balt., 248 A.3d 336, 389 Educ. L. Rep. 867 (Md. 2021).

the ALJ had the authority to issue an order effectively increasing the state university system's budget. The union appealed, and a special appellate court held that the ALJ lacked jurisdiction because the dispute was not grievable. The union appealed, and the Maryland Supreme Court affirmed the order vacating and remanding the case to the ALJ for dismissal.

A community college faculty union sued for a review of the public labor relations commission's decision to defer consideration of unfair labor practice (ULP) charges against the community college until an arbitrator could resolve underlying questions of contract interpretation.[65] At the heart of the issue are the means of calculation used to apportion back pay for past wage increases that had been authorized but unfunded by the state legislature since 2008. On appeal, the union argued for a narrowed conception of commission authority to determine when to defer to arbitration, with which the Washington appellate court disagreed. The union also argued that the decision to defer was arbitrary and capricious on grounds the commission "fails to explain its decision's inconsistency" with precedent. Still, the court found that the decision was reasonable, given the college's assertion that a colorable waiver-by-contract defense might impact the union's two statutory claims. In the end, the court affirmed the commission's deferment on the ULP claims until after arbitration determines if those claims are waived by contract.

A public university sought judicial review of an order from the state public employee labor relations agency finding the university violated obligations under state collective bargaining law to bargain in good faith.[66] A union member shared concerns with a steward about job description changes, and his supervisor's hostile treatment, and the steward sought access to an HR report. The university shared a redacted version that allegedly violated the contractual grievance procedure, claiming that redacted portions were unrelated to the grievance at issue and were confidential. On review, the Oregon appellate court identified the crux of the case as whether the nature of the information requested qualified as confidential. The board found that the university had not met its burden to establish a confidentiality interest arising from a faculty records policy and that the policy required disclosure of information

---

[65] American Fed'n of Teachers, Local 1950 v. Pub. Emp't Relations Comm'n, 493 P.3d 1212, 394 Educ. L. Rep. 374 (Wash. Ct. App. 2021).

[66] Service Emps. Int'l Union Local 503 v. Univ. of Or., 494 P.3d 993, 394 Educ. L. Rep. 1084 (Or. Ct. App. 2021).

to effectuate other state laws, including the state law governing collective bargaining. Because balancing is required in consideration of the totality of circumstances, the appellate court reversed the board report and remanded for further proceeding.

Torts

This case involves a university seeking indemnification from a contractor for the wrongful death of a participant in a sleep diagnostic study.[67] The university entered into a Sleep Diagnostics Services Agreement with the contractor. The contractor settled with the plaintiff. At trial, the jury returned a verdict against the contractor assigning 60% fault. The jury further found the university liable for the contractor's negligence. The university soon after settled with the plaintiff. The university filed in federal court claiming contractual and common law indemnification. The Georgia federal district court granted summary judgment in favor of the contractor, but the Eleventh Circuit vacated and remanded, holding that the indemnification bar does not apply in this unique circumstance.

In another North Carolina case, the plaintiff worked for a public university in one state as a college recruiter in another. Plaintiff alleged that he was sexually harassed by two co-workers and reported the behavior to appropriate university officials.[68] After filing the complaint against his supervisor, one of the participants in his report suspended him from work for poor performance. The supervisor terminated his employment with the university. The plaintiff brought a lawsuit in the state where he worked, alleging wrongful discharge, negligent retention, and-or supervision of an employee. The defendants claimed sovereign immunity. During the trial, the U.S. Supreme Court decided *Franchise Tax Board of California v. Hyatt* which held that states retain sovereign immunity from private suits filed in other states. The trial court granted the defendant's motion to dismiss. The plaintiff appealed. The North Carolina appellate court affirmed the trial court's order, finding that the university had not waived its immunity.

A worker was injured while climbing stairs when he hit his head on a beam erected to support a scaffold. The worker fell backward

---

[67] Emory Univ., Inc. v. Neurocare, Inc., 985 F.3d 1337, 386 Educ. L. Rep. 34 (11th Cir. 2021).
[68] Farmer v. Troy Univ., 855 S.E.2d 801, 388 Educ. L. Rep. 975 (N.C. Ct. App. 2021).

approximately ten feet down the stairs. The construction site was the renovation of the university's physical science building. A public benefit corporation addressing state university construction planning needs was one of the named defendants, in addition to a construction and contracting company. The New York appellate court applied a dangerous conditions theory, holding that the lower court prematurely awarded contractual indemnification to the public benefit corporation at the summary judgment phase.[69]

A spectator to a university women's basketball game tripped over a four-to-five-inch riser in front of the stands at the end of the court and broke her shoulder. Two years later, she sued the university, alleging that the university negligently failed to maintain a safe and unobstructed floor and failed to warn of the floor's "defective condition."[70] At the deposition, the associate athletic director testified that she believed tables and chairs were on the riser at the time of the accident. However, a video was later found that the tables were not on the riser. It wasn't until the trial that the mistake about the tables being present was uncovered, which would have presented a view of the change in height. The jury returned a verdict against the plaintiff. The plaintiff filed a motion to correct the error. The trial court vacated the judgment and ordered a new trial. The university appealed. The Indiana appellate court found for the university, asserting that the change in testimony at the trial did not prevent the plaintiff from presenting her case. In another Indiana appellate case, the plaintiff filed a complaint against a public university for a slip and fell outside of the library.[71] The appeals court described it as the beginning of a "tortuous history." In this iteration of the case, the Indiana appellate court noted that all the issues raised by the plaintiff had been litigated and resolved adversely to him. The public university sought sanctions against the plaintiff for his latest appeal, restrictions on future filings related to the case, and award of attorneys' fees and expenses. The appellate court agreed with the Indiana trial court that "enough is enough" and imposed the filing restrictions request.

---

[69] Edwards v. State Univ. Const. Fund, 151 N.Y.S.3d 464, 394 Educ. L. Rep. 1036 (N.Y. App. 2021).

[70] Univ. of Notre Dame v. Bahney, 158 N.E.3d 809, 384 Educ. L. Rep. 988 (Ind. Ct. App. 2021).

[71] Holland v. Trs. of Ind. Univ., 171 N.E.3d 684, 393 Educ. L. Rep. 431 (Ind. Ct. App. 2021).

Conclusion

Among the cases presented, a handful latch onto ongoing political and cultural concerns and movements. The Sixth Circuit case from Ohio concerning a professor's refusal to use a transgender student's pronouns has since been resolved in a settlement that prevents the university from dictating the use or non-use of pronouns that the professor believes conflict with the assumed biological sex of a student, and which resulted in a $400,000 payment to the professor. The Massachusetts case concerning a tenured faculty member at a religiously affiliated HEI has resulted in a denial of certiorari. Still, the denial was accompanied by a written statement from Justice Samuel Alito that seemed to lay a path to a full hearing at the highest court. This could portend a possible extension of the "ministerial exception" into higher education by broadening the concepts embodied by the phrase "teachers in church-operated schools," thus affecting the employment relationships between religiously-affiliated HEIs and their staff and faculty.[72] We presented only one case concerning COVID-19 mitigation efforts by an HEI, though the changing nature of the virus and uncertain future of the pandemic response mean challenges yet remain, and cases have continued into the 2022-2023 academic year as lower court decisions find their way into the appellate level.[73] As task forces devoted to COVID-19 responses know all too well at the end of the Spring 2022 semester, much is still unknown about emerging variants and how they will move through populations over the summer and into the fall; even now, mask mandates are being reconsidered and reinstated on some campuses. So, the hot buttons do not all burn at the same temperature, but underlying issues remain inflamed.

---

[72] *NLRB v. Catholic Bishop of Chicago*, 440 US 490, 500 (1979).
[73] *See* Avalon Zoppo, *'Watching the Outcome Like a Hawk': COVID-19 Tuition Refund Fights Heat Up in Appeals Court*, THE NATIONAL L. J. (Feb. 1, 2022),

Alphabetical List of Cases

Am. Fed'n of Teachers, Loc. 1950 v. Pub. Emp't Relations Comm'n
Arkansas Times LP v. Waldrip
Baker v. Ferris State Univ.
Ballard v. Dir., Dept. of Workforce Servs.
Bd. of Regents, Univ. of S. Fla. Bd. of Trs. v. Rowsey
Bd. of Regents, Univ. of S. Fla. Bd. of Trs. v. Rowsey
Bibliotechnical Athenaeum v. Am. Univ. of Beirut
Briggs v. Univ. of Cincinnati
Britt v. Univ. of Louisville
Burnett Int'l Coll. v. Bd. of Nursing
City of Bloomington Bd. of Zoning App. v. UJ-Eighty Corp.
Creswick v. Univ. of S.C.
DeWeese-Boyd v. Gordon Coll.
DiCoby v. Syracuse Univ.
Doe v. Coll. of N.J.
Edwards v. State Univ. Const. Fund
Emory Univ., Inc. v. Neurocare, Inc.
Esposito v. Suffolk Cnty. Cmty. Coll.
Fac. v. N.Y. Univ.
Farmer v. Troy Univ.
Farzinpour v. Berklee Coll. of Music
Firmand v. Univ. of Mo
Freyd v. Univ. of Or.
Halva v. Minn. State Colleges and Universities
Harrison v. Harris-Stowe State Univ.
Holland v. Trs. of Ind. Univ.
Holmes v. Cuyahoga Cmty. Coll.
Jones v. Bd. of Trs. for Ala. Agr. & Mech. Univ.
Jorgensen v. Loyola Marymount Univ.
Joshi v. Trs. of Columbia Univ. in City of N.Y
Kalan v. MedStar-Georgetown Med. Ctr., Inc
Kalan v. MedStar-Georgetown Med. Ctr., Inc.
Kaplan v. Univ. of Louisville
Lindquist v. Freedom of Info. Comm'n.
Mammen v. Thomas Jefferson Univ.
McGruder v. Curators of Univ. of Mo.
Meriwether v. Hartop
Merryman v. Univ. of Balt.
Miller v. Sam Hous. State Univ.
Monroe v. Columbia Coll. Chicago
Mont. State Univ.-Northern v. Bachmeier

Newman v. Univ. of Dayton
Ohio State Univ. v. Redbubble, Inc
Onyiah v. St. Cloud State Univ.
Pagano v. Case Western Reserve Univ.
People for Ethical Treatment of Animals v. Hinckley
Prairie Mountain Pub. Co., LLP v. Regents of Univ. of Colo.
Prunty v. Unemp't Comp. Bd. of Rev.
Sacerdote v. N.Y. Univ.
Schires v. Carlat
Service Emps. Int'l Union Loc. 503 v. Univ. of Or.
Sinha v. Bradley Univ.
So. Cal. Sch. of Theology v. Claremont Graduate Univ.
State ex rel. Schmitt v. Choi
Sullivan v. Tex. A&M Univ. Sys.
Taite v. Bridgewater State Univ. Bd. of Trs.
Tarrant Cnty. Coll. Dist. v. Sims
Taylor-Travis v. Jackson State Univ.
Tercero v. Tex. Southmost Coll. Dist.
Throupe v. Univ. of Denver
Tudor v. Se. Okla. State Univ.
U.S. Right to Know v. Univ. of Vt.
U.S. v. Avalos
U.S. v. Dawkins
U.S. v. Yale Univ.
Univ. of Notre Dame v. Bahney
Univ. of the Dist. of Columbia Fac. Ass'n / Nat. Educ. Ass'n v. Bd. of Trs. of Univ. of the Dist. of Columbia
Wille v. Curators of Univ. of Mo.

Cases by Jurisdiction

FEDERAL CASES

D.C. Circuit
Kalan v. MedStar-Georgetown Med. Ctr., Inc.
Univ. of the Dist. of Columbia Fac. Ass'n / Nat. Educ. Ass'n v. Bd. of Trs. of Univ. of the Dist. of Columbia

First Circuit
Taite v. Bridgewater State Univ. Bd. of Trs.

Massachusetts
Farzinpour v. Berklee Coll. of Music

Second Circuit
Fac. v. N.Y. Univ.
Sacerdote v. N.Y. Univ.
U.S. v. Dawkins

Connecticut
U.S. v. Yale Univ.
New York
Bibliotechnical Athenaeum v. Am. Univ. of Beirut
Esposito v. Suffolk Cnty. Cmty. Coll.
Joshi v. Trs. of Columbia Univ. in City of N.Y

Third Circuit
Doe v. Coll. of N.J.

Pennsylvania
Mammen v. Thomas Jefferson Univ.

Fifth Circuit
Miller v. Sam Hous. State Univ.
Sullivan v. Tex. A&M Univ. Sys.
Taylor-Travis v. Jackson State Univ.
Tercero v. Tex. Southmost Coll. Dist.

Texas
People for Ethical Treatment of Animals v. Hinckley

Sixth Circuit
Briggs v. Univ. of Cincinnati
Kaplan v. Univ. of Louisville
Meriwether v. Hartop
Ohio State Univ. v. Redbubble, Inc

Michigan
Baker v. Ferris State Univ.
Ohio
Pagano v. Case Western Reserve Univ.

Seventh Circuit
Monroe v. Columbia Coll. Chicago
Sinha v. Bradley Univ.

Eighth Circuit
Arkansas Times LP v. Waldrip
Onyiah v. St. Cloud State Univ.
U.S. v. Avalos

Ninth Circuit
Freyd v. Univ. of Or.

Alaska
Jones v. Bd. of Trs. for Ala. Agr. & Mech. Univ.

Tenth Circuit
Throupe v. Univ. of Denver
Tudor v. Se. Okla. State Univ.

Eleventh Circuit
Emory Univ., Inc. v. Neurocare, Inc.

Florida
Bd. of Regents, Univ. of S. Fla. Bd. of Trs. v. Rowsey

STATE & D.C COURT CASES

Arizona
Schires v. Carlat

Arkansas
Ballard v. Dir., Dept. of Workforce Servs.

California
Jorgensen v. Loyola Marymount Univ.
So. Cal. Sch. of Theology v. Claremont Graduate Univ.

Colorado
Prairie Mountain Pub. Co., LLP v. Regents of Univ. of Colo.

Connecticut
Lindquist v. Freedom of Info. Comm'n.

Florida
Bd. of Regents, Univ. of S. Fla. Bd. of Trs. v. Rowsey
Burnett Int'l Coll. v. Bd. of Nursing

Indiana
City of Bloomington Bd. of Zoning App. v. UJ-Eighty Corp.
Holland v. Trs. of Ind. Univ.
Univ. of Notre Dame v. Bahney

Kentucky
Britt v. Univ. of Louisville

Maryland
Merryman v. Univ. of Balt.

Massachusetts
DeWeese-Boyd v. Gordon Coll.

Minnesota
Halva v. Minn. State Colleges and Universities

Missouri
Firmand v. Univ. of Mo
Harrison v. Harris-Stowe State Univ.
McGruder v. Curators of Univ. of Mo.
Wille v. Curators of Univ. of Mo.
State ex rel. Schmitt v. Choi

Montana
Mont. State Univ.-Northern v. Bachmeier

New York
DiCoby v. Syracuse Univ.
Edwards v. State Univ. Const. Fund

North Carolina
Farmer v. Troy Univ.

Ohio
Holmes v. Cuyahoga Cmty. Coll.
Newman v. Univ. of Dayton
Pagano v. Case Western Reserve Univ.

Oregon
Service Emps. Int'l Union Loc. 503 v. Univ. of Or.

Pennsylvania
Prunty v. Unemp't Comp. Bd. of Rev.

South Carolina
Creswick v. Univ. of S.C.

Texas
Tarrant Cnty. Coll. Dist. v. Sims

Vermont
U.S. Right to Know v. Univ. of Vt.

Washington
Am. Fed'n of Teachers, Loc. 1950 v. Pub. Emp't Relations Comm'n

District of Columbia
Kalan v. MedStar-Georgetown Med. Ctr., Inc

Chapter 9

STUDENTS IN HIGHER EDUCATION

Elizabeth T. Lugg, J.D., Ph.D.,[1] Joy Blanchard,[2] and Gillian P. Foss[3]

Introduction 305
Academic and Curriculum Matters 305
   Authority Over Curricular Requirements 305
   Challenges to Managerial Authority 306
      Admissions 306
      General 307
Student Misconduct 309
   Academic Misconduct 309
   Non-Academic Misconduct 310
Torts 313
COVID-19 314
Discrimination 317
   First Amendment 317
   National Origin, Race, and Ethnicity 320
   Disability 322
   Sex Discrimination/Harassment 323
   Other Discrimination 328
Tuition and Student Financial Aid 329

---

[1] Associate Professor, Educational Law, Illinois State University, Normal, Ill.
[2] Associate Professor, Higher Education, School of Education, Louisiana State University, Baton Rouge, La.
[3] School of Education, Louisiana State University, Baton Rouge, La.

Conclusion 332
Alphabetical List of Cases 333
Cases by Jurisdiction 334

Introduction

This chapter reviews cases reported in 2021 involving student-related matters in higher education. These cases dealt with academic and curricular issues; misconduct on academic and non-academic grounds; admissions; torts; crimes; discrimination claims involving race, gender, and disability; and financial aid.

Academic and Curriculum Matters

Authority Over Curricular Requirements

The Ninth Circuit heard the plaintiff's international student's appeal from the Idaho district court after he was dismissed from a doctoral program in clinical psychology for failing to satisfy the requirement that all students complete a 2,000-hour clinical internship. The student claimed that the public university violated Title VI by discriminating against him based on race or national origin based on comments from his supervisors regarding his English fluency and repeated dismissals from clinical placements for communication issues.[4] However, the court emphasized the importance of being able to communicate effectively in the clinical psychology field. The Ninth Circuit affirmed a jury's finding in favor of the institution, finding that adequate evidence supported the university's claim that it dismissed the student because of poor clinical performance.

In a Washington D.C. appellate case, a former doctoral student at a private university filed suit for breach of contract after he was dismissed for failing to complete his degree requirements in the time specified in the graduate student handbook.[5] The superior court dismissed his suit along with three subsequent filings of a similar nature. The D.C. appellate court upheld the judgments in favor of the university, maintaining that courts should defer to academic decisions barring any conduct that is arbitrary and capricious.

---

[4] Yu v. Idaho State Univ., 11 F.4th 1065, 394 Educ. L. Rep. 470 (9th Cir. 2021).
[5] Colvin v. Howard Univ., 257 A.3d 474, 394 Educ. L. Rep. 938 (D.C. 2021).

Challenges to Managerial Authority

Admissions

The Third Circuit affirmed a New Jersey federal district court's decision to grant summary judgment in favor of the defendant university on the plaintiff applicant's claims for discrimination based on religion, national origin, age, and disability against the public university after it rejected her numerous times for a clinical residency program.[6] The plaintiff, who was over the age of 40, from Serbia, and suffered a number of disabilities, had practiced psychiatry previously and was attempting to become licensed in the U.S. Despite passing examinations, the institution denied the plaintiff, claiming to base its denial on the fact that there were discrepancies in her educational and work history, she had little experience working in the U.S., and her application support materials were lacking. The federal trial court dismissed those claims for failing to meet the prima facie burden of proving that she was otherwise qualified for the position she sought and for failing to sufficiently rebut the non-discriminatory rationale offered by the university for her denial. The Third Circuit affirmed that ruling.

Despite losing a similar case before the U.S. Supreme Court, a nonprofit organization filed a lawsuit disputing race-based admissions at the defendant university.[7] A group of eight plaintiffs—all students of color at the defendant university—and three special-interest groups filed a motion to intervene. Under Federal Rule of Civil Procedure (FRCP) 24(a) governing motions for intervention, the motion must be timely, the movants must state a sufficient interest in the subject being challenged, and the disposition of the issue may interrupt their ability to protect that interest, and that the parties of the suit must inadequately represent the movants' interests. A federal district court in Texas granted that motion, citing that the motion satisfied the four requirements set forth by FRCP 24(a) and that the plaintiffs had pled sufficient interest in preserving race-based admissions to promote diversity at the institution.

A Georgia appellate court affirmed a ruling dismissing a student's breach of contract claim after she was dismissed from a

---

[6] Buj v. Psych. Residency Training, 860 F. App'x 241, 395 Educ. L. Rep. 174 (3d Cir. 2021).
[7] Students for Fair Admissions, Inc. v. Univ. of Texas at Austin, 338 F.R.D. 364, 392 Educ. L. Rep. 849 (W.D. Tex. 2021).

nursing program at a public university.[8] The lower court dismissed the claim, noting that it was barred under sovereign immunity. The student contended that the offer of admission and the student handbook constituted a contract that superseded sovereign immunity. In its review, the appellate court cited that both parties signed none of the documents in question, and there was no evidence that the university intended the student handbook to be construed as a binding contract.

General

The Third Circuit affirmed a Pennsylvania federal trial court's grant of attorney fees and court costs associated with a suit filed by a former student who sought to obtain a transcript certifying she completed her degree requirements, even though she owed the institution more than $6,000.[9] Though the student had filed for bankruptcy protection, the university claimed that the debt could not be discharged in bankruptcy court. The court ruled that the institution could not collect on debt accumulated before filing for bankruptcy. Thus, the university's appeal failed.

In another case, a California federal district court heard a claim where the plaintiff and defendant were former roommates on a university's campus.[10] The plaintiff had established a substantial presence via Internet social media platforms; the defendant, a computer science major, assisted the plaintiff in maintaining her accounts. During their time as roommates, their friendship began to deteriorate. The defendant told campus security that the plaintiff had threatened to poison her food. The plaintiff filed suit, claiming that her roommate had violated federal computer fraud law by accessing her accounts without her knowledge or permission (though she had given the roommate the passwords to her accounts). A federal court in California granted summary judgment in favor of the defendant, citing that the claim was barred by a two-year statute of limitations.

A group of students filed a Title IX lawsuit alleging sexual harassment against a private university in the D.C. federal district

---

[8] Patrick v. Bd. of Regents of Univ. of Ga., 855 S.E.2d 746, 388 Educ. L. Rep. 970 (Ga. Ct. App. 2021).
[9] In re Aleckna, 13 F.4th 337, 395 Educ. L. Rep. 88 (3d Cir. 2021).
[10] West v. Ronquillo-Morgan, 526 F. Supp. 3d 737, 395 Educ. L. Rep. 253 (C.D. Cal. 2021).

court.[11] During the discovery process, the plaintiffs learned that the institution had emails between the plaintiffs and their attorneys. They filed a motion for a protective order, requiring the institution to destroy all emails between the plaintiffs and their attorneys, citing attorney-client privilege. The federal district court denied the petition, noting that the institution did not come into possession of the emails during the discovery process but discovered the emails while searching its computing system for discoverable information. The court also noted that university policy did not place a caveat on university email accounts for personal use and that there was no inherent expectation of privacy.

The Supreme Court of Connecticut heard a case brought by a group of plaintiffs, including a private corporation that owned the house that housed a campus fraternity.[12] When the university implemented a policy requiring any Greek on-campus housing to become co-educational and later rescinded recognition of the fraternity as an official campus organization and forbade students from living, convening, or dining at the fraternity house, the plaintiffs filed suit claiming promissory estoppel, negligent misrepresentation, and tortious interference with business expectancies. Following a jury trial, the plaintiffs were awarded damages, attorney fees and costs, and an injunction mandating the university allow the corporation to house students and give the fraternity three years to transition to a coeducational arrangement. On appeal, the court reversed the trial court's decision, noting that the contract between the parties easily allowed the university to rescind recognition of the organization and that the jury should have been instructed accordingly. Further, given the contract's language, the corporation did not expect that it would perpetually be guaranteed the right to house students.

A student at a public university filed an open records request under New Jersey state law to obtain, among other things, any documents, paper or electronic, created during a certain time frame that contained his name or initials; employment, professional, and salary information related to a specified list of university officials; and all documents, with names redacted, related to any other graduate students charged with a separable offense during a

---

[11] Doe 1 v. George Washington Univ., 480 F. Supp. 3d 224, 385 Educ. L. Rep. 740 (D.D.C. 2021).
[12] Kent Literary Club of Wesleyan Univ. at Middletown v. Wesleyan Univ., 257 A.3d 874, 394 Educ. L. Rep. 980 (Conn. 2021).

specified time frame.[13] The student filed suit after his request was denied. A trial court dismissed the student's claim, but a New Jersey appellate court reversed, finding that the student was entitled to access to his records, and remanded the issue to determine if he was eligible to recoup attorney fees.

Student Misconduct

Academic Misconduct

An Indiana student claimed breach of contract—along with a violation of the Americans with Disabilities Act ("ADA"), false advertising, and defamation—after suspension from his institution on academic misconduct grounds and subsequent denial of reapplication. The Seventh Circuit affirmed the Indiana District Court in upholding the disciplinary measures taken by the institution following the plaintiff's extensive record of duplicating peers' assignments and no evidence of a breach of contract sufficient to satisfy Indiana's legal standard.[14] Moreover, the ADA complaint was dismissed because the institutional defendants showed clear documentation of accommodations to help the plaintiff succeed in their studies.

In another academic dismissal case, the Eighth Circuit ruled that the university officials had reasonably pursued their termination efforts against a first-year medical resident who had discharged a pulmonary embolism patient without following protocol on prescribing medication or following up with superiors.[15] The 57-year-old student sued the university for wrongful termination, claiming her firing was due to factors such as age and a preliminary disability diagnosis from a psychologist that her information retention skills were of fair concern to her future in the program. The court affirmed the Nebraska district court's holding, however, that reasons for termination were not indicative of discrimination; rather, the patient safety mistake and history of dubious progress in the medical program were reason enough for termination, and the institution followed protocol when making this decision.

---

[13] Doe v. Rutgers State Univ. of N. J., 245 A.3d 261, 387 Educ. L. Rep. 803 (N.J. Super. Ct. App. Div. 2021).
[14] Castelino v. Rose-Hulman Inst. of Tech., 999 F.3d 1031, 391 Educ. L. Rep. 436 (7th Cir. 2021).
[15] Canning v. Creighton Univ., 995 F.3d 603, 389 Educ. L. Rep. 50 (8th Cir. 2021).

A student in New York brought forth an Article 78 proceeding, which challenges due process rights under state law after they were expelled from their institution following a multiyear disciplinary process for violating the academic honor code.[16] The student argued that the initial accusations and subsequent hearings regarding his alleged cheating did not follow the procedures explicitly set by the institutional handbook, including the provision of witnesses. The Supreme Court of New York dismissed these claims and upheld the expulsion after concluding that the institutional disciplinary processes and the student's history of academic misconduct were operationally sound.

Following the dismissal from a Texas law school after a first-year academic performance that failed to meet grade point average (GPA) requirements, a student brought suit against the school, arguing that the dismissal constituted a breach of contract and a due course of law violation for a constitutionally protected property interest.[17] The Supreme Court of Texas affirmed the initial trial court ruling that such academic dismissal did not satisfy the property interest argument, as removal from the law program would not substantially impede the plaintiff's ability to find a job nor pursue future endeavors without a damaging stigma attached. Moreover, the student not only had notice of the law school GPA requirement and related academic standards before and during his dismissal process but also had the option of reenrolling at that same school after two years; thus, all due process considerations were satisfied in favor of the university defendants.

Non-Academic Misconduct

The Second Circuit heard the appeal of a military academy cadet who had amassed an extensive history of behavioral demerits pursuing legal recourse after mandated separation from the academy in his final year.[18] The cadet argued his dismissal had violated his due process rights; specifically, he was not granted the opportunity to utilize all disciplinary hearing processes, nor was the preponderance evidentiary standard employed by academy officials sufficient considering the facts of his case. Although the court took note of the six-figure recoupment that the plaintiff was ordered to

---

[16] Doe v. Trs. of Union Coll., 150 N.Y.S.3d 347, 393 Educ. L. Rep. 797 (N.Y. App. Div. 2021).
[17] Tex. S. Univ. v. Villarreal, 620 S.W.3d 899, 390 Educ. L. Rep. 422 (Tex. 2021).
[18] Doolen v. Wormuth, 5 F.4th 125, 393 Educ. L. Rep. 13 (2d Cir. 2021).

pay back to the government after the separation results, the Second Circuit affirmed the New York district court's holding that the student had been given ample opportunities spanning multiple years to mitigate his many demerits, and the intra-military immunity doctrine prevented further consideration of whether the preponderance standard was effectively applied.

Another unsuccessful due process complaint arose in the Sixth Circuit after a student was expelled for multiple counts of sexual assault. The expulsion outcome followed numerous rounds of disciplinary proceedings, including a three-day in-person proceeding, but the plaintiff filed suit under the premise that his procedures violated his due process rights, Title IX, and the Equal Protection Clause.[19] The plaintiff later narrowed the suit to a due process complaint, specifically arguing that university officials allowed the alleged victims to avoid certain questions during the cross-examination process. A Michigan district court dismissed both the due process claim and subsequent amendments to the complaint, and the Sixth Circuit affirmed this decision, noting that there were substantiative due process measures taken to ensure a fair proceeding.

A California appellate court reversed a lower court decision ruling in favor of a male student plaintiff with disabilities who faced suspension from campus after accusations of sexual misconduct from two female students.[20] The student, whose possible suspension was later reduced to a disciplinary notation on his college records, argued his due process rights were violated after campus disciplinary officials did not allow him the ability to cross-examine witnesses for his defense. The appellate court ruled that the initial hearing and notice of his charges (i.e., first-level due process) were sufficient enough to satisfy the plaintiff's due process rights and argued the trial court had erred in their ruling that the plaintiff was entitled to that second level of the process once the suspension outcome had been removed as a possibility instead of a warranted reprimand. In another California case, a national fraternity challenged the decision of a California institution to suspend their local chapter for six years after a fact-finding mission yielded a pattern of hazing incongruent with campus policies. The fraternity petitioned the university to appeal the suspension, followed by an attempted writ of administrative mandamus to a California trial court on the basis

---

[19] Doe v. Mich. State Univ., 989 F.3d 418, 387 Educ. L. Rep. 70 (6th Cir. 2021).
[20] Knight v. S. Orange Cmty. Coll. Dist., 275 Cal. Rptr. 3d 139, 386 Educ. L. Rep. 902 (Cal. Ct. App. 2021).

that the fact-finding mission violated proper evidentiary and administrative guidelines.[21] Both attempts at appeal were denied, and the California appellate court affirmed the earlier judgments that the university had conducted a thorough investigation without any indication of bias.

A string of three nonacademic misconduct cases took place in New York, albeit with somewhat varying outcomes. In one case, a student filed an Article 78 proceeding following campus disciplinary proceedings that determined he violated the institution's code of conduct via accusations of stalking and noncompliance.[22] The New York appellate court affirmed the lower court's ruling that the institution had diligently followed its disciplinary procedures leading to the outcome of suspension. In the second case, an appellate court reversed three previously granted Article 78 petitions from students who faced campus suspensions for their conduct found in violation of the Fall 2020 COVID-19 precautions.[23] The students argued that the institution had ineffectively communicated the potential disciplinary ramifications of partaking in unmasked, non-socially distanced gatherings during the pandemic; thus, they had no formal directives that participating in such environments could result in sanctions. The state appellate court's determination ran contrary to the lower court for two major reasons: (a) the appellate court recognized that the institution's status as a private institution precluded it from extensive judicial oversight of the conduct process, and (b) the student's argument about clear, a prior warning was marred in large part due to their violation of New York's executive order at the time. The third case from New York emerged when a state appellate court affirmed in part and denied in part the appeal of university defendants to dismiss a former student's breach of contract and defamation suit.[24] The student had been expelled from the defending institution after student conduct officials found him responsible for extensive sexual misconduct. Still, a jury later found him not guilty in criminal proceedings. Despite an eventual settlement and agreement between the expelling institution and the student that his

---

[21] Alpha Nu Ass'n of Theta Xi v. Univ. of S. Cal., 276 Cal. Rptr. 3d 623, 388 Educ. L. Rep. 282 (Cal. Ct. App. 2021).
[22] Rodriguez v. State Univ. of N.Y. at Buffalo, 145 N.Y.S.3d 725, 391 Educ. L. Rep. 352 (N.Y. App. Div. 2021).
[23] Storino v. N.Y. Univ., 146 N.Y.S.3d 594, 391 Educ. L. Rep. 927 (N.Y. App. Div. 2021).
[24] Bisimwa v. St. John Fisher Coll., 149 N.Y.S.3d 428, 393 Educ. L. Rep. 413 (N.Y. App. Div. 2021).

disciplinary record would be expunged in future transcripts, the assistant dean of students shared the student's disciplinary outcome and reasoning with two other institutions to which the student applied. The court dismissed the argument from the defendants that their settlement agreement permitted them to share non-expunged records with other entities but affirmed their argument that the defamation suit was without merit and, thus, the plaintiff was not entitled to punitive damages for the misstep by a private institution.

Torts

Although many of the tort cases in higher education are reviewed in the torts chapter, two cases this past year reflect ongoing concerns for legal concerns of college students and are noted in this section. The parents of a student who died from an alcohol-fueled hazing incident filed suit against numerous fraternity members in Louisiana federal district court.[25] The court considered whether amended allegations against members of the executive committee of the fraternity were time-barred. Before the hazing ritual, executive committee members met with a fraternity member over concerns about dangerous activities involving new members. On the night in question, the deceased student was forced to drink excessive amounts of alcohol and left on a sofa unresponsive. Fraternity members did not seek care for him until the next morning when new members were told to take him to the hospital and said they discovered him in his dorm room. He died at the hospital. The district court declined to dismiss claims against members of the executive committee, finding that facts existed that could render them joint tortfeasors, which expands the statute of limitations on filing claims.

The family of a student injured in an automobile accident following a campus party sued, alleging negligence against the student hosts, resident advisors, and the university. A New Jersey appellate court affirmed summary judgment in favor of the hosts but reversed summary judgment in favor of the resident advisors and university.[26] The student attended a party where he brought and consumed alcohol. He had indicated to his parents and the hosts his

---

[25] Gruver v. Louisiana *ex rel.* Bd. of Sup'rs of La. State Univ. and Agr. and Mech. Coll., 510 F. Supp. 3d 367, 391 Educ. L. Rep. 721 (M.D. La. 2021).
[26] Franco v. Fairleigh Dickinson Univ.,248 A.3d 1254, 390 Educ. L. Rep. 322 (N.J. Super. App. Div. 2021).

intent to spend the night but woke up and left around 5:00 a.m. when he was in an accident. The court did not find the hosts liable for the injuries the student sustained after he woke up and left. The court found a question of fact for a jury as to whether the resident assistants at the party were grossly negligent in not reporting underage drinking on campus, violating university policy.

COVID-19

In 2021, numerous suits were filed against institutions concerning the shift from on-campus to online instruction due to the COVID-19 pandemic—and with varying results and rationales. The First Circuit upheld a Maine district court's determination that granted a private company's motion to dismiss the plaintiff student's breach of contract claims when it shifted the final weeks of a study abroad experience to online instruction.[27] The plaintiff claimed she was owed a refund for the canceled excursions and activities because of this shift. Still, the court looked to the provision in the contract that the company would provide reasonable alternative arrangements for students to complete coursework should a program be canceled after the start date. Based on this provision and the court's refusal to find the contract procedurally or substantively unconscionable, the First Circuit affirmed that the plaintiff was not entitled to a refund.

In another instance, a Rhode Island federal district court reviewed five lawsuits brought against four universities in tandem.[28] All of the suits claimed that the institutions' decision to transition from on-campus learning to online instruction constituted a breach of contract. The plaintiffs alleged that "university publications, including websites, marketing materials, course catalogs, and other resources," constituted promises for on-campus experiences that could not be replicated online. The court granted the universities' motion to dismiss the claims, finding that there was no evidence of an existing contract that promised on-campus instruction; the publications referenced by the plaintiffs were general advertisements that were "vague and more akin to puffery, rather than enforceable promises."

---

[27] Zhao v. CIEE Inc., 3 F.4th 1, 391 Educ. L. Rep. 555 (1st Cir. 2021).
[28] Burt v. Bd. of Trs. of Univ. of R.I., 523 F. Supp. 3d 214, 394 Educ. L. Rep. 771 (D.R.I. 2021).

Similarly, a federal district court in New York granted an institution's motion to dismiss the plaintiff student's breach of contract claims related to a shift to online instruction.[29] The plaintiff's primary evidence was a catalog identifying "courses offered, instructors, and the times and locations of classes," with the location category "identifying the campus, building, and room" for each course, and students could sort classes by "online" or "in-person." The plaintiff also points to statements in the university's Academic Policies and Procedures regarding attendance and transfer policies. However, the court did not find that any published materials pointed to a promise of on-campus instruction.

A federal district court in Illinois dismissed claims against an institution for breach of contract and unjust enrichment when it failed to reimburse students prorated tuition and fees following the transition from on-campus to online instruction due to the COVID-19 pandemic.[30] The plaintiffs point to many documents describing "course offerings and residential life" at the university and the difference in tuition between in-person and online programs. However, the court did not find that any of the published materials related to on-campus programs made a contractual promise for on-campus instruction, and the difference in tuition for in-person and online programs was insufficient to prove a specific promise. However, regardless of the merits, the plaintiffs' breach of contract claims are barred by the educational malpractice doctrine, which prohibits courts from evaluating the quality of education or the "professional judgment" of a university.

Meanwhile, in some jurisdictions, the federal courts were more sympathetic to students' claims related to campus shutdowns. In a federal district court in Vermont, a class of students sued their university for breach of contract and unjust enrichment after the university switched to online learning due to COVID-19.[31] The students sought a partial refund of tuition, alleging the universities course catalog and website created actionable promises for in-person instruction. They also sought a refund for housing and meal plans; however, the housing and meal plans included a clause stating that "[i]n the event that the [university] closes due to a calamity or

---

[29] Hassan v. Fordham Univ., 515 F. Supp. 3d 77, 392 Educ. L. Rep. 704 (S.D.N.Y. 2021).

[30] Gociman v. Loyola Univ. of Chi., 515 F. Supp. 3d 861, 392 Educ. L. Rep. 801 (N.D. Ill. 2021).

[31] Patel v. Univ. of Vt. And State Agric. Coll., 526 F.Supp.3d 3, 395 Educ. L. Rep. 201 (D. Vt. 2021).

catastrophe beyond its control that would make continued operation of student housing infeasible, such as...widespread pandemic flu, room, and meal plan fees will not be refunded." The court ruled that the plaintiffs were not entitled to prorated refunds for housing and meals because of the "emergency closing" provision in the university's contract; however, the court denied a motion to dismiss claims related to a prorated refund for tuition.

In two separate cases filed against the same university, a federal district court in Arizona ruled that certain claims could move forward. Both cases involved class actions brought by students for breach of contract, unjust enrichment, and conversion due to the university's switch to online learning in response to COVID-19 and its failure to issue any refunds. In one case, the court rejected the institution's defense that it was impossible to provide the services in question due to the restrictions in place because of the pandemic.[32] The court denied the university's motion to dismiss the claims related to reimbursement of fees and prorated amounts for housing and meals. It dismissed with the ability to amend the contractual claims regarding the shift to online instruction. In the other case, the Arizona district court likewise found the plaintiffs had pled grounds to pursue contract and unjust enrichment claims when the institution failed to return portions of the money charged for meals, housing, and fees.[33]

In Florida, two federal district courts denied institutions' motions to dismiss claims against them for breach of contract. In the first case, a student sued his university, alleging breach of contract and unjust enrichment after changing its policies regarding academics and student life due to COVID-19.[34] In Florida, the contract terms between a student and a private university "may be derived from university publications such as the student handbook and catalog." Therefore, the court found that published materials equated to an implied contract promising students they would receive on-campus instruction. In the second case, another Florida district court heard a claim from students against their private university, alleging breach of contract and unjust enrichment after

---

[32] Hannibal-Fisher v. Grand Canyon Univ., 523 F. Supp. 3d 1087, 394 Educ. L. Rep. 846 (D. Ariz. 2021).
[33] Little v. Grand Canyon Univ., 516 F. Supp. 3d 958, 393 Educ. L. Rep. 297 (D. Ariz. 2021).
[34] Rhodes v. Embry-Riddle Aeronautical Univ., Inc., 513 F. Supp. 3d 1350, 392 Educ. L. Rep. 623 (M.D. Fla. 2021).

the university switched to online learning due to COVID-19.[35] Because contractual terms between a student and their private university "may be found in university catalogs, student manuals, student handbooks, and other university policies and procedures," the court agreed that the plaintiffs stated plausible claims that their contractual right to on-campus instruction had been breached and, thus, denied the university's motion to dismiss.

Discrimination

First Amendment

As was the case in 2020, among the discrimination-based claims in 2021 that emerged from the higher education context, violations of the First Amendment and-or viewpoint discrimination represented a significant grouping.

In a Fifth Circuit case on appeal from Texas, the plaintiff was removed from a graduate program in epidemiology after failing a required examination three times.[36] He filed suit alleging viewpoint discrimination and retaliation, failure to provide due process, and various state claims. He claimed he was dismissed because he was critical of current vaccine research. The district court dismissed his claim for lack of jurisdiction and failure to state a claim. In affirming the lower court, the Fifth Circuit held that the plaintiff failed to allege that the defendants were aware of his views on vaccines and, therefore, could not allege that such views were the motivating factor in his dismissal. In another Fifth Circuit case, the plaintiff, a postdoctoral fellow, claimed that his boss and named defendant promised to promote him to assistant professor contingent on his publishing two first-author research papers.[37] He published one in 2016. Two years later a colleague published a paper where the plaintiff was not listed as the first author. The plaintiff complained to the defendant, saying the other researcher was not permitted to publish the paper. In the response in which his complaint was denied, the plaintiff claimed that he was defamed. A meeting was held where the plaintiff was told to accept the decision, but he couldn't and ultimately was transferred to a different lab. The

---

[35]*In re* Univ. of Miami COVID-19 Tuition and Fee Refund Litig., 524 F. Supp. 3d 1346, 394 Educ. L. Rep. 901 (S.D. Fla. 2021).
[36]Doe v Harrell, 841 F.App'x 663, 388 Educ. L. Rep. 188 (5th Cir. 2021).
[37] Huang v Huang, 846 F.App'x 224, 389 Educ. L. Rep. 737 (5th Cir. 2021).

plaintiff filed suit, but it was dismissed by the Texas district court. On appeal, the Fifth Circuit held that the plaintiff's claims were barred by the Eleventh Amendment as to the university and university officials. As to his First Amendment free speech claims, the plaintiff's rights were not violated when he reported alleged scientific misconduct regarding the publication of the paper when he was told not to use "I think" in emails or by being told to sit by the supervisor's desk.

Two cases brought against the same university successfully challenged the application of a human rights policy against student organizations. In one case, students formed a registered student organization ("RSO") with the stated purpose of being a religious organization.[38] The university had a policy that RSOs must comply with its human rights policy and allow all students to join but it did not have an "all-comers policy" requiring RSOs to accept any student as a member or leader of a group. The university has also permitted religious groups to require members and leaders to adhere to a certain religious ideology. The issue arose when a gay man filed a complaint with the university after being denied a leadership position in an RSO because he refused to support and protect the group's religious mission, which included the belief that homosexual relationships were outside of God's design. The organization sued after the university revoked its RSO status, alleging violations of the First and Fourteenth Amendments, the federal Higher Education Act, and Iowa state laws. Ultimately, the Eighth Circuit reversed the Iowa district court's grant of qualified immunity for the individual administrators on the free speech and association claims because the law forbidding viewpoint discrimination was clearly established at the time but held that the individuals were entitled to qualified immunity on the free exercise claim. In the second case, the plaintiff's claim was based on the action of the defendant university following a court order to stop selectively enforcing a policy against student groups based on viewpoint.[39] When one religious RSO was required to be recognized, the university deregistered another, the current plaintiff. The plaintiff, a Christian RSO, had been active at the university for over 25 years until, during the above litigation, the university decided that the plaintiff violated its human rights policy and deregistered it as an RSO. It was not until the other RSO

---

[38]Business Leaders in Christ v Univ. of Iowa, 991 F.3d 969, 388 Educ. L. Rep. 79 (8th Cir. 2021).
[39]Intervarsity Christian Fellowship/USA v Univ. of Iowa, 5 F.4th 855, 393 Educ. L. Rep. 53 (8th Cir. 2021).

prevailed that the university reinstated the plaintiff, but damage to membership had already been done. The plaintiff sued the university and named administrators for violating the First Amendment speech and religion protections and damages. The defendants sought qualified immunity. The court found in favor of the plaintiff, once again finding a blatant case of viewpoint discrimination. Regarding qualified immunity, the Eighth Circuit affirmed the Iowa district court's denial of the defendants' motion for summary judgment, finding that the law was clearly established and that a policy that is viewpoint neutral on its face can still be unconstitutional if not applied uniformly.

In another Eighth Circuit case on appeal from Minnesota, a political student organization ("PSO") brought a conservative media personality to speak on campus at an event funded by a conservative youth foundation.[40] The PSO was advised to use the university's Large Scale Event Process (LSEP) policy to arrange the visit. The PSO did not use the LSEP, instead requesting a reservation for a large auditorium. The university president made clear in communications that he did not want the event located in the middle of campus. The PSO attempted to secure a larger venue further from the center of campus but could not do so and continued with its plans despite being told that security concerns made the auditorium unsuitable for the event. The event was held without any major disruptions. The plaintiffs sued the defendants in their official and individual capacities alleging First and Fourteenth Amendment violations. Specifically, the plaintiffs alleged the university LSEP policy was unconstitutional on its face and as applied. The defendants moved to dismiss and were subsequently granted summary judgment. On appeal, the court held that the challenges to the LSEP policy were moot as the university had adopted a new policy; further, the plaintiffs lacked standing.

A district court in Virginia heard a case where the plaintiff, a second-year medical student, attended a professor's presentation on microaggressions and proceeded to get involved in a question-and-answer session where the plaintiff monopolized the floor and persistently challenged the presentation until another faculty member stepped in.[41] Another faculty member who witnessed the altercation filed a complaint about professionalism with the university regarding the plaintiff's behavior. After an escalated

---

[40] Young America's Found. v Kaler, 14 F.4th 879, 395 Educ. L. Rep. 157 (8th Cir. 2021).
[41] Bhattacharya v Murry, 515 F.Supp.3d 436, 392 Educ. L. Rep. 748 (W.D. Va. 2021).

formal meeting, the plaintiff was suspended from the program over behavioral concerns. A no-trespass order was also issued against him. The plaintiff filed suit claiming retaliation for exercising his First Amendment right to free speech and violation of his due process rights. The defendant filed a motion to dismiss. The district court granted the motion in part and denied it in part. The court held that the plaintiff's comments at the panel discussion and at the hearing were protected speech. In addition, the plaintiff sufficiently alleged retaliation, showing temporal proximity such as to allege causality. However, the plaintiff was provided sufficient due process at the hearing and failed to state a cognizable claim under the civil rights conspiracy statute.

In the final case claiming violation of the First Amendment, the plaintiffs filed suit alleging that the procedure in which mandatory student-services fees were distributed was not viewpoint neutral.[42] The defendant university has adopted a policy governing the distribution of the fees, which included, in relevant part, that the allocation of fees will be done in a viewpoint-neutral manner. The plaintiffs contended that media groups were given preferential treatment and that the process used to fund media groups violated the First Amendment. Specifically, media groups were allowed to apply for unlimited funding, whereas RSOs have annual limits. The viewpoint discrimination allegedly occurred when the university established a public forum limited to media groups, thereby discriminating against RSOs that are not media groups. The defendants moved to dismiss. The Minnesota district court held that the preferential treatment given to media groups was not viewpoint discrimination; however, the process used to determine who could apply for media-group funding did violate the First Amendment by vesting unbridled discretion in one individual. Claims regarding processes for using the student union stated a potential constitutional issue, but refusing funding to partisan political organizations and requiring they provide financial documents were not viewpoint discrimination.

National Origin, Race, and Ethnicity

Discrimination based on national origin was the allegation in the next case, which was decided by the Tenth Circuit on appeal from a

---

[42] *Viewpoint Neutrality Now! v Regents of Univ. of Minn.*, 516 F.Supp.3d 904, 393 Educ. L. Rep. 269 (D. Minn. 2021).

federal district court in Colorado. The plaintiff, a doctoral student from the United Arab Emirates, filed suit against the defendant's board of trustees for national origin discrimination under Title VI.[43] When the plaintiff sat for his doctoral exam, he failed the theory part of the exam. He complained that he was given a method rather than a theory or question, and such an irregularity was absent with any other student's exam. In addition, one of the individuals grading the exam had conflicted with the plaintiff earlier in his studies and was to have no further contact with him. The district court dismissed the case. On appeal, the Tenth Circuit affirmed the dismissal, holding that the plaintiff failed to allege a link between the failing grade on his exam and discrimination based on national origin. While the court does not require the pleading to contain specific facts, the plaintiff must include enough information to connect the adverse action with a discriminatory or retaliatory motive. This was not done here.

Race discrimination and a violation of the first amendment were both alleged in an Eleventh Circuit case from Georgia.[44] The plaintiff, a public university cheerleader, kneeled during the pre-game national anthem at a university football game. Counsel informed state university presidents that the First Amendment protected the right to kneel so long as they were not disruptive. A state legislator and the county sheriff told the university that the cheerleaders must not be allowed to kneel. The university adopted the "tunnel rule," quickly abolished after public outcry, where the cheerleaders would remain in the tunnel during the national anthem. The plaintiff sued university leadership, state legislators, and the county sheriff, alleging First Amendment violations and conspiracy to commit a civil rights violation by denial of First Amendment rights. On appeal, the Eleventh Circuit affirmed the dismissal of the conspiracy claim against the sheriff, finding that the plaintiff failed to plausibly plead that the sheriff's actions were motivated by race. Additionally, the court held that when the cheerleaders were on the field, they were representing the school and, therefore, engaged in government speech, not individual speech that the First Amendment would cover.

---

[43] Al Ghareeb v Bd. of Trs. at Univ. of N. Colo., 849 F.App'x 746, 390 Educ. L. Rep. 912 (10th Cir. 2021).
[44] Dean v Warren, 12 F.4th 1248, 395 Educ. L. Rep. 51 (11th Cir. 2021).

Disability

The three cases alleging disability discrimination were based on failure to provide reasonable accommodations. In the Third Circuit, a former graduate student had ADHD and a sleep disorder.[45] When he enrolled in the defendant's private university, he sought and was granted disability accommodations. Unfortunately, even with the accommodations, he had difficulties; he was granted additional accommodations but continued to fail academically and was ultimately dismissed. He filed suit against the university under the Americans with Disabilities Act ("ADA"), alleging that the university discriminated against him when he was dismissed for his grades falling below the required standard and not being provided reasonable accommodations. The case was dismissed in the Pennsylvania district court. On appeal, the Third Circuit affirmed the lower court's decision, finding that the plaintiff was not "otherwise qualified" to continue in the program and, therefore, his dismissal was not due to bias for requesting ADA accommodations. The qualifications to enter a program may differ from those to stay enrolled. Even with reasonable accommodations, the student was unable to do the latter.

In the second suit, the plaintiffs were two blind students.[46] When they enrolled at the defendant community college, they each registered for disability accommodations. Even with such accommodations, they encountered accessibility problems for textbooks, in-class materials, educational technology, website and computer applications, and research databases at the college library. They sued the community college, alleging ADA and Section 504 violations. At trial, the students were awarded a permanent injunction against the defendant. On appeal, the Ninth Circuit found that the California district court had erroneously limited the scope of the plaintiffs' disability discrimination claims. Specifically, the court stated that a private right of action exists to enforce disparate impact claims under Title II but that the district court had improperly required the students to present some of their claims under disparate impact rather than failure to accommodate. "The important difference between these two theories is that a reasonable accommodation claim is focused on an accommodation based on an

---

[45] Jain v Carnegie Mellon Univ., 846 F. App'x 156, 389 Educ. L. Rep. 732 (3rd Cir. 2021).
[46] Payan v L.A. Cmty. Coll. Dist., 11 F.4th 729, 394 Educ. L. Rep. 138 (9th Cir. 2021).

individualized request or need, while a reasonable modification in response to a disparate impact finding is focused on modifying a policy or practice to improve systemic accessibility."[47]

The remaining case was an issue of lack of access. In a Florida district court case, the plaintiffs, deaf Florida residents and an advocacy group for Floridians with disabilities, sued the governor and a public university, alleging violations of the ADA for failing to provide in-frame American Sign Language interpreters on television channels operated by the university that broadcast the governor's press briefings.[48] The plaintiffs sought declaratory and injunctive relief. The request was denied, and the defendants moved to dismiss. In response, the plaintiffs moved to strike declarations attached to the dismissal. Both motions were denied. On the topic of the attached declarations, the court held that the plaintiffs sufficiently alleged facts to support standing, and issues of federal funding were relevant to the issue of immunity. Regarding the defendant's motion to dismiss, the court held that the plaintiffs had alleged a concrete and particularized injury, that their injury was traceable to and redressable by the defendants, and that they had made sufficient allegations to overcome Eleventh Amendment immunity.

Sex Discrimination/Harassment

The topics of deliberate indifference and gender bias in reporting, investigation, and discipline under Title IX were seen in several cases this year. In a Third Circuit case from Pennsylvania, the plaintiff, a former radiology resident, filed a Title IX suit against the defendant hospital alleging the creation of a hostile environment, retaliation, and quid pro quo harassment.[49] She alleged that an individual continually followed her, told her he loved her, and suggested they take trips together. She claimed that her residency was terminated because she refused his advances. Emails sent during this time contradict this narrative, as the plaintiff spoke of being in love with him. Even when the hospital administration attempted to intervene, the plaintiff continued to be the primary instigator of the conflict. Ultimately her residency was terminated. The hospital was granted summary judgment. On appeal, summary judgment was affirmed when the court held that the retaliation

---

[47] Payan, 11 F. 4th at 738.
[48] Yelapi v DeSantis, 525 F.Supp.3d 1317, 394 Educ. L. Rep. 921 (N.D. Fla. 2021).
[49] Doe v Mercy Catholic Med. Ctr., 855 F. App'x 842, 393 Educ. L. Rep. 178 (3rd Cir. 2021).

claim was not actionable, a prima facie case of quid pro quo harassment was not established, and due process was not denied. Regarding the retaliation claim, the hospital provided a legitimate reason for the plaintiff's termination, and she was unable to prove that such reasons were pretextual.

In a Fourth Circuit case from Virginia, the plaintiff's lawsuit arose from a conflict with a former girlfriend after she had taken some items from his dorm room.[50] When the resident assistants would not help him regain his property, he did it himself. While trying to retrieve his keys from her, he inadvertently pushed her. She filed a complaint. While the plaintiff was off campus, his ex-girlfriend took out a no-contact order against him. Unaware of the order, it was extended, and the plaintiff was suspended from school. The plaintiff filed suit against the university alleging that he was treated differently from his ex-girlfriend, who ultimately was found responsible for theft based on sex. The district court granted the university's motion to dismiss, finding that he failed to show he was treated less favorably than a similarly situated student on the basis of gender. In affirming the lower court's decision, the appellate court held that the plaintiff failed to state a plausible Title IX or equal protection claim that his treatment was based on his sex and that the university was entitled to qualified immunity regarding the due process claim.

In the first of three Eighth Circuit cases, the question was whether the plaintiff had engaged in a protected activity to trigger federal law. The plaintiff was a student-athlete at the university.[51] During her first year, her coach took a leave of absence because she was being investigated for sexual harassment. The plaintiff participated in the investigation, supporting the coach, who ultimately resigned. When a new coach was appointed, the plaintiff told him she was injured and couldn't compete. She was given the option of competing or leaving the team. Eventually, the plaintiff transferred and sued the defendant, alleging retaliation for participating in the sexual harassment investigation to support the coach, specifically by not allowing her to redshirt and sex discrimination under Title IX. The Minnesota district court granted the defendant's motion to dismiss. On appeal, the court affirmed that the plaintiff failed to allege that she engaged in protected activity

---

[50] Sheppard v Visitors of Va. State Univ., 993 F.3d 230, 388 Educ. L. Rep. 540 (4th Cir. 2021).
[51] DuBois v Bd. of Regents of Univ. of Minn., 987 F.3d 1199, 386 Educ. L. Rep. 581 (8th Cir. 2021).

under Title IX because she had never complained of sex discrimination. Participation in a sexual harassment investigation supporting the accused is not protected. Therefore, the plaintiff failed to plead facts sufficient to support her claim of a Title IX violation.

In another Eight Circuit case from Minnesota, eleven African-American football players filed suit against the university alleging sex discrimination and retaliation under Title IX, race discrimination under Title VI and the Equal Protection Clause, and violation of their due process rights.[52] The suit arose from the university's investigation into allegations of sexual assault against the men. Their suspension was lifted when the county attorney declined to file charges. The district court granted the university's motion for summary judgment, and ten of the men appealed. On appeal, the court held that although the players failed to state a retaliation or Title VI race discrimination claim, they did state a claim under Title IX. The 2011 "Dear Colleague Letter," combined with allegations of external pressure on the university from public attention, the threat of losing federal funding, and other evidence, created a plausible claim. In addition, the court held that the players failed to exhaust their state law remedies on deprivation of pre-hearing and post-hearing procedural due process.

In the third Eighth Circuit case from Minnesota, a student claimed she was assaulted in the dormitories by two male students.[53] The college learned of the alleged assault when the plaintiff student was hospitalized on suicide watch after seeing athletics posters featuring a photo of the first attacker. The plaintiff refused to identify her attacker or file a complaint. She did ask for several accommodations, which were granted, but they did not seem sufficient. She brought an action against her college alleging Title IX violations, intentional infliction of emotional distress, negligence per se, statutory social host liability, and breach of contract. The plaintiff alleged that the college mishandled disciplinary proceedings against the two male students accused of sexual assault. Summary judgment was granted to the defendant's college. On appeal, the appellate court affirmed, holding that how the disciplinary proceedings were conducted did not constitute deliberate indifference. Not only had the college urged the plaintiff to file her complaint, but it also did so upon learning the alleged attacker's name; its actions were not

---

[52] Does 1-2 v Regents of the Univ. of Minn. 999 F.3d 571, 391 Educ. L. Rep. 74 (8th Cir. 2021).
[53] Shank v Carleton Coll., 993 F.3d 567, 388 Educ. L. Rep. 562 (8th Cir. 2021).

clearly unreasonable in light of the known circumstances. In addition, the plaintiff was not denied reasonable accommodations.

In a Tenth Circuit case from Colorado, the plaintiff, a former male student, was expelled following an investigation of a sexual assault claim filed against him.[54] He filed suit against the defendant university, alleging sex discrimination arising from the university's investigation. The facts in the record provide very different views on what exactly took place. The plaintiff alleged that the investigation was tainted by anti-male bias to such a degree that it was reasonable to infer that sex was a motiving factor for its decision. The defendant emphasized that its policies are pro-sexual-assault complainant, rather than pro-female. Despite these conflicting accounts, the lower court entered summary judgment for the university. On appeal, the Tenth Circuit held that the plaintiff had made a prima facie case that the defendant's investigation and its decision to expel him was motivated by sex. In addition, the defendant had proffered legitimate reasons for its behavior. Therefore, a question remained as to whether the reasons given were pretextual and whether granting summary judgment was improper.

In South Carolina federal district court, the plaintiff brought a Title IX action against the defendant university, alleging gender bias in disciplinary proceedings, resulting in his permanent dismissal from the university.[55] The investigation and two disciplinary hearings occurred after the plaintiff and his roommate engaged in sexual intercourse with the alleged victim, who claimed she could not consent due to intoxication. At the first hearing, the plaintiff was found not in violation. At a second hearing, he was found in violation. What caused the Title IX director to review the files and hold a second hearing is unclear. The university was denied summary judgment because the different outcomes following the first and second disciplinary hearings created a genuine issue of material fact regarding the accuracy of the outcome. Although the difference in treatment between the alleged victim and plaintiff and small talk between the victim and members of the student conduct board was not evidence of gender bias, the questions surrounding the decision to grant the alleged victim a second hearing did create a question of material fact as to whether the university was motivated by gender bias.

---

[54]Doe v Univ. of Denver, 1 F.4th 822, 391 Educ. L. Rep. 506 (10th Cir. 2021).
[55]Doe v Coastal Carolina Univ., 522 F.Supp.3d 173, 394 Educ. L. Rep. 598 (D.S.C. 2021).

A New York federal district court heard a case brought by female students against the defendant university alleging violation of Title IX and common law negligence and breach of contract.[56] The allegations stemmed from physical and verbal sexual harassment of female swim team members by male members and sexual assault by a male member of a non-swimmer. Such behavior was reported to coaches and administrators, but nothing was done. The Title IX office discouraged the plaintiffs from filing a complaint. Dismissal of the suit was granted to the university in part and denied in part. On appeal, the district court found that the plaintiffs met their burden to allege facts in addition to the harassment and assaults on campus, specifically that the university had actual notice of the risk of sexual assault and that deliberate indifference had been sufficiently pled. The breach of contract claim failed. The court held that the physical violence, biting and holding a woman's head underwater, was a far cry from the type of behavior that is not actionable under Title IX.

The Supreme Court of Rhode Island heard a rather complicated case in which a student from one university sued another university under the Rhode Island Civil Rights Act ("RICRA") and state constitution alleging mishandling of sexual assault allegations against a student at the second university.[57] The plaintiff alleged she was drugged at a bar and transported to the defendant's university, where three football players sexually assaulted her. The defendant's university informed the plaintiff that they would investigate and discipline the students under its code of conduct, which the plaintiff took as an insufficient Title IX response. The court dismissed the issue because, as a non-student, her claim did not fall under Title IX's private-cause-of-action and dismissed the Title IX suit. The plaintiff filed this suit under state law and was dismissed for failing to state a claim. The state Supreme Court held that RICRA was barred by collateral estoppel on the claims alleging Title IX violations and was inapplicable since the university being sued did not intentionally interfere with the plaintiff's education with her college as required. Finally, the antidiscrimination clause in the state constitution did not create a private cause of action.

The highest state court in New York explored the definition of consent.[58] Here, the plaintiff was accused of sexual assault by a fellow student with whom he had sexual intercourse. The female

---

[56] Posso v Niagra Univ., 518 F.Supp.3d 688, 393 Educ. L. Rep. 623 (W.D.N.Y. 2021).
[57] Doe v Brown Univ., 253 A.3d 389, 392 Educ. L. Rep. 920 (R.I. 2021).
[58] Doe v Purchase Coll. State Univ. of N.Y., 145 N.Y.S.3d 562, 391 Educ. L. Rep. 335 (N.Y. App. Div. 2021).

student stated that, although she had not told the plaintiff to stop, she could not consent because she consumed alcohol and-or her PTSD. The plaintiff disagreed, stating that she had consented to sexual activity through her actions. Despite conflicting and concerning discrepancies in the alleged victim's statements, the plaintiff was found in violation of the student code of conduct. The plaintiff was suspended, after which he filed suit. The court found that substantial evidence did not support the university's decision. While both agreed that no verbal consent was obtained, consent may be given by words or actions. To find that there was no consent was speculation. The plaintiff's Article 78 petition was granted, the determination was annulled, penalties were vacated, and it was directed that all references to the findings be expunged.

Other Discrimination

In a Seventh Circuit case on appeal from Indiana, the university enacted a policy for attendance requiring all students to be vaccinated against COVID-19 unless they had a recognized exemption for religious or health reasons.[59] Those exempted students were required to wear a mask and submit to testing twice a week. The plaintiff students filed suit alleging that the defendant's vaccination and testing requirements violated their right to due process. The district court denied their request for a preliminary injunction. On appeal, the Seventh Circuit held that the university's policy did not violate their due process. Unlike previous cases, the policy at the university allowed individuals to be granted exemptions. In addition, the policy only affected attendance to that one institution, allowing individuals who disagreed with the policy to choose to attend a different institution.

The Missouri Court of Appeals decided that the constitutionality of a university rule regarding firearms on campus was questioned. An employee of the university brought a suit against the university alleging that a university rule prohibiting the employee's possession of a firearm in his vehicle on campus violated state law.[60] The state of Missouri intervened and filed a parallel action under its name but raised the same claims. The plaintiff and the state argued that the university regulation prohibiting even the possession of a firearm in the employee's locked vehicle on campus was preempted by state

---

[59] Klaassen v Trs. of Ind. Univ., 7 F.4th 592, 393 Educ. L. Rep. 117 (7th Cir. 2021).
[60] State ex rel. Schmitt v Choi, 627 S.W.3d 1, 393 Educ. L. Rep. 962 (Mo. Ct. App. 2021).

law. In addition, the constitutionality of the rule was questioned. The state trial court found in favor of the university, finding that the rule satisfied strict scrutiny review. On appeal, the state appellate court held that the university rule directly conflicted with state law. On the question of constitutionality, the court held that the burden of proving that the university rule clearly and undoubtedly violated the state constitution rested with the plaintiffs. However, the rule was narrowly tailored to achieve the compelling governmental interest of promoting safety and reducing crime and therefore survived a strict scrutiny review.

Tuition and Student Financial Aid

A slew of student loan borrowers filed suit under the premise of undue hardship and had varying results. In one of those cases on appeal from New York, the Second Circuit held that a 52-year-old woman with no dependents, an income in excess of the federal poverty level, and no evidentiary support of a disability that would prevent said income failed to satisfy the undue hardship stipulations needed to discharge the remaining loan debt.[61]

In the Sixth Circuit, on appeal from Ohio, another student loan borrower presented the argument that her new student loan servicer violated the Fair Debt Collection Practices Act (FDCPA). The plaintiff, who had recently moved out of default status due to a "Rehabilitation Agreement" with her prior servicer, pursued legal recourse after the new servicer took over her loans and presented her with a balance and repayment plan which she felt was inaccurate and indicative of debt collecting practices.[62] The Sixth Circuit disagreed, however, affirming the earlier trial court ruling that because she was no longer classified as in default when this new servicer took over her existing balance, there was no violation of the FDCPA.

Another unsuccessful undue hardship claim arose in Illinois federal bankruptcy court when the Chapter 7 debtor sought to discharge nearly $245,000 in student loans. The plaintiff claimed the undue hardship prongs were satisfied due to a prior criminal conviction and status as a registered sex offender, which resulted in expulsion midway through law school; specifically, he argued that his job options under such restrictions were not high-paying enough

---

[61] *In re* Tingling, 990 F.3d 304, 387 Educ. L. Rep. 127 (2d Cir. 2021).
[62] Willison v. Nelnet, Inc., 850 F. App'x 389, 391 Educ. L. Rep. 143 (6th Cir. 2021).

to maintain the legally recognized baseline for a standard of living in addition to loan repayment.[63] Based on the calculated net monthly income, the state bankruptcy court did find that the plaintiff would never be able to pay off the loans in his current financial predicament; yet, they ultimately denied the plaintiff's undue hardship claim via arguments that (a) he had still successfully found full-time employment even with a criminal record, and that trend would likely continue; and (b) future expenditures that the plaintiff foresaw, such as caring for aging parents, were not associated with any dependents and were solely predictions.

In Maryland federal bankruptcy court, a Chapter 7 debtor had slightly more success with her undue hardship claim when the court ruled to discharge a portion of her six-figure student loan debt.[64] The court considered various factors in this determination, but particularly salient was the plaintiff's age (68), documented attempts at making payments while living within her means, and small likelihood of ever-increasing annual income to the point of making progress on student loans and general living expenses. As such, the court ruled that the plaintiff should only be responsible for paying $12,000 (plus interest) of the remaining debt over ten years.

Another case also resulted in a somewhat positive outcome for the plaintiff. A 64-year-old North Dakota woman with an extensive history of unfinished postsecondary coursework at several institutions cited an even longer history of sole part-time employment and considerable physical disability for her inability to repay her remaining student loan balance.[65] Given these factors, along with no assets nor the likelihood of financial advancement, the North Dakota federal bankruptcy court ruled that repayment of the loans would inflict undue hardship upon the plaintiff and ordered them discharged as a result.

Conversely, a Florida federal bankruptcy court held in favor of a defendant who argued the plaintiff—his ex-wife—still owed him nondischargeable student loan repayments after they divorced.[66] She stopped payments toward the loan agreement she had originally filed with his grandmother. The agreement for federal student loan repayment originally transpired to help the plaintiff pay off her private student loans, but upon the grandmother's death, the remaining balance of that loan agreement shifted to her ex-husband.

---

[63] *In re* Promisco, 625 B.R. 715, 388 Educ. L. Rep. 223 (Bankr. N.D. Ill. 2021).
[64] *In re* Randall, 628 B.R. 772, 391 Educ. L. Rep. 880 (Bankr. D. Md. 2021).
[65] *In re* Marchus, 630 B.R. 91, 393 Educ. L. Rep. 711 (Bankr. D.N.D. 2021).
[66] *In re* Mallett, 625 B.R. 553, 387 Educ. L. Rep. 788 (Bankr. M.D. Fla. 2021).

The court held that the defendant successfully proved these loans were nondischargeable due to a multiyear history of the plaintiff claiming tax deductions to the loan interest paid to the grandmother, thereby meeting the stipulations of a "qualified education loan."

In South Carolina, a federal bankruptcy court denied a Chapter 13 relief plan presented by a plaintiff who sought to alleviate some of her six-figure student loan debt amid even more debt owed due to a contentious divorce and sale of a previously shared asset.[67] Part of the court's decision stemmed from the plaintiff adding her new fiancé and stepdaughter as dependents under the plan, despite an existing no-contact order with said stepdaughter; moreover, the plaintiff was unable to dredge up proof needed to successfully contest the defendant's claim that her monthly disposable income figure was inaccurate.

In another case involving a student loan servicer, a New York federal trial court found that a loan servicer had been criminally sanctioned after a bankruptcy court presiding over a borrower's Chapter 7 claim imposed a six-figure fine on the servicer for noncompliance with court appearances and proceedings over a multiyear period.[68] That fine was to be paid to the Department of Education, yet, the borrower had failed to recognize that the Department of Education was the central loan servicer in this situation rather than the loan servicer held in contempt. As such, the appellate court vacated the considerable sanction.

A district court in Pennsylvania deliberated over a borrower's claim that her student loan creditor violated the Fair Credit Reporting Act (FCRA); the plaintiff had successfully whittled her remaining balance to $0 but concurrently received notice of 120-day delinquency for payments she had struggled to repay on time during a prior year.[69] The court held that the dichotomous loan statuses, while odd, were not inaccurate nor intentionally unclear based on the facts of the borrower's repayment history, and granted summary judgment to the defendants accordingly.

The U.S. Court of Appeals for the Federal Circuit affirmed an earlier ruling by the U.S. Court of Appeals for Veterans Claims on the grounds that a veteran borrower was no longer entitled to educational benefits after mistakenly being awarded enough Post-

---

[67] *In re* Pizzo, 628 B.R. 811, 391 Educ. L. Rep. 897 (Bankr. D.S.C. 2021).
[68] Great Lakes Educ. Loan Servs., Inc. v. Leary, 629 B.R. 360, 392 Educ. L. Rep. 859 (S.D.N.Y. 2021).
[69] Bibbs v. Trans Union LLC, 521 F. Supp. 3d 569, 394 Educ. L. Rep. 300 (E.D. Pa. 2021).

9/11 benefits to pursue a second graduate degree.[70] The court argued that stipulations of the Post-9/11 benefits prevented the veteran from utilizing another set of benefits simultaneously; additionally, the plaintiff was not required to repay the errant loan due to his lack of fault in its original dissemination, diminishing the salience of the claim.

The Supreme Court of Rhode Island granted summary judgment to the plaintiff, a bank, following their suit against a defendant who defaulted on approximately $40,000 of student loans and pursued damages as a Native American tribal member.[71] The bank had undergone several name and merger changes since the time of the original loan agreement, and the borrower also argued he had sovereign immunity from this suit as a member of a Native American tribe. The court disagreed, finding instead that the bank was entitled to summary judgment following the borrower's documented knowledge of the merger, and that the sovereign immunity argument would have only succeeded had the defendant been in his official capacity as a tribal officer when the original loan agreement transpired.

An extensive class action lawsuit arose between a for-profit institution and a former student who contested their considerable tuition balance after multiple attempts at withdrawing from courses that they considered misleading and ineffective. The institutional defendants attempted to remedy the lawsuit via court-ordered arbitration, but an appellate court in Georgia overturned a prior trial court ruling and denied the defendant's pursuit of remedying the issue in this way—the court argued that the plaintiff's claims fell within the stipulations of a borrower's defense classification, thereby preventing the institution from forcing arbitration.[72]

Conclusion

Cases involving students in higher education continued to occupy both state and federal courts. This chapter, through its summary of the sixty-eight cases in the past year, this chapter illustrates the balance courts strike in weighing students' rights and those of the institution and other governing bodies.

---

[70] Vollono v. McDonough, 991 F.3d 1381, 388 Educ. L. Rep. 125 (Fed. Cir. Ct. 2021).
[71] Citizens Bank, N.A. v. Palermo, 247 A.3d 131, 389 Educ. L. Rep. 388 (R.I. 2021).
[72] Grand Canyon Educ., Inc. v. Ward, 855 S.E.2d 415, 388 Educ. L. Rep. 370 (Ga. Ct. App. 2021).

Alphabetical List of Cases

Al Ghareeb v Bd. of Trs. at Univ. of N. Colo.
Alpha Nu Ass'n of Theta Xi v. Univ. of S. Cal.
Bhattacharya v Murry
Bibbs v. Trans Union LLC
Bisimwa v. St. John Fisher Coll.
Buj v. Psych. Residency Training
Burt v. Bd. of Trs. of Univ. of R.I.
Business Leaders in Christ v Univ. of Iowa
Canning v. Creighton Univ.
Castelino v. Rose-Hulman Inst. of Tech.
Citizens Bank, N.A. v. Palermo
Colvin v. Howard Univ.
Dean v Warren
Doe 1 v. George Washington Univ.
Doe v Brown Univ.
Doe v Coastal Carolina Univ.
Doe v Harrell
Doe v Mercy Catholic Med. Ctr.
Doe v Purchase Coll. State Univ. of N.Y.
Doe v Univ. of Denver
Doe v. Mich. State Univ.
Doe v. Rutgers State Univ. of N. J.
Doe v. Trs. of Union Coll.
Does 1-2 v Regents of the Univ. of Minn.
Doolen v. Wormuth
DuBois v Bd. of Regents of Univ. of Minn.
Franco v. Fairleigh Dickinson Univ.
Gociman v. Loyola Univ. of Chi.
Grand Canyon Educ., Inc. v. Ward
Great Lakes Educ. Loan Servs., Inc. v. Leary
Gruver v. Louisiana ex rel. Bd. of Sup'rs of La. State Univ. and Agric. and Mech. Coll.
Hannibal-Fisher v. Grand Canyon Univ.
Hassan v. Fordham Univ.
Huang v Huang
In re Aleckna
In re Mallett
In re Marchus
In re Pizzo
In re Promisco
In re Randall

In re Tingling
In re Univ. of Miami COVID-19 Tuition and Fee Refund Litig.
Intervarsity Christian Fellowship/USA v Univ. of Iowa
Jain v Carnegie Mellon Univ.
Kent Literary Club of Wesleyan Univ. at Middletown v. Wesleyan Univ.
Klaassen v Trs. of Ind. Univ.
Knight v. S. Orange Cmty. Coll. Dist.
Little v. Grand Canyon Univ.
Miles v. Simmons Univ.
Oyoque v. DePaul Univ.
Patel v. Univ. of Vt. And State Agric. Coll.
Patrick v. Bd. of Regents of Univ. of Ga.
Payan v L.A. Cmty. Coll. Dist.
Posso v Niagra Univ.
Rhodes v. Embry-Riddle Aeronautical Univ.
Rodriguez v. State Univ. of N.Y. at Buffalo
Shank v Carleton Coll.
Sheppard v Vistors of Va. State Univ.
State ex rel. Schmitt v Choi
Storino v. N.Y. Univ.
Students for Fair Admissions, Inc. v. Univ. of Texas at Austin
Tex. S. Univ. v. Villarreal
Viewpoint Neutrality Now! v Regents of Univ. of Minn.
Vollono v. McDonough
Vollono v. McDonough
West v. Ronquillo-Morgan
Willison v. Nelnet, Inc.
Yelapi v DeSantis
Young America's Found. v Kaler
Yu v. Idaho State Univ.
Zhao v. CIEE Inc.

Cases by Jurisdiction

FEDERAL CASES

D.C. Circuit
Colvin v. Howard Univ.

District of Columbia
Doe 1 v. George Washington Univ.

First Circuit
Zhao v. CIEE Inc.

Second Circuit
Doolen v. Wormuth
In re Tingling

> ***New York***
> Hassan v. Fordham Univ.
> Posso v Niagra Univ.
> Great Lakes Educ. Loan Servs., Inc. v. Leary
> ***Vermont***
> Patel v. Univ. of Vt. And State Agric. Coll.
> ***Rhode Island***
> Burt v. Bd. of Trs. of Univ. of R.I.

Third Circuit
Buj v. Psych. Residency Training
In re Aleckna
Doe v Mercy Catholic Med. Ctr.
Jain v Carnegie Mellon Univ.

> ***Pennsylvania***
> Bibbs v. Trans Union LLC

Fourth Circuit
Sheppard v Vistors of Va. State Univ.

> ***Maryland***
> *In re* Randall
> ***South Carolina***
> Doe v Coastal Carolina Univ.
> *In re* Pizzo
> ***West Virginia***
> Bhattacharya v Murry

Fifth Circuit
Doe v Harrell
Huang v Huang

Louisiana
Gruver v. Louisiana *ex rel.* Bd. of Sup'rs of La. State Univ. and Agric. And Mech. Coll.
Texas
Students for Fair Admissions, Inc. v. Univ. of Texas at Austin

Sixth Circuit
Doe v. Mich. State Univ.
Willison v. Nelnet, Inc.

Seventh Circuit
Castelino v. Rose-Hulman Inst. of Tech.
Klaassen v Trs. of Ind. Univ.

Illinois
Gociman v. Loyola Univ. of Chi.
Oyoque v. DePaul Univ.
In re Promisco

Eighth Circuit
Business Leaders in Christ v Univ. of Iowa
Intervarsity Christian Fellowship/USA v Univ. of Iowa
Shank v Carleton Coll.
Does 1-2 v Regents of the Univ. of Minn.
DuBois v Bd. of Regents of Univ. of Minn.
Young America's Found. v Kaler
Canning v. Creighton Univ.

Minnesota
Miles v. Simmons Univ.
Viewpoint Neutrality Now! v Regents of Univ. of Minn.
North Dakota
In re Marchus

Ninth Circuit
Payan v L.A. Cmty. Coll. Dist.
Yu v. Idaho State Univ.

Arizona
Hannibal-Fisher v. Grand Canyon Univ.
Little v. Grand Canyon Univ.
California
West v. Ronquillo-Morgan

Tenth Circuit
Al Ghareeb v Bd. of Trs. at Univ. of N. Colo.
Doe v Univ. of Denver

Eleventh Circuit
Dean v Warren

Arizona
In re Univ. of Miami COVID-19 Tuition and Fee Refund Litig.
Rhodes v. Embry-Riddle Aeronautical Univ.
Yelapi v DeSantis
In re Mallett

Federal Circuit
Vollono v. McDonough

STATE & D.C. COURT CASES

California
Alpha Nu Ass'n of Theta Xi v. Univ. of S. Cal.
Knight v. S. Orange Cmty. Coll. Dist.

Connecticut
Kent Literary Club of Wesleyan Univ. at Middletown v. Wesleyan Univ.

Georgia
Grand Canyon Educ., Inc. v. Ward
Patrick v. Bd. of Regents of Univ. of Ga.

Missouri
State ex rel. Schmitt v Choi

New Jersey
Doe v. Rutgers State Univ. of N. J.
Franco v. Fairleigh Dickinson Univ.

New York
Bisimwa v. St. John Fisher Coll.
Doe v Purchase Coll. State Univ. of N.Y.
Doe v. Trs. of Union Coll.
Rodriguez v. State Univ. of N.Y. at Buffalo
Storino v. N.Y. Univ.

Rhode Island
Citizens Bank, N.A. v. Palermo
Doe v Brown Univ.

Texas
Tex. S. Univ. v. Villarreal

Chapter 10

FEDERAL AND STATE LEGISLATION

Amy L. Dagley[1] and David L. Dagley[2]

Introduction 340
Federal Legislation... 342
State Legislation 343
   Accountability and School Reform.. 343
   Athletics 348
   Attendance, Promotion, and Graduation 351
   Buildings and Grounds... 362
   Curricular Requirements 366
   Employment.. 377
   Finance and School Business... 394
   Governance and School Leadership.. 405
   Parental and Student Rights 417
   Program Development.. 428
   School Choice 442
   School Safety... 445
   Students with Disabilities... 460
   Technology 466
   Transportation 467
   Higher Education.. 470
Conclusion 506

---

[1] Assistant Professor, Educational Leadership, University of Alabama at Birmingham, Birmingham, Ala.
[2] Professor Emeritus, Educational Leadership, University of Alabama, Tuscaloosa, Ala.

Introduction

This chapter describes federal and state-level legislation from the 2021 calendar year, which directed, controlled, or impacted public and private schools and universities, from prekindergarten through postsecondary levels of education. The acts reported in this chapter result from searches for education-related bills passed by the United States Congress and the legislatures and general assemblies of the fifty states.

When the secondary author first produced this chapter for *The Yearbook of Education Law* in 1998, the search for records of legislative acts began in the stacks of local law libraries where the legislative service bulletins for many states could be pulled from the shelves. If law libraries did not subscribe to legislative service bulletins for the state, they typically subscribed to the printed statutory volumes so physical searches could be conducted by visually scanning the pages of the education code or the "pocket parts" for new legislation. This methodology for finding the previous year's legislation began to fail with the economic downturn in 2007 when law libraries began canceling their subscriptions to legislative service bulletins and statute books from distant states.

Electronic record keeping existed six years ago but was in its infancy at this time. Consequently, various states had lists of enrolled acts on their legislative websites or passed them on to the offices of their secretaries of state or state archivists. Occasionally, we could access legislative reports compiled by state school board associations, state school administrator associations, or postsecondary institutions. We visually scanned database providers such as Legiscan, Hein Online, and TheLAW.net for education-related legislation in the last seven years. Those materials and newsletters from state associations have been the primary sources for the laws described in this chapter.

After locating legislative acts, we reviewed them for language describing policy changes directed toward educational institutions. Appropriation acts were not typically reported in these materials, whether for general appropriations acts,[3] for state departments of education,[4] for school boards and charter schools,[5] for state special

---

[3] *See, e.g.*, 2021 Ga. Laws Act 505, HB 80, 2021 Mont. Laws Ch. 573, HB 2, or 2021 N.M. Laws Ch. 137, HB 2.
[4] *See, e.g.*, 2021 Ark. Acts 842, SB 111 or 2021 Idaho Sess. Laws Ch. 315, H. 372.
[5] *See, e.g.*, 2021 Colo. Sess. Laws SB 268.

schools,[6] for public community and junior colleges,[7] or for colleges or universities.[8] We did not include most acts about state retirement systems unless they had policy outcomes such as approval for retired teachers to return to service without financial penalties to help schools staff hard-to-fill positions, as occurred in Oklahoma.[9] Because resolutions represent the sentiment of legislative bodies but do not direct particular actions or policy outcomes, they are also not reported in this chapter.[10]

For each act, we tried to summarize policy changes in one sentence, if at all possible. A single-sentence summary greatly saves printing space but can also misinterpret or misrepresent what legislative bodies actually intended to do. Each act reviewed in this chapter has therefore been cited as fully as was provided by the general assembly or legislature that passed it to assist readers in finding the original bills as introduced and as ultimately enrolled or passed. We then sorted summary descriptions of laws into one of the two main categories of "Federal" and "State" Legislation with subcategories such as "Athletics," "Employment," or "Higher Education" in the latter.

The categories dividing this chapter have generally remained static. "Professional Development" was a viable category with multiple entries each year until 2010, when no acts related to it were enrolled. Thus, items that might fit under the "Professional Development" heading were folded into the "Employment" section. Within each category of state-level legislation, we then sorted each of the acts qualitatively into subcategories. "Sorting qualitatively" meant moving acts from across the states into subcategories within the main categories. For example, in the last legislative year, fourteen states passed twenty-two acts about professional development needs for school employees, all arranged together within the main employment category.

This chapter provides a snapshot of issues legislative bodies addressed during the prior calendar year. Sorting the new acts into constant categories from year to year can serve to assist readers in identifying new policy initiatives that arose in the calendar year.

---

[6] *See, e.g.*, 2021 Ark. Acts 859, SB 374.
[7] *See, e.g.*, 2021 Miss. Laws SB 2914.
[8] *See, e.g.*, 2021 Miss. Laws SB 2905.
[9] 2021 Okla. Sess. Laws S.B. No. 267.).
[10] *See, e.g.*, an Arizona house resolution which encouraged schools to use various distance learning tools, to keep suspended or expelled students engaged with their schools (2021 Ariz. HR 2004), or a Utah concurrent resolution which emphasized the importance of civics education (2021 Utah Laws HCR 15).

Adding the data from each calendar year to data from earlier years can provide readers with a potential database of long-term legislative trends and the means of comparing educational policy initiatives within those subcategories from state to state.

Federal Legislation

Education-related legislation was again exceedingly sparse for the first session of the 117th Federal Congress in 2021. This section describes four acts that appeared to be related to education at the elementary, secondary, or postsecondary levels.

Congress created the Alyce Spotted Bear and Walter Soboleff Commission on Native Children in 2016,[11] tasking it with studying federal programs and funding to support Native American children and youth and with making recommendations for improving those efforts to help Native children and youth thrive. Staff representing the Departments of Education, Health and Human Services, Interior, and Justice were made available to confer with the commission. This 2021 act amended the 2016 version by giving the commission two additional years to complete its work.[12]

The Consider Teachers Act of 2021 amended the Higher Education Act of 1965 to improve the service obligation verification process for the Teacher Education Assistance for College and Higher Education (TEACH) grant program. The TEACH grant program provides grants of up to $4,000 for postsecondary students who intend to teach in high-need fields in low-income schools. If recipients do not perform their service obligations, the grants are converted to Federal Direct Unsubsidized Stafford Loans. The Consider Teachers Act of 2021 extended the time for completing the service obligation to eight years while authorizing recipients to seek discharges of their loans for years they met their service obligations.[13]

The Colonel John M. McHugh Tuition Fairness for Survivors Act of 2021 directed the Department of Veterans Affairs to disapprove payment for courses offered by public institutions of higher learning that do not charge veterans the in-state tuition rate for purposes of survivors' and dependents' educational assistance programs.[14]

---

[11] Pub. L. 114-244, S. 246 (October 14, 2016).
[12] Pub. L. 117-41, S. 325 (September 24, 2020).
[13] Pub. L. 117-49, S. 848 (October 13, 2021).
[14] Pub. L. 117-68, S. 1095 (November 30, 2021).

Federal and State Legislation 343

Congress authorized the National Medal of Honor Museum Foundation to establish a commemorative work on Federal land in the District of Columbia and its environs to honor the extraordinary acts of valor, selfless service, and sacrifice displayed by Medal of Honor recipients. The law anticipates that the foundation will solicit private funds for the memorial while the balance of funds remaining after the memorial is completed will be transferred to a separate account with the National Park Foundation to be available to the Secretary of the Interior or the Director of the General Services Administration for maintenance and upkeep. Insofar as museums and memorials serve an educative function, this act is included in these materials.[15]

State Legislation

Accountability and School Reform

Legislation on accountability and school reform addresses setting standards, measuring progress toward those standards, and reporting those matters to the public. This section details accountability and school reform legislation passed in 2021, beginning with eight acts from six states about the COVID-19 pandemic's impact on accountability.

Arizona delayed repeal of a provision permitting suspension of school performance evaluations for the 2020-21 school year to allow a continued pause in the accountability system.[16] Arkansas suspended its school rating system for the 2020-21 academic year.[17] Indiana directed its state board to assign a "null" or "no letter grade" for school corporations for the 2020-21 school year.[18] Indiana then ordered its state department of education to conduct a learning loss study for students in grades K-10 during the first two years of the COVID pandemic.[19]

Nevada suspended the requirement of establishing learning goals for students during the 2020-21 and 2021-22 school years.[20] Nevada also authorized its state department of education (DOE) to

---

[15] Pub. L. 117-80, H.R. 1664 (December 27, 2021).
[16] 2021 Ariz. Sess. Laws Ch. 68, SB 1165.
[17] 2021 Ark. Acts 89, HB 1151.
[18] 2021 Ind. Acts Pub. Law 211, § 36, HB 1514.
[19] 2021 Ind. Acts Pub. Law 211, §15, HB 1514.
[20] 2021 Nev. Stat. Ch. 255, AB 57.

waive or pause requirements related to the statewide system of accountability for public schools and examinations or assessments during the COVID-19 pandemic temporarily.[21] North Carolina suspended school performance grading and annual report cards for the 2021-22 school year.[22] Utah suspended accountability requirements, including identifying schools as not achieving state-established levels of student performance, assigning each school a letter grade, or publishing a report card on the state board's website, for the 2020-21 school year.[23]

Other accountability and school reform-related legislation adopted in 2021 follow. Colorado funded a thorough, independent, third-party review of its existing 2009 statewide system of standards and assessments along with its statewide educational accountability system for information about the efficacy of its current systems and areas needing improvement.[24] Idaho created a commission on continuous improvement plans and student achievement measures, directing it to revise provisions about staff evaluations, college and career advising, and literacy intervention.[25] To a report about the number of teachers who are National Board Certified Teachers, Illinois added that the information must be disaggregated by race and ethnicity.[26] Further, Illinois required the report cards released by its state board of education (BOE) to include data on the number of incidents of violence that occurred on school grounds or during school-related activities that resulted in out-of-school suspensions, expulsions or placements in alternative settings.[27]

Indiana obligated its state BOE to establish a compilation of longitudinal data indicating school performance success in various selected and enumerated program areas, along with providing an online dashboard to convey indicators of school performance to the broader community.[28] Indiana mandated the creation of a benchmark, formative, interim, or similar assessment administered to students in grades K-2 to meet screening requirements and show alignment with academic standards for English and language arts and for numeracy; it created similar directions for assessments for

---

[21] 2021 Nev. Stat. Ch. 5, SB 83.
[22] 2021 N.C. Sess. Laws Ch. 130, S. 654.
[23] 2021 Utah Laws H.B. 184.
[24] 2021 Colo. Sess. Laws HB 1294.
[25] 2021 Idaho Sess. Laws Ch. 207, H. 222.
[26] 2021 Ill. Laws Pub. Act 102-0594, HB 2438.
[27] 2021 Ill. Laws Pub. Act 102-0294, SB 633.
[28] 2021 Ind. Acts Pub. Law 211, § 23, HB 1514.

students in grades 3-7.[29] In a third act, Indiana called on its state DOE to adopt and provide schools with an early warning system that provides actionable data on students as early as elementary school; metrics based on student-level data to assist in identifying potential learning loss at the student, school, and district level; and, research-proven predictive analytics for on-time high school graduation using local data to determine threshold-based indicators.[30]

Kansas called for the development and display of a foster care children's annual academic report card.[31] Louisiana ordered its department of elementary and secondary education to conduct site visits each year in order to observe the learning environment at schools that fail to meet minimum standards for academic performance for the purpose of addressing their failures to prepare students to qualify for scholarship programs.[32] Maine discontinued the use of the SAT standardized test as a method for assessing student performance.[33] Maine next directed educators in the middle, junior high, and secondary schools to provide electronic links to the Department of Labor's statewide employment projections to assist students in preparing for opportunities to live and work there.[34] Maryland added personally identifiable data such as name, birth date, and identification number, as well as industry certification to be included in the state longitudinal data system.[35]

Nevada ordered the disclosure of information about management organizations, if applicable, and contracts of the members of the governing bodies of charter schools.[36] Nevada then required the sponsors of charter schools that received one of the two lowest performance ratings under the statewide system of accountability for public schools in each of the last three consecutive years and has not requested a change in sponsorship to report to the legislative committee on education about changes to reconstitute their governing bodies or terminate their charter contracts.[37] Nevada directed its state DOE to review the examinations and assessments administered to students about costs, educational benefits, and redundancy of information, allowing it to grant waivers

---

[29] 2021 Ind. Acts Pub. Law 211, § 33, HB 1514.
[30] 2021 Ind. Acts Pub. Law 164 § 1; Sen. Enr. Act No. 414 § 1.
[31] 2021 Kan. Sess. Laws HB 2134.
[32] 2021 La. Acts No. 196, H.B. 280.
[33] 2021 Me. Laws Ch. 462, H.P. 193, L.D. 277.
[34] 2021 Me. Laws Ch. 75, H.P. 417, L.D. 572.
[35] 2021 Md. Laws Ch. 586, HB 320.
[36] 2021 Nev. Stat. Ch. 374, AB 419.
[37] 2021 Nev. Stat. Ch. 374, AB 419.

on examination requirements.[38] Moreover, Nevada tasked its state BOE with adopting a uniform grading scale for dual credit courses and international baccalaureate classes.[39]

New Jersey mandated that school report cards include the number of mental health professionals and school safety specialists employed by each school board.[40] North Carolina changed the mandatory testing of ninth-grade students in private church schools to measure either achievement in the areas of English grammar, reading, spelling, and mathematics or competencies in the verbal and quantitative areas.[41] Ohio added assessment scores for science, American history, and the American government in computing the performance index scores for accountability reporting. In the same act, Ohio altered the computation for accountability report cards.[42] Oklahoma now expects reporting on student data as needed to include information about tribal affiliations and American Indian heritages.[43] Rhode Island directed officials in public schools to provide written notice annually to parents, guardians, and/or caretakers of students, inviting them to attend orientation meetings within thirty days from the beginning of school years.[44] South Carolina revised its accountability measures for public schools and boards, defining chronically underperforming schools as either receiving unsatisfactory ratings for three consecutive years on their annual school report cards or in the absence of report cards. The state DOE applies the same metrics as noted in the state and federal combined accountability model under the Every Students Succeeds Act. The state DOE must then implement a tiered system for providing technical and other assistance, professional development, and monitoring for schools and boards. On notice from the state DOE of their placements on tiers, boards, superintendents, in consultation with school and community stakeholders, must review and revise their strategic plan with the assistance of their School Improvement Councils described in existing statute[45] to include a turnaround plan component for any under-performing schools or district.[46]

---

[38] 2021 Nev. Stat. Ch. 475, SB 353.
[39] 2021 Nev. Stat. Ch. 169, SB 172.
[40] 2021 N.J. Laws c. 339, S. 2811.
[41] 2021 N.C. Sess. Laws Ch. 111, H. 78.
[42] 2021 Ohio Laws HB 82.
[43] 2021 Okla. Sess. Laws H.B. No. 1104.
[44] 2021 R.I. Pub. Laws S. 999, H. 5698.
[45] S.C. CODE ANN. § 59-20-60.
[46] 2021 S.C. Act No. 44, S. 201.

South Dakota authorized its state secretary of education to waive, due to the nationally declared emergency, designated accountability requirements[47] through December 31, 2024.[48] Tennessee amended provisions related to the achievement school district (ASD), a part of the state accountability program, generally limiting the time schools can remain in the ASD to ten years, with some exceptions, calling for the creation of transition plans for schools to move out of the ASD.[49] Tennessee enacted a school turnaround pilot program obligating officials in schools identified in need of intervention to construct turnaround plans, affording them three years to implement and show improvement.[50] Also, Tennessee prohibited its state BOE from using textbooks or instructional materials in the public schools that were created to align exclusively with the common core state standards.[51]

In a separate but similar act, Tennessee prohibited teachers or principals in public schools from using or permitting the adoption of textbooks or other instructional materials created to align exclusively with the common core state standards.[52] Tennessee ordered its state DOE to submit a report to two legislative committees regarding the high school graduation rate and data from the report card on student readiness for college.[53] Tennessee tasked its commissioner of education with obtaining approval from its state BOE for changes to the formula used to calculate school or school district performance goals and measures, calling on its commissioner to convene a working group for studying changes to the formula.[54]

Texas informed its state education agency to add a performance indicator for students who successfully completed programs of study in career and technical education when evaluating the performance of high school campuses and districts including high school campuses.[55] Further, Texas adopted new procedures for assigning accountability ratings, interventions, sanctions, and fiscal management for open-enrollment charter schools. The lengthy accountability act includes provisions for investigations, performance ratings, the appeal of adverse decisions, including

---

[47] S.D. CODIFIED LAWS. ANN. §§ 13-3-55 and 13-3-62 to 13-3-65, inclusive.
[48] 2021 S.D. Laws HB 1083.
[49] 2021 Tenn. Pub. Acts Ch. No. 490, H.B. No. 74, S.B. No. 737.
[50] 2021 Tenn. Pub. Acts Ch. No. 578, S.B. No. 122, H.B. No. 1501.
[51] 2021 Tenn. Pub. Acts Ch. No. 205, S.B. No. 769, H.B. No. 782.
[52] 2021 Tenn. Pub. Acts Ch. No. 471, S.B. No. 630, H.B. No. 755.
[53] 2021 Tenn. Pub. Acts Ch. No. 323, H.B. No. 462, S.B. No. 1340.
[54] 2021 Tenn. Pub. Acts Ch. No. 299, H.B. No. 1570, S.B. No. 1579.
[55] 2021 Tex. Gen. Laws H.B. No. 773.

judicial review, alternative methods for determining ratings during the COVID-19 pandemic, and appointment of a conservator or management team.[56] Utah requires for each grading period that public school officials provide students with grades or performance reports for each course in which they are enrolled reflecting their work, including progress based on mastery, during the grading period.[57] Vermont obligates officials in all schools, technical centers, and supervisory entities to adopt the shared school district data management system, with quarterly reports on implementation due as of June 30, 2021.[58]

Athletics

This section describes the laws adopted in 2021 related to athletics, beginning with two about governance over athletic contests in K-12 schools. Nevada called on governing boards over interscholastic sports to include at least three members who are parents or guardians of students who participate in sanctioned sports.[59] North Carolina restructured oversight of public high school interscholastic athletic activities by obligating its state BOE to set rules for them and allowing the organization to enter into memoranda of understanding for a term of four years with nonprofit organizations to administer and enforce the rules it adopts.[60]

The most numerous types of legislation in the category of athletics addressed participation. Eight states enacted prohibitions on participation based on whether students' genders printed on their birth certificates agreed with their gender identities. Alabama specified that officials in public K-12 schools might not allow biological females to participate on male teams if there are female teams in sports and may never allow biological males to participate on female teams.[61] Arkansas created a legal cause of action for what it labeled a violation of gender integrity reinforcement through its Gender Integrity Reinforcement Legislation for Sports (Girls) Act; the act bans males from interscholastic, intercollegiate, intramural, or club athletic teams or sports expressly designated for females,

---

[56] 2021 Tex. Gen. Laws S.B. No. 1365.
[57] 2021 Utah Laws S.B. 148.
[58] 2021 Vt. Laws Act 66, S. 115.
[59] 2021 Nev. Stat. Ch. 511, AB 105.
[60] 2021 N.C. Sess. Laws Ch. 184, H. 91.
[61] 2021 Ala. Acts No. 2021-285, HB 391.

women, or girls.⁶² Florida required that sports activities must be identified as male, female, or co-ed sports, directing that females may participate in male sports, but males may not take part in female sports; gender must be defined by students' birth certificates.⁶³ Mississippi ordered officials in public schools belonging to interscholastic associations to designate their athletic teams or sports according to biological sex.⁶⁴ Montana obligated interscholastic athletes to participate under their sexes as assigned at birth.⁶⁵ Tennessee mandated that students' genders for the purposes of participation in public middle or high school interscholastic athletic activities or events is determined by their sexes at birth as stated on their birth certificates.⁶⁶ Texas directed public school students to compete in interscholastic athletic competitions based on their biological sexes.⁶⁷ West Virginia forbade athletic teams or sports designated for females, women, or girls, in interscholastic, intercollegiate, intramural, or club athletic teams or sports to be open to males where selection for such teams is based on competitive skills or the activities are contact sports.⁶⁸

Six states added eight laws about participation in student athletics in other categories. Arkansas enabled children of members of military families to attend school and participate in interscholastic sports when veterans transition to National Guard membership or citizen employment above the benefits provided by interstate compacts.⁶⁹ Georgia adopted rules and procedures permitting students who are homeschooled to participate in extracurricular or interscholastic activities.⁷⁰ Montana allowed students attending nonpublic or home schools to participate in extracurricular activities offered by their resident districts.⁷¹ Oregon authorized students in GED programs to participate in interscholastic athletics after they passed at least one of its practice tests.⁷² South Carolina waived its four academic course

---

[62] 2021 Ark. Acts 953, SB 450. *See also*, 2021 Ark. Acts 461, SB 354.
[63] 2021 Fla. Laws ch. 35, Subst. S.B. No. 128, at footnote 61.
[64] 2021 Miss. Laws SB 2536.
[65] 2021 Mont. Laws Ch. 405, HB 112.
[66] 2021 Tenn. Pub. Acts Ch. 40, S.B. No. 228, H.B. No. 3.
[67] 2021 Tex. Gen. Laws H.B. No. 25 (3rd Spec. Sess.).
[68] 2021 W. Va. Acts Ch. 105, H.B. 3293.
[69] 2021 Ark. Acts 1031, SB 638.
[70] 2021 Ga. Laws Act 245, SB 42.
[71] 2021 Mont. Laws Ch. 297, SB 157.
[72] 2021 Or. Laws Ch. 70, HB 2817.

requirements so that students who are home-schooled can be eligible to participate in public school interscholastic activities for the 2021-22 and 2022-23 school years.[73]

Texas, in the first of four laws, afforded eligible students who have homeschooled the opportunity to participate in interscholastic league activities as if they were enrolled in school districts.[74] Texas clarified that students receiving outpatient mental health services may not be prohibited from taking part in interscholastic leagues based solely on their receipt of mental health services or their absence during the instructional time while receiving outpatient mental health services.[75] Texas directed officials in interscholastic leagues to ensure that students with disabilities have opportunities to participate in team athletic activities by establishing and maintaining inclusive sports programs.[76] Texas created a cause for banning students from participating in interscholastic competitions in future leagues or school-sponsored extracurricular activities for up to a full year if the league's state executive committee determines that they intentionally, knowingly, or recklessly caused bodily injury to referees or other officials in retaliation for or as a result of the latter's actions taken in performing their duties.[77]

Three states addressed media access to athletic contests. Alabama granted officials in K-12 schools the sole authority to decide media organizations or organizations can cover or broadcast regular season sporting events and to contract for such broadcasts of their regular season sporting events.[78] Oklahoma directed that in all regular season high school athletic competitions visiting teams shall have the same rights to the radio broadcast, video stream, and telegraphic play-by-play accounts as the home teams except where local BOEs have valid applicable agreements with media organizations.[79] South Dakota mandated that no school board, association, or media contractor may interfere with the rights of news media to attend and engage in journalism about interscholastic high school activities or events; no association or media contractor may charge a fee to news media to engage in journalism at such activities or events; school boards must prevent officials in schools

---

[73] 2021 S.C. Act No. 101, H. 3925.
[74] 2021 Tex. Gen. Laws H.B. No. 547.
[75] 2021 Tex. Gen. Laws H.B. No. 1080.
[76] 2021 Tex. Gen. Laws S.B. No. 776.
[77] 2021 Tex. Gen. Laws H.B. No. 2721.
[78] 2021 Ala. Acts No. 2021-452, HB 248.
[79] 2021 Okla. Sess. Laws S.B. No. 302.

under their authority from interfering with the right of news media to engage in journalism at any such activities or events; and, that the above provisions are inapplicable to state championship interscholastic events.[80]

Two states negated the adoption of specific categories of mascots. Nevada directed local school boards and officials in charter schools to change from or adopt policies prohibiting the use of any names, logos, mascots, songs, or other identifiers that are racially discriminatory or contain racially discriminatory language or imagery, or identify with the Confederate States of America or a federally-recognized Indian tribe. The law makes an exception with respect to federally-recognized Indian tribes with their permission.[81] Washington forbade the use of Native American names, symbols, or images as public school mascots or team names.[82]

In the first of two final acts on school athletics. Indiana required governing bodies planning to close high schools to develop plans to preserve or transfer memorabilia, trophies or other property with historical significance.[83] Then, Indiana added a list of symptoms of sudden cardiac arrest to the information sheet provided for parents of students participating in extracurricular activities.[84]

Attendance, Promotion, and Graduation

This category captured the migration of instructional methodology from face-to-face to virtual and hybrid instruction during the COVID-19 pandemic as well as the necessary change in attendance rules which also impacted school funding. Movement through programs was impacted, requiring legislative bodies to look for ways to keep students on track, keeping in mind standards for high school graduation. This section describes attendance, promotion, and graduation-related legislation.

Virginia embraced a preference for face-to-face instruction in directing school boards to provide in-person instruction in a manner that adheres, to the maximum extent practicable, to currently-applicable mitigation strategies to reduce the transmission of COVID-19 that had been provided by the Centers for Disease

---

[80] 2021 S. D. Laws SB 128.
[81] 2021 Nev. Stat. Ch. 348, AB 88.
[82] 2021 Wash. Laws Ch. 128, H.B. 1356.
[83] 2021 Ind. Acts Pub. Law 216 § 14; H. B. No. 1549.
[84] 2021 Ind. Acts Pub. Law 56, H.B. 1040.

Control and Prevention.[85] Three other states added acts about virtual instruction.

Arkansas directed public school officials to adopt attendance policies for their students who attend class virtually or remotely.[86] Texas allowed school boards and open-enrollment charter schools with overall performance ratings of C or higher to operate local remote learning programs to offer virtual courses outside of the state virtual school network.[87] Utah permitted certified online course providers the state BOE approves to offer courses directly through the statewide online education program.[88] Utah also limited the number of middle school course credits students in private schools may enroll in each year through the statewide online education program.[89]

Twelve states adopted fifteen laws about school schedules and calendars. Arizona provided direction for constructing school calendars by including models for instructional time.[90] Arkansas amended a school calendar provision, specifying that the first day of school cannot be earlier than the Monday two weeks before Labor Day; the act also permitted public boards to select alternative school calendars with at least 1,068 hours of instructional time and 30 make-up hours due to weather or emergency circumstances.[91] Colorado supported the development of an academically-enriching environment on the fifth day of a four-day school week; the bill related that 111 of the state's 178 districts, involving more than 80,000 schoolchildren, were on four-day school weeks.[92] Kansas declared that only local governing boards had the authority to close schools and make changes in the means of instruction, including in-person attendance, hybrid, or remote learning during the COVID-19 pandemic; in addition, the act laid out hearing rights for aggrieved employees, parents, and students over governing boards decisions relating to the pandemic.[93]

Kentucky enabled school boards to request approval for more than ten student attendance days, the previous limit allowed by statute, under a nontraditional instruction plan due to the COVID-

---

[85] 2021 Va. Acts Ch. 456, S. 1303 (1st Spec. Sess.).
[86] 2021 Ark. Acts 897, SB 576.
[87] 2021 Tex. Gen. Laws S.B. No. 15 (2nd Spec. Sess.).
[88] 2021 Utah Laws S.B. 226.
[89] 2021 Utah Laws S.B. 234.
[90] 2021 Ariz. Sess. Laws Ch. 299, HB 2862. *See*, Ariz. Rev. Stat. §15-901.08.
[91] 2021 Ark. Acts 688, HB 1237.
[92] 2021 Colo. Sess. Laws HB 1006.
[93] 2021 Kan. Sess. Laws SB 40.

19 emergency, directing officials to submit nontraditional instruction plans for the 2021-22 year.[94] Kentucky then established a supplemental school year program for the 2021-22 year, permitting students enrolled in a public school in grades K-12 to request to use that year as a supplemental year to retake or supplement the courses or grades they had already taken; courses that students have retaken do not count as additional credit towards graduation unless they failed the original class.[95] Maine ordered its state DOE to conduct a feasibility study of a 30-minute lunch period for students.[96] Montana allowed instruction to occur on Saturdays to make up for instructional time lost due to emergencies.[97]

North Dakota authorized school boards to satisfy the calendar for instruction by providing virtual instruction.[98] Next, North Dakota removed both a beginning date from a 2009 provision authorizing the delivery of summer school and a reference to its use for remediation for the teaching of reading and mathematics.[99] South Dakota enabled its secretary of education to waive the minimum number of instructional hours required by state statute[100] if the Governor or the American President declares a state of emergency and affected schools are located within the areas to which a state of emergency is applicable.[101] Tennessee allowed local boards and officials in private or church-related schools to use excess instructional time accumulated over the years due to serious outbreaks of illnesses affecting or endangering students or staff without needing approval from its commission on education.[102] Tennessee indicated that local boards and governing bodies of charter schools have the sole authority to open or close schools during public health emergencies but may delegate it to their directors or superintendent as to whether to stay open, close or move to in-person learning and instruction.[103]

Virginia permitted public school officials to declare unscheduled remote learning days when severe weather conditions or other emergencies result in school closings, subject to a limit of ten

---

[94] 2021 Ky. Acts Ch. 9, HB 208.
[95] 2021 Ky. Acts Ch. 108, SB 128.
[96] 2021 Me. Laws Ch. 74, H.P. 482, L.D. 655.
[97] 2021 Mont. Laws Ch. 151, SB 75.
[98] 2021 N.D. Laws H.B. No. 1232.
[99] 2021 N.D. Laws H.B. No. 1436.
[100] S.D. CODIFIED LAWS ANN. § 13-26-1.
[101] 2021 S.D. Laws SB 46.
[102] 2021 Tenn. Pub. Acts Ch. No. 180, H.B. No. 587, S.B. No. 596.
[103] 2021 Tenn. Pub. Acts Ch. No. 96, S.B. No. 103, H.B. No. 225.

unscheduled remote learning days in school years; the bill empowers the superintendent of public instruction to suspend the limit on the number of days.[104] Washington allowed its state BOE to adopt rules allowing private schools to maintain their approval status when they are unable to fulfill 180-day calendars of instruction due to emergencies.[105] Wyoming directed its state BOE to establish minimum pupil-teacher contact time requirements for grades K-12, which may include in-person, virtual, and other methods of instruction.[106]

Ten states enacted seventeen bills defining additional excused absences. California included mental or behavioral health in the definition of student illnesses for purposes of permitting excused school absences.[107] California added excused absences for attendance at cultural ceremonies or events to its attendance law.[108] Delaware added a provision in its attendance law explicitly requiring school officials to excuse student absences for observance of religious holidays.[109] Delaware also allowed one excused absence per school year for students in grades 6-12 to attend civic engagements.[110]

In the first of four laws, Illinois obligated school boards to adopt written policies related to absences and missed homework or classwork assignments as a result of or related to student pregnancies.[111] Illinois removed a requirement that boards prescribe rules about absences for religious holidays, instead directing that children may be absent from public schools due to religious reasons, including the observance of religious holidays or participation in religious instruction.[112] Illinois amended its compulsory attendance law, mandating that absence for cause by illness shall include the mental or behavioral health of students for up to five days, for which they must not need to obtain medical notes, and they must be given opportunities to make up missed school work.[113] Illinois also directed that after a second excused absence for mental health reasons, students must be referred to appropriate school support

---

[104] 2021 Va. Acts Ch. 19, H. 1790; Ch. 293, S. 1132 (1st Spec. Sess.).
[105] 2021 Wash. Laws Ch. 8, H.B. 1131.
[106] 2021 Wyo. Sess. Laws Enr. Act No. 42, Ch. 82, S.F. 115.
[107] 2021 Cal. Stat. Ch. 672, SB 14.
[108] 2021 Cal. Stat. Ch. 281, AB 516.
[109] 2021 Del. Ch. 78, HB 163.
[110] 2021 Del. Ch. 77, HB 175.
[111] 2021 Ill. Laws Pub. Act 102-0471, HB 3272.
[112] 2021 Ill. Laws Pub. Act 102-0406, HB 169.
[113] 2021 Ill. Laws Pub. Act. 102-0321, SB 1577.

personnel.[114] Maine eliminated the need for prior approval for school absences for recognized religious holidays.[115]

Minnesota ordered boards to provide notice annually to parents about their policies relating to a student's absences for religious observances.[116] Tennessee called on public schools officials to credit student who participates in activities or programs sponsored by 4-H as present for attendance purposes.[117] Texas informed school boards to excuse students for absences resulting from serious or life-threatening illnesses or related treatment, making their attendance infeasible.[118] Texas then provided a one-day, one-time excused absence for students fifteen or older to obtain driver's or learner's licenses.[119] Utah added mental or behavioral health as a valid excuse for a school absence[120] while prohibiting officials from requiring documentation from medical professionals for absences due to mental or physical illnesses.[121] Virginia ordered public school officials to permit one day as an excused absence each year for middle and high school students to participate in civic events, also allowing educators to grant additional excused absences for those absent for civic events.[122]

Four states addressed truancy. Illinois directed officials on school boards, charter schools, alternative schools, or any schools receiving public funds to develop absenteeism and truancy policies to be communicated to students and parents or guardians annually; policies must be reviewed every two years and filed with the state BOE.[123] Maine ordered its advisory committee on truancy, dropouts, and alternative education to study truancy and attendance while developing recommendations to improve student attendance.[124] Tennessee amended provisions on student truancy, noting that progressive truancy plans adopted by local boards must be applied prior to referral to juvenile courts for adjudication as truant.[125] Utah imposed a moratorium for truancy enforcement during the COVID-

---

[114] 2021 Ill. Laws Pub. Act 102-0266, HB 576.
[115] 2021 Me. Laws Ch. 25, H.P. 21, L.D. 55.
[116] 2021 Minn. Laws Ch. 13, H.F. no. 2.
[117] 2021 Tenn. Pub. Acts Ch. No. 116, S.B. No. 203, H.B. No. 332.
[118] 2021 Tex. Gen. Laws H.B. No. 699.
[119] 2021 Tex. Gen. Laws S.B. No. 289.
[120] 2021 Utah Laws H.B. 81.
[121] 2021 Utah Laws H.B. 116.
[122] 2021 Va. Acts Ch. 104, H. 1940; Acts Ch. 105, S. 1439 (1st Spec. Sess.).
[123] 2021 Ill. Laws Pub. Act 102-0157, SB 605.
[124] 2021 Me. Laws Ch. 57, H.P. 182, L.D. 261.
[125] 2021 Tenn. Pub. Acts Ch. No. 223, H.B. No. 206, S.B. No. 273.

19 emergency until 2022.[126] Wyoming modified its truancy law, recognizing the following circumstances as excused absences, those pre-approved by officials; due to illnesses, injuries, or other health care needs of students; due to a death or serious illness in a student's family; and, for attending the state fair as an exhibitor.[127]

Fourteen states spoke to attendance policies and residency for the children of military personnel. Alabama mandated that military service members stationed in the state, as well as their spouses and minor children, have resident status, regardless of whether they are under orders to attend school.[128] Colorado tasked officials in local boards and charter schools with providing easier matriculation for students who are dependents of members of the military by allowing their enrollment prior to arrival in districts, allowing them to matriculate in the next grade.[129] Connecticut permitted military orders to be accepted as proof of residency, enabling children of members of the armed forces to enroll in public schools.[130] Illinois provided a longer time for a dependent of military service members to begin enrollment in public districts while still located outside of the state from six months instead of just sixty days.[131] Louisiana authorized remote public school registration and enrollment of children of military personnel transferring to the state.[132]

Montana permitted early school enrollment for children of relocated military families.[133] New York allowed students whose parents or guardians are being relocated under military orders to be considered state residents who may transfer their educational records to state schools.[134] North Carolina authorized students who are dependents of active-duty military personnel to attend local schools without being domiciled in a district.[135] Ohio directed local education agencies to permit children of military families to participate in technology-based education as soon as the service member received orders to relocate, allowing children to pre-enroll to ease the transition to their new schools.[136] Oklahoma granted

---

[126] 2021 Utah Laws S.B. 219.
[127] 2021 Wyo. Sess. Laws Enr. Act No. 66, Ch. 163, S.F. 68.
[128] 2021 Ala. Acts no. 2021-881, S.B. 83.
[129] 2021 Colo. Sess. Laws HB 1217.
[130] 2021 Conn. Acts 21-86 (Reg. Sess.), HB 6483.
[131] 2021 Ill. Laws Pub. Act 102-0126, HB 557.
[132] 2021 La. Acts No. 208, S.B. 114.
[133] 2021 Mont. Laws Ch. 20, HB 68.
[134] 2021 N.Y. Laws Ch. 605, A. 6528.
[135] 2021 N.C. Sess. Laws Ch. 9, H. 53.
[136] 2021 Ohio Laws HB 244.

school district residency status to children whose parents are on active military duty and receive orders to report to a new location in the state.[137] Oklahoma also enabled virtual charter school enrollment for children whose parents are on active military duty.[138]

South Dakota authorized students from military families who are subject to relocation to be eligible for registration with state-approved distance learning providers.[139] Texas permitted school systems operated by general academic teaching institutions to place military-connected students on priority lists for enrollment.[140] Utah obligated local education agencies to permit children of members of the uniformed services relocating to or out of the state to enroll in public schools there in the same manner as those residing in-state while remaining enrolled after their parents relocate out of the state.[141] Wyoming called for advanced enrollment of K-12 students who are children of transferred or transferring military personnel.[142]

Two states changed the beginning dates for kindergarten. Louisiana amended its compulsory attendance law to mandate kindergarten attendance beginning at age five.[143] Nevada required children to be five on or before September 30 to be admitted to kindergarten, six for first grade, and seven for second grade. Nevada changed the relevant date for all three years from September 30 to the first day of school for that year.[144]

Five states addressed grade retention matters. California ordered school board and charter school officials to implement supplemental policies on the retention of students who received deficient grades in the 2020-21 academic year.[145] Florida enabled parents or guardians to request that their children in grades K-5 student be retained at grade level for academic reasons following specified procedures.[146] New Jersey permitted parents and guardians to request grade retention for students during the 2021-22 school year.[147] Tennessee amended a provision on mandatory retention in third grade for students who fail reading assessments,

---

[137] 2021 Okla. Sess. Laws S.B. No. 68.
[138] 2021 Okla. Sess. Laws S.B. No. 69.
[139] 2021 S.D. Laws HB 1055.
[140] 2021 Tex. Gen. Laws H.B. No. 4124.
[141] 2021 Utah Laws S.B. 145.
[142] 2021 Wyo. Sess. Laws Enr. Act No. 33, Ch. 71, H.B. 57.
[143] 2021 La. Acts No. 386, S.B. 10.
[144] 2021 Nev. Stat. Ch. 221, AB 102.
[145] 2021 Cal. Stat. Ch. 41, AB 104.
[146] 2021 Fla. Laws ch. 228, H. 1159.
[147] 2021 N.J. Laws c. 141, A. 5365.

pointing out that if appeals are filed, they must be made by the student's parents or guardians.[148] Texas repealed grade promotion standards tied to the State of Texas Assessment and Academic Readiness (STAAR) mathematics and reading tests for grades 5 and 8, along with a provision for the development and option to administer the Algebra II and English III examinations.[149] In a second law, Texas allowed parents to ask that their children repeat grades or retake courses with the creation of retention committees led by principals to work with them to discuss their requests while affording them the final decisions on retention.[150]

Two states passed legislation about withdrawal from school. Arkansas repealed a requirement for a waiting time before parents or guardians can withdraw their children from school.[151] Connecticut enabled parents to withdraw their children from school at age seventeen, but parents must personally appear at school and sign a withdrawal and enrollment form, receive information about adult education, and enroll their students in adult education.[152]

Nine states adopted fourteen acts changing graduation standards. Arkansas changed the score needed on the U.S. citizenship test to receive high school diplomas to sixty percent.[153] California added a one-semester course in ethnic studies as a graduation requirement as of the 2029-30 school year, including students in charter schools.[154] Florida revised its social studies high school graduation credit requirement to accommodate the added study of civics.[155] Indiana permitted science, technology, engineering, and mathematics (STEM) courses to replace dual credit courses for academic honors-designated courses.[156] Indiana next allowed its state BOE to allow organizations to provide credit under Core 40 curricular models it adopted for alternative programs in which students obtain credit counting toward graduation from non-school educational experiences that apply or incorporate content area knowledge in lieu of a mandatory or elective course in this model.[157]

---

[148] 2021 Tenn. Pub. Acts Ch. No. 367, S.B. No. 1156, H. B. No. 1591.
[149] 2021 Tex. Gen. Laws H.B. No. 4545.
[150] 2021 Tex. Gen. Laws S.B. No. 1697.
[151] 2021 Ark. Acts 623, HB 1429.
[152] 2021 Conn. Acts 21-199 (Reg. Sess.), SB 1032.
[153] 2021 Ark. Acts 730, HB 1744.
[154] 2021 Cal. Stat. Ch. 661, AB 101.
[155] 2021 Fla. Laws ch. 158, H. 5.
[156] 2021 Ind. Acts Pub. Law 216 § 28; H. B. No. 1549.
[157] 2021 Ind. Acts Pub. Law 73, S.B. 196.

Montana decreed that students who experienced disruptions in schooling could receive diplomas if they meet its minimum high school credit requirement even if their resident district boards call for more credit than the state standard.[158] New Hampshire imposed a civics competency assessment as necessary for high school graduation.[159] In the first of three laws, Ohio enabled students who successfully complete driver's education courses offered by their boards or through organizations with which it contracts to earn a one-half unit of high school elective credit toward graduation. Ohio allowed students in career-technical education programs to receive up to two points toward their high school diplomas for completing driver's education courses.[160] Ohio authorized students to fulfill one unit of mathematics toward graduation by completing one-half of a unit on financial literacy and one-half of a unit on mathematics courses except in Algebra II; the exception is bounded for students who take one unit of advanced computer science in lieu of Algebra II.[161]

Oregon allowed credit in language arts to meet high school diploma requirements in English.[162] Oregon then directed its state DOE to review its standards for high school diplomas, making recommendations about them.[163] Oregon informed students to complete at least one-half credit of civics and demonstrate proficiency in it to receive high school diplomas.[164] Texas allowed graduation committees to determine whether students are qualified to graduate without considering the performance on any end-of-course examination if they are seniors during the 2020-21 school year, with an expiration date for this provision of September 1, 2022.[165] Texas repealed the expiration date for the use of individual graduation committees, enabling its commissioner of education to authorize special accreditation investigations when ten percent or more of students graduating in a year from the same high school are awarded diplomas based on the decisions of individual graduation committees.[166]

---

[158] 2021 Mont. Laws Ch. 80, SB 18.
[159] 2021 N.H. Laws Ch. 157, HB 320.
[160] 2021 Ohio Laws Subs. SB 166.
[161] 2021 Ohio Laws SB 1.
[162] 2021 Or. Laws Ch. 178, HB 2056.
[163] 2021 Or. Laws Ch. 495, SB 744.
[164] 2021 Or. Laws Ch. 175, SB 513.
[165] 2021 Tex. Gen. Laws H.B. No. 999.
[166] 2021 Tex. Gen. Laws H.B. No. 1603.

Three states moved toward adopting alternative measures for graduation. Montana empowered its superintendent of public instruction to create a process for students to demonstrate proficiency in high school content standards through alternative means and thereby receive a state high school diploma.[167] Nevada ordered its state DOE to adopt regulations about the eligibility of those at least eighteen and are eligible for educational programs for incarcerated persons as well as individuals who are at least seventeen and attended at least four years of high school to enroll in adult education courses to earn high school diplomas.[168] North Dakota granted discretion to local boards and officials in nonpublic schools to develop eligibility criteria or programmatic requirements to allow passing scores on individual units of credit on the GED assessment.[169]

Three states addressed the acceleration of students through their programs to achieve early graduation. Tennessee obligated local school boards and officials in public charter schools to develop and adopt academic acceleration policies for enrolling students in grades 7-12 into available advanced English language arts, mathematics, or science courses.[170] Texas established an early high school completion program to allow students who demonstrate early readiness for college to graduate early while adopting a "Texas First" scholarship program to fund early high school graduates' tuition in higher education.[171] Louisiana added language to assure that students move smoothly to graduation, specifying that they meet with school counselors and their parents or legal guardians, either in person or virtually, to explain the possible impact of a revision to their graduation plan before revising them.[172]

Other legislation related to attendance, promotion, and graduation enacted in 2021 is described as follows. Connecticut amended a statute directing local and regional school boards to adopt policies for calculating grade point averages (GPAs), expecting them to specify whether these are weighted, not just in advanced placement courses, but also in International Baccalaureate programs, Cambridge International programs, dual enrollment

---

[167] 2021 Mont. Laws Ch. 223, HB 556.
[168] 2021 Nev. Stat. Ch. 198, AB 215.
[169] 2021 N.D. Laws S.B. No. 2147.
[170] 2021 Tenn. Pub. Acts Ch. No. 170, S.B. No. 414, H.B. No. 973.
[171] 2021 Tex. Gen. Laws S.B. No. 1888.
[172] 2021 La. Acts No. 458, S.B. 214.

programs, dual credit courses, and early college courses.¹⁷³ Illinois changed its rules for playtime for students in elementary grades, first to make them applicable to grades K-5 rather than to K-8, then to require their length to be thirty, rather than sixty, minutes on any day that is at least five clock hours long; the new rules no longer call for equity in playtime for students with disabilities, leaving required play time subject to their Individuals with Disabilities Education Act (IDEA) mandated Individualized Education Programs (IEPs) or plans under Section 504 of the Rehabilitation Act (Section 504) plans.¹⁷⁴

Maine adopted a bill to increase high school graduation rates for students experiencing educational disruption, adopting a community approach for assisting them to receive diplomas issued through the state DOE, identifying public and private sector resources that can assist in the project, and adding homeless and immigrant students to those targeted for assistance.¹⁷⁵ Nebraska prohibited discrimination in admission or attendance at denominational or parochial high schools, not just in public or private schools.¹⁷⁶ New Hampshire requires the principal or other administrator of high schools to grant credit for courses and programs that have been completed at other approved schools.¹⁷⁷ Rhode Island directed principals to report annually on the number of both graduating students and how many apply for admission to college or vocational training.¹⁷⁸

In the first of four changes. Texas directed parents to provide updated contact information to officials within two weeks of the beginning of the school year or within two weeks if it changes during years.¹⁷⁹ Texas directed its state education agency, the higher education coordinating board, and the workforce commission to develop and make available a model data-sharing agreement to evaluate electronic student records systems.¹⁸⁰ Texas approved the movement toward the electronic administration of the STAAR test and end-of-course examinations, particularly for purchases of

---

[173] 2021 Conn. Acts 21-199 (Reg. Sess.), SB 1032.
[174] 2021 Ill. Laws Pub. Act 102-0357, SB 654.
[175] 2021 Me. Laws Ch. 445, S.P. 424, L.D. 1318; 2021 Me. Laws Ch. 61, H.P. 229, L.D. 325.
[176] 2021 Neb. Laws LB 92.
[177] 2021 N.H. Laws Ch. 82, HB 182.
[178] 2021 R.I. Pub. Laws S. 998, H. 5076.
[179] 2021 Tex. Gen. Laws S.B. No. 746.
[180] 2021 Tex. Gen. Laws S.B. No. 788.

technology and test administration programs.[181] Texas extended eligibility for free prekindergarten to children residing in the state or has ever been in foster care in another state or territory.[182]

Washington amended a provision that permits school officials to withhold diplomas from students who destroy school property, tasking local boards with publishing information on their websites about the numbers they withheld by each graduating class, aggregated to count the number of pupils eligible for free- and reduced-price meals.[183] In lieu of one-time end-of-year assessments, Virginia called on its BOE to establish, to provide measures of individual student growth over school years, a through-year growth assessment system aligned with the standards of learning for the administration of reading and mathematics assessments in grades 3-8.[184] West Virginia permitted county boards to provide electronic notice of school attendance to its DMV in lieu of a paper notice.[185] Also, West Virginia allowed students from other states, or who are eligible to enroll in its public schools, to enroll in the same grades in public schools in which they were enrolled in the schools from which they transferred.[186]

Buildings and Grounds

This section describes buildings and grounds-related legislation passed in 2021. Two states addressed the nature of the agencies with authority over state property. Alabama conferred authority over managing and renovating a property that is part of state educational institutions to its state DOE rather than its state finance department.[187] Hawai'i renamed its School Facilities Agency, now calling it the Schools Facility Authority, while describing its powers and responsibilities.[188]

Two states altered the law about eminent domain, often a precursor to governmental ownership of buildings and grounds. Arkansas codified eminent domain law to specify that "public use" does not include the taking of private property for the economic

---

[181] 2021 Tex. Gen. Laws H.B. No. 3261.
[182] 2021 Tex. Gen. Laws H.B. No. 725.
[183] 2021 Wash. Laws Ch. 120, H.B. 1176.
[184] 2021 Va. Acts Ch. 443, H. 2027 (1st Spec. Sess.).
[185] 2021 W. Va. Acts Ch. 184, S.B. 431.
[186] 2021 W. Va. Acts Ch. 100, H.B. 2785.
[187] 2021 Ala. Acts No. 2021-476, HB 220.
[188] 2021 Haw. Sess. Laws Act 217, SB 808.

benefit of the general public, noting that this is without limitation for the purposes of increases in tax bases, tax revenues, or employment.[189] Texas permitted school boards in counties with populations of less than 25,000 to confirm the accuracy of their prior-year eminent domain reports but removed this directive if there were no changes.[190]

Seven states enacted bills about property acquisition, conveyance, or disposal. California repealed a provision that the state lands commission must obtain a statement from the U.S. Land Office after federal government officials survey any township; the act also informed the commission to notify by letter and by posting on its website a conveyance of state lands to a private party or governmental agency.[191] Connecticut conveyed a parcel of state land in the town of North Haven to a board of cooperative educational services to develop a magnet school.[192] Hawai'i directed its state attorney general to institute proceedings on behalf of its DOE to acquire land owned by the Mililani Town Association by voluntary action or condemnation.[193]

Illinois declared that unless school buildings are unsafe, unsanitary, or unfit for occupancy and notice has been served or provided by a licensed entity able to determine its safety. Boards must conduct at least three public hearings solely to discuss closing such a building and receive community input.[194] Indiana added to the procedures for selling, exchanging, leasing, demolishing, holding without operating, or disposing of school buildings, especially receiving prior certifications from the state attorney general.[195] New Mexico provided funding for the demolition of abandoned schools.[196] North Dakota permitted county committees, with state board approval, to sell, exchange, or donate property or assets after the dissolution of school districts for less than fair market value if the dissolving board has sufficient property and assets to satisfy liquidation requirements.[197]

Three states enacted four provisions for modernizing and improving school facilities. California ordered its superintendent of

---

[189] 2021 Ark. Acts 945, SB 334.
[190] 2021 Tex. Gen. Laws S.B. No. 157.
[191] 2021 Cal. Stat. Ch. 715, AB 1390.
[192] 2021 Conn. Acts 21-33 (Reg. Sess.), HB 6685.
[193] 2021 Haw. Sess. Laws Act 165, SB 806.
[194] 2021 Ill. Laws Pub. Act 102-0204, HB 1785.
[195] 2021 Ind. Acts Pub. Law 155; S.B. 358.
[196] 2021 N.M. Laws Ch. 27, SB 43.
[197] 2021 N.D. Laws H.B. No. 1337.

public instruction to create a list of schools identified as requiring comprehensive, targeted support and improvement while revising the duties of county superintendents to include annual inspection of schools on this list/[198] New York granted authority to the city of Rochester and its BOE to modernize school facilities.[199] Also, New York sought a report of building projects and the computation of costs to modernize schools in Syracuse.[200] Oklahoma allowed funds from the federal Coronavirus Response and Relief Supplemental Appropriation Act of 2021 (CRRSA) and the federal American Rescue Plan Act of 2021 (ARP) to be allocated to local boards through the public common school building equalization fund.[201]

Two states directed changes to the contours of construction contracts. Maryland amended its law for construction projects receiving state funding for annual payments from the supplemental school construction financing fund, calling for four-party memoranda of understanding.[202] Texas made contractors not responsible for the consequences of design defects while prohibiting them from granting warranties of accuracy, adequacy, sufficiency, or suitability of plans, specifications, or other design documents provided to them by persons other than their own contractors, fabricators, suppliers, or consultants.[203] Further, Texas permitted local boards to adopt uniform general conditions to be incorporated in all district building construction contracts.[204]

Four states expressed concerns about air quality in school facilities. Colorado transferred funds from its general fund to the public-school capital construction assistance fund to provide grants for public school air quality improvement.[205] Maine directed its state BOE to amend rules for major capital school construction projects as well as for basic approval standards for public schools and administrative units to improve air quality and ventilation for all public schools.[206] Nevada obligated the boards of trustees of school districts and governing bodies of charter schools to assess and improve ventilation and filtration systems of schools by extending

---

[198] 2021 Cal. Stat. Ch. 667, AB 599.
[199] 2021 N.Y. Laws Ch. 614M A. 993.
[200] 2021 N.Y. Laws Ch. 617, A. 6258.
[201] 2021 Okla. Sess. Laws S.B. No. 1037.
[202] 2021 Md. Laws Ch. 698, SB 551.
[203] 2021 Tex. Gen. Laws S.B. No. 219.
[204] 2021 Tex. Gen. Laws S.B. No. 338.
[205] 2021 Colo. Sess. Laws SB 202.
[206] 2021 Me. Laws Ch. 114, H.P. 517, L.D. 705.

available financing.²⁰⁷ Virginia ordered officials in its public schools to provide carbon monoxide detectors for buildings built before 2015 and housing student classrooms.²⁰⁸

Two states enacted legislation to improve charter schools' ability to occupy other public-school buildings. Indiana created a panel to study charter school funding and methods for improving used by school corporations.²⁰⁹ New Hampshire made unused school facilities available to chartered public schools.²¹⁰

Two states prompted energy savings in the operation of school facilities. Maine redefined its school energy savings program as a decarbonization program.²¹¹ Maryland directed school boards to adopt or update their energy policies using specified content.²¹²

Other buildings and grounds-related legislation adopted last legislative year are described as follows. California excluded residential housing for school employees from requirements related to supervision of the design and construction of school buildings.²¹³ Maryland ordered the school board in Howard County to report annually to the general assembly on program capacity at its permanent school facilities.²¹⁴ New Mexico directed its legislative council service to publish on the legislature's website a searchable list of capital projects that it passed, the name of legislators or the governor who allocated a portion of the appropriation or bond authorization for each project, and the amount of the allocation.²¹⁵

New York banned hate symbols on state-owned property.²¹⁶ North Dakota permitted local boards to lease property for the installation of wireless telecommunications facilities which may be leased for up to twenty years.²¹⁷ Rhode Island decreed that school officials comply with composting and recycling laws.²¹⁸ Vermont directed its secretary of education, in consultation with the chair of the state BOE and the executive director of the state superintendents' association, to update its school construction

---

[207] 2021 Nev. Stat. Ch. 307, AB 257.
[208] 2021 Va. Acts Ch. 165, H. 1823 (1ˢᵗ Spec. Sess.).
[209] 2021 Ind. Acts Pub. Law 163, S.B. 413.
[210] 2021 N.H. Laws Ch. 186, HB 278.
[211] 2021 Me. Laws Ch. 152, S.P. 184, L.D. 815.
[212] 2021 Md. Laws Ch. 608, HB 630.
[213] 2021 Cal. Stat. Ch. 49, AB 306.
[214] 2021 Md. Laws Ch. 396, HB 1190.
[215] 2021 N.M. Laws Ch. 122, HB 55.
[216] 2021 N.Y. Laws Ch. 5, A. 962.
[217] 2021 N.D. Laws H.B. No. 1370.
[218] 2021 R.I. Pub. Laws H. 5328, S. 104.

facilities standards, reflecting changes in educational delivery models and standards for healthy and resource-efficient school facilities.[219] Wyoming tasked its school facilities commission with conducting annual evaluations of the adequacy of school buildings and facilities while prioritizing school building and facility needs while calling for follow-up inspections as needed.[220]

Curricular Requirements

This section describes curricular matters added or changed in the 2021 legislative year. The most numerous legislation about curricular requirements addressed teaching about civics and patriotism, either standing alone or embedded in history programs, with eighteen states enacting twenty-four pieces of legislation in those subject areas. Arkansas directed public school officials to have students recite the Pledge of Allegiance at assemblies and sporting events as well as to observe a moment of silence following the daily recitation of the Pledge of Allegiance.[221] California designated September 11 each year as September 11 Remembrance Day, mandating a moment of silence at an appropriate time when school is in session.[222] Colorado added explicit components on teaching civics, including the three branches of government and the formation and development of civil government using foundational documents; the bill ordered the state DOE to review curricular standards and revise them to comply with its terms while encouraging officials in local school boards to partner with local service organizations to improve the quality of civics education.[223]

Florida tasked its state DOE with developing or approving an integrated civic education curriculum and curating oral history resources to be used in it.[224] Illinois obligated officials in high school to include in a unit of instruction in their curriculum about the process of naturalization by which foreign citizens or nationals becomes U.S. citizens.[225] Indiana informed its state BOE to establish standards for civics education which are subject to review only by

---

[219] 2021 Vt. Laws Act 72, H. 426.
[220] 2021 Wyo. Sess. Laws Enr. Act No. 58, Ch. 131, S.F. 2.
[221] 2021 Ark. Acts 959, HB 1832.
[222] 2021 Cal. Stat. Ch. 102, SB 254.
[223] 2021 Colo. Sess. Laws SB 67.
[224] 2021 Fla. Laws ch. 158, H. 5.
[225] 2021 Ill. Laws Pub. Act 102-0472, HB 3281.

the general assembly.²²⁶ Louisiana ordered the playing or singing of the national anthem before competitive athletic events in venues constructed by, operated by, or maintained by the state or its political subdivisions.²²⁷ Montana changed the size requirements for U.S. flags displayed on school property from 3' x 5' to 16" x 24" for classroom flags, and 4' x 6' to 3' x 5' for outdoor flags, while declaring that all flags must be manufactured in the U.S.²²⁸ Montana next directed school district trustees to ensure that all students in grades 3-12 receive instruction about the U.S. Constitution and the Pledge of Allegiance; the act also dictated that the Pledge of Allegiance must be followed with a moment of silence.²²⁹

Nevada added civics to its social studies curriculum, established a state seal for excellence in civics, and obligated its superintendent of public instruction to establish criteria for designating schools, pupils, teachers, or other school employees as a school, student, or educator civic leaders.²³⁰ In a separate act Nevada removed government from the list of subjects included in the social studies curriculum, replacing it with civics, financial literacy, and multicultural education.²³¹ New Hampshire prohibited the state or any of its political subdivision restricting school officials from displaying the national or state motto.²³² New Jersey specified the delivery of civics instruction in middle school, using a curriculum provided by the state center for civic education.²³³

North Dakota allowed a youth patriotic society, defined as a youth group that promotes patriotism, civic education, and civic involvement, to speak to students during regular class hours during the first quarter of each academic school year, to inform them about the society and explain how they may participate in it.²³⁴ North Dakota authorized school officials to permit students to recite the Pledge of Allegiance.²³⁵ Oklahoma decreed that U.S. government courses, history, or social studies must include study of important, named historical documents.²³⁶ Effective 2022, Rhode Island

---

[226] 2021 Ind. Acts Pub. Law 39, H.B. 1384.
[227] 2021 La. Acts No. 224, S.B. 124.
[228] 2021 Mont. Laws Ch. 253, HB 611.
[229] 2021 Mont. Laws Ch. 239, HB 543.
[230] 2021 Nev. Stat. Ch. 327, SB 194.
[231] 2021 Nev. Stat. Ch. 192, AB 19.
[232] 2021 N.H. Laws Ch. 161, HB 69.
[233] 2021 N.J. Laws c. 185, S. 854.
[234] 2021 N.D. Laws H.B. No. 1356.
[235] 2021 N.D. Laws S.B. No. 2308.
[236] 2021 Okla. Sess. Laws H.B. No. 2030.

amended its civil literacy act to require middle and high school students in public schools to demonstrate proficiency, as defined by their local boards, in civics education, which would satisfy half credit or course requirement in history and social studies.[237] South Carolina enacted the Reinforcing College Education on America's Constitutional Heritage (REACH) Act, directing officials in public high schools to provide instruction about the U.S. Constitution, the Federalist Papers, and the Declaration of Independence to all student for at least one year.[238]

In the first of four actions, Texas directed its state BOE to adopt essential knowledge and skills for each grade level from K-12 regarding civics in its social studies curriculum.[239] Texas then rewrote an objective for public education to cultivate in students informed American patriotism and lead them in a close study of the founding documents of the U.S. and Texas.[240] Third, Texas ordered officials in public elementary and secondary schools to display in conspicuous places in each building durable posters or framed copies of the U.S. national motto, "In God We Trust."[241]

Finally, in an act about U.S. history Texas directed that the social studies curriculum the state BOE adopted must include an understanding of various areas of inquiry including the fundamental moral, political, and intellectual foundations of the American experiment in self-government; the history, qualities, traditions, and features of civic engagement in the U.S.; the history of Native Americans; the founding documents; the history of white supremacy; the history and importance of the civil rights movement; the history of women's suffrage; and, important persons and events in Latino culture. The act explains that teachers not be compelled to discuss particular current events or issues but those who do must strive to explore the topics from diverse and contending perspectives without giving deference to any one perspective. The act also prohibits training, orientation, or therapy representing any form of race or sex stereotyping or blame on the basis of race or sex, while prohibited inclusion of the idea that individual, by virtue of race or sex, are inherently racist, sexist, or oppressive; the act further supported teaching an understanding of the 1619 Project.[242]

---

[237] 2021 R.I. Pub. Laws H. 5028, S. 76.
[238] 2021 S.C. Act No. 26, S. 38.
[239] 2021 Tex. Gen. Laws S.B. No. 3 (2nd Spec. Sess.).
[240] 2021 Tex. Gen. Laws H.B. No. 4509.
[241] 2021 Tex. Gen. Laws S.B. No. 797.
[242] 2021 Tex. Gen. Laws H. B. 3979.

Utah informed the Utah Valley University to establish a civic thought and leadership initiative.[243] Utah next changed its definition of the basic civics test to reflect changes in the version used by the U.S. citizenship and immigration services.[244] West Virginia mandated that officials in all public, private, parochial, and denominational schools provide at least one year of instruction in civics and the history of the state prior to the completion of grade 8.[245]

Five states sought more coverage of Black, or African-American, history. Delaware directed school boards to develop and implement curricula in Black History for students in grades K-12.[246] Illinois amended references to what it calls Freedom Schools and changes references to Black students, addressing them as historically disadvantaged, including African American and other students of color.[247] New Jersey required public school officials to include instruction on accomplishments and contributions of African Americans to American society.[248] New Mexico mandated that public education and higher education departments cooperate in developing programs, curricula, and instructional materials recognizing and teaching Black culture and anti-racism while improving job opportunities for Black candidates in public and higher education.[249] Rhode Island called for the implementation of courses in African American history in elementary and secondary schools commencing with the 2022-23 school year.[250]

Four states added acts prohibiting teaching what they regarded as a consequence of critical race theory. In a budget reconciliation bill, Arizona forbade instruction about the blame or judgment on the basis of race, ethnicity, or sex, or that individuals should feel discomfort, guilt, anguish, or any other form of psychological distress because of their race, ethnicity or sex.[251] Arkansas banned the propagation of divisive concepts related to race or sex by state entities and employees including in its state DOE; the proscribed concepts include a prohibition against teaching that individuals should feel discomfort, guilt, anguish, or any other form of

---

[243] 2021 Utah Laws H.B. 327.
[244] 2021 Utah Laws H.B. 124.
[245] 2021 W. Va. Acts Ch. 96, S.B. 636.
[246] 2021 Del. Ch. 51, HB 198.
[247] 2021 Ill. Laws Pub. Act 102-0209, SB 820.
[248] 2021 N.J. Laws c. 153, S. 1028.
[249] 2021 N.M. Laws Ch. 51, HB 43.
[250] 2021 R.I. Pub. Laws S. 458, H. 5697.
[251] 2021 Ariz. Sess. Laws Ch. 404, HB 2898, Sec. 21.

psychological distress on account of their race or sex.[252] Idaho prohibited officials in public institutions of higher education, school boards, public schools, or public charter schools to direct or otherwise compel students personally to affirm, adopt, or adhere to any of a list of tenets described as belonging to "critical race theory."[253]

Tennessee adopted a provision banning teachers or other employees in school boards and public charter schools from teaching or using materials that include or promote concepts such as that one race is inherently superior to another race or sex; individuals, by virtue of their race or sex, are inherently privileged, racist, sexist, or oppressive, whether consciously or subconsciously; persons should be discriminated against or receive adverse treatment because of their races or sexes; one's moral character is determined by one's race or sex; meritocracy is inherently racist or sexist or designed by a particular race or sex to oppress members of another race or sex; and other race or sex-related topics.[254]

Seven states amended their sex education curricula with three granting parents the right to excuse their children from parts or all of the sex education curriculum. Alabama revised provisions about sexual health education, specifying that the subject matter must be age-appropriate; that educators must provide parents or guardians advanced written notification of the teaching of sex education or of the human reproductive process; and afford parents or guardians, on request and prior to the distribution to students, the sex education curriculum. The act also struck down an admonition that homosexuality is not a lifestyle acceptable to the general public and that homosexual conduct is a criminal offense under state law.[255] Florida stipulated that the health education program for grades 6-12 must include an awareness of the benefits of sexual abstinence as the expected standard and the consequences of teenage pregnancy.[256] Illinois mandated that sex education course materials and instruction in grades 6-12 include age-appropriate discussions on sexting.[257] Montana allowed parents or guardians to remove their child from human sexuality instruction.[258]

---

[252] 2021 Ark. Acts 1100, SB 627.
[253] 2021 Idaho Sess. Laws Ch. 293, H. 377.
[254] 2021 Tenn. Pub. Acts Ch. No. 493, S.B. No. 623, H.B. No. 580.
[255] 2021 Ala. Acts No. 2021-293.
[256] 2021 Fla. Laws ch. 83, H. 519.
[257] 2021 Ill. Laws Pub. Act 102-0412, HB 24.
[258] 2021 Mont. Laws Ch. 316, SB 99.

Tennessee amended its standards about contraceptives and the family life curriculum, now calling for information about contraception and condoms to be presented in a manner that clearly informs students that while such methods may reduce the risk of acquiring sexually transmitted diseases or becoming pregnant, only abstinence removes all risk; that governing boards review and approve the information used in family life curricula for medical accuracy, age-appropriateness; are aligned to academic standards; and that parents are allowed to review and opt their children out of receiving the information as part of a family life curriculum.[259] Texas directed school boards to adopt policies for a process to adopt curricular materials for human sexuality instruction.[260] Wisconsin ordered that its curriculum for human growth and development must include information about the process under which parents of newborn children may relinquish custody of them to a law enforcement officers, emergency medical services practitioners, or hospital staff members.[261]

Five states increased requirements for their health curricula, with three focusing more on mental health issues. Maine added information about common cancer symptoms, the bone marrow registry, and organ donation to the health education curriculum at elementary and high school levels.[262] Oklahoma passed a new provision obligating officials in public schools to have courses taught in health education, which must include physical health, mental health, social and emotional health, and intellectual health.[263] Oregon declared that boards must provide age-appropriate instruction in oral health as part of health education curricula.[264] Oregon tasked boards with providing instruction on organ and tissue donation and the lifesaving potential of organ and tissue donations, in grades 9-12 in their health education curricula.[265]

Texas ordered that the health curricula at appropriate grade levels to include instruction about child abuse, family and violence, sex trafficking, directing publishers to sell to parents, on request and at a minimum price, copies of instructional materials for those subjects for their inspection.[266] Virginia informed the

---

[259] 2021 Tenn. Pub. Acts Ch. No. 380, S.B. No. 1392, H.B. No. 577.
[260] 2021 Tex. Gen. Laws H.B. No. 1525.
[261] 2021 Wis. Laws Act 90, S.B. 555.
[262] 2021 Me. Laws Ch. 41, H.P. 778, L.D. 1049.
[263] 2021 Okla. Sess. Laws S.B. 89.
[264] 2021 Or. Laws Ch. 245, HB 2969.
[265] 2021 Or. Laws Ch. 373, HB 3234.
[266] 2021 Tex. Gen. Laws S.B. No. 9 (2nd Spec. Sess.).

commonwealth's BOE to include advanced directive education in its curricular framework for health standards of learning for high school students.[267]

Arizona decreed that all health education instruction must include mental health instruction.[268] California ordered officials in local school boards, county offices of education, state special schools, and charter schools that offers one or more courses in health education in middle or high schools to include instruction in mental health.[269] Oklahoma directed the inclusion of mental health instruction in school boards' health education curricula.[270]

Five states sought more coverage on the Holocaust and/or genocide in their curricula. Arizona directed its state BOE to ensure that students are taught about the Holocaust and other genocides at least twice between the grades 7-12.[271] Arkansas mandated the teaching of Holocaust Education in all public schools.[272] Massachusetts created a fund to be used by its commissioner of elementary and secondary education to promote the teaching of human rights issues in all public schools and districts, with particular attention to the study of the inhumanity of genocide.[273] Nevada directed its state BOE to appoint a subcommittee to review and make recommendations about the manner of providing information about the Holocaust and other genocides.[274] Rhode Island created a commission to study and make recommendations about teaching the Holocaust and genocide.[275]

Two states addressed Asian American history. Illinois obligated officials in public elementary and high schools to include a unit of instruction studying the events of Asian American history in their curriculum; the act specifically directs that curricula must include instruction about the wrongful incarceration of Japanese Americans during World War II and the heroic service of the 100th Infantry Battalion and the 442nd Regimental Combat Team of the U.S. Army during World War II.[276] New Jersey ordered local boards to include

---

[267] 2021 Va. Acts Ch. 294, S. 1190 (1st Spec. Sess.).
[268] 2021 Ariz. Sess. Laws Ch. 445, SB 1376.
[269] 2021 Cal. Stat. Ch. 675, SB 224.
[270] 2021 Okla. Sess. Laws H.B. No. 1568.
[271] 2021 Ariz. Sess. Laws Ch. 418, HB 2241.
[272] 2021 Ark. Acts 611, SB 160.
[273] 2021 Mass. Acts Ch. 98, S. 2557.
[274] 2021 Nev. Stat. Ch. 242, AB 231.
[275] 2021 R.I. Pub. Laws S. 840, H. 5650.
[276] 2021 Ill. Laws Pub. Act 102-0044, HB 376.

the history and contributions of Asian Americans and Pacific Islanders in their social studies curricula.[277]

Six states addressed the teaching of financial literacy. Arkansas created a financial education commission to develop financial literacy education programs to all geographic areas and socioeconomic backgrounds while promoting the importance of saving for education.[278] Colorado set standards for financial literacy programs in high schools, specifying that they include the costs associated with obtaining postsecondary degrees or credentials in and out of state, how to assess the affordability for postsecondary degrees or credentialing, the means of paying for higher education expenses, the types of loan programs for higher education, the federal and state loan application processes, the repayment of student loans, potential career earnings in various fields, common methods for saving for retirement, the use of credit cards, and home ownership and mortgages.[279]

Illinois directed that of the two years of social studies required to receive high school diplomas, one semester, or part of one semester, may include financial literacy courses beginning in Grade 9 as of the 2021-22 school year.[280] Nevada added financial literacy to the list of required subjects in its curriculum.[281] Texas ordered its state BOE to develop a new economics course, which allocates two-thirds of instructional time to personal financial literacy and one-third to general economic matters.[282] Virginia amended a provision calling for economic education and financial literacy education in middle and high school grades, now specifying that "employment arrangements" include full-and part-time employment, independent contract work, gig work, piece work, contingent work, day labor work, freelance work, and 1099 work.[283]

Four states increased requirements for reading literacy. Arkansas prohibited instruction in grades K-2 based on practices or intervention programs using "three-cueing" systems of reading.[284] Colorado ordered local education agencies to submit to information to its department of education about producing transparency in the delivery of reading programs: a detailed description of reading

---

[277] 2021 N.J. Laws c. 416, S. 4021.
[278] 2021 Ark. Acts 1025, SB 599.
[279] 2021 Colo. Sess. Laws HB 1200.
[280] 2021 Ill. Laws Pub. Act 102-0366, SB 1830.
[281] 2021 Nev. Stat. Ch. 192, AB 19.
[282] 2021 Tex. Gen. Laws S.B. No. 1063.
[283] 2021 Va. Acts Ch. 25, H. 1905 (1st Spec. Sess.).
[284] 2021 Ark. Acts 606, SB 349.

curricula, by grade, used at each of their schools; the targeted, evidence or scientifically-based core and supplemental reading instructional programs and interventions; an accounting of the reading deficiencies among students; and, a website to make the information submitted available to the general public.[285] Louisiana created a literacy program for students in grades K-3 reading below grade level, for those in grades 4-5 scoring below master in English language arts on the state assessment, and pupils recommended by their English-language arts teachers for participation.[286] Tennessee enacted the Literacy Success Act stipulating that local boards must provide foundational literacy skills instruction, reading interventions and supports, and the administration of universal reading screeners to students in grades K-3.[287]

Five states enacted bills about the teaching of computer science. Hawai'i declared that public and charter schools must include classes in computer science in their curricula.[288] Mississippi obligated its state DOE to implement a mandatory K-12 computer science curriculum based on the state's college and career-readiness standards for computer science which includes instruction on cyber-related programming, cyber security, data science, robotics and other computer science and cyber-related content.[289] Oklahoma tasked all public high and charter schools with offering a minimum of one computer science course to students beginning in the 2024-2025 school year. Also, in that year, all public and charter middle and elementary schools must offer instruction aligned with academic standards for computer science.[290] Virginia called on its DOE to perform a comprehensive review of the ongoing implementation of mandatory computer science standards in elementary and middle schools and their alignment with course pathways.[291] Washington obligated officials to offer elective computer science course to all high school students by the 2022-23 school year which could be used for graduation credit in computer science or mathematics retroactively back to the 2019-20 year.[292]

Driver's education was the subject of six acts. Illinois ordered the inclusion of law enforcement procedures during traffic stops in

---

[285] 2021 Colo. Sess. Laws SB 151.
[286] 2021 La. Acts No. 415, H.B. 85.
[287] 2021 Tenn. Pub. Acts Ch. 3, S.B. No. 3, H.B. No. 2 (First Extra. Sess.).
[288] 2021 Haw. Sess. Laws Act 158, SB 242.
[289] 2021 Miss. Laws HB 633.
[290] 2021 Okla. Sess. Laws S.B. No. 252.
[291] 2021 Va. Acts Ch. 22, H. 1885 (1st Spec. Sess.).
[292] 2021 Wash. Laws Ch. 307, S.B. 5299.

driver's education courses.²⁹³ Montana allowed the classroom component of driver's education to be provided by distance learning, also permitting the hands-on driving component to be offered by students' parents or guardians.²⁹⁴ Utah extended the term of a driver's education learner permits from one year to eighteen months.²⁹⁵ The previous two acts were adopted in response to constraints in instruction due to COVID-19. Ensured that driver's education programs include instruction on the dangers of speeding and distracted driving.²⁹⁶ Virginia waived the mandatory, minimum ninety-minute parent and student driver component of the driver's education for pupils who are at least eighteen, emancipated, or unaccompanied minors not in the physical custody of their parents or guardians.²⁹⁷ West Virginia approved of having written driver's examinations to be administered in school driver's education courses.²⁹⁸

Four states addressed curricular requirements about substance abuse. Illinois amended a provision on instruction, study, and discussion in grades K-8 on effective methods for the prevention and avoidance of drugs and the dangers of opioid and substance abuse; the added language underscores the importance of discussing opioid addiction.²⁹⁹ Louisiana added information on the health risks associated with vapor products to its curriculum on alcohol, tobacco, drug, and substance abuse.³⁰⁰ Maryland authorized its state DOE to coordinate with its department of health to establish procedures for administering the youth risk behavior survey and youth tobacco survey for the Centers for Disease Control.³⁰¹ Tennessee specified that its department of health, in cooperation with its state DOE, provide information to middle, junior, and senior high school students on the dangers of vapor products.³⁰²

Five states adopted laws about standards or learning outcomes. Arizona ordered its state BOE to establish learning outcomes beginning with mathematics.³⁰³ Arkansas removed references to the

---

²⁹³ 2021 Ill. Laws Pub. Act 102-0455, HB 3097.
²⁹⁴ 2021 Mont. Laws Ch. 450, SB 300.
²⁹⁵ 2021 Utah Laws H.B. 18.
²⁹⁶ 2021 Va. Acts Ch. 74, H. 1918; Ch. 75, S. 1169 (1ˢᵗ Spec. Sess.).
²⁹⁷ 2021 Va. Acts Ch. 28, H. 2119 (1ˢᵗ Spec. Sess.).
²⁹⁸ 2021 W. Va. Acts Ch. 183, S.B. 356.
²⁹⁹ 2021 Ill. Laws Pub. Act 102-0195, HB 1162.
³⁰⁰ 2021 La. Acts No. 230, H.B. 368.
³⁰¹ 2021 Md. Laws Ch. 569, HB 771; 2021 Md. Laws Ch. 570, SB 548.
³⁰² 2021 Tenn. Pub. Acts Ch. No. 157, S.B. No. 20, H.B. No. 789.
³⁰³ 2021 Ariz. Sess. Laws Ch. 289, HB 2135.

"common core" for state academic standards in its materials about curricula in its state BOE.[304] New Jersey ordered local boards to include instruction on diversity and inclusion as part of their learning standards.[305] Oregon directed its state BOE to initiate a review of state academic standards for social studies.[306] Tennessee forbade teachers or principals in public schools from using or permitting the use of, whether as adopted or supplemental sources, textbooks or instructional materials created to align exclusively with the common core standards or marketed or identified as common core textbooks.[307]

Two states included the potential addition of hunter safety in their curricula. Arkansas permitted officials to offer a hunter safety course as part of school curriculum.[308] Oklahoma adopted a resolution encouraging public school authorities to incorporate the department of wildlife conservation's approved hunter education course in middle or high school curricula.[309]

Other curriculum-related acts adopted in 2021 are detailed as follows. Alabama enabled local school boards to offer yoga to students in grades K-12.[310] Arkansas clarified that students in grades 5-6 in public schools not configured as elementary schools must participate in visual art and music classes.[311] Florida changed the grade levels for which boards are encouraged to provide first aid training from grades 6 and every two years thereafter to grades 8-11; the act also stipulated that the training should include cardiopulmonary resuscitation.[312] Illinois required that history courses include the study and contributions made by Muslims and Muslim Americans to society, and added January 17, the birthday of Muhammad Ali, to the list of commemorative holidays.[313] Illinois ordered public high schools to include a unit of instruction on media literacy in their curricula.[314]

Maine obligated its state DOE to develop a process and timeline for reviewing prior legislation that proposes to mandate instruction

---

[304] 2021 Ark. Acts 544, SB 64.
[305] 2021 N.J. Laws c. 32, A. 4454.
[306] 2021 Or. Laws Ch. 406, SB 702.
[307] 2021 Tenn. Pub. Acts Ch. No. 205, S.B. No. 769, H.B. No. 782.
[308] 2021 Ark. Acts 536, SB 161.
[309] 2021 Okla. Sess. Laws S.C.R. 5.
[310] 2021 Ala. Acts No. 2021-475, HB 246.
[311] 2021 Ark. Acts 644, SB 451.
[312] 2021 Fla. Laws ch. 141, H. 157.
[313] 2021 Ill. Laws Pub. Act 102-0411, SB 564.
[314] 2021 Ill. Laws Pub. Act 102-0055, HB 234.

or training for students.³¹⁵ New Hampshire included environmental science, with biological, physical, and earth sciences, in curricular standards, for science.³¹⁶ Oklahoma obligated officials in public and charter schools to provide students in grades 10-12 opportunities to take the Armed Services Vocational Aptitude Battery (ASVAB) test and consult with a military recruiter.³¹⁷ Rhode Island called on its department of elementary and secondary education to make educational resources available about litter prevention and recycling awareness to elementary and middle school students.³¹⁸

Tennessee informed local school boards to publish their curricula on their websites and update changes at the beginning of each semester.³¹⁹ Tennessee decreed that its state DOE develop a rubric to assist its education commission in reviewing and scoring textbooks and instructional materials proposed for adoption.³²⁰ Texas allowed local boards to offer electives on the Old and New Testament, or both combined, to middle school students, taught by certified teachers in language arts, social studies, or history who successfully completed specified training on the nature of the courses.³²¹ At the same time, Texas authorized its state BOE to add personal skills to the essential skills for positive character traits for grades K-12, as appropriate; among those personal skills, the act mandated the inclusion of self-management skills, interpersonal skills, and responsible decision-making skills.³²²

Employment

During the 2021 calendar year, legislatures and general assemblies focused first and foremost on measures designed to understand and address the continuing and growing shortage of teachers available to fill multiple vacancies across the nation. Alabama provided additional compensation for teachers of mathematics and science who elect to serve in hard-to-staff

---

[315] 2021 Me. Laws Ch. 65, H.P. 194, L.D. 278; 2021 Me. Laws Ch. 58, H.P. 381, L.D. 518.
[316] 2021 N.H. Laws Ch. 210, SB 148.
[317] 2021 Okla. Sess. Laws S.B. No. 642.
[318] 2021 R.I. Pub. Laws S. 210, H. 6418.
[319] 2021 Tenn. Pub. Acts Ch. No. 519, H.B. No. 210, S.B. No. 1147.
[320] 2021 Tenn. Pub. Acts Ch. No. 342, H.B. No. 1537, S.B. No. 1036.
[321] 2021 Tex. Gen. Laws H.B. No. 2681.
[322] 2021 Tex. Gen. Laws S.B. No. 123.

schools.³²³ Alabama included computer science teachers in a student loan repayment program, to allow teachers to return to college to obtain certification in mathematics, science, or computer science and serve in failing schools.³²⁴ Next, Alabama authorized its state BOE to establish and issue alternative teaching certificates to qualified former members of the U.S. armed forces.³²⁵ Alaska directed its department of commerce, community, and economic development to prepare an annual report that describes the number of temporary courtesy licenses distributed to military spouses for each previous fiscal year.³²⁶

Arizona extended the life of an alternative teacher development program for schools with low-income students until July 1, 2030.³²⁷ Arkansas amended standards for a recruitment and retention, calling for three-year plans, adding that they must set goals for the recruitment and retention of teachers and administrators to increase diversity to reflect the racial and ethnic diversity of their student bodies.³²⁸ Arkansas permitted its division of elementary and secondary education to grant teaching licenses to noncitizens with valid employment authorization documents from immigration services and approved exemptions under the deferred action for childhood arrivals policy.³²⁹

In the first of four acts Colorado directed its state departments of higher education and public education to study barriers to and effective strategies for preparing, recruiting, and retaining a diverse educator workforce, reflecting the diversity of state students.³³⁰ Colorado extended the licensing period for professional teacher licenses from five to seven years.³³¹ Colorado expanded provisions creating adjunct instructor authorization, calculated to provide more teachers in rural areas, explaining that they must work under the general supervision of educators with professional teacher licenses.³³² Colorado established a fund to be used to increase base salaries for teachers and principals.³³³

---

[323] 2021 Ala. Acts No. 2021-340, S.B. 327.
[324] 2021 Ala. Acts No. 2021-389, H.B. 175.
[325] 2021 Ala. Acts No. 2021-111, S.B. 16.
[326] 2021 Alaska Sess. Laws Ch. 34, SB 12.
[327] 2021 Ariz. Sess. Laws Ch. 446, SB 1401.
[328] 2021 Ark. Acts 646, SB 524.
[329] 2021 Ark. Acts 513, HB 1594.
[330] 2021 Colo. Sess. Laws HB 1010.
[331] 2021 Colo. Sess. Laws HB 1104.
[332] 2021 Colo. Sess. Laws SB 185.
[333] 2021 Colo. Sess. Laws SB 172.

Delaware created a teacher candidate residency program whereby those enrolled in education preparation programs receive year-long, practice-based learning experiences working directly with students in a manner mirroring the experience of teachers in that school.[334] Delaware directed its state DOE to identify a list of critical need teaching areas and publish annually it on its website; from this list, institutions of higher education can seek reimbursement for programs providing standard teaching certificates in high-need areas.[335] Hawai'i allowed dependents of military service members to meet state residency standards for government employment if the service member is in Hawai'i on bona fide military orders, also allowing their spouses with equivalent licensure in other states to practice there. The legislation listed by title mostly medically-related specialties, such as physician, dentist, nurse, and optician but might be read to include school employees in the "other" category.[336]

Maine included career and technical education teachers in a minimum $40,000 salary initiative to increase its pool of candidates.[337] Minnesota allocated funds for a marketing campaign for teacher recruitment.[338] Minnesota created a program to support boards and schools recruiting and offering hiring bonuses for licensed teachers who are American Indian or person of colors from other states or countries to meet staffing needs in shortage areas in its economic development regions.[339] Minnesota also allocated grant funds for a "grow-your-own" teacher preparation program by collaboration between local boards and standards board-approved teacher education programs.[340] Mississippi renewed its Critical Teacher Shortage Act of 1998 plus provisions promoting teacher recruitment and retention plus the employer-assisted housing teacher program.[341] Mississippi then created a teacher loan repayment program which would allow students who received baccalaureate degrees, obtained standard five-year teacher licenses, and signed first-year contracts to have their undergraduate educational loans repaid.[342]

---

[334] 2021 Del. Laws Ch. 117, HB 178.
[335] 2021 Del. Ch. 46, HB 89.
[336] 2021 Haw. Sess. Laws Act 18, HB 961.
[337] 2021 Me. Laws Ch. 441, H.P. 886, L.D. 1188.
[338] 2021 Minn. Laws Ch. 13, H.F. no. 2 (1st Spec. Sess.).
[339] 2021 Minn. Laws Ch. 13, H.F. no. 2 (1st Spec. Sess.).
[340] 2021 Minn. Laws Ch. 13, H.F. no. 2 (1st Spec. Sess.).
[341] 2021 Miss. Laws HB 135.
[342] 2021 Miss. Laws HB 1179.

Montana created a "grow your own" teacher grant program to develop teacher pipelines aimed at serving rural and reservation school districts.[343] Montana established a scholarship program to support the teaching of computer programming in educational institutions on tribal lands.[344] Third, Montana provided an increase in the quality educator payment in its funding formula as an incentive for public school board to increase the base pay for teachers.[345] Nevada called on its commission on professional standards in education to adopt regulations allowing persons currently employed as paraprofessionals and enrolled in teacher education programs to complete accelerated programs, adopting regulations allowing its state DOE to accept student teaching experiences completed in other state or foreign countries, if its officials determines that they fulfilled its requirements.[346] New Jersey provided loan redemption for teachers working in hard-to-staff fields or in low-performing schools.[347] Moreover, New Jersey allowed individuals enrolled in institutions of higher education who completed thirty semester-hour credits to serve as substitute teachers.[348]

New Mexico expanded the list of those who qualify for scholarships under its grow your own teachers program,[349] providing professional leave for public school employees who are recipients of such scholarships.[350] North Carolina allowed adjunct instructors with bachelors' or graduate degrees who have taken a semester of courses in pedagogy from a community college or educator preparation program to teach high school-level core academic subjects, fine and performing arts, and foreign language courses in their areas of specialized knowledge or work experience.[351] Oklahoma enabled student teachers to be eligible to receive compensation beginning on the first day of their internships for up to one full school year, but does not treat it as compensation for purposes of teacher retirement or placement on the teacher salary schedule.[352] For a period of three years beginning July 1, 2021,

---

[343] 2021 Mont. Laws Ch. 514, HB 403.
[344] 2021 Mont. Laws Ch. 416, HB 644.
[345] 2021 Mont. Laws Ch. 60, HB 143.
[346] 2021 Nev. Stat. Ch. 529, SB 352.
[347] 2021 N.J. Laws c. 384, S. 969.
[348] 2021 N.J. Laws c. 87, S. 2832.
[349] N.M.S.A. § 21-21P-2 (1978).
[350] 2021 N.M. Laws Ch. 11, HB 22.
[351] 2021 N.C. Sess. Laws Ch. 48, S. 582.
[352] 2021 Okla. Sess. Laws S.B. No. 1038.

Oklahoma made teachers who retired as of July 1, 2020, received retirement benefits for at least one year, and were not employed by public schools during that time, eligible to be reemployed as active classroom teachers in common or career tech school districts with no limitations on their earnings.[353]

Oregon obligated educational employers to provide information for eligible employees who might be interested in the public service loan forgiveness program.[354] Pennsylvania allowed retired teachers to serve up to twenty days as substitutes without impacting their retirement pay, even if not certified for the assignments.[355] Utah extended bonuses for teachers to work in high-poverty schools through the 2020-21 school year.[356] Utah then ensured that teachers whom local education agencies assigned to teach in online settings or work in online-only districts or charter schools are eligible for the supplemental educator COVID-19 salary supplement.[357] Utah created a grow your own teacher and school counselor pipeline program to provide scholarships for persons wishing to pursue those positions.[358] West Virginia terminated extracurricular contracts of retired school employees but allowed them to apply for extracurricular contracts and, if successful, to be employed consistent with the rules for employment of retirees established by its public retirement board; this provision appears to be designed to address a shortage of coaches and extracurricular sponsors.[359]

Twenty-two states changed certification standards, in many cases to speed up authorization for teacher candidates to enter the classroom. Arizona established an endorsement as a requirement for teacher certification in literacy in grades K-5.[360] Arkansas created a pathway for college faculty members to be recognized as highly qualified professors or teachers by certification from its state BOE.[361] California added to teacher certification standards to support education specialist teaching credentials, especially for the effective means of teaching literacy.[362] California directed that baccalaureates or higher degrees for school nurse-teacher

---

[353] 2021 Okla. Sess. Laws S.B. No. 267.
[354] 2021 Or. Laws Ch. 261, HB 3255.
[355] 2021 Pa. Laws Act No. 91, HB 412.
[356] 2021 Utah Laws H.B. 323.
[357] 2021 Utah Laws H.B. 450.
[358] 2021 Utah Laws H.B. 381.
[359] 2021 W. Va. Acts Ch. 245, H.B. 3266.
[360] 2021 Ariz. Sess. Laws Ch. 434, SB 1572.
[361] 2021 Ark. Acts 657, HB 1678.
[362] 2021 Cal. Stat. Ch. 678, SB 488.

credentials, authorizing its credentialing commission to approve programs offered by local education agencies for one year of coursework beyond baccalaureate degrees.[363]

Connecticut adjusted standards for those in bilingual education programs to allow the teaching of courses with specified numbers of credit hour courses in various subject areas.[364] Idaho retained teachers at the category three contract status, regardless of whether the same districts have continuously employed them for more than three years until they met nontraditional route program standards and received five-year renewable certificates.[365] Illinois amended its requirements for licensure of teacher candidates, providing that individuals may not be obligated to submit test materials by video.[366] Indiana permitted speech-language pathologists to practice with licenses from other states through a reciprocity agreement.[367] Indiana enabled those who are at least twenty-six and have bachelor's degrees to receive initial teacher certification through an alternative program which includes a one-year clinical experience during one's first year in classrooms while employed full-time.[368]

Kentucky directed its educational professional standards board to issue ten-year emeritus certificates to applicants who retired a year or less ago and received emeritus certificates for one year. The same law called on the board to issue a one-time five-year exception certificate for persons who held Rank I or II certificates, taught at least three years, and met other requirements for an exception certificate.[369] Kentucky joined the audiology and speech-language therapy interstate compact with other jurisdictions in the compact.[370] Maine directed its commissioner of education to issue emergency teaching certificates to teachers, specialists, and administrators, and adopted alternative certification procedures when educator staffing shortages exist there.[371]

Michigan created two exceptions to a provision requiring teachers to have a certificate. The first is for school counselors with master's degrees who passed the guidance counselor examination and are recommended by approved counseling programs. The second

---

[363] 2021 Cal. Stat. Ch. 668, AB 815.
[364] 2021 Conn. Acts 21-144 (Reg. Sess.), SB 945.
[365] 2021 Idaho Sess. Laws Ch. 96, H. 111.
[366] 2021 Ill. Laws Pub. Act 102-0301, SB 808.
[367] 2021 Ind. Acts Pub. Law 216 § 52; H. B. No. 1549.
[368] 2021 Ind. Acts Pub. Law 96, S.B. 205.
[369] 2021 Ky. Acts Ch. 187, HB 163.
[370] 2021 Ky. Acts Ch. 45, SB 47.
[371] 2021 Me. Laws Ch. 228, H.P. 867, L.D. 1189.

concerns certified school counselors with five years of experience in those jobs in other states who have passed the certification examination.[372] Mississippi obligated its state DOE to grant teaching licenses within twenty-one days from the completion of an application to teachers if they possess a valid standard teaching license from another state.[373] Nebraska directed its state BOE to authorize the issuance of teaching certificates to military spouses who had them in other states.[374] Nebraska adopted the audiology and speech-language pathology interstate compact.[375]

Nevada ordered its commission on professional standards in education to consider alternative means of demonstrating competency when adopting regulations governing examinations for teacher licensure.[376] Nevada mandated that boards of trustees of school districts report the number of teachers participating in alternative routes to licensure to the legislative committee on education.[377] While Nevada previously permitted teachers in specified content areas to teach in charter schools without licenses, it now requires that eighty percent of those who teach at charter schools must have licenses or endorsements; the act also specifies that all teachers of core academic subjects must have licenses or endorsements.[378] New Hampshire exempted persons applying to teach courses in career technology education specialty areas from having to have a bachelor's degree to obtain a one-year certificate.[379]

In the first of four new laws, New Jersey established an alternate route for certification of teachers through early college high school programs to expedite an earlier certification.[380] New Jersey informed its state DOE to create a five-year pilot program under which it may offer limited certificates of eligibility to teach for shorter periods to speed up full certification.[381] In its state DOE, New Jersey established a five-year alternative route interstate reciprocity pilot program whereby teachers from other states may be issued certificates prior to meeting full requirements and where students in teacher education programs may earn credits from that

---

[372] 2021 Mich. Pub. Acts No. 149, H.B. 4294.
[373] 2021 Miss. Laws SB 2267.
[374] 2021 Neb. Laws LB 389.
[375] 2021 Neb. Laws 14.
[376] 2021 Nev. Stat. Ch. 405, AB 225.
[377] 2021 Nev. Stat. Ch. 355, AB 266.
[378] 2021 Nev. Stat. Ch. 115, AB 109.
[379] 2021 N.H. Laws Ch. 28, SB 20.
[380] 2021 N.J. Laws c. 279, S. 3253.
[381] 2021 N.J. Laws c. 224, A. 2826.

program.[382] New Jersey allowed alternative evaluation to replace basic skills testing requirements for teacher certification.[383]

New Mexico provided a teacher license endorsement for secondary computer science.[384] New Mexico next created a path for persons seeking alternative level one special education licenses; this appears to allow educators to begin teaching while pursuing courses in pedagogy.[385] North Dakota added to the criteria needed for teacher certification, now obligating those in special education to operate in accordance with the procedures and program approval standards and requirements set by the board for teacher education programs for educator licensure.[386] Further, North Dakota added to the credentials for which the state superintendent of public instruction is authorized to issue to school employees to include certification of completion for special education technicians.[387]

In the first of four changes, Oklahoma permitted persons with advanced degrees, such as Ed.Ds., Ph.Ds., and/or masters of fine arts degrees, to participate in an alternative teacher certification program for service as an early childhood or elementary education teacher.[388] Oklahoma required its state DOE, in coordination with its commission for educational quality and accountability, to permit teacher candidates or teachers with certificates to teach to complete additional coursework and thereby earn micro-credentials in STEM endorsement areas and computer science.[389] Oklahoma authorized its state BOE, in consultation with its commission for educational quality and accountability, to grant an exception for subject area examinations for initial certification in fields not necessitating advanced degrees where candidates earned them in those fields.[390] Oklahoma allowed its state BOE to grant an exception to the examination requirement for certification for teacher candidates who are deaf and use American Sign Language.[391]

Rhode Island specified that only certified nurse teachers may be employed as school nurses in elementary and secondary schools.[392]

---

[382] 2021 N.J. Laws c. 57, S. 2831.
[383] 2021 N.J. Laws c. 420, S. 4074.
[384] 2021 N.M. Laws Ch. 102, HB 188.
[385] 2021 N.M. Laws Ch. 129, HB 266.
[386] 2021 N.D. Laws S.B. No. 2332.
[387] 2021 N.D. Laws H.B. No. 1188.
[388] 2021 Okla. Sess. Laws H.B. No. 2748.
[389] 2021 Okla. Sess. Laws H. B. 2752.
[390] 2021 Okla. Sess. Laws H.B. No. 1796.
[391] 2021 Okla. Sess. Laws H.B. No. 2329.
[392] 2021 R.I. Pub. Laws S. 87, H. 5197.

Tennessee directed that when issuing licenses to teach in public schools to individuals with active teaching licenses in other jurisdictions, its state BOE must issue licenses as held in the other stated if both have reciprocal agreements.[393] In the first of three changes, Texas allowed teacher candidates to satisfy internship requirements through local remote learning programs or the state virtual school network.[394] Texas directed its state board for educator certification to develop a certificate for teaching bilingual special education.[395] Texas ordered its state board for educator certification to propose rules giving flexible options for the field-based experience or internships required for certification, including a mix of in-person and virtual observations.[396] Virginia obligated its state BOE to grant a two-year extension of teaching licenses set to expire on June 30, 2021, due to the COVID-19 emergency.[397]

Two states addressed generating more data and information about the teacher shortage. Colorado informed its state DOE to provide an annual report on the number of licensed and employed school psychologists in school districts.[398] Tennessee required its state DOE to survey all local school districts, public charter schools, and state special schools to determine whether there is a sufficient number of licensed speech-language pathologists in the schools to meet student needs.[399]

Four states added legislation about certificate revocation or suspension pending revocation. Arizona mandated that investigators related to investigating certificated persons, those seeking certification, and non-certificated individuals for immoral or unprofessional conduct be housed within and be employees of the state BOE.[400] Arkansas prohibited the issuance or renewals of teaching licenses to those who plead guilty or *nolo contendere* or were found guilty of sexually grooming a child.[401] Oklahoma required that when teachers have certificates suspended by its state BOE pending revocation, they must be placed on suspension from their classrooms.[402] Texas amended provisions in its law about the role of

---

[393] 2021 Tenn. Pub. Acts Ch. No. 125, S.B. No. 479, H.B. No. 533.
[394] 2021 Tex. Gen. Laws S.B. No. 15 (2nd Spec. Sess.).
[395] 2021 Tex. Gen. Laws H.B. No. 2256.
[396] 2021 Tex. Gen. Laws S.B. No. 1590.
[397] 2021 Va. Acts Ch. 394, H. 1776 (1st Spec. Sess.).
[398] 2021 Colo. Sess. Laws HB 1273.
[399] 2021 Tenn. Pub. Acts Ch. 34, S.B. No. 233, H.B. No.23.
[400] 2021 Ariz. Sess. Laws Ch. 404, HB 2898, Sec. 5.
[401] 2021 Ark. Acts 985, HB 1837.
[402] 2021 Okla. Sess. Laws S.B. No. 13.

its state board for educator certification in sanctioning school professionals who abandon teaching contracts by prohibiting it from suspending or revoking their certification as a sanction for failure to file timely written resignations if the individuals file written resignations to the board of trustees or their designees in their districts at least thirty days before the first day of instruction of the following school year.[403]

Fifteen states passed twenty-three acts about professional development.[404] Arizona opened up participation in its Arizona Teachers Academy to schools that serve primarily public school students with disabilities.[405] Arkansas called for the development of education programs for school nurses, mandating that they participate in such activities.[406] California required the state DOE to recommend best practices and identify evidence-based and evidence-informed training programs for schools to address youth behavioral health.[407] Colorado added a year, to the beginning of the 2022-23 school year, to the time by which teachers must receive training in teaching reading.[408] Connecticut directed its state DOE to implement the recommendations of a task force, regarding the adoption of laws governing dyslexia instruction and training.[409]

Illinois delayed the training of staff and students in trauma-informed practices from the 2022-23 school year to the 2034-24 school year.[410] Illinois next informed its state BOE to establish a competitive grant program to support a new principal mentoring program and to approve one or more eligible entities to provide services to new principals under the program.[411] Louisiana required in-service training for teachers and other school personnel regarding adverse childhood experiences and trauma-informed education.[412] In

---

[403] 2021 Tex. Gen. Laws S.B. No. 2519.

[404] Although resolutions are not usually reported in these materials, a theme discovered in the qualitative analysis across categories was legislation in support of culture wars. Oklahoma adopted a resolution discouraging schools from mandating professional development for teachers that covers critical race theory, Project 1619, or other issues in Enrolled House Bill No. 11775 of the 1st Regular Session of the 58th Oklahoma Legislature. 2021 Okla. Sess. Laws H.R. 1038.

[405] 2021 Ariz. Sess. Laws Ch. 43, HB 2832.

[406] 2021 Ark. Acts 1089, HB 1826.

[407] 2021 Cal. Stat. Ch. 672, SB 14.

[408] 2021 Colo. Sess. Laws HB 1129.

[409] 2021 Conn. Acts 21-168, (Reg. Sess.), HB 6517.

[410] 2021 Ill. Laws Pub. Act 102-0638, SB 2109.

[411] 2021 Ill. Laws Pub. Act 102-0521, SB 814.

[412] 2021 La. Acts No. 353, S.B. 211.

the first of three laws Maine created a pilot program to provide grants for professional development for computer science instruction.[413] Maine ordered its state DOE to review diversity, equity, and inclusion training and other professional development for school staff.[414] Maine specified that its state DOE must devise training and professional development for school counselors on family or intimate partner violence.[415]

Mississippi required school boards to provide four hours of awareness training for dyslexia and related disorders to all licensed educators and paraprofessionals.[416] New Jersey directed arbitrators in its state DOE to have training about issues related to cultural diversity and bias.[417] Oklahoma initiated professional development for teachers in prekindergarten through grade five in the science of how students learn to read as well as exposure to instructional materials necessary for its implementation.[418] Oklahoma added professional development for teachers in digital teaching, mental health training, workplace safety training, and alcohol and drug abuse training.[419] Tennessee changed, from one time to once every three years, the mandated in-service training for teachers on the detection, intervention, prevention, and treatment of human trafficking.[420]

In the first of five new laws Texas obligated its commissioner of education to develop and make available a civics training program for teachers and administrators.[421] Texas extended the deadline for K-3 principals and teachers to complete reading academy training by no later than the 2022-23 school year.[422] Texas specified that only a school board's cybersecurity coordinator must complete annual cybersecurity training.[423] Texas directed its state education agency to study the effect of teacher participation in a mathematics achievement academy on student performance in mathematics.[424] Texas required its state board for educator certification to develop

---

[413] 2021 Me. Laws Ch. 102, S.P. 60, L.D. 127.
[414] 2021 Me. Laws Ch. 94, S.P. 247, L.D. 633.
[415] 2021 Me. Laws Ch. 89, H.P. 470, L.D. 639.
[416] 2021 Miss. Laws HB 754.
[417] 2021 N.J. Laws c. 51, S. 699.
[418] 2021 Okla. Sess. Laws H.B. No. 2749.
[419] 2021 Okla. Sess. Laws H.B. 1593.
[420] 2021 Tenn. Pub. Acts Ch. No. 287, H.B. No. 117, S.B. No. 337.
[421] 2021 Tex. Gen. Laws S.B. No. 3, (2nd Spec. Sess.).
[422] 2021 Tex. Gen. Laws H.B. No. 1525.
[423] 2021 Tex. Gen. Laws S.B. No. 1267.
[424] 2021 Tex. Gen. Laws S.B. No. 1267.

and publish a comprehensive clearinghouse of information regarding continuing education and training requirements for educators and other student personnel; under this provision officials on school boards and in charter schools must annually review the clearinghouse information and adopt professional development policies.[425]

Utah broadened the intended audience and the content of training that its state BOE must prepare and make available for school resource officers (SROs).[426] Washington added continuing education elements focused on equity-based school and classroom practices for administrator and teacher certificate renewal.[427]

Six states adopted eight acts on educator evaluations. Delaware suspended its evaluation system during the 2020-21 school year, replacing it with an observation and feedback cycle that provides educators with coaching and support related to hybrid and remote learning practices.[428] Delaware then replaced its former teacher performance appraisal system with a pilot program, the Teacher Growth and Support System, dedicated to student improvement; the newer model is apparently formative rather than summative in its evaluative aspect and consists of two parts. The first must contain at least one individual professional learning goal created jointly by teachers and administrators focused on the continuous improvement skills aligned to a rubric on the teacher observation document. The second must contain at least two individual student improvement goals demonstrating teachers' contribution to student growth for their current cohort of pupils.[429] Illinois directed school boards to implement, rather than establish, informal teacher observation plans.[430]

Maine waived teacher and principal evaluations mandated by state law[431] during the 2021-22 school year.[432] Additionally, Maine informed its state DOE to create a study group to determine best practices and accountability standards for school boards to measure the performance of superintendents.[433] Nevada blunted the use of pupil growth data as part of teacher and administrator evaluations

---

[425] 2021 Tex. Gen. Laws S.B. No. 1267.
[426] 2021 Utah Laws H.B. 345.
[427] 2021 Wash. Laws Ch. 77, H.B. 1426.
[428] 2021 Del. Ch. 5, SB 42.
[429] 2021 Del. Laws Ch. 116, HB 133.
[430] 2021 Ill. Laws Pub. Act 102-0252. HB 18.
[431] ME. REV. STAT. tit. 20-A, sec. 1055, subs. 10, and tit. 20-A, sec. 13701, subs. 1.
[432] 2021 Me. Laws Ch. 180, H.P. 850, L.D. 1172.
[433] 2021 Me. Laws Ch. 73, H.P. 474, L.D. 643.

in the 2021-22 school year so that none of it is deployed in the formula but allowed the percentage to rise to fifteen in 2022-23.[434] New York set aside a requirement for an annual teacher or principal evaluation during the 2020-21 school year.[435] Tennessee excluded data generated by state assessments administered in the 2020-21 school year as well as data generated by alternative growth models used by local school boards in the same year to evaluate teachers in non-tested grades and subjects.[436]

Five states adopted acts about employee leaves. Maine granted up to fifteen sick leave days for public school employees affected by infection with the coronavirus, which causes COVID-19.[437] Illinois decreed that school board employees who worked at least twelve months and at least 1,000 hours in the previous year be eligible for family and medical leave under the same terms and conditions under the federal Family and Medical Leave Act.[438] New York granted time off for public employees to receive COVID-19 vaccinations.[439] Tennessee specified, for purposes concerning sick leave and leaves of absence, that schools or boards are not considered to be closed when teachers are required to work remotely and provide virtual instruction.[440] Virginia obligated teachers, principals, and division superintendents to be evaluated on cultural competency.[441]

Two states expressed concern about out-of-pocket expenses for teachers. Arkansas doubled the amount of income tax deduction teachers may claim for classroom investment expenses to $500 per taxpayer or $1,000 for taxpayers who are married and filing jointly, if each taxpayer is a teacher.[442] North Dakota sought a legislative management study of out-of-pocket expenses incurred by its teachers for classroom supplies and the feasibility and desirability of creating a teacher reimbursement program.[443]

Six states passed eight laws on salaries and benefits. Alabama repealed a provision directing the BOE in Dale County to determine and fix the annual salary to be paid to its county superintendent of

---

[434] 2021 Nev. Stat. Ch. 255, AB 57.
[435] 2021 N.Y. Laws Ch. 112, S. 5576.
[436] 2021 Tenn. Pub. Acts Ch. No. 2, S.B. No. 1, H.B. No. 3 (First Extra. Sess.).
[437] 2021 Me. Laws Ch. 378, H.P. 731, L.D. 993.
[438] 2021 Ill. Laws Pub. Act 102-0335, HB 12.
[439] 2021 N.Y. Laws Ch. 77, A. 3354.
[440] 2021 Tenn. Pub. Acts Ch. No. 261, S.B. No. 636, H.B. No. 1342.
[441] 2021 Va. Acts Ch. 23, H. 1904; Ch. 24, S. 1196 (1st Spec. Sess.).
[442] 2021 Ark. Acts 971, HB 1157.
[443] 2021 N.D. Laws H.B. No. 1210.

education.[444] Arizona informed officials on school boards and charter schools to provide each employee a full annual listing of all salaries, benefits, and any payments they received.[445] Louisiana directed its office of group benefits, which manages insurance policies for governmental agencies, including public schools, to cover bariatric surgery in their benefits packages.[446] Louisiana included a reasonable time during pregnancy in its definition of a disability under state employment law, directing employers to make reasonable accommodations for pregnant six-week periods.[447]

Maryland required officials in its school for blind to operate a uniform pay plan for teachers and professional personnel with the secretary of budget and management to establish the pay plan.[448] Utah permitted staff members with professional deaf education licenses issued by its state BOE to be eligible for the teacher salary supplement program.[449] West Virginia added titles for school service personnel for Aide V and Aide VI classifications.[450] West Virginia next re-enacted its state salary schedule, allowing its state superintendent of schools to define classroom teachers certified to teach in special education.[451]

Five states enacted laws about employee working conditions. Colorado authorized education support professionals to participate in the legislatively-required teaching and learning conditions survey.[452] Louisiana first stressed that the forty-five minute planning time established by state statute[453] is uninterrupted time.[454] Louisiana then provided free tools for teachers, school bus drivers, and other school employees on the Louisiana Highway 1 Bridge.[455] Maine obligated local school boards to adopt and implement policies to address the negative effects of bullying of school employees by administrators, school employees, parents, students, or other individuals associated with the public school and to ensure the safety of employees and an inclusive environment for

---

[444] 2021 Ala. Acts No. 2021-135, H.B. 250.
[445] 2021 Ariz. Sess. Laws Ch. 260, HB 2268.
[446] 2021 La. Acts No. 388, S.B. 150.
[447] 2021 La. Acts No. 393, S.B. 215.
[448] 2021 Md. Laws Ch. 423, HB 1054; 2021 Md. Laws Ch. 424, SB 720.
[449] 2021 Utah Laws S.B. 154.
[450] 2021 W. Va. Acts Ch. 243, H.B. 2145.
[451] 2021 W. Va. Acts Ch. 241, S.B. 680.
[452] 2021 Colo. Sess. Laws HB 1087.
[453] LA. REV. STAT. § 17:434(A).
[454] 2021 La. Acts No. 392, S.B. 128.
[455] 2021 La. Acts No. 392, S.B. 128.

all employees and students in the public school. Policies must include a clear statement that bullying, harassment, and retaliation for reporting such behavior are prohibited, provide a procedure for reporting incidents, and initiate procedure for promptly investigating and responding to bullying, including written document of reported occurrences.[456] Virginia amended a provision banning bullying and abusive work environments in schools to specify a prohibition against abusive conduct by school board employees in the workplace that a reasonable person would find hostile, and that is severe enough to cause physical or psychological harm to other board employees.[457] Washington informed its state superintendent of education to produce a model policy and procedure for dealing with stress experienced by the K-12 workforce due to secondary trauma.[458]

In five laws, three states addressed teacher/student ratios. Nevada directed the boards of trustees of school districts to develop plans to improve pupil-to-personnel ratios to conform with state BOE standards.[459] Nevada ordered the boards of trustees of school districts to determine the number of job vacancies based on the teacher/student ratio recommended by its state BOE.[460] In a third law, Nevada precluded administrators, counselors, coaches, and other licensed personnel present in the classroom but not teaching every pupil therein from being counted in computing teacher/student ratio for reporting to the state DOE.[461] Texas extended the maximum class size requirement of 22 students for pre-K classes, the same limit as for grades K-4 classes.[462] Virginia obligated school boards to provide at least three specialized student support positions per 1,000 students; the act includes school social workers, school psychologists, school nurses, and other licensed health and behavioral personnel in the list of specialized student support positions.[463]

Three states amended their collective bargaining law for school employees. Maine now requires public employers to give written notice to the bargaining agents of teachers when they change their educational policies.[464] Maryland created a separate bargaining unit

---

[456] 2021 Me. Laws Ch. 471, S.P. 294, L.D. 880.
[457] 2021 Va. Acts Ch. 450, H. 2176 (1st Spec. Sess.).
[458] 2021 Wash. Laws Ch. 129, H.B. 1363.
[459] 2021 Nev. Stat. Ch. 167, SB 151.
[460] 2021 Nev. Stat. Ch. 355, AB 266.
[461] 2021 Nev. Stat. Ch. 355, AB 266.
[462] 2021 Tex. Gen. Laws S.B. No. 2081.
[463] 2021 Va. Acts Ch. 454, S. 1257 (1st Spec. Sess.).
[464] 2021 Me. Laws Ch. 96, H.P. 18, L.D. 52.

for faculty at the state school for deaf students, including after-school program counselors, American sign language specialists, athletic trainers, behavior specialists, clerical aids, dorm counselors, employment specialists, instructional technology resource specialists, librarians, literacy and reading specialists, occupational therapists, orientation and mobility specialists, physical therapists, school counselors, school IEP coordinators, school nurses, school social workers, speech-language pathologists, student support specialists, teacher aides, transition coordinators, work-to-learn specialists, and teachers.[465] West Virginia prohibited the closure of schools due to work stoppages or strikes, specifying that engaging in such behavior is a cause for dismissal; if boards do not dismiss employees, their salaries must be prorated.[466]

Two states added provisions about ethics. Illinois prohibited guidance counselors from intentionally soliciting or accepting gifts from prohibited sources or soliciting or accepting gifts that would violate a federal or state law.[467] New Mexico added a duty to report ethical misconduct, including a means of training school personnel in the requirements, investigating reports, and barring violators from school employment.[468]

Other employment-related legislation enacted last calendar year were as follows. Arizona permitted public school boards that provide or contract for child care services to reduce the fee for employees if what they pay is not grossly disproportionate to the total consideration received from the employees.[469] Arkansas struck a provision about the employment of instructors for the state school for mathematics and science, stipulating that instructors could not carry professional ranks.[470] Arkansas amended procedures for the investigation of ethical violations by educators, mandating that complaint forms must bear the original signatures of complainants.[471] California provided permanent classified school employees with the same rights to notice and hearing with respect to layoffs as afforded certificated school board employees.[472] California ordered all full-time peace officers or public safety

---

[465] 2021 Md. Laws Ch. 804, SB 556.
[466] 2021 W. Va. Acts Ch. 207, S.B. 11.
[467] 2021 Ill. Laws Pub. Act 102-0327, SB 1640.
[468] 2021 N.M. Laws Ch. 94, HB 128.
[469] 2021 Ariz. Sess. Laws Ch. 91, HB 2020.
[470] 2021 Ark. Acts 354, HB 1472.
[471] 2021 Ark. Acts 96, SB 71.
[472] 2021 Cal. Stat. Ch. 665, AB 438.

dispatchers employed by school boards to serve probationary periods of one year before receiving permanent classified service status.[473]

Oregon required school boards to make reductions in force to retain teachers with less seniority if their dismissals would result in a lesser proportion of those with cultural or linguistic expertise.[474] Illinois obligated the superintendent of its school for the deaf to have a degree in educational administration and at least ten years of experience in either deaf or hard-of-hearing education, the administration of deaf or hard-of-hearing education, or a combination of the two; the act places parallel requirements for the superintendent for the school for the visually impaired.[475] Indiana permitted school employees to resign from and end any financial obligations to their employee organizations at any time.[476] Louisiana changed the job title of school guidance counselor to school counselor.[477]

In the first of five laws, Maine created privacy protections for those teaching through remote instruction by prohibiting others from distributing or re-transmitting recorded sessions of these sessions or any part thereof with the express written consent of officials of the public or private school.[478] Maine protected the retirement stipend for school employees who lost compensation due to the cancellation or elimination of their extracurricular or co-curricular positions during the COVID-19 pandemic.[479] Maine permits a member of school boards or their spouses to serve as a "stipend employee" on contractual bases if doing so is in the best interest of students, a summation of potential conflicts of interest is documented, and *a priori* mitigations are described in the signed contract. The act defines a "stipend employee" as one who receives limited monetary payment or benefits, through a series of payments or in a lump sum, for personal services performed in an advisory, mentoring, or coaching capacity for a school administrative unit.[480] Maine directed its state retirement system to study options and make recommendations for a plan to allow teachers to contribute, accumulate credit, and collect benefits under the social security

---

[473] 2021 Cal. Stat. Ch. 666, AB 486, Sec. 37.
[474] 2021 Or. Laws Ch. 445, HB 2001.
[475] 2021 Ill. Laws Pub. Act 102-0196, HB 1710.
[476] 2021 Ind. Acts Pub. Law 98, S.B. 251.
[477] 2021 La. Acts No. 275, H.B. 156.
[478] 2021 Me. Laws Ch. 383, H.P. 632, L.D. 864.
[479] 2021 Me. Laws Ch. 225, H.P. 372, L.D. 509.
[480] 2021 Me. Laws Ch. 242, H.P. 975, L.D. 1323.

program.[481] Maine amended its teacher retirement law to cover educational technicians not needing certificates for employment.[482]

New York altered its tenure law to allow the imposition of a longer probationary period for teachers in specified circumstances during the pandemic.[483] Oklahoma ordered local boards of education to adopt policies to assist employees who are lactating.[484] Oklahoma also required local boards to pay support employees for time lost when schools are closed on account of epidemics or otherwise when order for such closing is issued by health officers authorized by law to do so.[485] Texas directed school boards to post their employment policies on their websites, the full texts of regulations referenced therein, and any forms they reference. If boards do not maintain internet websites, their employment policy information must be available at district administration offices.[486] Moreover, Texas applied the same provisions related to severance payments for traditional public-school administrators to superintendents and administrators of charter schools.[487]

Finance and School Business

Besides the usual topics occurring in finance and school business-related legislation each year, such as budgets, accounting, audits, and reporting, adjustments to school foundation programs figured prominently in legislative activity in the last calendar year. The attention to funding formulae, including how attendance impacts funding, demonstrated that legislative bodies understood and acted admirably to assure that local school boards and charter schools were held harmless financially during the COVID-19 pandemic.[488] However, legislators were of two minds during the pandemic. On the one hand, they wanted to help and protect their schools. On the other hand, once they recognized the political power of using the pandemic to wage the culture war, some legislators may have used legislation to score points with their constituencies. For example, Arizona declared that the use of public resources, including email, equipment, or compensated work time, to organize, plan, or

---

[481] 2021 Me. Laws Ch. 72, H.P. 456, L.D. 620.
[482] 2021 Me. Laws Ch. 6, H.P. 191, L.D. 275.
[483] 2021 N.Y. Laws Ch. 112, S. 5576.
[484] 2021 Okla. Sess. Laws S.B. No. 121.
[485] 2021 Okla. Sess. Laws S.B. No. 807.
[486] 2021 Tex. Gen. Laws H.B. No. 750.
[487] 2021 Tex. Gen. Laws H.B. No. 189.
[488] *See, e.g.*, text accompanying fn. 83 to fn.125, *supra*.

execute activities impeding or preventing public schools from operating for periods would be considered illegal use of public monies unless educators acted in good faith in furtherance of their official duties.[489] Knowing that charges of fiscal mismanagement can end careers, many administrators might have tilted decisions toward face-to-face instruction too early during the pandemic.

This section describes legislation related to finance and school business during 2021 legislative year, beginning with acts on school funding. Alabama revised its school foundation funding program to allow payments for both in-person and virtual instructional delivery and to provide funding increases based on an increase in average daily membership in the current school year.[490] Arizona directed its state superintendent of public instruction to adjust state aid for local boards when their officials request recalculations due to a change in assessed valuation resulting from decisions by county or state boards of equalization or the correction of property tax errors. Prior to this act, the recalculation could only arise by court judgments.[491] Arkansas amended its school finance law to allow boards with declining average daily membership in their schools to receive both declining enrollment funding and special needs isolated funding.[492] Colorado convened an interim committee to study changes to the method for funding public schools to improve student achievement.[493]

Delaware established an additional source of educational funding called the opportunity fund to support the increased needs of low-income and English learner students.[494] To provide a financial cushion during the pandemic, Idaho struck a limitation on the number of support units given to charter schools during the 2020-21 school year.[495] Illinois created a High-Cost Special Education Funding Commission to make recommendations to its Governor and the General Assembly for an alternative funding structure for expensive special education placements.[496] Illinois adjusted its funding formula in recognition of the impact of COVID-19, particularly by using the enrollment figure representing the 2020-

---

[489] 2021 Ariz. Sess. Laws Ch. 404, HB 2898, Sec. 50.
[490] 2021 Ala. Acts No. 2021-166, S.B. 9.
[491] 2021 Ariz. Sess. Laws Ch. 156, SB 1449.
[492] 2021 Ark. Acts 909, SB 629.
[493] 2021 Colo. Sess. Laws HB 1325.
[494] 2021 Del. Ch. 53, SB 56.
[495] 2021 Idaho Sess. Laws Ch. 127, H. 22.
[496] 2021 Ill. Laws Pub. Act 102-0150, SB 517.

21 school year as the greater of the enrollment for 2020-21 or the 2019-20 school year.[497]

Maine passed an act to protect school funding for the 2021-22 school year if the count of enrolled students fell by ten percent or more by using a prior year count of those enrolled in the formula.[498] Maine required its state DOE to report to the state's joint standing committee on education regarding funding methods and reporting protocols for public charter schools.[499] Further, Maine directed its state DOE to analyze funding to address student achievement gaps.[500] Mississippi required its state DOE to hold school boards harmless when calculating average daily attendance for the 2020-21 school year by providing funding equal to that provided for the prior year.[501]

In the first of five changes, Montana increased the multiplier in its school funding formula to increase appropriations while accounting for the expected revenue from the legalization of marijuana with a twenty percent sales tax.[502] Montana obligated its office of public instruction plus its department of public health and human services to collaborate in supporting school boards seeking reimbursement for school-based eligible services under Medicaid and the state children's health insurance program.[503] Montana allowed students in nonpublic or home schools who participated in extracurricular activities for six or more weeks to be counted in the pupil count for funding purposes.[504] Montana added to its school funding formula to adjust for inflation.[505] Finally, Montana informed its legislative finance committee to study funding for K-12 enrollment increases and report to the interim education committee by September 1, 2022.[506]

The first of four changes in New Hampshire repealed the directive that its commission study school funding remains active until the general court addresses its recommendations.[507] New Hampshire established a committee to study the funding of tuition

---

[497] 2021 Ill. Laws Pub. Act 102-0033, SB 813.
[498] 2021 Me. Laws Ch. 428, L.D. 651.
[499] 2021 Me. Laws Ch. 39, H.P. 440, L.D. 604.
[500] 2021 Me. Laws Ch. 35, H.P. 197, L.D. 281.
[501] 2021 Miss. Laws SB 2149.
[502] 2021 Mont. Laws Ch. 560, HB 663.
[503] 2021 Mont. Laws Ch. 562, HB 671.
[504] 2021 Mont. Laws Ch. 269, SB 72.
[505] 2021 Mont. Laws Ch. 23, HB 15.
[506] 2021 Mont. Laws Ch. 562, HB 671.
[507] 2021 N.H. Laws Ch. 64, HB 464.

and transportation for career technical education.[508] New Hampshire deleted a requirement that private schools must be nonsectarian to be approved as participants in its school tuition program.[509] New Hampshire permitted the apportionment formula for cooperative school districts to be subject to review five years after the passage of the article to continue the current formula.[510] New York acted to ensure that schools experienced no loss of financial resources needed to operate for full 180-day academic years during the COVID-19 pandemic.[511] Oklahoma passed the Redbud School Funding Act, which apportioned to school boards the taxes collected for the retail sale of medical marijuana.[512]

South Carolina appropriated $9 million to its state DOE to distribute to its public charter school district to make up for funding shortfalls due to financial uncertainties in connection with the COVID-19 pandemic.[513] South Dakota adjusted tax levies to support the general fund for school boards while revising state aid for general and special education formulas.[514] In the event that students in school districts are admitted to out-of-state residential mental health facilities, Tennessee requires their boards to allocate a prorated daily amount of funds to cover those expenses.[515] Texas allowed a graduate's enrollment in the National Guard as an indicator of "military readiness" to compute an outcomes bonus under the foundation school program.[516] Texas also expanded eligibility for the Jobs and Education for Texans (JET) grant program to open-enrollment charter schools.[517]

Utah directed its state BOE to use the fiscal year 2019 data for the distribution of state appropriations for student transportation for fiscal years 2021 and 2022.[518] Vermont created a task force to implement the 2019 pupil weighting factors report for the purpose of rebuilding the state's school funding model.[519] Wyoming allowed

---

[508] 2021 N.H. Laws Ch. 11, HB 304.
[509] 2021 N.H. Laws Ch. 106, HB 282.
[510] 2021 N.H. Laws Ch. 80, HB 152.
[511] 2021 N.Y. Laws Ch. 130, S. 897.
[512] 2021 Okla. Sess. Laws S.B. No. 229.
[513] 2021 S.C. Act No. 8, H. 3608.
[514] 2021 S.D. Laws SB 49.
[515] 2021 Tenn. Pub. Acts Ch. No. 589, H.B. No. 713, S.B. No. 449.
[516] 2021 Tex. Gen. Laws H.B. No. 1147.
[517] 2021 Tex. Gen. Laws S.B. No. 346.
[518] 2021 Utah Laws H.B. 402.
[519] 2021 Vt. Laws Act 59, S. 13.

local boards to seek reimbursements for school-based health services for students eligible for Medicaid payments.[520]

Three states adopted measures regarding donations. Georgia allowed the nonprofit corporation created by its foundation for public education to receive private donations to be used for grants for public schools.[521] Rhode Island permitted school boards to assess or request voluntary donations from students' parents or guardians to help pay for the cost of school-sponsored field trips, dances, and clubs.[522] Texas obligated school boards to accept donations designated to fund supplemental educational staff positions at school campuses from PTAs or PTOs.[523]

Two states adopted measures adjusting means of measuring average daily attendance or membership, impacting funding. Indiana ordered that pupil enrollment be determined during the spring counts of average daily membership during spring sessions.[524] Kentucky allowed school boards to include nonresident pupils in their average daily attendance, directing them to adopt nonresident policies while forbidding discrimination among nonresident students.[525]

Four states, through nine acts, addressed bonded debt. Illinois authorized Iroquois County Community Unit School District 9 to issue bonds with an aggregate principal amount not to exceed $17.125 million, and Field Community Consolidated School District 3 to issue bonds with an aggregate principal amount not to exceed $2.6 million, subject to voter approval and procedural steps required of the school boards.[526] Nevada enabled governing boards over school districts with prior voter approval to issue general obligation bonds for a second ten-year period for school facilities without another approval of the voters.[527]

Rhode Island empowered the Town of Westerly to issue bonds and notes in an amount not exceeding $2 million to finance the construction, renovation, improvement, alteration, repair, furnishing, and equipping of schools and school facilities in the town.[528] In a second act, Rhode Island permitted the schools in

---

[520] 2021 Wyo. Sess. Laws Enr. Act No. 20, Ch. 60, S.F. 79.
[521] 2021 Ga. Laws Act 157, SB 66.
[522] 2021 R.I. Pub. Laws H. 5079.
[523] 2021 Tex. Gen. Laws H.B. No. 1525.
[524] 2021 Ind. Acts Pub. Law 164 § 3; Sen. Enr. Act No. 414 § 3.
[525] 2021 Ky. Acts Ch. 167, HB 563.
[526] 2021 Ill. Laws Pub. Act 102-0316, SB 1305.
[527] 2021 Nev. Stat. Ch. 493, SB 450.
[528] 2021 R.I. Pub. Laws H. 5181, S. 53.

Central Falls to issue bonds for $5.76 million for the same purposes as above.[529] Further, Rhode Island allowed Providence to issue up to $140 million in bonds to finance the construction, renovation, improvement, alteration, repair, landscaping, furnishing, and equipping of schools and school facilities in the city.[530] Rhode Island next granted the town of South Kingston the authority to issue up to $85 million bonds and notes.[531] Tennessee authorized Deptford Independent School District to issue bonds and notes in an amount not to exceed $2.35 million[532] while permitting the Franklin Special School District to issue bonds or notes in an amount not to exceed $45 million.[533] Finally, Tennessee enabled the Gibson County Special School District to issue bonds in the amount of $5 million or less to provide funds for the district.[534]

Five states adopted laws on budget requirements. Arizona specified the number of years for which common school (K-8) districts may continue to calculate their budgets and equalization assessments while in transition to joining unified districts.[535] Kansas permitted school boards to be late in approving budgets that exceed the revenue rate, with certification occurring by September 20 rather than August 25.[536] For the four fiscal years between 2021 and 2025, Maine permitted local school administrative units to carry over unallocated balances in excess of 9% instead of 5% of the previous fiscal year's school budget.[537] New Jersey enabled local school boards to maintain surpluses of four percent of their budgets for the 2020-21 and 2021-22 school years.[538] Rhode Island allowed school committees to budget funds for field trips when creating their budgets.[539]

Alabama allowed three entities to seek approval from the voters to renew existing taxes, starting with authorizing voters in the Gardendale City tax district in Jefferson County to decide whether an existing ad valorem taxation should be renewed.[540] Alabama

---

[529] 2021 R.I. Pub. Laws S. 951, H. 6408.
[530] 2021 R.I. Pub. Laws H. 5534, S. 224.
[531] 2021 R.I. Pub. Laws H. 5696, S. 374.
[532] 2021 Tenn. Priv. Acts Ch. No. 35, S.B. No. 1652, H.B. No. 1632.
[533] 2021 Tenn. Priv. Acts Ch. No. 6, H.B. No. 701, S.B. No. 573.
[534] 2021 Tenn. Priv. Acts Ch. No. 3, H.B. No. 665, S.B. No. 1393.
[535] 2021 Ariz. Sess. Laws Ch. 11, HB 2259.
[536] 2021 Kan. Sess. Laws HB 2104.
[537] 2021 Me. Laws Ch. 213, H.P. 876, L.D. 1198.
[538] 2021 N.J. Laws c. 35,S. 2691.
[539] 2021 R.I. Pub. Laws S. 936.
[540] 2021 Ala. Acts No. 2021-394, H.B. 546.

allowed voters in the Trussville City tax district in Jefferson County to determine whether an existing ad valorem taxation should be renewed.[541] Alabama enabled voters in the Midfield City tax district in Jefferson County to address whether an existing ad valorem taxation should be renewed.[542]

Georgia provided a homestead exemption from ad valorem taxes for residents of the city school district for Decatur in the amount of $200,000 of the assessed valuation of the homestead.[543] It also granted a homestead exemption from school district ad valorem taxes in Early County for residents who are 70 or older.[544] Then Georgia authorized a homestead exemption for ad valorem taxes in the amount of $15,000 of the assessed value of the homestead for residents of the independent school district in Atlanta.[545]

Four states adopted other tax exemptions and credits. Arkansas provided sales tax exemptions for school fundraisers[546] along with including electronic equipment in the definition of "instructional materials" in the statute allowing sales tax exemptions for schools for expenditures for such equipment.[547] Delaware permitted local school boards to authorize a full credit against taxation for property owned and occupied as a dwelling by a veteran on 100% military-related disability.[548] New York allowed a refund of taxes levied by local boards to municipal public libraries and special district public libraries.[549] Texas provided a property tax exemption for real property leased to a school board, charter school, or community college and used for educational purposes.[550]

Nine states enrolled twelve acts on purchasing, including purchasing through lease-purchase agreements. Alabama included leases and lease-purchase agreements, along with purchases, in a provision excluding the need for competitive bids when accomplished through a cooperative purchase agreement.[551] Arizona raised the limit of the value of a lease-purchase agreement for school boards in

---

[541] 2021 Ala. Acts No. 2021-217, H.B. 515.
[542] 2021 Ala. Acts No. 2021-8, H.B. 522.
[543] 2021 Ga. Laws Act 154, SB 292.
[544] 2021 Ga. Laws Act 283, SB 305.
[545] 2021 Ga. Laws Act 107, HB 732.
[546] 2021 Ark. Acts 873, HB 1023.
[547] 2021 Ark. Acts 914, SB 244.
[548] 2021 Del. Laws Ch. 124, HB 214.
[549] 2021 N.Y. Laws Ch. 503, A. 6489.
[550] 2021 Tex. Gen. Laws H.B. No. 3610.
[551] 2021 Ala. Acts No. 2021-485, HB 187.

a county with a population of 750,000 persons.[552] Arizona added to the list of discretionary powers given to boards, allowing them to provide food and beverages at events, including official school functions and training.[553] California amended provisions on lease-purchase agreements in schools to allow the governing boards of school districts to lease property for a minimum rental of $1 per year if the instruments by which the property is leased require the lessee to construct or provide for the construction of, a building to be used by the board and directs that the title to the building must vest in it at the end of the lease.[554]

Hawai'i called on each of its departments to ensure that a percentage of the products they purchase consists of fresh local agricultural products or local value-added, processed, agricultural, or food products.[555] Idaho allowed funds from the advanced opportunities account to be used for college entrance examinations and preliminary college entrance examinations.[556] Indiana permitted a public school or school corporation to purchase up to $7,500 of food per fiscal year from a youth agricultural program.[557] Kansas ordered its state BOE to provide a list of approved at-risk educational programs to each school board; expenditures for a board's at-risk education program or service can only be made for items on the list.[558]

Tennessee set the limit for purchases without competitive bids at $10,000 for school boards in a county with a population of 40,000 or less and at $25,000 for those in counties with populations of more than 40,000.[559] Tennessee enabled local boards to purchase technology using state school funds for textbooks and instructional materials in the academic year immediately following a textbook adoption cycle in which is textbook and instructional materials quality commission did not list or recommend career and technical education textbooks or instructional materials.[560] Texas obligated local boards to notify vendors of disputed amounts in invoices not later than 21 days after officials receive them, prohibiting officials

---

[552] 2021 Ariz. Sess. Laws Ch. 38, SB 1012.
[553] 2021 Ariz. Sess. Laws Ch. 437, HB 2210.
[554] 2021 Cal. Stat. Ch. 666, AB 486, Sec. 5, 6.
[555] 2021 Haw. Sess. Laws Act 176, HB 817.
[556] 2021 Idaho Sess. Laws Ch. 210, H. 250.
[557] 2021 Ind. Acts Pub. Law 175, HB 1119.
[558] 2021 Kan. Sess. Laws HB 2134, sec. 20.
[559] 2021 Tenn. Pub. Acts Ch. No. 310, H.B. No. 235, S.B. No. 1125.
[560] 2021 Tenn. Pub. Acts Ch. No. 276, S.B. No. 1377, H.B. No. 795.

from withholding more than 110 percent of the disputed invoices.[561] Texas authorized political subdivisions, including schools, to finance the purchase of cloud computing services through the Public Property Finance Act.[562]

Seven states adopted laws on school accounting. Louisiana amended language relevant to its Caddo Educational Excellence Fund to allow for the Caddo Parish School Board to withdraw money from it under specified conditions.[563] Maine directed its state DOE plus its department of health and human services to study a centralized billing process for developmental and school-based services covered by the MaineCare Program and other insurers while reporting on updates to the child find process.[564] North Carolina created rules for cash management in local school boards.[565] North Carolina also changed requirements about fund transfers from local school administrative units to a charter schools to speed them up.[566] Oregon permitted the payment of student fees, costs, and instructors for career and technical education courses from the student investment account.[567]

Utah allowed local education agencies to transfer 35% of state-restricted funds to their general funds to be used without restriction during the COVID-19 emergency.[568] Utah also created a charter school closure-reserve account to pay outstanding debts of charter schools that cease operations.[569] Vermont directed all supervisory unions, school boards, and independent technical centers to utilize the same shared data management system, eFinancePlus, by a deadline extended to December 31, 2022, for statewide adoption.[570] Wyoming revised the dates when county treasurers must make "recapture" payments to school boards to the second Monday of each month and on June 20 or the last business day immediately preceding each June 20. "Recapture" refers to the redistribution of taxes gained by richer school districts given to poorer districts.[571]

---

[561] 2021 Tex. Gen. Laws H.B. No. 1476.
[562] 2021 Tex. Gen. Laws S.B. 58.
[563] 2021 La. Acts No. 295, SB 238.
[564] 2021 Me. Laws Ch. 109, H.P. 91, L.D. 135.
[565] 2021 N.C. Sess. Laws Ch. 170, S. 695.
[566] 2021 N.C. Sess. Laws Ch. 79, H. 335.
[567] 2021 Or. Laws Ch. 227, HB 2537.
[568] 2021 Utah Laws S.B. 178.
[569] 2021 Utah Laws H.B. 425.
[570] 2021 Vt. Laws Act. 66, S. 115.
[571] 2021 Wyo. Sess. Laws Enr. Act No. 5, Ch. 24, S.F. 57.

Six states passed acts about financial audits. Arizona specified that its auditor general must detail in writing the deficiencies of school board accountings system in a general's report to its DOE and state BOE.[572] Hawai'i directed charter school authorizing bodies to provide the schools they oversee with a list of approved independent auditors.[573] Illinois stipulated that charter school officials could not retain outside, independent contractors to audit their finances if the individual is one of its employees or is affiliated with it or its authorizing entity in any way.[574] Indiana mandated that financial audits of school corporations must include examinations of revenue spending plans and funds for operating referenda tax levies or school safety referenda.[575] New Jersey extended the deadline for school boards to submit their annual audit reports for the 2020-21 school year.[576] Oklahoma called on school boards to post their most recent audit for public inspection on their websites.[577]

Seven states added laws about reporting and financial accountability. Arizona obligated its DOE to develop a transparent and easily-accessible school financial transparency portal, including school-level data for charter schools and individual schools operated by local boards.[578] Colorado repealed a provision that its state auditor must report annually on the uses of state education funds for school capital construction to specified committees of the general assembly.[579] Illinois directed trustees of schools in Class II county school units to maintain internet websites with investments reports.[580] Nevada obligated the governing boards of each charter school entering into contracts with educational management organizations to submit to their sponsor reports on the amount paid to those firms on November 1 of each even-numbered year.[581]

Oklahoma deleted special reporting requirements for gifted and talented programs receiving $1 million or more in state aid.[582] In lieu of filing paper reports, West Virginia permitted county boards of

---

[572] 2021 Ariz. Sess. Laws Ch. 7, HB 2018.
[573] 2021 Haw. Sess. Laws Act 166, SB 813.
[574] 2021 Ill. Laws Pub. Act 102-0445, HB 2795.
[575] 2021 Ind. Acts Pub. Law 136, S.B. 55.
[576] 2021 N.J. Laws c. 256, S. 3881.
[577] 2021 Okla. Sess. Laws H.B. No. 1046.
[578] 2021 Ariz. Sess. Laws Ch. 404, HB 2898.
[579] 2021 Colo. Sess. Laws SB 198.
[580] 2021 Ill. Laws Pub. Act 102-0346, HB 1725.
[581] 2021 Nev. Stat. Ch. 214, SB 363.
[582] 2021 Okla. Sess. Laws H.B. No. 1968.

education to publish financial statements on their websites.[583] Wisconsin mandated that detailed information about the receipt and expenditure data collected through its uniform accounting system and other financial data must be made available on its state department of public instruction's website.[584]

Other finance and school business-related acts adopted in 2021 are described as follows. Alabama permitted the Elmore County BOE to insure school buildings and property in the state insurance fund or with an insurance company.[585] Arizona authorized the production of special license plates for education and community enrichment; this act awarded the right to design the plates to a person who pays $32,000 for the privilege, which will be reimbursed from the initial fees paid for the license plates.[586] Arizona amended a provision allowing its state BOE to impose penalties on testing contracts for scores received after dates supplied by statute, directing that, if the state board alters the testing window for assessments, it may adjust the dates by which local education agencies must receive those scores and assessment data, and a penalty may not be imposed unless the information is received after the adjusted dates.[587] Florida enabled its state DOE to hold patents, copyrights, trademarks, and service marks, directing its department of education to notify the department of state when it secures property rights under the new provision.[588]

Georgia permitted local school boards and charter schools to make agreements for sharing federal funds.[589] Hawai'i excluded housing developed by the department of home lands from school impact fees for three years.[590] Indiana prohibited contracts between charter school organizers from entering into nepotistic contracts under which officers or employees of the organizers or their relatives receive compensation or proceeds.[591] Indiana also required its state DOE to request information to explore potential opportunities to improve the efficiency of non-instructional school services.[592]

---

[583] 2021 W. Va. Acts Ch. 97, S.B. 651.
[584] 2021 Wis. Laws Act 89, S.B. 373.
[585] 2021 Ala. Acts No. 2021-149, S.B. 271.
[586] 2021 Ariz. Sess. Laws Ch. 253, HB 2031.
[587] 2021 Ariz. Sess. Laws Ch. 19, HB 2402.
[588] 2021 Fla. Laws ch. 157, S. 1108.
[589] 2021 Ga. Laws Act 158, SB 59.
[590] 2021 Haw. Sess. Laws Act 197, HB 753.
[591] 2021 Ind. Acts Pub. Law 216; H.B. No. 1549.
[592] 2021 Ind. Acts Pub. Law 186, H.B. 1266.

Maryland forbade local school systems from charging fees for enrollment in summer school programs if students attend classes if credit for it is required for graduation and if the pupils previously took them but did not complete or receive credit for doing so.[593] Montana directed school boards of residence to contribute a portion of the tuition costs for pupils placed in group homes or foster care and for part of the educational costs of eligible children in in-state residential facilities.[594] Montana clarified that boards may waive tuition for students, regardless of whether they are residents of elementary districts unified with county high schools.[595]

Governance and School Leadership

This section describes governance and school leadership-related legislation enacted in 2021, beginning with acts related to state-level entities, including state BOEs, DOEs, plus state-level commissions and committees. Alabama redrew the representational districts for members of its state BOE.[596] Hawai'i directed that members of its charter school commission must collectively represent experience and expertise in a variety of fields.[597] Idaho established a school safety and security program in the office of its state BOE.[598] Illinois added state policy advocates, early childhood administrators, and other stakeholders to committee members appointed by the state superintendent to a committee on kindergarten readiness standards.[599] In its sick leave bank act for educators, Illinois declared that its state BOE is not an agency under the act.[600] Indiana established the Cambridge international program under the administration of its state DOE.[601]

Kentucky legislated that membership on the state BOE shall reflect the equal representation of the two sexes, as far as possible, reflect no less than proportional representation of the two leading political parties of the Commonwealth based on voter registration, and reflect the minority racial population using census data.[602]

---

[593] 2021 Md. Laws Ch. 218, HB 394.
[594] 2021 Mont. Laws Ch. 371, HB 206.
[595] 2021 Mont. Laws Ch. 238, HB 454.
[596] 2021 Ala. Acts No. 2021-559, SB 2.
[597] 2021 Haw. Sess. Laws Act 167, SB 814.
[598] 2021 Idaho Sess. Laws Ch. 98, H. 173.
[599] 2021 Ill. Laws Pub. Act 102-635, SB 2088.
[600] 2021 Ill. Laws Pub. Act 102-0539, SB 2043.
[601] 2021 Ind. Acts Pub. Law 216; H.B. No. 1549.
[602] 2021 Ky. Acts Ch. 178, HB 178.

Kentucky created a DOE advisory committee to advise its department on assessment and accountability in place of existing structures.[603] Louisiana amended a provision on the advisory council on historically Black colleges and universities, adding a student member and directing it to submit annual reports to the legislative committees on education.[604] Nebraska set new boundaries for state BOE districts.[605]

Nevada changed the districts from which members of the state BOE are elected.[606] Nevada also changed the name of its Office of the Western Regional Education Compact to the Nevada Office of the Western Interstate Commission for Higher Education, updating the signatories to it with the changing name of the administrator.[607] Nevada removed the office of the Western Regional Education Compact from the governor's office, moving it to the office of the Nevada State Commission.[608] New Jersey established a commission on Asian American heritage in its state DOE[609] along with creating the office of school bus safety in its state DOE.[610]

Texas required that at least two members of its state board for educator certification must serve in a school district classified as a small or mid-sized in its allotment system.[611] Texas established an industry-based certification advisory council to advise the workforce commission on alignment of public high school career and technology education programs with current and future workforce needs in communities, regions, and the state.[612] Utah established new district boundaries for its state BOE, adopting election dates for board members to have staggered terms.[613] Virginia created a STEM advisory board to develop a unified vision on STEM educational goals and standards.[614] Virginia decreed that its nine-member state BOE include at least five members appointed by the governor and who reside in different superintendents' regions in the commonwealth.[615]

---

[603] 2021 Ky. Acts Ch. 79, SB 129.
[604] 2021 La. Acts No. 417, H.B. 119.
[605] 2021 Neb. Laws LB 7 (1st Spec. Sess.).
[606] 2021 Nev. Stat. Ch. 1, SB 1 (1st Spec. Sess.).
[607] 2021 Nev. Stat. Ch. 407, AB 247.
[608] 2021 Nev. Stat. Ch. 422, SB 446.
[609] 2021 N.J. Laws c. 410, S. 3764.
[610] 2021 N.J. Laws c. 471, A. 5814.
[611] 2021 Tex. Gen. Laws S.B. No. 2519.
[612] 2021 Tex. Gen. Laws H.B. 3938.
[613] 2021 Utah Laws S.B. 2005 (2nd Spec. Sess.).
[614] 2021 Va. Acts Ch. 291, H. 2058 (1st Spec. Sess.).
[615] 2021 Va. Acts Ch. 21, H. 1827 (1st Spec. Sess.).

Twelve states passed fifteen acts changing in the authority or duties given to a state agency. Arizona changed the number and representation on its school facilities board, initiating changes in capital and maintenance audits.[616] Arkansas transferred the duties of its state and public school life and health insurance board to its state board of finance.[617] Arkansas clarified the authority of its career education and workforce development board, noting that it would be given to the division of career and technical education in its state BOE.[618] Delaware transferred responsibility for early intervention services for children to age three, from its department of health and social services to its DOE.[619] Next, Delaware transferred responsibility for the Parents Right to Know Act from its department of services for children, youth, and their families, to its state DOE; the act creates a duty to provide information about child care facilities in the state.[620]

Florida deleted the office of early learning in its office of independent education and parental choice, instead establishing the division of early learning within the DOE.[621] Hawai'i relocated its farm-to-school program, from its department of agriculture to its DOE, establishing a programmatic goal for it that at least 30% of food served in public schools shall consist of locally-sourced products.[622] Hawai'i moved budgetary control for the conference center revolving fund at the University of Hawai'i at Hilo, from the dean of the college of continuing education and community service, to the chancellor of the university or the chancellor's designee.[623] Indiana replaced references to its state superintendent of public instruction, now referring to its secretary of education, a position apparently no longer held by an elected state official.[624] Louisiana amended the governance and funding of its special schools, the schools for the deaf and visually impaired, removing them from the DOE's control and establishing a special school district governed by a board of directors.[625]

---

[616] 2021 Ariz. Sess. Laws Ch. 404, HB 2898, Sec. 60.
[617] 2021 Ark. Acts 1004, SB 693.
[618] 2021 Ark. Acts 545, SB 235.
[619] 2021 Del. Laws Ch. 213, SB 136.
[620] 2021 Del. Laws Ch. 194, HB 196.
[621] 2021 Fla. Laws ch. 10, H. 419.
[622] 2021 Haw. Sess. Laws Act 175, HB 767.
[623] 2021 Haw. Sess. Laws Act 171, SB 1222.
[624] 2021 Ind. Acts Pub. Law 43, H.B. 1564.
[625] 2021 La. Acts No. 468, HB 253.

Maine directed its state DOE to establish a process to transition the delivery of early childhood special education services for children ages four to six from the regional child development services system to school administrative units.[626] Maryland moved responsibility for educational programs for juveniles in residential facilities from its state DOE to its department of juvenile services.[627] Oregon granted authority to its state DOE to disburse or expend money to it consistent with the purpose of the allocation when the funding statute fails to direct explicitly where the monies should go.[628] Tennessee extended the life of its state textbook and instructional materials quality commission to June 30, 2023.[629] Texas transferred functions of its state BOE and school land board to oversee the permanent school fund to a newly-created government corporation called the Texas Permanent School Fund Corporation.[630]

Ten states enacted seventeen local school board governance laws, including boundaries, the number of members, trustee districts, term lengths, and whether individuals are elected or appointed. California permitted county committees, by resolution, to establish trustee areas and elect governing board members using district-based elections without submitting the resolution to the electors for approval.[631] Delaware decreased the term of board members elected after December 31, 2021, from five to four years.[632]

Georgia continued the existence of the city school district in Gainesville, provided for the powers of the continued board, and set the number of members at five, with each representing an election ward.[633] Georgia changed the number of members for the school board in Carroll County from three to five.[634] Georgia clarified that the boundaries of the Atlanta school system would not become extended by annexation into the boundaries of the school district in DeKalb County, except by local act of the general assembly.[635] Georgia added provisions designating the districts for the election of members of the County BOE for DeKalb County while adopting

---

[626] 2021 Me. Laws Ch. 106, H.P. 270, L.D. 386.
[627] 2021 Md. Laws Ch. 147, SB 497.
[628] 2021 Or. Laws Ch. 511, HB 2057.
[629] 2021 Tenn. Pub. Acts Ch. No. 159, S.B. No. 76, H.B. No. 297.
[630] 2021 Tex. Gen. Laws S.B. No. 1232.
[631] 2021 Cal. Stat. Ch. 139, SB 442.
[632] 2021 Del. Laws Ch. 251, HB 92.
[633] 2021 Ga. Laws Act 87, HB 742.
[634] 2021 Ga. Laws Act 58, HB 456.
[635] 2021 Ga. Laws Act 281, SB 209.

agreements for student attendance and school finance for the county board and the school system in the city of Decatur.[636]

Illinois abolished the terms of all members of the Chicago BOE effective January 15, 2025, putting new rules in place permitting it to have both elected and appointed members.[637] Maryland altered the boundaries of the residence districts for the Montgomery County BOE[638] while increasing the number of terms a voting member of the board in Cecil County may serve to three.[639] Further, Maryland altered the procedures for school redistricting plans where the one proposed by the board of Howard County was different from what the superintendent suggested, such that the board must now allow a specified number of the members of a household whose school assignment is changed only in its plan to offer public testimony before the final vote on redistricting.[640] Massachusetts amended the charter of the city of Amesbury to authorize changes in the position of school committee chair.[641] New Jersey required school district BOEs and charter school boards of trustees serving -12 to appoint student representatives to their boards.[642]

North Carolina changed the school board from appointed to elected membership in Asheville City while increasing the number of members from five to seven.[643] South Carolina consolidated Bamberg-Ehrhardt School District 1 with Denmark-Olar School District 2, creating the Bamberg County Consolidated School District;[644] it also consolidated Clarendon County School District No. 2 and Clarendon County School District No. 4 into one district to be known as Clarendon County School District.[645] At the same time, South Carolina suspended the duty of the school board in Orangeburg County to adopt attendance zones if it determines that a school building or structure is an imminent threat to the health or safety of students or staff, if the needed upgrades and repairs to maintain a school building or structure are economically unfeasible, or if a school building or structure is underutilized and the use of

---

[636] 2021 Ga. Laws Act 282, SB 293.
[637] 2021 Ill. Laws Pub. Act 102-0177, HB 2908.
[638] 2021 Md. Laws Ch. 3, HB 3, SB 3.
[639] 2021 Md. Laws Ch. 571, HB 692; 2021 Md. Laws Ch. 572, SB 823.
[640] 2021 Md. Laws Ch. 187, HB 1142.
[641] 2021 Mass. Acts Ch. 46, S. 2450.
[642] 2021 N.J. Laws c. 446, A. 3392.
[643] 2021 N.C. Sess. Laws Ch. 187, H. 400.
[644] 2021 S.C. Act No. 104, S. 771.
[645] 2021 S.C. Act No. 106, S. 648.

another school building or structure is feasible.[646] Virginia enabled school board members in Loudoun County to serve staggered terms.[647]

Nine states adopted acts about school board elections. Illinois changed the election date for members of the Chicago BOE, beginning with the 2024 general election rather than beginning on November 5, 2024.[648] Maryland modified the manner of election for members of the school board in Charles County with members now elected from county commissioner districts.[649] New Hampshire directed that any vacancies occurring on school district governing boards between the beginning of the filing period and the election shall not be filled by official ballot until the following year.[650] New York allowed voters in school district elections to apply for absentee ballot during the pandemics.[651] North Carolina changed the method of election for members of the board in Craven County to partisan electoral districts,[652] in Lincoln County from nonpartisan to partisan,[653] in Burke County and Caldwell County from nonpartisan to partisan, adding that the elections for the board in Burke County will occur in even-numbered years.[654]

South Carolina changed election procedures for the BOE of Georgetown County to conform to a 2008 consent decree while setting the number of board members to nine.[655] Tennessee permitted elections for school board members to be conducted on partisan bases.[656] Texas required boards to post the results of each board election or votes for or against proposed measures on their websites.[657] Virginia amended its school board member election law, specifying that in localities imposes district-based or ward-based residency requirements for members, those elected from each district or ward must be elected by the qualified voters of the district or ward and not by the district at large.[658]

---

[646] 2021 S.C. Act No. 112, S. 515.
[647] 2021 Va. Acts Ch. 166, H. 1838 (1st Spec. Sess.).
[648] 2021 Ill. Laws Pub. Act 102-0691, SB 1784.
[649] 2021 Md. Laws Ch. 404, HB 1060; 2021 Md. Laws Ch. 405, SB 749.
[650] 2021 N.H. Laws Ch. 42, HB 409.
[651] 2021 N.Y. Laws Ch. 60, S. 5545.
[652] 2021 N.C. Sess. Laws Ch. 140, H. 3.
[653] 2021 N.C. Sess. Laws Ch. 99, HB 244.
[654] 2021 N.C. Sess. Laws Ch. 51, S. 288.
[655] 2021 S.C. Act No. 107, H. 4241.
[656] 2021 Tenn. Pub. Ch. No. 1, S.B. No. 9009, H.B No. 9072.
[657] 2021 Tex. Gen. Laws S.B. No. 1116.
[658] 2021 Va. Acts Ch. 225, H. 2198 (1st Spec. Sess.).

Nine stated adopted laws setting school board member compensation. Colorado noted that board members may set their compensation by written resolution within statutory limits, but it may not be increased during a term in which a member has been elected or appointed.[659] In the first of six acts Georgia changed the compensation for members of the board in Bacon County to $200 per month, $50 for attendance at each board meeting, and $50 for each day that the member is outside the county on official board business; compensation for the chair of the board was set at $250 per month, $75 for attendance at each board meeting, and $75 for each day that the board member is outside the county on official board business.[660] Georgia permitted the board in Clayton County to set its own compensation and expenses, by providing notice in a required manner and delaying the change in compensation until January 1 of the year following the next general election[661] while modifying the compensation for board members in Terrell County to $300 per meeting and $350 per meeting for the chair.[662] Georgia changed the compensation for members of the board in Hall County to $1,000 per month,[663] for board members in Baldwin County to $500 per month plus reimbursement of actual expenses,[664] and for board members of Clay County to $300 per month plus reimbursement of actual expenses.[665]

Maryland increased the annual compensation for members of the school board in St. Mary's County to $10,000 and to $11,000 for the chair.[666] Virginia removed the board from Brunswick County, an elected body, from a list of approved member salaries for appointed boards.[667]

Three states adopted four laws on filling vacant local school board positions. Arkansas amended the number of days by which a board may appoint an individual to fill a vacancy to 30 for one classification and 60 for another classification of school board.[668] For school districts with ten percent or greater minority populations, Arkansas increased the time frame, from 90 to 120 days for boards

---

[659] 2021 Colo. Sess. Laws HB 1055.
[660] 2021 Ga. Laws Act 98, HB 376.
[661] 2021 Ga. Laws Act 43, HB 251.
[662] 2021 Ga. Laws Act 97, HB 196.
[663] 2021 Ga. Laws Act 128, SB 297.
[664] 2021 Ga. Laws Act 99, HB 103.
[665] 2021 Ga. Laws Act 100, HB 595.
[666] 2021 Md. Laws Ch. 650, HB 1097.
[667] 2021 Va. Acts Ch. 20, H. 1798; Ch. 81, S. 1175 (1st Spec. Sess.).
[668] 2021 Ark. Acts 261, HB 1193.

to pass resolutions to elect new members.[669] North Carolina permitted the board in Cleveland County to fill a vacancy on a partisan level in consultation with the county executive committee and based on the latter's recommendation.[670] Oklahoma empowered its governor to appoint a sufficient number of board members to have a quorum in situations where a BOE or a board of a technology center school district have vacancies resulting in the loss of a majority.[671]

Two states adopted laws on the removal of a school board member. Kentucky removed a provision allowing its chief commonwealth school officer to recommend to its state BOE the suspension or removal of a local school board member.[672] South Carolina rewrote the causes for removal as a member of a charter school board of directors, specifying the reasons as both causes or types of incapacity.[673]

Four states set more requirements for local school board training. Arkansas mandated extra training on school safety and student discipline for board members.[674] Nevada required sponsors of charter schools to provide training on governance for members of their governing boards with similar expectations for members of the state public charter school authority.[675] Texas directed board trustees to complete training on school safety, using curricula and materials developed by its state BOE in coordination with its school safety center.[676] Washington declared that the school directors' association will provide directors training, using an equity, diversity, inclusion, anti-racism, and cultural competency training program while instructing them to dismantle institutional racism by examining district policies with an equity lens;[677] directors are school board members in Washington.

"Sunshine" laws encompass open meetings and open records laws for school boards. Sixteen states added open meeting laws as follows. California extended a temporary provision allowing for school board meetings by teleconference during the pandemic,

---

[669] 2021 Ark. Acts 511, HB 1540.
[670] 2021 N.C. Sess. Laws Ch. 28, H. 85.
[671] 2021 Okla. Sess. Laws H.B. No. 1963.
[672] 2021 Ky. Acts Ch. 144, HB 331.
[673] 2021 S.C. Act No. 32, S. 607.
[674] 2021 Ark. Acts 182, HB 1102.
[675] 2021 Nev. Stat. Ch. 374, AB 419.
[676] 2021 Tex. Gen. Laws H.B. No. 690.
[677] 2021 Wash. Laws Ch. 197, S.B. 5044.

permitting such arrangements during other emergencies.[678] California also amended a provision on public meetings by local agencies, calling for internet access to their agendas.[679] Colorado clarified its open meetings law by pointing out that emails that not relating to the substance of public business need not be disclosed.[680] Connecticut inserted a limitation on the authority of school boards to conduct public hearings such that hearings may only relate to the delivery of education under their auspices.[681]

Hawai'i amended its open meeting law to allow public boards to gather by interactive conference technology for remotely-conducted meetings.[682] Idaho mandated that school board hearings for student discipline must be conducted in executive session.[683] Illinois changed its open meetings act to require public bodies to meet periodically, every six months or as soon after that as is practicable, to review minutes of all closed meetings.[684] Indiana permitted school employers to allow governing body members or the public to participate in public hearings via electronic communications.[685] Minnesota amended its open meetings law call for the recording of votes in board meetings, not only in journals, while changing references to permission to meet via interactive technology rather than electronic means and enabling board members to attend from a private location more than three times in the calendar year 2021.[686] Nebraska amended its open meetings act to allow virtual conferencing in conducting school board meetings.[687] Nevada made hearings or proceedings related to disciplinary exclusions for students who commit battery, distribute controlled substances, or possess a firearm or dangerous weapons on school premises not subject to provisions of the open meeting law.[688]

New Hampshire prohibited its superior court from allowing special school meetings for a collective bargaining agreement that was voted down at a regular session.[689] New York amended its open

---

[678] 2021 Cal. Stat. Ch. 669, AB 824.
[679] 2021 Cal. Stat. Ch.763, SB 274.
[680] 2021 Colo. Sess. Laws HB 1025.
[681] 2021 Conn. Acts 21-95 (Reg. Sess.), SB 6621.
[682] 2021 Haw. Sess. Laws Act 220, SB 1034.
[683] 2021 Idaho Sess. Laws Ch. 290, S. 1043.
[684] 2021 Ill. Laws Pub. Act 102-0653, SB 2356.
[685] 2021 Ind. Acts Pub. Law 216 § 23; H. B. No. 1549.
[686] 2021 Minn. Laws Ch. 14, H.F. no. 820.
[687] 2021 Neb. Laws LB 83.
[688] 2021 Nev. Stat. Ch. 384, AB 67.
[689] 2021 N.H. Laws Ch. 77, HB 71.

meeting law to require minutes taken at a public meeting to be posted one week after executive sessions and two weeks after open meetings.[690] Rhode Island authorized the board of trustees members to attend open public board meetings remotely.[691] South Dakota enabled official meetings to be conducted by teleconferences, adding provisions to assure that voice votes are recorded; the act also provided that members are deemed present if they answer present to roll calls conducted by teleconferences to determine quora; each vote at official meetings conducted by teleconference may be taken by voice, and if any member votes in the negative, it shall proceed to a roll call vote.[692] Utah modified provisions on convening electronic public meetings by directing public bodies to provide facilities at anchor locations for the public to attend.[693] Utah prohibited votes in closed meetings, except to end the closed portions of the sessions.[694]

Four states added more open records laws. California re-codified and reorganized its public records act with the intent of making no substantive changes in its content.[695] Companion legislation provided conforming and technical changes to assure that state and local agencies continue to make their records available for public inspection.[696] Kansas added exceptions to the disclosure of public records under its act by creating exemptions for cyber security assessments, plans, and vulnerabilities.[697] Tennessee made records of minor students created by a school resource officer or other law enforcement officer confidential and not subject to disclosure under public records requests.[698] Texas entered a memorandum of understanding between school boards and its school safety center, making safety issues confidential and not subject to disclosure under its open records law.[699]

Two states-initiated changes regarding organizational meetings for school boards. California modified the time frame for the annual organizational meetings after the elections of governing board members, now to convene within fifteen days beginning with the

---

[690] 2021 N.Y. Laws Ch. 587, A. 1108.
[691] 2021 R.I. Pub. Laws H. 5887, S. 715.
[692] 2021 S.D. Laws HB 1127.
[693] 2021 Utah Laws S.B. 125.
[694] 2021 Utah Laws S.B. 72.
[695] 2021 Cal. Stat. Ch. 614, AB 473.
[696] 2021 Cal. Stat. Ch. 615, AB 474.
[697] 2021 Kan. Sess. Laws HB 2390.
[698] 2021 Tenn. Pub. Acts Ch. No. 391, H.B. No. 368, S.B. No. 1598.
[699] 2021 Tex. Gen. Laws H.B. No. 3597.

second Friday in December after the elections.[700] New York allowed the Great Neck school district to move the date of its annual meeting and election for 2021 to avoid a conflict with religious observances.[701]

Two states adopted legislation, one permitting an assessment of civil liability against school boards, the other bestowing immunity for a wide variety of entities and persons involved in public education. New Hampshire re-enacted a provision allowing actions against boards or chartered public schools for gross negligence or willful misconduct.[702] North Dakota provided immunity for the state superintendent of public instruction, boards, and individual board members, governing boards, and individual governing board members, administrators, principals, teachers, and other board employees for civil liability for damage, loss, or injury resulting from individuals' contracting, being exposed to, or potentially being exposed to COVID-19 while in public schools or in vehicles they own or lease; this immunity is pierced by individuals' gross negligence or willful misconduct.[703]

Three states enacted legislation on entities below the level of school boards. Illinois amended its school code relating to Chicago to provide that if the number of members serving on local school councils falls below seven, then four serving members constitute a quorum.[704] Illinois directed, effective the amending act's passage date, local school council elections to occur in each Chicago Attendance Center that serves seventh and eighth graders.[705] Illinois also amended the membership requirements of local councils for secondary attendance centers in Chicago, now calling for three, rather than one, student member.[706] Montana changed representation on county transportation boards to allow one member from each school district within a county, except that various school districts are limited to one representative.[707] Oregon obligates local boards to establish educational equity advisory committees, to advise them and administrators about the educational equity impacts of policy decisions.[708]

---

[700] 2021 Cal. Stat. Ch. 666, AB 486, Sec. 24.
[701] 2021 N.Y. Laws Ch. 99, S. 5669.
[702] 2021 N.H. Laws Ch. 164, HB 140.
[703] 2021 N.D. Laws S.B. No. 2278.
[704] 2021 Ill. Laws Pub. Act. 102-0296, SB 652.
[705] 2021 Ill. Laws Pub. Act 102-0677, SB 101.
[706] 2021 Ill. Laws Pub. Act 102-0194, HB 1158.
[707] 2021 Mont. Laws Ch. 53, SB 74.
[708] 2021 Or. Laws Ch. 493, SB 732.

Other governance and school leadership-related legislation passed in the prior legislative year is detailed as follows. Alabama submitted a constitutional amendment to the voters which would permit the school superintendent in Cullman County to be elected.[709] Arkansas allowed its commissioner of elementary and secondary education to appoint a designee to appear on his or her behalf at a meeting of a board or commission of which the commissioner is a member in an official capacity.[710] Georgia enabled the teacher of the year to be invited to serve as an advisor ex officio to the state BOE.[711] Delaware increased the qualifications for local and state school board members by disqualifying persons who were convicted of various crimes against children and those involving drug abuse; the act also mandates reporting to entire board when a member is charged with one of the crimes identified under its provisions.[712]

Maine added to regulatory duties for private schools enrolling sixty percent or more publicly-funded students to align their curricula with learning standards while meeting health and safety standards applicable to public schools. The act also required officials in schools enrolling eight-five percent of publicly-funded students to enroll all students, including those with disabilities, who must be served in accordance with applicable state and federal law.[713] Maine substituted the word "policies" for the word "rules" in a provision directing boards to adopt rules.[714] Maine ordered local boards to communicate regularly with employees in their administrative units and members of the public who reside within their boundaries.[715]

New Jersey supported the move toward what it called school district "regionalization," suggesting the desire to reverse the regional consolidation of districts by establishing a grant program to conduct feasibility studies and providing financial incentives for "regionalization."[716] New York provided payment of expenses incurred by monitors of the East Ramapo Central School District.[717] New York also allowed the creation of an insurance reserve fund in

---

[709] 2021 Ala. Acts No. 2021-343, HB 622.
[710] 2021 Ark. Acts 321, SB 63.
[711] 2021 Ga. Laws Act 159, SB 88.
[712] 2021 Del. Laws Ch. 187, Senate Substitute 2 for SB 78.
[713] 2021 Me. Laws Ch. 386, H.P. 1243, L.D. 1672.
[714] 2021 Me. Laws Ch. 157, H.P. 779, L.D. 1050.
[715] 2021 Me. Laws Ch. 281, S.P. 185, L.D. 816.
[716] 2021 N.J. Laws c. 402, S. 3488.
[717] 2021 N.Y. Laws Ch. 173, S. 6052.

the Maine-Endwell,[718] Owego Apalachin,[719] Carmel,[720] Depew,[721] and in Liverpool school districts.[722] Oklahoma elected to stop publication and distribution of its biennial school laws book under the direction of the state superintendent of public education.[723] Rhode Island prohibited the use of school board listservs to distribute political advertisements, invitations, and/or propaganda.[724]

Utah removed provisions related to English being the sole language of state government, as well as requirements that official government documents, transactions, proceedings, meetings, or publications must be in English.[725] Utah directed its state BOE to inform its office of the legislative fiscal analyst when a bill impacts reporting for local education agencies.[726] Utah informed its state BOE to work with local education agencies to develop a process to review reports mandated by statute and state board rule.[727] Utah obligated its state BOE to adopt a policy to evaluate the impact that a report required in a proposed rule may have on reporting standards for local schools.[728] Vermont called on its state BOE and state education agency to identify and document federal and state statutory mandates while adopting an agreement on the roles and duties of the two entities to carry out their responsibilities in a professional and timely manner.[729]

Parental and Student Rights

This section describes rights and privileges accruing to students and their parents arising from state legislative acts. Those rights can be based on constitutional rights, such as First Amendment speech or religion, a privacy interest vested in parents' right to direct their children's upbringing, or the right to be free from discrimination under federal and state civil rights law. The rights

---

[718] 2021 N.Y. Laws Ch. 354, S. 5381.
[719] 2021 N.Y. Laws Ch. 353, S. 5380.
[720] 2021 N.Y. Laws Ch. 290, S. 4481.
[721] 2021 N.Y. Laws Ch. 212, S. 2675.
[722] 2021 N.Y. Laws Ch. 215, S. 4431.
[723] 2021 Okla. Sess. Laws H.B. No. 1018.
[724] 2021 R.I. Pub. Laws S. 89, H. 5830.
[725] 2021 Utah Laws S.B. 214.
[726] 2021 Utah Laws H.B. 134.
[727] 2021 Utah Laws H.B. 300.
[728] 2021 Utah Laws H.B. 42.
[729] 2021 Vt. Laws Act 66, S. 115.

discussed in this section can include protecting students by providing for needs that must be fulfilled for them to thrive, controlling others who can take advantage of them financially or otherwise, or protecting them from disciplinary overreach in their schools. This last example is exemplified by a 2021 act in Oregon,[730] which prohibited suspensions and expulsions of very young students; as an act with a disciplinary component, it is recorded primarily in the School Safety section of this chapter. However, the act also addresses racial justice in discipline, positive social-emotional development, and trauma-informed service to the child.

Sixteen states enacted twenty bills to secure the right for schoolchildren to be free of hunger in a climate of food security. Arkansas enabled public schools or open-enrollment public charter schools to distribute excess food to students to consume on their campuses or at home.[731] Arkansas enabled students in grades 7-12 to have in-school access to vending machines offering food and beverages meeting the nutrition standards of the federal Smart Snacks in School program.[732] Next, in its Healthy Active Schools Act, Arkansas called on its division of elementary and secondary education to consult with its department of health in creating the opportunity for students to walk more between classes, to provide more school gardens, to raise nutritional standards, and to promote the use of local farm or food products in school lunches.[733] California allowed its state superintendent to seek injunctive relief against boards not in compliance with standards for delivering meals for needy students.[734]

Illinois directed local boards to create food-sharing plans for unused food with a focus on needy students.[735] Louisiana amended how student information is recorded so it can be used to administer federal food assistance as well as contribute to the financial profile of those seeking student loans.[736] Maine encouraged the use of local foods in school food service programs by more than doubling the reimbursement for local food purchased in the program and expanding to include dairy products, protein, and local foods from a food processor or food service distributor, and not just produce.[737]

---

[730] 2021 Or. Laws Ch. 518, H.B. 2166.
[731] 2021 Ark. Acts 141, HB 1009.
[732] 2021 Ark. Acts 1070, HB 1783.
[733] 2021 Ark. Acts 1074, HB 1848.
[734] 2021 Cal. Stat. Ch. 666, AB 486, Sec. 45.
[735] 2021 Ill. Laws Pub. Act 102-0359, SB 805.
[736] 2021 La. Acts No. 366, H.B. 322.
[737] 2021 Me. Laws Ch. 426, S.P. 2500, L.D. 636.

Maine obligated its state DOE to make its free school lunch application form available on its website in an understandable and uniform format and, to the maximum extent practicable, in a language parents and legal guardians can understand.[738] Maine ordered its state DOE to report to its joint standing committee on education on using alternative data bases and family income measures to determine eligibility of students for the public school nutrition programs.[739] Minnesota decreed that students receiving school lunch aid must receive respectful treatment.[740]

Nebraska directed its state DOE to develop a farm-to-school program so that its elementary and secondary public and nonpublic schools receive fresh and minimally-processed food for inclusion in school meals and snacks.[741] New Jersey provided supplemental funds for "breakfast after the bell" meals[742] and summer food service programs.[743] To reduce school food waste and address child hunger, New Hampshire permitted schools to partner with a nonprofit entity to freeze leftover food that was never served and send it home with children who participate in a free or reduced price meals program.[744] New York prohibited schools or boards from suing students' parents or guardians for unpaid school meals.[745]

Oregon supplemented the federal school lunch and breakfast programs with state funds to make the meals free for students coming from households with incomes not exceeding 300 percent of the federal poverty guidelines.[746] Texas allowed packaged, unserved food packaged on the campuses of school boards or charter schools that have not been removed from the cafeteria to be donated to nonprofit organizations.[747] Utah moved back the time by which high-poverty schools are required to serve breakfast to students after the instructional day begins.[748] Virginia forbade boards from initiating legal actions against students or their parents if they cannot pay for meals at school or owes money for the meals.[749] Washington

---

[738] 2021 Me. Laws Ch. 212, H.PP. 707, L.D. 961.
[739] 2021 Me. Laws Ch. 37, H.P. 260, L.D. 362.
[740] 2021 Minn. Laws Ch. 13, H.F. no. 2 (1st Spec. Sess.).
[741] 2021 Neb. Laws LB 396.
[742] 2021 N.J. Laws c. 247, A. 5883.
[743] 2021 N.J. Laws c. 246, A. 5882.
[744] 2021 N.H. Laws Ch. 45, HB 500.
[745] 2021 N.Y. Laws Ch. 315, S. 5151.
[746] 2021 Or. Laws Ch. 119, HB 2536.
[747] 2021 Tex. Gen. Laws S.B. No. 1351.
[748] 2021 Utah Laws H.B. 372.
[749] 2021 Va. Acts Ch. 106, H. 2013 (1st Spec. Sess.).

eliminated lunch co-payments for students who qualify for reduced-price school lunches.[750] Wyoming provided grants for boards to increase the use of state meat products in school nutrition programs.[751]

Ten states mandated the availability of menstrual hygiene products for students who need them, free of charge.[752] Arkansas permitted public schools and open-enrollment public charter schools to use the funding to provide feminine hygiene products at no charge.[753] California adopted the Menstrual Equity for All Act of 2021, requiring public schools serving grades 6 to 12 to stock free menstrual products in all women's restrooms, in all "all-gender" restrooms, and at least one men's restroom, rather than in 50% of all restrooms.[754] Delaware directed all public and charter schools with students in grades 6-12 to provide free feminine hygiene products in 50% of the bathrooms used by students who can have menstrual cycles.[755] Illinois amended a provision ordering boards to make menstrual, rather than feminine, hygiene products available at no cost in every school building;[756] A similar Illinois bill replaced references to feminine products with menstrual products.[757]

Maryland obligated county boards to ensure that their public schools provide menstrual hygiene products via dispensers in restrooms for women at no charge to students.[758] Nevada called on public and charter middle, junior, and high schools to provide menstrual products at no cost to pupils; this duty was embedded in an existing statute mandating a detailed annual report for accountability purposes.[759] Oregon directed public education providers to provide tampons and sanitary pads at no cost to students.[760] Rhode Island ordered that feminine hygiene products be provided in all public schools.[761] Vermont declared that boards and approved independent schools make menstrual products available at no cost in a majority of gender-neutral bathrooms designated for

---

[750] 2021 Wash. Laws Ch. 74, H.B. 1342.
[751] 2021 Wyo. Sess. Laws Enr. Act No. 47, Ch. 74, H.B. 52.
[752] Alabama urged local school boards to provide feminine hygiene products in certain schools at no cost to students, by resolution. 2021 Ala. HR 262.
[753] 2021 Ark. Acts 933, HB 1611.
[754] 2021 Cal. Stat. Ch. 664, AB 367.
[755] 2021 Del. Ch. 11, HB 20.
[756] 2021 Ill. Laws Pub. Act 102-0340, HB 156.
[757] 2021 Ill. Laws Pub. Act 102-0250, HB 641.
[758] 2021 Md. Laws Ch. 705, HB 205; 2021 Md. Laws Ch.706, SB 427.
[759] 2021 Nev. Stat. Ch. 503, AB 224.
[760] 2021 Or. Laws Ch. 635, HB 3294.
[761] 2021 R.I. Pub. Laws S. 86, H. 5083.

female students generally used by those eight years of age or older and the school nurse's office.[762] Washington obligated boards, private schools, and institutions of higher education to make menstrual hygiene products available at no cost in all gender-neutral bathrooms and bathrooms designed for female students, for students in grade 6 and above in K-12 schools.[763]

Five states adopted six laws on First Amendment speech rights. Florida enacted a parental bill of rights stipulating that it is their fundamental right to direct the upbringing, education, and care of their minor children. The act detailed such rights as the rights to information and records; to direct the education and care of their minor children; to direct the upbringing and moral or religious training of minor children; to apply to enroll minor children in public schools, alternatives to public schools, private schools, religious schools, home education programs, or other available options authorized by law; consent before biometric scans of minor children; to consent in writing before making videos or voice records of children except during court proceedings or forensic interviews; and other rights. Each BOE was directed to pass a policy implementing the act.[764] Florida also removed a provision ordering local boards to require a brief moment of silence, instead requiring principals in public schools to direct teachers in first-period classrooms in all grades to set aside at least one minute, but no more than two minutes daily, for a moment of silence, during which students may not interfere with the participation of peers. First-period teachers may not make suggestions as to the nature of reflections during the moment of silence but must encourage parents or guardians to discuss the moment of silence with their children and make recommendations as to the best use of this time.[765]

New Jersey ordered local boards to adopt written policies concerning freedom of expression for student journalists that must include reasonable provisions for manner, place, and time restrictions, and may include limitations on profane, harassing, threatening, or intimidating language.[766] New Mexico prohibited the imposition of discipline, discrimination, or disparate treatment in public and charter schools based on the hair or cultural or religious

---

[762] 2021 Vt. Laws Act 66, S. 115.
[763] 2021 Wash. Laws Ch. 163, H.B. 1273.
[764] 2021 Fla. Laws ch. 199, HB 241.
[765] 2021 Fla. Laws ch. 89, H. 529.
[766] 2021 N.J. Laws c. 309, S. 108.

headdresses of a student.[767] New York forbade the selling or displaying of hate symbols by municipalities, fire districts, volunteer fire companies, police departments, and school districts.[768] Washington passed the uniform public expression protection act creating a private cause of action against government entities, presumably including schools, to protect communication on issues under consideration or review in legislative, executive, judicial, administrative, or other governmental proceedings.[769]

Four states passed acts that addressed rights in First Amendment religion clauses. Illinois directed that pupils shall be excused from engaging in physical education courses during a period of religious fasting if their parents or guardians notify the school principals in writing that their children are participating in religious fasting.[770] Montana adopted a religious freedom restoration act obligating state courts to use the compelling governmental interest test in cases on the free exercise of religion.[771] North Dakota permitted local boards to display the ten commandments along with other historical documents in schools and classrooms.[772] Texas encouraged the display of the Ten Commandments in public educational institutions.[773]

Three states initiated parental notice regarding the sex education curriculum, affording them the right to excuse their children from participating. Florida required each school board to provide notice on their websites explaining parental rights to exempt their children from reproductive health and disease education as well as to approve instructional materials related to these topics annually.[774] Tennessee ordered local boards or officials in public charter schools to notify parents or guardians prior to commencing instruction on a sexual orientation or gender identity curriculum, permitting them to excuse their children from these classes.[775] Texas called for the board to provide parents with annual written notice about plans to provide human sexuality instruction to students.[776]

---

[767] 2021 N.M. Laws Ch. 37, HB 29. *See also,* 2021 N.M. Laws Ch. 19, SB 80.
[768] 2021 N.Y. Laws Ch. 554, S. 4615.
[769] 2021 Wash. Laws Ch. 259, S.B. 5009.
[770] 2021 Ill. Laws Pub. Act 102-0405, HB 160.
[771] 2021 Mont. Laws Ch. 276, SB 215.
[772] 2021 N.D. Laws S.B. No. 2308.
[773] 2021 Tex. Gen. Laws H.C.R. 1.
[774] 2021 Fla. Laws ch. 69, H. 545.
[775] 2021 Tenn. Pub. Acts Ch. No. 281, S.B. No. 1229, H.B. No. 529.
[776] 2021 Tex. Gen. Laws H.B. No. 1525.

Four states addressed gender issues or gender identity. The Arkansas Save Adolescents from Experimentation (SAFE) Act, among other provisions, prohibits referrals for gender transition procedures for persons younger than eighteen under the penalty of discipline from licensing entities or review boards and compensatory damages plus other relief in judicial or administrative proceedings.[777] California replaced gendered language in its public school code with non-gendered terms.[778] California also amended a provision allowing gender-specific programming for Boys State and Girls State conferences to provide participation opportunities for students who do not identify as either male or female or with their assigned birth genders.[779] Colorado added a provision mandating equal access to services related to out-of-home placements, including gender expression and gender identity as protected classes.[780] Oregon ordered its DOE to develop and implement a statewide education plan for students who may be lesbian, gay, bisexual, transgender, queer, two-spirit, intersex, asexual, non-binary, or other minority gender identity or sexual orientation.[781]

Six states adopted eight laws about financial aid and the free application for federal student aid (FAFSA), and protection from abuses by loan service providers. California obligated its student aid commission and state DOE to facilitate the completion of the FAFSA through data sharing and comparison of roster data.[782] Connecticut first directed local and regional school boards to adopt policies to improve completion rates of FAFSA by students in grade 12.[783] Connecticut next created a private cause of action against student loan service providers who engage in abusive acts or practices while servicing student education loans.[784] Maryland informed county school boards to encourage and assist as many high school seniors as possible in completing a submitted financial aid application annually by a date set by the higher education commission.[785]

Nevada required boards of trustees of school districts and governing bodies of charter schools and private schools to provide support and assistance to pupils and their parents and guardians in

---

[777] 2021 Ark. Acts 626, HB 1570.
[778] 2021 Cal. Stat. Ch. 666, AB 486.
[779] 2021 Cal. Stat. Ch. 676, SB 363.
[780] 2021 Colo. Sess. Laws HB 1072.
[781] 2021 Or. Laws Ch. 644, SB 52.
[782] 2021 Cal. Stat. Ch. 560, AB 469.
[783] 2021 Conn. Acts 21-199 (Reg. Sess.), SB 1032.
[784] 2021 Conn. Acts 21-190 (Reg. Sess.), SB 716.
[785] 2021 Md. Laws Ch. 577, SB 664.

completing FAFSA.[786] Rhode Island allowed students who are legally unable to complete FAFSA to use a comparable form created by colleges.[787] Texas ordered local boards and charter school officials to adopt a form that provides students or their parents or guardians the opportunity to decline to complete and to submit a financial aid application that is generally needed for high school graduation; high school guidance counselors can sign off on the waivers.[788] Texas then delayed the implementation of a duty of its higher education coordinating board to available an electronic version of the application for state financial aid (TASFA) until the 2023-24 school year.[789]

Five states spoke to liaison services for children who are homeless, in foster care, or are English language learners. California required the identification of the official in local education agencies designated to serve as liaisons for children and youth who are homeless.[790] Illinois directed local boards to appoint at least one employee to act as the liaison to facility enrollment and the transfer of records of students in the legal custody of its department of children and family services.[791] Rhode Island called on school superintendents to create annual reports on the progress and status of academic achievement of students in foster care.[792] Vermont permitted school boards and towns or cities to act jointly to fund the services of one or more cultural liaisons to support students and families with limited English proficiency.[793] Washington obligated officials in public schools to identify persons to serves as points of contact for students in foster care.[794]

Two states passed laws stressing that students have protected rights in their hair and clothing styles associated with race or religion. Illinois prohibited nonpublic elementary or secondary schools registered with the state BOE from not allowing ethnic hair styles, or hair texture.[795] Oregon amended disciplinary standards to permit students to wear religious clothing in accordance with their sincerely held religious beliefs consistent with safety and health

---

[786] 2021 Nev. Stat. Ch. 241, AB 235.
[787] 2021 R.I. Pub. Laws S. 993, H. 5826.
[788] 2021 Tex. Gen. Laws S.B. No. 369.
[789] 2021 Tex. Gen. Laws S.B. No. 1860.
[790] 2021 Cal. Stat. Ch. 400, SB 400.
[791] 2021 Ill. Laws Pub. Act 102-0199, HB 1746.
[792] 2021 R.I. Pub. Laws S. 989, H. 5157.
[793] 2021 Vt. Laws Act 66, S. 115.
[794] 2021 Wash. Laws Ch. 95, S.B. 5184.
[795] 2021 Ill. Laws Pub. Act 102-0360, SB 817.

standards while balancing their health, safety, and reasonable accommodation needs on activity-by-activity bases; the act also recognized the need to protect hairstyles, braided hair, natural hair, and hair texture related to physical characteristics historically associated with race.[796]

Two states specified that tribal symbols qualify as graduation regalia. Arizona directed that local boards and charter school officials may not prohibit graduating students who are members of federally-recognized Indian tribes from wearing traditional regalia or objects of cultural significance, including eagle feathers, at graduation ceremonies.[797] Oregon directed local boards to allow students to wear Native American items of cultural significance at public school events, including high school graduation.[798]

Five states adopted the Purple Star program, which provides a military liaison for student support. Delaware empowered its state DOE to designate Purple Star Schools when military-connected students are enrolled in their classes; officials in these schools must identify a staff member as a military liaison to provide information and other services to families of military-connected students.[799] Florida obligated its state DOE to establish the Purple Star Campus program.[800] Nebraska adopted the Purple Star Schools Act recognizing schools serving military-connected students while expecting officials to name staff member as military liaison to assist students in registration, enrollment, relocation, records transfer, and academic planning.[801] New Mexico adopted the Purple Star public school program to identify schools that demonstrate a commitment to students and families connected to the U.S. military.[802] Oklahoma joined the Purple Star school recognition program.[803]

Three states added provisions about student records. Arizona set standards for identifying who has access to student-level data in school records.[804] Illinois determined that school student records or information may be shared under intergovernmental agreements between elementary and high school districts if their attendance

---

[796] 2021 Or. Laws Ch. 239, HB 2935.
[797] 2021 Ariz. Sess. Laws Ch. 268, HB 2705.
[798] 2021 Or. Laws Ch. 45, HB 2052.
[799] 2021 Del. Laws Ch. 120, SB 117.
[800] 2021 Fla. Laws ch. 65, H. 429.
[801] 2021 Neb. Laws LB 5.
[802] 2021 N.M. Laws Ch. 75, SB 271.
[803] 2021 Okla. Sess. Laws S.B. No. 54.
[804] 2021 Ariz. Sess. Laws Ch. 404, HB 2898, Sec. 37.

boundaries overlap.[805] New Hampshire permitted its state DOE to collect student address information for the purpose of distributing assessment results.[806]

Two states prohibited mask mandates during the COVID-19 pandemic. As part of a budget reconciliation bill, Arizona forbade school boards and charter school officials from mandating the use of a face covering by students or staff during class hours and on school property.[807] Utah banned the adoption of face covering requirements in its system of higher or public education.[808]

Two states specified that parents have the right to review instructional materials. Texas afforded parents the authority to observe virtual instruction and review materials or other teaching aids while their children are participating in virtual or remote learning.[809] Utah ordered public school officials to provide parents with access to the curricula that they use.[810]

Other parental and student rights-related legislation enacted in 2021 is described as follows. Arkansas recognized the last Wednesday of September of each year as a day of prayer for Arkansas students, directing the governor to proclaim the day publicly annually and to call on citizens, in accordance with their own faith and consciences, to pray, meditate, or otherwise reflect on the following individuals of this state: students, teachers, school administrators, and schools.[811] The Arkansas Student Protection Act then forbade school personnel from making abortion referrals or engaging in formal or informal agreements between a public school and private entities in this regard; the act does not seem to be bounded by the subject of agreements between schools and private entity. In other words, the subject of agreements could arguably be on any matter.[812]

Connecticut amended the obligation that local and regional school boards adopt student success plans, now expecting them to be created collaboratively with parents.[813] Second, Connecticut created a pilot program to enable families participating in inter-district public school attendance programs to move to the towns where their

---

[805] 2021 Ill. Laws Pub. Act 102-0557, SB 2434.
[806] 2021 N.H. Laws Ch. 20, HB 194.
[807] 2021 Ariz. Sess. Laws Ch. 404, HB 2898, Sec. 12.
[808] 2021 Utah Laws H.B. 1007 (1st Spec. Sess.).
[809] 2021 Tex. Gen. Laws S.B. No. 358.
[810] 2021 Utah Laws S.B. 148.
[811] 2021 Ark. Acts 902, SB 662.
[812] 2021 Ark. Acts 820, HB 1592.
[813] 2021 Conn. Acts 21-199 (Reg. Sess.), SB 1032.

children attend school.⁸¹⁴ In the first of three laws, Louisiana added to a provision allowing school boards to share student data with other entities, granting permission for the company with which the state contracted to develop unique student identifiers to have access.⁸¹⁵ Louisiana passed a Foster Youth's Bill of Rights for those aged 14-18 in foster care, including the right to attend the school of origin, participate in extracurricular activities, attend driver's education classes, and access school materials, including an electronic device and internet connection.⁸¹⁶ Louisiana extended academic support in 2021-22 and 2022-23 through accelerated learning committees for students in grades 4-8 who failed to achieve mastery on prior-year statewide assessments.⁸¹⁷

Maryland decreed that contracts for sales of single-family residential real property in Montgomery County must contain a notice that school boundaries designated for the property may be subject to change.⁸¹⁸ In a second law, Maryland directed its state DOE to establish a model policy to support the educational and parenting goals to improve educational outcomes for pregnant and parenting students.⁸¹⁹ Nevada dictated that school boards electronically publish statements of rights of parents and guardians of pupils who are English language learners.⁸²⁰ New Jersey permitted local boards to administer student health surveys after prior written notification to their parents and legal guardians.⁸²¹ New York prohibited the use of biometric identifying technology in schools until July 1, 2022, or until its commissioner of education authorizes such use.⁸²²

Ohio enabled parents or guardians of students to notify their school boards that their children will not take nationally-standardized assessments; boards must comply with these requests.⁸²³ Oregon forbade education providers from displaying symbols of hate on school property or in educational programs.⁸²⁴ Texas informed school boards and officials in open-enrollment

---

⁸¹⁴ 2021 Conn. Acts 21-26 (Reg. Sess.), HB 6436.
⁸¹⁵ 2021 La. Acts No. 407, H.B. 711.
⁸¹⁶ 2021 La. Acts No. 351, S.B. 151.
⁸¹⁷ 2021 La. Acts No. 294, S.B. 234.
⁸¹⁸ 2021 Md. Laws Ch. 593, HB 541.
⁸¹⁹ 2021 Md. Laws Ch. 345, HB 401; 2021 Md. Laws Ch. 346, SB 438.
⁸²⁰ 2021 Nev. Stat. Ch. 263, AB 195.
⁸²¹ 2021 N.J. Laws c. 156, A. 5825.
⁸²² 2021 N.Y. Laws Ch. 2, A. 954.
⁸²³ 2021 Ohio Laws HB 82.
⁸²⁴ 2021 Or. Laws Ch. 147, HB 2697.

charter schools that they must use a learning management system or online learning portal to provide login credentials to all parents.[825] West Virginia empowered persons other than superintendents, including principals of private schools, to issue work permits for students aged fourteen or fifteen.[826] Wisconsin allowed students who are home-schooled to serve as election inspectors.[827]

Program Development

This section reviews 2021 legislation on program development. As legislative bodies add program initiatives, it is possible to gauge growth in the types of programs across the states. When legislatures adopt novel initiatives, it serves to alert the authors and readers to the possibilities of entirely new trends. Such was the case with a 2021 law from Tennessee which required its state BOE to approve a process for school boards, for when two or more work together, to establish their own teacher training programs.[828] Legislative direction about teacher training programs is uniformly reported in the chapter section on higher education because that is where it almost always occurs. While the authors can recall the passage of laws for pilot programs for teacher training created and operated by one or a few boards cooperatively with university initiatives, this is, in our memory, the first statewide occurrence of a statewide directive wholly within school systems that their state BOR must approve.

Of existing programs, career and technical education, vocational technical, apprenticeship programs, and other measures designed to help students gain awareness of various career paths received a boost in 2021, with nineteen states adopting twenty-five acts in those areas. Arizona permitted payment from the career and technical education projects fund for expenses of approved career and technical student organizations, including costs associated with events, conferences, or competitions.[829] Arkansas amended its description of the federal law funding vocational education programs to simply provide its name, the Carl D. Perkins Career and Technical Education Act of 2006.[830] Colorado appropriated funds to support

---

[825] 2021 Tex. Gen. Laws S.B. No. 3 (2nd Spec. Sess.).
[826] 2021 W. Va. Acts Ch. 168, S.B. 435.
[827] 2021 Wis. Laws Act 34, S.B. 102.
[828] 2021 Tenn Pub. Acts Ch. No. 571, S.B. No. 653, H.B. No. 1534.
[829] 2021 Ariz. Sess. Laws Ch. 95, HB 2055.
[830] 2021 Ark. Acts 1027, SB 618.

increased access in high school credentials in its career development success program.[831] Delaware required its advisory council on career and technical education to add to the information needed in its annual report. The annual report must address advocacy efforts to provide students and families with information about educational, employment, and training opportunities.[832]

Florida created the office of "reimagining" education and career help, charging it with revising workforce services including the labor market estimating conference, the workforce opportunity portal, and the credential review committee.[833] Hawai'i first obligated its state board for career and technical education to review processes, requirements, and rules related to student attainment of industry-recognized credentials annually.[834] Hawai'i next granted priority for enrollment in career and technical education programs for students who live within the service areas of the school or were enrolled therein during the previous academic year.[835] Idaho adopted the award of a workforce readiness and career technical education diploma.[836] Idaho also authorized, subject to appropriations, the expenditure of $750 per student to assist those not enrolled in public schools for dual credits, postsecondary credit-bearing examinations, and career technical education certificate examinations.[837] Illinois replaced references to vocational education in its school code, now referring to career and technical education.[838]

Kentucky mandated that when local boards initiate management of state-operated vocational education and technology centers, the latter shall receive 100% of the funding they have commonwealth-operated facilities from the annual general fund appropriation.[839] New Hampshire clarified that students attending private schools or who are homeschooled may attend career and technical education centers for the areas of their public school residency with transportation costs repaid by its state DOE.[840] New Mexico included secondary school students working in apprenticeship programs for coverage under its state minimum

---

[831] 2021 Colo. Sess. Laws SB 119.
[832] 2021 Del. Laws Ch. 135, SB 86.
[833] 2021 Fla. Laws ch. 165, H. 1507.
[834] 2021 Haw. Sess. Laws Act 163, SB 516.
[835] 2021 Haw. Sess. Laws Act 157, SB 224.
[836] 2021 Idaho Sess. Laws Ch. 287, S. 1039.
[837] 2021 Idaho Sess. Laws Ch. 259, S. 1045.
[838] 2021 Ill. Laws Pub. Act 102-0403, HB 3218.
[839] 2021 Ky. Acts Ch. 40, SB 101.
[840] 2021 N.H. Laws Ch. 210, SB 148.

wage law.[841] North Dakota directed its superintendent of public instruction to permit local boards and charter school governing boards to adopt policies allowing students in grades 6-12 to enroll in educational opportunities, which it defined as instruction outside of classrooms that meet course content standards and include work-based learning, pre-apprenticeships, apprenticeships, internships, industry certifications, and community programs.[842]

Oklahoma permitted sophomores sixteen or older, not just juniors and seniors, to participate in apprenticeship, internship, or mentorship programs.[843] Oklahoma next informed its commission on educational quality and accountability to study and issue a report to its governor and legislative leadership on factors in the state's public education system contributing to improvements in the common education system, higher education, and career and technology education systems, workforce and career readiness, and employment availability.[844] Rhode Island guaranteed students the right to enroll in approved career technical education programs outside of their districts of residence.[845] Tennessee directed its state DOE to begin preparing students in middle school grades for career and technical education pathways by introducing them to career exploration opportunities that allow pupils to explore a wide variety of high-skill, high-wage, or in-demand career fields.[846]

Texas established the Tri-Agency Workforce Initiative to coordinate and improve information and resources necessary to ensure the efficient use of funds to achieve workforce development goals; align career education and training programs to workforce demands; and enable local and state policy makers to identify workforce outcomes to participants in career education and training programs.[847] In a related act Texas obligated agency officials to appoint an existing employee to lead the development of a framework as well as a report including thirteen specific components.[848] Moreover, Texas called on local boards to notify parents of students in ninth grade or above annually about the availability of career and technology programs or other work-based

---

[841] 2021 N.M. Laws Ch. 10, SB 35.
[842] 2021 N.D. Laws H.B. No. 1478.
[843] 2021 Okla. Sess. Laws S.B. No. 619.
[844] 2021 Okla. Sess. Laws H.B. No. 2691.
[845] 2021 R.I. Pub. Laws S. 212, H. 5836.
[846] 2021 Tenn. Pub. Acts Ch. No. 271, S.B. No. 1240, H.B. No. 1446.
[847] 2021 Tex. Gen. Laws H.B. 3767.
[848] 2021 Tex. Gen. Laws H.B. No. 1247.

education opportunities in their systems, including those with internships or apprenticeships.[849]

West Virginia directed county boards to empower students who are homeschooled or who attend private schools to enroll and take classes at county vocational schools at no additional cost beyond those charged to their peers in public school.[850] Wisconsin mandated that its youth apprenticeship program administered by its department of workforce development must be included in the list of educational options schools provide parents and guardians, including them on board websites.[851] Wyoming allowed school boards, community colleges, technical schools, and employers to enter into learner agreements for providing vocational work and training opportunities; these agreements enable students to receive coverage for workers' compensation.[852] Wyoming also changed references in its K-12 school code from vocational education to career and technical education.[853]

Early childhood programs continued to be established and to grow across twelve states enacting thirteen bills. Colorado established a unified state system of early childhood education, creating its department of early childhood to lead that effort.[854] Florida obligated its office of early learning to coordinate with university centers for early childhood studies in giving priority for students to participate in early learning programs based on initiatives for supplemental nutrition assistance, Medicaid assistance, and the housing choice voucher program.[855] At the same time, Florida obligated its state DOE, in consultation with its office of early learning, to implement a coordinated screening and progress monitoring system for early childhood through grade eight.[856] Hawai'i permitted its DOE to accept private funding to create public prekindergarten programs.[857] Idaho created a kindergarten jump-start program and training for parents.[858]

Illinois declared that children who receive early intervention services prior to their third birthdays, are eligible for individualized

---

[849] 2021 Tex. Gen. Laws S.B. No. 1095.
[850] 2021 W. Va. Acts Ch. 101, H.B. 2791.
[851] 2021 Wis. Laws Act 83, A.B. 220.
[852] 2021 Wyo. Sess. Laws Enr. Act No. 78, Ch. 160, H.B. 239.
[853] 2021 Wyo. Sess. Laws Enr. Act No. 29, Ch. 66, S.F. 108.
[854] 2021 Colo. Sess. Laws HB 1304.
[855] 2021 Fla. Laws ch. 87, H. 1349.
[856] 2021 Fla. Laws ch. 9, H. 7011.
[857] 2021 Haw. Sess. Laws Act 210, HB 1362.
[858] 2021 Idaho Sess. Laws Ch. 326, S. 1075.

education programs, and whose birthdays falls between May 1 and August 31 may continue to receive early intervention services until the beginning of the school year following their third birthdays.[859] Indiana allowed the enrollment period for its prekindergarten pilot program to begin after April 1, 2021.[860] Louisiana directed its state board of elementary and secondary education to coordinate and report data about its early childhood care and education network to assists legislators in evaluating its effectiveness while determining the most efficient and effective allocation of funding and services to maximize opportunities for children aged birth through five to achieve kindergarten readiness.[861] Maine mandated that its state DOE develop a plan for the provision of early intervention services along with an advisory committee to study what is needed for children from birth to under age three.[862]

Maryland added to a directive for the state DOE to study its infant and early childhood mental health consultation project specifying that it assess the costs and benefits associated with current project staffing qualifications and potential alternative models, including the capacity to continue to provide needed services under these alternative models.[863] New York clarified that kindergartens or pre-kindergartens operated by public school boards are not to be considered child daycare facilities if they are not located on the campus of those schools.[864] North Dakota reenacted authorization for early childhood education, renaming it as a program for four-year-old's.[865] Virginia amended provisions about its school readiness committee, setting a goal for it to provide recommendations for and track progress on the financing of a comprehensive birth-to-five early childhood care and education system.[866]

Six state legislatures, through nine acts, addressed school-based health services. Arizona increased, from five to six, the number of area health education centers, with one designated as focusing on the health care delivery system for Native Americans.[867] Arkansas amended a provision on vision screening, pointing out that its

---

[859] 2021 Ill. Laws Pub. Act 102-0209, SB 820.
[860] 2021 Ind. Acts Pub. Law 216.
[861] 2021 La. Acts No. 198, H.B. 304.
[862] 2021 Me. Laws Ch. 110, H.P. 176, L.D. 255.
[863] 2021 Md. Laws Ch. 430, HB 776.
[864] 2021 N.Y. Laws Ch. 328, A. 7176.
[865] 2021 N.D. Laws H.B. No. 1416.
[866] 2021 Va. Acts Ch. 446, H. 2105 (1st Spec. Sess.).
[867] 2021 Ariz. Sess. Laws Ch. 142, SB 1301.

division of elementary and secondary education will work with its commission on eye and vision care of school-age children to adopt rules for such screenings.[868] Maryland directed its secretary of health to consult with its state DOE to develop guidelines supporting the expansion of school-based health centers.[869] Maryland called on its state DOE, along with its department of health, to authorize health care practitioners at approved school-based health centers to provide health care services through telehealth.[870]

New York ordered its state education department to collect information from healthcare professionals licensed, certified, registered, or authorized to work in school settings for the purpose of providing its department of health with information to evaluate access to needed services, including, but not limited to, the locations and types of settings in which the professionals practice and other relevant information.[871] Oregon required its health authority to provide planning grants to ten school districts or education service districts to evaluate the need and develop plans for school-based health services.[872] Oregon also provided reimbursement for vision screenings of students through the state DOE.[873] Rhode Island specified that only certified nurse teachers might be employed as school nurses in elementary and secondary schools.[874] Washington created a school-based health center program office within the department of health to award grants and coordinate with other agencies and entities to provide support, training, and technical assistance to school-based health centers.[875]

Five states adopted seven acts about virtual education. Colorado added a provision stipulating that nothing in a statute on the purchasing, leasing, construction, maintenance, or operation of facilities can be construed to block students, teachers, staff members, or member districts of the board of cooperative services from accessing school-owned and operated networks to facilitate remote learning.[876] Florida changed the calculation for establishing the number of state funds to be received by the Florida Virtual School for operating purposes; the apparent change is the addition

---

[868] 2021 Ark. Acts 320, SB 60.
[869] 2021 Md. Laws Ch. 605, HB 1148.
[870] 2021 Md. Laws Ch. 347, HB 34; 2021 Md. Laws Ch. 348, SB 278.
[871] 2021 N.Y. Laws Ch. 701. S. 3543.
[872] 2021 Or. Laws Ch. 619, HB 2591.
[873] 2021 Or. Laws Ch. 648, SB 222.
[874] 2021 R.I. Pub. Laws S. 87, H. 5197.
[875] 2021 Wash. Laws Ch. 68, H.B. 1225.
[876] 2021 Colo. Sess. Laws HB 1114.

of targeted allocations such as for instructional materials, mental health assistance, and teacher salary increments to the equation.[877]

In the first of a trilogy of laws Indiana defined and funded virtual instruction in public schools for the 2020-21 academic year.[878] Indiana then decided that virtual instruction or remote learning must be of the same quality and rigor as what students would receive if they attended in-person instruction in schools.[879] Indiana also permitted school corporations to enter or renew contracts with vendors to operate virtual education schools if the latter submits the contracts to its state DOE.[880] Kansas placed a limit of forty total school term hours of remote learning for the 2021-22 academic year; this limit can be set aside in identified situations including individual student needs or authorization by its state BOE if boards seeking such waivers.[881] Nevada revised provisions on the delivery of distance education, allowing its use in special schools for gifted programs and permitting students to complete courses they began before moving outside of the state.[882]

Ten states enacted bills about learning loss due to the COVID-19 pandemic. Colorado directed its state DOE to identify best practices for addressing learning loss and effective strategies for overcoming learning loss due to the pandemic.[883] Nevada authorized the board of trustees of school districts and its public charter school authority to submit plans to its superintendent of public instruction addressing the loss of learning that occurred because of the pandemic.[884] Texas informed its state education agency to establish programs to assist boards and charter school officials to ensure that students perform at grade level while demonstrating academic core requirements, along with supports to regional service centers, boards, and charter schools to assist students not performing adequately along with funding for tutoring programs.[885]

Maine directed its state DOE to report to its joint standing committee on summer educational programs, including summer school and extended year programs, by November 15, 2021, and each

---

[877] 2021 Fla. Laws ch. 44, H. 5101.
[878] 2021 Ind. Acts Pub. Law 3, S.B. 2.
[879] 2021 Ind. Acts Pub. Law 216 § 27; H. B. No. 1549.
[880] 2021 Ind. Acts Pub. Law 216; H.B. No. 1549.
[881] 2021 Kan. Sess. Laws HB 2134.
[882] 2021 Nev. Stat. Ch. 524, SB 215.
[883] 2021 Colo. Sess. Laws SB 13.
[884] 2021 Nev. Stat. Ch. 494, SB 173.
[885] 2021 Tex. Gen. Laws H.B. No. 1525.

year after that.⁸⁸⁶ New Mexico specified how instructional time is calculated, thereby providing additional appropriations for K-5 extended learning time programs.⁸⁸⁷ Oklahoma created an out-of-school time task force to identify, evaluate, and recommend a set of best practices for children, youth, and families, to improve and increase the number of quality, affordable out-of-school programs in the state.⁸⁸⁸ Tennessee ordered local boards and public charter school officials to implement programs of after-school learning mini-camps, learning loss bridge camps, and summer learning campuses, to assist students who had learning losses due to the pandemic.⁸⁸⁹ Virginia permitted public schools with at least 50% free and reduced lunch services to also offer after-school or enrichment programs.⁸⁹⁰

Another strategy for addressing learning loss was through tutoring, an approach two states adopted. Colorado appropriated funds to provide incentives to local education providers to implement high-impact tutoring as one of the interventions schools have access to as they create plans to recover from learning loss or unfinished learning due to the pandemic.⁸⁹¹ Texas mandated that its state education agency establish a tutoring program available to private schools plus nonprofit teacher organizations to provide supplemental instruction to students in grades K-12 on individualized or small-group bases.⁸⁹²

COVID-19 changed the workplace for many industries, including education. The move from face-to-face to virtual to hybrid schooling opened the door for legislatures to think about innovative methodologies and other types of programming for schools. Fifteen laws in twelve states prompted rethinking about schools and schooling as follows. In its state DOE, Florida created an innovative blended learning and real-time weekly student assessment educational model to improve the educational processes of students while helping to close achievement gaps; the act defines innovative blended learning as a model where in-person and remote students are combined in one classroom environment; where the education, instruction, and engagement occur simultaneously with the same teacher and other students physically present in the classroom; and,

---

⁸⁸⁶ 2021 Me. Laws Ch. 32, H.P. 10, L.D. 44.
⁸⁸⁷ 2021 N.M. Laws Ch. 134, SB. 40.
⁸⁸⁸ 2021 Okla. Sess. Laws H.B. No. 1882.
⁸⁸⁹ 2021 Tenn. Pub. Acts Ch. No. 1, H.B. No. 4, S.B. No. 2 (First Extra. Sess.).
⁸⁹⁰ 2021 Va. Acts Ch. 292, H. 2135 (1ˢᵗ Spec. Sess.).
⁸⁹¹ 2021 Colo. Sess. Laws HB 1234.
⁸⁹² 2021 Tex. Gen. Laws S.B. No. 1356.

for given courses, students learn in part through online delivery of content and instruction with some element of student control over time, place, path, or pact, and in part, traditional supervised classroom locations away from their homes.[893]

Idaho added a new chapter in its school code enabling students in public schools to be eligible for extended learning opportunities outside of traditional classrooms and to earn academic credit while receiving credit for prior knowledge.[894] Idaho also appropriated additional funds to create innovative classrooms in which alternative curricula are to be taught.[895] Indiana adopted the Cambridge international program under the administration of its state DOE.[896] Montana encouraged greater variety in instructional practices through directed, distributive, collaborative, work-based, or other experiential learning activities provided, supervised, guided, facilitated, or coordinated under the supervision of teachers that are conducted purposely to achieve content proficiency while facilitating the acquisition of knowledge, skills, and abilities by pupils in public schools.[897]

North Carolina permitted a range of methods for delivering instruction, including remote and homebound programming as well as abbreviated calendars during the pandemic.[898] North Dakota allowed its state board of public school education to establish a learning continuum for approved mastery framework policies to award required class units on the recommendation of its K-12 education coordination council.[899] North Dakota also launched a legislative management study of competency-based learning initiatives implemented in schools under innovative education programs.[900] Oklahoma adopted the Play to Learn Act to focus on the importance of child-centered, play-based learning as the most rigorous and most developmentally-appropriate way for children in early childhood grades to learn literacy, science, technology, engineering, art, and mathematics; the act blocked local boards from prohibiting teachers from utilizing play-based learning in early childhood education.[901]

---

[893] 2021 Fla. Laws ch. 157, S. 1108.
[894] 2021 Idaho Sess. Laws Ch. 138, H. 172.
[895] 2021 Idaho Sess. Laws Ch.302, S. 1046.
[896] 2021 Ind. Acts Pub. Law 216; H.B. No. 1549.
[897] 2021 Mont. Laws Ch. 247, HB 246.
[898] 2021 N.C. Sess. Laws Ch. 140, H. 3.
[899] 2021 N.D. Laws S.B. No. 2196.
[900] 2021 N.D. Laws H.B. No. 1111.
[901] 2021 Okla. Sess. Laws H.B. No. 1569.

Texas called for the creation of accelerated learning committees to develop individual educational plans for students who do not perform satisfactorily on grades three, five, and eight mathematics and reading STAAR tests not later than the beginning of the next school year; the act enables parents to request that their unsuccessful children be assigned to particular classrooms in the applicable subject areas for the following school year.[902] Texas further directed its state education agency to study the implementation of competency-based programs in its public schools; the study must address funding that does not rely on average daily attendance; the performance of competency-based programs under the current accountability system; and the efficacy of providing competency-based programs to nontraditional students, including adult students.[903] Utah replaced references to "competency-based education" in its school code with "personalized, competency-based learning."[904] Washington directed an existing work group on mastery learning to develop a state profile of graduates, describing the cross-disciplinary skills students should have developed by the time they graduate high school, with a focus on under-served pupils as well as transition to addressing workforce development.[905]

Two states embraced community schools as a means of educational renewal. Arkansas encouraged the adoption of a community schools' approach by mandating the creation of plans describing how educators, governmental entities, and community partners use and leverage all available assets to meet specific student and family needs while improving opportunities and outcomes for children.[906] Vermont adopted a statement supporting community schools where learning extends beyond the walls of schools through active engagement with community partners. The act supports equitable access to high-quality education through community schools and funded support for beginning the implementation of this vision with the designation of community school coordinators in eligible schools, districts, and-or supervisory unions.[907]

Three states sought improvements in the delivery of counseling programs. Arkansas added a subsection to its school counseling

---

[902] 2021 Tex. Gen. Laws H.B. No. 4545.
[903] 2021 Tex. Gen. Laws H.B. No. 572.
[904] 2021 Utah Laws H.B. 181.
[905] 2021 Wash. Laws Ch. 144, S.B. 5249.
[906] 2021 Ark. Acts 744, SB 291.
[907] 2021 Vt. Laws Act 67, H. 106.

improvement act authorizing its state BOE to promulgate rules for its implementation.[908] Texas ordered the boards of trustees of local districts to adopt policies requiring school counselors to spend at least 80% of their total work time on duties that are components of counseling programs.[909] Washington obligated local boards to develop and implement written plans for comprehensive school counseling programs based on regularly-updated standards developed by national organizations representing school counselors.[910]

Four states enacted five laws on dual language or English language learner programs. Arkansas allowed public school boards or open-enrollment public charter schools to adopt approved bilingual or dual-immersion programs.[911] California amended provisions defining quality in preschool programs to include data on dual language learners.[912] Minnesota increased funding for English learner aid by $2 million per year for fiscal years 2022-25.[913] Texas replaced references to students of limited English proficiency with the terms "emergent bilingual" students.[914] Texas also directed its state education agency, in conjunction with its higher education coordinating board and workforce commission, to develop a strategic plan to increase the number of educators certified in bilingual education instruction, the number of program models, and the number of bilingual and multilingual high school graduates.[915]

Six states adopted eight laws about dual credit programs. Colorado authorized the use of funds for a pilot program for low-income students to graduate from high school. The program allows funds for a fourth year for those who graduate in three years to pursue their career and postsecondary training and education.[916] Louisiana removed the sunset provision from its dual enrollment framework task force.[917] Nevada directed officials at the College of Southern Nevada to create a pilot program for dual credit courses for students.[918] Additionally, Nevada informed officials at a

---

[908] 2021 Ark. Acts 650, SB 120.
[909] 2021 Tex. Gen. Laws S.B. No. 179.
[910] 2021 Wash. Laws Ch. 174, S.B. 5030.
[911] 2021 Ark. Acts 663, HB 1451.
[912] 2021 Cal. Stat. Ch. 498, AB 1363.
[913] 2021 Minn. Laws Ch. 13, H.F. no. 2 (1st Spec. Sess.).
[914] 2021 Tex. Gen. Laws S.B. No. 2066.
[915] 2021 Tex. Gen. Laws S.B. No. 560.
[916] 2021 Colo. Sess. Laws SB 106.
[917] 2021 La. Acts No. 147, H.B. 60.
[918] 2021 Nev. Stat. Ch. 541, AB 319.

university school for the gifted to enter into a cooperative agreement to provide dual credit courses.[919] Oklahoma opened the opportunity for eleventh graders to take advantage of opportunities to participate in and contract with its higher learning access program.[920] Oklahoma also created a task force to study its concurrent enrollment needs.[921] Texas mandated that dual-credit agreements or memoranda of agreement between local boards and public institution of higher education designate at least one employee of either entity as the person responsible for providing academic advising to students.[922] Washington adopted a college in the high school program, governed by a contract between institutions of higher education and local boards, charter schools, or state-tribal compact schools.[923]

Two states adopted acts for gifted and talented programming. Connecticut required local and regional school boards to adopt policies for the equitable identification of gifted and talented students.[924] Montana made delivery of gifted and talented programs mandatory rather than permissive.[925] New Hampshire directed officials in all public schools to submit annual reports in a standardized format to its state DOE detailing the policies, programs, and procedures in place to identify and accommodate the needs of gifted and talented students.[926]

Five states adopted six laws supporting mental health programming. Delaware created a mental health services unit for elementary students in its school funding mechanism with a unit set as a ratio of 250 full-time equivalent pupils in grades K-5 for a full-time school counselor, school social worker, or licensed clinical social worker.[927] New Jersey created a mental health screening in schools grant program in its DOE, appropriating $1 million for its operations.[928] New Jersey established a pilot program in its state DOE to provide school-based social-emotional learning to students in grades K-5 at selected public schools.[929] Tennessee created a K-12

---

[919] 2021 Nev. Stat. Ch. 237, SB 160.
[920] 2021 Okla. Sess. Laws S.B. No. 132.
[921] 2021 Okla. Sess. Laws S.B. No. 292.
[922] 2021 Tex. Gen. Laws S.B. No. 1277.
[923] 2021 Wash. Laws Ch. 71, H.B. 1302.
[924] 2021 Conn. Acts 21-199 (Reg. Sess.), SB 1032.
[925] 2021 Mont. Laws Ch. 150, SB 109.
[926] 2021 N.H. Laws Ch. 139, HB 321.
[927] 2021 Del. Laws Ch. 126, HB 100.
[928] 2021 N.J. Laws c. 237, A. 970.
[929] 2021 N.J. Laws c. 85, S. 2486.

mental health trust fund act to offer mental health support to students in primary and secondary schools in the state.[930]

Texas empowered its collaborative task force on public school mental health services to obtain information from school boards, charter schools, and other entities, and to enter into agreements with institutions of higher education as needed.[931] Washington modified its workforce education investment act by mandating the development of a behavioral health workforce pilot program for community mental health providers including, but not limited to, clinical social workers, licensed mental health counselors, licensed marriage and family therapists, clinical psychologist, and substance abuse treatment providers.[932]

Three states added to their reading literacy programs. North Carolina established an early literacy program within its department of public instruction, using the science of reading for children in the prekindergarten program and requiring more teacher training in the science of reading.[933] Vermont continued the ongoing work to improve literacy for all students with an act that provided technical support and professional development learning modules for teachers in teaching literacy in its five key areas.[934] Virginia added that reading intervention services must be evidence-based, including services grounded in the science of reading, including the components of effective reading instruction and explicit, systematic, sequential, and cumulative instruction, to include phonemic awareness, systematic phonics, fluency, vocabulary development, and text comprehension as appropriate, based on the student's demonstrated reading deficiencies.[935]

In the first of two acts on dropout recovery, Texas amended eligibility standards for open-enrollment charter schools to be designated by its commissioner of education as a dropout recovery school if it serves students in grades 9-12 and has enrollments of which at least sixty percent of the students are at least sixteen years or older as of the fall semester.[936] Texas amended a provision on dropout recovery schools, stipulating that students at risk of dropping out include those under twenty-six who are in schools,

---

[930] 2021 Tenn. Pub. Acts. Ch. No. 595, S.B. No. 739, H.B. No. 73.
[931] 2021 Tex. Gen. Laws H.B. No. 2287.
[932] 2021 Wash. Laws Ch. 170, H.B. 1504.
[933] 2021 N.C. Sess. Laws Ch. 8, S. 387.
[934] 2021 Vt. Laws Act 28, S. 114.
[935] 2021 Va. Acts Ch. 167, H. 1865 (1st Spec. Sess.).
[936] 2021 Tex. Gen. Laws S.B. No. 879.

districts, or charter schools designated as dropout recovery schools.[937]

The first of two laws from Montana on Native languages revitalized the Indian language preservation program that had been set for termination.[938] Then Montana required its legislative finance committee to study Indian language preservation and report to its interim education committee by September 1, 2022.[939]

Other program development-related acts adopted by state legislatures are detailed as follows. Florida directed school boards to allocate funds to prepare students to enroll in Advanced International Certificate of Education courses.[940] Louisiana repealed a provision creating an international language immersion school.[941] Minnesota rewrote a provision to promote the establishment of a new international baccalaureate (IB) program, or expand existing IB programs, ordering officials in schools or boards to approve three-year plans for IB programming within ninety days of receiving grants.[942]

New Jersey obligated its state DOE to develop an outreach program to encourage young women and minorities to pursue postsecondary degrees and careers in STEM.[943]

Oregon provided permanent funding for student foreign exchange programs and small school system grants.[944] Rhode Island informed its council on elementary and secondary education, in consultation with its state DOE, to develop and approve academic standards on consumer education in public schools.[945] Texas ordered its state education agency to develop an agriculture education program for elementary school students to encourage appreciation and improve their understanding of agriculture.[946] Vermont dictated that its state education agency update and distribute a model wellness program policy using the expanded definition of "wellness program" to local boards[947]

---

[937] 2021 Tex. Gen. Laws H.B. No. 572.
[938] 2021 Mont. Laws Ch. 562, HB 671.
[939] 2021 Mont. Laws Ch. 562, HB 671.
[940] 2021 Fla. Laws ch. 84, H. 827.
[941] 2021 La. Acts No. 110, S.B. 246.
[942] 2021 Minn. Laws Ch. 13, H.F. no. 2 (1st Spec. Sess.).
[943] 2021 N. J. Laws c. 239, A. 1625.
[944] 2021 Or. Laws Ch. 355, HB 2330.
[945] 2021 R.I. Pub. Law H. 5491, S. 349.
[946] 2021 Tex. Gen. Laws S.B. No. 801.
[947] 2021 Vt. Laws Act 66, S. 115.

School Choice

This section describes laws related to school choice that states adopted in 2021. The most numerous types of school choice acts addressed charter schools, revocations, renewal, and-or enrollment preference. Alabama authorized the formation of public charter schools near military installations focused on serving military dependents.[948] Arkansas removed a requirement that officials in open-enrollment public charter schools must list the waivers granted with their petition to their chartering school districts, instead requiring them to list the waivers on their websites annually by August 1.[949] Georgia permitted the designation of alternative charter schools, which provide alternative educations program and services focused on dropout recovery or high school credit recovery.[950] Indiana repealed sections related to the renewal of charter schools' authorizations, substituting new procedures for repeals or authorizations of charters as well as for assessments and evidence of improvement.[951]

Nevada authorized the sponsors of charter schools to eliminate their elementary, middle, or high school campuses meeting the criteria for termination of their contracts or reopening under new charters.[952] New Hampshire revoked possible consequences of charter school officials' failure to submit mandated reports to its state DOE.[953] New Mexico granted enrollment preferences for students whose parents are employees of charter schools.[954] Oregon enabled officials in public charter schools to use weighted lotteries favoring historically-underserved students when the number of enrollment applications exceeded program capacity.[955] Tennessee extended the life of its public charter school commission to June 30, 2023.[956] Utah repealed standards related to its state charter school board's reviews of applications for charter schools seeking authorization from the boards of trustees of institutions of higher education.[957] West Virginia amended its charter school code to

---

[948] 2021 Ala. Acts No. 2021-117, S.B. 103.
[949] 2021 Ark. Acts 774, SB 251.
[950] 2021 Ga. Laws Act 156, SB 153.
[951] 2021 Ind. Acts Pub. Law 211, HB 1514.
[952] 2021 Nev. Stat. Ch. 80, AB 68.
[953] 2021 N.H. Laws Ch. 44, HB 442.
[954] 2021 N.M. Laws Ch. 28, SB 51.
[955] 2021 Or. Laws Ch. 364, HB 2954.
[956] 2021 Tenn. Pub. Acts Ch. No. 49, S.B. No. 88, H.B. No. 308.
[957] 2021 Utah Laws S.B. 148.

prohibit conversion of private schools to charter schools while forbidding elected officials from considering profit or monetary considerations in decisions related to charter schools.[958]

Six states adopted legislation supporting open enrollment or open transfers in public schools. Arizona directed its state BOE to adopt a model format for describing open enrollment options.[959] Oklahoma modified its education open transfer act by directing local boards to adopt policies determining the number of transfer students they have the capacity to accept in each grade level for each school site no later than January 1, 2022.[960] Tennessee informed local boards of their duty to establish open enrollment periods during which parents or guardians may seek to transfer their children to schools in their districts for which they are not zoned to attend.[961] If boards deliver instruction primarily over the Internet for more than one grading period during a school year, Texas allows students to transfer tuition-free to other districts offering in-person instruction, and the latter accepts the transfers.[962] West Virginia forbade county boards from refusing transfers because students are moving from private, parochial, church, or religious schools.[963] Wisconsin allowed students to attend fully virtual options offered by nonresident school boards or charter schools in their district under a full-time enrollment program during the 2021-22 school year.[964]

Waivers from state rules remained a relatively popular means of exercising choice, as five states chose this methodology last year. Georgia adopted the Learning Pod Protection Act, which allows voluntary associations of parents choosing to group their children in grades K-12 for common learning activities or remote learning options offered by primary educational programs; the act appears to provide waiver privileges from multiple regulatory requirements which might have limited the utility of learning pods.[965] Louisiana allowed public school boards to establish learning pods for offering small group instruction for students.[966] New Hampshire enabled boards to develop plans for waiving rules to establish innovation

---

[958] 2021 W. Va. Acts Ch. 98, H.B. 2012.
[959] 2021 Ariz. Sess. Laws Ch. 404, HB 2898, Sec. 26.
[960] 2021 Okla. Sess. Laws S.B. No. 783.
[961] 2021 Tenn. Pub. Acts Ch. No. 479, S.B. No. 788, H.B. No. 1305.
[962] 2021 Tex. Gen. Laws S.B. No. 481.
[963] 2021 W. Va. Acts Ch. 95, S.B. 375.
[964] 2021 Wis. Laws Act 18, S.B. 109.
[965] 2021 Ga. Laws Act 246, SB 246.
[966] 2021 La. Acts No. 400, H.B. 421.

schools.⁹⁶⁷ South Carolina re-designated schools of choice as being of innovation, providing a means of exempting them from state statutes, regulations, and policies to enhance academic achievement for their students.⁹⁶⁸ Texas exempted learning pods from ordinances, rules, regulations, policies, and-or guidelines adopted by local governmental entities applied to school board campuses or child-care facilities, including standards regulating staff-to-child ratios, staff certification, background checks, physical accommodations, and-or building or fire codes.⁹⁶⁹

Three states provided tax benefits for donations to pay private school tuition. Louisiana excluded amounts deposited into education savings accounts for tuition expenses for elementary and secondary schools from the state income tax.⁹⁷⁰ Missouri created an empowerment scholarship accounts program which appears to be based on tax benefits provided for private entities making donations to it.⁹⁷¹ Montana revised its tax credit scholarship program, which provides tax credits for donations to its innovative education program fund while extending its statutory termination date from 2023 to 2029.⁹⁷²

Other 2021 school choice-related legislation is described as follows. Arkansas amended its public school choice act to specify that transfer requests to choice schools may be made no earlier than January 1 of the academic year before the ones in which students intend to transfer.⁹⁷³ Indiana permitted school corporations to enter or renew contracts with vendors to operate virtual education schools if they first submit the contract to its state DOE.⁹⁷⁴ Louisiana developed an appeals process for denials of participation in the public school choice program.⁹⁷⁵ New Hampshire added approved private schools along with public schools or academies to the types of schools to which superintendents may change students' placements due to manifest educational hardship.⁹⁷⁶ Wisconsin dictated that when its department of public instruction waives some requirements for students to participate in its parental choice

---

[967] 2021 N.H. Laws Ch. 27, HB 609.
[968] 2021 S.C. Act No. 20, H. 3589.
[969] 2021 Tex. Gen. Laws S.B. No. 1955.
[970] 2021 La. Acts No. 52, S.B. 5.
[971] 2021 Mo. Laws HB 349.
[972] 2021 Mont. Laws Ch. 480, HB 279.
[973] 2021 Ark. Acts 490, SB 147.
[974] 2021 Ind. Acts Pub. Law 216; H.B. No. 1549.
[975] 2021 La. Acts No. 420, H.B. 211.
[976] 2021 N.H. Laws Ch. 84, HB 388.

program, officials must specify the school year or years to which the waivers apply.[977] South Dakota amended its compulsory school attendance law to provide parental choice through a procedure for them to receive an acknowledgment that their children are receiving alternative educations.[978]

School Safety

School safety remained one of the most active education-related areas of legislative activity in the 2021 calendar year. The public health crisis caused by the COVID-19 pandemic was certainly a safety concern of legislative bodies but did not necessarily translate into the adoption of significant measures to protect student health from this disease, as only eight states passed laws. Alabama prohibited vaccine mandates unless required by the federal government, created an exemption for vaccinations for medical and religious reasons, and imposed parental consent for minors to receive COVID-19 vaccines.[979] A companion bill in Alabama called for the submission of a form requesting exemptions for medical or religious reasons.[980] Arkansas banned vaccine or immunization mandates for COVID-19.[981] Hawai'i directed its DOE to publish a weekly report on schools reporting positive COVID-19 cases.[982]

In the first of two laws, Idaho clarified that school boards, in consultation with local health departments, can close schools or programs or limit their activities to stop the spread of infectious diseases.[983] Idaho then ratified both virtual and in-person instruction as a means of providing educational services but placed a priority on in-person instruction when possible during emergencies.[984] North Carolina adopted plans for minimal social distancing or six-feet social distancing during in-person learning for K-12 students.[985] Oklahoma obligated its state DOE to ensure that local boards maintain current information about immunization requirements for attendance and enrollment on their websites.[986]

---

[977] 2021 Wis. Laws Act 56, S.B. 302.
[978] 2021 S.D. Laws SB 177.
[979] 2021 Ala. Acts No. 2021-560, SB 15.
[980] 2021 Ala. Acts No. 2021-561, SB 9.
[981] 2021 Ark. Acts 977, HB 1547.
[982] 2021 Haw. Sess. Laws Act 4, SB 811, Special Session 7/6/2021.
[983] 2021 Idaho Sess. Laws Ch. 14, H. 67.
[984] 2021 Idaho Sess. Laws Ch. 201, H. 175.
[985] 2021 N.C. Sess. Laws Ch. 4, S. 220.
[986] 2021 Okla. Sess. Laws S.B. No. 658.

However, Oklahoma prohibited boards from requiring vaccinations against COVID-19 or vaccines passport while banning them from independently issuing mask mandates absent emergency orders from the governor, in consultation with the local health departments, and continuing review of the standards for doing so at each of their subsequent meetings.[987]

Tennessee declared that for any communication from school, nursery schools, preschool, child care facilities, or public institutions of higher education regarding immunization requirements to students and-or parents, the materials must include information about exemption.[988] Utah called on its department of health to support widespread testing of public-school students for COVID-19 to facilitate in-person instruction.[989]

Eight states addressed the management of medications in the schools. Alabama permitted the administration of medication by school personnel to students with seizure disorders.[990] Arkansas allowed students to self-administer stress dose medication for adrenal insufficiency or adrenal crisis.[991] Colorado made it mandatory, rather than permissive, for school boards to adopt policies enabling students to possess and administer medical marijuana in a non-smokeable form based on prescriptions detailing dosing, timing, and delivery routes.[992] Illinois directed its state BOE, in consultation with its department of public health, to establish an anaphylactic policy for school boards.[993] New Jersey expanded authorization for persons or entities, including public and private schools, to obtain, distribute, and administer opioid antidotes.[994]

New York authorized trained unlicensed school personnel to administer prescribed glucagon or epinephrine auto-injectors in emergencies.[995] Rhode Island empowered public school students to possess and use FDA-regulated over-the-counter sunscreen without prescriptions or physicians' notes. Students in grades K-5 need notes from parents or guardians.[996] Virginia obligated local boards to adopt and implement policies for the possession and administration of

---

[987] 2021 Okla. Sess. Laws S.B. No. 658.
[988] 2021 Tenn. Pub. Acts Ch. No. 369, S.B. No. 1175, H.B. No. 1403.
[989] 2021 Utah Laws S.B. 107.
[990] 2021 Ala. Acts No. 2021-519, HB 76.
[991] 2021 Ark. Acts 1050, SB 569.
[992] 2021 Colo. Sess. Laws SB 56.
[993] 2021 Ill. Laws Pub. Act 102-0413, HB 102.
[994] 2021 N.J. Laws c. 152, S. 3491.
[995] 2021 N.Y. Laws Ch. 339, S. 1239.
[996] 2021 R.I. Pub. Laws S. 34, H. 5164.

undesignated stock albuterol inhalers and valved holding chambers in public schools to be administered by school nurses or other personnel trained in their administration and use.[997]

Seventeen states passed twenty-eight laws on student discipline including such topics as seclusion and restraint, anti-bullying, suspensions, and expulsions. Arizona set limits on suspensions or expulsions of students in grades K-4.[998] Arkansas required school employees to receive training in and adopt school-wide positive behavioral support programs while limiting the use of restraint or seclusion in behavior interventions; the law mandates the development of individualized behavior intervention plans for students.[999] Colorado amended provisions related to the prevention of bullying and harassment, calling for planning functions to include stakeholders in fashioning model anti-bullying policies and addressing cyber-bullying.[1000] Colorado also addressed disciplinary procedures for students in online instruction, including a provision that parents must be in a room separate from where their children attend online classes if the adults actively engage in behavior that disrupts children or class after the teacher asks them parent to discontinue their behavior.[1001]

Florida banned the use of seclusion of students, particularly as a disciplinary consequence, in addition to limiting the use of restraints, set personnel standards, and enabled the use of video cameras in specified classrooms.[1002] Idaho added possession of a deadly or dangerous weapon or firearm on school property as a cause for expulsion but granted boards discretion in deciding whether reasonable conditions apply and students' presence may not be detrimental to the health and safety of others.[1003] In the first of a pair of laws, Illinois directed its state BOE to adopt rules on the use of time out, isolation, and physical restraint in public schools as well as special education non-public facilities.[1004] Illinois amended provisions about bullying prevention, defining "restorative measures" as including alternatives to exclusionary discipline to increase student accountability if incidents are based on religion, race, ethnicity, or any other category identified in the state's human

---

[997] 2021 Va. Acts Ch. 508, H. 2019 (1st Spec. Sess.).
[998] 2021 Ariz. Sess. Laws Ch. 373, HB 2123.
[999] 2021 Ark. Acts 1084, HB 1610.
[1000] 2021 Colo. Sess. Laws HB 1221.
[1001] 2021 Colo. Sess. Laws HB 1059.
[1002] 2021 Fla. Laws ch. 140, H. 149.
[1003] 2021 Idaho Sess. Laws Ch. 182, S. 1116.
[1004] 2021 Ill. Laws Pub. Act 102-0339, HB 219.

rights act; the law provided additional funds for counselors to support mediation as a restorative measure.[1005]

Louisiana obligated public school officials to endeavor to address student behavior with a focus on evidence-based interventions and supports and to prioritize classroom and school-based interventions in lieu of out-of-school disciplinary removals.[1006] In the first of a trilogy of laws, Maine restricted the use of seclusion in public and private schools, highlighting physical, mechanical, and chemical restraints, the use of physical prompts or escorting the student, the use of seclusion, and required a report of annual data on the use of seclusion and restraint.[1007] Maine banned boards from authorizing school principals to issue out-of-school suspension of students enrolled in grades five or below with limited exceptions including imminent danger of serious physical injury to the pupils themselves or others and less restrictive interventions would be ineffective.[1008] Maine stipulated that a district-wide disciplinary policies must address whether expulsion procedures are in line with state standards, allowing boards to grant superintendent the authority to impose alternative consequences to expulsions on case-by-case bases.[1009]

Montana amended a provision for expulsion of students who bring firearms, extending it to those who have possessed one at school while affording administrators discretion in impose another consequence besides expulsion.[1010] Nebraska ordered its state BOE to implement a statewide system by August 1, 2022 to track individual student discipline, using an identifier of the department that can be aggregated to track incidents by type and demographic characteristic while provides data about disciplinary consequences.[1011]

Nevada, in the first of three laws, required its state DOE to obtain data on public schools to reduce the frequency of suspensions, expulsions, or removals of pupils from school in its statewide accountability system along with develop plans of action based on restorative justice.[1012] Nevada made hearings or proceedings about disciplinary exclusions for students who commit battery, distribute

---

[1005] 2021 Ill. Laws Pub. Act 102-0241, SB 673.
[1006] 2021 La. Acts No. 473, H.B. 411.
[1007] 2021 Me. Laws Ch. 453, H.P. 1007, L.D. 1373.
[1008] 2021 Me. Laws Ch. 295, H.P. 348, L.D. 474.
[1009] 2021 Me. Laws Ch. 320, H.P. 1067, L.D. 1451.
[1010] 2021 Mont. Laws Ch. 303, SB 283.
[1011] 2021 Neb. Laws LB 154.
[1012] 2021 Nev. Stat. Ch. 530, SB 354.

controlled substances, or possess firearm or dangerous weapons at schools not subject to provisions of its open meetings law.[1013] Nevada revised its procedures about student suspensions or expulsions, calling for annual accountability reports to include information related to the application of restorative justice.[1014] New Jersey dictated that boards report discipline data on their websites and to its commissioner of education.[1015] At the same time, New Jersey obligated public and private high schools and middle schools to adopt anti-hazing policies.[1016]

North Dakota amended provisions related to seclusion and restraint of persons with disabilities in institutions, facilities, or individualized settings from public or private agencies or organizations, banning the use of shock treatment.[1017] Oregon informed school officials to notify the parents or guardians of students who were harassed, intimidated, or bullied in person or online; the act also directs officials to notify the parents or guardians of students who may have conducted the acts at issue.[1018] Oregon then adopted an early childhood suspension and expulsion prevention program to reduce the use of exclusions in early childhood care and education programs while reducing disparities in exclusions of students based on race, ethnicity, language, ability, or any other protected class identified by its early learning council.[1019] Oregon, in a third law, applied preexisting applicability of education policies related to teen dating violence, domestic violence, and sexual harassment to private schools.[1020]

The first of these laws from Tennessee allowed local boards to remove students from regular programs without assigning them to alternative schools or programs if they were suspended or expelled for offenses that may threaten the safety of themselves or others.[1021] Tennessee amended provisions on the use of seclusion and restraint for students receiving special education services, specifying that behavior intervention training, the use of restraints for medical immobilization, adaptive support, or medical protection, or a seat belt or other belting system to secure a child with a disability during

---

[1013] 2021 Nev. Stat. Ch. 384, AB 67.
[1014] 2021 Nev. Stat. Ch. 196, AB 194.
[1015] 2021 N.J. Laws c. 387, S. 1020.
[1016] 2021 N.J. Laws c. 208, S. 84.
[1017] 2021 N.D. Laws H.B. No. 1089.
[1018] 2021 Or. Laws Ch. 232, HB 2631.
[1019] 2021 Or. Laws Ch. 518, HB 2166.
[1020] 2021 Or. Laws Ch. 479, SB 197.
[1021] 2021 Tenn. Pub. Acts Ch. No. 229, H.B. No. 890, S.B. No. 1223.

transit are not prohibited.[1022] Tennessee established rules and procedures for teachers to discipline students in their classrooms, including relocating them.[1023] Texas added minimum standards to be adopted for board policies on bullying.[1024] Vermont created a task force on equitable and inclusive school environments to make recommendations to end suspensions and expulsions for all but the most serious misbehaviors while compiling data on discipline in public and approved independent schools.[1025]

Two states added provisions for immunity if school personnel must assert control over students. Tennessee conferred immunity from civil liability for teachers, principals, school employees, or school bus drivers using reasonable force in exercising their lawful authority to control students unless their actions are grossly negligent, reckless, or intentional misconduct.[1026] Texas granted immunity to school district peace officers, school marshals, SROs, and retired peace officers hired by boards or charter schools officials for damages resulting from their reasonable actions to maintain school safety.[1027]

Because student suicide continues to be a serious concern, eight states adopted eleven laws on point. Arizona required officials in public and charter schools to post signs displaying the telephone number for a hotline for reporting suspected abuse and neglect of children, instructions to call 911 in emergencies, and directions for accessing the website for the department of child safety.[1028] Illinois obligated officials in schools serving pupils in grades 6-12 that issue identifications card to them to include information about the National Suicide Prevention Lifeline, the Crisis Text Line, and either the Safe2Help Illinois helpline or a local suicide hotline or both on the cards.[1029] Illinois added to a provision for youth suicide awareness and prevention by listing characteristics of students at an increased risk of suicide.[1030] Finally, Illinois directed local boards to provide contact information on the National Suicide Prevention

---

[1022] 2021 Tenn. Pub. Acts Ch. No. 134, S.B. No. 738, H.B. No. 770.
[1023] 2021 Tenn. Pub. Acts Ch. No. 77, H.B. No. 16, S.B. No. 230.
[1024] 2021 Tex. Gen. Laws S.B. No. 2050.
[1025] 2021 Vt. Laws Act 35, S. 16.
[1026] 2021 Tenn. Pub. Acts Ch. No. 188, H.B. No. 1096, S.B. No. 109.
[1027] 2021 Tex. Gen. Laws H.B. No. 1788.
[1028] 2021 Ariz. Sess. Laws Ch. 123, SB 1114.
[1029] 2021 Ill. Laws Pub. Act 102-0416, HB 1778.
[1030] 2021 Ill. Laws Pub. Act 102-0267, HB 577.

Hotline and the Crisis Text Line on the back of school-issued student identification (ID) cards.[1031]

New Jersey ordered officials in public schools serving students in grades 7-12 that issue ID cards to include telephone numbers for its suicide prevention hotline (NJ Hopeline), an on-campus crisis center, or other mental health support services.[1032] Oklahoma mandated the biennial administration of mental health prevention surveys for public school students in grades 6, 8, 10, and 12 managed by its department of mental health and substance abuse services.[1033] Oklahoma required, rather than allowed, boards to adopt policies on suicide awareness training.[1034] Rhode Island called for the training of teachers, students, and school personnel on suicide awareness and prevention as well as adopting a conflict resolution processes between teachers, students, and school personnel.[1035]

Texas required that ID cards issued to students in grade 6 or higher in public schools must contain the contact information for the national suicide prevention lifeline and the crisis text line along with contact information for a local suicide prevention hotline.[1036] Utah amended its suicide prevention provisions, creating separate elements for elementary and secondary grades.[1037] Washington directed officials in public schools with websites to post on them the contact information for suicide prevention organizations and resources for adolescents about depression, anxiety, counseling, eating disorders, substance abuse, and mental health.[1038]

Four states added provisions about potable water. Arkansas called on newly constructed and renovated public schools to provide for water bottle filling stations.[1039] Louisiana dictated that newly-constructed public school buildings and those undergoing major plumbing renovations must be equipped with water bottle filling stations.[1040] Rhode Island declared that all new school buildings and those undergoing major renovations or substantial repairs or replacements to their plumbing systems must install water bottle

---

[1031] 2021 Ill. Laws Pub. Act 102-00134, HB 597.
[1032] 2021 N.J. Laws c. 261, S. 550.
[1033] 2021 Okla. Sess. Laws H.B. No. 1103.
[1034] 20212 Okla. Sess. Laws S.B. No. 21.
[1035] 2021 R.I. Pub. Laws S. 31, H. 5353.
[1036] 2021 Tex. Gen. Laws S.B. No. 279.
[1037] 2021 Utah Laws H.B. 93.
[1038] 2021 Wash. Laws Ch. 167, H.B. 1373.
[1039] 2021 Ark. Acts 775, SB 532.
[1040] 2021 La. Acts No. 363, H.B. 132.

filling stations.[1041] New York set minimum quality standards for potable water in school buildings, permitted building aid for remediation measures.[1042]

Arkansas adopted four acts and Wisconsin added one about coordination between school and law enforcement coordination. Arkansas permitted school superintendents to inform SROs of the suspensions of teachers or recommendations for termination their dismissals.[1043] Next, Arkansas informed school boards and local law enforcement agencies of their duties to enter into memoranda of understanding governing the work of SROs, adding that they receive specialized training.[1044] Arkansas amended its 2015 School Safety Act, directing boards and officials in open-enrollment charter schools to conduct comprehensive school safety audits every three years to assess the safety, security, accessibility, and emergency preparedness of their buildings and grounds in collaboration with local law enforcement, fire, and emergency management authorities, and to create an advisory board for the Arkansas Center for School Safety of the Criminal Justice Institute.[1045] Arkansas next allowed private schools to appoint institutional law enforcement officers.[1046] Wisconsin expanded a provision that public and private schools provide law enforcement officials with blueprints for security purposes to create grant programs to permit them to give law enforcement officials critical incident mapping data.[1047]

Two states enacted bills about specialized training for SROs. Connecticut added a training requirement for SROs in social-emotional learning and restorative practices.[1048] Maine called for training for SROs in diversity, equity, and inclusion.[1049]

Four, states passed five bills on firearms in schools. Montana enacted a school marshal program that allows persons with concealed carry weapons permits which meet the requirements for peace officers or are active or retired peace officers to be hired as independent contractors or as employees of boards to protect the health and safety of persons and to maintain order on public school

---

[1041] 2021 R.I. Pub. Laws S. 459, H. 5738.
[1042] 2021 N.Y. Laws Ch. 771, Approval Memo 126, S. 2122A.
[1043] 2021 Ark. Acts 964, HB 1591.
[1044] 2021 Ark. Acts 622, HB 1510; 2021 Ark. Acts 551, SB 407.
[1045] 2021 Ark. Acts 620, HB 1549.
[1046] 2021 Ark. Acts 535, SB 159.
[1047] 2021 Wis. Laws Act 109, S.B. 449.
[1048] 2021 Conn. Acts 21-95 (Reg. Sess.), SB 6621.
[1049] 2021 Me. Laws Ch. 156, S.P. 330, L.D. 1040.

property.¹⁰⁵⁰ Rhode Island banned the possession of firearms on school grounds except by peace officers, retired law enforcement officers, persons under contract to provide security services, and unloaded firearms in locked containers or locked racks on motor vehicles.¹⁰⁵¹ Texas first permitted school marshals appointed by boards to carry concealed handguns on their person and in the schools.¹⁰⁵² Texas clarified that its definition of SROs does not include peace officers providing law enforcement in public school or at their event only for extracurricular activities.¹⁰⁵³ Virginia empowered boards to declare building or property that they own or lease, where their employees are regularly present as gun-free zones.¹⁰⁵⁴

Six states added provisions about performing safety drills. Arkansas transferred the duty to conduct tornado safety drills from its division of emergency management to its division of elementary and secondary education, adding that officials must conduct earthquake safety drills in designated areas of the state.¹⁰⁵⁵ California directed its state DOE to post information on its website about COVID-19 safety in school settings.¹⁰⁵⁶ Illinois maintained that before law enforcement school safety drills can be conducted, officials must notify parents or guardians at least five days before doing so and that the drills may not include simulations that mimic actual school shooting incidents. Additionally, active shooter events must be announced to school communities before their commencements, include age and developmentally appropriate content, involve school personnel including mental health professionals, and include trauma informed approaches addressing the concerns and well-being of students and employees.¹⁰⁵⁷

New Jersey called for age-appropriate communications with students and parents in announcing the initiation of school security drills before and after the drills.¹⁰⁵⁸ Texas directed its commissioner of education, in consultation with its school safety center and state fire marshal, Texas directed its commissioner of education to adopt rules for best practices for emergency school drills and exercises. The

---

¹⁰⁵⁰ 2021 Mont. Laws Ch. 541, HB 572.
¹⁰⁵¹ 2021 R.I. Pub. Laws S. 73, H. 5555.
¹⁰⁵² 2021 Tex. Gen. Laws S.B. No. 741.
¹⁰⁵³ 2021 Tex. Gen. Laws S.B. No. 1191.
¹⁰⁵⁴ 2021 Va. Acts Ch. 439, H. 1909 (1ˢᵗ Spec. Sess.).
¹⁰⁵⁵ 2021 Ark. Acts 422, SB 249.
¹⁰⁵⁶ 2021 Cal. Stat. Ch. 123, AB 856.
¹⁰⁵⁷ 2021 Ill. Laws Pub. Act 102-0395, HB 2400.
¹⁰⁵⁸ 2021 N.J. Laws c. 365, A. 5727.

act requires that before boards conduct active threat exercises, including active shooter situations, they must provide adequate notice to students and communities while announcing to students and staff before initiating exercises.[1059] Virginia reduced the number of mandatory annual lock-down safety drills in public elementary and elementary schools from three to two drills.[1060]

Seven states adopted laws on other types of safety planning. Arkansas amended its 2015 School Safety Act to establish a center for school safety with its criminal justice institute advisory board.[1061] Colorado mandated the creation of individualized seizure action plans for children at risk of seizure disorders to provide a safer environment for K-12 students diagnosed with such conditions.[1062] Connecticut obligated officials in public and private schools to develop and implement emergency action plans for responding to serious and life-threatening sports-related injuries that occur during interscholastic and intramural athletic events.[1063] Maine required school emergency management plans to include health and safety, adding school nurses, physicians, and public health staff to the list of professionals who should be involved in formulating comprehensive plans.[1064]

Nevada changed the name of the bodies of school boards or charter schools charged with developing plans for responding to crises, emergencies, or suicides, naming them emergency operations plan development committee.[1065] New Hampshire obligated boards, along with officials in chartered public school and nonpublic schools to establish emergency action plans to respond to co-curricular related injuries and emergencies includes the locations of equipment and supplies such as automated external defibrillators.[1066] Oklahoma amended a provision on emergency medical services at athletic practices, broadened its content to address emergency action plans for facilities, athletic practices, events, or activities conducted at board-owned facilities.[1067]

Four states passed legislation on mental health needs. California directed its state DOE to develop model referral protocols

---

[1059] 2021 Tex. Gen. Laws H.B. No. 168.
[1060] 2021 Va. Acts Ch. 26, H. 1998 (1st Spec. Sess.).
[1061] 2021 Ark. Acts 648, SB 394.
[1062] 2021 Colo. Sess. Laws HB 1133.
[1063] 2021 Conn. Acts 21-92 (Reg. Sess.), HB 6534.
[1064] 2021 Me. Laws Ch. 464, H.P. 309, L.D. 429.
[1065] 2021 Nev. Stat. Ch. 146, SB 36.
[1066] 2021 N. H. Laws Ch. 210, SB 148.
[1067] 2021 Okla. Sess. Laws H.B. No. 1801.

for addressing pupil mental health concerns.[1068] As a result of the COVID-19 pandemic, Nebraska initiated a school safety and security reporting system to obtain data on the concerning behavior of students, including suicide; bullying; stalking; cyber or electronic harassment; bomb threats; family violence; physical or sexual abuse; threats to property; behavior indicative of terrorism; assaults or attacks; inappropriate weapons use; concern about mental health associated with substance abuse; sexual exploitation or predation; and, direct or indirect threatening statements.[1069] Nevada decreed that the school district boards of trustees and the governing bodies of charter schools must ensure that information on mental health resources appears on the back of ID cards issued to students.[1070] Utah created an education and mental health coordinating council to study and make recommendations about behavioral health support for youth and families in the state.[1071]

Six states adopted laws about criminal background checks. Colorado amended a provision imposing criminal background checks for public school employees to include charter schools, adding that they must seek information about whether individuals were subject to allegations of sexual acts involving students eighteen years of age or older, regardless of whether they consented to the acts.[1072] Florida directed its state DOE to maintain a list of individuals whose employment was terminated in public and private schools and so disqualified from working in educational activities.[1073] Indiana ordered school corporations to conduct criminal background checks for bus drivers, even those hired by corporations with which they enter agreements to transport students.[1074]

Maryland permitted the emergency hiring of employees by county school boards or nonpublic schools for sixty days, pending reviews of their employment history if they will have direct contact with minors.[1075] New Hampshire added a superintendent's designee to those persons charged with the duty to be trained and to perform the interpretation of criminal background checks.[1076] Tennessee modified its criminal background check law to cover employees who

---

[1068] 2021 Cal. Stat. Ch. 662, AB 309.
[1069] 2021 Neb. Laws LB 322.
[1070] 2021 Nev. Stat. Ch. 495, SB 249.
[1071] 2021 Utah Laws H.B. 288.
[1072] 2021 Colo. Sess. Laws SB 17.
[1073] 2021 Fla. Laws ch. 138, H. 131.
[1074] 2021 Ind. Acts Pub. Law 216 §§ 18-19; H. B. No. 1549.
[1075] 2021 Md. Laws Ch. 192, HB 373.
[1076] 2021 N.H. Laws Ch. 71, HB 401.

may come in direct contact with students if their criminal history records check indicate that they were convicted of misdemeanor offenses that occurred more than ten years preceding the dates they applied and did not involve minors.[1077]

Five states adopted laws about the development of inappropriate relationships between school personnel and students. Illinois directed local school boards to include definitions of prohibited grooming behaviors and boundary violations for school personnel in their policies and how to report such behaviors, along with mandating training on specified child sexual abuse and grooming behaviors no later than January 31 of each year.[1078] Maine amended its ban against teachers, employees, and other officials from engaging in sexual activity with students, including substitutes with instructional, supervisory, and-or disciplinary authority over pupils at any time during the twelve months before the sexual acts.[1079]

Tennessee enabled school child abuse coordinators, teachers, officials, and other personnel to provide information about suspected or actual child abuse to parents when federal laws or regulations require them to do so.[1080] Texas amended its law prohibiting improper relationships between educators and students to include public and private schools along with proscribing the persons or entities operating them from releasing to the public the names of employees who allegedly committed such offenses until they are indicted on the charges; this does not inhibit communications related to investigating or communications as mandatory reporters of child abuse.[1081] New Hampshire added human trafficking to the offenses that render individuals ineligible from working for school administrative units, boards, chartered public schools, or public academies.[1082]

Four states adopted six laws on internet safety. Indiana directed school corporations and officials in charter schools to adopt and implement internet use policies banning the sending, receiving, viewing, or downloading materials harmful to minors on computers or other school owned devices; policies must address the use of filters and appropriate disciplinary measures against violators.[1083]

[1077] 2021 Tenn. Pub. Acts Ch. No. 417, H.B. No. 1131, S.B. No.1424.
[1078] 2021 Ill. Laws Pub. Act 0610, HB 3461.
[1079] 2021 Me. Laws Ch. 360, S.P. 549, L.D. 1715.
[1080] 2021 Tenn. Pub. Acts Ch. No. 161, S.B. No. 124, H.B. No. 475.
[1081] 2021 Tex. Gen. Laws H.B. No. 246.
[1082] 2021 N.H. Laws Ch. 142, HB432.
[1083] 2021 Ind. Acts Pub. Law 164 § 2; Sen. Enr. Act No. 414 § 2.

Minnesota prohibited children in publicly funded preschool or kindergarten programs from working on individual-use screens such as tablets, smartphones, or other digital media without engagement from teachers or peers; this provision does not apply to children with IEPs or Section 504 plans in effect.[1084] Minnesota directed its commissioner of education to award a grant to Live More Screen Less, an organization that collaborates with communities to promote digital well-being.[1085]

Texas ordered its state education agency and department of information resources to establish and maintain a system to coordinate the anonymous sharing of information about cyberattacks or other cybersecurity incidents against public or charter schools based on information reported by their officials.[1086] Texas obligated its state education agency, in consultation with its commission for health and human services, to develop and distribute model health and safety guidelines for local boards and charter schools to devise best practices for the effective integration of digital devices in their schools.[1087] Utah mandated that the digital resources provided by its educational television network to the public schools must block obscene or pornographic material.[1088]

Six states addressed policies on seizure management. Minnesota informed school boards and charter school officials that after they notify parents or guardians of students whose children are diagnosed with seizure disorders and take medication when they develop individualized plans for them.[1089] Nebraska adopted a seizure safe schools act obligating officials in public, private, denominational, and-or parochial schools to develop action plans for addressing the needs of students who suffer seizures.[1090] Oklahoma, too, adopted a seizure safe schools act calling for training in seizure management and addressing the administration of medication for seizures.[1091] Pennsylvania obligated training in seizure recognition and related first aid training for school staff.[1092] Virginia extended immunity for persons providing emergency care, now including school personnel rendering care in accordance with seizure

---

[1084] 2021 Minn. Laws Ch. 13, H.F. no. 2 (1st Spec. Sess.).
[1085] 2021 Minn. Laws Ch. 13, H.F. no. 2 (1st Spec. Sess.).
[1086] 2021 Tex. Gen. Laws S.B. No. 1696.
[1087] 2021 Tex. Gen. Laws H.B. No. 3489.
[1088] 2021 Utah Laws H.B. 38.
[1089] 2021 Minn. Laws Ch. 13, H.F. no. 2 (1st Spec. Sess.).
[1090] 2021 Neb. Laws LB 639.
[1091] 2021 Okla. Sess. Laws S.B. No. 128.
[1092] 2021 Pa. Laws Act No. 84, HB 416.

management and action plans.[1093] Washington directed board to adopt and periodically revise policies for assisting students with epilepsy or other seizure disorders including the storage and administration of medication.[1094]

As the first of two states approving laws on concussion management, Maine informed its commissioner of education, in consultation with school principal groups to report annually to its standing committee on the incidence of concussions sustained by student-athletes.[1095] New Jersey declared that local boards must implement six-step return-to-competition processes for student-athletes who sustain concussions, noting that they may not return to competition prior to resuming to regular school activities.[1096]

In the first of three pieces of legislation defining school zones, Rhode Island exempted two plots on Douglas Avenue in Providence from an ordinance about permitting alcoholic beverages retail licenses within 200 feet of schools and churches.[1097] Rhode Island passed similar provisions exempting proximity requirements from alcohol sales in Barrington.[1098] and on Hartford Avenue in Providence.[1099]

Other school safety-related legislation occurring in the 2021 calendar year is described as follows. Alabama approved school speed zones on both public and private property.[1100] Arkansas amended the list of mandatory reporters in its Child Maltreatment Act[1101] to include full and part-time public and private school employees, coaches, volunteers, social workers, surgeons, and persons employed in institutions of higher education.[1102] Illinois called for disclosure by multiple entities, but especially public school boards and officials, on the use of coal tar-based sealants or high polycyclic aromatic hydrocarbon sealant products; the law further called on boards to consider the cost-benefits of using alternative sealing products.[1103]

[1093] 2021 Va. Acts Ch. 514, S. 1322 (1st Spec. Sess.).
[1094] 2021 Wash. Laws Ch. 29, H.B. 1085.
[1095] 2021 Me. Laws Ch. 12, H.P. 70, L.D. 104.
[1096] 2021 N.J. Laws c. 222, S. 225.
[1097] 20212 R.I. Pub. Laws H. 6397, S. 556.
[1098] 2021 R.I. Pub. Laws S. 969, H. 6421.
[1099] 2021 R.I. Pub. Laws H. 6422, S. 440.
[1100] 2021 Ala. Acts No. 2021-305, H.B. 280.
[1101] ARK. CODE §12–18-402(b).
[1102] 2021 Ark. Acts 556, HB 1100.
[1103] 2021 Ill. Laws Pub. Act 102-0242, SB 692.

Indiana directed its state DOE to provide informational material on its website to help teachers and other school employees to identify students who may have been impacted by traumas.[1104] Indiana next ordered that the list of symptoms of sudden cardiac arrest be added to the information sheets provided to parents whose children are participating in extracurricular activities.[1105] Maine obligated officials at educational institutions conducting outdoor educational trips to provide at least one trip leader with a permit for such a position and is associated with it or a person with a state guide license for every twelve participants.[1106] In the first of a pair of laws, Maryland made it a criminal act to introduce ransomware on computers or computer networks at healthcare facilities or public schools without authorization to do so.[1107] Maryland prohibited the operation of electric retractable room partitions in public and nonpublic schools with limited exceptions.[1108] New Jersey authorized civil liability for parents of minors who are adjudicated delinquent for harassment or cyber-harassment.[1109]

Tennessee, in the first of three laws, made communicating threats to commit acts of mass violence on school property or at school activities a Class A misdemeanor and made knowingly failing to report such threats a Class B misdemeanor.[1110] Tennessee allowed local boards to develop "stop the bleed" programs, granting limited civil immunity to boards, schools, and their employees for personal injuries resulting from the use of items in the bleeding control list.[1111] Tennessee adopted standards for school youth athletic activities to improve safety by ordering coaches to receive training in concussion recognition, cardiopulmonary resuscitation training, sudden cardiac arrest prevention, and anaphylaxis prevention.[1112] Texas obligated its state education agency to give all school boards and open-enrollment charter schools inkless, in home fingerprint and DNA identification kits to be distributed to the parents or guardians of students in grades K-8 who request them.[1113] Washington directed boards to collect information about school

---

[1104] 2021 Ind. Acts Pub. Law 216 § 9; H. B. No. 1549.
[1105] 2021 Ind. Acts Pub. Law 56, H.B. 1040.
[1106] 2021 Me. Laws Ch. 162, H.P. 1089, L.D. 1474.
[1107] 2021 Md. Laws Ch. 146, SB 623.
[1108] 2021 Md. Laws Ch. 434, HB 83.
[1109] 2021 N.J. Laws c. 338, S. 1790.
[1110] 2021 Tenn. Pub. Acts Ch. No. 395, H.B. No. 534, S.B. No. 627.
[1111] 2021 Tenn. Pub. Acts Ch. No. 389, H.B. No. 212, S.B. No. 634.
[1112] 2021 Tenn. Pub. Acts Ch. No. 272, S.B. No. 1259, H.B. No. 1410.
[1113] 2021 Tex. Gen. Laws S.B. No. 2158.

security personnel and security contractors working in their schools and report it to the office of its state superintendent to address the school-to-prison pipelines.[1114]

Students with Disabilities

This section details laws adopted in 2021 related to students with disabilities beginning with legislative intent to provide extended time for services for students with disabilities due to the COVID-19 pandemic. Delaware extended special education and related services to students with disabilities who turned twenty-one during the 2020-21 school year to address unfinished learning as a result of the pandemic.[1115] Illinois dictated that if students with IEPs reach the age of twenty-two during the time in which their in-person instruction, services, or activities are suspended for periods of three months or more during school years as a result of the COVID-19 pandemic, then they are eligible for services up to the end of the regular 2021-22 school year unless they are no longer residents of the districts providing programming.[1116] In a parallel bill, Illinois directed that students whose twenty-second birthdays occur during the school year maintain eligibility for services through the end of the current school year rather than until the day before their twenty-second birthdays.[1117]

Montana extended school funding for special education students over nineteen but not yet twenty-one who are likely to be eligible for adult services to provide them with transition services.[1118] New Jersey extended the age of eligibility for special education and related services during the 2023-24 school year for students with disabilities who reach twenty-one during the 2022-23 school year.[1119] New York permitted boards to provide educational services during the 2021-22 and 2022-23 school years to students who turned twenty-one during the 2019-20 and 2020-21 academic years and had IEPs; these students may continue to receive services until they become twenty-three.[1120] Pennsylvania allowed students with disabilities to continue to receive special education after the age of

---

[1114] 2021 Wash. Laws Ch. 38, H.B. 1214.
[1115] 2021 Del. Ch. 39, HB 128.
[1116] 2021 Ill. Laws Pub. Act 102-0173, HB 2748.
[1117] 2021 Ill. Laws Pub. Act 102-0172, HB 40.
[1118] 2021 Mont. Laws Ch. 406, HB 233.
[1119] 2021 N.J. Laws c. 109, S. 3434.
[1120] 2021 N.Y. Laws Ch. 167, A. 8021.

twenty-one enabling them to recover services they lost during the COVID-19 pandemic.[1121]

Five states added supplemental directions for those creating IEPs through seven laws. Illinois obligated school boards to provide copies of a guide titled "Understanding PUNS: A Guide to Prioritization for Urgency of Need for Services" to parents or guardians at annual IEP review meetings.[1122] Maryland mandated that IEPs include learning continuity plans to be implemented for students with disabilities during emergency conditions beginning October 1, 2021.[1123] Minnesota obligated boards to schedule IEP meetings no later than December 1, 2021, to determine whether special education services and supports are necessary to address lack of progress on IEP goals or loss of learning or skills due to disruptions related to the COVID-19 pandemic.[1124]

Texas declared that behavior intervention plans included in students' IEP must be reviewed at least once per year and more frequently to address changes in their circumstances or their safety or that of others; the law additionally called for written notice to parent for each use of restraint on their children giving them specific details about incident. The act further ordered that when boards take disciplinary actions constituting changes in placement for students with IEPs, not later than the tenth school day after making the change, officials must seek parental consent to conduct functional behavior assessments and develop or revise behavior intervention plans.[1125] Texas called for the development of supplement to IEPs to address compensatory education beginning during the 2019-20 and 2020-21 school years as a result of the COVID-19 pandemic.[1126]

In the first of a pair of changes, Virginia called on the commonwealth's BOE to develop a mandatory training module for participants in IEP meetings.[1127] Virginia then required its BOE to amend its regulations governing the review and approval of IEPs to assure that team members understand their duties and roles while updating special education eligibility worksheets.[1128]

[1121] 20212 Pa. Laws Act No. 66, SB 664.
[1122] 2021 Ill. Laws Pub. Act 102-0057, HB 290.
[1123] 2021 Md. Laws Ch. 214, HB 714.
[1124] 2021 Minn. Laws Ch. 13, H.F. no. 2 (1st Spec. Sess.).
[1125] 2021 Tex. Gen. Laws H.B. No. 785.
[1126] 2021 Tex. Gen. Laws S.B. No. 89.
[1127] 2021 Va. Acts Ch. 451, H. 2299; Ch. 452, S. 1288 (1st Spec. Sess.).
[1128] 2021 Va. Acts Ch. 173, H. 2316 (1st Spec. Sess.).

Four states enacted five laws on private residential placements. Illinois declared that before children can be placed in out-of-state special education residential facilities, the agencies, boards, or courts initiating the moves must afford students' parents or guardians the option to place them in comparable in-state facilities.[1129] New Jersey eliminated the obligation that its state DOE set tuition rates for approved private school placements for students with disabilities.[1130] Oregon expanded its definition of students in eligible residential treatment programs to include institutions providing disability-related supports under licenses issued by its department of human services; a residential program that continues and was under license by it when the law became effective in 2021; and a program that has students being provided by local boards that received money under the same funding sources and had average daily memberships of 15,000 or less.[1131]

Virginia directed the commonwealth's BOE to require private schools for students with disabilities licensed by it, as a condition for renewal of their initial licenses to operate, to obtain accreditation from an agency recognized by its council for private education within three years of the issuance of their initial triennial licenses.[1132] In a second law, Virginia limited the use of funds for private special education services to be spent on educational programs licensed by its BOE.[1133]

Five states addressed dyslexia. Arkansas created a network of certified academic language therapists to provide dyslexia instructional programs for public school students by authorizing funds to employ and organize such specialists.[1134] Indiana added a time limit of ninety days from the start of school years to the time when school corporations must conduct dyslexia screening for students deemed at risk for dyslexia.[1135] Louisiana directed local boards to report to its state DOE by the end of October each year on the number of students of all grade levels identified as dyslexic.[1136] Mississippi explained the steps school officials must take for the education and care of students with dyslexia and related

---

[1129] 2021 Ill. Laws Pub. Act 102-0254, HB 41.
[1130] 2021 N.J. Laws c. 487, A. 6207.
[1131] 2021 Or. Laws Ch. 304, HB 3254.
[1132] 2021 Va. Acts Ch. 172, H. 2238 (1st Spec. Sess.).
[1133] 2021 Va. Acts Ch. 70, H. 2117 (1st Spec. Sess.).
[1134] 2021 Ark. Acts 1016, HB 1891.
[1135] 2021 Ind. Acts Pub. Law 211, § 34, HB 1514.
[1136] 2021 La. Acts No. 419, H.B. 170.

disorders.[1137] Oklahoma called on its state DOE to develop and maintain a dyslexia handbook.[1138]

Two states added acts about brain injury. Maine established a task force to study the coordination of services and expansion of educational programs and vocational opportunities for young adults with intellectual or developmental disabilities or acquired brain injury.[1139] Virginia amended its definition of traumatic brain injury with respect to the identification and delivery of special education services for students; the definition referred to an acquired injury to the brain caused by external physical force or by other medical conditions, including stroke, anoxia, infectious disease, aneurysm, brain tumors, and neurological insults resulting from medical or surgical treatments, resulting in total or partial functional disability or psychosocial impairment, or both, that adversely affects a child's educational performance.[1140]

Two states changed procedural aspects of dispute resolution. Illinois staked out the position that complaints about delays and denials of special education services in Chicago during the 2016-2017 and 2017-2018 school years due to policies and procedures identified by its state BOE as unlawful must be filed on or before September 30, 2022.[1141] New Hampshire established a committee to study special education dispute resolution options and the burden of proof in due process hearings conducted by its state DOE.[1142]

Other acts related to students with disabilities adopted in 2021 are discussed as follows. Alabama amended a provision providing tuition for students with disabilities who are children of military veterans with disabilities to include the Space Force in the list of armed forces, indicating that the definition of students with intellectual disabilities conforms with federal law.[1143] Arkansas created a committee to study compliance with the Americans with Disabilities Act in its public schools.[1144] California amended standards for speech-language pathologists to assess students' eligibility for special education, directing them to evaluate their difficulties in understanding or using language results from sound

---

[1137] 2021 Miss. Laws HB 754.
[1138] 2021 Okla. Sess. Laws H.B. No. 2223.
[1139] 2021 Me. Laws Ch. 116, H.P. 680, L.D. 924.
[1140] 2021 Va. Acts Ch. 170, H. 2182 (1st Spec. Sess.).
[1141] 2021 Ill. Laws Pub. Act 102-0429, HB 2425.
[1142] 2021 N.H. Laws Ch. 158, HB 581.
[1143] 2021 Ala. Acts No. 2021-444, H.B. 554. The federal definition of "students with disabilities" is codified at 20 U.S.C. § 1140.
[1144] 2021 Ark. Acts 987, HB 1863.

speech disorders, voice disorders, fluency disorders, language disorders, or hearing impairments or deafness.[1145] Colorado amended standards for special education child find responsibilities, differentiating between the duties of its department of human services and DOE, and to mandate interagency agreements between the departments about those duties.[1146] Delaware increased funding for K-3 students identified as eligible for basic special education services.[1147] Delaware next made home-schooled students eligible for the same services as children with disabilities who attend private schools in a manner that allows federal funds to pay for their educations.[1148] Georgia expanded the availability of its special needs scholarship for students on IEPs to cover those receiving accommodations or services under Section 504.[1149]

Illinois conferred power on its state superintendent of education to decide whether the locations of the parents or guardians of students with disabilities are unknown, based on evidence and affidavits provided by local superintendents.[1150] Louisiana called on public school boards to adopt policies to install video cameras in classrooms serving special education, but not for gifted, students.[1151] Maine established the Help Maine Grow System as a comprehensive, statewide, coordinated approach to early identification, referral, and follow-up for all children from prenatal care up to eight years of age and their families; the system stresses early screening, diagnosis, and treatment services through Medicaid, and by state department child-find efforts and early intervention services.[1152]

Maryland increased the state contribution to the cost of educating children with disabilities in nonpublic programs by four percent in fiscal year 2023.[1153] Nebraska amended a provision on transition services for students with developmental disability, initiating them by the age of fourteen rather than sixteen.[1154] New Hampshire designated $250,000 for communities of 1,000 or fewer

---

[1145] 2021 Cal. Stat. Ch. 666, AB 486, Sec. 99.
[1146] 2021 Colo. Sess. Laws SB 275.
[1147] 2021 Del. Laws Ch. 89, HB 86.
[1148] 2021 Del. Laws Ch. 87, SB 106.
[1149] 2021 Ga. Laws Act 243, SB 47.
[1150] 2021 Ill. Laws Pub. Act 102-0514, HB 3906.
[1151] 2021 La. Acts No. 456, S.B. 86.
[1152] 2021 Me. Laws Ch. 457, S.P. 533, L.D. 1712.
[1153] 2021 Md. Laws Ch. 700, HB 1365.
[1154] 2021 Neb. Laws LB 527.

residents to mitigate the impact of special education costs when emergency assistance is necessary to prevent significant financial harm to locales.[1155] New Hampshire placed the burden of proof for the appropriateness of special education placements on school boards or other public agencies.[1156] New Jersey mandated that websites and web services offered by local boards, charter schools, renaissance schools, and its school for the deaf must be accessible to persons with disabilities.[1157]

New Mexico created the office of the state special education ombud to investigate and resolve concerns while offering potential courses of actions for noncompliance.[1158] Oregon ordered parents of children who are deaf or deafblind or who are hard of hearing to be given information about relevant services and placements offered by their school boards, education service centers, regional programs, and state school for the deaf.[1159] Oregon called on local boards to provide students with disabilities and their parents with information about supported decision-making and strategies to remain engaged in the secondary education and post-school outcomes of their children.[1160]

Tennessee amended provisions on the use of seclusion and restraint for students on IEPs, services, noting that behavior intervention training, restraints for medical immobilization, adaptive support, medical protection, and the use of seat belts or other belting systems to secure these children during transit are not prohibited.[1161] Tennessee directed that the instructions provided to students identified for intervention through the response to instruction and intervention framework developed by its DOE must be set by their local education agencies based on their individual needs.[1162] Texas established a grant program to purchase $1,500 in supplemental services and materials for students receiving special education.[1163]

[1155] 2021 N. H. Laws Ch. 209, SB 147.
[1156] 2021 N.H. Laws Ch. 158, HB 581.
[1157] 2021 N.J. Laws c. 461, A. 4856.
[1158] 2021 N.M. Laws Ch. 53, HB 222.
[1159] 2021 Or. Laws Ch. 255, HB 3183.
[1160] 2021 Or. Laws Ch. 210, HB 2105.
[1161] 2021 Tenn. Pub. Acts Ch. No. 134, S.B. No. 738, H.B. No. 770.
[1162] 2021 Tenn. Pub. Acts Ch. No. 57, S.B. No. 235, H.B. No. 5.
[1163] 2021 Tex. Gen. Laws S.B. No. 1716.

Technology

This section includes technology-related bills passed in the 2021 calendar year. Five states adopted six acts supporting improvements in broadband and internet connectivity. Illinois required that school districts, rather than the state BOE, must ensure that the internet service in schools must comply with Level AA of web content accessibility guidelines.[1164] Nevada directed the boards of trustees for all school districts and its state public charter school authority to submit information to the office of science, innovation, and technology related to the extent to which students have access to the internet at home.[1165] New Mexico amended its statute for public school capital outlay to include expenditures for internet connectivity in rural areas.[1166]

Texas first obligated its state education agency to provide technical assistance for broadband technical support for students with limited or no access, and reimbursement funds for technology acquisitions.[1167] Texas next adopted a law aimed at expanding broadband services through a newly-created broadband development office in the comptroller's office; a grant program informs the development office to award grants with a priority to applications that will expand broadband service in public and private primary and secondary schools and institutions of higher education.[1168] Virginia permitted public bodies, such as school boards, to appropriate funds to promote, facilitate, and encourage the development, expansion, provision, and operation of broadband services for educational purposes.[1169]

Other technology-related bills enacted last year are described as follows. Montana ordered its legislative finance committee to study the state digital academy and report to the interim education committee by September 1, 2022.[1170] New Jersey created a pilot program in its state DOE to support robotics programs in school systems.[1171] Washington provided access to internet-accessible

---

[1164] 2021 Ill. Laws Pub. Act 102-0238, HB 26.
[1165] 2021 Nev. Stat. Ch. 193, SB 66.
[1166] 2021 N.M. Laws Ch. 49, SB 144.
[1167] 2021 Tex. Gen. Laws H.B. No. 1525.
[1168] 2021 Tex. Gen. Laws H.B. No. 5.
[1169] 2021 Va. Acts Ch. 496, S. 1225 (1st Spec. Sess.).
[1170] 2021 Mont. Laws Ch. 562, HB 671.
[1171] 2021 N.J. Laws c. 320, A. 2455.

learning devices for students, plus training and technical assistance on using them to support their learning.[1172]

Transportation

This section details transportation-related legislation adopted in the 2021 legislative year. Five states enacted six acts about passing stopped school buses. Arkansas amended state prohibitions against passing stopped school buses to include violations on public and private roads; on public or private property open to the general public; or on public or private roads, driveways, or parking lots belonging to public or private schools.[1173] Delaware created a pilot program in 2020 to allow one school board to place video cameras on the outside of school buses to catch drivers who pass stopped buses[1174] while adding a stipulation that drivers caught in this manner face civil, rather than criminal, penalties.[1175] Montana revised it promoted to promote vehicle operators approaching or passing school buses preparing to stop or that have stopped, particularly prohibiting the vehicle from passing a stopped school bus on the right and to ban drivers from actuating flashing red lights when the buses are stopped outside of roadways and children will not enter roadways, mandating the use of extended mechanical arms across roadways where students must cross.[1176] New York allowed part of the money derived from fines for illegally passing school buses to pass to its school bus driver safety program.[1177] Pennsylvania increased the consequences for failure to stop for school buses that have flashing red lights operating from three years to five years.[1178]

Three states authorized the use of alternative vehicles other than a regular school bus, in specified circumstances. Georgia enabled local school boards to transport students who receive special education or homeless services in vehicles with capacities of eight persons or less.[1179] Maryland added to a provision allowing county school boards to transport students in vehicles other than Type I or Type II vehicles, identifying the categories of students for which this

---

[1172] 2021 Wash. Laws Ch. 301, H.B. 1365.
[1173] 2021 Ark. Acts 264, HB 1265.
[1174] 21 Del. C. § 4101(d).
[1175] 2021 Del. Ch. 67, HB 120.
[1176] 2021 Mont. Laws Ch. 478, HB 267.
[1177] 2021 N.Y. Laws Ch. 536, S. 4661.
[1178] 2021 Pa. Laws Act No. 80, SB 859.
[1179] 2021 Ga. Laws 155, SB 159.

is allowable.[1180] Montana approved the use of eight to fifteen passenger vehicles for transporting students to and from school-sponsored functions or activities but not to or from schools on regular bus routes.[1181]

Two states revised their laws about lights on school buses. Montana permitted buses to have additional red flashing lights, which must be mounted thirty-six to seventy-two inches from the ground and actuated if vehicles are stopped.[1182] Texas allowed school bus operators to use flashing warning signal lights and other equipment on the vehicles to warn other drivers that their buses are stopped or being stopped to permit the distribution of food or technological equipment for student use.[1183]

Other transportation-related bills enacted in 2021 are detailed as follows. Arizona authorized school bus drivers to possess commercial driver licenses issued by other state if applicant will drive school buses for boards adjacent to that state.[1184] Colorado fostered greater cooperation for transportation for students in out-of-home placement between school boards county departments of human services by calling for consistent procedures and standardized forms along with invoices to bill for transportation services.[1185] Idaho increased the state's share of transportation costs due to emergencies.[1186] Louisiana permitted immediate family members of local school board member to be employed as certified school bus operators.[1187] Michigan replaced a state-level waiver process to now permit bus drivers with insulin-treated diabetes to work instead opting for the process described by federal regulations.[1188]

Nevada mandated that written notice must be submitted to superintendents of schools when bus need repairs inspection.[1189] New Hampshire permitted school boards to enter agreements with contract passenger carriers to transport students to and from school activities on vehicles designed to carry sixteen or more persons,

---

[1180] 2021 Md. Laws Ch. 197, HB 72; 2021 Md. Laws Ch. 198, SB 448.
[1181] 2021 Mont. Laws Ch. 292, HB 300.
[1182] 2021 Mont. Laws Ch. 246, HB 207.
[1183] 2021 Tex. Gen. Laws S.B. No. 445.
[1184] 2021 Ariz. Sess. Laws Ch. 100, HB 2159.
[1185] 2021 Colo. Sess. Laws SB 117.
[1186] 2021 Idaho Sess. Laws Ch. 248, H. 265.
[1187] 2021 La. Acts No. 199, H.B. 306.
[1188] 2021 Mich. Pub. Acts No. 131, H.B. 4861. The citation for the regulation is 49 C.F.R. 391.41-391.49.
[1189] 2021 Nev. Stat. Ch. 92, AB 417.

including drivers.[1190] New Jersey first created the office of school bus safety in its state DOE.[1191] New Jersey next increased the penalty for school boards or bus contractors who knowingly approve or assign unauthorized individuals as bus drivers from $5,000 to $15,000.[1192] New York allowed the use of signs, placards, or other displays to give notice that school buses use photo violation monitoring systems.[1193] North Dakota directed its superintendent of public instruction to reimburse local boards for the costs of school bus transportation, including for students in special as well as vocational and technical education plus those in open enrollment programs.[1194] Rhode Island banned school committees from contracting with bus services unless agreements provide for payments to school bus drivers, monitors, and aides for 180 days or the length of school years.[1195]

Tennessee raised the maximum period for contracts for school transportation services from four to six years.[1196] Texas allows local boards to establish and operate public school transportation outside their districts if the students reside outside the district; they have policies prohibiting the screening of transfer students based on performance, disciplinary history, or attendance records; and they have performance ratings of C or higher and accountability score of seventy or higher.[1197] Utah required local boards to establish written policies that school bus drivers must inspect the entire interior of vehicles at the end of every route.[1198] Washington permitted school board transportation programs to transition to creative ways of serving students during the COVID-19 pandemic, temporarily suspending the traditional rider eligibility criteria for funding.[1199] West Virginia authorized school boards to create bus operator training programs without offering guarantees of employment to participants.[1200]

[1190] 2021 N.H. Laws Ch. 209, SB 147.
[1191] 2021 N.J. Laws c. 471, A. 5814.
[1192] 2021 N.J. Laws c. 306, A. 5817.
[1193] 2021 N.Y. Laws Ch. 325, A. 6155.
[1194] 2021 N.D. Laws H.B. No. 1027.
[1195] 2021 R.I. Pub. Laws S. 635, H. 6118.
[1196] 2021 Tenn. Pub. Acts Ch. No. 146, S.B. No. 1116, H.B. No. 497.
[1197] 2021 Tex. Gen. Laws S.B. No. 204.
[1198] 2021 Utah Laws H.B. 369.
[1199] 2021 Wash. Laws Ch. 234, S.B. 5128.
[1200] 2021 W. Va. Acts Ch. 244, H.B. 2267.

Higher Education

Higher education-related legislation is perennially the category with the most acts, and that state of affairs persisted in 2021. This section categorizes and describes last year's legislation. Seventeen states, through thirty-three laws, changed the names of higher education institutions, altered their designations or missions, or modified the programs and degrees they offer. California extended the operation of its statewide baccalaureate degree pilot program indefinitely with its operation no longer limited to the fifteen original community college districts.[1201] Then California defined regionally accredited institutions of higher education as including community and junior colleges authorized to confer baccalaureate degrees and to specified schools with teacher preparation programs.[1202] Colorado removed the word junior from the name of multiple community colleges.[1203] Georgia permitted the state board of its technical college system to award high school diplomas.[1204]

Maryland directed officials at the medical school at the University of Maryland to provide clinical services at its Capital Regional Medical Center.[1205] Nevada designated the Universities of Nevada Las Vegas, Nevada Reno, and the Desert Research Institute as state land grant institutions.[1206] New Hampshire authorized Signum University to grant degrees subject to the approval of its higher education commission.[1207] New Jersey designated Kean as a public urban research university.[1208] New Mexico designated New Mexico State University-Carlsbad as a community college.[1209] New York established the State University of New York educational opportunity centers which provide an integrated system of education, vocational training, and student support services targeted to higher education access and the development of a quality workforce.[1210] Oklahoma renamed the University Center of Southern Oklahoma to Murray State College at Ardmore.[1211]

[1201] 2021 Cal. Stat. Ch. 565, AB 927.
[1202] 2012 Cal. Stat. Ch. 663, AB 320.
[1203] 2021 Colo. Sess. Laws SB 8.
[1204] 2021 Ga. Laws Act 253, SB 204.
[1205] 2021 Md. Laws Ch. 44, SB 433; 2021 Md. Laws Ch. 418, HB 173.
[1206] 2021 Nev. Stat. Ch. 413, SB 287.
[1207] 2021 N.H. Laws Ch. 159, HB 513.
[1208] 2021 N.J. Laws c. 282, S. 3811.
[1209] 2021 N.M. Laws Ch. 104, HB 212.
[1210] 2021 N.Y. Laws Ch. 13, S. 874.
[1211] 2021 Okla. Sess. Laws H.B. No. 2943.

Oregon approved an order from its higher education coordinating commission to transfer the northernmost portion of Lake County from the Central Oregon Community College Service District to the Klamath Community College Service District.[1212] South Carolina designated the Dean of the University of South Carolina Lancaster Campus as an *ex officio* member of the county commission for higher education in that locale while changing the range of courses it can offer from first and second-year classes to secondary courses.[1213] Tennessee authorized the colleges of medicine at the University of Tennessee and East Tennessee State to administer additional resident training opportunities.[1214] In addition, Tennessee added William R. Moore College of Technology as an eligible institution for receipt of dual enrollment grants.[1215]

Texas, in the first of a dozen changes, allowed a federal work college as defined by federal law[1216] to participate in a library resource-sharing consortium, thereby allowing Paul Quinn College to take part in it.[1217] Texas moved Midwestern State University to the Texas Tech University system.[1218] Texas re-established the regional campus at Laredo as a multi-institution center overseen by the University of Texas system.[1219] Texas created the Texas Woman's University system as a woman-focused university system under the Texas Woman's University and other institutions assigned by law to the governance of the new system; branch locations in Dallas and Houston were assigned to the new system.[1220] Texas removed references in the code to the University of Texas at Brownsville and Pan American, replacing them with references to the University of Texas Rio Grande Valley. At the same time, the act clarified and harmonized student fee structures which had been different at the two constituent universities.[1221]

Texas permitted the board of regents of its university system to offer joint graduate degree programs at the health science center at Houston and the Anderson cancer center.[1222]Texas transferred the

---

[1212] 2021 Or. Laws Ch. 52, HB 2089.
[1213] 2021 S.C. Act No. 110, H. 3740.
[1214] 2021 Tenn. Pub. Acts Ch. No. 587, S.B. No. 298, H.B. No. 443.
[1215] 2021 Tenn. Pub. Acts Ch. No. 392, H.B. No. 471, S.B. No. 1157.
[1216] 20 U.S.C. § 1087-58.
[1217] 2021 Tex. Gen. Laws H.B. No. 4202.
[1218] 2021 Tex. Gen. Laws H.B. No. 1522.
[1219] 2021 Tex. Gen. Laws S.B. No. 884.
[1220] 2021 Tex. Gen. Laws S.B. No. 1126.
[1221] 2021 Tex. Gen. Laws S.B. No. 1467.
[1222] 2021 Tex. Gen. Laws S.B. No. 1251.

administration of its rural veterinarian incentive program from Texas A&M University to its animal health commission; the incentive program provides funds for veterinarians in rural areas to reduce their student loan debt.[1223] Texas previously permitted a community college district with a taxable property valuation of at least $4 billion but lacked a four-year institution of higher education to offer a baccalaureate program; this act struck down the property valuation requirement for community college districts to offer baccalaureate programs in nursing.[1224]

Texas allowed community colleges to offer no more than five baccalaureate programs at a time; previously, the limit was three, with four specific community colleges enabled to offer up to five.[1225] Texas made the medical school at the University of Houston and the College of Osteopathic Medicine at Sam Houston State University eligible for the joint admissions medical program.[1226] Texas created a commission on community college finance to recommend state formula funding levels for public junior colleges; this charge included a focus on workforce development.[1227] Texas transferred control over its postsecondary education and career counseling academies from the Center for Teaching and Learning at UT-Austin to the higher education coordinating board.[1228] Texas directed its higher education coordinating board to study the feasibility of establishing a religious studies program offering bachelors, masters, and doctoral degrees at Texas Southern University.[1229]

In the first of three laws, Utah changed the name of Dixie State University to Utah Tech University.[1230] Utah authorized institutions of higher education to form nonprofit corporations or foundations related to technical education within their roles and missions.[1231] Utah obligated its state board of higher education to set five-year goals for its state system of education and degree-granting institutions and technical colleges aligned with each system.[1232] Washington enables community and technical colleges to offer

---

[1223] 2021 Tex. Gen. Laws H.B. No. 1259.
[1224] 2021 Tex. Gen. Laws H.B. No. 885.
[1225] 2021 Tex. Gen. Laws H.B. No. 3348.
[1226] 2021 Tex. Gen. Laws H.B. No. 1325.
[1227] 2021 Tex. Gen. Laws S.B. No. 1230.
[1228] 2021 Tex. Gen. Laws H.B. No. 2827.
[1229] 2021 Tex. Gen. Laws H.B. No. 981.
[1230] 2021 Utah Laws H.B. 2001 (2nd Spec. Sess.).
[1231] 2021 Utah Laws H.B. 318.
[1232] 2021 Utah Laws SB 193.

baccalaureate degrees in computer science.[1233] Wyoming created the Gillette community college district in Campbell County.[1234]

Through ten acts, five states revised matters about the governing boards of state institutions of higher education. Alabama permitted one of the members on the board of trustees for the University of Montevallo to be a nonresident, appointed at-large.[1235] Colorado deleted a requirement that the student member of the board of trustees at Western Colorado University must be a state resident.[1236] Missouri changed the representation of members of the board of governors of Southeast Missouri State University.[1237] Tennessee extended the legal authority for the boards of trustees for its public institutions of higher education as follows for the University of Memphis to June 30, 2027,[1238] Tennessee Technological University to June 30, 2025,[1239] East Tennessee State University to June 30, 2027,[1240] Middle Tennessee State University to June 30, 2027,[1241] and Austin Peay State University to June 30, 2027.[1242] Virginia directed officials at all of its public institutions of higher education to establish and maintain listings of all board members, including the name of the Governor who made the appointments, the dates of the appointments, and other information about members and board meeting schedules on their websites.[1243]

Three states adjusted geographic boundaries for the areas represented by governing board members. Nebraska set new district boundaries for members of the Board of Regents of the University of Nebraska.[1244] Nevada changed the districts from which the members of the board of regents for the University of Nevada are elected.[1245] Oregon established a time limit of ninety days from the first signature on petitions to their presentation to its higher education coordinating commission in its role as the entity that sets geographic boundaries for community college districts.[1246]

[1233] 2021 Wash. Laws Ch. 147, S.B. 5401.
[1234] 2021 Wyo. Sess. Laws Enr. Act No. 47, Ch. 120, SF 83.
[1235] 2021 Ala. Acts No. 2021-382, S.B. 66.
[1236] 2021 Colo. Sess. Laws SB 191.
[1237] 2021 Mo. Laws HB 297.
[1238] 2021 Tenn. Pub. Acts Ch. No. 317, H.B. No. 315, S.B. No. 95.
[1239] 2021 Tenn. Pub. Acts Ch. No. 316, H.B. No. 312, S.B. No. 92.
[1240] 2021 Tenn. Pub. Acts Ch. No. 313, H.B. No. 278, S.B. No. 53.
[1241] 2021 Tenn. Pub. Acts Ch. No. 314, H.B. No. 284, S.B. No. 59.
[1242] 2021 Tenn. Pub. Acts Ch. No. 312, H.B. No. 258, S.B. No. 32.
[1243] 2021 Va. Acts Ch. 447, H. 2120 (1st Spec. Sess.).
[1244] 2021 Neb. Laws LB 8 (1st Spec. Sess.).
[1245] 2021 Nev. Stat. Ch. 2, AB 1, (1st Spec. Sess.).
[1246] 2021 Or. Laws Ch. 53, HB 2090.

Six states enacted new provisions about First Amendment free speech rights on college campuses. Florida prohibited its state BOE and the board of governors from shielding students, staff, and faculty from free speech protected under the First Amendment to the Constitution. Florida also directed its state BOE to require each college system institution to conduct annual assessments of the intellectual freedom and viewpoint diversity on their campuses.[1247] Montana directed officials at its public postsecondary institutions to provide for freedom of association and speech on campuses, banned discrimination against student organizations, and mandated that they adopt anti-harassment policies.[1248] Moreover, Montana designated outdoor areas of campuses as public fora, enabling the application of manner, place, and time restrictions to those areas while calling for training for campus personnel on implementing free speech.[1249]

North Dakota enhanced free speech provisions for policies by public institutions of higher education by creating protections for faculty speech in classrooms germane to the subject matter at hand, prohibiting student-on-student discriminatory harassment, adopting provisions for open fora on campuses, and the ability of officials to set manner, place, and time restrictions in open fora.[1250] Utah banned institutions of higher education from sanctioning or disciplining acts of speech not constituting discriminatory harassment, created a cause of action for its attorney general related to discriminatory harassment, and enacted provisions related to free expression at an institution of higher education.[1251] West Virginia protected expressive activities within public institutions of higher education, identifying outdoor areas to be public fora.[1252] Washington passed an act protecting public expression, which provided private causes of action against government entities, presumably including universities, to protect communication on issues under consideration or review in legislative, executive, judicial, administrative, or other governmental proceedings.[1253]

Nine states adopted twelve laws altering admission criteria for institutions of higher education. It should be noted that where states

---

[1247] 2021 Fla. Laws ch. 159, H. 233.
[1248] 2021 Mont. Laws Ch. 234, HB 349.
[1249] 2021 Mont. Laws Ch. 231, HB 218.
[1250] 2021 N.D. Laws H.B. No. 1503.
[1251] 2021 Utah Laws H.B. 159.
[1252] 2021 W. Va. Acts Ch. 156, S.B. 657.
[1253] 2021 Wash. Laws Ch. 259, S.B. 5009.

decrease admission standards, especially teacher education programs, the purposes appeared to attempts to address teacher shortages in their state. California extended a priority enrollment model for its university systems and community colleges for foster youth.[1254] Colorado forbade the governing boards of state-supported institutions of higher education from considering legacy preferences as eligibility criteria for admission.[1255] In companion legislation, Colorado permitted, but did not require, state-support institutions of higher education to rely on national assessment test score as eligibility criteria.[1256]

Illinois directed officials at the University of Illinois to admit community college transfer students under a pilot program, specifying that they offer multiple pathways to transfer and to guarantee admission when students meet standards identified in the act, including a GPA of 3.0, 36 semester hours that are transferable and other requirements.[1257] Illinois prohibited officials at public institutions of higher education from obligating applicants who are state residents from having to submit standardized college admissions test scores as a part of their applications.[1258] Maryland prohibited institutions of higher education from using third-party admissions application information about the criminal backgrounds of the applicant and from denying admission on this bases.[1259]

Nevada created an enrollment preference for military veterans for admission into college programs in teaching and nursing.[1260] New York removed the requirement of a minimum score on an examination such as the graduate record examination for admission to graduate-level teacher and educational leader programs at campuses of the State University of New York.[1261] New York next increased the percentage of students, from no more than 15% to no more than 50%, who can be exempt from admission standards for graduate-level teacher and educational leader programs.[1262] Oregon prohibited public or private postsecondary institutions of higher education from directing prospective students to disclose whether

---

[1254] 2021 Cal. Stat. Ch. 574, SB 512.
[1255] 2021 Colo. Sess. Laws HB 1173.
[1256] 2021 Colo. Sess. Laws HB 1067.
[1257] 2021 Ill. Laws Pub. Act 102-0187, HB 796.
[1258] 2021 Ill. Laws Pub. Act 102-0067, HB 3139.
[1259] 2021 Md. Laws Ch. 676, SB 127.
[1260] 2021 Nev. Stat. Ch. 211, SB 193.
[1261] 2021 N.Y. Laws Ch. 620, A. 7491.
[1262] 2021 N.Y. Laws Ch. 626, S. 5666.

they had criminal convictions before they make final decisions on whether to admit applicants.[1263]

Virginia forbade public institutions of higher education from utilizing institution-specific applications containing questions about individuals' criminal histories or denying admissions solely on this basis except for entry to law school or reserve officers training corps programs.[1264] West Virginia prohibited institutions of higher education from discriminating against graduates of home, private, or nonpublic schools, by expecting them to undergo alternative testing as a condition for acceptance.[1265]

Twenty-five states added thirty-eight laws designed to assist students with scholarships and grants. Alabama raised the cap on the student grant program from $1,200 to $3,000 per academic year.[1266] Arizona called on public postsecondary institutions to implement state-supported promise scholarship programs to assist students in receiving baccalaureate degrees.[1267] California provided exemptions from tuition and fees at public postsecondary institutions for survivors of persons who died as a result of providing medical or emergency services during the COVID-19 state of emergency.[1268] Colorado first funded an opportunity scholarship for displaced workers from funds appropriated to its department of higher education.[1269] Colorado then permitted local school boards to create scholarship programs for their graduates with their locally-received money.[1270]

Delaware created the Student Excellence Equals Degree (SEED) Act to provide funding for college tuition for adult students seeking an associate of arts degrees at community colleges or universities.[1271] In a separate act, Delaware provided for scholarship funds to cover the full cost of tuition for SEED students at Delaware State University.[1272] Georgia first allowed individuals with disabilities, as defined by the Americans with Disabilities Act,[1273] to apply to its student finance commission for a limited waiver from the time limit

---

[1263] 2021 Or. Laws Ch. 341, SB 713.
[1264] 2021 Va. Acts Ch. 440, H. 1930, (1st Spec. Sess.).
[1265] 2021 W. Va. Acts Ch. 157, H.B. 2529.
[1266] 2021 Ala. Acts No. 2021-442, HB 424.
[1267] 2021 Ariz. Sess. Laws Ch. 410, SB 1825.
[1268] 2021 Cal. Stat. Ch. 569, AB 1113.
[1269] 2021 Colo. Sess. Laws SB 232.
[1270] 2021 Colo. Sess. Laws HB 1112.
[1271] 2021 Del. Laws Ch. 239, SB 12.
[1272] 2021 Del. Laws Ch. 97, SB 95.
[1273] 42 U.S.C. § 12102.

for receipt of scholarships.[1274] Georgia added the independent school association to the list of accrediting agencies for high schools for which students are eligible for its HOPE scholarship, thereby making them available to more pupils in private schools.[1275] Hawai'i created a fourth possible criterion for displaying evidence of academic excellence to receive state scholarships applicable to high school students with GPAs of 3.0 and receive special education services for two or more years during grades 7-12.[1276]

Illinois clarified the priority of award of student scholarships in fiscal years where funding is insufficient to award all scholarships.[1277] Indiana permitted high school students achieving GPAs of at least 3.5 on a 4.0 scale to be eligible for its Hoosier educators scholarship.[1278] In a second law, Indiana declared that students who are at least seventeen and accepted awards from the Hoosiers education scholarship program to defray the expense of attending postsecondary educational institutions have full legal capacity to act on their behalf and are subject to any obligations arising from these agreements.[1279] Kansas extended its promise scholarship act to offer postsecondary educational scholarships for two-year associate's degree programs, career and technical education certificates, and other programs.[1280] Louisiana adopted the M.J. Foster Promise Program, a financial assistance award for eligible students to enroll in two-year public postsecondary educational institutions or accredited proprietary schools licensed by its board of regents.[1281]

Maine provided tuition waivers for individuals who graduated from high schools in the state during the 2019-20 and 2020-021 academic years who completed applications for federal student aid and are eligible for Pell grants for the either academic year; the stated purpose of the laws is to help students catch up and keep up via remedial and compensatory assistance in the face of educational disruptions.[1282] Maryland permitted tenth, not just ninth, graders to prequalify for the guaranteed access grants scholarship program.[1283]

[1274] 2021 Ga. Laws Act 229, SB 187.
[1275] 2021 Ga. Laws Act 201, HB 606.
[1276] 2021 Haw. Sess. Laws Act 156, HB 1291.
[1277] 2021 Ill. Laws Pub. Act 102-0621, SB 661.
[1278] 2021 Ind. Acts Pub. Law 63, H.B. 1553.
[1279] 2021 Ind. Acts Pub. Law 9, S.B. 101.
[1280] 2021 Kan. Sess. Laws HB 2064.
[1281] 2021 La. Acts No. 457, S.B. 148.
[1282] 2021 Me. Laws Ch. 372, H.P. 238, L.D. 334.
[1283] 2021 Md. Laws Ch. 578, HB 1245.

In the first of a trilogy of laws, Maryland allowed applicants who graduated from high school five or more years before the date of applications not to be subject to GPA requirements to be eligible for the state's community college Promise Scholarship Program.[1284] Maryland changed the definition of the eligible student to include those enrolled in registered apprenticeship programs partnering with public community colleges to be eligible for workforce development sequence scholarships.[1285]

Michigan, in the first of three new laws, provided tuition assistance for higher education for the children of police officers and firefighters killed on duty.[1286] Michigan changed the qualifications for the state competitive scholarship based on scholastic achievement instead of standardized test scores.[1287] Michigan amended its tuition grant act to allow undergraduates enrolled in private colleges and universities for the 2020 spring term and the 2020-21 academic year to have two extra semesters of eligibility.[1288] Nevada directed its state treasurer to study the effectiveness of its publicly funded scholarship and grant programs.[1289] New Mexico permitted students who are homeschooled to receive college and university scholarships funded by the state lottery.[1290] North Dakota created a tuition scholarship program for students taking dual-credit courses while in high school.[1291] North Dakota next made minor changes in the eligibility criteria for students to receive career and technical education scholarships and academic scholarships, including an option for integrated mathematics in the former scholarship as well as an option for education subject areas in the latter scholarship.[1292]

South Carolina expanded the use of its Palmetto Fellows Scholarship by including two-year institutions of higher learning and technical colleges among those whose students may be eligible to pursue awards.[1293] Tennessee ordered its higher education commission to establish a four-year pilot program to award completion grants to promise scholarship students who have

---

[1284] 2021 Md. Laws Ch. 344, SB 308.
[1285] 2021 Md. Laws Ch. 96, HB 905; 2021 Md. Laws Ch. 97, SB 845.
[1286] 2021 Mich. Pub. Acts No. 127, H.B. 4247.
[1287] 2021 Mich. Pub. Acts No. 40, H.B. 4055.
[1288] 2021 Mich. Pub. Acts No. 41, H.B. 4056.
[1289] 2021 Nev. Stat. Ch. 324, SB 128.
[1290] 2021 N.M. Laws Ch. 73, SB 234.
[1291] 2021 N.D. Laws H.B. No. 1375.
[1292] 2021 N.D. Laws H.B. No. 1135; 2021 N.D. Laws SB No. 2136.
[1293] 2021 S.C. Act No. 36, H. 3017.

immediate financial needs or hardships that may impede their ability to finish college programs.[1294] Tennessee also increased the amount of the middle college scholarship award from $1,000 to $1,250 per semester.[1295] In the third law, Tennessee removed the expectation that students who are homeschooled must be enrolled in this status for a full year to be eligible for a state lottery scholarship.[1296] Texas included a nationally-accredited post-doctor of podiatric medicine program in the definition of graduate medical education program for purposes of participation in graduate medical education grant programs.[1297]

In the first of three new laws, Utah closed off new applications for new century scholarships after the 2021-22 academic year.[1298] Utah then expanded eligibility and availability of technical education scholarships[1299] along with replaced its regent's scholarship program with the opportunity scholarship program for degree-granting institutions.[1300] Virginia created an enslaved-ancestors scholarship program to promote college access.[1301] Washington offered scholarships for more students to attend institutions of higher education, community, and technical colleges, plus to receive industry certification.[1302] West Virginia made scholarships available to students wanting to obtain industrial certifications or degrees from technical and community colleges.[1303] Wyoming permitted courses taken before ninth grade that are the functional equivalent of classes taken in grades 9-12 to be used to meet standards for scholarship programs.[1304]

Four states enrolled six acts about student fees. Louisiana authorized the board of supervisors of Louisiana State University to impose course fees for aviation classes at Louisiana State University at Alexandria.[1305] Maryland directed the presidents of the higher education institutions in its university system to ensure that their student fees committees of record are presented with proposed fees

---

[1294] 2021 Tenn. Pub. Acts Ch. No. 512, H.B. No. 6, S.B. No. 229.
[1295] 2021 Tenn. Pub. Acts Ch. No. 529, H.B. No. 542, S.B. No. 9.
[1296] 2021 Tenn. Pub. Acts Ch. No. 467, S.B. No. 458, H.B. No. 646.
[1297] 2021 Tex. Gen. Laws H.B. No. 2509.
[1298] 2021 Utah Laws S.B. 136.
[1299] 2021 Utah Laws S.B. 136.
[1300] 2021 Utah Laws S.B. 136.
[1301] 2021 Va. Acts Ch. 442, H. 1980 (1st Spec. Sess.).
[1302] 2021 Wash. Laws Ch. 133, H.B. 1425.
[1303] 2021 W. Va. Acts Ch. 155, S.B. 335.
[1304] 2021 Wyo. Sess. Laws Enr. Act No. 29, Ch. 43, H.B. 120.
[1305] 2021 La. Acts No. 412, HB 410.

for their review.[1306] Nevada prohibited the assessment of registration, enrollment, laboratory, and other mandatory fees by its university board of regents against Native American students who are members of federally-recognized Indian tribes or nations.[1307] Nevada authorized the board of regents of its university system to waive fees for spouses or children of members of the active Nevada National Guard who reenlisted.[1308] Oregon revised a provision about student fees in public institutions of higher education, directing their recognized student governments to make good faith efforts to collaborate with their boards and presidents in assuring that fees support the education, instruction, service, and recreation of students.[1309] In a second new law, Oregon obligated officials in public universities and community colleges to make prominent displays of the mandatory fees they charge students.[1310]

Nineteen states enacted laws providing scholarships and resident tuition for military service members, veterans, and their families, as well as other perquisites based on their relationships with the armed forces. Alabama specified that students who are minor children of military service members stationed in the state qualify for resident tuition at public institutions of higher education.[1311] Arkansas adopted tuition waivers for veterans to attend in-state private, nonprofit institutions of higher education.[1312] Arkansas then authorized a scholarship program for children of members of the uniformed services.[1313] Delaware declared spouses and children of active-duty military members to be in-state residents for tuition purposes at public colleges, universities, and community colleges.[1314] Nebraska provided resident tuition status for military veterans, their spouses, and dependents who graduated from state high schools or if they served in the state during their military service between 2001 and 2021.[1315]

Nevada extended free tuition to postsecondary institutions for dependents of military veterans.[1316] New Jersey provided resident

---

[1306] 2021 Md. Laws Ch. 217, SB 895.
[1307] 2021 Nev. Stat. Ch. 349, AB 262.
[1308] 2021 Nev. Stat. Ch. 353, AB 156.
[1309] 2021 Or. Laws Ch. 163, HB 3012.
[1310] 2021 Or. Laws Ch. 158, HB 2542.
[1311] 2021 Ala. Acts no. 2021-881, S.B. 83.
[1312] 2021 Ark. Acts 988, HB 1879.
[1313] 2021 Ark. Acts 689, HB 1446.
[1314] 2021 Del. Laws Ch. 119, SB 125.
[1315] 2021 Neb. Laws LB 669.
[1316] 2021 Nev. Stat. Ch. 211, SB 193.

tuitions rate for non-resident dependent children of U.S. military personnel who attend state public institutions of higher education.[1317] New York extended in-state residency for university tuition for dependents of active-duty service members.[1318] North Dakota offered free tuition to state institutions of higher education for spouses, widows, widowers, or stepchildren of veterans killed in action or from service-connected deaths or those on full disability.[1319] South Carolina removed the three-year window during which veterans or their dependents must enroll in institutions of higher learning in order to be eligible for in-state tuition rates.[1320]

South Dakota classified all of the following as resident students without having to meet the twelve-month residency requirement: veterans, active duty members of the armed forces, the spouses or children of veterans who established in-state residency, and, the spouses or children of an active duty member.[1321] Tennessee extended tuition reimbursement for members of the National Guard to include not just university programs but also technical certificates, diplomas, and other graduate programs.[1322] West Virginia provided in-state residency tuition rates for nonresident members of reserve units as well as current members of the U.S. armed services residing there.[1323]

Other military-related perquisites are described as follows. California required its two university systems to develop consistent policies to award military personnel and veterans courses equivalent to their military education, training, and service.[1324] Louisiana directed officials at public and private postsecondary education institutions to adopt and implement a military-friendly matriculation and transfer process aligned with national-recognized standards for evaluating educational experiences in the U.S. armed forces.[1325] New Jersey extended additional attendance rights at its public institutions of higher education for members of the military, including permitting them to register late for courses.[1326] Texas amended a provision on excused absences from public institutions of

---

[1317] 2021 N.J. Laws c. 49, S. 275.
[1318] 2021 N.Y. Laws Ch. 604, A. 6249.
[1319] 2021 N.D. Laws H.B. No. 1125.
[1320] 2021 S.C. Act No. 29, S. 241.
[1321] 2021 S.D. Laws HB 1057.
[1322] 2021 Tenn. Pub. Acts Ch. No. 216, H.B. No. 83, S.B. No. 755.
[1323] 2021 W. Va. Acts Ch. 154, S.B. 307.
[1324] 2021 Cal. Stat. Ch. 567, AB 1002.
[1325] 2021 La. Acts No. 429, S.B. 27.
[1326] 2021 N.J. Laws c. 174, S 278.

higher education for students called to active military service, instead using the term required military service.[1327] Utah allowed veterans who are state residents to audit classes at its institutions of higher education.[1328]

Six states granted resident tuition status to non-military students. Colorado provided in-state tuition classification for members of American Indian tribes with historical ties to the state, especially those living in other states.[1329] Oregon made resident tuition status available to undergraduate and graduate students who legally entered the U.S. under the Compact of Free Association treaty between it, the Republic of Palau, the Republic of the Marshall Islands, and the Federated States of Micronesia who have not previously established residency in another state or the District of Columbia.[1330] Rhode Island adopted the Student Success Act, which provides students who are not U.S. citizens but who have attended at least three consecutive years in and graduated from an in-state high school with resident tuition status at community colleges and public universities.[1331]

South Dakota provided free tuition and fees to students who are visually impaired for courses at state institutions of higher education that are not subsidized by the state general fund under programs such as distance education.[1332] Texas conferred educational benefits at public institutions of higher education for survivors of public servants, including those listed as a dependent on tax forms in the year before the public servant's death, age twenty-five or younger, and not just biological and adopted children.[1333] Virginia granted students eligibility for in-state tuition and financial assistance programs at public institutions of higher education regardless of their immigration or citizenship status if they attended at least two years in commonwealth schools and met other general admission standards.[1334]

Two states adopted laws about awarding transfer credits. Maryland ordered its higher education commission to establish procedures directing officials at public institutions of higher education that refuse to transfer credits or courses to enrolled

---

[1327] 2021 Tex. Gen. Laws S.B. No 937.
[1328] 2021 Utah Laws S.B. 45.
[1329] 2021 Colo. Sess. Laws SB 29.
[1330] 2021 Or. Laws Ch. 652, SB 553.
[1331] 2021 R.I. Pub. Laws S. 990, H. 5328.
[1332] 2021 S.D. Laws HB 1196.
[1333] 2021 Tex. Gen. Laws H.B. No. 133.
[1334] 2021 Va. Acts Ch. 107, H. 2123 (1st Spec. Sess.).

students to report their actions to them and school officials within set time limit.[1335] Wyoming obligated officials at state institution of higher education to accept college level credit from other state institutions of higher education unless they can demonstrate that there is no application to its current educational standards, subject to an appeals process.[1336]

In efforts toward gathering and sharing information about educational costs, assisting students to recognize available career paths, and provide for more efficient workforce development, twelve states adopted eighteen laws. Arkansas called on its division of higher education to provide students, parents, and guidance counselors with information about the most in-demand jobs in the state, starting salaries for jobs in the state, the completion rate for graduation, the costs of education, and student loans.[1337] California mandated that eligibility criteria for the state's supplemental nutrition program at community colleges and state universities include a linkage between them and student employability in food service occupations.[1338] Colorado allocated federal funds from the American Rescue Plan Act of 2021,[1339] to deliver direct and indirect support to students to re-enroll and complete postsecondary credentials as well as on how to improve their employment prospects.[1340]

Connecticut ordered its university board of trustees and board of regents for higher education to study workforce development issues related to the insurance industry, including an audit of courses and programs of study relating to it.[1341] Indiana called on its department of workforce development to maintain a course catalog of classes for life-long learning on its website.[1342] Indiana also directed its commissioner for higher education and state DOE, in consultation with state educational institutions, to prepare a model guidance and informational resources on postsecondary enrollment opportunities incorporating work-based learning experiences.[1343] Kansas adopted a students' right to know act, mandating the publication of information about postsecondary education, including the degree

---

[1335] 2021 Md. Laws Ch. 188, HB 460; 2021 Md. Laws Ch. 189, SB 886.
[1336] 2021 Wyo. Sess. Laws Enr. Act No. 83, Ch. 146, H.B. 231.
[1337] 2021 Ark. Acts 1066, HB 1700.
[1338] 2021 Cal. Stat. Ch. 461, AB 396.
[1339] Pub. L. 117-2, 135 STAT. 4, H.R. 1319 (March 11, 2021).
[1340] 2021 Colo. Sess. Laws HB 1330.
[1341] 2021 Conn. Acts 21-21, (Reg. Sess.), SB 193.
[1342] 2021 Ind. Acts Pub. Law 216 § 2; House Enr. Act No. 1549.
[1343] 2021 Ind. Acts Pub. Law 216 § 46; H. B. No. 1549.

prospectus information published by its state board of regents, the training information program report, and other data relevant to students' understanding of potential earnings as determined by its department of labor and each branch of the U.S. armed services.[1344] Louisiana obligated the governing boards for postsecondary education institutions under its control to provide information about student loans, including total loans taken out, percentage borrowing rate, monthly repayment amounts.[1345]

Maine reestablished its commission charged with studying college affordability and college completion.[1346] Missouri informed its department of higher education and workforce development to collect and compile data annually about the most in-demand jobs in the state, including salary and education level required for such jobs; the average cost at its public institution of higher education and vocational school; the average monthly student loan payment for those attending such in-state schools; the average three-year student loan default rate; the average graduation rate for these in-state schools; the completion rate for apprenticeship programs, high school credential programs, career and technical education programs, and military first-term enlistments; and the average starting salaries for graduates from its in-state public institutions of higher education and vocational schools.[1347]

Nevada required officials at postsecondary educational institutions to provide various types of information to recruited students, including course catalogs before signing agreement to enroll.[1348] In the first of two new laws New Jersey mandated that students receive data about loans for postsecondary education, including debt and demographic data.[1349] New Jersey next directed institutions of higher education to provide new graduates with information on income-contingent student loan repayment programs.[1350] Tennessee dictated that its higher education commission make available a publicly-accessible web-based platform to assist current and prospective students in making informed decisions about possible postsecondary credential pathways and

---

[1344] 2021 Kan. Sess. Laws HB 2085.
[1345] 2021 La. Acts No. 413, H.B. 42.
[1346] 2021 Me. Laws Ch. 103, S.P. 108, L.D. 247.
[1347] 2021 Mo. Laws HB 297.
[1348] 2021 Nev. Stat. Ch. 123, AB 169.
[1349] 2021 N.J. Laws c. 349, S. 3683.
[1350] 2021 N.J. Laws c. 357, S. 2286.

outcomes; the information must include program costs, financial aid options, highest-need occupations, and salary estimates.[1351] The Texas Reskilling and Upskilling Through Education (TRUE) program, the first of four new laws there, was a new grant administered by the state's higher education coordinating board to be awarded to community colleges, technical schools, and other entities to create, redesign, or expand workforce training programs leading to industry certifications or other workforce credentials in high-demand fields.[1352] Texas then obligated its higher education coordinating board, in its recommendation to the legislature about community colleges, to include success measures achieved by students in qualified continuing workforce education courses.[1353] Texas ordered its workforce commission to adopt a strategic plan for improving the quality of its infant, toddler, preschool, and school-age children workforce; plans must address recommendations to public and private institutions of higher education to increase the use of matriculation agreements with school boards and open-enrollment charter schools to assist the education and training of childcare workers.[1354] Fourth, Texas permitted institutions of higher education to enter into agreements with employers to provide off-campus workforce education or lower-division programs at sites requested by employers without needing approval of higher education regional councils.[1355]

Six states addressed apprenticeship programs. Arizona called on its university cooperative extension service to establish a workforce development program to provide incentives to food-producing agriculture organizations to hire apprentices.[1356] Colorado created a state apprenticeship agency to register and oversee in-state programs and agreements.[1357] Montana directed that the wages of apprentices must begin on the dates they register with sponsors.[1358] Tennessee stipulated that high school officials designate persons as apprenticeship training program contact, obligating its state DOE to compile and publish a list of the apprenticeship program contacts.[1359] Utah modified the duties of its commissioner of apprenticeship

---

[1351] 2021 Tenn. Pub. Acts Ch. No. 507, S.B. NO. 1521, H.B. No. 1246.
[1352] 2021 Tex. Gen. Laws S.B. No. 1102.
[1353] 2021 Tex. Gen. Laws S.B. No. 959.
[1354] 2021 Tex. Gen. Laws H.B. No. 619.
[1355] 2021 Tex. Gen. Laws H.B. No. 4361.
[1356] 2021 Ariz. Sess. Laws Ch. 410, SB 1825.
[1357] 2021 Colo. Sess. Laws HB 1007.
[1358] 2021 Mont. Laws Ch. 114, HB 213.
[1359] 2021 Tenn. Pub. Acts Ch. No. 206, S.B. No. 844, H.B. No. 842.

programs while added definitions for the terms "apprenticeship," "pre-apprenticeship," and "youth apprenticeship."[1360] Washington allowed apprenticeship programs to issue substance use disorder professional certifications for persons training in them.[1361]

Three states authorized bills addressing timely progress toward program completion. California decreed that officials in community colleges adopt common course numbering systems for all general education required and transfer pathway classes, incorporating these numbers into their course catalogs.[1362] Illinois directed the governing boards of its public universities to provide enrolled students when they declare or change their academic majors or programs of study with reports containing relevant, independent, and accurate data about their choices and the current occupational outlook data associated with their majors or programs of study.[1363] Oregon directed that its higher education coordinating commission adopt a common course numbering system for introductory and other lower-division courses with similar learning outcomes that are taught in accelerated college credit programs, public and participating nonpublic postsecondary educational institutions.[1364]

Four states attempted to reduce college costs by relying upon open-source or low-cost instructional materials. Colorado continued and expanded its practice of using open-resource materials for courses and zero-textbook cost degree programs in its institutions of higher education.[1365] Oregon declared that officials at its public universities and community colleges must display prominently or establish links to websites revealing estimated costs of all required course materials and directly-related course fees for no less than seventy-five percent of the total for-credit courses they offer.[1366] Texas obligated public institutions of higher education to disclose information about course schedules as well as required and recommended course materials, also mandating that private or independent institutions disseminate course and textbook information.[1367] Washington directed its state and regional universities and the Evergreen State College to designate whether

---

[1360] 2021 Utah Laws H.B. 391.
[1361] 2021 Wash. Laws Ch. 165, H.B. 1311.
[1362] 2021 Cal. Stat. Ch. 568, AB 1111.
[1363] 2021 Ill. Laws Pub. Act 102-0214, SB 1638.
[1364] 2021 Or. Laws Ch. 575, SB 233.
[1365] 2021 Colo. Sess. Laws SB 215.
[1366] 2021 Or. Laws Ch. 162, HB 2919.
[1367] 2021 Tex. Gen. Laws H.B. No. 1027.

courses use open educational resources or low-cost required instructional materials in their online course descriptions.[1368]

Nine states responded to concerns about student loan issues while imposing greater oversight on lenders. Colorado required the registration of private education lenders while promoting standards for them.[1369] Connecticut obligated service providers of federal student loans to register with its Department of Banking in addition to complying with its record and consumer protection mandates.[1370] Illinois directed private educational lenders to obtain information from institutions of higher education at which borrowers will use loan proceeds about cost, enrollment status, and financial assistance available to the students; the act further informs lenders to file quarterly reports with its Department of Financial and Professional Regulation, placing a duty on institutions of higher education to certify compliance to their governance boards.[1371] Maine called on its postsecondary educational institutions to review student debt and develop plans to limit it, focusing on targeted goals such as matching student debt to allowable four-year loans.[1372]

New Jersey enabled public institutions of higher education to reduce students' financial aid from them as a result of awards of private scholarships if the total exceeds their actual needs.[1373] New York created a private student loan refinance task force to study and report on ways lending institutions offering private student loans to graduates of institutions of higher education can be encouraged to establish loan refinancing programs.[1374] Oklahoma created a student borrower's bill of rights, directing its attorney general to draft a statement banning student loan service providers from engaging in fraud, unfair or deceptive practices in connection with servicing loans, failing to apply loan payments to loan balances, and other practices that violate the rights of student borrowers.[1375] Oregon called on persons who service student loans to be licensed by the state while adopting a review process for licensing these individuals.[1376] Texas ordered its higher education coordinating

---

[1368] 2021 Wash. Laws Ch. 152, H.B. 1119.
[1369] 2021 Colo. Sess. Laws SB 57.
[1370] 2021 Conn. Acts 21-130 (Reg. Sess.), SB 890.
[1371] 2021 Ill. Laws Pub. Act 102-0583, HB 2746.
[1372] 2021 Me. Laws Ch. 79, H.P. 830, L.D. 1152.
[1373] 2021 N.J. Laws c. 223, S. 985.
[1374] 2021 N.Y. Laws Ch. 774, Approval Memo 132, S. 2767A.
[1375] 2021 Okla. Sess. Laws S.B. No. 261.
[1376] 2021 Or. Laws Ch. 651, SB 485.

board to include data about student loan repayment in its annual reports.[1377]

Eleven states adopted twelve laws creating greater oversight for private proprietary schools. Arizona amended a section creating a student tuition recovery fund at private postsecondary institutions, limiting the annual assessment to $10 per student and an aggregate of $25,000 per school.[1378] California amended its statute about regulating private postsecondary institutions, specifying that continuing education expressly excludes instruction leading to degrees, to create a student tuition recovery fund, and to afford the agency with regulatory power over them the authority to refund tuition expenses.[1379] Colorado amended provisions related to oversight of private postsecondary educational institutions, detailing institutional or programmatic accreditation requirements by accrediting agencies such as the Council for Higher Education or the U.S. DOE.[1380] Connecticut changed the threshold at which private occupational schools are subject to oversight from those enrolling fewer than ten students those receiving less than $50,000 in tuition revenue.[1381]

Georgia revised exemptions provided to nonpublic postsecondary institutions operating on military installations or bases while permitted alternative review methods including audiovisual remote reviews for renewal applications and inspection of facilities.[1382] Kansas created a structure by which institutions that are exempt from its private and out-of-state postsecondary educational institution act may choose to seek certificates of approval to submit themselves to the jurisdiction of its state board. Under this structure, issues such as student complaints, record management, plus management of scholarships and grants can be addressed through existing procedures and produce some protection from liability for the institutions.[1383] Maine created protections for students who obtain loans for postsecondary education by informing providers of public and private postsecondary education and student finance companies to register with its office of consumer credit protection within its department of professional and financial

---

[1377] 2021 Tex. Gen. Laws S.B. No. 1019.
[1378] 2021 Ariz. Sess. Laws Ch. 242, SB 1308.
[1379] 2021 Cal. Stat. Ch. 552, SB 802.
[1380] 2021 Colo. Sess. Laws HB 1306.
[1381] 2021 Conn. Acts 21-45, SB 998.
[1382] 2021 Ga. Laws Act 230, HB 152.
[1383] 2021 Kan. Sess. Laws SB 64.

regulation, provide information and data to the office, and serve as a regulator of the industry.[1384]

Michigan amended its Proprietary Schools Act, adding language that schools that exclusively offer registered and approved apprenticeship programs or approved pre-apprenticeship or apprenticeship readiness programs administered by registered apprenticeship programs are not proprietary schools.[1385] New Jersey directed institutions of higher education and proprietary degree-granting institutions to be transparent as to tuition and fees for prospective and current students.[1386] New Jersey added regulatory controls over private proprietary schools, private career schools, and institutions of higher education, including an approval process for branch campuses, a review process for new academic programs, and a process for the closure of the schools.[1387]

Along with public schools and universities, New York included in the definition of "educational institutions" in its executive law[1388] as applicable to for-profit entities operating colleges, universities, licensed private career schools, or certified English-as-second-language schools which hold themselves out as non-sectarian and which are not exempt from taxation pursuant to the provisions of article four of its real property tax law.[1389] Texas forbade its higher education coordinating board from approving certificates of authorization for state schools to offer professional degrees except under reciprocity agreements; the certificates of authorization refer to the process for accredited private postsecondary institutions and out-of-state public postsecondary schools seeking to offer degrees in Texas.[1390]

Eight states changed their teacher education programs in higher education through twelve laws. Delaware ordered teacher preparation programs preparing elementary school, early childhood education, special education teachers, and reading specialists to provide instruction in evidence-based reading instruction as part of implementing the 2019 Delaware Literacy Plan.[1391] Kentucky allowed its college of university programs involved in preparing teachers and other professional school personnel to be approved for

---

[1384] 2021 Me. Laws Ch. 357, S.P. 530, L.D. 1645.
[1385] 2021 Mich. Pub. Acts No. 32, H. B. 4040.
[1386] 2021 N.J. Laws c. 211, S. 1877.
[1387] 2021 N.J. Laws c. 27, S. 1271.
[1388] N.Y. EXEC. LAW § 292, subd. 37.
[1389] 2021 N.Y. Laws Ch. 654, A. 7390.
[1390] 2021 Tex. Gen. Laws S.B. No. 1490.
[1391] 2021 Del. Ch. 80, SB 133.

regional or national level accreditation and eligible to receive federal funding under 20 U.S.C. §§ 1061-1063.[1392] Maine directed its state DOE to review course work standards on autism spectrum disorder for special education certification.[1393] Maine changed the name of an elementary education-level course of study, from career and education development readiness, to life and career readiness.[1394]

In the first of two new laws, New Jersey obligated teacher preparation programs to provide culturally-responsive teaching training for certification.[1395] New Jersey authorized educator preparation programs to report passing rates of students who complete identified tests, to disseminate information on test fee waivers, and to collect student fees for the costs of mandated testing.[1396] Oklahoma required teacher candidates in early childhood, elementary, secondary, and special education to study the philosophy, overarching framework, components, and implementation of a multi-tiered system of support designed to address their core academic and nonacademic needs; the act also obligated programs to provide for training utilizing evidence-based assessments, interventions, and data-based decision-making procedures within a tiered system of support to identify students at risk for academic or nonacademic outcomes.[1397] Oregon decreed that in the approval process for educator preparation programs, candidates must be evaluated using multiple measures to determine whether their knowledge, skills, and competencies qualify them for teaching licenses and must include at least one measure determined locally and adopted by program officials with the approval of its teacher standards and practices commission.[1398]

The first of a trilogy of new laws from Texas informed its state board for educator certification to make information available about educator preparation programs for instructing emergent bilingual students.[1399] Texas then changed the standards for certification for primary and secondary education, particularly for those working with students with disabilities; certification in this area must include basic knowledge of each category of disability under the IDEA and conditions that may be considered disabilities under

---

[1392] 2021 Ky. Acts Ch. 204, SB 270.
[1393] 2021 Me. Laws Ch. 89, H.P. 470, L.D. 639.
[1394] 2021 Me. Laws Ch. 190, H.P. 34, L.D. 68.
[1395] 2021 N.J. Laws c. 311, S. 2834.
[1396] 2021 N.J. Laws c. 393, S. 2830.
[1397] 2021 Okla. Sess. Laws H.B. No. 1773.
[1398] 2021 Or. Laws Ch. 637, HB 3354.
[1399] 2021 Tex. Gen. Laws S.B. No. 2066.

Section 504 as well as competence in the use of proactive instructional planning techniques and evidence-based inclusive instructional practices.[1400] Texas next obligated those seeking teaching certificates to receive training on virtual learning.[1401] As of September 1, 2022, Washington directed that all education standards board-approved teacher preparation programs must implement procedures for evaluating and recommending candidates for residency teacher certification consistent with the model procedure, including a tool or rubric to consider whether and to what extent they demonstrate the knowledge, skills, and competencies expected under a prior law.[1402]

Sixteen states allowed student-athletes to receive compensation for their names, images, or likenesses (NILs). Maryland added legislation specifying exceptions to what it considered NILs. Alabama restricted postsecondary education institutions from prohibiting student-athletes from receiving compensation for their NILs.[1403] Arizona permitted postsecondary education institutions competing in an intercollegiate sport to allow a student-athlete to earn compensation from their NILs under NCAA rules.[1404] Arkansas adopted the Student-Athlete Publicity Rights Act to guide compensation agreements for college-level student-athletes regarding their NILs.[1405] California extended to community college student-athletes the ability to receive compensation for the use of their NILs.[1406] Georgia enables student-athletes in postsecondary schools to receive compensation for the use of their NILs.[1407]

Illinois adopted a student-athlete endorsement rights act which set forth conditions under which individuals may earn compensation for the use of their NILs or voices while enrolled at postsecondary educational institutions.[1408] Louisiana empowered intercollegiate athletes to earn compensation for the use of their NILs.[1409] Maryland clarified that student-athletes could not make commercial use of names, trademarks, logos, or other intellectual property owned or

---

[1400] 2021 Tex. Gen. Laws H.B. No. 159.
[1401] 2021 Tex. Gen. Laws S.B. No. 226.
[1402] 2021 Wash. Laws Ch. 198, H.B. 1028. The prior statute is cited as WASH. REV. CODE § 28A.410.270.
[1403] 2021 Ala. Acts no. 2021-227, H.B. 404.
[1404] 2021 Ariz. Sess. Laws Ch. 141, SB 1296.
[1405] 2021 Ark. Acts 810, HB 1671.
[1406] 2021 Cal. Stat. Ch. 159, SB 26.
[1407] 2021 Ga. Laws Act 228, HB 617.
[1408] 2021 Ill. Laws Pub. Act 102-0042, SB 2338.
[1409] 2021 La. Acts No. 479, S.B. 60.

controlled by public institutions of higher education; the same act authorizes athletic programs to prohibit student-athletes from engaging in in-person advertising for third-party sponsors during official and mandatory team activities without prior approval from their athletic departments.[1410] Mississippi allowed, through its Intercollegiate Athletics Compensation Rights Act, student-athletes to earn remuneration for their NILs.[1411]

Missouri prohibited postsecondary educational institutions from upholding rules, requirements, standards, or other limitations preventing their students from fully participating in intercollegiate athletics without penalty and earning compensation as a result of the use of their NILs or athletic reputation.[1412] Montana adopted a provision ensuring that student-athletes can earn compensation for the use of their NILs.[1413] Nevada forbade institutions of higher education to deny student-athletes opportunities to receive compensation for the use of their NILs.[1414] New Mexico prohibited the imposition of limitations against student-athletes from earning compensation for the use of their NILs.[1415] Oregon enabled students participating in intercollegiate sports to earn compensation for the use of their NILs and to retain professional representation or athletic agents.[1416] South Carolina permitted intercollegiate athletes to earn compensation for the use of their NILs.[1417] Tennessee allowed intercollegiate athletes at public or private institutions of higher education to earn compensation for the use of their NILs.[1418] Texas authorized student-athletes at public and private institutions of higher education to earn compensation for the use of their NILs.[1419]

Other athletics-related acts passed last year were as follows. Colorado prohibited the adoption of American Indian mascots in state athletic programs.[1420] Nevada directed universities to adopt a policy forbidding the use of named, logos, mascots, songs, or other identifiers that are racially discriminatory or containing racially discriminatory language or imagery, or identifies with the

---

[1410] 2021 Md. Laws Ch. 138, SB 439.
[1411] 2021 Miss. Laws SB 2313.
[1412] 2021 Mo. Laws HB 297.
[1413] 2021 Mont. Laws Ch. 396, SB 248.
[1414] 2021 Nev. Stat. Ch. 202, AB 254.
[1415] 2021 N. M. Laws Ch. 124, SB 94.
[1416] 2021 Or. Laws Ch. 422, SB 5.
[1417] 2021 S.C. Act No. 35, S. 685.
[1418] 2021 Tenn. Pub. Acts Ch. No. 400, H.B. No. 1351, S.B. No. 1000.
[1419] 2021 Tex. Gen. Laws S.B. No. 1385.
[1420] 2021 Colo. Sess. Laws SB 116.

Confederate States of America or a federally-recognized Indian tribe; the law grants an exception with respect to a federally-recognized Indian tribe, with its permission.[1421] Maryland required intercollegiate athletic programs at public institutions of higher education to adopt and implement guidelines to prevent, assess, and treat serious sports-related conditions, including brain injury, heat illness, rhabdomyolysis; to enact exercise and supervision guidelines for any student-athlete who is identified with potential life-threatening health conditions, including sickle cell trait and asthma; and to devise return-to-play protocols for athletes who experience injury or illness during practice or play.[1422] Mississippi directed that public institutions of higher learning that are members of intercollegiate associations must designate their athletic teams or sports according to biological sex.[1423]

Five states addressed support students who are homeless students or in foster care. Arkansas permitted state-supported two- or four-year institutions of higher education to designate staff persons as homeless and foster student liaisons.[1424] Delaware provided tuition, fees, and room and board at public institutions of higher education for students who spent all or part of their teen years in foster care.[1425] Georgia provided waiver of tuition and fees for homeless students to attend postsecondary institutions in its university and technical college systems.[1426] Tennessee directed its department of children's services as well as its higher education commission, board of regents, and public institutions of higher education to establish a foster care youth outreach liaison pilot program at a minimum of five of its public institutions to assist educational progress for youth in foster care.[1427] Texas ordered its department of family and protective services to address barriers for youth with disabilities to participate in the preparation for adult living program, and to establish a work group to plan to ensure foster youth who complete the preparation for adult living program to receive college credit.[1428]

Seven states passed ten laws about campus violence and sexual crimes. Connecticut protected students from retaliation for reporting

---

[1421] 2021 Nev. Stat. Ch. 348, AB 88.
[1422] 2021 Md. Laws Ch. 138, SB 439.
[1423] 2021 Miss. Laws SB 2536.
[1424] 2021 Ark. Acts 355, HB 1462.
[1425] 2021 Del. Laws Ch. 255, HB 123.
[1426] 2021 Ga. Laws Act 139, SB 107.
[1427] 2021 Tenn. Pub. Acts Ch. No. 547, S.B. No. 722, H.B. No. 139.
[1428] 2021 Tex. Gen. Laws H.B. No. 700.

being victims or witnesses of sexual assaults, stalking or violence in its institutions of higher education.[1429] Connecticut next ordered institutions of higher education, to report accidental deaths that occur on their campuses.[1430] Illinois informed its higher education institutions to conduct annual sexual misconduct climate surveys of their students.[1431]

Louisiana created the power-based violence review panel under the jurisdiction of its board of regents to evaluate policies and practices of its institutions of public postsecondary education about reporting, investigating, and adjudicating power-based violence by and against students and recommend revisions to improve such policies and practices.[1432] Louisiana obligated officials at its postsecondary educational institutions to provide information about campus security policies and crime statistics on their websites.[1433] In a third act, Louisiana mandated that public postsecondary education institutions report instances of "power-based" violence occurring on their campuses; the law defined . "power-based" violence as including dating violence, domestic abuse and family violence, sexual violence, voyeurism, video voyeurism, and nonconsensual disclosure of a private image.[1434]

Nevada created a task force to study sexual misconduct at its institutions of higher learning.[1435] Oklahoma permitted its state regents for higher education to allow, if offered by nonprofit organizations specializing in outreach and educational programs on sex trafficking and exploitation, a series of in-depth prevention and education programs on point to all of their first-year students.[1436] Texas directed that if victims of sexual harassment, sexual assault, dating violence, or stalking at institutions of higher education choose to make reports using pseudonyms, the report made by campus peace officers shall not include their names, phone numbers, addresses, or other identifying information.[1437] Utah ordered law enforcement authorities on the campuses of its institutions of higher education to report crimes occurring outside of their campus

---

[1429] 2021 Conn. Acts 21-81 (Reg. Sess.), HB 6374.
[1430] 2021 Conn. Acts 21-184, (Reg. Sess.), SB 954.
[1431] 2021 Ill. Laws Pub. Act 102-0325, SB 1610.
[1432] 2021 La. Acts No. 441, S.B. 232.
[1433] 2021 La. Acts No. 447, H.B. 394.
[1434] 2021 La. Acts No. 439, S.B. 230.
[1435] 2021 Nev. Stat. Ch. 542, SB 347.
[1436] 2021 Okla. Sess. Laws H.B. No. 2396.
[1437] 2021 Tex. Gen. Laws S.B. No. 1371.

jurisdiction with local law enforcement officials and create reports of crime statistics aggregated by type of housing facility.[1438]

Two states addressed jurisdictional issues between campus police and local municipalities. North Dakota reenacted provisions describing the jurisdiction of police officers in the employ of the state's universities.[1439] Rhode Island authorized institutions of higher education to enter into agreements with cities or towns to provide police assistance in non-emergency situations.[1440]

Four states adopted acts to make it easier and quicker to contact suicide-prevention groups. Arkansas mandated that student ID cards include information on them about a national domestic violence hotline, sexual assault hotline, suicide prevention hotline, and campus-related contact information.[1441] Illinois declared that if public higher education institutions issue student identification cards, they must contain contact information for suicide prevention and mental health assistance.[1442] Maryland directed colleges to provide first-year student ID cards that must include telephone numbers of helplines or on-campus crisis centers.[1443] South Carolina ordered public and private institutions of higher learning that issue student ID cards to print the telephone number for the national suicide prevention lifeline and contact information for at least one other crisis resource serving its community.[1444]

Two states adopted three acts on mental health issues. Nevada called on the governing boards of universities, state colleges, or community colleges to ensure that information relating to mental health resources appears on the back of ID cards they issue to students.[1445] New Jersey obligated institutions of higher education to provide students with access to mental health care programs and services as well as to establish a hotline to provide information on the availability of these services.[1446] In a second act, New Jersey funded a grant program to encourage school boards to partner with institutions of higher education in training school-based mental health service providers.[1447]

[1438] 2021 Utah Laws S.B. 163.
[1439] 2021 N.D. Laws S.B. No. 2168.
[1440] 2021 R.I. Pub. Laws S. 717, H. 5815.
[1441] 2021 Ark. Acts 1069, HB 1770.
[1442] 2021 Ill. Laws Pub. Act 102-0373, SB 2014.
[1443] 2021 Md. Laws Ch. 212, SB 405.
[1444] 2021 S.C. Act No. 45, S. 231.
[1445] 2021 Nev. Stat. Ch. 495, SB 249.
[1446] 2021 N.J. Laws c. 445, A. 3007.
[1447] 2021 N.J. Laws c. 322, A. 4433.

A pair of states commented on officials' authority at postsecondary institutions to close operations due to COVID-19. Idaho empowered its community college boards of trustees and its institution of higher education to adopt policies for measures and procedures to prevent the spread of contagious or infectious disease, including temporary closure of their entire schools or any of their buildings or campuses.[1448] Kansas noted that only the governing boards of its community colleges and technical schools have the authority to close them and make changes in the means of instruction, including in-person attendance, hybrid, or remote learning during the COVID-19 pandemic; in addition, the established hearing rights for aggrieved employees, parents, and students about decisions these boards made about the pandemic.[1449]

Utah adopted two other measures about COVID-19. Utah first prohibited its state board of higher education and institutions within its system from requiring proof of vaccination unless exemptions were available. Moreover, the act also forbade institutions of higher education and local education agencies that offer both remote and in-person learning from obligating vaccine-exempt students from participating remotely rather than in-person.[1450] In the second act, Utah directed its Department of Health to support widespread testing of students in public institutions of higher education for COVID-19, to facilitate the requirement for in-person instruction.[1451]

Two states added provisions about the management of medications. Delaware allowed institutions of higher education to acquire and stock supplies of epinephrine auto-injectors once employees are trained in their use.[1452] New Jersey expanded authorization for persons or entities to obtain, distribute, and administer opioid antidotes, including public and private schools as well as public or private institutions of higher education.[1453]

A pair of states directed postsecondary schools to address hazing. Georgia added to its anti-hazing law, applicable to public and private postsecondary schools, defining it as including coercing students through the use of social or physical pressure to consume food, liquid, alcohol, drugs, or other substances which subjects them

---

[1448] 2021 Idaho Sess. Laws Ch. 15, H. 68.
[1449] 2021 Kan. Sess. Laws SB 40.
[1450] 2021 Utah Laws H.B. 233.
[1451] 2021 Utah Laws S.B. 107.
[1452] 2021 Del. Laws Ch. 122, SB 55.
[1453] 2021 N.J. Laws c. 152, S. 3491.

to the likely risk of vomiting, intoxication, or unconsciousness.[1454] New Jersey called on its public and private institutions of higher education to adopt anti-hazing policies.[1455]

On a different issue, Hawai'i added its university system to the list of agencies authorized to conduct criminal background checks for positions or duties related to campus security.[1456]

Because postsecondary institutions of higher education are often one of the larger organizations in their states, they typically have large numbers of employees. As such, higher education employment-related legislation adopted in 2021 is described as follows.

California passed three laws on employment actions. California amended its higher education employer-employee relations act directing institutions to devise procedures for all medical and dental interns and residents and other postgraduate medical and dental trainees to challenge the terminations of their employment or disciplinary actions except when dismissals are based on academic or clinical matters.[1457] California again amended its higher education employee relations act, this time clarifying that if its university system has an existing job classification that was previously subject to its academic senate but is now not so covered, employees in impacted positions who were represented by exclusive bargaining representatives would continue to be covered under the previous terms of their jobs.[1458] California added a provision about discipline of academic employees in community colleges, specifying that the ninety-day period for officials to complete investigations of accused misconduct and initiate disciplinary proceedings against them or reinstate employees.[1459]

Delaware directed that laborers and mechanics working on construction and renovation projects on its university campus must be paid prevailing wages as set by its Department of Labor Division of Industrial Affairs.[1460] Illinois decreed that employees of public universities or community college districts who worked for at least twelve months and at least 1,000 hours in the previous year are eligible for family and medical leave under the same terms and conditions as under the federal Family and Medical Leave Act of

---

[1454] 2021 Ga. Laws Act 144, SB 85.
[1455] 2021 N.J. Laws c. 208, S. 84.
[1456] 2021 Haw. Sess. Laws Act 170, SB 1220.
[1457] 2021 Cal. Stat. Ch. 563, AB 615.
[1458] 2021 Cal. Stat. Ch. 754, AB 1550.
[1459] 2021 Cal. Stat. Ch. 29, AB 1383.
[1460] 2021 Del. Laws Ch. 130, SB 156.

1993.[1461] Illinois ordered the governing boards of its public universities and community college districts to determine, at least thirty, and again fourteen, days before the beginning of terms, the status of the classes adjunct faculty members were hired to teach.[1462]

New Jersey prohibited public institutions of higher education from entering into subcontracts which may impact the jobs of employees in collective bargaining units during the terms of those agreements.[1463] Oregon provided health benefits for part-time faculty members at public postsecondary institutions of higher education who worked at least half-time in at least three of the four previous academic terms.[1464] South Dakota banned preferential treatment in higher education employment by adopting a provision forbidding individuals from being employed or dismissed or accorded preferential, adverse, or unequal treatment concerning their applications, hiring, training, apprenticeships, tenure, promotions, upgrading, compensation, layoffs, or any term or condition of employment because of their ideological, political, or sectarian opinions or perspectives or due to their races, colors, creeds, religions, sexes, ancestries, disabilities, or national origins.[1465]

Insofar as postsecondary institutions are also massive business entities, acts relevant to their operations are described as follows. Four states adopted five laws about prepaid college tuition savings programs. Tennessee abandoned its college savings program that allowed tuition units to be purchased under tuition contracts.[1466] Texas allowed funds accumulated for prepaid tuition contracts to be used for tuition and fees for registered apprenticeship programs[1467] but adopted a sunset date of September 1, 2033, for its tax-advantage prepaid higher education tuition program.[1468] Washington amended its formula for adopting a unit price for tuition at its institutions of higher education in its prepaid college tuition payment program.[1469] Utah repealed income tax incentives related to its Student Prosperity Savings Program.[1470]

[1461] 2021 Ill. Laws Pub. Act 102-0335, HB 12.
[1462] 2021 Ill. Laws Pub. Act 102-0260, HB 375.
[1463] 2021 N.J. Laws c. 104, S. 2932.
[1464] 2021 Or. Laws Ch. 583, SB 551.
[1465] 2021 S.D. Laws HB 1254.
[1466] 2021 Tenn. Pub. Acts Ch. No. 469, S.B. No. 501, H.B. No. 1396.
[1467] 2021 Tex. Gen. Laws S.B. No. 1094.
[1468] 2021 Tex. Gen. Laws S.B. No. 702.
[1469] 2021 Wash. Laws Ch. 248, S.B. 5430.
[1470] 2021 Utah Laws H.B. 46.

Federal and State Legislation 499

South Dakota authorized new building construction of three projects beginning by authorizing its board of regents to contract for the construction of a new Mineral Industry Building on the campus of the South Dakota School of Mines and Technology.[1471] It next authorized its board of regents to contract for the redesign and renovation plus an addition to the Sanford Jackrabbit Athletic Complex at South Dakota State University[1472] while empowering it to contract for the design and construction of a new dairy research and extension farm on the same campus.[1473]

Connecticut was the first of two states addressing the use of bids in purchasing when it directed its university health center to obtain approval from its general assembly before soliciting bids or requesting proposals for privatization or public-private partnership contract.[1474] Maryland placed Baltimore City Community College in a category of the state procurement law, making it unnecessary for its officials to obtain approval from its board of public works for contracts with values in excess of $500,000.[1475]

Two states enacted three measures about rates for tuition and fees. South Dakota directed that all courses offered at off-campus locations, not including online or other remote technology offerings, to be at self-support tuition rates established by the board of regents with the exception of nursing classes offered at Pierre.[1476] Texas enabled institutions of higher education to charge higher tuition rates for students taking more than fifteen semester credit hours beyond those required for degrees up to the tuition rate for out-of-state residents.[1477] Texas allowed officials at the University of Houston to spend funds collected through the student union fee for programming at the student union building; although not specified in it provisions, the purported purpose of act was to increase mental health services for students.[1478]

As the first of two states addressing financial audits, Nevada directed its legislative auditor to conduct an audit of the state system of higher education.[1479] North Dakota specified that working papers of internal auditors for state higher education institutions are

---

[1471] 2021 S.D. Laws SB 156.
[1472] 2021 S.D. Laws SB 28.
[1473] 2021 S.D. Laws HB 1153.
[1474] 2021 Conn. Acts 21-198 (Reg. Sess.), SB 1076.
[1475] 2021 Md. Laws Ch. 732, SB 326.
[1476] 2021 S.D. Laws SB 27.
[1477] 2021 Tex. Gen. Laws S.B. No. 1531.
[1478] 2021 Tex. Gen. Laws S.B. No. 480.
[1479] 2021 Nev. Stat. Ch. 467, AB 416.

private until final reports are issued, or work ceases on audits, at which point the papers enter the public domain.[1480]

Other business-related acts passed in 2021 with respect to postsecondary schools are detailed as follows. Nevada called on the director of its agricultural extension department to conduct all of its business while administering its funds.[1481] North Dakota reenacted a provision directing the state to pay oil and gas royalties on leases owned and managed by the boards of university and school lands.[1482] Texas first adopted an outcomes-based funding model for comprehensive regional universities by providing $500,000 in basic funding plus $1,000 for each at-risk student receiving degrees there.[1483] Texas added institutions of higher education to the definition of "governmental entities" in the Government Code, thereby requiring that construction and installation projects they enter must use iron or steel products manufactured in the United States.[1484]

Virginia authorized the issuance of bonds in up to $34 million for revenue-producing capital projects at Virginia Tech University.[1485] Wyoming directed officials in its school of energy resources at the University of Wyoming to submit its biennial budget independently from the university's budget.[1486] Moreover, Wyoming enabled officials at the University of Wyoming to establish a water system on its property without restriction from city or county governments.[1487]

Five states fostered the development of specific programs on campuses. In the first of two laws on inmate education, Washington amended provisions to put increased emphasis on postsecondary education beyond community college or technical schools for eligible individuals.[1488] Washington next obligated world language and American sign language proficiency tests along with general education development tests for students in or released from institutional education facilities, thereby permitting the granting of

---

[1480] 2021 N.D. Laws H.B. No. 1346.
[1481] 2021 Nev. Stat. Ch. 413, SB 287.
[1482] 2021 N.D. Laws H.B. No. 1080.
[1483] 2021 Tex. Gen. Laws S.B. No. 1295.
[1484] 2021 Tex. Gen. Laws S.B. No. 783.
[1485] 2021 Va. Acts Ch. 108, S. 1387 (1st Spec. Sess.).
[1486] 2021 Wyo. Sess. Laws Enr. Act No. 55, Ch. 132, S.F. 111.
[1487] 2021 Wyo. Sess. Laws Enr. Act No. 65, Ch. 93, H.B. 198.
[1488] 2021 Wash. Laws Ch. 200, H.B. 1044.

academic credit and assisting their transition from institutional to public education.[1489]

California, as the first of two states addressing student housing, required the chancellor's office for its state university system and the president's office for its university system to conduct a needs assessment in this area on their campuses.[1490] Illinois authorized non-exempt local governments to develop affordable housing for community college students in coordination with nonprofit affordable housing developers and housing authorities.[1491]

Other program-development activities supported by legislatures were as follows. Connecticut directed officials at its state university to study the feasibility of establishing a food and agricultural education program.[1492] Maryland ordered its higher education commission to administer the Hunger-Free Campus Grant program to address student hunger and basic food needs on campus.[1493]

During 2021 legislatures also enacted measurers, some of which might be construed as "hot-button" topics, representative of culture wars, articulating the rights and privileges of students and employee are described as follows. California directed officials in public and private universities as well as community colleges to stock free menstrual products, making them available in at least one centralized location.[1494] Idaho prohibited officials in public institutions of higher education from directing or otherwise compelling students personally to affirm, adopt, or adhere to any of a list of tenets described as those often found in critical race theory.[1495]

Illinois mandated that the governing boards of its institutions of higher education must permit personal support workers appointed through its home-based support services program for adults with mental disabilities to accompany them to classes.[1496] At the same time, Illinois obligated the governing board of its public universities and community college district to designate specific employees as undocumented student resource liaisons to be available on campus to help those them and their peers with mixed status to streamline access to financial aid and academic support to matriculate

---

[1489] 2021 Wash. Laws Ch. 164, H.B. 1295.
[1490] 2021 Cal. Stat. Ch. 571, AB 1377.
[1491] 2021 Ill. Laws Pub. Act 102-0062, HB 374.
[1492] 2021 Conn. Acts 21-27 (Reg. Sess.), HB 6580.
[1493] 2021 Md. Laws Ch. 579, HB 891; 2021 Md. Laws Ch. 580, SB 767.
[1494] 2021 Cal. Stat. Ch. 664, AB 367.
[1495] 2021 Idaho Sess. Laws Ch. 293, H. 377.
[1496] 2021 Ill. Laws Pub. Act 102-0568, HB 3359.

successfully toward degree completion.[1497] North Dakota permitted officials in its state institutions of higher education to issue students voting cards containing private data about them and information about voter eligibility.[1498] New Jersey directed its secretary of higher education to develop guidance for institutions of higher education to identify cultural barriers in the recruitment and retention of underrepresented students for STEM programs.[1499]

Oklahoma banned state institutions of higher education from requiring students to engage in any form of mandatory gender or sexual diversity training or counseling but did not prohibit voluntary counseling. The law also proscribes any sessions presenting any form of race or sex stereotyping or a bias due to race or sex.[1500] In a second law, Oklahoma empowered institutions to designate student directories as public notice of the release information unless their parents or guardians inform officials not to release it; institutions which receive access to student records for educational purposes may not sell it to others.[1501] Oregon obligated officials in community colleges and public universities to hire benefits navigators to assist students in determining eligibility and in applying for federal, state, and local benefits programs.[1502]

Texas directed officials in public institutions of higher education to display in conspicuous places in each building durable posters or framed copies of the U.S. national motto, "In God We Trust."[1503] In a second law Texas permitted students to exceed the statutory limit of no more than six dropped courses during their enrollments after a declaration of a disaster by the governor results in limits on class attendance; institutions often drop classes due to insufficient students enrollment.[1504] Washington mandated anti-racism, diversity, equity, and inclusion training at institutions of higher education as well as professional development for employees.[1505] Wyoming banned officials at the University of Wyoming and community colleges from spending funds on abortions or insurance coverage for abortions.[1506]

[1497] 2021 Ill. Laws Pub. Act 102-475, HB 3438.
[1498] 2021 N.D. Laws H.B. No. 1447.
[1499] 2021 N.J. Laws c. 76, A. 1070.
[1500] 2021 Okla. Sess. Laws H.B. No. 1775.
[1501] 2021 Okla. Sess. Laws H.B. No. 1875.
[1502] 2021 Or. Laws Ch. 621, HB 2835.
[1503] 2021 Tex. Gen. Laws S.B. No. 797.
[1504] 2021 Tex. Gen. Laws S.B. No. 165.
[1505] 2021 Wash. Laws Ch. 275, S.B. 5227.
[1506] 2021 Wyo. Sess. Laws Enr. Act No. 89, Ch. 148, H.B. 253.

Three states enacted bills asking officials at postsecondary institutions for additional reports. California directed its state university system to provide reports on the proficiency levels of first-year students on their campuses concerning general education written communications, mathematics, and quantitative reasoning.[1507] Indiana informed its commissioner of higher education to study and issue reports on the three topics of cost reductions, free speech on campus, and protection from foreign malfeasance reports.[1508] Oregon required public universities to report annually to its attorney general on their use of outside counsel for legal matters including the types of issues they cover, the number of topics, and the total amount spent for outside counsel.[1509]

Other higher education-related legislation adopted in the 2021 calendar year are detailed as follows. Arkansas directed its division of higher education to develop an asynchronous module on the concepts of personal finance and macroeconomics for students enrolled in its institutions.[1510] California ordered institutions of higher education to update the legal names and gender information in student records, noting that diplomas must be conferred in their chosen names.[1511] Illinois required its board of higher education to prepare forms to have each institution of higher education collect demographic data on the parental or legal guardian status of students based on a newly-revised definition of "parent."[1512]

Maryland repealed the termination date of its higher education outreach and college access pilot program, which it created to increase the number of low-income students attending and succeeding in college.[1513] Maryland then forbade institutions of higher education from paying commissions, bonuses, or other incentives based on success in securing enrollments or awards of financial aid to persons or entities engaged in student recruitment or admissions.[1514] New Jersey removed eligibility of postsecondary students to receive student assistance, training, and employment services, if schools or training providers obligate them to consent to arbitration as part of agreement for their attendance.[1515]

[1507] 2021 Cal. Stat. Ch. 564, AB 914.
[1508] 2021 Ind. Acts Pub. Law 216 § 53; H. B. No. 1549.
[1509] 2021 Or. Laws Ch. 675, HB 2214.
[1510] 2021 Ark. Acts 1038, SB 694.
[1511] 2021 Cal. Stat. Ch. 555, AB 245.
[1512] 2021 Ill. Laws Pub. Act 102-0088, SB 267.
[1513] 2021 Md. Laws Ch. 403, HB 98.
[1514] 2021 Md. Laws Ch. 735, SB 927.
[1515] 2021 N.J. Laws c. 53, S. 1851.

North Dakota permitted its board of higher education to conduct an executive session to consider the appointment or removal of its commissioner, or a president or other faculty head, professor, instructor, teacher, officer, or other employee of an institution of higher education under the board's control, unless the individual involved requests the meeting to be open to other individuals or the public. The act further addressed what constitutes a quorum of a committee created by its board of higher education and conditions for when such sessions are closed or open to the public.[1516] Oklahoma decreed that a course credit policy for advanced placement examinations must be posted on campus websites, specifying that the minimum required scores on these measures for earning course credit for lower division classes at state institutions of higher education shall not require examination scores of more than three with a few exceptions.[1517]

Oregon, in the first of a trilogy of laws, created a task force on success for underrepresented students in higher education, directing it to develop policy and funding to help them achieve success.[1518] Oregon ordered officials in its public institutions of higher education to have the same developmental and educational requirements while ordering the same placement tests for each subject area for incoming students who completed high school and who they decide are college ready after having received high school equivalency for passing General Educational Developments tests.[1519] Oregon permitted community college officials to allow criminal justice courses approved by their curriculum committees to be eligible for classes in the social science cluster portion of associates' degrees.[1520]

South Carolina enacted the Reinforcing College Education on America's Constitutional Heritage (REACH) Act, obligating officials in institutions of higher learning to provide three-semester hours of instruction about the U.S. Constitution, the Federalist Papers, and the Declaration of Independence for undergraduates.[1521] Tennessee forbade officials in its public institutions of higher education from hosting Confucius Institutes and accepting gifts from or entering contracts with foreign sources with some exceptions.[1522] Tennessee

---

[1516] 2021 N.D. Laws H.B. No. 1220.
[1517] 2021 Okla. Sess. Laws H.B. 2750.
[1518] 2021 Or. Laws Ch. 533, HB 2590.
[1519] 2021 Or. Laws Ch. 68, HB 2589.
[1520] 2021 Or. Laws Ch. 277, SB 416.
[1521] 2021 S.C. Act No. 26, S. 38.
[1522] 2021 Tenn. Pub. Acts Ch. No. 344, H.B. No. 1238, S.B. No. 1191.

next designated sports facilities at private universities as sports authority facilities for purposes of consumption of alcoholic beverages on their premises.[1523]

In the first of three laws, Texas specified that officials in institutions of higher education may not require scores on college-level examinations greater than the minimum recommended by the American Council on Education in awarding course credit for lower-division classes; this provides an exception if institutional chief academic officers decide that higher scores are necessary to demonstrate that students are sufficiently prepared for more advanced courses for which the lower-division classes are prerequisites.[1524] Texas allowed the services provided by licensed vocational nursing students in licensed facilities to be permitted at all times, including during declared states of disaster.[1525] Texas expanded its innovative adult career education grant program to include nonprofit organizations that provide training to veterans.[1526]

[1523] 2021 Tenn. Pub. Acts Ch. No. 267, S.B. No. 1004, H.B. No. 1082.
[1524] 2021 Tex. Gen. Laws S.B. No. 1227.
[1525] 2021 Tex. Gen. Laws S.B. No. 1856.
[1526] 2021 Tex. Gen. Laws H.B. No. 626.

Conclusion

This chapter identifies and categorizes legislative acts adopted by the United States Congress and each of the fifty state legislatures and general assemblies during the 2021 calendar year. The secondary author began researching and reporting for this chapter with the 1998 legislative year when only 253 education-related acts at federal and state levels were adopted nationally. This chapter, which reported 799 education-related laws for the 2020 legislative year, covered 1,480 acts in 2021. These trends represent the acceleration of education-related acts since 1998, with peaks in 2011, 2019, and 2021.

Years	Number of Acts Reported
1998	253 acts
1999-2001	430 acts on average annually
2022-2006	630 acts on average annually
2007-2009	890 acts on average annually
2010	1,050 acts
2011	1,225 acts
2012	830 acts
2013	922 acts
2014	819 acts
2015	864 acts
2016	671 acts
2017	960 acts
2018	919 acts
2019	1,233 acts
2020	799 acts
2021	1,480 acts

These data demonstrate that legislative bodies produced more education-related legislation in 2021 than recorded in earlier years, going back to 1998. The following chart tabulates the number of acts reported in each category of education-related legislation passed in 2021.

Categories	Number of Acts Reported
Federal Legislation	4
State Legislation	
Accountability and School Reform	41
Athletics	26
Attendance, Promotion, and Graduation	100
Buildings and Grounds	32
Curricular Requirements	100
Employment	156
Finance and School Business	107
Governance and School Leadership	134
Parental and Student Rights	93
Program Development	123
School Choice	31
School Safety	135
Student with Disabilities	48
Technology	9
Transportation	27
Higher Education	314

Higher education-related legislation in 2021 again represented the area with the greatest activity in this chapter, with 314 acts. In 1998 thirteen states enrolled eighteen acts about higher education. In 1999, sixteen states added thirty-five more such acts. From 2000 to 2005, on average, twenty-nine states added fifty-four acts on higher education. Then the amount of higher education-related legislation accelerated dramatically each year until 2011, with 94 acts in 2006; 170 acts in 2007; 151 acts in 2008; 141 acts in 2009; 218 acts in 2010; and 257 acts in 2011.

The first decade of the new century marked a change in higher education-related legislation because legislatures treated these institutions more like K-12 schools with more direct involvement in their operations. Subsequently, the number of higher education-related acts remained relatively high, as follows: 150 in 2012; 147 in 2013; 151 in 2014; 173 in 2015; 102 in 2016; 147 in 2017; 167 in 2018;

263 in 2019; 152 in 2020; and, 314 in 2021. In this last and current decade, higher education-related legislation was the most numerous category of legislation every year, except in 2016, when it was surpassed by school safety.

In 2021 higher education-related legislation continued to be dominated by concerns about its costs. States continued to add scholarship programs and financial aid for targeted groups of students, including the homeless, foster youth, undocumented immigrants, children of firefighters and police officers, visually-impaired students, and students eligible through a treaty with various Pacific Island governments. Again, states broadened assistance to military members, veterans, and their dependents in the form of tuition scholarships, resident-tuition status, academic credit for military training, and fee reductions or waivers. Military personnel also benefited from friendly transfer processes, excused absences for military service, and the ability to register late for courses.

Various states addressed the issue of student debt by requiring institutions to foster open-source educational materials. An increasingly-occurring requirement was for institutions to provide more information projecting the actual education costs, the likelihood of employment for graduates from various academic programs, and counseling about related decisions. In recent years, more states added increasing regulatory oversight over private proprietary schools, initiating regulatory control over businesses that service student loans similar to the oversight provided by proprietary schools.

During the last legislative year, more states directed officials in technical centers, colleges, and universities to do more to make students aware of careers not requiring a college education. States ordered officials in these entities to gather more data and make it available in brochures and websites while creating greater student counseling opportunities.

States continued to promote career and technology courses, workforce training, apprenticeship, and internship programs, arranged in what many states describe as "pathways" for specialized degrees, industry certification, or other means of indicating readiness for particular careers. New apprenticeship statutes included state-level oversight of the program, direction concerning wages during participation in the program, and support for industry certification relevant to perceived need within the state. The association of these elements into "pathways" for career and technology courses, beginning in middle school and continuing through high school and on to postsecondary schools, is a trend that was first noted in 2019 and continues to accelerate today.

Legislative bodies continued to place additional emphasis on campus safety issues on various fronts of concern, including violence, sexual violence, sexual misconduct, suicide, mental health, hazing, bullying, and athletic injury. Many states ordered information and data about violent acts on campuses, sought stronger relationships between city and campus police, and required campus-wide interventions to address suicide, mental health issues, and hazing. Maryland directed public institutions of higher education to adopt policies and procedures dealing with a range of conditions such as brain injury, heat illness, and rhabdomyolysis. [1527] While it is common for K-12 schools to receive legislative direction on student-athlete safety, it is uncommon to see it directed at colleges and universities.

An emerging trend in 2019 was the adoption in seventeen states of legislation allowing student-athletes in postsecondary institutions to earn compensation for the commercial use of the student-athlete's name, image, or likeness (NIL). Permission was implicitly, and in one state explicitly, extended to include student-athletes in community colleges. This trend accelerated in 2021.

One of the most remarkable changes in legislative activity related to higher education over the last twenty-one years has been for legislators to intercede directly in program decisions in academic programs in public higher education institutions, as they have done for many decades for K-12 schools. The 2000 legislative year was the first during which such behavior was observed for higher education institutions. The year 2021 had much to say about the academic aspect of teacher preparation programs, including what was to be taught, what was a preferred model of instruction, and how it was to be evaluated. Remarkably, each of the acts directing teacher preparation programs last year ratcheted up requirements for them in a labor environment where teacher shortages were occurring and for which legislative bodies were responding by simultaneously finding ways to get persons into a classroom but without standard certifications.

Legislation related to school employment was the second most common category of legislation in 2021, with 156 acts recorded. The number of employment-related acts averaged 65 acts annually from 2000-2005; 85 in 2006; 157 in 2007; 107 in 2008; 113 in 2009; 151 in

---

[1527] 2021 Md. Laws Ch. 138, SB 439.

2010; 183 in 2011; 127 in 2012; 95 in 2013; 94 in 2014; 102 in 2015; 57 in 2016; 124 in 2017; 155 in 2018; 148 in 2019; 98 in 2020; and, 156 in 2021. In recent years school employment-related legislation competed with school safety legislation for second place for most numerous.

For the third year in a row, the leading issue covered by school employment-related legislation in 2021 was the need to address teacher shortages. Financial incentives played a role, including salary increases, bonuses for teachers in STEM, tuition reimbursement and grants, student loan reimbursement, and loan forgiveness.

The policy goal of honoring military personnel and veterans for their service was combined in many states with the goal of filling empty teaching positions by granting instant reciprocity to military members, veterans, and their spouses with out-of-state teaching certificates. States sped up the process of preparing teachers by dropping requirements for admission and testing, reducing requirements for certification, opening up more alternative certificate programs, allowing teachers to teach while working on alternative certificates, affording teacher trainees full pay while they student teach, and creating "adjunct" certificates for those who may lack academic or pedagogic training or either. Selected states allowed retired educators to return to work without financial penalties from their retirement systems or awarded certificates to those from other countries.

States passed eleven laws changing requirements for admission to academic programs. One state removed the requirement for a minimum score on an entrance examination for admission to graduate-level teacher and educational leader programs and also raised the percentage of students, from 15% to 50%, who can be exempt from admission requirements for graduate-level teacher and educational leader programs. This example of decreasing admission requirements illustrates the increasing the number of teacher education candidates and alleviating the shortage of available teachers.

State legislative bodies adopted 135 school safety-related acts in 2021, making it the third-most numerous categories of legislation. By comparison, 107 school safety-related acts were enrolled in 1999, the year of violence at Columbine High School, and 100 more were adopted in the next two years. From 2002 to 2004, approximately fifty school safety acts were passed annually. The following number of acts were signed into law in subsequent years: 81 in 2005; 70 in 2006; 122 in 2007; 81 in 2008; 97 in 2009, 54 in 2010; 87 in 2011; 55

in 2012; 88 in 2013; 88 in 2014; 110 in 2015; 115 in 2016; 120 in 2017; 155 in 2018; 190 in 2019; 100 in 2020; and, 135 in 2021. School safety was the most-numerous type of legislation adopted only once during this decade, in 2016. In the other years of this decade, it exchanged second and third place with employment.

The most legislation enacted last year in the category of school safety focused on student discipline. States added provisions limiting restraints and seclusion, especially for students with disabilities, and a number of prohibited exclusions, such as suspensions and expulsions for younger students. Reducing bullying continued to be pressed through legislation. There was growing support for building equitable and inclusive school environments, with the introduction of behavioral supports and a commitment to restorative justice. Acts seeking reduction of suicide incidents continued to increase in number, as did laws on internet safety. Bills designed to stop inappropriate relationships between school employees and students were added, including more on using criminal background checks to screen out who should not be working with children; other acts targeted grooming behaviors, inappropriate relationships, and sex with students.

The authors reported last year in *The Yearbook of Education Law* that in 2020 both federal and state legislatures performed yeoman work in helping schools make their way through the first year of the COVID-19 pandemic. Legislatures continued in 2021 to find ways to help schools and children through the pandemic's second year. More legislatures in 2021 paused the operation of their accountability and school reform programs, such as assigning school letter grades while seeking ways to address learning loss, as some temporarily halted evaluation programs for teachers and administrators. Increasing numbers of states noted the migration of instructional methodology from face-to-face to virtual and to hybrid models as they changed funding and school foundation programs to safeguard local boards from funding losses due to changing attendance profiles.

A few states created study groups or directed professional associations to re-imagine how schooling should be provided and asked for new models of instruction. Ten states added sixteen types of excused absences which would often help to protect school funding. Fourteen states passed fifteen laws allowing children of members of the military to enroll in schools where their parents or guardians are being transferred before they move and, in many cases, allowing them to attend schools virtually from the moment the military member receives transfer orders. Through fourteen acts, nine states changed graduation requirements to allow students to graduate on time despite the impact of the pandemic on attendance and course progression. Five states adopted alternative paths or accelerated promotion with early graduation.

The year 2021 saw many legislative bodies actively working to protect schools. Yet, the political climate concurrent with the pandemic's second year had a dark side as states could not resist enlisting in the culture wars, introducing and passing legislation to score political points through the public schools. Public health requirements became grist for the mill, with two states blocking mask mandates in schools and a third only permitting them when initiated by emergency orders from the governor. Seven states enacted ten laws on COVID-19 vaccinations, with legislatures adding provisions such as prohibiting school boards from mandating inoculations without orders from the governor or requiring the inclusion of exemptions appended to the orders.

In the category of Curricular Requirements, seven states added requirements for their sex education curricula, with three underscoring parental rights to excuse their child from sex education topics. Civics and patriotism figured prominently in 2021 legislation, with twenty-five acts bolstering the teaching of civics while mandating or permitting the Pledge to the Flag or displays of the national motto. Five (blue) states initiated the teaching of African-American history, two added instructions on Asian American history, and Illinois included material on the contributions of Muslims along with placing the January 17 birthday of Muhammad Ali on the list of its commemorative holidays. Three (red) states prohibited teaching in public schools what the legislatures perceived as based on critical race theory.

The authors' state of residence repealed a provision admonishing that homosexuality is not a lifestyle acceptable to the general public and that homosexual conduct is a criminal offense under state law. The legislature may have been surprised by *Dobbs v. Jackson Women's Health Organization*,[1528] and did not anticipate the possibility of its fostering anti-gay progeny in the future. Another surprise is that the same legislature permitted K-12 schools to offer the teaching of yoga.

The legislation also addressed gender-related issues last year. Three (blue) states added laws to protect students based on gender identity or expression. Seven (red) states directed students to

---

[1528] 142 S. Ct. 2228 (2022).

participate in athletics on boys' or girls' teams that conform to the biological sexes printed on their birth certificates. One of those states prohibited personnel with licenses to practice in the state from referring persons younger than eighteen for gender transition procedures under penalty of license revocation and damages.

Four states adopted five acts about firearms in schools, with two supporting more persons, with or without applicable training, present in schools with firearms and two prohibiting individuals from carrying firearms unless they are properly-trained police officers. Two more states called for additional training for SROs, one championing restorative justice practices and the other promoting diversity, equity, and inclusion.

One state permitted all of its school board elections to be partisan. The authors are unaware of partisan school board elections preexisting in the nation before 1998, do not recall such legislation since 1998, and have not encountered them in their practice.[1529] Such laws are "local acts," which generally do not become recorded in school codes. The expressions "all politics are local" and "all elections are local" are in the tradition of our democracy. However, partisanship invites more culture wars into the business of schools. Excessive partisanship with red and blue teams in school board elections may benefit the teams but not the schoolchildren they were created to serve.

[1529] Authors' note: an email to the membership of the Council of School Attorneys elicited responses that, while rare, a few states have partisan elections based on local laws involving school boards in a small number of states.

Made in United States
North Haven, CT
31 July 2023